THE SUNDAY TIMES
ILLUSTRATED HISTORY OF
FOOTBALL

THE SUNDAY TIMES
ILLUSTRATED HISTORY OF
FOOTBALL

CHRIS NAWRAT & STEVE HUTCHINGS

HAMLYN

To Jules Rimet and Henri Delaunay, the men who
founded the World Cup and ensured that football became
a truly global game

Editors: David Heslam, David Ballheimer, Peter Arnold
Designers: Ian Muggeridge, Christopher Matthews
Design Manager: Bryan Dunn
Picture Researcher: Judy Todd
Production: Michelle Thomas

First published in Great Britain in 1994
by Hamlyn an imprint of Reed Consumer Books Limited
Michelin House, 81 Fulham Road, London SW3 6RB
and Auckland, Melbourne, Singapore and Toronto

Produced by Mandarin Offset
Printed and bound in Great Britain by
Butler & Tanner Ltd, Frome and London

Half-title Ultimate triumph: England, Bobby Moore and the World Cup
given a lift in 1966
Title pages Spot the ball: defence in depth in the 1994 World Cup final,
Brazil v Italy
This page Best and worst: Diego Maradona, genius in the 1986 World
Cup, bad boy in 1994

Contents

Introduction

The world is round

THERE IS no question that football is the biggest sport in the world. When Pele called it "the beautiful game" he also had in mind its beguiling simplicity. This simple game that captivated the world has become a global, complex business that has political, social and economic repercussions that nobody could have anticipated a century ago.

Yet in Britain, which gave the game to the world, football is not properly celebrated for the wondrous thing it is. Who could have imagined when the Football Association was established that the self-confidence the British would enjoy for more than 100 years would be supplanted by a cultural neurosis of self-denigration in the last quarter of the 20th century?

There are some good reasons for this lack of self-esteem: our track record on hooliganism at home and abroad was appalling for over a generation; our inability to modernise our stadiums led to major disasters; our international record since winning the World Cup in 1966 has never lived up to expectations; and our emphasis on the athletic aspect of the game over the artistic causes us to doubt our own abilities as a footballing nation.

But how true is this? England came within a penalty whisker of reaching the 1990 World Cup final; within a sending-off of qualifying for the 1994 finals; within a Maradona hand-ball of the 1986 World Cup semi-finals. Every country in Europe is respectful of both the national side and our club sides. This is not surprising given that a British club either won a European trophy, or appeared in a final, every single year from 1965 to 1985. Continental clubs import our players at great cost precisely because of our British athleticism, heart and skill. They cannot for the life of them fathom why we have such a low opinion of ourselves, particularly as the hooligan problems experienced in Holland, Germany, Spain and Italy were every bit as bad as ours during the dark days of 1980s.

But where did this self-imposed low self-esteem come from? Partly from the specific nature of British society and partly from the origins of the professional game in England.

Britain was, and is, the most class-riven society in Western civilisation. Football, or soccer as the public schools called it, was hijacked from the snooty establishment by the northern horny-hands of toil in the last quarter of the 19th century and turned into a full-time job. For the working class football became a symbol of their defiance of the governing class and, incidentally, coincided with the rise of the Labour party.

The establishment pigeon-holed football as a working class diversion. This label still persists today. Never mind that the urban working class has virtually disappeared from British society and that, since the early 1960s, it was obvious to anybody who had eyes to see that the popularity of football in Britain cut across every class, sex, race and religious divide.

This categorisation of following football as peculiarly working-class, if not a downright yobbish activity, permeates all aspects of British society, despite the evidence to the contrary. Football's popularity was such that England's World Cup semi-final against West Germany in 1990 was seen on TV by 26m, 12m more than voted for the Tories in the 1992 General Election. What's more important: who runs the country? or can England win the World Cup? The nation voted accordingly.

Yet still national newspapers have a split personality in dealing with the people's game. On the one hand they recognise that they have to cover it in their sports pages, rather like they understand that they have to have extensive television listings – after all both sell millions of newspapers. But on the other hand, there are very few national newspaper editors that would have football anywhere on their list of priorities. Strange when you consider that huge numbers of people buy newspapers just for their sports coverage, and in particular football.

One of the most extraordinary examples of this contradiction comes from the tabloids, largely Tory papers sold to the masses. The Sun is one of the few papers that understands the importance of football. Yet after the Hillsborough disaster in 1989 it ran a front-page story accusing Liverpool fans of being drunk and urinating over dead bodies. There was outrage in Liverpool. The story turned out to be untrue and The Sun's sales in Merseyside have never recovered.

Football often does not get the press it deserves. But what happens when it is left to its own devices? Fans on the terraces, tired of being misunderstood and misrepresented, desired their own voice and fanzines, written by fans for fans, have mushroomed in the past few years.

Yet even fanzines have a one-eyed view of the world, reflecting a tribal hate of rival teams and the scorn that supporters heap on their own players, particularly the unfortunate individual singled out for mockery and disdain for the most spurious of reasons. Ian Branfoot, Southampton's manager, was hounded out after the most vitriolic hate campaign by the club's own supporters. A so-called fanzine even called for his death. Thus

Hand of fate: Diego Maradona fists the ball past Peter Shilton and Argentina lead in Mexico 1986

the alternative press had come full circle.

Football, like politics, is populated by people who remember every failing, every statistic, every player's name, but learn nothing from what has gone before. The media explosion has fed our thirst for the latest facts and our demands seem insatiable. However it appears that the better informed we are about today and tomorrow, the less we understand about yesterday.

This book seeks to redress that balance: to take you through this century by analysing and reporting the significant events of each year. We have tried to choose our words and our interpretations carefully and to use the benefit of hindsight to record how football developed in Britain in the 20th century.

When we sat down to write this book we had in mind three different sets of readers: the young, whom we hoped to introduce to the fascinating tapestry of football's history; the old, who would want to be reminded of great moments from the past; and the obsessives, who, when they are standing on the terraces on a freezing cold winter's night would want something to keep them warm and explain to them why they are there.

This is a book of record: there are comprehensive statistics and League tables for each season and reports of all the big matches. But it is also more than a reference book, it is something to be read, whether you dip into it or gulp, and read it from cover to cover in one sitting. Interspersed throughout the book are 18 essays on the key figures we believe shaped the game as we know it today. We hope we have made everybody happy with our efforts. However, we apologise for any errors that may have accidentally crept in.

A project of this magnitude would not have been possible without the help and encouragement freely given by friends and some colleagues. As well as the people who contributed articles and suggestions for this book we would particularly like to thank the following for their support: Arthur Appleton, Peter Arnold, Christine Boyle, Antony Dalgleish, John Duncan, Mike Hammond, David Heslam, Sally Hibbin, Roddy Mackenzie, Tony Moss, Sue Mott, Sandy Sutherland and Carolyn Wigoder. Last, but not least, there are the thousands of footballers who have brought joy to all of our lives. Without them this book would not exist.

On level terms: Gary Lineker equalises against West Germany in Italy in 1990

Paying the penalty: Stuart Pearce misses in the shoot-out and England miss out on the 1990 final

Turning point: Koeman escapes being sent off and England are on their way out of the 1994 finals

Football begins with a bang

THE FORMATION of the Football Association, at the Freemason's Tavern in London on October 26, 1863, was not regarded as earth-shattering news – a report of the monumental occasion warranted a mere 35 lines in The Times the next day.

But the delegates who agreed to pay a subscription of a guinea a year had no doubt about the importance of the task facing them. As football had grown in popularity, and spread throughout England, the need for a common set of rules was becoming more pressing.

In some places the goal was the width of the pitch, in others it was only 12ft across. Some goals were 8ft tall, others were 20ft, and still more had no height restriction whatsoever. And according to The Laws of Football as Played at Rugby School, published in 1846, all matches were declared draws after five days, or three days if no goal had been kicked.

A meeting at Cambridge in 1848 had set about establishing a common standard, although the Cambridge rules allowed the ball to be caught (providing it was promptly placed on the ground and kicked) and offside was defined as any player being in front of the ball.

Yet another set of rules had been drawn up in Sheffield in the mid-1850s. These rules, although not that dissimilar to the Cambridge ones, had been drawn up independently and even contained innovations such as opposing teams having to wear different coloured caps so they could be identified.

But the greatest stumbling blocks, which nearly tore the newly-established FA apart, were the thorny questions of whether carrying the ball and hacking should be allowed.

Football's future hung in the balance at a series of stormy and indecisive meetings. The game could just as easily have become the one we know today as rugby until Sheffield FC tipped the scales. Applying to join the FA, they outlined their rules and said that if carrying the ball and hacking were allowed then the game would be more like wrestling than football.

This letter almost certainly proved to be decisive in helping the no-carrying and no-hacking camp finally win the day on December 1 by 13 votes to four. As a result, Blackheath, who had championed the cause of hacking, resigned and soon became one of the founders of the Rugby Football Union.

Queen's Park's exploits set the ball rolling in Scotland

QUEEN'S PARK'S adventures in the first FA Cup were the catalyst for the formation of the Scottish FA and the start of a Scottish Cup competition. The club's players discussed the idea on the way home from London, which led to an inaugural meeting in Glasgow on March 13, 1873.

Eight clubs attended, but one notable absentee was Rangers. Their application for membership arrived to late for them to take part in the first competition, which involved 16 clubs. Not surprisingly, Queen's Park won the Cup for the first three years and the first goal they ever conceded in a competitive match was when they lost to Vale of Leven in the semi-final of the 1876-77 competition.

But the single greatest influence on Scottish football was the presumptuous English. In 1870 Charles Alcock, the secretary of the English FA, arranged a series of four matches between England and "Scotland" in London in 1870.

England won three matches and drew one, but the Scots were not satisfied. They did not regard a team picked by an Englishman, composed of exiles, as truly representative.

So in 1872, Queen's Park, on behalf of Scotland, challenged England to come to Glasgow for an official international. More than 2,000 people packed into the West of Scotland Cricket Club, whose ground was the biggest in Glasgow, to see the 0-0 draw on November 30.

The gate receipts were £102 19s 6d and the match made a profit of just over £38. The money enabled the Scots to send a team to England the following March, establishing the future of the world's oldest international fixture.

QUEEN'S PARK FOOTBALL CLUB
SEASON 1873-74.

The pride of Scotland: Queen's Park led the move for a Scottish FA

Professionalism casts shadow

THE SUCCESS of the first FA Cup caught the imagination of clubs throughout the country, and the number of entries increased nearly five-fold in a decade.

It was not long before regional associations started to spring up, many of which ran their own tournaments modelled on the FA Cup. But the rapid expansion of the game soon brought yet another dispute, this time between the rich south and the poor, but fast expanding north.

The labourers of the north could not afford to have their wages docked for taking time off to play football. And Scots, the first exponents of the passing rather than the dribbling game, were flooding across the border, lured by newspaper advertisements and under-the-counter payments.

When Blackburn Olympic took the Cup out of London for the first time in 1883, the FA was still very much dominated by the gentlemen of the south, who thought that sport should only be played by amateurs. Matters came to a head in the next competition when Accrington and Preston were expelled from the FA Cup for professionalism.

The north and Midlands were incensed and Preston's suggestion of forming a breakaway British Football Association received support from 28 clubs. Motivated by the desire to keep control of the game, and after a good deal of politicking, the FA gave in to professionalism before the 1885 season started.

With professionalism legalised, and accepted by all but a few of the old guard, the last piece of the jigsaw was about to drop into place – the formation of the Football League.

The people's game comes of age with the launch of the FA Cup

THE newly-formed FA, having finally voted to outlaw handling the ball and kicking opponents, busied itself with defining how the game should be played.

Sheffield, meanwhile, although members of the FA, persevered with their own rules. But enough headway had been made for London and Sheffield to play two representative matches in 1866.

Soon after, when it was convinced that it had finally got all the details right, the FA staged an exhibition match, Middlesex v Kent and Surrey, to unveil its new-look rules to the world.

Although the fixture was declared a success, something was still needed to kick-start the game. Enter Charles Alcock the newly-elected secretary of the FA. Alcock remembered that when he had attended Harrow all the houses at the school competed in a knockout competition for the honour of being the "Cock House".

So he suggested that clubs should contribute towards the £20 cost of buying a cup to be played for by all the members of the FA. The decision to stage the FA Challenge Cup competition was taken on October 16, 1871, and 15 clubs entered – 13 of them from the London area, plus Donington school, Lincolnshire, and Queen's Park, Glasgow.

Queen's Park's motivation for throwing in their lot with the English was straightforward. They wanted to play a better standard of football than it was possible to play in Scotland.

The club was the first to be founded in Scotland, in 1867, and in all the matches they had played since then they had still not conceded a goal. They found it so hard to find suitable competition that they often had to resort to playing matches between their own players.

Thanks to two byes and one opponent scratching, Queen's Park reached the semi-final without having played a match. They had a 0-0 draw with Wanderers at The Oval but could not afford the cost of another trip to London for the replay, so they withdrew. Wanderers went on to beat the Royal Engineers 1-0 in the final at The Oval in front of a crowd of 2,000, who paid a not inconsiderable shilling each.

Accrington's ledger recording their results from the 1878-79 season gave few clues to the storm that was about to break about the club paying their players

---

Other milestones on the way to the Football League

1862: J C Thring published "The Simplest Game", 10 rules adopted by many public schools. Violence was not allowed and players were not allowed in front of the ball.

1863: The Cambridge rules were rewritten to encompass 14 points including the size of the pitch and the banning of tripping and kicking opponents' shins. These rules were the foundation of the ones adopted by the FA.

1866: Players were no longer offside providing three opponents were between them and the goal.

1867: Sheffield formed its own Football Association, the forerunner of the regional structure of the FA.

1869: Goal kicks were introduced.

1872: Corner kicks were introduced.

1874: Samuel Widdowson of Nottingham Forest is credited with inventing shinguards.

1876: The Welsh FA was formed.

1877: Sheffield changed its rules to be consistent with the FA.

October 14, 1878: More than 20,000 people watched a match played under floodlights at Bramall Lane, Sheffield.

October 24, 1878: The first match was played in Northern Ireland, an exhibition between Queen's Park and Caledonians.

A star is born: first floodlit match

1878: Wanderers won the FA Cup for the third year running and the fifth time in seven years.

1878: A referee used a whistle for the first time.

1879: England played their first match against Wales.

1879: Rangers refused to play in the replay for the Scottish Cup Final because they had had a goal disallowed in the first match. The Cup was awarded to Vale of Leven.

1880: The Irish Football Association was formed in Belfast.

1881: The first special train was to the Scottish Cup final between Dumbarton and Queen's Park, who scored the winning goal during a pitch invasion. Dumbarton appealed and were granted a replay, which they also lost.

February 18, 1882: Ireland lost 13-0 to England at Knock. A week later, they lost 7-1 to Wales at Wrexham.

December 6, 1882: The English, Scottish, Welsh and Irish FAs met in Manchester, unified their rules and formed the International Football Association Board to control the laws of the game.

1882: Scotland played Wales for the first time.

1882: Throw-ins had to be made two-handed.

1883: Scotland v Ireland also became a regular fixture, creating the first home nations' championship.

September 5, 1885: Arbroath beat Bon Accord 36-0 in the first round of the Scottish Cup, which is still a record for an official match. On the same day Dundee Harp beat Aberdeen Rovers 35-0.

1886: Blackburn Rovers repeated Wanderers' feat of winning the FA Cup three years running.

1886: International caps were awarded for the first time.

First of three: Blackburn Rovers won the FA Cup in successive seasons

1888-99
POST-FOOTBALL LEAGUE

Invincible Preston

THE first season of the Football League was dominated by Preston. The club had been founded in 1881 by members of the North End cricket club, and Major William Suddell was determined that his team would rival Blackburn Rovers, then the most powerful side in Lancashire.

He recruited heavily from Scotland, where players were adept at the passing game, made little secret of the fact that his team was paid, and led the campaign to force the FA to accept professionalism.

Preston's strength grew to the point where they were so confident of winning the 1888 FA Cup final that they wanted their photograph taken with the FA Cup before the match started, so as not to spoil the victory picture with their muddy clothes. They lost 2-1 to West Bromwich in what was described as "the greatest upset in the history of the competition."

But they did not make any mistakes in the 1888-89 season. They won the League by 11 points without losing a match, and only once failed to score, against Accrington. Preston completed the Double by taking the FA Cup without conceding a goal in the competition. These performances, earned them the name "The Old Invincibles".

The following season Preston did not fare quite so well. They went out of the FA Cup in the third round but still won the League, albeit after four defeats. Although they finished runners-up in the League for the next two years the club was clearly in decline, and in 1894 they just escaped relegation.

England write the script . . .

CLUBS needed a way to make enough money to pay their players. Apart from the FA Cup and some county tournaments, there was still no organised football and clubs had to organise ad hoc fixtures as best they could.

The idea of having regular fixtures had been raised several times but not pursued before William McGregor, a director of Aston Villa, wrote to Blackburn, Bolton, Preston and West Bromwich on March 2, 1888.

He was worried that attendances were declining because spectators did not know when matches were taking place, or even whether they would be played – re-arranged Cup matches and replays meant that many friendlies were called off with little or no notice.

In response to McGregor's letter a meeting was held on March 23, 1888, in Anderton's hotel, London, on the eve of the Cup final. A name was chosen – the Football League was preferred to the Association Football Union – and another meeting was arranged for April 17. This time the venue was Manchester, at the Royal hotel, because not one southern club had expressed any interest in the Football League.

After careful study of the calendar, to allow for the Cup matches, it was decided that there were 22 free days in the season. With teams playing home and away, that meant there was only room for 12 clubs in the League.

So Halliwell, Nottingham Forest and The Wednesday missed out while Accrington, Aston Villa, Blackburn Rovers, Bolton, Burnley, Derby County, Everton, Notts County, Preston North End, Stoke, West Bromwich Albion and Wolverhampton Wanderers became founder members of the oldest league in the world.

. . . and Scotland dance to their tune

SCOTLAND wasted no time in following England's example and 11 clubs – Abercorn, Celtic, Cowlairs, Cambuslang, Dumbarton, Hearts, Rangers, St Mirren, Renton, Third Lanark and Vale of Leven – formed the Scottish League in time for the start of the 1890-91 season.

But it was not long before the Scottish League was riven by the same dispute that had nearly split the game in England – paying players. Renton had only played five matches when they were expelled from the League. Their only offence was to play a match against Edinburgh Saints, a team that the Scottish FA decided was professional.

The Scots were even more determined than the English to keep their game "pure" and amateur. Rangers had entered the English FA Cup in 1885 (they were drawn against Rawtenstall and, ironically, then scratched rather than play against professionals, a decision that cost them a 10-shilling fine from the English FA). The next season, Rangers entered the English FA Cup again (and reached the semi-final, beating Cowlairs in the process). This was too much for the Scottish FA to stomach, and they promptly forbade all of their clubs from entering the English competition.

And with more and more of the best Scottish players being poached by big-spending clubs from England, clubs were forced to make secret payments to the members of their team just to keep their side together. The practice became so widespread that the Scottish FA was powerless, so they virtually ignored the problem.

When the Scottish League was announced, the amateur camp were furious. One commentator denounced it in a newspaper, saying: "The rules stink of money-grabbing."

In 1893 the Scottish FA bowed to the inevitable and finally allowed professionalism.

With the politicking over, clubs were free to concentrate on trying to win the championship. Then, as now, the story was much the same – Celtic and Rangers battling for the title with Hearts and Hibs snapping at their heels. Not that there was much of a contest in 1899, when Rangers took the the title with a perfect record – played 18 won 18. Celtic, though, did pull off a shock 2-0 defeat of Rangers in the Cup final.

Invincible Preston							
Football League							
	P	W	D	L	F	A	Pts
Preston	22	18	4	0	74	15	40
Aston Villa	22	12	5	5	61	43	29
Wolverhampton	22	12	4	6	50	37	28
Blackburn	22	10	6	6	66	45	26
Bolton	22	10	2	10	63	59	22
West Brom	22	10	2	10	40	46	22
Accrington	22	6	8	8	48	48	20
Everton	22	9	2	11	35	46	20
Burnley	22	7	3	12	42	62	17
Derby	22	7	2	13	41	60	16
Notts County	22	5	2	15	39	73	12
Stoke	22	4	4	14	26	51	12

FA Cup

First round: Bootle 0 Preston 3. Second round: Grimsby Town 0 Preston 2. Third round: Preston 2 Birmingham St George's 0. Semi-final: Preston 1 West Bromwich 0. Final: Preston 3 Wolverhampton 0.

Sunderland and Villa leave Preston trailing

As Preston went into decline, the balance of power shifted to two clubs, Sunderland and Aston Villa. Sunderland joined the League in 1890 to replace Stoke, who had twice finished bottom. Like Preston, they made great use of Scottish imports. After taking one season to find their feet they went on to dominate the League, winning it three times in the next four years and finishing runners-up on the other occasion.

The 1892 champions won 13 matches in a row between November and April and were known as the "Team of All Talents". A better description would be the team of all countries because they only had one English player – their captain.

The one time Sunderland did not win the championship, 1894, the title went to Aston Villa. Like Sunderland, they topped the table three times in four years. Then, for good measure, they were the champions twice in the next three years as well.

Along the way, they also won the FA Cup twice. Unfortunately, they also became the first club to win and lose the Cup in the same season. After their victory over West Bromwich in 1895 the put the silver on display in a local shoe shop, from where it was stolen. Nearly 60 years later the thief admitted that the Cup had been melted down to make counterfeit half-crowns. The FA fined Aston Villa £25 and used the money to purchase a replacement trophy.

Arsenal and Millwall spearhead the southern revolution as game's boom sweeps the nation

THE success of the Football League led to the introduction of a Second Division in 1892, which helped to give the game much-needed impetus in the south of England. It wasn't that there weren't any clubs in the south, or that they didn't want to play in the League, it was that London, and other county associations, still refused to recognise professional players.

Woolwich Arsenal, despairing of this hidebound attitude were the first to make the break, abandoning the London FA and joining the Second Division of the Football League in 1893. A year later more clubs jumped ship and Millwall were instrumental in the formation of the Southern League, for some time almost as important as the Football League itself.

While all this was going on, the finishing touches were being put to the rules. A blatant handball on the goal-line by a Notts County player in the the FA Cup quarter-final against Stoke led to the introduction of penalties in 1891. Then Stoke were again the victims of an injustice that led to time being added on for stoppages.

Trailing 1-0 and awarded a penalty with two minutes remaining, they could only watch in horror as the Aston Villa goalkeeper kicked the ball out of the ground. By the time it was recovered, 90 minutes had elapsed and the match was over.

These, and other minor indiscretions apart, football was in fine fettle. In a little óver 50 years it had gone through an enormous revolution, coming from virtually nowhere to be the national pastime. Football was talked about the length and breadth of the nation. Teams were followed with a passion and, thanks to newspapers, individual players were household names. Everything was set fair for the new century.

Tender for building a Grandstand at Anfield dated 25 September 1886. The estimated cost: £64! Scrawled across the letter is a 'penalty clause' required by the Liverpool chairman John Houlding: 'To be complete and ready for use by 8 Oct 1886; forfeit one pound per day incomplete after.'

Stand and deliver: (far left) the builders at Anfield could not be late

First foot: the British Ladies' Football Club's first match in 1895

THE
1900-01
SEASON

Tottenham's historic triumph

Southern revolt: Tottenham were held at Crystal Palace but overturned Sheffield United in the replay at Bolton

Queen's Park swallow their pride to sign up with the professionals

QUEEN'S PARK finally made their debut in the Scottish League, but the circumstances surrounding their election to the First Division were shrouded in mystery.

Queen's Park had declined to join the League when it was formed because the strictly amateur club did not want to be associated with professional teams. As the League grew Queen's Park found it harder to arrange friendlies, but they were not prepared to swallow their pride and ask directly for admission.

When a pre-season dispute between two groups of clubs threatened to tear the League apart Queen's Park offered to act as unofficial negotiators. Their intervention headed off the revolt and they were subsequently invited to join the First Division.

TOTTENHAM turned the established order upside down when they became the only non-League side to win the FA Cup.

The Southern League side's defeat of a powerful Sheffield United team was hailed as further proof that the South was becoming a force to be reckoned with in a sport that, until now, had been dominated by teams from the North and Midlands. Ironically, though, none of their team were born within 100 miles of London – and five came from Scotland, two from Wales and one from Ireland.

John Cameron, Tottenham's player-manager, had recruited wisely and his team beat four First Division sides, including Bury, the Cup holders. They owed a great deal to their striker Sandy Brown, who scored in every round.

Tottenham were unlucky to be taken to a replay in the final, which drew a record crowd of

more than 110,000 to Crystal Palace. Brown scored both of Tottenham's goals and film of the match proved that Sheffield United's equaliser was not a goal. The ball had not been within a foot of the line and a corner should have been awarded, as the linesman indicated at the time.

The replay, at Burnden Park, Bolton, was a more low-key affair. The weather was bad, and the Lancashire and Yorkshire

Rail Company refused to issue any cheap tickets. With many supporters unable to travel to the match the attendance was a mere 20,000.

Tottenham trailed 1-0 at half time but three goals in the second half, the third from Brown, won them the Cup. At the celebration dinner Tottenham officials tied ribbons in the club's colours to the handle of the Cup, starting a tradition that has continued ever since.

Liverpool start the century with a bang

LIVERPOOL also showed that the balance of power was shifting when they won the League for the first time with a dramatic finishing burst.

Aston Villa, who had been champions five times in the past seven years, were going for a hat-trick of titles for a second time. But they spent most of the season flirting with relegation and it looked as if the championship was going to return to Sunderland.

Liverpool looked to be destined for a mid-table finish until they went to Sunderland in February and won 1-0. That started a run of 12 matches without defeat and Liverpool slowly narrowed the gap on Sunderland, finally taking the title by beating West Bromwich in their final match.

Bloomer: leading marksman

■ Rangers won the Scottish League for the third year running, and went out of the Scottish Cup to Celtic for the

FOR THE RECORD

■ The maximum wage was raised to £4 a week. The FA limited signing-on fees to £10 and banned match bonuses, but did allow players to be given a benefit every five years or when they retired.

■ Steve Bloomer, the Derby and England inside-forward, was the First Division's leading goalscorer for the fourth time in six years.

third time in a row. But Celtic's hope of a hat-trick of Cups was dashed by Hearts, who won the final 4-3.

■ Scotland beat Ireland 11-0 in February, their highest international score, but finished second to England in the home internationals when they drew at Crystal Palace. The Scottish League XI gained some measure of revenge when they beat the Football League XI 6-2 in Glasgow, the most goals they had ever scored.

■ Football matches were cancelled when places of public entertainment were closed during the mourning for the death of Queen Victoria in January.

■ Bristol City became the third Southern League club to be elected to the Second Division.

■ The FA gave permission for Surrey Wanderers and Southampton to make tours of Germany and Austria.

■ The rules were changed so that the goalkeeper could only be charged when he was holding the ball. Previously, he could be charged when he was playing the ball.

THE
1901-02
SEASON

English cream turns Germans extremely sour

A GERMAN touring team played two matches against England Amateurs and England Professionals in the autumn. Although the fixtures were not generally regarded as full internationals they were given representative status.

In the first game, R E Foster of Corinthians, who also played first-class cricket for Worcestershire, scored six goals as the amateurs won 12-0 in front of a 6,000 crowd at Tottenham. Foster went on to captain both the England football and cricket teams, and score a record 287 runs in a Test match against Australia.

Four days later, the England Professional XI, which contained several members of the full international team, won 10-0 at Manchester City's Hyde Road ground, watched by 8,000 people.

Ibrox suffers as stand crashes

TWENTY-FIVE people died and more than 500 were injured when a section of terracing collapsed during the match between Scotland and England at Ibrox Park on April 5.

Rangers were determined to have the finest facilities in Glasgow and they employed Britain's leading engineers to build Ibrox Park. The stadium had only been open a few years and was chosen to stage the home internationals because it was so modern.

But the capacity crowd exposed a fatal flaw in the design – the wooden steps supported on pillars could not withstand the weight of a crowd swaying back and forth to try to get a better view of the action. The planks gave way and hundreds of people plunged through a gaping hole.

The match was only a few minutes old when the disaster happened, and play was continued to prevent any further panic. Amazingly, many people in the ground did not know what had happened and the first they knew of the terrible events was when they read about them in the newspapers that evening.

The result, a 1-1 draw, was declared unofficial and the match was replayed at Villa Park in May, with the receipts going to the disaster fund.

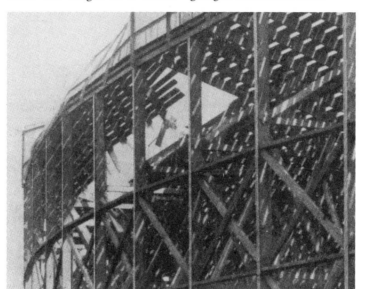

Death traps: 25 people died and 500 were injured in the disaster

Sunderland profit from border raids

SUNDERLAND made up for the disappointment of just being pipped for the League title last season by rediscovering some of the form that had earned them the label "Team of all the Talents" in the 1890s. Once again, their rivals came from Merseyside, but this time it was Everton who were their nearest challengers, finishing second by three points.

Only Ted Doig, the goalkeeper, and Jimmy Millar, the centre-forward, remained from the team that had won the last title. Both men were Scottish internationals, and Sunderland once again relied heavily on players imported from north of the border although they bolstered their side by signing Alf Common from Sheffield United.

Both Doig and Millar collected their fourth championship medal and Millar enjoyed the distinction of winning two titles on each side of the border – two with Sunderland and two with Rangers – and two Cup medals, both in Scotland.

Sheffield United also made amends for last season's setback when, as their players had promised, they won the FA Cup.

However, they were taken to a replay again by another Southern League side Southampton, who had the great amateur all-rounder C B Fry playing at right back.

We felt we'd let the North down and vowed to make amends

ERNEST "NUDGER" NEEDHAM
Sheffield United wing-half,
after they had lost to
Tottenham in the 1901
Cup final

Needham: fulfilled his promise

THE
1902-03
SEASON

Sunderland blow the title at Newcastle

SUNDERLAND'S 1-0 home defeat by Sheffield Wednesday in March finished on a sour note, when some of their fans stoned the referee as he left the ground. Sunderland were ordered to shut Roker Park for a week, but the defeat turned out to be a bigger punishment because it cost them the League title.

For the second time in three years everything hinged on Sunderland's last match of the season. Sheffield Wednesday had completed their fixtures a week before and led the table by one point. Sunderland needed to win at Newcastle; a draw would not suffice because of their inferior goal average.

The omens were good: Sunderland had won their last four League matches at Newcastle. But they were undone by Bob McColl, and the 1-0 defeat did not even leave them in second place. Aston Villa snatched the runners-up spot on goal average with a remarkable finish, scoring 15 goals as they won their last five matches all in the space of 15 days.

McColl: decisive goal

Curse haunts Derby

DERBY fans had plenty of cause to think that their club was indeed damned. Legend had it that they were being punished by a gypsy curse, imposed when the club had built their ground on the site of a Romany camp.

There was enough evidence for people who wanted to believe the story. In the past 10 years they had reached the semi-final of the Cup three times and the final twice, and had lost every time. After five cases of misfortune they had to be due a change of luck. But no, on the sixth occasion they were routed 6-0 by Bury in the Cup final.

Derby had only conceded one goal on the way to the final, to Small Heath in the first round. Bury had gone one better, not allowing any of their opponents to score. They became only the second team to win the Cup without letting in a goal.

Derby were without their ace marksman Steve Bloomer but his absence could not excuse their lacklustre performance. They were sunk in one short spell in the second half when Bury hit four goals in a little over 10 minutes.

Then, to add to Derby's apparently never-ending tale of woe, they lost Fryer, their goalkeeper, with an injury. Not that his absence made a great deal of difference because they were already five goals down at the time.

Jinxed: Derby are demolished 6-0 by Bury in the Cup final

Ireland upset the established order

IRELAND broke England and Scotland's monopoly on the Home International championship when they took a share of the title for the first time.

Such a result was beyond their wildest dreams after the first match, a 4-0 defeat by England at Wolverhampton. They were undone by a tactical switch by England who moved Jack Sharp, the Everton outside right, to inside forward, strengthening the centre of their attack to telling effect.

Ireland had never beaten Scotland, so their 2-0 victory at Parkhead was cause for celebration in itself. Connor's header early in the game gave Scotland the jitters and as their anxiety increased under Ireland's relentless pressure Kirwan was able to add a second goal.

Ireland had never won two matches in a row in the tournament, so when they defeated Wales 2-0 there was even more celebration. The match, in Belfast, was halted for 15 minutes by a violent hailstorm. Wales, without many of their best players who had not been released by English clubs, could not cope with the treacherous conditions when play resumed. One of Ireland's goals came from a speculative 40-yard shot which the Welsh goalkeeper could not control.

Even after two great results, Ireland had no thoughts of the title because England only needed a draw against Scotland. The Scots understood the importance of the match and their goalkeeper and two full-backs all defied their club, Sunderland, by choosing to play for their country.

England took the lead early, with a goal from Woodward, but Doig, McCombie and Watson, the three Sunderland men, stopped them extending their advantage. The second half was the opposite of the first as Scotland applied all the pressure. Goals from Speedie and Walker gave Scotland a 2-1 win and a share of the title with England and Ireland, the first time there had been a three-way tie.

Europe leaves FA in the cold

THE rest of Europe had grown tired of waiting for England to take the lead in the establishment of an international governing body. Robert Guerin, of the Union of French Sports Clubs, summed up their frustration.

After he tried to interest Frederick Wall, the secretary of the FA, in the idea he wrote: "His head in his hands, Mr Wall listened to my story. He said he would report back to his council. I waited a few months. I travelled to London once more and had a meeting with the FA president Lord Kinnaird. However, that, too, was of no avail.

"Tired of the struggle and recognising that the Englishmen, true to tradition, wanted to wait and watch, I undertook to invite delegates myself."

The FA did stir itself into writing a round-robin to several countries in January, suggesting talks about talks. But it was too little too late.

Fifa was born in Paris on May 21. The meeting was timed to coincide with the Congress of Paris, and apart from France there were representatives from Holland and Belgium (both of whom had also had approaches to the FA rebuffed), Switzerland, Denmark, Sweden and Spain.

The FA was finally moved to appoint a committee to review this development, though within days the FA had rejected another invitation, this time to an international tournament to be held over Easter.

England's perennial suspicion of the rest of the world, and Europe's despair at British inertia were to have far-reaching implications for many years to come.

Quinn rewards Maley's gamble with hat-trick

CELTIC put paid to their reputation as the nearly men (twice the runners-up in the League and twice beaten finalists in the Cup in the past three seasons) with a stirring performance against Rangers in the Scottish Cup final.

The first Cup final to be staged at Hampden Park attracted 65,000 spectators to what turned out to be a thrilling game. But, at first, it looked as if Celtic were going to miss out once again as Finlay Speedie gave Rangers a 2-0 lead early in the match.

Willie Maley, the Celtic manager, was far from popular with many of the club's supporters. He had got rid of many of the established players and, instead of buying replacements, had staked his reputation on developing the talent of Celtic's young players.

Jimmy Quinn had struggled to make an impact on the left wing and more than a few eyebrows were raised when Maley chose to play him at centre-forward for the final, particularly because Quinn, at only 5ft 8in, hardly had the build of an out-and-out striker.

But Quinn's bustling style had Celtic back in the match before half-time. His first goal proved he did not lack courage or strength and his second showed that he packed a fearsome shot.

Driven on by Quinn, Celtic threatened to over-run Rangers in the second half. But they had to wait until the last 10 minutes for the winning goal. Quinn's hat-trick justified the faith that Maley had shown in him, and showed that the manager had successfully built a team that was to go on to dominate the rest of the decade.

FOR THE RECORD

■ The International Board ruled that goals could be scored direct from free kicks awarded for intentional fouls. Referees were also given the discretion to play the advantage.

■ David Lindsay scored three penalties and one other goal, all in the second half, as St Mirren came back from 2-1 down to beat Rangers 5-4 in January.

■ Manchester City won the FA Cup managed by Tom Maley, the brother of Willie, the manager of the Scottish Cup winners Celtic.

■ Sheffield Wednesday won the League for the second year running despite only scoring 48 goals, one less than Liverpool who were relegated.

■ Arsenal won promotion, the first southern club to reach the First Division.

■ Manchester United set a record of 14 consecutive victories in the League, but still missed out on promotion by one point.

■ Third Lanark won the Scottish League, the last time the title was won by a club other than Rangers or Celtic until 1932.

■ The FA finally gave up attempts to control financial agreements between clubs and players, agreeing that the rules should be determined by the League. However, the FA did try to impose dress standards, ruling that "footballers' knickers must cover the knee".

Sharpshooter Bloomer leaves the opposing defences stricken

STEVE BLOOMER was the First Division leading scorer for the fifth time, eight years after he had first achieved the feat. The Derby inside-right and captain was a regular member of the England team, for whom he scored 28 times in 23 appearances.

Despite his slender build and anaemic appearance – he was nicknamed "Paleface" – he was always prepared to take on opposing teams, either with surging runs or incisive passes.

His greatest attribute was his determination to shoot on sight,

and he packed an equally powerful shot in either foot, something that was very rare. Bloomer's determination to go

The purpose of play is the scoring of goals
STEVE BLOOMER

for goal brought him a total of 352 goals in a career that lasted 21 seasons and only ended when he was interned in Germany during the war.

Keeping it in the family: Tom Maley's Manchester City won the FA Cup

Foulke adds his weight to the Stamford Bridge speculators

A DECISION to expand the League next season led to the creation of Chelsea in a matter of months. However, the football team was formed as an afterthought by Gus Mears.

Mears and his brother were businessmen who had watched with interest the development of the big stadiums in Glasgow. They wanted to do the same thing in London – create a venue as grand as Hampden Park that attracted money-spinning Cup finals and international matches.

Stamford Bridge, built on the site of the London Athletic Club, had a capacity not far short of 100,000, with 5,000 spectators seated. Its football team, which only signed its first player a month before Chelsea talked its way into the Second Division, also owed much to Scotland.

John Robertson, the manager, was a former Rangers and Scotland international, and he recruited many of his side from north of the border. But his most famous signing was Bill "Fatty" Foulke, the giant Sheffield United goalkeeper.

Despite his enormous girth (he weighed more than 22st) he was adept at saving shots. However, Foulke was remarkably temperamental; he had been known to walk off in the middle of a match if he thought his defence was not trying hard enough, and opposing forwards who tangled with him were likely to be picked up by the scruff of the neck and bodily thrown into the goal.

Foulke: weighed 22st

But Foulke was a great crowd-puller and Chelsea decided to exploit this. They stood two small boys behind the goal to draw attention to Foulke's size and distract opposing forwards. Thus, quite accidentally, ball-boys came into being.

Newcastle ride their luck but take a tumble in the Cup final

IF NEWCASTLE cursed themselves for not being the third side to capture the League and FA Cup Double, they should spare a thought for poor Everton. The Merseyside club finished championship runners-up behind Newcastle by a solitary point. However, they were deprived of two points earlier in the season when fog had caused their match with Arsenal to be abandoned with minutes remaining. Everton had been leading 3-1. When the re-arranged fixture was played Everton lost 2-1.

Newcastle's first Cup final must have been a great disappointment to them. Harry Hampton scored after two minutes when Newcastle failed to clear a cross from Hall. And 14 minutes from time Hampton wrapped the game up when Lawrence, the Newcastle goalkeeper, could only parry Hall's shot into his path. Thus Villa won their fourth Cup in five finals.

Quick strike: Hampton gives Villa the lead after two minutes

Common deal stuns nation

MIDDLESBROUGH'S purchase of Alf Common from Sunderland scandalised the country. They were struggling to avoid relegation from the First Division and had not won an away game for more than two years but, so many people thought, that did not justify them spending the unheard of sum of £1,000 on the England inside-forward.

W C Pickford, who was later to become president of the FA,

fulminated: "It is a painful commentary upon this club's boasted astuteness that it holds the record for transfer fees. This questionable distinction is a truly sensational transaction that is likely to stand unchallenged for some time."

Charles Clegg of Sheffield United was not pleased either. His club had sold Common to Sunderland for a few hundred pounds, and then Common

scored against Sheffield United on his debut to bring Middlesbrough a long-awaited away win.

Clegg was instrumental in the FA passing a rule limiting transfer fees to £350 and fining Middlesbrough for making unauthorised payments to players. But the Middlesbrough fans were not bothered – Common's arrival helped their team to escape relegation by two points.

THE
1905-06
SEASON

FA discover rest of the world

THE FA had belatedly given Fifa its blessing in April the year before and in July a British delegation led by Frederick Wall, the FA secretary, and Daniel Woolfall attended a Fifa conference in Berne. Woolfall was elected as the world body's first president.

Fifa were heartened by England's decision to finally recognise the fledgling world body, but they were also suspicious of their motives. The Scottish and Irish associations were refused membership because it was thought they would merely be puppets of the FA.

Liverpool's winning formula

NEWLY promoted Liverpool won their second League title and became the first club to win promotion to the First Division and the championship in successive seasons.

Tom Watson, their secretary manager, should take much of the credit. He had largely been responsible for moulding the 1901 championship-winning side, in particular the astute signing of the centre-half Alex Raisbeck from Scotland. He used the season in the Second Division to graft new players on to his old team and they romped away with the title, scoring 93 goals and winning 27 of their 34 fixtures.

The key to Watson's and Liverpool's success was the importance they placed on their goalkeeper. To stem the flood of goals Watson had bought the veteran Teddy Doig from Sunderland in 1904. But as they

Up and coming: newly-promoted Liverpool took the title

launched their assault on the League title, Watson felt Doig, in his mid-thirties needed to be replaced.

Amazingly he bought Sam Hardy, the young Chesterfield goalkeeper who had conceded six goals when they had played Liverpool in the Second Division. Hardy was an immediate hit with his new team con-

ceding just 22 goals in 35 games.

Their championship campaign had its hiccups, a string of injuries led to some poor results, but – as in 1901 – Liverpool mounted a late spurt losing only two of their last four games. A 3-1 victory away to Preston North End in March was decisive and Liverpool eventually finishing four points clear of Preston.

Everton prove there are two Merseyside teams

MERSEYSIDE could truly call itself the home of English football when Everton added the FA Cup to Liverpool's League championship success. However Everton's first victory in the Cup final – they had lost in 1893 and 1897 – was not as stirring a match as had been anticipated.

Newcastle, who had lost the final to Aston Villa the year before, never lived up to their reputation at Crystal Palace and their famed midfield of Aitken, Gardner and McWilliam never imposed their authority on

Everton. The only goal was scored in the 75th minute when Jack Sharp crossed to centre-forward Sandy Young.

By contrast, Everton's semi-final victory at Villa Park over Liverpool was a dramatic affair, especially as Liverpool had the Double in their sights. Everton had already lost to their rivals 4-2 at Goodison in the League and were the underdogs. But in a see-saw match where neither side got the upper hand, it was luck that proved decisive.

In the second half Sam Hardy, Liverpool's goalkeeper, was left

First blood: Everton took the FA Cup after two failures

stranded as a tame shot from Abbott was deflected by Dunlop into the net. Before they could compose themselves Liverpool were suddenly 2-0 down

when Hardy could only palm Hardman's shot into the path of Sharp. Instantly Sharp crossed to Hardman and the winger snapped up the chance.

ALF COMMON
The £1,000 transfer that set the ball rolling

Sue Mott

TWO OLD MEN, miners perhaps, are leaning on a bar in Teesside, each nursing a pint of ale. They are animated, incredulous, overawed. Something beyond the scope of their imagination has happened. Public opinion has been gripped like a vice and on this day in 1905, people are talking of little else.

No, it wasn't the uprising in St Petersburg, the return of Sherlock Holmes, the fall of Balfour's Tory government, the first aspirin going on sale nor even Lillie Langtry's 52nd birthday. It was in the realm of sport, but though May Sutton had stunned Wimbledon with a skirt of such brevity it almost showed her knees, though the All Blacks went unbeaten in 27 games on tour in Britain and though President Roosevelt declared American Football too dangerous after 18 deaths on the field … it was something closer to home that captivated the nation.

It was, in fact, the transfer of Alf Common, inside-forward and goalscorer extraordinaire, from Sunderland to Middlesbrough for the ridiculously handsome sum of £1,000.

1947: Tommy Lawton, first £20,000 transfer

"Seemingly, every club has its price. But what a price!" exclaimed the Athletic News on February 20, 1905. It went on to ponder the propriety of paying such an inflated sum (the average transfer fee was a mere £400 at the time) even for an England international forward.

"But fancy a young club like Middlesbrough, with their resources, paying £1,000 for a single player. As a matter of commerce, 10 young recruits at £100 apiece might have paid better, and as a matter of sport the Second Division would be more honourable than retention of place by purchase."

The football world was scandalized at the effrontery of Middlesbrough buying their way out of trouble. They were a mere six years old, having been elected to the League in 1899 and promoted in 1902. They had enjoyed great success in their infancy but by February 1905 they stood second from bottom in the First Division and without an away win in the League for two years.

They tried buying a Stockport striker, known only to posterity as T Green, but a more urgent response was needed. Alf Common, a 13 stone, 5ft 8in goalscoring machine, was summoned to the rescue.

The transfer was vigorously opposed. Many felt that it would presage spiralling inflation in the transfer market with who knows what results. Perhaps one day a player would move for the unthinkable sum of £20,000. (He did – Tommy Lawton from Chelsea to Notts County in 1947). Or £100,000. (He did – Denis Law from Manchester City to Torino in 1961). But even Charles Clegg, the enraged chairman of the Football Association in those far off pre-Titanic days, could never have guessed that one day transfer fees would swell to multi-million pound deals.

He had quite enough to occupy his rage in the contemplation of Common's move. For not only did he strenuously object as chief mandarin of the FA, he had more personal grounds for hurt.

Clegg's own club, Sheffield United, only months before had sold the uncommonly talented Common back to Sunderland when the player declared himself homesick for his native North-East. He had business to attend to, he said. So Common was sold for the relatively modest fee of £375.

Clegg was beside himself to find out that he could have made a monumental profit on the sale and Common made matters considerably worse when he tactlessly scored the goal that beat

United at Bramall Lane in his debut match for Middlesbrough.

Had Common been a modern player, with obligations to smile into the television eye, to squeeze up to the tabloids and to satisfy the demands of his agent, his manager and the fans, he might have found the going harder at Ayresome Park. But he was a tough character.

He is remembered as a talkative humourist, vastly fond of practical jokes and a man well able to absorb whatever pressures his transfer placed upon him. He presented a typically Edwardian face to the camera of the day, all stern features and the ubiquitous moustache. But those that knew him well describe him as possessing a jovial, ruddy face – all the ruddier for his famous exertions to lose weight. Like Gazza, Common found it hard to keep to a fighting weight.

There is no doubt, however, that he saved Middlesbrough from relegation that season. He took over the captaincy from another forward, Joe Cassidy, and went on to play for England again the next season.

1905: Alf Common, first £1,000 transfer

Common: 5ft 8in goalscoring machine

But, for all that, Middlesbrough were to become embroiled in trouble of the type that remains familiar to this day. They had cooked the books. They had cause to regret the ostentation of the Common transfer when the searchlight of an FA commission of inquiry discovered irregular payments to players.

Players were not permitted to receive more than £208 a year in this era. But the inquiry proved that under-the-table bonuses had been paid to players during an FA Cup run in 1904 and the relegation battles of 1905. Whether money changed hands in brown paper bags on the bridleways of Britain was never discussed, but Middlesbrough certainly felt themselves fortunate to escape suspension from the League.

Exposure, censure and a £250 fine were deemed sufficient punishment – quite wrongly as it happened. No sooner had Middlesbrough squirmed off the hook than they embarked on a spending spree and the irregular payments continued unabated.

Despite the wonderful Common in attack, the new manager of the club, Alex Mackie (chosen from 70 applicants) stunned the sport yet again, extracting the legendary Steve Bloomer from Derby County and an England international outside-right by the apt name of Brawn from Aston Villa.

Once again, Middlesbrough had spent their way to safety. Perhaps Common was marginally past his prime by now. For most of his career – beginning at South Hylton Juniors before going on to Jarrow as a 17-year-old, then Sunderland, Sheffield United, Sunderland, Middlesbrough – he had shuttled between centre and inside-forward. In either role, his aggression and power made him a permanent threat.

By the time he moved to Woolwich Arsenal in 1910 Common was 30. The Gunners had yet to reach their prime and had purchased Common (not for a record fee this time) as much for his name as for his talent. His first season with them was wretched.

Relegation, so adroitly avoided by Middlesbrough, soon became a certainty in 1912 as Arsenal finished bottom of the First Division with 18 points from 38 matches, five points behind Notts County who also went down. The Reds were aptly named. Their bank balance was reputed to be £19 and, despite Common's best efforts, they only scored 26 goals all season.

Common, on a personal level, was the very opposite of deflated. His practical jokes continued unabated and Arsenal were forced to devise all sorts of physical tortures to keep down his inflation-prone weight. Road walks were highly esteemed by the Arsenal training staff. Common invariably brought up the rear. He would also return to Plumstead, the seat of Arsenal in those days, every afternoon to wrestle and shadow box.

These latter activities were to prove very useful when, after a brief stop with Preston North End, he took up his second successful career, as a publican. For 11 years he was mine host at the Alma Hotel, Cockerton. He must have made a formidable bouncer.

1979: Trevor Francis, the first British transfer to break the £1m barrier

1992: Gianluigi Lentini moved from Torino to AC Milan for a world record £13m

Celtic sweep past Hibs and Hearts in relentless march to first Double

CELTIC had to battle past the pride of Edinburgh to finally become the first club to achieve the Double of the League and Cup in Scotland.

Hibernian put up a titanic struggle in the semi-finals of the Scottish Cup forcing two 0-0 draws before being demolished 3-0. Then Hearts, Hibs' cross-town rivals, lost by the same score in the final. Celtic's third championship in succession had been won at a canter: they lost only twice, conceded less than a goal a game and finished seven points clear of Dundee.

Celtic had come close to the elusive Double on no fewer than three occasions in the previous 15 years. But the 1907 team should be extremely grateful to the 1899 side. That was the year Rangers seemed to be sweeping all before them as they marched to the championship having won all of their League matches. They only lost one game all season – the Cup final 2-0 to Celtic.

Celtic's previous near-misses		
	League	Cup
1892	runners-up	winners
1893	champions	finalists
1894	champions	finalists

No-hopers Palace defy the doubters

CRYSTAL PALACE'S FA Cup exploits once again demonstrated the quality of the Southern League. Six years earlier Tottenham had shocked their northern counterparts when they became the first non-League club to win the Cup. Palace, languishing near the bottom of the table, proved this was not a flash in the pan. Indeed, their first-round victory was more startling than Tottenham's eventual triumph.

When Palace were drawn against Newcastle at St James's Park nobody gave them the slenderest of chances, and many suggested that the long trek to the north-east was a waste of time and money. Mighty Newcastle had played in the two previous Cup finals, and having lost both of them were determined to make amends. Instead they went down 1-0 in one of the most remarkable upsets.

Palace did not rest on their laurels. In successive rounds they beat Fulham 1-0 after a replay and Brentford 1-0, also in a replay, before holding Everton – the Cup-holders – to a 1-1 draw. Sadly the bubble burst at Goodison and the Southern League minnows succumbed 4-0.

Another scalp: Palace knocked Fulham out in a replay

England's blunder lets Wales in

BILLY MEREDITH, Manchester United's inspirational winger, led Wales to their first Home international championship when Scotland forced a 1-1 draw with England at St James's Park in April.

Wales had earlier beaten Ireland 3-2 in Belfast, Scotland 1-0 at Wrexham, and held England to a 1-1 draw at Craven Cottage, and they hoped their fellow Celts would stop England and give them the outright championship. They need not have worried, an own goal from Bob Crompton – the right back and England captain no less – did the trick, cancelling out Steve Bloomer's strike.

Amateur revolt fails to turn tide of progress

THE London, Middlesex and Surrey associations acrimoniously broke away from the FA and established the Amateur Football Association. The schism was ostensibly about an FA resolution that counties should allow professional clubs to affiliate to their associations. In reality it was a rearguard action by traditionalists against the modernisation of the game.

Their leader was N Lane "Pa" Jackson, the founder of the Corinthians and a man who was utterly opposed to professionalism, innovation or anything that would "taint" the amateur ethos. Indeed, when the penalty kick was introduced in 1891 the public school Old Boys' teams initially refused to accept it.

The split lasted until 1914 and rebounded on the breakaway associations as virtually all the other associations remained loyal to the FA. If anything, in fact, it reinforced the FA's authority. The one lasting damage it did cause was in the public schools, where a number switched to rugby union, which was now seen as the real "amateur" sport.

FOR THE RECORD

■ Woolwich Arsenal, with 11 points from their first seven matches, became the first southern club to lead the First Division. However, as the season progressed they slipped back to finish seventh in table, seven points behind the champions Newcastle, who only dropped one point at home all season.

■ The honour of being the highest-ever placed southern club at the end of the season went to Bristol City. Newly promoted from the Second Division, they finished in second place.

■ Vivian Woodward scored eight times when the England amateur team beat France.

■ Chelsea, in only their second season in the League, won promotion to the First Division. They started the season with a 9-2 victory over Glossop (George Hilsdon scored five of the goals on his debut for the club) and won 18 of their 19 home matches.

■ Arsenal went on a post-season tour of Europe and won seven of the eight games they played in 16 days. They scored nine goals twice, winning 9-1 in Berlin and 9-0 in Budapest.

■ The fee paid to international players by the FA was quadrupled to £4.

■ Numbering players' shirts was suggested, but the idea was rejected.

THE 1907-08 SEASON

Meredith: idiosyncratic

United race past rest of the field

MANCHESTER UNITED impressively won their first League title in only their second season back in the top flight. The team was built around the rock-solid defending of Charlie Roberts, their captain and centre-half. They began the season like a team racing to put out a fire, driven by the goal-scoring genius of Billy Meredith, their Welsh international winger. Meredith was a popular, but idiosyncratic personality: he always played with a toothpick in his mouth. So attached was he to the pick that it was said he took it to bed.

They won 13 of their first 14 games and scored 48 goals – including a 6-1 thrashing of the champions Newcastle at St James's Park. With a virtually unassailable lead and the fire doused, Manchester United understandably eased up, eventually sauntering to the title nine points clear of Aston Villa and Manchester City.

Meredith driving force behind players' union

IN BETWEEN spurring Manchester United to the championship Billy Meredith was merrily forging another team. In the Imperial Hotel in Manchester on December 2 he chaired the inaugural meeting of the Players' Union. More than 500 players, mostly from the Midlands and the North, attended and agreed to make approaches to their southern brethren to form a national union.

Their grievances were the maximum wage, unchanged since it was set in 1900 at £4 a week, and freedom of contract whereby players could not choose their place of work. As the game had become more popular, generating higher attendances and admission charges, the maximum wage had become the norm. The big clubs agreed with the players, but the small clubs always voted them down.

Meredith and five others were elected to draw up a constitution and conduct negotiations with the southern footballers in London. This proved successful and in January 1908 the Players' Union was officially christened in Sheffield. Players flocked to join the union.

However their efforts at militancy came to naught. Despite threats by Manchester United and other well-off clubs to break away and pay better wages, the smaller clubs had their way and the maximum wage stayed. In fact, these threats were counterproductive. The FA insisted that all players' contracts had a loyalty clause and that clubs had no truck with the Players' Union.

The revolt collapsed. A year later the Manchester United players refused to sign the loyalty clause and attempted to organise a strike. That too collapsed.

Newcastle haunted

CRYSTAL PALACE. Two words that will forever haunt Newcastle supporters. For the third time in four years Newcastle had made it to an FA Cup final at Crystal Palace. And once again they were beaten. The odd year they did not progress to the final they were surprisingly knocked out in the first round by a struggling Southern League team: Crystal Palace.

Their opponents, Wolves, were a middling Second Division side who had enjoyed an easy run to the final and were seen as cannon-fodder for the big guns from Tyneside, a team studded with internationals from the Home countries.

But Goliath met his David and Newcastle went down 3-1. Two goals just before the interval, the first from the Reverend Kenneth Hunt, an Oxford Blue, Corinthian and amateur international, in the 40th minute and the second from the centre-forward George Hedley three minutes later were the killing sling-shots.

Jim Howie pulled one back for Newcastle with 17 minutes remaining, but then 12 minutes later Billy Harrison, the Wolves right-winger, popped up to end the contest. And so Wolves became only the second Second Division side since Notts County in 1894 to win the FA Cup.

Newcastle had 90% of the play. But our 10%, plus our dash and directness, was enough for victory

REV KENNETH HUNT

Kings of the Palace: Wolves extended Newcastle's misery

Unsung heroes Olympic champions

THE 1908 Olympics, held in London, was the first to have football as competition proper – in the first three Olympic Games it had only been an exhibition sport. The competition was played in October, after the rest of the Games had finished in July. This meant it was competing with the League programme and, as a result, it received scant coverage in the press.

The England team, led by Tottenham's Vivian Woodward, was composed entirely of amateurs but still proved far too strong for the other entrants.

Only four other countries were represented, Denmark, France, Holland and Sweden, though France fielded two teams. England swept to the final against Denmark, where goals from Chapman and Woodward gave them the tenuous title of world champions.

Whisky fuels Cup final riot

THERE WAS mayhem at the Scottish Cup final replay at Hampden when hundreds of spectators rioted at the end of the match. It was the second time that Rangers and Celtic had finished all-square and most of the players and most of the crowd assumed there would be extra time. However, under the SFA rules extra time was only permissible for the second replay.

As the players finally left the pitch, the 60,000 crowd were furious and many believed the two draws, 2-2 and 1-1, had been stage-managed to bring in additional revenue. Hundreds of spectators poured on to the pitch, tore down the goals, cut up the turf and set fire to the pay-boxes and the stand using whisky as fuel. Action by the police had escalated the situation and when the fire brigade

Replay rumpus: furious fans set the pay-boxes alight

arrived their hoses were cut. More than 100 people, many policeman and fireman, were injured.

The Cup and the players' medals were withheld and both clubs agreed to pay Queen's Park compensation for the damage. The disorder had also

wrecked Celtic's hopes of a third consecutive Double. They had won the championship in a breath-taking finish. Faced with a huge fixture pile-up Celtic were forced to play eight games in 12 days. They won six, drew two and edged out Dundee by a single point.

■ **Manchester United,** last season's League champions, played Queen's Park Rangers, the Southern League champions, in the first ever Charity Shield in September. United won the replay 4-0 after a 1-1 draw. Charity matches were the only exception to the rule introduced last year that a match had to be kicked off by one of the players involved.

■ **Leicester Fosse** lost 12-0 to Nottingham Forest on April 21 and three Nottingham players, West, Hooper and Spouncer, all scored hat-tricks. The First Division's record score was regarded with some suspicion because Leicester were already relegated while Forest needed to win to stay in the First Division. After an investigation by the League the margin of victory was attributed to the fact that most of the Leicester team had spent the night before the match celebrating a player's wedding.

■ **The Football League** ruled that goalkeepers should wear a different coloured jersey to the rest of their team. Scotland followed a year later.

Turnbull repays his captain's faith

ALTHOUGH the two FA Cup finalists, Manchester United and Bristol City, had never played in a final before, both had shown their pedigree in the League. United had won the championship the year before and Bristol City had finished runners-up in 1907.

Bristol City's team revolved around their international centre-half Billy Wedlock, who at 5ft 4½in was the smallest centre-half to play for England. Wedlock was a resilient, no-nonsense defender but with an even temperament, so much so that he was nicknamed "Smiler". In the final at Crystal

Palace Wedlock lived up to his reputation. Unfortunately it seemed the rest of his team were overawed by the occasion.

The only goal of the game was scored by United's Sandy Turnbull in the 22nd minute when he opportunely stabbed the ball into the net after it had rebounded from the crossbar. Manchester United had taken a gamble on playing Turnbull as he was suffering from a bad knee injury. However Charlie Roberts, the United captain, had recommended: "Let him play. He might get a goal, and if he does we can afford to carry him." And so it proved.

Turnbull (front left): hero

Newcastle's crazy year

AT first glance the final First Division table contained no surprises: Newcastle were the champions, seven points clear of Everton having scored 65 goals and conceded 41 in their 38 matches. However their march to the title was not as serene as it appeared.

Against Sunderland they managed to lose 9-1 at home. And against Liverpool at Anfield they let slip a 5-2 half-time lead and eventually lost 6-5. After the Sunderland debacle they won 10 of their next 11 fixtures and had put themselves back on course for their third championship in five years.

THE
1909-10
SEASON

Dundee's marathon run

IT CAN only take five matches to win the Scottish Cup, as Celtic demonstrated as recently as 1908. However, when Dundee began their Cup campaign against little Beith they seemed to have decided they had entered a marathon, not a sprint. By the time Dundee finally got their hands on the trophy for the first time they had slogged their way through a staggering 10 matches.

It took a replay to dispose of Beith. Falkirk and Motherwell were convincingly beaten in the next two rounds. Then came the endurance tests. The semi-final against Hibs was more like a war of attrition with two goalless draws before Dundee prevailed 1-0 in the second replay.

Clyde, Dundee's opponents in the final, had had their own private war with Queen's Park in the third round which stretched into two replays. But when Clyde found themselves 2-0 up with seven minutes left they could hardly have contemplated yet more replays. Goals from John Hunter and Johnny Langland forced the inevitable replay – a goalless draw. At long last the second replay provided a winner: Dundee 2-1.

Veitch vindicated

Success at last: Newcastle eventually triumphed in a replay

TWO YEARS earlier Colin Veitch, the Newcastle captain, had vowed when they lost their third FA Cup final in four years: "Never mind. Our turn will come some day." But if he thought Newcastle were finally about to beat their Crystal Palace jinx he was wrong.

With seven minutes remaining, and trailing 1-0 to a 37th minute goal from Harry Tufnell, it looked as if Second Division Barnsley were going to dash Newcastle's hopes. Then Rutherford popped up to head the equaliser.

The final had been criticised for fierce, relentless tackling and for the proliferation of fouls. The replay at Goodison five days later was much worse.

Mearns, the Barnsley goalkeeper, was laid out early on by Alex Higgins. In the second half Dicky Downs, the Barnsley right-back who was limping from an earlier foul, was kicked in the stomach and had to be taken off for treatment. Clearly Newcastle's desperation to get their hands on the Cup had brought out the worst in them.

Two second-half goals from Albert Shepherd, Newcastle's centre-forward, the second a penalty – the first conceded in a Cup final – ended their drought. But even before the end of the match cries of "Dirty Newcastle" were heard from many of the 60,000 crowd.

■ **Vivian Woodward (above), the Tottenham centre-forward, scored six goals for the England amateur team when they beat Holland 9-1 at Stamford Bridge on December 11. It was the second double hat-trick of his career (he had scored eight goals in the 15-0 defeat of France in 1906), the first time anybody had managed such a feat.**

■ **The recently launched newspaper The Racing and Football Outlook started offering a prize of five guineas a week in a competition to correctly forecast six teams that would win away from home. If the prize was not won it was carried forward to the following week.**

■ **When the draw for the first round of the FA Cup was made both Notts County and Nottingham Forest received home ties. Notts County, desperate for cash, feared that their match against Bradford City would be overshadowed by Nottingham Forest's game against Sheffield United. So Notts County agreed to switch their game to Bradford in exchange for £1,000. But the deal backfired on both clubs; Notts County lost 4-2 and Bradford did not attract a big enough crowd to cover the payment.**

■ **Manchester United moved to Old Trafford on February 19. Their new home was hailed as one of the most modern stadiums in the country.**

■ **Aston Villa equalled the First Division record of 53 points to win their sixth League title. It was the first time they had won the championship in a decade.**

■ **The FA, keen to strengthen its links with the Empire, staged a tour of South Africa.**

Oldham: from ridiculous to sublime

IN ONE of the most dramatic turnarounds ever witnessed, Oldham soared from the depths of mediocrity to the heights of promotion to the First Division.

On Boxing Day Oldham had lost 6-2 to Glossop and were contemplating on a miserable first half of the season in which they had accumulated a mere 17 points from 17 matches. Then, in the New Year, they miraculously transformed themselves, suffering only one defeat as they amassed 36 points from the next 21 games.

The drama of their storm up the table continued to the very last Saturday of the season. Any one of three clubs could go up with Manchester City, who were already assured of promotion. Hull, with 53 points, needed a draw at Oldham, who had 51 points but a superior goal average. Derby, with 52 points and the worst goal average, needed Oldham to beat Hull.

Oldham duly beat Hull 3-0 but Derby's goalless draw at West Bromwich meant all three sides finished with 53 points, so Oldham's superior goal average put them into the First Division for the first time. Much of the credit for Oldham's success lay with the goalscoring feats of James Fay, who notched up 26 in 38 matches.

LEADING TABLES AND RESULTS 1900–1910

LEAGUE TABLES AND RESULTS 1900 –1910

1900-01 | 1901-02 | 1902-03 | 1903-04 | 1904-05

FA CUP

1900-01	1901-02	1902-03	1903-04	1904-05
Tottenham Hotspur 3	Sheffield United 2	Bury 6	Manchester City 1	Aston Villa 2
Sheffield United 1, after 2-2	Southampton 1, after 1-1	Derby County 0	Bolton Wanderers 0	Newcastle United 0

FIRST DIVISION

1900-01
	P	W	D	L	F	A	Pts
Liverpool	34	19	7	8	59	35	45
Sunderland	34	15	13	6	57	26	43
Notts C	34	18	4	12	54	46	40
Nottm F	34	16	7	11	53	36	39
Bury	34	16	7	11	53	37	39
Newcastle	34	14	10	10	42	37	38
Everton	34	16	5	13	55	42	37
Wednesday	34	13	10	11	52	42	36
Blackburn	34	12	9	13	39	47	33
Bolton	34	13	7	14	39	55	33
Man City	34	13	6	15	48	58	32
Derby	34	12	7	15	55	42	31
Wolves	34	9	13	12	39	55	31
Sheff Utd	34	12	7	15	35	52	31
Aston Villa	34	10	10	14	45	51	30
Stoke City	34	11	5	18	46	57	27
Preston	34	9	7	18	49	75	25
West Brom	34	7	8	19	35	62	22

1901-02
	P	W	D	L	F	A	Pts
Sunderland	34	19	6	9	50	35	44
Everton	34	17	7	10	53	35	41
Newcastle	34	14	9	11	48	34	37
Blackburn	34	15	6	13	52	48	36
Nottm F	34	13	9	12	43	43	35
Derby	34	13	9	12	39	41	35
Bury	34	13	8	13	44	38	34
Aston Villa	34	13	8	13	42	40	34
Wednesday	34	13	8	13	48	52	34
Sheff Utd	34	13	7	14	53	48	33
Liverpool	34	10	12	12	42	38	32
Bolton	34	12	8	14	51	56	32
Notts C	34	14	4	16	51	57	32
Wolves	34	13	6	15	46	57	32
Grimsby	34	13	6	15	44	60	32
Stoke City	34	11	9	14	45	55	31
Small Heath	34	11	8	15	47	45	30
Man City	34	11	6	17	42	58	28

1902-03
	P	W	D	L	F	A	Pts
Wednesday	34	19	4	11	54	36	42
Aston Villa	34	19	3	12	61	40	41
Sunderland	34	16	9	9	51	36	41
Sheff Utd	34	17	5	12	58	44	39
Liverpool	34	17	4	13	68	49	38
Stoke City	34	15	7	12	46	38	37
West Brom	34	16	4	14	54	53	36
Bury	34	16	3	15	54	43	35
Derby	34	16	3	15	50	47	35
Nottm F	34	14	7	13	49	47	35
Wolves	34	14	5	15	48	57	33
Everton	34	13	6	15	45	47	32
Middlesbro	34	14	4	16	41	50	32
Newcastle	34	14	4	16	41	51	32
Notts C	34	12	7	15	41	49	31
Blackburn	34	12	5	17	44	63	29
Grimsby	34	8	9	17	43	62	25
Bolton	34	8	3	23	37	73	19

1903-04
	P	W	D	L	F	A	Pts
Wednesday	34	20	7	7	48	28	47
Man City	34	19	6	9	71	45	44
Everton	34	19	5	10	59	32	43
Newcastle	34	18	6	10	58	45	42
Aston Villa	34	17	7	10	70	48	41
Sunderland	34	17	5	12	63	49	39
Sheff Utd	34	15	8	11	62	57	38
Wolves	34	14	8	12	44	66	36
Nottm F	34	11	9	14	57	57	31
Middlesbro	34	9	12	13	46	47	30
Small Heath	34	11	8	15	39	52	30
Bury	34	7	15	12	40	53	29
Notts C	34	12	5	17	37	61	29
Derby	34	9	10	15	58	60	28
Blackburn	34	11	6	17	48	60	28
Stoke City	34	10	7	17	54	57	27
Liverpool	34	9	8	17	49	62	26
West Brom	34	7	10	17	36	60	24

1904-05
	P	W	D	L	F	A	Pts
Newcastle	34	23	2	9	72	33	48
Everton	34	21	5	8	63	28	47
Man City	34	20	6	8	66	37	46
Aston Villa	34	19	4	11	63	43	42
Sunderland	34	16	8	10	60	44	40
Sheff Utd	34	19	2	13	64	56	40
Small Heath	34	17	5	12	54	38	39
Preston	34	13	10	11	42	37	36
Wednesday	34	14	5	15	61	57	33
Arsenal	34	12	9	13	36	40	33
Derby	34	12	8	14	37	48	32
Stoke City	34	13	4	17	40	58	30
Blackburn	34	11	5	18	40	51	27
Wolves	34	11	4	19	47	73	26
Middlesbro	34	9	8	17	36	56	26
Nottm F	34	9	7	18	40	61	25
Bury	34	10	4	20	47	67	24
Notts C	34	5	8	21	36	69	18

SECOND DIVISION

1900-01	1901-02	1902-03	1903-04	1904-05
Champions: Grimsby Town	Champions: West Bromwich Albion	Champions: Manchester City	Champions: Preston North End	Champions: Liverpool
Also promoted: Small Heath	Also promoted: Middlesbrough	Also promoted: Small Heath	Also promoted: Royal Arsenal	Also promoted: Bolton Wanderers

SCOTTISH CUP

1900-01	1901-02	1902-03	1903-04	1904-05
Hearts 4	Hibernian 1	Rangers 2	Celtic 3	Third Lanark 3
Celtic 3	Celtic 0	Hearts 0, after 1-1 and 0-0	Rangers 2	Rangers 1, after 0-0

SCOTTISH FIRST DIVISION

1900-01
	P	W	D	L	F	A	Pts
Rangers	20	17	1	2	60	25	35
Celtic	20	13	3	4	49	28	29
Hibernian	20	9	7	4	29	22	25
Morton	20	9	3	8	40	40	21
Kilmarnock	20	7	4	9	35	47	18
T Lanark	20	6	6	8	20	29	18
Dundee	20	6	5	9	36	35	17
Queen's P	20	7	3	10	33	37	17
St Mirren	20	5	6	9	33	43	16
Hearts	20	5	4	11	22	30	14
Partick	20	4	2	14	28	49	10

1901-02
	P	W	D	L	F	A	Pts
Rangers	18	13	2	3	43	29	28
Celtic	18	11	4	3	38	28	26
Hearts	18	10	2	6	32	21	22
T Lanark	18	7	5	6	30	26	19
St Mirren	18	8	3	7	29	28	19
Hibernian	18	6	4	8	36	24	16
Kilmarnock	18	5	6	7	21	25	16
Queen's P	18	5	4	9	21	32	14
Dundee	18	4	5	9	16	31	13
Morton	18	1	5	12	18	40	7

1902-03
	P	W	D	L	F	A	Pts
Hibernian	22	16	5	1	48	18	37
Dundee	22	13	5	4	31	12	31
Rangers	22	12	5	5	56	30	29
Hearts	22	11	6	5	46	27	28
Celtic	22	8	10	4	36	30	26
St Mirren	22	7	8	7	39	40	22
T Lanark	22	8	5	9	34	27	21
Partick	22	6	7	9	34	50	19
Kilmarnock	22	6	4	12	24	43	16
Queen's P	22	5	5	12	33	48	15
P Glasgow	22	3	5	14	26	49	11
Morton	22	2	5	15	22	55	9

1903-04
	P	W	D	L	F	A	Pts
T Lanark	26	20	3	3	61	26	43
Hearts	26	18	3	5	62	34	39
Celtic	26	18	2	6	68	27	38
Rangers	26	16	6	4	80	33	38
Dundee	26	13	2	11	54	45	28
St Mirren	26	11	5	10	45	38	27
Partick	26	10	7	9	46	41	27
Queen's P	26	6	9	11	28	47	21
P Glasgow	26	8	4	14	32	49	20
Hibernian	26	7	5	14	29	40	19
Morton	26	7	4	15	32	53	18
Airdrie	26	7	4	15	32	62	18
Motherwell	26	6	3	17	26	61	15
Kilmarnock	26	4	5	17	24	63	13

1904-05
	P	W	D	L	F	A	Pts
Celtic	26	18	5	3	68	31	41
Rangers	26	19	3	4	83	28	41
T Lanark	26	14	7	5	60	28	35
Airdrie	26	11	5	10	38	45	27
Hibernian	26	9	8	9	39	39	26
Partick	26	12	2	12	36	56	26
Dundee	26	10	5	11	38	32	25
Hearts	26	11	3	12	46	44	25
Kilmarnock	26	9	5	12	29	45	23
St Mirren	26	9	4	13	33	36	22
P Glasgow	26	8	5	13	30	51	21
Queen's P	26	6	8	12	28	45	20
Morton	26	7	4	15	27	50	18
Motherwell	26	6	2	18	28	53	14

SCOTTISH SECOND DIVISION

1900-01	1901-02	1902-03	1903-04	1904-05
Champions (not promoted): St Bernard's	Champions: Port Glasgow Athletic	Champions: Airdrie	Champions (not promoted): Hamilton Academical	Champions (not promoted): Clyde
Runners-up (not promoted): Airdrie	Also elected to First Division: Partick Thistle	Also elected to First Division: Motherwell	Runners-up (not promoted): Clyde	Falkirk (runners-up) and Aberdeen (seventh) elected to the First Division

---

FOR THE RECORD: WINNERS 1872-1900

1872 FA CUP: Wanderers 1
Royal Engineers 0

1873 FA CUP: Wanderers 2
Oxford University 0

1874 FA CUP: Oxford University 2
Royal Engineers 0
SCOTTISH CUP: Queen's Park 2
Clydesdale 0

1875 FA CUP: Royal Engineers 2
Old Etonians 0 (after 1-1)
SCOTTISH CUP: Queen's Park 3
Renton 0

1876 FA CUP: Wanderers 3
Old Etonians 0 (after 1-1)
SCOTTISH CUP: Queen's Park 2
Third Lanark 0 (after 1-1)

1877 FA CUP: Wanderers 2
Oxford University 1
SCOTTISH CUP: Vale of Leven 3
Rangers 2 (after 0-0 and 1-1)

1878 FA CUP: Wanderers 3
Royal Engineers 1
SCOTTISH CUP: Vale of Leven 1
Third Lanark 0

1879 FA CUP: Old Etonians 1
Clapham 0
SCOTTISH CUP: Vale of Leven awarded the Cup when Rangers refused to play a replay after a 1-1 draw

1880 FA CUP: Clapham 1
Oxford University 0
SCOTTISH CUP: Queen's Park 3
Thornlibank 0

1881 FA CUP: Old Carthusians 3
Old Etonians 0
SCOTTISH CUP: Queen's Park 3
Dumbarton 1 (after a protest, Queen's Park won the first match 2-1)

1882 FA CUP: Old Etonians 1
Blackburn Rovers 0
SCOTTISH CUP: Queen's Park 4
Dumbarton 1 (after 2-2)

1883 FA CUP: Blackburn Olympic 2
Old Etonians 1
SCOTTISH CUP: Dumbarton 2
Vale of Leven 1 (after 2-2)

1884 FA CUP: Blackburn Rovers 2
Queen's Park 1
SCOTTISH CUP: Queen's Park awarded the Cup when Vale of Leven scratched

1885 FA CUP: Blackburn Rovers 2
Queen's Park 0
SCOTTISH CUP: Renton 3
Vale of Leven 1 (after 0-0)

1886 FA CUP: Blackburn Rovers 2
West Brom 0 (after 0-0)
SCOTTISH CUP: Queen's Park 3
Renton 1

1887 FA CUP: Aston Villa 2
West Brom 0
SCOTTISH CUP: Hibernian 2
Dumbarton 1

1888 FA CUP: West Brom 2 Preston 1
SCOTTISH CUP: Renton 6
Cambuslang 1

1889 FA CUP: Preston 3
Wolverhampton 0
FOOTBALL LEAGUE: Preston
SCOTTISH CUP: Third Lanark 2 Celtic 1
(replayed because weather affected the first match, which Third Lanark won 3-0)

1890 FA CUP: Blackburn Rovers 6
The Wednesday 1
FOOTBALL LEAGUE: Preston
SCOTTISH CUP: Queen's Park 2
Vale of Leven 1 (after 1-1)

1905-06 · 1906-07 · 1907-08 · 1908-09 · 1909-10

1905-06

FA CUP: Everton 1 / Newcastle United 0

FIRST DIVISION

	P	W	D	L	F	A	Pts
Liverpool	38	23	5	10	79	46	51
Preston	38	17	13	8	54	39	47
Wednesday	38	18	8	12	63	52	44
Newcastle	38	18	7	13	74	48	43
Man City	38	19	5	14	73	54	43
Bolton	38	17	7	14	81	67	41
Birmingham	38	17	7	14	65	59	41
Aston Villa	38	17	6	15	72	56	40
Blackburn	38	16	8	14	54	52	40
Stoke City	38	16	7	15	54	55	39
Everton	38	15	7	16	70	66	37
Arsenal	38	15	7	16	62	64	37
Sheff Utd	38	15	6	17	57	62	36
Sunderland	38	15	5	18	61	70	35
Derby	38	14	7	17	39	58	35
Notts C	38	11	12	15	55	71	34
Bury	38	11	10	17	57	74	32
Middlesbro	38	10	11	17	56	71	31
Nottm F	38	13	5	20	58	79	31
Wolves	38	8	7	23	58	99	23

SECOND DIVISION: Champions: Bristol City / Also promoted: Manchester United

SCOTTISH CUP: Hearts 1 / Third Lanark 0

SCOTTISH FIRST DIVISION

	P	W	D	L	F	A	Pts
Celtic	30	24	1	5	76	19	49
Hearts	30	18	7	5	64	27	43
Airdrie	30	15	8	7	53	31	38
Rangers	30	15	7	8	58	48	37
Partick	30	15	6	9	44	40	36
T Lanark	30	16	2	12	62	39	34
Dundee	30	11	12	7	40	33	34
St Mirren	30	13	5	12	41	37	31
Motherwell	30	9	8	13	50	62	26
Morton	30	10	6	14	35	54	26
Hibernian	30	10	5	15	35	40	25
Aberdeen	30	8	8	14	36	48	24
Falkirk	30	9	5	16	52	68	23
Kilmarnock	30	8	4	18	46	68	20
P Glasgow	30	6	8	16	38	68	20
Queen's P	30	5	4	21	39	87	14

SCOTTISH SECOND DIVISION: Champions (not promoted): Leith Athletic / Clyde (runners-up) and Hamilton (fourth) elected to the First Division

1906-07

FA CUP: The Wednesday 2 / Everton 1

FIRST DIVISION

	P	W	D	L	F	A	Pts
Newcastle	38	22	7	9	74	46	51
Bristol C	38	20	8	10	66	47	48
Everton	38	20	5	13	70	46	45
Sheff Utd	38	17	11	10	57	55	45
Aston Villa	38	19	6	13	78	52	44
Bolton	38	18	8	12	59	47	44
Arsenal	38	20	4	14	66	59	44
Man Utd	38	17	8	13	53	56	42
Birmingham	38	15	8	15	52	52	38
Sunderland	38	14	9	15	65	66	37
Middlesbro	38	17	6	17	56	63	36
Blackburn	38	14	7	17	56	59	35
Wednesday	38	12	11	15	49	60	35
Preston	38	14	7	17	44	57	35
Liverpool	38	13	7	18	64	65	33
Bury	38	13	6	19	58	68	32
Man City	38	10	12	16	53	77	32
Notts C	38	8	15	15	46	50	31
Derby	38	9	9	20	41	59	27
Stoke City	38	8	10	20	41	64	26

SECOND DIVISION: Champions: Nottingham Forest / Also promoted: Chelsea

SCOTTISH CUP: Celtic 3 / Hearts 0

SCOTTISH FIRST DIVISION

	P	W	D	L	F	A	Pts
Celtic	34	23	9	2	80	30	55
Dundee	34	18	12	4	53	26	48
Rangers	34	19	7	8	69	33	45
Airdrie	34	18	6	10	59	44	42
Falkirk	34	17	7	10	73	58	41
T Lanark	34	15	9	10	57	48	39
St Mirren	34	12	13	9	50	44	37
Clyde	34	15	6	13	47	52	36
Hearts	34	11	13	10	47	43	35
Motherwell	34	12	9	13	45	49	33
Aberdeen	34	10	10	14	48	55	30
Hibernian	34	10	10	14	40	49	30
Morton	34	11	6	17	41	50	28
Partick	34	9	8	17	40	60	26
Queen's P	34	9	6	19	51	66	24
Hamilton	34	8	5	21	40	64	21
Kilmarnock	34	8	5	21	40	72	21
P Glasgow	34	7	7	20	30	67	21

SCOTTISH SECOND DIVISION: Champions (not promoted): St Bernard's / Runners-up (not promoted): Vale of Leven

1907-08

FA CUP: Wolverhampton Wanderers 3 / Newcastle United 1

FIRST DIVISION

	P	W	D	L	F	A	Pts
Man Utd	38	23	6	9	81	48	52
Aston Villa	38	17	9	12	77	59	43
Man City	38	16	11	11	62	54	43
Newcastle	38	15	12	11	65	54	42
Wednesday	38	19	4	15	73	64	42
Middlesbro	38	17	7	14	54	45	41
Bury	38	14	11	13	58	61	39
Liverpool	38	16	6	16	68	61	38
Nottm F	38	13	11	14	59	62	37
Bristol C	38	12	12	14	58	61	36
Everton	38	15	6	17	58	64	36
Preston	38	12	12	14	47	53	36
Chelsea	38	14	8	16	53	62	36
Blackburn	38	12	12	14	51	63	36
Arsenal	38	12	12	14	51	63	36
Sunderland	38	16	3	19	78	75	35
Sheff Utd	38	12	11	15	52	58	35
Notts C	38	13	8	17	39	51	34
Bolton	38	14	5	19	52	58	33
Birmingham	38	9	12	17	40	60	30

SECOND DIVISION: Champions: Bradford City / Also promoted: Leicester Fosse

SCOTTISH CUP: Celtic 5 / St Mirren 1

SCOTTISH FIRST DIVISION

	P	W	D	L	F	A	Pts
Celtic	34	24	7	3	86	27	55
Falkirk	34	22	7	5	102	40	51
Rangers	34	21	8	5	74	40	50
Dundee	34	20	8	6	70	27	48
Hibernian	34	17	8	9	55	42	42
Airdrie	34	18	5	11	58	41	41
St Mirren	34	13	10	11	50	59	36
Aberdeen	34	13	9	12	45	44	35
T Lanark	34	13	7	14	45	50	33
Motherwell	34	12	7	15	61	53	31
Hamilton	34	10	8	16	54	65	28
Hearts	34	11	6	17	55	62	28
Morton	34	9	9	16	43	66	27
Kilmarnock	34	6	13	15	38	61	25
Partick	34	8	9	17	43	69	25
Queen's P	34	9	6	19	51	66	24
Clyde	34	5	8	21	36	75	18
P Glasgow	34	5	7	22	39	98	17

SCOTTISH SECOND DIVISION: Champions (not promoted): Raith Rovers / Runners-up (not promoted): Dumbarton

1908-09

FA CUP: Manchester United 1 / Bristol City 0

FIRST DIVISION

	P	W	D	L	F	A	Pts
Newcastle	38	24	5	9	65	41	53
Everton	38	18	10	10	82	57	46
Sunderland	38	21	2	15	78	63	44
Blackburn	38	14	13	11	61	50	41
Wednesday	38	17	6	15	67	61	40
Arsenal	38	14	10	14	52	49	38
Aston Villa	38	14	10	14	58	56	38
Bristol C	38	13	12	13	45	58	38
Middlesbro	38	14	9	15	59	53	37
Preston	38	13	11	14	48	44	37
Chelsea	38	14	9	15	56	61	37
Sheff Utd	38	14	9	15	51	59	37
Man Utd	38	15	7	16	58	68	37
Nottm F	38	14	8	16	66	57	36
Notts C	38	14	8	16	51	48	36
Liverpool	38	15	6	17	57	65	36
Bury	38	14	8	16	63	77	34
Bradford C	38	12	10	16	47	47	34
Man City	38	15	4	19	67	69	34
Leicester F	38	8	9	21	54	102	25

SECOND DIVISION: Champions: Bolton Wanderers / Also promoted: Tottenham Hotspur

SCOTTISH CUP: Cup withheld after a riot, following 1-1 and 2-2

SCOTTISH FIRST DIVISION

	P	W	D	L	F	A	Pts
Celtic	34	23	5	6	71	24	51
Dundee	34	22	6	6	70	32	50
Clyde	34	21	6	7	61	37	48
Rangers	34	19	7	8	91	38	45
Airdrie	34	16	9	9	67	46	41
Hibernian	34	16	7	11	40	32	39
St Mirren	34	15	6	13	53	45	36
Aberdeen	34	15	6	13	61	53	36
Falkirk	34	13	7	14	58	56	33
Kilmarnock	34	13	7	14	47	61	33
T Lanark	34	11	10	13	56	49	32
P Glasgow	34	10	8	16	39	52	28
Motherwell	34	11	6	17	47	73	28
Queen's P	34	6	13	15	42	65	25
Hamilton	34	6	12	16	42	72	24
Morton	34	8	7	19	39	90	23
Partick	34	2	4	28	38	102	8

SCOTTISH SECOND DIVISION: Champions (not promoted): Abercorn / Runners-up (not promoted): Raith

1909-10

FA CUP: Newcastle United 2 / Barnsley 0, after 1-1

FIRST DIVISION

	P	W	D	L	F	A	Pts
Aston Villa	38	23	7	8	84	42	53
Liverpool	38	21	6	11	78	57	48
Blackburn	38	18	9	11	73	55	45
Newcastle	38	19	7	12	70	56	45
Man Utd	38	19	7	12	69	61	45
Sheff Utd	38	16	10	12	62	41	42
Bradford C	38	17	8	13	64	47	42
Sunderland	38	18	5	15	66	51	41
Notts C	38	15	10	13	67	59	40
Everton	38	16	8	14	51	56	40
Wednesday	38	15	9	14	60	63	39
Preston	38	15	5	18	52	58	35
Bury	38	12	9	17	62	66	33
Nottm F	38	11	11	16	54	72	33
Tottenham	38	11	10	17	53	69	32
Bristol C	38	12	8	18	45	60	32
Middlesbro	38	11	9	18	56	73	31
Arsenal	38	11	9	18	37	67	31
Chelsea	38	11	7	20	47	70	29
Bolton	38	9	6	23	44	71	24

SECOND DIVISION: Champions: Manchester City / Also promoted: Oldham Athletic

SCOTTISH CUP: Dundee 2 / Clyde 1, after 2-2 and 0-0

SCOTTISH FIRST DIVISION

	P	W	D	L	F	A	Pts
Celtic	34	24	6	4	63	22	54
Falkirk	34	22	8	4	71	28	52
Rangers	34	20	6	8	70	35	46
Aberdeen	34	16	8	10	44	29	40
Clyde	34	14	9	11	47	40	37
Dundee	34	14	8	12	52	44	36
T Lanark	34	13	8	13	62	44	34
Hibernian	34	14	6	14	33	40	34
Airdrie	34	12	9	13	46	57	33
Motherwell	34	12	8	14	59	60	32
Kilmarnock	34	12	8	14	53	60	32
Hearts	34	12	7	15	59	50	31
St Mirren	34	13	5	16	49	58	31
Queen's P	34	12	6	16	54	74	30
Hamilton	34	11	6	17	50	67	28
Partick	34	8	10	16	47	59	26
Morton	34	11	3	20	38	60	25
P Glasgow	34	3	5	26	25	95	11

SCOTTISH SECOND DIVISION: Champions (not promoted): Leith Athletic / Runners-up (elected to First Division): Raith Rovers

---

FOR THE RECORD: WINNERS 1872-1900

1891 FA CUP: Blackburn Rovers 3 Notts County 1
FOOTBALL LEAGUE: Everton
SCOTTISH CUP: Hearts 1 Dumbarton 0
SCOTTISH FIRST DIVISION: Dumbarton

1892 FA CUP: West Brom 3 Aston Villa 0
FOOTBALL LEAGUE: Sunderland
SCOTTISH CUP: Celtic 5 Queen's Park 1 (after both sides protested about the first match, which Celtic won 1-0).
SCOTTISH FIRST DIVISION: Dumbarton

1893 FA CUP: Wolverhampton 1 Everton 0
FIRST DIVISION: Sunderland
SECOND DIVISION: Small Heath

SCOTTISH CUP: Queen's Park 2 Celtic 1
SCOTTISH FIRST DIVISION: Celtic

1894 FA CUP: Notts County 4 Bolton 1
FIRST DIVISION: Aston Villa
SECOND DIVISION: Liverpool
SCOTTISH CUP: Rangers 3 Celtic 1
SCOTTISH FIRST DIVISION: Celtic
SCOTTISH SECOND DIVISION: Hibernian

1895 FA CUP: Aston Villa 1 West Brom 0
FIRST DIVISION: Sunderland
SECOND DIVISION: Bury
SCOTTISH CUP: St Bernard's 2 Renton 1
SCOTTISH FIRST DIVISION: Hearts
SCOTTISH SECOND DIVISION: Hibernian

1896 FA CUP: The Wednesday 2 Wolverhampton 1
FIRST DIVISION: Aston Villa
SECOND DIVISION: Liverpool
SCOTTISH CUP: Hearts 3 Hibs 1
SCOTTISH FIRST DIVISION: Celtic
SCOTTISH SECOND DIVISION: Abercorn

1897 FA CUP: Aston Villa 3 Everton 2
FIRST DIVISION: Aston Villa
SECOND DIVISION: Notts County
SCOTTISH CUP: Rangers 5 Dumbarton 1
SCOTTISH FIRST DIVISION: Hearts
SCOTTISH SECOND DIVISION: Partick

1898 FA CUP: Nottingham Forest 3 Derby 1
FIRST DIVISION: Sheffield United
SECOND DIVISION: Burnley

SCOTTISH CUP: Rangers 2 Kilmarnock 0
SCOTTISH FIRST DIVISION: Celtic
SCOTTISH SECOND DIVISION: Kilmarnock

1899 FA CUP: Sheffield United 4 Derby 1
FIRST DIVISION: Aston Villa
SECOND DIVISION: Manchester City
SCOTTISH CUP: Celtic 2 Rangers 0
SCOTTISH FIRST DIVISION: Rangers
SCOTTISH SECOND DIVISION: Kilmarnock

1900 FA CUP: Bury 4 Southampton 0
FIRST DIVISION: Aston Villa
SECOND DIVISION: The Wednesday
SCOTTISH CUP: Celtic 4 Queen's Park 3
SCOTTISH FIRST DIVISION: Rangers
SCOTTISH SECOND DIVISION: Partick

THE
1910-11
SEASON

Palace jinx still plagues Newcastle

THAT Crystal Palace jinx just would not lie down. For the fifth time in seven years Newcastle had battled through to an FA Cup final at Crystal Palace and for the fifth time they failed to win. The only blot on the famous ground's record of dashing Newcastle's aspirations was the previous year when Newcastle had won a bruising replay at Goodison. This year they could not even do that.

The match at Crystal Palace was a dire, dismal affair. Newcastle laboured in attack and sorely missed Albert Shepherd, whose two goals had brought them the Cup a year ago. Bradford City's two giant full-backs, Campbell and Taylor, easily blunted the ultra-cautious Newcastle forwards. Significantly, Bradford, appearing in their first final, were neither overawed by the occasion or the reputation of their illustrious opponents.

The story was much the same in the replay at Old Trafford four days later, except that Bradford strengthened their defence with Torrance as their centre-half. Campbell and Taylor continued in much the same vein as the first match and Newcastle simply could not rise to the occasion, even after Bradford had gone ahead in the 15th minute.

A bad mistake by Lawrence, Newcastle's goalkeeper in all five of their Cup final appearances, let in Jimmy Spiers to to take a simple goal and once again Newcastle went away empty-handed and Bradford had captured their first trophy.

United snatch title from careless Villa

ASTON VILLA, the defending champions, had only themselves to blame as Manchester United came through on the rails on the last Saturday of the season to clinch their second League title. Villa seemed to have done the hard work the week before when an ill-tempered 4-2 defeat of Manchester United at Villa Park pushed them into pole position on goal average. But then in two disastrous games the League title slipped out of their hands.

On the Monday Villa could only draw at Blackburn, leaving them needing a victory at Anfield while Manchester United needed a resounding win over third-placed Sunderland at Old Trafford. United romped to a 5-1 victory as Villa crashed 3-1, so United were champions by a single point.

The team that had won the title three years earlier was still largely intact with Charlie Roberts and Billy Meredith still pulling the strings. The most significant change had been the acquisition of Enoch "Knocker" West, a consistent striker whose 19 goals were the foundation for their championship success. West was an engaging player, a bundle of energy and the perfect foil for Meredith.

New Cup goes straight back home to Bradford

NEWCASTLE never stood a chance. The FA Cup they were playing for was a new one, the third to have been commissioned. It was the handiwork of Messrs Fattorini & Sons, a Bradford silversmiths.

The FA received a large number of offers to produce the new trophy and they chose to break with tradition. Fattorini's design was much more striking than the others — an urn 19 inches high standing on a plinth. The total cost was 50 guineas, and 175oz of silver were used.

The second FA Cup had been almost identical to the first one and had, in fact, been modelled on the original design. When the first trophy was stolen in 1895 the replacement had been modelled on replicas presented by Wolverhampton to their victorious players in 1893.

The FA changed the design for the new Cup because the original had been pirated. They had not claimed copyright – an oversight they rectified with the latest design. The second trophy was presented to Lord Kinnaird to mark his 21st year as the FA president.

Made in Bradford: the winning team and the new trophy

■ James Gordon (above) made his debut for Rangers. During the course of his 20-year career with the club he played in every position, including in goal.

■ After non-League Northampton Town had held First Division Newcastle to a 1-1 draw in the second round of the FA Cup they sold their right to stage the replay. The second match was also staged at St James's Park. Newcastle won 1-0 but Northampton went home £900 richer.

■ Celtic's six-year stranglehold on the League title was comprehensively broken. They could only finish in fifth place as Rangers beat Aberdeen to the championship by four points. Celtic's only consolation was a 2-1 defeat of Hamilton in the Scottish Cup final replay.

■ Bradford City fielded a record eight Scotsmen in their team for the FA Cup final against Newcastle, who had four themselves. The attendance for the replay, 66,646, was also a record for a midweek match.

■ The FA abolished its maximum-wage rule, but the League changed its regulation to stop clubs paying players more than £208 a year without special permission. The League also introduced talent and place money for the clubs finishing in the top places in each Division.

■ The amount of money on offer from the competitions that were the forerunners of the pools rose dramatically when The Umpire magazine offered a first prize of £300 for correctly predicting the scores of six matches.

■ Cardiff City were the first club from the south of Wales to win the Welsh Cup in the history of the competition.

Players' union loses with a legal own goal

SINCE being formed in 1907, the players' union had been slowly growing in size and influence but had been unable to make any dent in the retain and transfer system.

Unfortunately when they took the test case of Kingaby and his dispute with Aston Villa to the King's Bench division the judge ruled in favour of the club. On the face of it Kingaby had a strong case: Villa had posted a ludicrously high sum for his transfer and effectively kept him out of the game for two years.

The union's lawyers based their case on Villa's motives, accusing them of malice, rather than the system itself. The defeat was a political setback for the union as they had now enshrined the transfer system in law.

Gritty Barnsley win the war

BATTLING BARNSLEY became the third Second Division club to win the FA Cup when they eventually wore down West Bromwich Albion in extra time in the replay at Bramall Lane. It was yet another typical, gritty performance from a Yorkshire club that had slogged through 10 Cup ties to reach the final.

En route to Crystal Palace Barnsley only conceded three goals and participated in five goalless draws, three of which were with the holders Bradford. As expected, the Cup final was a goalless draw as Barnsley's immaculate defence snuffed out West Brom's attacking forays

and for the third year in succession a replay was necessary.

At Bramall Lane four days later the replay carried on where the first match ended, with Barnsley yet again smothering Albion's attacks. With two minutes of extra time remaining the stalemate was broken.

As West Brom pressed forward in profuse numbers, Utley broke up an attack and found Harry Tufnell unmarked on the half-way line. The striker made a bee-line for goal with only Jesse Pennington and the goalkeeper to beat. As Tufnell swerved past Pennington the defender, always a gentleman,

disdained the "professional" foul and the Barnsley forward ran on to score a glorious goal.

The epic saga of the final was notable for two rule changes that followed. First, Cup finals were to play extra time from the 1913 season. Second, a player wishing to return to the field of play had to have the referee's permission.

The latter alteration came about because Glendinning, a Barnsley midfielder, was having treatment for a foot injury on the touchline when he suddenly dashed on to the pitch wearing only one boot and whacked the ball away from his goalmouth.

Long and winding road: Barnsley had to play 10 matches to reach the FA Cup final

FOR THE RECORD

■ The laws of the game were changed so that goalkeepers could only handle the ball in their penalty area. The change was prompted by a match in 1910, when both the Third Lanark and Motherwell goalkeepers took advantage of being able to handle the ball anywhere on the pitch to both score a goal. This was the only time in first-class football that both goalkeepers had scored in the same match.

■ An agreement between the Football Association and the Football League in December defined more clearly the two organisations' powers. The FA had authority over the laws of the game and Cup competitions, while the League was responsible for the financial affairs and conduct of the First and Second Division clubs.

■ Tottenham won their League match at Liverpool 2-1 and did not win again at Anfield until 1985.

■ Blackburn won the League for the first time in their history, but their total of 46 points was the lowest since the First Division was expanded to 20 teams.

■ Both Rangers and Celtic retained the trophies they had won the previous season. Rangers won the League by six points from Celtic, and Celtic beat Clyde 2-0 in the Cup final.

■ Derby County suggested promoting and relegating four clubs rather than two, but the idea was rejected.

Woodward and England waltz through Olympics

IN STOCKHOLM England comfortably retained the Olympic football title they had won four years earlier. Once again their opponents in the final were Denmark, who were beaten 4-2, and again Vivian Woodward was to prove an inspirational

leader of the amateur side as they waltzed to the final without conceding a goal.

In their semi-final against Finland, the England team chose to demonstrate their notion of fair play by ostentatiously lofting a penalty they considered too

severe handsomely over the bar.

The Swedish hosts had initially been reluctant to include football, doubting its worldwide popularity. The fact that there were only 11 entries, all from Europe, confirmed their reservations. To compensate the

seven teams eliminated in the first and second rounds a consolation tournament was organised which Hungary won. Germany's Gottfried Fuchs set a scoring record against Czarist Russia when he scored 10 of his country's 16 goals.

Villa enjoy dream final

ASTON VILLA swaggered into their sixth final while Sunderland had to battle to reach their first. But for the first time the two teams at the top of the First Division contested the final and the nation was agog. A world record attendance of 120,081 watched on April 19.

Villa had an edge: Clem Stephenson, their inside left, already knew the result and he told Sunderland's Charlie Buchan early on as they were waiting for a throw-in. "1-0. Dreamt it last night. Tommy Barber with a header."

When Clem Stephenson was brought down by Charlie Gladwin and only the second penalty in a Cup final was awarded, the result looked right but the scorer wrong as Villa's Charlie Wallace stepped up to take the kick. Wallace, the only Sunderland-born player on the pitch, unbelievably sliced the ball 10 yards wide. Such was the shock that Jackie Mordue, Sunderland's penalty-taker remonstrated with the disconsolate Wallace. At half-time he locked himself in the toilet.

In the second half the pendulum swung Sunderland's way when Sam Hardy, the Villa goalkeeper, left the field for 10 minutes to receive treatment. Despite twice hitting the woodwork Sunderland were unable to seize their opportunity.

Then with 15 minutes left came the dream ending. Wallace fired a corner from the right to the edge of the penalty area and there was right-half Barber, who had suddenly advanced from midfield, to meet it with his head. 1-0. Sunderland's dreams of a Double were in tatters.

Honours even in an epic duel

World record crowd: 120,000 people jammed into Crystal Palace for the eagerly-anticipated FA Cup final

Sunderland capture impossible title

IF AFTER Sunderland's first seven League fixtures anybody had predicted they would win the title with a record number of points they would have promptly been locked up. Sunderland had lost five of those games and drawn two, they had two points and had conceded 18 goals. Relegation beckoned.

However after two raids into the transfer market in October they were a completely different team. Joe Butler, a goalkeeper, was bought from Glossop and Charlie Gladwin, a full-back, from Blackpool. With the defence now sorted the rest of the team could play. And they did. Five quick victories put them back on course for the League championship.

Sunderland's great strengths lay in their "Terrible Trio" of Jackie Mordue and Charlie Buchan on the right wing with Frank Cuggy at right-half; it was a triangular combination that truly was the terror of the land. George Holley, at inside-left, a robust, clever and grafting forward perfectly complemented them as other First Division sides began to discover.

Aston Villa were beaten 3-1 and Liverpool 7-0, Buchan helping himself to five goals. Since their disastrous start to the season Sunderland had only lost three times. Then after Christmas they lost only once more in their final 17 matches.

But their most difficult task was to pick themselves up four days after their Cup final defeat and go to Villa Park to bolster their championship hopes and end Villa's thoughts of a Double. Bravely, young Walter Tinsley who had been picked for the Cup final to replace the injured Holley but had cried off because of stage fright, played the game of his life. His goal earned a 1-1 draw and put Sunderland in the championship driving seat. Three days later Sunderland beat Bolton 3-1 to land a title that had seemed impossible in October.

FOR THE RECORD

■ In order to favour attacking play the FA decided that the distance an opposing player had to retreat from a free kick would be increased from six yards to ten.

■ Ireland beat England for the first time with a heroic comeback in Belfast. England led 1-0 when Ireland were reduced to 10 men by an injury to one of their forwards. But two goals from Billy Gillespie lifted them to an historic victory.

■ Rangers completed a hat-trick of Scottish championships but neither they nor Celtic reached the final of the Cup, only the second time this had happened. Neither of the two finalists, Falkirk, who won 2-0, or Raith Rovers, had been in a Cup final before.

■ Every player to appear for Morton in the Scottish First Division scored at least once, including their goalkeeper, who successfully took a penalty.

■ A Bill to ban cash betting on football matches was introduced in the House of Commons, but did not become law until 1920.

■ Dumbarton were elected to the Scottish First Division, despite only finishing sixth in the Second Division.

■ Fifa were granted two representatives on the International Board, and Ireland also became a member.

THE 1913-14 SEASON

Ireland win the Home championship the hard way — with a mere 10 men

IT SHOULD not have been a surprise that Ireland at last won the Home championship outright. After all, they had beaten England for the first time in an international the season before, and with only 10 men for well over an hour. So losing a man in two of their three games in 1914 was almost par for the course.

Ireland opened their campaign in January in Wrexham against Wales, whom they had never beaten away, with a makeshift side. It became even more makeshift when Everton's Harris went off with a torn ligament. However Ireland took the lead against the run of play when Young got behind their defence to hook in an overhead lob. Billy Gillespie added a second and, despite an Evan Jones penalty, Ireland finished as 2-1 winners.

England were the next victims a month later in Middlesbrough. Ireland were a goal up after five minutes when Lacey pounced on a loose ball and blasted it into the net through a melee of players.

Although England seemingly had an incomparable midfield and defence, the rag-bag Irish team were running them ragged. Their second goal from Gillespie exemplified this as he swept past both Frank Cuggy and Jesse Pennington as if they weren't there. Lacey completed the 3-0 rout in the second half. It was Ireland's first victory on English soil.

All that stood between Ireland and destiny were the Scots at Belfast on March 14 – and the usual injury problems. Their centre-half, O'Connell, had to leave the field early on when Wilson stepped on his arm. After that their right-back McConnell was carried off injured. To complete the misery McKee, Ireland's goalkeeper, collided with Wilson and played on in a terrible state until he was forced to retire early in the second half. Fortunately the first half was scoreless.

The Irish wounded regrouped: the injured McConnell went in goal and O'Connell returned. Now it was 9½ battling Irishmen versus 11 Scots. The Irish held out for 25 minutes until McConnell ill-advisedly dashed off his line to present Donnachie with an open goal.

The Irish still would not give in and eight minutes from time their centre-forward Young snatched the equaliser. As the final whistle blew the record crowd surged on to the pitch and carried their heroes off shoulder-high.

King sees Burnley crowned at Palace

ALTHOUGH the FA Cup final between Burnley and Liverpool was neither a particularly dramatic nor an entertaining match, it was certainly historic. For among the 72,778 spectators at the Crystal Palace was the reigning monarch, George V.

It was the first time the sovereign had attended the Cup final and it caused more of a stir than the final. When the King left Buckingham Palace by car just before 3pm on April 25 to travel to Sydenham the length of the royal route was thronged with cheering crowds.

In the first half Liverpool attempted to set up a royal feast and Nicholl had two great chances. The first, with a yawning open goal, he ran over the byeline. The second was a shot so fierce that when Taylor just got his head in the way he was concussed for more than a minute. Lacey and Miller had further good chances, but luck and the bounce of the ball favoured the Burnley defence.

The only goal of the game came in the 58th minute when Burnley's England international Bertie Freeman, from a throw-in near the corner flag, volleyed the ball into the Liverpool goal with such power that hardly anybody saw the shot. In the final 30 minutes Liverpool threw everything at Burnley but Sewell, with a string of fine saves, kept Liverpool at bay to win the last Cup final at Crystal Palace.

Let us hope that the King's appearance will put an end to the snobbish notion that true-blue sportsmen ought to ignore games played by men who earn their money at it

NATIONAL NEWSPAPER

Royal salute: the King went to the FA Cup final for the first time

FOR THE RECORD

■ The 10-yard rule was extended to include corner kicks.

■ Arsenal moved to Highbury, built on the grounds of a theological college, on September 6. The building work was only just finished in time and all the facilities were still not in place for the first match, a 2-1 defeat of Leicester Fosse. The teams had to use bowls of water in which to wash and an injured player was wheeled away on a milk cart.

■ Norman Wood was in the thick of the action for Stockport on October 4. He scored an own goal, gave away a penalty, which Fulham scored, and then missed a penalty himself. Hardly surprisingly, Fulham won 3-1.

■ Aston Villa finished runners-up in the League for the third time in four seasons, finishing seven points behind Blackburn Rovers. This was the last time that Blackburn were to win the championship.

■ Celtic, inspired by Patsy "Mighty Atom" Gallagher, won the Double for the third time. Gallagher was the leading scorer in the League, where Celtic finished six points clear of Rangers. Celtic only conceded 14 goals in 38 matches, a record that still stands, and kept a clean sheet 25 times.

■ Albert Iremonger, the ever-present Notts County goalkeeper, kept up his remarkable run of appearances. Since February 9, 1907, he had only missed four League matches, all in the 1912-13 season.

■ The dispute between the breakaway Amateur Football Association and the FA ended when the amateurs agreed to affiliate to the FA.

FIRST
1914-18
WORLD WAR

Cook leaves ref steaming

BILLY COOK, the Oldham left-back, forced the referee to abandon his team's match with Middlesbrough on Easter Monday 1915 when he refused to leave the pitch after being sent off.

The match was of vital importance to Oldham, who were challenging for the First Division title, but were 3-0 down after 20 minutes at Ayresome Park. The Oldham players thought one of the goals should not have been allowed, and they were further annoyed when they had a penalty appeal turned down. Early in the second half Cook fouled Carr and Middlesbrough scored the penalty to extend their lead to 4-1. Soon after, Cook fouled Carr again and the referee had no hesitation in sending Cook off. The Oldham players surrounded the referee to protest but he refused to change his decision, and gave Cook one minute to leave the field.

The referee pulled out his watch and when 60 seconds had elapsed and Cook was still on the pitch, the official walked off, abandoning the game.

Oldham compounded the offense by playing Cook again in their next match. The League fined the club £350, banned Cook for a year and allowed the result to stand.

Football rises to challenge

WHEN BRITAIN went to war with Germany on August 4, 1914 everybody thought that the fighting would be over before Christmas. There did not appear to be any reason to suspend the League and FA Cup. But when the British Expeditionary Force was all but wiped out, a fierce debate about the morality of playing football raged in the pages of The Times. A F Pollard wrote: "We view with indignation and alarm the persistence of Association football clubs in doing their best for the enemy. There is no excuse for diverting from the front thousands of athletes in order to feast the eyes of crowds of inactive spectators, who are either unfit to fight or else unfit to be fought for."

In consultation with the War Office, the FA appealed for single men to volunteer and decided to stage recruiting drives at matches. When only one person enlisted at Arsenal's match, and nobody at Nottingham Forest's game, The Times mocked football's efforts.

The FA hit back by pointing out that the game had produced 100,000 recruits in four months and only 600 single men who earned their living from football had not volunteered, compared with the two million people who could have enlisted.

As the season continued, interest in football declined rapidly. Attendances virtually halved and entertainment tax was imposed on matches, forcing the League to cut player's wages to keep clubs afloat. The War Office sanctioned the staging of the Cup final and 50,000 people, so many of them in uniform that the game was known as the Khaki Cup, saw Sheffield United beat Chelsea at Old Trafford.

After Lord Derby had presented the trophy and medals he said: "The clubs and their supporters had seen the Cup played for and it was now everybody's duty to play a sterner game for England." Football bowed to the inevitable. The League, the Cup and internationals were suspended and replaced by regional competitions. In England players were not allowed to be paid, but Scotland allowed payments of £2 a week providing that players did not earn their living from the game. All players who had not enlisted were also required to take jobs that helped the war effort.

When the war ended there were suggestions that a scaled down FA Cup should be staged in the 1918-19 season. But with the country still struggling to recover the authorities decided that the idea was not practicable.

Match fixing scandal

RUMOURS about matches having been fixed started to surface at the end of the 1914-15 season. The most serious claim, made by a bookmaker, was that a match in Manchester during the Easter holiday had been rigged in favour of the home team. The bookmaker claimed that the result of the game had been arranged in advance so that a betting coup could be staged.

Liverpool had been accused twice before in the past four years of being involved in fixed matches but had been cleared both times because of a lack of evidence. On Good Friday they had lost 2-0 to Manchester United, putting on a display that was widely reported as having been staggeringly inept. And there had been a flood of bets, at odds of 7-1 on that score.

The bookmaker refused to pay out on the bets and the Football League started an official investigation in May. Under intense questioning one of the Liverpool players finally confessed, and the inquiry's report just before Christmas told a sorry tale.

The plot had been hatched in a Manchester pub and had involved several players from each team. Bets had secretly been placed throughout the country and many of the other players knew what was going on, and although they were not involved they said nothing. Eight players, four from each club, were banned for life – Tom Fairfoul, Tommy Miller, Bob Purcell and Jackie Sheldon of Liverpool, and Laurence Cook, Sandy Turnbull, Enoch "Knocker" West and Arthur Whalley of Manchester United. Sheldon, a former Manchester United player, was alleged to be the ringleader.

The punishment on seven of them was lifted at the end of the war to reflect the fact that they had made amends by fighting for their country. However, the pardon came too late for Turnball, who was killed in action. West was the only one of the four Manchester United men to have actually played in the match and his ban was not lifted until 1945, despite his continued insistence that he was innocent.

THE 1919-20 SEASON

Secret plot promotes Arsenal

TOTTENHAM were a club with a mission when they began their Second Division campaign. They had every right to claim that they should have been in the First Division instead of Arsenal, who had finished fifth in the Second Division.

Although Tottenham had fin-ished bottom of the First Division in 1915, the League had decided to increase the two divisions from 20 to 22 clubs. The last time the League had accepted extra clubs, in 1905, there had been no relegation.

However, this time Derby and Preston, first and second in the Second Division, were pro-moted, while Chelsea, second from bottom in the First Division, were elected separately. There was a ballot for the final place and seven clubs applied.

Behind the scenes Sir Henry Norris, the Machiavellian chair-man of Arsenal, had been con-spiring with John McKenna, the Liverpool chairman and League president. So transparent was this plot that before the election McKenna urged the clubs to vote for Arsenal using the spe-cious argument that they had been in the League longer than Tottenham. However he conve-niently ignored the fact that two other candidates, Wolverhamp-ton and Birmingham, had been members even longer – Wolves in fact were founder members of the League, and had also fin-ished above Arsenal.

Having lost the vote, Spurs took the Second Division by storm finishing as champions with 70 points – six points clear of Huddersfield – and scoring 102 goals. They even reached the quarter-finals of the FA Cup where they lost by conceding an own-goal to Aston Villa, the eventual winners.

Huddersfield's revival borders on a miracle

BY any standards Huddersfield experienced the most remark-able of seasons. They began by facing extinction, amalgama-tion and re-location, lost many of their best players and ended by winning promotion to the First Division and reaching their first FA Cup final.

On October 4, Leeds City were expelled from the League for making irregular payments to players during the war years. Although it was known that other clubs had been up to the same tricks, Leeds City were seen as the worst example, a perception they made worse when they refused to produce their accounts.

Port Vale replaced them in the Second Division taking over their fixtures and their results. The Leeds City players were sold off in a bizarre auction a week later fetching some £10,000.

Meanwhile two directors demanded that Huddersfield repay the £40,000 owed to them. When it was discovered that Huddersfield were basically insolvent, the League decreed that Huddersfield either go into liquidation or move to Elland Road and amalgamate with the newly-formed Leeds United.

Amazingly, there was an out-cry in Huddersfield, a town more renowned for rugby league. By dint of public sub-scriptions, appeals and the wholesale transfer of players the club found enough money to satisfy the League and stay afloat.

Because Tottenham had run away with the Second Division

Kirton: ended the dream

championship, Huddersfield's achievement in winning promo-tion was to some extent over-shadowed. But they were runaway runners-up, scoring 97 goals and winning 28 matches. They confirmed their pedigree in the Cup eliminating Newcas-tle and Liverpool en route to the final against Aston Villa, who had won the Cup five times.

Despite being the underdogs up against an elite side, Hudders-field comfortably held their own for 90 minutes. Then the ghosts of Leeds City's demise came to haunt them.

In the 10th minute of extra time a Villa corner from Dorrell was flicked on by Billy Kirton as the other players rose. The ball flew into net. Was it deflected by a defender? Accounts differ, but Kirton was credited with the match-winner. Kirton was an inside-right who was picked up by Aston Villa in the Leeds City auction for £250.

LEAGUE TABLES AND RESULTS 1910 – 1920

1910-11 | 1911-12 | 1912-13 | 1913-14 | 1914-15

FA CUP

1910-11	1911-12	1912-13	1913-14	1914-15
Bradford City 1	Barnsley 1	Aston Villa 1	Burnley 1	Sheffield United 3
Newcastle United 0, after 0-0	West Bromwich Albion 0, after 0-0	Sunderland 0	Liverpool 0	Chelsea 0

FIRST DIVISION

1910-11

	P	W	D	L	F	A	Pts
Man Utd	38	22	8	8	72	40	52
Aston Villa	38	22	7	9	69	41	51
Sunderland	38	15	15	8	67	48	45
Everton	38	19	7	12	50	36	45
Bradford C	38	20	5	13	51	42	45
Wednesday	38	17	8	13	47	48	42
Oldham	38	16	9	13	44	41	41
Newcastle	38	15	10	13	61	43	40
Sheff Utd	38	15	8	15	49	43	38
Arsenal	38	13	12	13	41	49	38
Notts C	38	13	11	14	37	45	38
Blackburn	38	13	11	14	62	54	37
Liverpool	38	15	7	16	53	53	37
Preston	38	12	11	15	40	49	35
Tottenham	38	13	6	19	52	63	32
Middlesbro	38	11	10	17	49	63	32
Man City	38	9	13	16	43	58	31
Bury	38	9	11	18	43	71	29
Bristol C	*38*	*11*	*5*	*22*	*43*	*66*	*27*
Nottm F	*38*	*9*	*7*	*22*	*55*	*75*	*25*

1911-12

	P	W	D	L	F	A	Pts
Blackburn	38	20	9	9	60	43	49
Everton	38	20	6	12	46	42	46
Newcastle	38	18	8	12	64	50	44
Bolton	38	20	3	15	54	43	43
Wednesday	38	16	9	13	69	49	41
Aston Villa	38	17	7	14	76	63	41
Middlesbro	38	16	8	14	56	45	40
Sunderland	38	14	11	13	58	51	39
West Brom	38	15	9	14	43	47	39
Arsenal	38	15	8	15	55	59	38
Bradford C	38	15	8	15	46	50	38
Tottenham	38	14	9	15	53	53	37
Man Utd	38	13	11	14	45	60	37
Sheff Utd	38	13	10	15	63	56	36
Man City	38	13	9	16	56	58	35
Notts C	38	14	7	17	46	63	35
Liverpool	38	12	10	16	49	55	34
Oldham	38	12	10	16	46	54	34
Preston	*38*	*13*	*7*	*18*	*40*	*57*	*33*
Bury	*38*	*6*	*9*	*23*	*32*	*59*	*21*

1912-13

	P	W	D	L	F	A	Pts
Sunderland	38	25	4	9	86	43	54
Aston Villa	38	19	12	7	86	52	50
Wednesday	38	21	7	10	75	55	49
Man Utd	38	19	8	11	69	43	46
Blackburn	38	16	13	9	79	43	45
Man City	38	18	8	12	53	37	44
Derby	38	17	8	13	69	66	42
Bolton	38	16	10	12	62	63	42
Oldham	38	14	14	10	50	55	42
West Brom	38	13	12	13	57	50	38
Everton	38	15	7	16	48	54	37
Liverpool	38	16	5	17	61	71	37
Bradford C	38	12	11	15	50	60	35
Newcastle	38	13	8	17	47	47	34
Sheff Utd	38	14	6	18	56	70	34
Middlesbro	38	11	10	17	55	69	32
Tottenham	38	12	6	20	45	72	30
Chelsea	38	11	6	21	51	73	28
Notts C	*38*	*7*	*9*	*22*	*28*	*56*	*23*
Arsenal	*38*	*3*	*11*	*23*	*26*	*74*	*18*

1913-14

	P	W	D	L	F	A	Pts
Blackburn	38	20	11	7	78	42	51
Aston Villa	38	19	6	13	65	50	44
Oldham	38	17	12	9	55	45	46
Middlesbro	38	19	5	14	77	60	43
West Brom	38	15	13	10	46	42	43
Bolton	38	16	10	12	65	52	42
Sunderland	38	17	6	15	63	52	40
Chelsea	38	16	7	15	46	55	39
Bradford C	38	12	14	12	40	40	38
Sheff Utd	38	16	5	17	63	60	37
Newcastle	38	13	11	14	39	48	37
Burnley	38	12	12	14	61	53	36
Man City	38	14	8	16	51	53	36
Man Utd	38	15	6	17	52	62	36
Everton	38	12	11	15	46	55	35
Liverpool	38	14	7	17	46	62	35
Tottenham	38	12	10	16	50	62	34
Wednesday	38	13	8	17	53	70	34
Preston	*38*	*12*	*6*	*20*	*52*	*69*	*30*
Derby	*38*	*8*	*11*	*19*	*55*	*71*	*27*

1914-15

	P	W	D	L	F	A	Pts
Everton	38	19	8	11	76	47	46
Oldham	38	17	11	10	70	56	45
Blackburn	38	18	7	13	83	61	43
Burnley	38	18	7	13	61	47	43
Man City	38	15	13	10	49	39	43
Sheff Utd	38	15	13	10	49	41	43
Wednesday	38	15	13	10	61	54	43
Sunderland	38	18	5	15	81	72	41
Bradford PA	38	17	7	14	69	65	41
West Brom	38	15	10	13	49	43	40
Bradford C	38	13	14	11	55	49	40
Middlesbro	38	13	12	13	62	74	38
Aston Villa	38	13	11	14	62	72	37
Liverpool	38	14	9	15	65	75	37
Newcastle	38	11	10	17	46	48	32
Notts C	38	9	13	16	41	57	31
Bolton	38	11	8	19	68	84	30
Man Utd	38	9	12	17	46	62	30
Chelsea	38	8	13	17	51	65	29
Tottenham	38	8	12	18	57	90	28

SECOND DIVISION

1910-11	1911-12	1912-13	1913-14	1914-15
Champions: West Bromwich Albion	Champions: Derby County	Champions: Preston North End	Champions: Notts County	Champions: Derby County
Also promoted: Bolton Wanderers	Also promoted: Chelsea	Also promoted: Burnley	Also promoted: Bradford Park Avenue	Also promoted: Preston North End

SCOTTISH CUP

1910-11	1911-12	1912-13	1913-14	1914-15
Celtic 2	Celtic 2	Falkirk 2	Celtic 4	
Hamilton Academical 1, after 0-0	Clyde 0	Raith Rovers 0	Hibernian 1, after 0-0	

SCOTTISH FIRST DIVISION

1910-11

	P	W	D	L	F	A	Pts
Rangers	34	23	6	5	90	34	52
Aberdeen	34	19	10	5	53	28	48
Falkirk	34	17	10	7	65	42	44
Partick	34	17	8	9	50	41	42
Celtic	34	15	11	8	48	18	41
Dundee	34	18	5	11	54	42	41
Clyde	34	14	11	9	45	36	39
T Lanark	34	16	7	11	59	53	39
Hibernian	34	15	6	13	44	48	36
Kilmarnock	34	12	10	12	43	45	34
Airdrie	34	12	9	13	49	53	33
St Mirren	34	12	7	15	46	57	31
Morton	34	9	11	14	49	51	29
Hearts	34	8	8	18	42	59	24
Raith	34	7	10	17	36	56	24
Hamilton	34	8	5	21	31	60	21
Motherwell	34	8	4	22	37	66	20
Queen's P	34	5	4	25	28	80	14

1911-12

	P	W	D	L	F	A	Pts
Rangers	34	24	3	7	86	34	51
Celtic	34	17	11	6	58	33	45
Clyde	34	19	4	11	56	32	42
Hearts	34	16	8	10	54	40	40
Partick	34	16	8	10	47	40	40
Morton	34	14	9	11	44	44	37
Falkirk	34	15	6	13	46	43	36
Dundee	34	13	9	12	52	41	35
Aberdeen	34	14	7	13	44	44	35
Airdrie	34	12	8	14	40	41	32
T Lanark	34	12	7	15	40	57	31
Hamilton	34	11	8	15	32	44	30
Hibernian	34	12	5	17	44	47	29
Motherwell	34	11	5	18	34	44	27
Raith	34	9	9	16	39	59	27
Kilmarnock	34	11	4	19	38	60	26
Queen's P	34	8	9	17	29	53	25
St Mirren	34	7	10	17	32	59	24

1912-13

	P	W	D	L	F	A	Pts
Rangers	34	24	5	5	76	41	53
Celtic	34	22	5	7	53	28	49
Hearts	34	17	7	10	71	43	41
Airdrie	34	15	11	8	64	46	41
Falkirk	34	14	12	8	56	38	40
Hibernian	34	16	5	13	63	54	37
Motherwell	34	12	13	9	47	39	37
Aberdeen	34	14	9	11	47	40	37
Clyde	34	13	9	12	41	44	35
Hamilton	34	12	8	14	44	47	32
Kilmarnock	34	10	11	13	37	54	31
St Mirren	34	10	10	14	50	60	30
Morton	34	11	7	16	50	59	29
Dundee	34	8	13	13	33	46	29
T Lanark	34	8	12	14	31	41	28
Raith	34	8	10	16	46	60	26
Partick	34	10	4	20	40	55	24
Queen's P	34	5	3	26	34	88	13

1913-14

	P	W	D	L	F	A	Pts
Celtic	38	30	5	3	81	14	65
Rangers	38	27	5	6	79	31	59
Hearts	38	23	8	7	70	29	54
Morton	38	26	2	10	76	51	54
Falkirk	38	20	9	9	69	51	49
Airdrie	38	18	12	8	72	43	48
Dundee	38	19	5	14	64	53	43
T Lanark	38	13	10	15	42	51	36
Clyde	38	11	11	16	46	46	33
Ayr	38	13	7	18	58	74	33
Raith	38	13	6	19	56	57	32
Kilmarnock	38	11	9	18	48	68	31
Hibernian	38	12	6	20	58	75	30
Aberdeen	38	10	10	18	38	55	30
Partick	38	10	9	19	37	51	29
Queen's P	38	10	9	19	52	84	29
Motherwell	38	11	6	21	49	66	28
Hamilton	38	11	6	21	46	65	28
Dumbarton	38	10	7	21	45	87	27
St Mirren	38	8	6	24	38	73	22

1914-15

	P	W	D	L	F	A	Pts
Celtic	38	30	5	3	91	25	65
Hearts	38	27	7	4	83	32	61
Rangers	38	23	4	11	74	47	50
Morton	38	18	12	8	74	48	48
Ayr	38	20	8	10	55	40	48
Falkirk	38	16	7	15	48	48	39
Hamilton	38	16	6	16	60	55	38
Partick	38	15	8	15	56	58	38
St Mirren	38	14	8	16	56	65	36
Airdrie	38	14	7	17	54	60	35
Hibernian	38	12	11	15	59	66	35
Kilmarnock	38	15	4	19	55	59	34
Dumbarton	38	13	8	17	51	66	34
Aberdeen	38	11	11	16	39	52	33
Dundee	38	12	9	17	43	61	33
T Lanark	38	10	12	16	51	57	32
Clyde	38	12	6	20	44	59	30
Motherwell	38	10	10	18	49	66	30
Raith	38	9	10	19	53	68	28
Queen's P	38	4	5	29	27	90	13

SCOTTISH SECOND DIVISION

1910-11	1911-12	1912-13	1913-14	1914-15
Champions (not promoted): Dumbarton	Champions (not promoted): Ayr United	Champions: Ayr United	Champions (not promoted): Cowdenbeath	Champions (not promoted): Cowdenbeath
Runners-up (not promoted): Ayr United	Runners-up (not promoted): Abercorn	Dumbarton (sixth) were also elected to the First Division	Runners-up (not promoted): Albion R	Runners-up (not promoted): Leith

There always will be a corner of a foreign field that will be forever England: officers and men of the 26th Divisional Train on Christmas Day 1915 in Salonika

1915-16 | 1916-17 | 1917-18 | 1918-19 | 1919-20

FA CUP

1919-20
Aston Villa 1
Huddersfield Town 0

FIRST DIVISION

1919-20

	P	W	D	L	F	A	Pts
West Brom	42	28	4	10	104	47	60
Burnley	42	21	9	12	65	59	51
Chelsea	42	22	5	15	56	51	49
Liverpool	42	19	10	13	59	44	48
Sunderland	42	22	4	16	72	59	48
Bolton	42	19	9	14	72	65	47
Man City	42	18	9	15	71	62	45
Newcastle	42	17	9	16	44	39	43
Aston Villa	42	18	6	18	75	73	42
Arsenal	42	15	12	15	56	58	42
Bradford PA	42	15	12	15	60	63	42
Man Utd	42	13	14	15	54	50	40
Middlesbro	42	15	10	17	61	65	40
Sheff Utd	42	16	8	18	59	69	40
Bradford C	42	14	11	17	54	63	39
Everton	42	12	14	16	69	68	38
Oldham	42	15	8	19	49	52	38
Derby	42	13	12	17	47	57	38
Preston	42	14	10	18	57	73	38
Blackburn	42	13	11	18	64	77	37
Notts C	*42*	*12*	*12*	*18*	*56*	*74*	*36*
Wednesday	*42*	*7*	*9*	*26*	*28*	*64*	*23*

SECOND DIVISION

1919-20
Champions: Tottenham Hotspur
Also promoted: Huddersfield Town

SCOTTISH CUP

1919-20
Kilmarnock 3
Albion Rovers 2

SCOTTISH FIRST DIVISION

1915-16

	P	W	D	L	F	A	Pts
Celtic	38	32	3	3	116	23	67
Rangers	38	25	6	7	87	39	56
Morton	37	22	7	8	86	35	51
Ayr	38	20	8	10	72	45	48
Partick	38	19	8	11	65	41	46
Hearts	37	20	6	11	66	45	46
Hamilton	38	19	3	16	68	76	41
Dundee	38	18	4	16	56	49	40
Dumbarton	38	13	11	14	54	64	37
Kilmarnock	38	12	11	15	46	49	35
Aberdeen	38	11	12	15	51	64	34
Falkirk	38	12	9	17	45	61	33
St Mirren	38	13	4	21	50	67	30
Motherwell	38	11	8	19	55	82	30
Airdrie	38	11	8	19	44	74	30
T Lanark	38	9	11	18	40	56	29
Clyde	38	11	7	20	49	71	29
Queen's P	38	11	6	21	53	100	28
Hibernian	38	9	7	22	44	71	25
Raith	38	9	5	24	30	65	23

1916-17

	P	W	D	L	F	A	Pts
Celtic	38	27	10	1	79	17	64
Morton	38	24	6	8	72	39	54
Rangers	38	24	5	9	68	32	53
Airdrie	38	21	8	9	71	38	50
T Lanark	38	19	11	8	53	37	49
Kilmarnock	38	18	7	13	69	46	43
St Mirren	38	15	10	13	49	43	40
Motherwell	38	16	6	16	57	59	38
Partick	38	14	7	17	44	43	35
Dumbarton	38	12	11	15	56	73	35
Hamilton	38	13	9	16	54	73	35
Falkirk	38	12	10	16	58	57	34
Clyde	38	10	14	14	41	53	34
Hearts	38	14	4	20	44	59	32
Ayr	38	12	7	19	47	59	31
Dundee	38	13	4	21	58	71	30
Hibernian	38	10	10	18	57	72	30
Queen's P	38	11	7	20	56	81	29
Raith	38	8	7	23	42	91	23
Aberdeen	38	7	7	24	36	68	21

1917-18

	P	W	D	L	F	A	Pts
Rangers	34	25	6	3	66	24	56
Celtic	34	24	7	3	66	26	55
Kilmarnock	34	19	5	10	69	41	43
Morton	34	17	9	8	53	42	43
Motherwell	34	16	9	9	70	51	41
Partick	34	14	12	8	51	37	40
Queen's P	34	14	6	14	64	63	34
Dumbarton	34	13	8	13	48	49	34
Clydebank	34	14	5	15	55	56	33
Hearts	34	14	4	16	41	58	32
St Mirren	34	11	7	16	42	50	29
Hamilton	34	11	6	17	52	63	28
T Lanark	34	10	7	17	56	62	27
Falkirk	34	9	9	16	38	58	27
Airdrie	34	10	6	18	46	58	26
Hibernian	34	8	9	17	42	57	25
Clyde	34	9	2	23	37	72	20
Ayr	34	5	9	20	32	61	19

1918-19

	P	W	D	L	F	A	Pts
Celtic	34	26	6	2	71	22	58
Rangers	34	26	5	3	86	16	57
Morton	34	18	11	5	76	40	47
Partick	34	17	7	10	62	43	41
Motherwell	34	14	10	10	51	40	38
Ayr	34	15	8	11	62	53	38
Hearts	34	14	9	11	59	52	37
Queen's P	34	15	5	14	59	57	35
Kilmarnock	34	14	7	13	61	59	35
Clydebank	34	12	8	14	54	65	32
St Mirren	34	10	12	12	43	55	32
T Lanark	34	11	9	14	60	62	31
Airdrie	34	9	11	14	45	54	29
Hamilton	34	11	5	18	49	75	27
Dumbarton	34	7	8	19	31	58	22
Falkirk	34	6	8	20	46	73	20
Clyde	34	7	6	21	45	75	20
Hibernian	34	5	3	26	30	91	13

1919-20

	P	W	D	L	F	A	Pts
Rangers	42	31	9	2	106	25	71
Celtic	42	29	10	3	89	31	68
Motherwell	42	23	11	8	73	53	57
Dundee	42	22	6	14	79	65	50
Clydebank	42	20	8	14	78	54	48
Morton	42	16	13	13	71	48	45
Airdrie	42	17	10	15	57	43	44
T Lanark	42	16	11	15	57	62	43
Kilmarnock	42	20	3	19	59	74	43
Ayr	42	15	10	17	72	69	40
Dumbarton	42	13	13	16	57	65	39
Queen's P	42	14	10	18	67	73	38
Partick	42	13	12	17	51	62	38
St Mirren	42	15	8	19	63	81	38
Hearts	42	14	9	19	57	72	37
Clyde	42	14	9	19	64	71	37
Aberdeen	42	11	13	18	46	64	35
Hibernian	42	13	7	22	60	79	33
Raith	42	11	10	21	61	82	32
Falkirk	42	10	11	21	45	74	31
Hamilton	42	11	7	24	56	86	29
Albion	42	10	8	24	42	77	28

War-time winners

1914-15
FA Cup: Sheffield United 3 Chelsea 0
First Division: Everton
Second Division: Derby
Scottish First Division: Celtic
Scottish Second Division: Cowdenbeath

1915-16
Lancashire Region: Manchester City
Lancashire Region Northern Division: Burnley
Lancashire Region Southern Division: Manchester City
London Region: Chelsea
London Region A Tournament: Chelsea
London Region B Tournament: West Ham United
Midland Region: Nottingham Forest
Midland Region Midland Division: Grimsby Town
Midland Region Northern Division: Leeds City
Midland Region Southern Division: Nottingham Forest
South-western Region: Portsmouth
Scottish Leage: Celtic

1916-17
Lancashire Region: Liverpool
Lancashire Region Subsidiary Tournament: Rochdale
London Region: West Ham United
Midland Region: Leeds City
Midland Region Subsidiary Tournament: Bradford Park Avenue
Scottish League: Celtic

1917-18
Region championship (two-leg play-off between the Lancashire and Midland champions): Leeds City
Lancashire Region: Stoke City
Lancashire Region Subsidiary Tournament: Liverpool
London Region: Chelsea
Midland Region: Leeds City
Midland Region Subsidiary Tournament: Grimsby Town
Scottish League: Rangers

1918-19
League championship (two leg play-off between the Lancashire Midland champions): Nottingham Forest
Lancashire Region: Everton
Lancashire Region A Tournament: Blackpool
Lancashire Region B Tournament: Oldham Athletic
Lancashire Region C Tournament: Manchester City
Lancashire Region D Tournament: Liverpool
London Region: Brentford
Midland Region: Nottingham Forest
Midland Region A Tournament: Sheffield United
Midland Region B Tournament: Birmingham
Midland C Tournament: Bradford Park Avenue
Midland Region C Tournament: Hull City
Scottish League: Celtic

THE
1920-21
SEASON

Fortune favours slick Spurs as Wolves sink in the swamp

Singing in the rain: Spurs won their second FA Cup final

League booms as more clubs join the fray

THE NEW Third Division was so successful that from next season there will be two: the Third Division South and the Third Division North. The top club from each division will be promoted in place of the bottom two clubs in the Second Division, who will be re-allocated according to their geographical location.

In the same fashion as last year's expansion, when the Southern League's First Division was accepted en bloc, 20 northern clubs were immediately accepted into the new division. With the addition of these two extra divisions the League has virtually doubled in size in two years.

The introduction of new blood into the League has already had positive results. Cardiff City, who were accepted into the Second Division last season to replace Grimsby, won immediate promotion to the First Division, having lost the Second Division championship on goal average. They will be the first Welsh club to play in the top flight in England.

THE RAIN ruined the FA Cup final. Tottenham, under the visionary management of the stern Peter McWilliam who had won the Cup with Newcastle in 1910, had played in the First Division the same, sweet football that had destroyed the Second Division the season before. However that depended on keeping the ball on the ground. In the quagmire that was Stamford Bridge on April 23 their skills were reduced to farce.

Before the match Spurs were overwhelming favourites to beat Second Division Wolves. But when the game kicked off it was thought it would be a lottery, and so it proved. Tottenham discovered they had the winning ticket in the 53rd minute when Jimmy Dimmock scored one of the luckiest goals to win a Cup final.

Dimmock received a pass near the half-way line and ran at Wolves down the left wing. He

Dimmock: lucky winner

rounded Gregory but lost the ball to Woodward. Sadly for the Wolves full-back, the ball bounced off his legs and Dimmock was off again and into the penalty area.

His left-foot shot from 15 yards skidded on the mud, kept deceptively low and slid under the arms of George, the Wolves goalkeeper, to nestle in the net by the far post. Thus Tottenham won the Cup for the second time.

Burnley go from zeros to heroes

THE TALE of Burnley's first championship success defied all fiction: it had a lousy beginning, a brilliant middle and a rotten end. Burnley started by losing their first three matches. Then, on September 6, they defeated Huddersfield 3-0 to launch an unbeaten run of 30 consecutive League matches. In that magical spell they won 21 games, drew nine, scored 68 goals while conceding nine, and amassed 51 points. It effectively won the title.

Little wonder they tailed off after Manchester City beat them 3-0 at Maine Road on March 25. They won their next two matches – including a 2-1 defeat of Manchester City – but failed to win any of their final six matches. It made no difference, Burnley were convincing First Division champions with 59 points, five points clear of Manchester City.

Burnley used 23 players in their campaign. The centre-forward Joe Anderson scored 25 goals, aided and abetted by the inside-right Bob Kelly (20) and Ben Cross (14). Even Tom Boyle, their captain and centre-half, chipped in with seven goals.

Cup final penalty sparks row

Immoral victory: the wrong decision produced the right result in the FA Cup final

Rangers slip up yet again

FOR the third consecutive year Rangers' League form inexplicably deserted them in the Scottish Cup. In 1920 bottom-placed Albion Rovers had had the temerity to knock them out in the semi-finals while they were coasting to the championship. The next year it was Partick Thistle, playing in their first final, who denied the runaway champions the Double.

It had seemed impossible that Rangers would make it a hat-trick of failures when they took on Morton in the Scottish Cup final. But they did and in the most naïve of ways. After 12 minutes Morton were awarded a free-kick outside the penalty area because William Robb, Rangers' goalkeeper, had carried the ball outside the box.

The Rangers players thought the free-kick was indirect, confusing it with a new rule that had recently been introduced.

Jimmy Gourlay, Morton's right-half, knew better. He thumped the ball past the hapless Robb for the only score of the match.

THE CLUB that was apparently dead two seasons ago is definitely alive and kicking. Huddersfield, now under the new management of Herbert Chapman, won their first major trophy, the FA Cup, and in the most controversial of circumstances: a penalty-kick.

The decision by the referee, J W D Fowler, divided the nation and was replayed endlessly on the news film at cinemas. "Was the offence inside or outside the penalty area? Should the culprit have been sent off? Even if it was outside the area wasn't the 'wrong' decision right? And what about the keeper? All that jumping around, shouldn't be allowed."

The Cup final between Preston and Huddersfield at Stamford Bridge, the last to be played there, was thoroughly dull until the 67th minute. Then Hamilton, the Preston full-back, deliberately brought down Billy Smith from behind when he had a clear opportunity to score. The referee instantly awarded a penalty amid furious protests from the Preston players.

Smith, also the England left-winger, picked himself up to take the kick. Whereupon Preston's bespectacled, amateur goalkeeper, J F Mitchell, began to dance about in the goal attempting to put Smith off. His antics were likened to "an excited monkey on a stick awaiting the offer of a bag of peanuts". Smith scored despite Mitchell and the Cup was won for the first time by a penalty.

It probably wasn't a penalty, but the right team won anyway, and Hamilton should have been sent off. As for the goalkeeper, his clowning around led to an important rule change: goalkeepers have to remain stationary when a penalty is taken.

Scott's mean net profit

LIVERPOOL'S third championship owed as much to their strong goalkeeping tradition laid down by Tom Watson at the turn of the century as anything else. Elisha Scott, their Irish keeper, was simply following the tradition of the legendary Sam Hardy and Teddy Doig. With Scott guarding the net, Liverpool could play a mean game.

In their 42 League games Liverpool conceded a mere 36 goals while the vast majority of the

rest of the First Division were letting in 50s, 60s and 70s. Scott was the secret. At 5ft 9in he was on the small side for a goalkeeper, but his agility more than made up for it.

Liverpool opened the season with a defeat, then, with Scott in ruthless form, reeled off 30 matches with only one defeat. They eventually cruised to the title on April 17 when they beat Burnley, the defending champions, 2-1.

FOR THE RECORD

■ Unhappy with Stamford Bridge, the FA toyed with investing in the old Crystal Palace ground, now relinquished by the army, but decided to associate themselves with a new development at Wembley.

■ Billy Walker of Aston Villa scored three penalties, a record for one match, against Bradford City in November.

■ Frank Barson, the Aston Villa centre-half, scored the winning goal with a 30-yard header in the match against Sheffield United on Boxing Day.

■ Syd Puddefoot was transferred from West Ham to Falkirk in February for the unbelievable sum of £5,000. Syd King, the West Ham manager, attempted to call Falkirk's bluff by

naming an outrageous fee. It was the first £5,000 transfer and prompted Arsenal to propose a transfer-fee limit of £1,650. The idea was rejected.

■ Southend only scored 34 League goals in the season. Their leading scorer was their full-back Jimmy Evans with 10, all of them penalties. Evans thus became the first full-back in the League to be a club's leading scorer.

■ Scotland continued its restructuring by changing the size of the two Divisions, relegating three teams and only promoting one. Queen's Park, one of the clubs to go down, were relegated for the first time since they had joined the League.

THE
1922-23
SEASON

West Ham come good in the end

TWO DAYS after the most extraordinary FA Cup final, West Ham had to put their disappointment and shattered nerves behind them if they wanted to escape from the Second Division. They travelled to Sheffield Wednesday and gained a brave 2-0 victory that put them back on top of the table on goal average, with Notts County and Leicester also on 51 points.

So on the final Saturday all three teams were vying for the two promotion places but with the added complication that West Ham were at home to Notts County while Leicester had a much easier challenge at Bury.

To West Ham's delight, Leicester fell at the final hurdle and lost to Bury, and Notts County's 1-0 defeat of West Ham was irrelevant. By virtue of goal average, the East London club were in the First Division for the first time.

Promotion on goal average was a just reward for their season's efforts. Away from home West Ham had a prodigious record, averaging two goals a game, including a 6-0 thrashing of Leicester.

> *I believe that all right-minded people have good reason to thank God for the great progress of this popular national game*
>
> LORD KINNAIRD
> president of the FA
> for 33 years

Copper steals show

Turning the tide: PC Scorey saved the day at the Cup final

THE FIRST FA Cup final at Wembley was at best a farce, at the worst a near disaster. Such was the interest in the new stadium, heightened by the grandiose boasts of the owners, that more than a quarter of a million people converged on a ground whose capacity was 127,000. Chaos ensued as they stormed the stadium, overturning barricades and pouring into the ground whether they had tickets or not. Inevitably the crowd overspilled and the pitch became a sea of people.

It was at this point that disaster and loss of life were narrowly averted. The arrival of King George V was the catalyst for order to be restored as the playing of the national anthem calmed the swirling crowd. Mounted police gained control with a nudge here, a little gentle shepherding there, until a space was cleared and the crowd drifted back to terraces.

The press decided that the hero of the hour was Constable George Scorey and his 13-year-old white horse, Billy. Obviously Scorey was just one of a team of mounted policeman who saved the day – but he was the only one on a white horse. The final has always been remembered as the "White horse final".

Ironically, PC Scorey wasn't much interested in football and when he returned home his girlfriend asked him what kind of day he'd had. "Just ordinary, lass," he said. "Just ordinary."

The match, between Bolton and Second Division West Ham, kicked off 45 minutes late with thousands of spectators standing on the touchlines and was effectively over in two minutes. The ball went out of play and West Ham's Tresarden dived into the human wall to retrieve it. Before he could return to the pitch David Jack had headed Bolton into the lead.

At half-time the players stayed on the field and eight minutes after the restart Bolton scored their second, and decisive, goal when John Smith smashed the ball into the back of the net. However, because there were bodies pressed up against the netting the ball instantly rebounded and many people mistakenly thought it had come back off the post.

Wembley and the FA had learnt their lesson, from then on Cup finals were made all-ticket.

Amazing amateurs: 85,000 people watched the Corinthians Cup exploits

THE
1923-24
SEASON

Newcastle do better at Wembley

THERE WAS just one question on the lips of the Newcastle fans as their team took the field for the FA Cup final: would Wembley be a happier hunting ground than Crystal Palace. Five times Newcastle had gone to the old Cup final venue (1905, 1906, 1908, 1910 and 1911) and only once had they returned with the trophy – and that was after a replay at Goodison in 1910. Aston Villa's Cup record was quite different: eight finals, six trophies including Newcastle's scalp in 1905.

With seven minutes remaining and the game scoreless it looked as if Newcastle's Cup final jinx was never going to go away. Then, whoosh, two goals in three minutes sent the Cup to Tyneside. Harris made, and scored, the first when Jackson, the Villa goalkeeper, could only parry the ball back to him. Seymour's drive for the second

Cardiff get their sums wrong

CARDIFF'S dizzy ascent in the Football League since they were accepted into the Second Division in 1920 was cruelly halted just as they had the ultimate prize – the championship – in their sights. On the final day of the season Cardiff, who were a point ahead of Huddersfield, only had to win at Birmingham to take the title.

With the score 0-0 Cardiff were awarded a penalty when the ball was punched off the goal-line. Amazingly, none of the Cardiff players wanted to take the kick and they allowed the responsibility to fall to Len Davies, who had never taken a penalty before. The home goalkeeper saved his effort and the match finished goalless.

Meanwhile Huddersfield beat Nottingham Forest to finish level on 57 points. However Huddersfield had scored 60 goals and conceded 33, while Cardiff's record was 61-34. Goal average was used to separate the two clubs and Huddersfield were champions by 0.0241 of a goal. If goal difference had been used instead (as it was from 1976) Cardiff would have been champions by virtue of having scored more goals.

Glory days: Hudspeth, Newcastle's full, rejoices back with the FA Cup

Airdrie owe it to Gallacher

IF there was one single explanation for the meteoric rise of Airdrie it was certainly Hughie Gallacher. The tenacious 5ft 5in centre-forward had so galvanised the little Lanarkshire club that the talk in Scotland was that at last there was a team to threaten Celtic and Rangers.

The previous season Gallacher had scored 10 goals in 18 games and pushed his side into the runners-up spot behind Rangers. It was no flash in the pan. Gallacher scored 33 times in 34 appearances as Airdrie again finished runners-up to Rangers. But this year they went one further and beat Hibernian 2-0 in the Scottish Cup final to win the trophy for the first time.

was unstoppable and the pain of those earlier defeats was instantly wiped away.

Wales sweep the rest aside

ONCE AGAIN Fred Keenor, the Cardiff captain, inspired Wales to the Home international championship. But unlike 1920, when they had had to rely on England beating Scotland, this season Wales did it by beating all three countries. They had begun with a businesslike 2-0 defeat of Scotland at Cardiff in February, but England at Blackburn in March were a different proposition.

Fortune seemed to favour the Welsh when the referee mistakenly blew for offside when David Jack had legitimately

scored, and then Roberts hit the bar and Jack the post. Roberts did head England into the lead from a free-kick only for Willie Davies to equalise from a deflection.

Keenor, the captain, decided to take matters into his own capable hands. The centre-half advanced upfield into the penalty area and passed to Nicholls. His shot was palmed down to Ted Vizard, who never missed from two yards. Twelve days later a penalty from Moses Russell in Belfast sealed the Triple Crown.

FOR THE RECORD

■ Sammy Wynne, Oldham's left back, was both hero and villain on October 6. Against Manchester United in the Second Division he scored four times, from a penalty and a free-kick for Oldham, and two own goals for United. Fortunately Oldham finished 3-2 winners.

■ Corinthian Casuals continued their exploits in the FA Cup, beating First Division Blackburn Rovers 1-0 in the first round before losing 5-0 to West Brom.

■ Four penalties were awarded in five minutes, a League record, during the Third Division North match between Crewe and Bradford Park Avenue on March 8.

■ Billy Meredith became the oldest man to play in the FA Cup when, at the

age of 49 years and eight months, he took the field for Manchester City against Newcastle in the semi-finals.

■ Hibernian proved themselves the replay specialists in the Scottish Cup, needing three games to beat Partick in the quarter-finals and another three games to dispatch Aberdeen in the semi-finals.

■ The Chesterfield goalkeeper, Birch, scored five penalties in the Third Division North to set a League scoring record for a goalkeeper. ·

■ Walter Hampson of Newcastle, at 41 years and 8 months, was thought to have been the oldest man to play in a Cup final so far this century.

■ The Scottish League continued its tinkering, creating a Third Division of 16 clubs.

37

THE
1924-25
SEASON

Arsenal steal Chapman from Huddersfield

HUDDERSFIELD'S joy at winning their second successive championship was tempered within a few weeks when Herbert Chapman, their manager, decided to take over the helm at Arsenal. It had been the appointment of Chapman in 1921 that had transformed Huddersfield from also-rans into one of the most successful clubs in the country. Apart from the two League titles he had also guided them to an FA Cup victory in 1922, the first major trophies they had won.

Chapman built well at Huddersfield and made some astute purchases in the transfer market. The most notable was his first signing, the veteran Clem Stephenson from Aston Villa for £4,000, who became Chapman's leader on the field.

Huddersfield had begun the season in cracking form, undefeated in their first 10 matches. Then they eased up, losing five times, as the rest of the First Division got their breath back, only to race home reeling off 17 games without defeat to win the title with two points to spare.

Tunstall: nightmare goal

Offside law turns game upside down

THE DECISION to alter the offside rule by the International Board in June changed the face of football forever. Although the new ruling might have appeared minor (after all only one word was amended) it would have unforeseen repercussions that would profoundly transform the way the game was played.

The rule change was straightforward. From the 1926-27 season instead of three men being required to be between a player and the goal when the ball was passed, only two would be necessary. The intention of the lawmakers was to cut down on the number of offside decisions and to prevent sterile defensive play. Matches with 40 offside decisions had become commonplace.

Newcastle, with their two international full-backs, Bill McCracken and Frank Hudspeth, had turned the offside trap into an art form. One of them would venture near the half-way line and suddenly sneak behind the attacking forwards, leaving the player in possession with nobody to pass to. Understandably, this infuriated the opposition. The standing joke for teams arriving at Newcastle railway station was to quip: "Blimey, offside already," when the guard blew his whistle.

The rule on corner kicks was also amended, making it clear that a player could not touch the ball again until it had been played by another player. Previously it had been thought that a player could dribble the ball from a corner kick.

Cardiff miss out again as Wake falls asleep

POOR Cardiff. Having suffered the agony of losing the championship by two-hundredths of a goal the previous season, they lost the FA Cup final to Sheffield United because of one split-second error.

In the 30th minute United's Pantling put a deep cross over to the left wing which Harry Wake, the right half, should have intercepted. However, Wake hesitated for a fraction of a second, enough for Fred Tunstall, United's brilliant winger, to latch on to the ball, race through a wide open defence and place a low shot beyond the reach of the diving Farquharson, Cardiff's goalkeeper. The headline in the South Wales Echo said it all: "Wake not Awake."

It was particularly disappointing for Cardiff because the first visit to the Cup final by a Welsh club turned the occasion into an international event. There were telegrams and cables from Welsh expatriates around the world wishing them well, partic-

ularly because of the battle they had fought to reach the final.

In the first round it had taken them two replays to get past Third Division Darlington. And in the quarter-finals Leicester, the Second Division pacesetters, put up a tremendous fight

FOR THE RECORD

■ After the change in the laws governing corner kicks, Billy Smith of Huddersfield Town was the first player to score a goal direct from a corner in the match against Arsenal on October 11.

■ Exeter finally ended a barren spell of 20 months (April 12, 1923 to November 7, 1924) during which time they did not score an away goal.

■ Arthur Chandler scored in 16 consecutive Second Division matches for Leicester City, the champions. He also finished as the division's leading scorer, with 33 goals.

■ Merthyr Town set a record in the Third Division South they would rather forget, losing 29 of their 42 matches.

■ Manchester United, the Second Division runners-up, only conceded 23 goals in 42 matches, an all-time low for the division.

■ Huddersfield never conceded more than two goals in a match on their way to the First Division title.

■ Patsy Gallagher scored an amazing equaliser for Celtic in the Scottish Cup final. At the end of a long run, which beat several players, Gallagher fell when a Dundee defender made a last-ditch tackle just in front of the goal. As Gallagher went down he managed to keep the ball wedged between his legs, and he somersaulted across the line to score. Celtic won the Cup for a record 11th time with a late goal from Jimmy McGrory.

until a last second goal by Willie Davies – direct from a corner kick – saw Cardiff through 2-1.

Welsh woes: Cardiff were caught napping yet again

THE
1925-26
SEASON

Barnstorming City end up as the fall guys

IT WAS a heartbreaking season for Manchester City. They stormed through to the FA Cup final, beating champions Huddersfield 4-0, trouncing Crystal Palace 11-4 and demolishing rivals Manchester United 3-0 in the semi-final. But in the final Bolton's Dick Pym, their ex-fisherman from Devon turned goalkeeper, kept the City's goal-scoring sharks at bay. The only goal came 13 minutes from time when Ted Vizard pulled the ball back perfectly for David Jack to score.

Losing the Cup final was bad enough, a week later they were relegated from the First Division, the first team to achieve this dubious feat. City went into the final Saturday needing only a draw at Newcastle to be certain of staying up. However, if either Leeds United or Burnley lost they would still be safe. City missed a penalty and lost 3-2.

Arsenal get their man

IT WAS very much Herbert Chapman's trademark to raid the transfer market for the very best players, whatever their age, so the only person surprised when he moved for Sunderland's 33-year-old Charlie Buchan, was the player himself. Buchan, who had walked out on Arsenal in 1909, thought he was joking when Chapman walked into his shop and told him he was joining Arsenal.

The financial arrangements were handled by the Arsenal chairman Sir Henry Norris, who refused to pay the £4,000 Sunderland wanted. When Bob Kyle, the Sunderland manager, justified the fee by claiming that Buchan would score 20 goals in his first season with Arsenal, Norris challenged him to put his money where his mouth was: £2,000 down and £100 per goal.

It was a perfect deal: Arsenal got great publicity – every time Buchan advanced on goal the crowd would shout: "There's another £100" – Buchan scored 19 goals in the League and two in the Cup, and Sunderland made £100 profit.

Burnley and Leeds both won so, despite scoring 89 goals, City returned to the Second Division for the first time since 1909.

Buchan on the ball

Seizing the time: Buchan transformed the way the game was played

THE ALTERATION in the offside law certainly shook things up. True, there were fewer offside decisions, but there were an awful lot of goals. On the opening day of the season Aston Villa scored 10 against Burnley; then Newcastle beat Arsenal 7-0; Arsenal retaliated by putting five past Cardiff; Tottenham and Huddersfield drew 5-5. By the end of the season the number of goals scored in the Football League had totalled 6,373. The year before it had been 4,700. The floodgates had opened and who would stem the tide?

Charlie Buchan, Arsenal's close-season signing, had been arguing to Herbert Chapman since the opening day of the season that a new tactical formation was needed. Buchan wanted the centre-half withdrawn from the middle of the field (where he was a roaming attacker) back into defence between the two full-backs. This would mean that an inside forward would have to move into midfield and the old 2-3-5 formation would become 3-3-4.

Chapman paid no attention to his new captain until Saturday October 3 when Newcastle, using their centre-half Charlie Spencer in a similar role to that advocated by Buchan, hammered Arsenal 7-0. In a Newcastle hotel that night Chapman and Buchan thrashed out how Arsenal could implement such a strategy. It was unveiled on the Monday after at West Ham, where Arsenal won 4-0. Chapman would refine the system as time went on, and as the right players for their new roles would be found, but essentially modern football had been conceived.

Local heroes: Bolton return in triumph with the FA Cup

Welsh blunder gifts Cardiff the FA Cup

FOR the first time since the FA Cup was started in 1871 the trophy left England when Cardiff beat Arsenal courtesy of one the most incredible goalkeeping blunders ever seen in a final.

With 15 minutes remaining Hugh Ferguson received the ball from a throw-in by Fred Keenor, his Cardiff captain. From 20 yards out Ferguson attempted a shot along the ground, but his effort was poor and Dan Lewis, Arsenal's Welsh goalkeeper, seemed to have comfortably gathered the ball. Suddenly it slipped out of his grasp and, perhaps distracted by the on-rushing Ferguson and Len Davies, the Arsenal keeper struck the ball with his elbow and could only watch helplessly as it slowly trickled over the line.

The sheen on Lewis's new jersey was blamed for the fumble and from then on Arsenal managers have insisted their goalkeepers wore jerseys that had been through the wash.

It was a cruel way for Arsenal to lose their first Cup final, although Cardiff could point out that a stupid blunder by their right-half, Harry Wake, had similarly cost them the 1925 final. Arsenal had dominated the match throughout, indeed they had won all eight of the corners awarded.

Arsenal even had a wonderful opportunity to equalise two minutes from time when Tom Farquharson, the Cardiff goalkeeper, misjudged Sid Hoar's centre and it sailed over his head. Jimmy Brain and Charlie Buchan both rushed in and either one of them could have headed the ball into the empty net, but they each left it to the other and the chance was missed.

Gallacher transforms Newcastle

NEWCASTLE'S raid into the transfer market in December 1925 paid excellent dividends when Hughie Gallacher, their £5,500 purchase from Airdrie, inspired them to their fourth League championship. Gallacher had worked miracles at the little Lanarkshire club: in three seasons they had won the Scottish Cup and been League runners-up each year. Gallacher had soon demonstrated that his magical powers also worked south of the border: in his 19 matches in 1925-6 he scored 23 goals.

Then he capped that feat by establishing a club record with 36 goals in 38 games as Newcastle comfortably won the title five points clear of Huddersfield. Bizarrely, Newcastle's home and away form bordered on the schizophrenic: at home they won 19 matches, losing once and drawing once, but away from St James's Park they could only muster six wins and five draws.

Miracle worker: Gallacher delivered Newcastle's fourth League title

FOR THE RECORD

■ Charles Clegg, the president of the FA since 1923, received a knighthood for services to football. He was the first person in the game to be given this honour.

■ The First Division match between Arsenal and Sheffield United on January 22 was the first to be broadcast on radio. A diagram of the pitch, divided up into numbered squares was printed in the Radio Times. One commentator described the play while another called out the number of the square, so listeners knew where the action was taking place. Thus, the famous phrase "back to square one" came into being.

■ Manchester United signed Hughie McLenahan, an amateur wing-half, from Stockport County in exchange for three freezers full of ice-cream, which Stockport sold at a fund-raising bazaar.

■ Dixie Dean scored twice on his debut for England, a 3-3 draw against Wales in the Home championships on February 12. He followed that up with another 10 goals in his next four matches, including two hat-tricks against Belgium and Luxembourg.

■ Two Second Division clubs reached the semi-finals of the FA Cup – Southampton and Reading. Southampton beat two First Division teams – Birmingham and Newcastle – in successive rounds. Reading also eliminated a First Division club, Manchester United, after two replays. It was clearly the year of the underdog as Second Division Chelsea, Swansea and Wolverhampton all reached the quarter-finals, as did Millwall, of the Third Division South.

■ Stockport had two points deducted for using an unregistered player in the Third Division North.

■ Jimmy McGrory scored 49 goals in 33 matches for Celtic but his team, who hit 101 in total, could only finish third in the League behind Rangers and Motherwell.

Sharpshooter Camsell shreds the record books

WHEN Middlesbrough began their Second Division campaign with three defeats, one draw and a single goal nobody could have predicted the achievements that unfolded in the subsequent 38 matches. Once George Camsell, the Middlesbrough centre-forward, got his eye in, goalscoring

records simply went tumbling.

Camsell scored nine hat-tricks (a record), 59 goals in 37 games (a record) as Middlesbrough amassed 122 goals (a record) and raced away with the Second Division title by eight points from Portsmouth and Manchester City, who were hav-

ing their own private scrap for the second promotion place.

So tight was this battle that it all boiled down to goal average on the final Saturday. Unfortunately for Manchester City, Portsmouth's match against Preston had kicked off a quarter of an hour after theirs, thus giv-

ing Portsmouth the advantage. With only minutes to go the Portsmouth players learnt that City had beaten Bradford City 8-0 and knew that their 4-1 lead over Preston was not enough. They duly scored a fifth and snatched promotion spot by five thousandths of a goal.

Payments dispute forces Britain to quit Fifa

THE SIMMERING dispute between Britain and the rest of the world about amateurism was brought to a head by the 1928 Olympics and led to the Home nations leaving Fifa.

The International Olympic Committee had earlier adopted Britain's strict definition of an amateur to determine eligibility for the Olympics. But, in 1926, Switzerland's proposal that countries could compensate amateurs for lost earnings was passed by 12 votes to eight.

The following year, Fifa demanded that the IOC should allow broken-time payments.

The IOC, faced with Fifa's threat to ban its members from taking part in the Olympics, backed down.

This was unacceptable to the British associations, who withdrew from the Olympics and resigned from Fifa several months later.

Dean tops Camsell

Just in time: Dean had eight minutes to spare as he broke the record

A YEAR after George Camsell had torn up the goalscoring record books, Dixie Dean shredded them again when he overhauled Camsell's 59 League goals in the last match of the season. But with three matches to go the 21-year-old Everton centre-forward was nine short of the record.

Dean scored two against Aston Villa, four against Burnley and required a hat-trick against Arsenal to reach 60. Although Everton had already won the championship, more than 48,000 packed Goodison on May 5 to see if he could pull it off.

Arsenal took the lead inside two minutes only for Dean to grab an equaliser virtually from the restart. The excitement mounted when, minutes later, Dean was brought down in the penalty area and casually converted the spot-kick.

He had equalled Camsell's feat before half-time, but it was a long, tense wait before the record fell. In the 82nd minute Alec Troup floated a corner towards the far post and Dean soared above the Arsenal defence to score his 40th header of the season.

Scots wizards cast a spell

ON PAPER, the match between England and Scotland on March 31 was fairly meaningless, with both countries playing for the wooden spoon in the Home championships. Yet when the game was over – and Scotland had trounced England 5-1 – it was immediately hailed as a classic. Scotland's heroes were immortalised as the Wembley Wizards for the spell they cast over the English dunces.

England had almost taken the lead in the opening minutes, but the ball came back off a post. Then Alex Jackson headed Scotland into the lead and nothing much happened until Alex James made it 2-0 just before half-time.

In the second half the Scots ran riot as they converted their midfield mastery into goals with a flowing exhibition of passing. They even slowed the game to walking pace, daring the harassed opposition to take the ball off them. Jackson completed his hat-trick, Gibson added the fifth, and Kelly scored a late consolation goal.

FOR THE RECORD

■ Ronnie Dix became the youngest player to score in the League, at the age of 15 years and 180 days. His goal for Bristol Rovers against Norwich in the Third Division South came a week after he had made his debut in the first team.

■ Dixie Dean was not the only person setting goalscoring records. Jimmy McGrory hit eight (a Scottish First Division record) when Celtic beat Dunfermline 9-0 on January 14. And Jim Smith of Ayr scored a British record 66 goals in the season.

■ When Huddersfield lost 3-1 to Blackburn in the FA Cup final they became the first team since Barnsley in 1910 (and Barnsley lost a replay 2-0) to score in a final and fail to win the trophy.

■ Tottenham were relegated from the First Division with 38 points, the highest total for a club to go down. The battle to beat the drop was a real dogfight. The seven teams that finished immediately above Tottenham all had 39 points, and only four points separated bottom of the table Middlesbrough (37 points) and tenth-placed Arsenal.

■ Millwall won the Third Division South championship with a League record 127 goals. They finished 10 points clear of second-place Northampton.

Rangers finally end their drought

RANGERS' dearth of victories in the Scottish Cup final was legendary, and they were the butt of many music-hall jokes. In 25 years they had appeared in the Cup final five times and had never received the trophy. There was persistent talk of a hoodoo and Rangers players had suffered constant taunts over the years.

So it was hardly surprising that when the referee awarded Rangers a penalty early in the second half of the final against Celtic with the game scoreless, nobody wanted to take it. Ignominy or glory beckoned. David Meiklejohn, the Rangers captain, accepted the burden.

Outwardly calm, but inwardly shaking like a leaf, Meiklejohn took five steps back and thundered the ball into the net. The terraces exploded in joy and Meiklejohn went into a daze.

"For 10 minutes I was hardly conscious of where I was," he said. "If Celtic had attacked up the middle they might have passed me by without my seeing them."

Meiklejohn had broken the drought. Rangers overran Celtic 4-0 and the jokes were over. A week later Rangers put the icing on the cake by winning the League and finally capturing their first Double.

DIXIE DEAN
Head and shoulders above the rest

Vince Wright

DIXIE DEAN

Born January 21, 1906, Birkenhead

PLAYING CAREER
Tranmere Rovers 1923-25
Everton 1925-37
Scored 349 goals for Everton
In the season of 1927-28 Dean scored 60 goals in 39 First Division matches beating George Camsell's record, set the previous season, by one goal. Dean's record still stands
Honours FA Cup: Winners 1933
League Championship: Winners 1928, 1932
Notts County 1938
Sligo Rovers 1939
Internationals England debut v Wales at Wrexham February 12, 1927 (scoring twice)
16 appearances, 17 goals (12 in his first five internationals)
Career goal scoring record 473 goals (including 37 hat-tricks) in 502 League, FA Cup, representative and international matches

Died March 1, 1980 at Goodison Park

THERE have been many footballers idolised on Merseyside. Billy Liddell, Kevin Keegan, Kenny Dalglish and Ian Rush of Liverpool, and Joe Mercer, Tommy Lawton, Alan Ball and Neville Southall of Everton come especially to mind. But nobody has been held in greater affection than Dixie Dean, goalscorer supreme and the best centre-forward of his generation.

Dean, Merseyside's first footballing superstar, began his career at Tranmere Rovers and ended it at Notts County, but it was at Everton that he made his name, breaking all kinds of scoring records between the two world wars. During his 13 years at Goodison Park, Dean scored 349 League goals in 399 matches, including 60 in the 1927-28 season – a record unlikely to be surpassed. Dean's career total was an astonishing 473 from 502 games, which included a record 37 hat-tricks. He had scored 100 League goals before he was 21 and managed 200 in his first 198 appearances for Everton. Dean also averaged more than a goal a game for England, netting 18 from only 16 outings.

Dean's goals were rich in quality as well as quantity. He was a Roy of the Rovers type of player long before Roy Race had been invented. A fine athlete with great power and suppleness, Dean possessed a fierce shot in either foot, a good turn of speed, was brave almost to the point of foolhardiness and put the fear of God into goalkeepers and defenders. Although opponents tried to rile Dean in the hope of putting him off his game they rarely succeeded. He was too single-minded to be sidetracked and of a sound enough temperament not to retaliate.

Dean is best remembered for his prowess in the air, and about half of his goals came from his head. Indeed, he could head a ball harder than many players could kick it. Dean's accuracy, timing and power were awesome and it is widely accepted that there has never been a better header of a ball in front of goal.

The late Bernard Joy, the former Arsenal centre-half and chief football writer of the Evening Standard, recalled that Dean had such a prodigious leap that he could jump from a standing position on to a billiard table. Sir Matt Busby, who played against Dean on many occasions, including the 1933 FA Cup final, said at the time that "he could out-jump, out-time and out-head any defender". It was not a bad epitaph for somebody who was only 5ft 10in. Although Dean played in an era when goals were more plentiful, when five forwards were the norm, when mark-ing was less tight and when winning was regarded as more important than simply avoiding defeat, his achievements were still remarkable.

Born in Birkenhead in 1907, his real name was William Ralph Dean, and he preferred to be called Bill. The nickname stuck to him from his youth, when he was playing schoolboy football in the Birkenhead area. The song "Dixie" was very popular at the time and Dean's black hair and swarthy skin went well with America's deep south.

From as early as eight, Dean's ambition was to play for Everton. His father was an engine driver

Sterling efforts: silver plates inserted in his skull after a motorcycle accident did not hamper Dean

and Dean joined the Wirral Railway as an apprentice fitter. After appearing for the Wirral Railway team and another local side he was persuaded to join Tranmere, with whom he turned professional at 16. Dean gave immediate notice that he was something special, for in the following season, 1924-25, he scored 27 goals in 27 appearances for a club that finished second from bottom of the Third Division North.

Most leading First Division clubs wanted him, but Everton won the race for his signature, capturing him for the then considerable fee of £3,000 shortly before the 1925-26 season. If Dean were up for transfer now his value would probably exceed £5m.

Dean's transfer coincided with a change in the offside law that was to have far-reaching effects. The FA's alteration to the law reduced the number of defenders who had to be nearer the goal line than an attacker from three to two and there was a dramatic increase in goals. Dean was perfectly equipped to take advantage.

He reached an unforgettable peak in 1927-28, beating by one the record 59 League goals scored by George Camsell of Middlesbrough the previous season. With three games left, Camsell's

Leadership: Dean was an inspirational captain

"He could out-jump and and out-head any defender." Dean leaves the Liverpool defence standing

total seemed out of reach as Dean was on the 50-goal mark. But he struck seven times in the next two matches to set up a fascinating finale.

The championship was already assured when Everton played Arsenal on the final Saturday of the season. More than 60,000 spectators crammed into Goodison Park to celebrate Everton's title success and to will Dean into the history books.

The great man did not disappoint them. He equalled Camsell's total by scoring twice early on – the second from the penalty spot – but Arsenal fought back well to draw level. Then, with time running out, came the moment for which every Everton supporter had been waiting. A corner by Alec Troup, the Scottish international winger, was aimed at Dean, who towered above Arsenal's defenders to send the ball hurtling into the net. Every Arsenal player shook Dean by the hand except Charlie Buchan, another prolific marksman whose farewell had been completely overshadowed. Not even a late Arsenal goal, which deprived Everton of a win, could dampen the joyous mood.

Dean's 60 League goals from 39 outings included seven hat-tricks. Another 22 in Cup and representative games brought a season's total of 82 that may never be equalled. As if this were not extraordinary enough, two years earlier Dean's life had been in danger after a motorcycle crash in north Wales. The crisis was averted but doctors were adamant that he

would never play football again after he had fractured his jaw and skull. How wrong they were.

Wearing silver plates in his skull, Dean continued to score regularly, if not quite so prolifically, for the rest of his glittering career. There were setbacks, most notably Everton's shock relegation in 1929-30. However, Everton were never down for long while Dean was playing for them. They regained their First Division place the next season and then won the championship and FA Cup in successive years. Dean captained them to a 3-0 victory in the final over Manchester City, as well as scoring one of the goals.

Injuries ended Dean's career in 1939 shortly after he was transferred, amid much controversy, to Notts County. On leaving football he became a publican in Chester and later had a long period working for Littlewoods pools. Dean's retirement was marred by ill-health and in 1976 he had his right leg amputated after unsuccessful operations for a blood clot. Four years later Dean collapsed and died while watching his beloved Everton lose 2-1 to Liverpool at Goodison Park. He was 73. Crowds lined the streets leading to the church where a 45-minute service was held before a private cremation in Dean's home town of Birkenhead. Joe Mercer, a close friend and former team-mate, read the lesson but the most fitting epitaph came from another Merseyside idol, Bill Shankly: "Today there is no red and blue, no black and white, no Protestants and Catholics – just mourning for a great footballer."

Fearsome shot: Dean scores against the hot favourites Manchester City in the 1933 Cup final

Chapman goes on a spending spree

HERBERT CHAPMAN made two stunning raids into the transfer market and for a little over £20,000 added two of Britain's leading players to the Arsenal roster. In October 1928 he swooped for Bolton's David Jack, doubling the transfer record in the process, and in June he stole Preston's Alex James from under the noses of all the other big clubs.

The retirement of Charlie Buchan had left Chapman with two holes in his Arsenal team: a goalscorer and a scheming leader on the field. He bought Jack to fill the former role, and James the latter.

Jack was a cultured England inside-forward whose goals had given Bolton two FA Cups. James was also a goalscorer, but had also been the inspiration behind the Wembley Wizards. Chapman wanted him for his vision and sent about turning him into the greatest midfield playmaker of his era.

James cost a mere £9,000. Jack was to be more expensive. Bolton originally asked for an outrageous £13,000, probably to get Chapman to go away. Chapman ensconced himself in the lounge bar of an hotel with his assistant and instructed a waiter to serve him gin and tonic without gin and his assistant whisky and dry ginger without whisky. The Bolton directors were to get double spirits. The fee came down to £11,500 and, by all accounts, the Bolton management left happy.

Jack: Arsenal's star signing

No player in the world is worth £10,000

SIR CHARLES CLEGG
FA president

Spain sink England

ENGLAND'S first defeat by non-British opposition was masterminded by an Englishman who used to play for Middlesbrough. Billy Pentland, Spain's coach, knew that his team would be vulnerable to the direct, athletic English style of play so, despite the FA requesting a later kick-off time, he ensured that the match in Madrid in May was played in the afternoon when the sun was at its hottest.

Spain had other advantages: England were without Dixie Dean and George Camsell, the two goalscoring phenomena of the Football League; it was England's third international in six days – and Ricardo Zamora, the world's finest goalkeeper.

Despite the Foreign Office advising England not to underestimate the Spaniards – they had recently beaten Portugal 5-0 and France 8-1 – the heat and the English complacency allowed a two-goal lead to become a 4-3 defeat.

Zamora: paid £20 a week

England began brightly enough, scoring twice early in the first half before the heat affected them. Refreshed by the interval they countered Spain's quick strike with another goal, but then they really began to wilt. At 3-3 a section of the 30,000 crowd invaded the pitch to celebrate and were dispatched with drawn swords by the Guardia Civil. Minutes later Spain had won their first international with England.

Butler's waiting game pays off

THE FA Cup final between Bolton and Portsmouth seemed something of an anti-climax. After all, Bolton were an established Cup side, having won the trophy in 1923 and 1926 and had seemed to have done all the hard work in just getting to Wembley.

They had disposed of Liverpool (who finished fifth in the League) 5-2 after a replay, then Leicester (runners-up) by 2-1 away, followed by Blackburn (seventh) after a replay, and then Huddersfield (the team of the decade).

For 79 minutes the final was an anti-climax as both sides played cat and mouse until Bolton's Billy Butler broke the deadlock with an unstoppable shot. Moments from time Butler set up the clinching second for Blackmore.

It was wonderfully appropriate that Butler played such a pivotal role in completing Bolton's hat-trick of FA Cups in the 1920s. Butler, along with Haworth, Nuttall, Dick Pym and the captain James Seddon had all played in the previous two finals – Pym enjoying the unusual record of never having conceded a goal in three finals.

FOR THE RECORD

■ Sir Henry Norris, the Machiavellian Arsenal chairman, finally got his comeuppance when he lost his libel case against the FA. Norris had been found guilty of a series of irregular payments and was banned from the game. He died in July 1934.

■ Numbered shirts were used in League matches for the first time on August 25.

■ Newcastle's team that played Leeds on October 6 only included one player who was not born in Scotland, the reserve centre-half Ted Wood, who was Welsh.

■ Scotland made a clean sweep in the Home internationals. Hughie Gallacher scored a record five goals in their 7-3 victory over Ireland in Belfast.

■ Rotherham suffered the embarrassment of being only the second team to concede 10 or more goals twice in the League in one season. After their thrashing by Bradford City on August 25, they lost 10-1 at South Shields on March 16. Those two defeats accounted for more than a quarter of the total number of goals which they conceded in the League, 77.

■ Arthurlie resigned from the Scottish Second Division after completing 32 of their 36 matches. Their results were allowed to stand.

■ Bradford City, the Third Division North champions, raised the League goalscoring record to 128. They scored 82 goals at home, including an 11-1 defeat of Rotherham in the first match of the season.

■ Cardiff finished bottom of the First Division despite conceding fewer goals (59) than any other team in the Division. Their problem was a lack of firepower – they only scored 43 goals, the worst performance in the League.

■ Jock Buchanan of Rangers was the first person to be sent off in a Scottish Cup final. Rangers lost 2-0 to Kilmarnock.

THE
1929-30
SEASON

Wednesday in clover with Seed

WHEN TOTTENHAM transferred Jimmy Seed, their inventive inside-right, to Sheffield Wednesday in 1927 they made one of their biggest blunders in the transfer market. For as Tottenham (relegated in 1928), declined Sheffield Wednesday prospered. For the second year in a row they won the League championship.

Seed's impact on the Sheffield club was immediate. Robert Brown, the manager, wisely installed Seed as his captain and he inspired Wednesday to escape relegation in 1928 with a late burst of form. Seed's influence continued the following season when, despite a mediocre away record, Wednesday were impregnable at Hillsborough. They managed to hold off a fierce challenge from Leicester to take the title by a point.

Then Wednesday truly hit a golden patch and coasted to the championship 10 points clear of Derby, scoring 105 goals in the process, a championship record. They were even close to winning the Double, but Huddersfield beat them 2-1 in the semi-final. Tottenham were still in the Second Division.

Seed: blossomed in Sheffield

James's great goal heralds golden era

Gatecrasher: the Graf Zeppelin hovers over Wembley at the Cup final

THE 1930 FA Cup final between Arsenal and Huddersfield on April 26 was indeed a memorable occasion. For the first time the two teams came out side-by-side; the Graf Zeppelin flew over Wembley during the match; Herbert Chapman, the Arsenal manager, had been the architect of Huddersfield's great days in the 1920s – and Alex James scored one of the cleverest goals ever seen in a Cup final.

For both teams the match was a watershed. Huddersfield had won a hat-trick of championships and the FA Cup in the previous decade. Arsenal had won nothing of consequence in their 47-year League history. By 4.45 pm Arsenal had rectified their lack of honours and were to embark on a glorious decade of success that would eclipse Huddersfield.

Arsenal's first goal was cred-ited to quick thinking by James. In fact, he had planned the move with Cliff Bastin on the team coach beforehand. James had told Bastin that if he won a free-kick in Huddersfield's half he would slip it to him on the wing, collect the return and have a crack at goal. In the 16th minute James won such a free-kick. He jumped up, got the referee's nod, took the free-kick without straightening up, then collected Bastin's return pass in his stride and slammed it into the corner of the net.

Soon after this the Zeppelin made its surprise appearance, hovering over the twin towers and apparently saluting the King. Newspaper reports give different accounts of the crowd's reaction. Some said the airship was booed, some that it was ignored and others that it was cheered. Clem Stephenson, the Huddersfield manager, who

been one of the few to know of the Zeppelin's arrival, had protested beforehand. However he could hardly claim it affected the outcome of the match. The opportunistic James did that.

Two minutes from the end, as Huddersfield pressed desperately for the equaliser, James hit a long ball out of defence and found his centre-forward, Jack Lambert, on the centre-circle. Lambert skipped round two defenders, raced virtually half the length of the pitch and beat the bewildered goalkeeper from the edge of the area.

LEAGUE TABLES AND RESULTS 1920–1930

| 1920-21 | 1921-22 | 1922-23 | 1923-24 | 1924-25 |

FA CUP

	1920-21	1921-22	1922-23	1923-24	1924-25
	Tottenham Hotspur 1	Huddersfield Town 1	Bolton Wanderers 2	Newcastle United 2	Sheffield United 1
	Wolverhampton Wanderers 0	Preston North End 0	West Ham United 0	Aston Villa 0	Cardiff City 0

FIRST DIVISION

1920-21

	P	W	D	L	F	A	Pts
Burnley	42	23	13	6	79	36	59
Man City	42	24	6	12	70	50	54
Bolton	42	19	14	9	77	53	52
Liverpool	42	18	15	9	63	35	51
Newcastle	42	20	10	12	66	45	50
Tottenham	42	19	9	14	70	48	47
Everton	42	17	13	12	66	55	47
Middlesbro	42	17	12	13	53	53	46
Arsenal	42	15	14	13	59	63	44
Aston Villa	42	18	7	17	63	70	43
Blackburn	42	13	15	14	57	59	41
Sunderland	42	14	13	15	57	60	41
Man Utd	42	15	10	17	64	68	40
West Brom	42	13	14	15	54	58	40
Bradford C	42	12	15	15	61	63	39
Preston	42	15	9	18	61	65	39
Huddersfld	42	15	9	18	42	49	39
Chelsea	42	13	13	16	48	58	39
Oldham	42	9	15	18	49	86	33
Sheff Utd	42	6	18	18	42	68	30
Derby C	*42*	*5*	*16*	*21*	*32*	*58*	*26*
Bradford PA	*42*	*8*	*8*	*26*	*43*	*76*	*24*

1921-22

	P	W	D	L	F	A	Pts
Liverpool	42	22	13	7	63	36	57
Tottenham	42	21	9	12	65	39	51
Burnley	42	22	5	15	72	54	49
Cardiff	42	19	10	13	61	53	48
Aston Villa	42	22	3	17	74	55	47
Bolton	42	20	7	15	68	59	47
Newcastle	42	18	10	14	59	45	46
Middlesbro	42	16	14	12	79	69	46
Chelsea	42	17	12	13	40	43	46
Man City	42	18	9	15	65	70	45
Sheff Utd	42	15	10	17	59	54	40
Sunderland	42	16	8	18	60	62	40
West Brom	42	15	10	17	51	63	40
Huddersfld	42	15	9	18	53	54	39
Blackburn	42	13	12	17	54	57	38
Preston	42	13	12	17	42	65	38
Arsenal	42	15	7	20	47	56	37
Birmingham	42	15	7	20	48	60	37
Oldham	42	13	11	18	38	50	37
Everton	42	12	12	18	57	55	36
Bradford C	*42*	*11*	*10*	*21*	*48*	*72*	*32*
Man Utd	*42*	*8*	*12*	*22*	*41*	*73*	*28*

1922-23

	P	W	D	L	F	A	Pts
Liverpool	42	26	8	8	70	31	60
Sunderland	42	22	10	10	72	54	54
Huddersfld	42	21	11	10	60	32	53
Newcastle	42	18	12	12	45	37	48
Everton	42	20	7	15	63	59	47
Aston Villa	42	18	10	14	64	51	46
West Brom	42	17	11	14	58	49	45
Man City	42	17	11	14	50	49	45
Cardiff	42	18	7	17	73	59	43
Sheff Utd	42	16	10	16	68	64	42
Arsenal	42	16	10	16	61	62	42
Tottenham	42	17	7	18	50	50	41
Bolton	42	14	12	16	50	58	40
Blackburn	42	14	12	16	47	62	40
Burnley	42	16	6	20	58	59	38
Preston	42	13	11	18	60	64	37
Birmingham	42	13	11	18	41	57	37
Middlesbro	42	13	10	19	57	63	36
Chelsea	42	9	18	15	45	53	36
Nottm F	42	13	8	21	41	70	34
Stoke	*42*	*10*	*10*	*22*	*47*	*67*	*30*
Oldham	*42*	*10*	*10*	*22*	*35*	*65*	*30*

1923-24

	P	W	D	L	F	A	Pts
Huddersfld	42	23	11	8	60	33	57
Cardiff	42	22	13	7	61	34	57
Sunderland	42	22	9	11	71	54	53
Bolton	42	18	14	10	68	34	50
Sheff Utd	42	19	12	11	69	49	50
Aston Villa	42	18	13	11	52	37	49
Everton	42	18	13	11	62	53	49
Blackburn	42	17	11	14	54	50	45
Newcastle	42	17	10	15	60	54	44
Notts C	42	14	14	14	44	49	42
Man City	42	15	12	15	54	71	42
Liverpool	42	15	11	16	49	48	41
West Ham	42	13	15	14	40	43	41
Birmingham	42	13	13	16	41	49	39
Tottenham	42	12	14	16	50	56	38
West Brom	42	12	14	16	51	62	38
Burnley	42	12	12	18	55	60	36
Preston	42	12	10	20	52	67	34
Arsenal	42	12	9	21	40	63	33
Nottm F	42	10	12	20	42	64	32
Chelsea	*42*	*9*	*14*	*19*	*31*	*53*	*32*
Middlesbro	*42*	*7*	*8*	*27*	*37*	*60*	*22*

1924-25

	P	W	D	L	F	A	Pts
Huddersfld	42	21	16	5	69	28	58
West Brom	42	23	10	9	58	34	56
Bolton	42	22	11	9	76	34	55
Liverpool	42	20	10	12	63	55	50
Bury	42	17	15	10	54	51	49
Newcastle	42	16	16	10	61	42	48
Sunderland	42	19	10	13	64	51	48
Birmingham	42	17	12	13	49	53	46
Notts C	42	16	13	13	42	31	45
Man City	42	17	9	16	76	68	43
Cardiff	42	16	11	15	56	51	43
Tottenham	42	15	12	15	52	43	42
West Ham	42	15	12	15	62	60	42
Sheff Utd	42	13	13	16	55	63	39
Aston Villa	42	13	13	16	58	71	39
Blackburn	42	11	13	18	53	66	35
Everton	42	12	11	19	40	60	35
Leeds	42	11	12	19	46	59	34
Burnley	42	11	12	19	46	75	34
Arsenal	42	14	5	23	46	58	33
Preston	*42*	*10*	*6*	*26*	*37*	*74*	*26*
Nottm F	*42*	*6*	*12*	*24*	*29*	*65*	*24*

SECOND DIVISION

	1920-21	1921-22	1922-23	1923-24	1924-25
	Champions: Birmingham	Champions: Nottingham Forest	Champions: Notts County	Champions: Leeds United	Champions: Leicester City
	Also promoted: Cardiff City	Also promoted: Stoke City	Also promoted: West Ham United	Also promoted: Bury	Also promoted: Manchester United
	Relegated: Stockport County	Relegated: Bradford Park Avenue, Bristol City	Relegated: Rotherham County, Wolverhampton Wanderers	Relegated: Nelson, Bristol City	Relegated: Crystal Palace, Coventry City

THIRD DIVISION SOUTH

	1920-21	1921-22	1922-23	1923-24	1924-25
	Champions: Crystal Palace	Champions: Southampton	Champions: Bristol City	Champions: Portsmouth	Champions: Swansea Town
	Runners-up (not promoted): Southampton	Runners-up (not promoted): Plymouth Argyle	Runners-up (not promoted): Plymouth Argyle	Runners-up (not promoted): Plymouth Argyle	Runners-up (not promoted): Plymouth Argyle

THIRD DIVISION NORTH

	1920-21	1921-22	1922-23	1923-24	1924-25
		Champions: Stockport County	Champions: Nelson	Champions: Wolverhampton Wanderers	Champions: Darlington
		Runners-up (not promoted): Darlington	Runners-up (not promoted): Bradford Park Avenue	Runners-up (not promoted): Rochdale	Runners-up (not promoted): Nelson

SCOTTISH CUP

	1920-21	1921-22	1922-23	1923-24	1924-25
	Partick Thistle 1	Morton 1	Celtic 1	Airdrie 2	Celtic 2
	Rangers 0	Rangers 0	Hibernian 0	Hibernian 0	Dundee 1

SCOTTISH FIRST DIVISION

1920-21

	P	W	D	L	F	A	Pts
Rangers	42	35	6	1	91	24	76
Celtic	42	30	6	6	86	35	66
Hearts	42	20	10	12	74	49	50
Dundee	42	19	11	12	54	48	49
Motherwell	42	19	10	13	75	51	48
Partick	42	17	12	13	53	39	46
Clyde	42	21	3	18	63	62	45
T Lanark	42	19	6	17	74	61	44
Morton	42	15	14	13	66	58	44
Airdrie	42	17	9	16	71	64	43
Aberdeen	42	14	14	14	53	54	42
Kilmarnock	42	17	8	17	62	68	42
Hibernian	42	16	9	17	58	57	41
Ayr	42	14	12	16	62	69	40
Hamilton	42	14	12	16	44	57	40
Raith	42	16	5	21	54	58	37
Albion	42	11	12	19	57	68	34
Falkirk	42	11	12	19	54	72	34
Queen's P	42	11	11	20	45	80	33
Clydebank	42	7	14	21	47	72	28
Dumbarton	42	10	4	28	41	89	24
St Mirren	42	7	4	31	43	92	18

1921-22

	P	W	D	L	F	A	Pts
Celtic	42	27	13	2	83	20	67
Rangers	42	28	10	4	83	26	66
Raith	42	19	13	10	66	43	51
Dundee	42	19	11	12	57	40	49
Falkirk	42	16	17	9	48	38	49
Partick	42	20	8	14	57	53	48
Hibernian	42	16	14	12	55	44	46
St Mirren	42	17	12	13	71	61	46
T Lanark	42	17	12	13	58	52	46
Clyde	42	16	12	14	60	51	44
Albion	42	17	10	15	55	51	44
Morton	42	16	10	16	58	57	42
Motherwell	42	16	7	19	63	58	39
Ayr	42	13	12	17	55	63	38
Aberdeen	42	13	9	20	48	54	35
Airdrie	42	12	11	19	46	56	35
Kilmarnock	42	13	9	20	56	83	35
Hamilton	42	9	16	17	51	62	34
Hearts	42	11	10	21	50	60	32
Dumbarton	*42*	*10*	*10*	*22*	*46*	*81*	*30*
Queen's P	*42*	*9*	*10*	*23*	*38*	*82*	*28*
Clydebank	*42*	*6*	*8*	*28*	*34*	*103*	*20*

1922-23

	P	W	D	L	F	A	Pts
Rangers	38	23	9	6	67	29	55
Airdrie	38	20	10	8	58	38	50
Celtic	38	19	8	11	52	39	46
Falkirk	38	14	17	7	44	32	45
Aberdeen	38	15	12	11	46	34	42
St Mirren	38	15	12	11	54	44	42
Dundee	38	17	7	14	51	45	41
Hibernian	38	17	7	14	45	40	41
Raith	38	13	13	12	31	43	39
Ayr	38	13	12	13	43	44	38
Partick	38	14	9	15	51	48	37
Hearts	38	11	15	12	51	50	37
Motherwell	38	13	10	15	59	60	36
Morton	38	12	11	15	44	47	35
Kilmarnock	38	14	7	17	57	66	35
Clyde	38	12	9	17	36	44	33
T Lanark	38	11	8	19	40	59	30
Hamilton	38	11	7	20	43	59	29
Albion	*38*	*8*	*10*	*20*	*38*	*64*	*26*
Alloa	*38*	*6*	*11*	*21*	*27*	*52*	*23*

1923-24

	P	W	D	L	F	A	Pts
Rangers	38	25	9	4	72	22	59
Airdrie	38	20	10	8	72	46	50
Celtic	38	17	12	9	56	33	46
Raith	38	17	13	56	38	43
Dundee	38	15	13	10	70	57	43
St Mirren	38	15	12	11	53	45	42
Hibernian	38	15	11	12	66	52	41
Partick	38	15	9	14	58	55	39
Hearts	38	14	10	14	61	50	38
Motherwell	38	15	7	16	58	63	37
Morton	38	16	5	17	48	54	37
Hamilton	38	15	11	12	51	57	37
Aberdeen	38	13	10	15	37	41	36
Ayr	38	12	10	16	38	60	34
Falkirk	38	13	6	19	46	53	32
Kilmarnock	38	12	8	18	48	65	32
Queen's P	38	11	9	18	43	60	31
T Lanark	38	11	8	19	54	78	30
Clyde	*38*	*10*	*9*	*19*	*40*	*70*	*29*
Clydebank	*38*	*10*	*5*	*23*	*42*	*71*	*25*

1924-25

	P	W	D	L	F	A	Pts
Rangers	38	25	10	3	77	27	60
Airdrie	38	25	7	6	85	31	57
Hibernian	38	22	8	8	78	43	52
Celtic	38	18	8	12	76	43	44
Cowdenb'th	38	16	10	12	76	65	42
St Mirren	38	18	4	16	65	63	40
Partick	38	14	10	14	60	61	38
Dundee	38	14	8	16	48	55	36
Raith	38	14	8	16	52	60	36
Hearts	38	12	11	15	65	69	35
St J'stone	38	12	11	15	56	71	35
Kilmarnock	38	12	9	17	53	64	33
Hamilton	38	15	3	20	50	63	33
Morton	38	12	9	17	46	69	33
Aberdeen	38	11	10	17	46	56	32
Falkirk	38	12	8	18	44	54	32
Queen's P	38	12	8	18	50	71	32
Motherwell	38	10	10	18	55	64	30
Ayr	*38*	*11*	*8*	*19*	*43*	*65*	*30*
T Lanark	*38*	*11*	*8*	*19*	*53*	*84*	*30*

SCOTTISH SECOND DIVISION

	1920-21	1921-22	1922-23	1923-24	1924-25
		Champions: Alloa	Champions: Queen's Park	Champions: St Johnstone	Champions: Dundee United
		Runners-up (not promoted): Cowdenbeath	Also promoted: Clydebank	Also promoted: Cowdenbeath	Also promoted: Clydebank

	1925-26	1926-27	1927-28	1928-29	1929-30
WORLD CUP					Uruguay 4 Argentina 2
FA CUP	Bolton Wanderers 1 Manchester City 0	Cardiff City 1 Arsenal 0	Blackburn Rovers 3 Huddersfield Town 1	Bolton Wanderers 2 Portsmouth 0	Arsenal 2 Huddersfield Town 0

FIRST DIVISION

1925-26	P	W	D	L	F	A	Pts
Huddersfld	42	23	11	8	92	60	57
Arsenal	42	22	8	12	87	63	52
Sunderland	42	21	6	15	96	80	48
Bury	42	20	7	15	85	77	47
Sheff Utd	42	19	8	15	102	82	46
Aston Villa	42	16	12	14	86	76	44
Liverpool	42	14	16	12	70	63	44
Bolton	42	17	10	15	75	76	44
Man Utd	42	19	6	17	66	73	44
Newcastle	42	16	10	16	84	75	42
Everton	42	12	18	12	72	70	42
Blackburn	42	15	11	16	91	80	41
West Ham	42	15	11	16	91	80	41

(First Division 1925-26 continued)

	P	W	D	L	F	A	Pts
West Ham	42	15	11	16	91	80	41
Birmingham	42	16	8	18	66	81	40
Tottenham	42	15	9	18	66	79	39
Cardiff	42	16	7	19	61	76	39
Leicester	42	14	10	18	70	80	38
West Ham	42	15	7	20	63	76	37
Leeds	42	14	8	20	64	76	36
Burnley	42	13	10	19	85	108	36
Man City	42	12	11	19	89	100	35
Notts C	42	13	7	22	54	74	33

1926-27	P	W	D	L	F	A	Pts
Newcastle	42	25	6	11	96	58	56
Huddersfld	42	17	17	8	76	60	51
Sunderland	42	21	7	14	98	70	49
Bolton	42	19	10	13	84	62	48
Burnley	42	19	9	14	91	80	47
West Ham	42	19	8	15	86	70	46
Leicester	42	17	12	13	85	70	46
Sheff Utd	42	17	10	15	74	86	44
Liverpool	42	18	7	17	69	61	43
Aston Villa	42	18	7	17	81	83	43
Arsenal	42	17	9	16	77	86	43
Derby	42	17	7	18	86	73	41
Tottenham	42	16	9	17	76	78	41
Cardiff	42	16	9	17	55	65	41
Man Utd	42	13	14	15	52	64	40
Wednesday	42	15	9	18	75	92	39
Birmingham	42	17	4	21	64	73	38
Blackburn	42	15	8	19	77	96	38
Bury	42	12	12	18	68	77	36
Everton	42	12	10	20	64	90	34
Leeds	42	11	8	23	69	88	30
West Brom	42	11	8	23	65	86	30

1927-28	P	W	D	L	F	A	Pts
Everton	42	20	13	9	102	66	53
Huddersfld	42	22	7	13	91	68	51
Leicester	42	18	12	12	96	72	48
Derby	42	17	10	15	96	83	44
Bury	42	20	4	18	80	80	44
Cardiff	42	17	10	15	70	80	44
Bolton	42	16	11	15	81	66	43
Aston Villa	42	17	9	16	78	73	43
Newcastle	42	15	13	14	79	81	43
Arsenal	42	13	15	14	82	86	41
Birmingham	42	13	15	14	70	75	41
Blackburn	42	16	9	17	66	78	41
Sheff Utd	42	15	10	17	79	86	40
Wednesday	42	13	13	16	81	78	39
Sunderland	42	15	9	18	74	76	39
Liverpool	42	13	13	16	84	87	39
West Ham	42	14	11	17	81	88	39
Man Utd	42	16	7	19	72	80	39
Burnley	42	16	7	19	82	98	39
Portsmouth	42	16	7	19	66	90	39
Tottenham	42	15	8	19	74	86	38
Middlesbro	42	11	15	16	81	88	37

1928-29	P	W	D	L	F	A	Pts
Wednesday	42	21	10	11	86	62	52
Leicester	42	21	9	12	96	67	51
Aston Villa	42	23	4	15	98	81	50
Sunderland	42	20	7	15	93	75	47
Liverpool	42	17	12	13	90	64	46
Derby	42	18	10	14	86	71	46
Blackburn	42	17	11	14	72	63	45
Man City	42	18	9	15	95	86	45
Arsenal	42	16	13	13	77	72	45
Newcastle	42	19	6	17	70	72	44
Sheff Utd	42	15	11	16	86	85	41
Man Utd	42	14	13	15	66	76	41
Leeds	42	16	9	17	71	84	41
Bolton	42	14	12	16	73	80	40
Birmingham	42	15	10	17	68	77	40
Huddersfld	42	14	11	17	70	61	39
West Ham	42	15	9	18	86	96	39
Everton	42	17	4	21	63	75	38
Burnley	42	15	8	19	81	103	38
Portsmouth	42	15	6	21	56	80	36
Bury	42	12	7	23	62	99	31
Cardiff	42	8	13	21	43	59	29

1929-30	P	W	D	L	F	A	Pts
Sheff Wed	42	26	8	8	105	57	60
Derby	42	21	8	13	90	82	50
Man City	42	19	9	14	91	81	47
Aston Villa	42	21	5	16	92	83	47
Leeds	42	20	6	16	79	63	46
Blackburn	42	19	7	16	99	93	45
West Ham	42	19	5	18	86	79	43
Leicester	42	17	9	16	86	90	43
Sunderland	42	18	7	17	76	80	43
Huddersfld	42	17	9	16	63	69	43
Birmingham	42	16	9	17	67	62	41
Liverpool	42	16	9	17	63	79	41
Portsmouth	42	15	10	17	66	62	40
Arsenal	42	14	11	17	78	66	39
Bolton	42	15	9	18	74	74	39
Middlesbro	42	16	6	20	82	84	38
Man Utd	42	15	8	19	67	88	38
Grimsby	42	15	7	20	73	89	37
Newcastle	42	15	7	20	71	92	37
Sheff Utd	42	15	6	21	91	96	36
Burnley	42	14	8	20	79	97	36
Everton	42	12	11	19	80	92	35

SECOND DIVISION

1925-26	1926-27	1927-28	1928-29	1929-30
Champions: The Wednesday Also promoted: Derby County Relegated: Stoke City, Stockport County	Champions: Middlesbrough Also promoted: Portsmouth Relegated: Darlington, Bradford City	Champions: Manchester City Also promoted: Leeds United Relegated: Fulham, South Shields	Champions: Middlesbrough Also promoted: Grimsby Town Relegated: Port Vale, Clapton Orient	Champions: Blackpool Also promoted: Chelsea Relegated: Hull City, Notts County

THIRD DIVISION SOUTH

1925-26	1926-27	1927-28	1928-29	1929-30
Champions: Reading Runners-up (not promoted): Plymouth Argyle	Champions: Bristol City Runners-up (not promoted): Plymouth Argyle	Champions: Millwall Runners-up (not promoted): Northampton Town	Champions: Charlton Athletic Runners-up (not promoted): Crystal Palace	Champions: Plymouth Argyle Runners-up (not promoted): Brentford

THIRD DIVISION NORTH

1925-26	1926-27	1927-28	1928-29	1929-30
Champions: Grimsby Town Runners-up (not promoted): Bradford Park Avenue	Champions: Stoke City Runners-up (not promoted): Rochdale	Champions: Bradford Park Avenue Runners-up (not promoted): Lincoln City	Champions: Bradford City Runners-up (not promoted): Stockport County	Champions: Port Vale Runners-up (not promoted): Stockport County

SCOTTISH CUP

1925-26	1926-27	1927-28	1928-29	1929-30
St Mirren 2 Celtic 0	Celtic 3 East Fife 1	Rangers 4 Celtic 0	Kilmarnock 2 Rangers 0	Rangers 2 Partick Thistle 1, after 0-0

SCOTTISH FIRST DIVISION

1925-26	P	W	D	L	F	A	Pts
Celtic	38	25	8	5	97	40	58
Airdrie	38	23	4	11	95	54	50
Hearts	38	21	8	9	87	56	50
St Mirren	38	20	7	11	62	52	47
Motherwell	38	19	8	11	67	46	46
Rangers	38	19	6	13	79	55	44
Cowdenb'th	38	18	6	14	87	68	42
Falkirk	38	14	14	10	61	57	42
Kilmarnock	38	17	7	14	79	77	41
Dundee	38	14	9	15	47	59	37
Aberdeen	38	13	10	15	49	54	36
Hamilton	38	13	9	16	68	79	35
Queen's P	38	15	4	19	70	81	34
Partick	38	10	13	15	64	73	33
Morton	38	12	7	19	57	84	31
Hibernian	38	12	6	20	72	77	30
Dundee	38	11	6	21	52	74	28
St J'stone	38	9	10	19	43	78	28
Raith	38	11	4	23	46	81	26
Clydebank	38	7	8	23	55	92	22

1926-27	P	W	D	L	F	A	Pts
Rangers	38	23	10	5	85	41	56
Motherwell	38	23	5	10	81	52	51
Celtic	38	21	7	10	101	55	49
Airdrie	38	18	9	11	97	64	45
Dundee	38	17	9	12	77	51	43
Falkirk	38	16	10	12	77	60	42
Cowdenb'th	38	18	6	14	74	60	42
Aberdeen	38	13	14	11	73	72	40
Hibernian	38	16	7	15	62	71	39
St Mirren	38	16	5	17	78	76	37
Partick	38	15	6	17	89	74	36
Queen's P	38	15	6	17	74	84	36
Hearts	38	12	11	15	65	64	35
St J'stone	38	13	9	16	55	69	35
Hamilton	38	13	9	16	60	85	35
Kilmarnock	38	12	8	18	54	71	32
Clyde	38	10	9	19	54	85	29
Dunfermline	38	10	8	20	53	85	28
Morton	38	12	4	22	56	101	28
Dundee	38	7	8	23	56	101	22

1927-28	P	W	D	L	F	A	Pts
Rangers	38	26	8	4	109	36	60
Celtic	38	23	9	6	93	39	55
Motherwell	38	23	9	6	92	46	55
St Mirren	38	18	8	12	77	76	44
Partick	38	18	7	13	85	67	43
Aberdeen	38	19	5	14	71	61	43
Kilmarnock	38	15	10	13	68	78	40
Cowdenb'th	38	16	7	15	66	68	39
Falkirk	38	16	5	17	76	69	37
St J'stone	38	14	8	16	66	67	36
Hibernian	38	13	9	16	73	75	35
Airdrie	38	12	11	15	59	69	35
Dundee	38	14	7	17	65	80	35
Clyde	38	14	6	18	46	72	34
Queen's P	38	12	9	17	69	80	33
Raith	38	11	7	20	60	89	29
Hamilton	38	11	6	21	67	86	28
Bo'ness	38	9	8	21	48	86	26
Dunfermline	38	4	4	30	41	126	12

1928-29	P	W	D	L	F	A	Pts
Rangers	38	30	7	1	107	32	67
Celtic	38	22	7	9	67	44	51
Motherwell	38	20	10	8	85	66	50
Hearts	38	19	9	10	91	57	47
Queen's P	38	18	7	13	100	69	43
Partick	38	17	7	14	91	70	41
Aberdeen	38	16	8	14	81	69	40
St Mirren	38	16	8	14	78	74	40
St J'stone	38	14	10	14	57	70	38
Kilmarnock	38	14	8	16	79	74	36
Falkirk	38	14	8	16	68	86	36
Hamilton	38	13	9	16	58	83	35
Cowdenb'th	38	14	5	19	55	69	33
Hibernian	38	13	6	19	54	62	32
Airdrie	38	12	7	19	56	65	31
Ayr	38	12	7	19	65	84	31
Clyde	38	12	6	20	47	71	30
Dundee	38	9	11	18	58	68	29
T Lanark	38	10	6	22	71	102	26
Raith	38	9	6	23	52	105	24

1929-30	P	W	D	L	F	A	Pts
Rangers	38	28	4	6	94	32	60
Motherwell	38	25	5	8	104	48	55
Aberdeen	38	23	7	8	85	61	53
Celtic	38	22	5	11	88	46	49
St Mirren	38	18	5	15	73	56	41
Partick	38	16	9	13	72	61	41
Falkirk	38	16	9	13	62	64	41
Kilmarnock	38	15	9	14	77	73	39
Ayr	38	16	6	16	70	92	38
Hearts	38	14	9	15	69	69	37
Clyde	38	13	11	14	64	69	37
Airdrie	38	16	4	18	60	66	36
Hamilton	38	14	7	17	76	81	35
Dundee	38	14	6	18	51	58	34
Queen's P	38	15	4	19	67	80	34
Cowdenb'th	38	13	7	18	64	74	33
Hibernian	38	9	11	18	45	62	29
Morton	38	10	7	21	67	95	27
Dundee	38	7	8	23	56	109	22
St J'stone	38	6	7	25	48	96	19

SCOTTISH SECOND DIVISION

1925-26	1926-27	1927-28	1928-29	1929-30
Champions: Dunfermline Athletic Also promoted: Clyde	Champions: Bo'ness Also promoted: Raith Rovers	Champions: Ayr United Also promoted: Third Lanark	Champions: Dundee United Also promoted: Morton	Champions: Leith Athletic Also promoted: East Fife

WORLD CUP 1930
Birth of the greatest show on earth

THE World Cup was conceived by two visionary Frenchmen in 1904, agreed at the Olympic Games at Antwerp in 1920, born amid chaos and confusion on the other side of the globe in Uruguay in 1930 and thrives today as the world's greatest single sports event. Yet at times it looked as if their child would be stillborn. Jules Rimet and Henri Delaunay, who were to hold high office in Fifa for more than 30 years, persuaded the fledgling world governing body that they should hold their own world championship outside of Olympic competition. However, the sporting politics of the day delayed and bedevilled their dream for nearly a decade.

The British associations, who had pioneered the game and formulated the rules, were extremely chary of this so-called international governing body which had established itself in dubious circumstances in Paris in 1904 without their presence. Only seven countries, all European, had been in attendance. Three of them did not even possess national federations. France had only played their first full international 20 days before the meeting. And, amazingly, Switzerland and Denmark would wait for another four years, while Spain dallied for 16 before competing internationally. By contrast, England and Scotland played each other in the very first full international in 1872.

However, the British associations co-operated with this new body after a fashion but walked out in 1928 over "shamateurism", an issue Fifa decided to duck because of political expediency. The British wanted a strict distinction between amateurs and professionals. The thorny problem of the fully employed player had been resolved in Britain as early as 1883, whereas in Europe and South America the distinction was blurred. "Broken time" payments (money for time off work) were either openly or covertly allowed, yet the players were still officially amateurs.

This was particularly important in the Olympic Games – the only kind of official football world championships that existed – where the British felt that, by adhering strictly to the Olympic amateur code, they were being cheated by other competing nations because they could not field their best players. To rub home the point, the Great Britain football team also withdrew from the 1928 Olympic Games.

Thus, the first World Cup took place without England, Scotland, Ireland or Wales, the very countries that gave the game to the world. The rift would be a long one, and not until after the Second World War would British football fully return to the world stage and realise what it had missed.

But the British teams were not the only European absentees. When the Fifa congress had to choose a host nation in 1929 it had five applicants: Italy, Holland, Spain, Sweden and Uruguay. The minuscule South American nation got the nod with an impassioned presentation: it was the centenary of their independence; they would build a new stadium and they would pay all the bills for the visiting teams. They had won the Olympic tournament in 1924 and 1928 and were the de facto world champions. Unsurprisingly, Uruguay's bid succeeded. Miffed, the four European aspirants then refused to attend, citing the three-week boat journey across the Atlantic and domestic commitments as their reasons.

Then four other European nations pulled out: Austria, Czechoslovakia, Germany and Switzerland, and the rest were lukewarm. The Latin American continent was incensed and threatened to resign from Fifa en bloc. The threat worked and Belgium, France, Romania and Yugoslavia were prevailed upon to participate. In all, 13 nations took part in the inaugural World Cup with the Americas providing Argentina, the host nation's arch rivals, Bolivia, Brazil, Chile, Mexico, Paraguay, Peru and the United States.

Interestingly, given the principled absence of the British teams, the United States team was largely composed of former Scottish and English professionals. They were to get to the semi-finals without conceding a goal, but then Argentina crushed them 6-1. The Romanian team had been hand-picked by their monarch, King Carol, who had also coerced the British oil company that employed many of the leading players to grant them paid leave. Yugoslavia, who were unfancied having been thrashed 7-1 by Uruguay in the 1924 Olympics, were the surprise of the tournament, beating Brazil and Bolivia to reach a semi-final with the hosts. This time they only lost 6-1, albeit scoring first.

While the tournament inevitably became a procession towards a repeat of the 1928 Olympic final between Uruguay and Argentina, which Uruguay had only won 2-1 after a replay, much of it was marred by poor refereeing and dirty play. France lost their goalkeeper after only 10 minutes in the opening game against Mexico when his jaw was kicked. Monti, Argentina's hard man, was allowed to get away with murder time after time.

In Argentina's match against France the referee blew for time six minutes early, just as France seemed likely to score the equaliser. After a near-riot the match was resumed but France could not score, and the best European team in the tournament never recovered from the setback. Then in Argentina's match against Mexico the referee awarded five penalties, most of them dubious.

The final, in the brand-new Centenario stadium in Montevideo on July 17, Uruguay's Independence day, was a wonderfully contested game befitting a match between the Olympic champions and the South American champions.

But the atmosphere surrounding this first World Cup final was extraordinary. It was if the entire futures of these neighbouring nations and bitter football rivals depended on the outcome. Boats had been hired to take thousands of Argentinians across the River Plate from Buenos Aires to Montevideo the night before, and the quaysides were packed as the Argentinians chanted: "Victory or Death". Security was tight as fans were searched for firearms, mounted police

New era: even the poster was stunning

escorted the Argentinian players, and soldiers with fixed bayonets patrolled the stadium.

Although Uruguay – with home advantage and most of the 90,000 crowd screaming them on – were the favourites, Argentina were a dangerous side. They had been playing neat, attractive football and had found in Guillermo Stabile a wonderful striker. And Uruguay's route to the final had not been as self-assured as had been expected. The match was finely balanced.

Pablo Dorado, their right wing, gave Uruguay the lead after 12 minutes. Peucelle equalised and Stabile put Argentina ahead eight minutes before the interval with a goal that Uruguay insisted was offside. In the second half, though, Uruguay came to life and started to play the football that had swept Europe aside at two Olympics. A wonderful solo goal from Pedro Cea 13 minutes after the restart inspired them and with two more goals, the last crashing into the roof of the net in the last minute, they became the winners of the first World Cup.

Montevideo went mad, cars hooted their horns, fireworks went off, boats sounded their sirens and the next day was declared a public holiday. In Buenos Aires they also went mad and stoned the Uruguayan embassy until the police opened fire on the angry mob. The World Cup was indeed born with a bang that eventually resounded throughout the globe.

FOR THE RECORD

GROUP ONE

	P	W	D	L	F	A	Pts
Argentina	3	3	0	0	10	4	6
Chile	3	2	0	1	5	3	4
France	3	1	0	2	4	3	2
Mexico	3	0	0	3	4	13	0

GROUP TWO

	P	W	D	L	F	A	Pts
Yugoslavia	2	2	0	0	6	1	4
Brazil	2	1	0	1	5	2	2
Bolivia	2	0	0	2	0	8	0

GROUP THREE

	P	W	D	L	F	A	Pts
Uruguay	2	2	0	0	5	0	4
Romania	2	1	0	1	3	5	2
Peru	2	0	0	2	1	4	0

GROUP FOUR

	P	W	D	L	F	A	Pts
USA	2	2	0	0	6	0	4
Paraguay	2	1	0	1	1	3	2
Belgium	2	0	0	2	0	4	0

SEMI-FINALS
Argentina 6   United States 1
HT 1-0 Att. 80,000
Uruguay 6   Yugoslavia 1
HT 3-1 Att. 93,000

FINAL
Uruguay 4   Argentina 2
HT 1-2 Att. 93,000

Teams
Uruguay Ballesteros; Nasazzi, Mascheroni, Andrade, Fernandez, Gestido, Dorado, Scarone, Castro, Cea, Iriarte
Argentina Botasso; Torre, Paternoster, Evaristo, Monti, Suarez, Peucelle, Varallo, Stabile, Ferreira, Evaristo
Referee Jean Langenus (Bel)

Leading goalscorers 8 Stabile (Arg) 5 Cea (Urg) 4 Subiabre (Chile)
Hat-tricks Stabile (Argentina v Mexico), Cea (Uruguay v Yugoslavia). Stabile was the first player to score a hat-trick in the World Cup finals
Fastest goal Desu (Romania v Peru), 1 minute
Total goals scored 70
Average per game: 3.88
Most appearances 5 Torre (Arg)
Sent off De Las Casas (Peru v Romania)

● Pedro Cea of Uruguay was the first person to score a goal in both the Olympic and the World Cup finals. He scored in the 1924 Olympic Final in Paris and in the inaugural World Cup six years later.
● Only two founder members of Fifa competed in the first World Cup, France and Belgium.
● Only three men played their club football in a country different from the one they represented. All three were Yugoslavians who played for French clubs; Stefanovic and Beck (Sete) and Seculic (Montpellier). In the 1990 World Cup more than 100 players played their League football abroad.

At long last the show gets on the road (left): the World Cup kicks off after 26 years
Founding father: Jules Rimet (above) presents the trophy to the president of the Uruguayan FA

Lacklustre United hit rock bottom

MANCHESTER UNITED, the club who had won two League championships at the start of the century (1908 and 1911) had fallen on hard times, and fallen hard.

United had regained their place in the First Division in 1925, but had struggled since then. They managed a couple of mid-table finishes, but most of the time the club was always hovering on the brink of relegation.

This season, their campaign began disastrously when they lost their first 12 matches to set an unenviable record that would stand for the rest of the century.

Things got even worse when they suffered their heaviest-ever defeat. United were beaten 7-0 by Aston Villa two days after Christmas. This equalled their 7-0 drubbing at the hands of Blackburn Rovers in 1926.

Relegation was inevitable and the pride of Manchester ended the season nine points adrift of Leeds United, having conceded the awesome figure of 115 goals and having scored a mere 53 times.

Not surprisingly, such a dismal set of results brought about a change of manager. Herbert Bamlett, who had been in charge since 1927, left the club and was replaced by Walter Crickmer. However, Crickmer fared little better. His time in charge only lasted one season.

United showed no signs of recovering their place in the First Division — finishing in twelfth place in the Second Division and suffering yet another record 7-0 defeat, at the hands of Wolverhampton, ironically also at Christmas.

West Brom toil to scale twin peaks

IN NAIL-BITING fashion West Bromwich Albion achieved a unique "double" – the first team to win the FA Cup and be promoted in the same season. But they certainly made it all look like hard work.

In the FA Cup it took them two replays in the third round to get past Charlton, after having been 2-0 down at home in the first match. Tottenham and Portsmouth were West Brom's next victims, but only by the slender margin of 1-0 victories. Wolves proved particularly stubborn opponents in the quarter-final only going down 2-1 in a replay. West Brom had only themselves to blame for the extra tie, Wolves' equaliser had come from a needlessly conceded own goal.

The semi-final against Everton was a titanic battle. Dixie Dean and Everton were always a formidable force and they were running away with the Second Division championship. The luck however favoured the Midlands side. In the 55th minute a Tommy Glidden cross was caught by the wind and pulled into the net. Despite the fact that Everton had virtually all the play they just could not equalise. Dean, of all people, missed a sitter.

West Brom's luck held in the final against Birmingham as well, when the referee dubiously disallowed an eighth-minute header from Gregg. William "W G" Richardson, who had been in prolific form all season, put West Brom ahead in

Richardson: prolific scorer

the 26th minute. Birmingham sensed it was never going to be their day when, having equalised in the 57th minute, W G Richardson scored again from the kick-off within 30 seconds. West Brom had won their third Cup.

However, in the League their form had been wavering as Tottenham battled them for promotion. Fortunately for West Brom, Spurs also stumbled in the closing matches and so, a week after the Cup final, it was still neck and neck.

West Brom had to beat to Charlton at home; if they drew and Tottenham beat Burnley 3-0 at Turf Moor then Spurs would be promoted. West Brom scraped home 3-2, thanks to W G Richardson, and Spurs went down 1-0. West Brom had their "double".

Arsenal stroll serenely to the title

HERBERT CHAPMAN'S expensively assembled Arsenal proved their worth as they utterly dominated the First Division and coasted to their first championship, the first Southern club to have won the League title. Having won the FA Cup last season, their first major trophy, Arsenal began

their League campaign in trophy-winning mood.

They won their first five games, were only beaten once in the first 18 and seemed to be setting about the record books with gusto. Their final tally of 66 points was a record; their 127 goals would also have been a record but Aston Villa, distant

runners-up seven points behind, had accumulated 128. Their 60 goals scored away from home were though, as were the 33 points they acquired on their travels.

The question for the rest of the First Division is: who can stop this latest Chapman wonder team?

THE
1931-32
SEASON

Striker haunted by tragic death of goalkeeper

SECTARIANISM in Scotland took a macabre, ghoulish turn when Celtic's brilliant young goalkeeper, John Thomson, died in hospital five hours after a collision in the match between Rangers and Celtic at Ibrox on September 5. Thomson, 22 years old and with four Scotland caps, fractured his skull when he dashed out of his area and dived at the feet of Sam English as they both went for a 50-50 ball.

Although neutral observers attached no blame to English for Thomson's death, bigoted crowds did and claimed the accident was deliberate. English, who had been devastated by the incident, was barracked mercilessly. In an attempt to escape the morbid taunts he moved to England a year later and played for Liverpool. However, the tragedy still haunted him and, disillusioned, he eventually returned to his native Ireland.

Referee ruins final with phantom goal

Caught in the act: film evidence of the goal that never was

IT WAS the most controversial goal in English football history and despite Adolf Hitler's electoral victory in Prussia it was front-page news as the goal that never was.

In the 38th minute of the FA Cup final between Arsenal and Newcastle, with Arsenal leading 1-0, Davison, the Newcastle centre-half struck a deep pass in front of Jimmy Richardson on the right wing. The inside forward just failed to connect with the ball before it went over the dead-ball line. Richardson crossed the ball anyway. The Arsenal players stood back and waited for the goal-kick as Jack Allen nonchalantly put the ball in the back of the net.

Amazingly the referee, Mr Harper, blew for a goal and defended his decision to the press: "It was a goal. As God is my judge, the man was in play. I was eight yards away. I do not mind what other people say." Sadly for Harper, modern technology had caught up with refer-

ees being somewhat cavalier with the truth, and film from British Movietone News proved his decision was wrong, and that he was a liar.

The photographic evidence clearly showed the whole of the ball beyond the goalline as Richardson prepared to centre it. Moreover, at the time of the incident Harper was a good five yards outside the penalty area and therefore 25 yards away from the incident. And thirdly "the man was in play" was irrelevant, *the ball* is the object that has to be in play.

The referee had ruined the final single-handedly. Arsenal came out for the second half a broken team and succumbed to another Allen goal in the 72nd minute. Newcastle thus became the first team to win the Cup having been a goal down since they did it themselves in 1910.

Charitably, Arsenal accepted the result without rancour. "The referee has made his decision and that is the end of it."

Everton capitalise on Arsenal's second lapse

ARSENAL'S hopes of a second League championship and a possible Double evaporated in two disastrous spells – at the start of the season and in two fateful weeks in March and April.

Arsenal lost their opening match to newly promoted West Bromwich Albion 1-0 at Highbury and went another three matches without a win. In the spring a five-match spell yielded only a meagre three points, all draws, as they seemed to be distracted by their second FA Cup final in two years.

Everton, who had stormed out of the Second Division the previous season, went on a goalscoring spree in the First, particularly at Goodison where they notched up 84. In total Everton amassed 116 goals with Dixie Dean on target 44 times.

Drawn matches did not seem to be in their vocabulary as they won 26 and lost 12 of their 42 matches to win the title two points clear of Arsenal, who had beaten them home and away.

FOR THE RECORD

■ Wigan Borough resigned from the Third Division North on October 26 after playing six matches. They were the first club to leave the League in mid-season and their results were deleted from the official records.

■ Newcastle United's 0-0 draw with Portsmouth on December 5 is believed to be the only first-class match in which neither side conceded a corner.

■ England avenged their 4-3 defeat in Madrid in 1929 with a 7-1 demolition of Spain at Highbury on December 9. Ricardo Zamora, the Spanish goalkeeper, was so shell-shocked that he was reduced to tears before the match had finished.

■ Stanley Matthews made his debut for Stoke in a 1-0 victory at Bury.

■ Rochdale finished rock bottom of the Third Division North, only winning four matches and drawing three. They lost a record 17 matches in a row between beating New Brighton on November 7 and drawing the return fixture on March 9. Oddly, New Brighton finished one place above Rochdale, with 13 more points, even though they scored 10 fewer goals.

Vanquished armada: Spain were sunk by England

THE
1932-33
SEASON

Old Firm return to break Motherwell's heart

MOTHERWELL, having broken the Old Firm's 28-year-old grip on the League title the season before, came heartbreakingly close to winning the Double but just missed out on the championship and the Scottish Cup by the narrowest of margins.

The Cup was the bigger disappointment. Motherwell had thundered through the early rounds, thrashing Montrose 7-1, Dundee 5-0, Kilmarnock (the winners in 1929) 8-3 after a replay, Clyde 2-0, but fell 1-0 in the final to a Celtic side determined to compensate for their failure to mount any challenge in the League.

Motherwell's prodigious goal-scoring was not confined to the Scottish Cup. In the Scottish First Division they accumulated 114 goals in 38 matches, outscoring Rangers by a goal and winning more matches than the Ibrox club, but missed the championship by three points largely because they lost games they could well have drawn.

Bank of England robbed by £69 outfit

WALSALL 2 ARSENAL 0. The third-round defeat of the champions-elect by Third-Division fodder was the greatest Cup upset of all time, a result that caused the nation to rejoice.

Arsenal were not a popular side: their players were costly imports and their style was seen as breakaway smash and grab. And they were a privileged London side when much of the North and Midlands was experiencing severe unemployment.

Consequently, the match had been built up by the press as the Bank of England team (the Arsenal side had cost £30,000) versus the little team that cost £69. "Arsenal enjoy champagne, gold and electrical massage in an atmosphere of prima donna preciousness. Walsall men eat fish and chips and drink beer."

Aside from this charged atmosphere, Arsenal's manager, Herbert Chapman had serious problems. Influenza had deprived him of three key players and injury of another two. He decided to blood four reserves, Tommy Black at left-back, Norman Sidey at left-half, Billy Warnes at right-wing and Charlie Walsh at centre-forward. Each of them were to contribute to the disaster and Black, Warnes and Walsh never played for the club again.

Walsall played the Cup-tie the way any Third Division club would against the cream of English football. "They could not have complained if five of their men had been sent off in the first 15 minutes," was Cliff Bastin's analysis of Walsall's tactics.

However, Arsenal also shot themselves in the foot.

Walsh missed a sitter and later took the ball off David Jack just as he was poised to score. After an hour and no score, Walsall could smell the upset. Lee took a corner, Black failed to get to the ball and Gilbert Alsop, Walsall's centre-forward, nodded home. "I'd been watching Dixie Dean," he said. Five minutes later Black was again the culprit when he brought Alsop down. Billy Sheppard converted the penalty.

Austria show England the proper way to play

ENGLAND'S match with Austria at Stamford Bridge in December was seen as the unofficial championship of Europe. Austria, under the visionary management of Hugo Meisl coupled with the training techniques of the former Blackpool and Bolton player Jimmy Hogan, arrived with impressive credentials. For the Austrian "Wunderteam" had already trounced Scotland 5-0, Germany 6-0, Switzerland 8-1 and Hungary 8-2.

England were 2-0 ahead at the interval, both goals coming from Blackpool's Jimmy Hampson. Despite their lead, England were being outplayed and this became apparent after half-time.

The Wunderteam put on a marvellous display of attacking, possession football. Although England eventually won 4-3 with goals from Houghton and

May the best team win

Crooks, in the second half Austria outscored them – and outplayed them. The press knew the truth: "Our visitors show us how to play!" was the headline in the Daily Herald.

FOR THE RECORD

■ Wales recorded their first victory in Scotland since 1906 with a 5-2 win on October 26, despite being reduced to 10 men after just 10 minutes. A goalless draw with England at Wrexham in November, and a 4-1 defeat of Northern Ireland on the same ground the following month won them the Home championship.

■ Tottenham, like Arsenal, went out of the FA Cup to a Third Division side, Luton. West Ham, who just avoided relegation from the Second Division, were left to carry the standard for London, beating two First Division teams on their way to the semi-finals.

■ Numbered shirts were used in the FA Cup final for the first time. The Everton players were numbered from one (their goalkeeper) to 11, and Manchester City sported 12 to 22 (their goalkeeper). Everton won 3-0, with goals from Stein, Dean and Dunn, to complete a hat-trick of successes – the Second Division championship in 1931, the First Division crown in 1932 and now the FA Cup.

■ Rangers, who only lost two matches on the way to the Scottish championship, boasted 13 international players in their squad, 10 Scots and three Irishmen.

Giant-killers: Luton bundle Tottenham out of the FA Cup

Rous steps up to top position

Rous: respected referee

STANLEY ROUS, the Cup final referee, was appointed secretary of the Football Association in June upon the retirement of Sir Frederick Wall, who had occupied the post since 1895.

Rous, the games master at Watford Grammar School, had had plenty of time to study the game both at home and abroad, where he had taken charge of several international matches.

His greatest concern was the development of the game and no sooner had he taken office than he started introducing a series of revolutionary plans. Rous encouraged former players to visit schools to teach youngsters how to play, and then set up a formal training scheme to produce properly qualified coaches.

I'm a bit of a mountaineer. I like to climb up to the pinnacle of whatever I undertake, be it work or play

STANLEY ROUS

Arsenal devastated by sudden death of visionary Chapman

HERBERT CHAPMAN, the greatest manager since the war, died suddenly in the early hours of Saturday January 6. The first that many of the Arsenal players knew of his death was when they arrived at Highbury for the match that afternoon. "As I approached the ground the newspaper sellers were shouting out the news," Cliff Bastin said. "It seemed just too bad to be true."

Chapman's drive for perfection undoubtedly brought about his death. After Arsenal had drawn at Birmingham the previous Saturday he travelled to Bury to watch a player he was interested in, and then went straight to Hillsborough to study Sheffield Wednesday, who he thought would be Arsenal's nearest rivals for the title.

By the time he returned home he had developed a heavy cold. Ignoring the club doctor's advice to go to bed, he went to watch Arsenal's third team, saying: "I don't get a chance to see the lads very often."

The cold appeared to be getting better by Friday, but it suddenly developed into pneumonia and by 3 am Chapman was dead. In a state of shock, the Arsenal team eked out a draw with Sheffield Wednesday that afternoon but then went to pieces, losing their next three games. But the team were driven on by a wave of emotion and rallied to win the championship for the second year running.

Chapman's legacy to the club he had transformed was the team that went on to win a record-equalling third successive title. His legacy to the game was equally impressive both on the pitch – novel tactics such as the defensive centre-half and forwards playing in a "W" formation – and off it.

Jittery Swift saved by Tilson's cool finishing

FRANK SWIFT, Manchester City's teenage goalkeeper, was terrified by the thought of playing in the FA Cup final. The night before the match he was so jumpy that Sam Cowan, the team's captain, spent most of the evening recounting tales of past matches to try to distract Swift from fretting about the match.

Portsmouth, too, were jumpy. Their manager, Jack Tinn, hired the comedian Bud Flanagan to crack jokes in the dressing-room before the kick-off to relax his players.

Tinn was laughing when Rutherford gave Portsmouth the lead in the 27th minute with a powerful shot. At half-time, while Tinn was happy Swift was distraught. He blamed himself for the goal, saying that he should have stopped the shot rather than just getting a hand to the ball.

Fred Tilson, the Manchester City centre-forward told Swift not to worry. He said that he was going to score two goals in the second half to make up for Manchester City's defeat by Everton in the previous year's final.

Tilson delivered on his promise, equalising in the 74th minute and putting Manchester City ahead in the 86th minute. With photographers crowding the pitch, counting down the final minutes, Swift's nerves returned.

When the referee blew for full-time Swift was so overcome that he fainted on his goal-line. He had to be revived by Cowan and helped up the steps to collect his medal.

Swift: survived stage fright

53

HERBERT CHAPMAN
The visionary manager of the century

Sue Mott

I T IS a fact not universally acknowledged (probably nobody dares) that a Spurs man made Arsenal.

He was sitting in the dressing-room baths, a roly-poly forward of marginal skill and many former clubs, with the Tottenham captain, Walter Bull, after their last match of the 1906-7 season. Bull had been offered the post of manager at Northampton Town but doubted his ability to flourish at the task.

"You take it Herbert," he said in a flash of inspiration and so Herbert Chapman, surely the greatest football manager of the century, took the path that would lead him to Highbury.

Some might think the only legacy of his eight-year reign at Arsenal – which saw them become the power in the land – is the famous bust in the marble entrance hall. But in many ways the ruthlessness, ambition and wisdom of the man pervade Highbury to this day.

He fostered a team of "winners", lightning strikers and a rocklike defence. He placed huge emphasis on team spirit as a shield against those who criticised Arsenal as a side whose paramount urge was to defend. The scoring of 127 goals in 1930-31 likewise deflated the critics.

He was an autocrat and a showman (he wore yellow boots in his playing days) and a visionary administrator. He advocated numbered shirts; the FA said no. He wanted a white ball; the FA were horrified. He was keen to introduce floodlights; the FA were dead set against them. Above all, Chapman wanted Arsenal to be the finest

Chapman: transformed Arsenal and the game

club in the world. His towering achievement was that he fulfilled his dream.

The son of an illiterate miner, Chapman was born eight years before Arsenal in 1878 in Kiveton Park, a small mining village in South Yorkshire. Most working-class children in such a situation could look forward to little except a pit helmet of their own in due course.

But Chapman was exceptionally bright. He took a course in mining engineering at Sheffield Technical College and was to hold jobs within the mining industry for many years even as his yellow boots were in evidence at Stalybridge Rovers, Rochdale, Grimsby, Swindon, Sheppey United, Worksop, Northampton, Sheffield United, Notts County and Spurs.

His two years at Tottenham (mostly in the reserves) was his longest spell anywhere, but by then he must have been one of the world's leading authorities on how not to manage a football club. Certainly, his arrival at Northampton as player-manager was to bring them radical success and so it proved wherever he went.

Chapman's next stop was Leeds City, who won virtually everything in the emergency competitions during the First World War. Huddersfield, within five years of his appointment, had won the first League hat-trick in history.

On May 11, 1925, an advertisement appeared in the Athletic News: "Arsenal Football Club is open to receive applications for the position of Team Manager. He must be experienced and possess the highest qualifications for the post, both as to ability and personal character."

This must have caught Chapman's eye, not least because he had already been offered the job and £2,000 a year for taking it. Brimful of ability and personal character, the miner's son came to London.

In his first season the London club, whose previous claim to fame was beating St Bartholomew's Hospital 6-0 in the London Senior Cup in 1891, came second in the League championship. A year later they reached the Cup final.

In 1931, Arsenal won the League, the first Southern club ever to perform the feat, much to Tottenham's chagrin. The next year they were runners-up in both the League and the Cup. Then followed the hat-trick of League titles and the conviction that Arsenal, the team that Chapman built, were all but invincible.

He pursued excellence relentlessly. Within the first two years he had spent the massive sum of

Confident: Chapman and James at Wembley

£25,000 gathering players of the calibre of Charlie Buchan, Tom Parker and Jack Lambert. But allied to the flourishing chequebook was the astuteness to mould unknowns into heroes.

Eddie Hapgood was a 19-year-old former milkman turned down by Bristol Rovers when he came into contact with Chapman. He sometimes suffered concussion from the repetitive heading of the heavy, leather ball. But Chapman had seen something he liked. Hapgood went on to become the captain of Arsenal and England.

Perhaps Chapman's greatest asset was his uncanny ability to impart a golden glow of confidence to those around him. Undoubtedly, his greatest purchase was Alex James, a wee Scots "Wembley Wizard" who had been placed on the transfer list by Preston to the fervent interest of Liverpool, Aston Villa, Birmingham and Manchester City. Preston were known as "Alex James and 10 others" at the time.

How Chapman beat them all to the quarry is not recorded by posterity. Perhaps he used the

Tribute to a legend: the memorial at Highbury

dastardly wiles that had helped extract David Jack from Bolton, namely doubling the quantity of alcohol in his visitors' drinks while himself quaffing gin and tonics entirely devoid of the gin.

Whatever his methods, James was duly installed at Highbury and his dominance of what we would call midfield today was the key to Arsenal's extravagant success. It had taken nerve, nous and vision to achieve, but when Chapman created a forward line of Hulme, Jack, Lambert, James and Bastin he had been blessed with the Midas touch.

But at first it appeared that James was dross. The wee man in the big, baggy shorts did not settle immediately into the side. After the changes in the offside law in 1925, Chapman had been at the forefront of sweeping tactical alterations, obliging his full-backs to swing wide, his centre-half to defend, his inside-forwards to drop back and his wingers ("the flying columns") to cut inside the opposing backs.

James was accustomed to playing as a goalscoring forward; now he was being asked to act as midfield playmaker. James lost crucial confidence and Chapman made the most courageous decision of his career. He dropped his star.

His recall was sensational. Early one Sunday morning, Chapman called personally at the James household, literally hauled his man out of bed and told him to get to Highbury to train. A vital FA Cup replay against Birmingham loomed and James was the only man for the job. The dramatic nature of the SOS appealed to the Scotsman, his confidence returned and his place in the Arsenal pantheon was assured.

Arguing against Chapman was hopeless. Cliff Bastin had not played at outside right since he was nine when the manager converted him to the wing. But Chapman was right and Bastin had won every honour in the game by the time he was 21.

George Male was a reserve right wing when Chapman told the flabbergasted player he was moving him to right back. The young man protested in vain. "By the time Chapman was finished with me I was convinced that I was not merely a full-back but the best in the country," Male said.

Through sheer force of personality and powers of persuasion, Chapman fashioned the club of his dreams. He even cajoled and bullied the London Electric Railway to change the name of Gillespie Road tube station to Arsenal.

In eight years he had created the modern Arsenal and even, in a state of apoplexy, watched the greatest giantkilling act in the history of English football. Walsall 2 Arsenal 0 was the score in 1933 in the third round of the FA Cup. It marked the nadir of Chapman's career: The Invincibles beaten by a Third Division Midlands team that cost £69 in all.

It was to be the last Cup-tie he ever saw Arsenal lose. By the time Aston Villa defeated them in the quarter-finals in 1934 Chapman was dead. A sudden attack of pneumonia carried him off at 3am on Saturday, January 6, 1934, exactly 12 hours before the kick-off against Sheffield

On the right track: Chapman had Gillespie Road tube station renamed

Wednesday at Highbury. "I suppose Arsenal gave quite a good display that day, considering the game was just an unimportant incident," Bastin recalled.

Huge crowds turned up to his funeral in Hendon where Jack, Hapgood, Hulme, Lambert, Bastin and James were the pallbearers. Perhaps the greatest obituary came from the Boy Bastin.

"There was an aura of greatness about him. His power of inspiration and gift of foresight were his greatest attributes. I think his qualities were worthy of an even better reward. He should have been Prime Minister."

It is doubtful that Chapman would have agreed. His heart belonged to the Arsenal he created and Bob Wall, his assistant who rose to become a powerful secretary at Highbury, insisted Chapman's spirit never left the club. For several years afterwards, he said, he heard Chapman's footsteps striding the corridors. And Wall, being an Arsenal man, was never the fanciful type.

Ahead of his time: Chapman's team making a "talkie" in 1930

WORLD CUP 1934

Italy deliver the goods for Mussolini

ITALY took full advantage of being the host nation for the second World Cup. Not only did they win and make a profit of a million lira, their victory was the perfect propaganda triumph for Mussolini. Italy had been awarded the tournament in 1932 when Fifa – sweetened by the offer of the Italian government to pick up all the bills – decided the World Cup was too large to hold in one city (as they had in Montevideo in 1930) and settled on a country with several imposing stadiums. The political spin-off for Il Duce and fascism was regarded as a small price to pay for a well-orchestrated tournament.

Internal politics also vitiated the event. Uruguay, the holders, still smarting from what they had perceived as a European boycott of the 1930 World Cup, and in dispute with Argentina, stayed at home. Then Argentina, furious that Italy had poached three of their best players, Guaita, Monti and Orsi claiming they were of Italian descent, deliberately sent a weakened squad. The British, still in splendid isolation, were again not in attendance.

The early stages of the 1934 World Cup hardly boded well for the success of the championship. In the qualifying rounds, as the 31 entrants were whittled down to the final 16, Peru and Chile withdrew and Yugoslavia, semi-finalists in 1930, were surprisingly eliminated. Bizarrely, even Italy had to qualify.

Cruelly, the finals were straight knock-out. By the end of the first round of the finals in Italy, all three representatives from the Americas were on the boat home and two of them, Argentina and Brazil, had only played one game in the entire competition because their qualifying opponents had pulled out. The United States had played twice in Italy, having knocked out Mexico in a qualifying match three days before the first round of the finals. Sadly, the Mexicans had come all the way to Rome and had not even played in the World Cup proper.

By the second round (the quarter-finals) the 1934 World Cup had become a purely European affair. The strongest teams were Austria, Czechoslovakia, Germany, Hungary and Italy. Four of these would contest the semi-finals. Austria were managed by Hugo Meisl, one of the great figures of European football, a co-founder of the Aus-

Let battle commence: the Italian and Czech captains shake hands

trian football federation whose legendary team in the 1930s was dubbed the "Wunderteam".

They knocked out Hungary, their old foes, 2-1 in the quarter-finals in a match Meisl described as "a brawl, not an exhibition of football". The trouble started when Austria took a 2-0 lead shortly after half-time, and then got worse when Hungary scored from a penalty. Just as Hungary were pressing for the equaliser their right-winger, Markos, was sent off and Austria came through against 10 men to face Italy in the semi-final.

Italy had not had the easiest of times getting there. Their first match was a 7-1 rout of the United States. But their quarter-final against Spain was extremely tough and required a replay.

Italy's manager, Vittorio Pozzo, was, alongside Meisl, the other revered coach in Europe. He needed all his wiles to defeat Spain. In the first match Spain had taken the lead with a freak goal when their centre-forward, Langara, swung at a free-kick, completely mis-hit it and utterly bamboozled the hapless goalkeeper. A fortunate equaliser

gave Italy the opportunity to redeem themselves the next day. After the match Pozzo summoned all of his players to see him in their hotel, and he read the riot act to each one individually. Three of them were dropped. Fortunately for the Italians, the Spaniards could only retain four of their team because of injuries. This time the Italians made no mistake with a 12th-minute headed goal from Meazza.

Their semi-final was played two days after the Spanish replay, whereas the Austrians had enjoyed a six-day break. So it was generally assumed that Meisl's Wunderteam, which had only lost to Czechoslovakia and England in the previous three years, were the favourites. Then the rains came and Austria were forced to play on a heavy pitch, completely unsuited to their style.

Despite playing their third game in four days, the Italians were not as tired as anticipated and, if anything, the Austrians were the more listless. A 19th-minute goal from Guaita, the former Argentinian, was enough to see them off. But not without a scare: a minute from time Zischek burst through the entire Italian defence and seemed certain to equalise. His shot went wide, the hosts breathed again and were in the final.

Italy's opponents were Czechoslovakia, who had beaten Switzerland 3-2 in a thrilling quarter-final that swung back and forth after the Swiss had taken the lead in the 18th minute. But the confident Czechs wrapped the game up seven minutes from time. Their semi-final against Germany was also a see-saw affair, but now it was the Czechs' complacency that let the Germans back into the match.

Germany had begun cautiously with both their inside forwards playing extremely deep, and they seemed out-classed by a superior ball-playing team. Oldrich Nejedly, a prolific striker, put Czechoslovakia ahead in the 21st minute, but then they seemed to treat the match as if it were a stroll. In the second half they were soon woken up when their goalkeeper, Planicka, stood leaden-footed as a speculative long shot from Noack sailed clean over his head. A fired-up Germany pressed for the winner and Czechoslovakia almost conceded an own goal. Then the Czechs hit the accelerator and two more goals from Nejedly ended the contest.

With home advantage and a powerful and hard team, Italy were the favourites to overcome the subtle and artistic skills of the Czechs in the final in Rome. However, the Italians seemed to freeze as the Czechs dazzled them with neat and accurate short passing tactics. Despite their superiority, the Czechs could not score until the 71st minute when from Puc's corner kick the ball was eventually returned to him and his long-range shot whistled past Combi, the Italian goalkeeper and captain, who seemed to have picked up the shot too late. Czechoslovakia then had two marvellous opportunities to seal the game – one hit the post – and become the first European winners of the World Cup. It was not to be.

Nine minutes from full time a coruscating goal from Orsi, one of the three Argentinians in the Italian team, turned the final on its head. He ran through the defence and feinted with his left foot while shooting with his right. The ball, swerving madly, was impossible to save, although the Czech goalkeeper did get his fingertips to it as it curled agonisingly into the net. So extraordinary was the goal that Orsi attempted to repeat it on an open field for the paparazzi the next day. Despite 20 attempts he could come nowhere near repeating his freak shot.

Extra time saw Pozzo's genius as he kept switching the positions of two of his forwards, Guaita and Schiavo, to bemuse the tiring Czech defence. And the winning goal came the second time these two changed roles, when they combined for Schiavio to shoot past Planicka. So, in the end, Pozzo's acumen and the raid Italy had made on the cream of Argentina's talent paid off handsomely and Mussolini had his propaganda coup: Italy were on top of the world. But would they have won if they had not been at home, or if the South American representation had been at full strength? We would find out some of the answers in four years' time.

Grand finale (from top): the Czech and Italian teams were deadlocked after 90 minutes. Pozzo's tactical switch in extra time paid off and his victorious players chaired him from the field

FOR THE RECORD

FIRST ROUND
Italy 7   United States 1
HT 3-0 Att. 30,000
Czechoslovakia 2   Romania 1
HT 0-1 Att. not recorded
Germany 5   Belgium 2
HT 1-2 Att. 8,000
Austria 3   France 2 aet
HT 1-1 90 mins. 1-1 Att. not recorded
Spain 3   Brazil 1
HT 2-0 Att. not recorded
Switzerland 3   Holland 2
HT 2-1 Att. not recorded
Sweden 3   Argentina 2
HT 1-1 Att. not recorded
Hungary 4   Egypt 2
HT 2-1 Att. not recorded

SECOND ROUND
Germany 2   Sweden 1
HT 0-0 Att. 3,000
Austria 2   Hungary 1
HT 1-0 Att. not recorded
Italy 1   Spain 1 aet
HT 0-1 90 mins. 1-1 Att. 35,000
Replay: Italy 1   Spain 0
HT: 1-0 Att. 43,000
Czechoslovakia 3   Switzerland 2
HT 1-1 Att. not recorded

SEMI-FINALS
Italy 1   Austria 0
HT 1-0 Att. 60,000
Czechoslovakia 3   Germany 1
HT 1-0 Att. 10,000

THIRD PLACE PLAY-OFF
Germany 3   Austria 2
HT 3-1 Att. 7,000

FINAL
Italy 2   Czechoslovakia 1 aet
HT 0-0 90 mins. 1-1 Att. 55,000

Teams
Italy Combi; Monzeglio, Allemandi, Ferraris IV, Monti, Bertolini, Guaita, Meazza, Schiavo, Ferrari, Orsi
Czechoslovakia Planicka; Zenisek, Ctyroky, Kostalek, Cambal, Krcil, Junek, Svoboda, Sobotka, Nejedly, Puc
Referee Ivan Eklind (Swe)

Leading goalscorers 5 Nejedly (Cz); 4 Schiavio (It), Conen (Ger); 3 Orsi (It), Kielholz (Swe)
Fastest goal Lehner (Germany v Austria), 30 seconds
Total goals scored 70
Average per game: 4.118
Most appearances 5 Allemandi, Combi, Meazza, Monti, Orsi (all Italy)
Sendings off Markos (Hun) v Austria. Referee: Francis Mattea (It)
Number of players used by finalists 17 Italy, 13 Czechoslovakia

● When Czechoslovakia reached the final their team consisted of 11 players from only two clubs – Sparta and Slavia. No other World Cup final team has contained such a small club representation.

Drake steers Arsenal to third title

ARSENAL'S third championship in a row equalled Huddersfield's record and was a fitting tribute to Herbert Chapman, who died last season after building both teams.

George Allison maintained Chapman's tradition at Arsenal, although much of the day-to-day running of the team was left in the hands of Joe Shaw and Tom Whittaker. Allison's greatest single contribution was the signing of Ted Drake, who won the title almost single-handedly.

Drake scored a hat-trick in Arsenal's first home game of the season, an 8-1 demolition of Liverpool, put four past Birmingham in a 5-1 win at Highbury in September, and scored another hat-trick in another 5-1 victory at home against Tottenham in October.

At home, Arsenal and Drake were formidable. Wolverhampton were beaten 7-0 (Drake scored four), Leicester 8-0 (Drake three) and Middlesbrough 8-0 (Drake four). Away from Highbury though, their form was indifferent with only one win before the turn of the year, 5-2 at Chelsea (four more goals for Drake).

Arsenal's erratic performances on their travels allowed Sunderland to briefly get their noses in front. But Drake kept on hitting the target as Arsenal eased to the title by four points. He was the League's leading goalscorer with 42 goals, and Arsenal hit 115, 25 more than Sunderland, the runners-up.

Battle of Highbury

Prince Arthur of Connaught greets the Italians

ENGLAND, despite spurning the World Cup, thought they were the best in the world. Italy, who had just won the World Cup, claimed that they were pre-eminent. The match between the two countries at Highbury on November 14 was billed as the showdown that would settle the argument.

England, with Ted Drake one of seven Arsenal players in the team, were hailed as Drake's Armada going to war with Mussolini. And it was some war. The fighting was so intense that the match was universally known as the Battle of Highbury.

The first skirmish came early, when Drake's tackle broke Luisito Monti's foot. Monti limped off, claiming that he had been injured deliberately. The rest of the Italian team went berserk, and spent the rest of the half determined to avenge Monti.

With the Italians more concerned with kicking their opponents than the ball England swept into a 3-0 lead in 15 minutes. Eric Brook scored twice after missing a penalty and Drake got the other goal while England were temporarily reduced to 10 men, their captain Eddie Hapgood receiving treatment for an elbow in the face.

In the second half Italy finally started to play good football. Giuseppe Meazza scored twice in five minutes and hit the bar. England's battered team clung grimly to their lead in pouring rain, with Frank Moss, the Arsenal goalkeeper denying the Italians an equaliser.

By the end of the match England were a team of walking wounded. Hapgood's nose was broken, Brook's arm was X-rayed because he feared it was fractured, Drake had a cut leg, Ray Bowden suffered an ankle injury, John Barker had his hand strapped, and several other players suffered severe bruising.

The press that had whipped up the hysteria before the match were, unsurprisingly, scathing about the Italians' conduct. There were even calls for the FA to stop playing internationals.

Wednesday's start and finish

SHEFFIELD WEDNESDAY won the FA Cup with a remarkable flourish in a thrilling match. No sooner had the game started than Sheffield Wednesday raced into the lead with a goal from Palethorpe. West Brom's riposte was a brilliant solo effort from Boyes to cap a run that took him half the length of the pitch.

Sheffield Wednesday restored their advantage in the second half, but West Brom struck back once again with another well-taken goal, Sandford crashing in a shot from the edge of the penalty area.

The balance of power was swinging back and forth until Ellis Rimmer decisively tipped it in Sheffield Wednesday's favour in two minutes. He had wasted one good chance early in the second half, but he made amends in the 88th minute when he beat Pearson, the West Brom keeper, to a loose ball.

That goal maintained Rimmer's tradition of scoring in every round. Virtually straight from the kick-off he struck again. Two goals in two minutes at the death took the Cup back to Hillsborough for the first time since 1907.

FOR THE RECORD

■ Public outcry persuaded the government to abandon legislation against football pools. The pools companies, using their mailing lists of customers, persuaded their clients to write to MPs objecting to the outlawing of the pools. The government, fearing that the entire Betting and Lotteries Act would be defeated, withdrew the clauses that would have stopped the pools.

■ Arsenal drew huge crowds wherever they played. Their match against Manchester City at Maine Road on February 23 broke the League's attendance record. The crowd was at least 77,582 – the number that paid at the turnstiles – and thought to be closer to 80,000 when season ticket holders were taken into account.

■ Frank Moss, the Arsenal goalkeeper, scored against Everton at Goodison Park on March 16. Moss, a useful forward earlier in his career, dislocated his shoulder during the match and spent the rest of the game as a "passenger" on the wing, as substitutes were not allowed. Despite his injury, he scored Arsenal's second goal in a 2-0 win.

■ Rangers won the Scottish Double for the second year running.

■ A total of 394 penalties were awarded in the 1,848 Football League matches and 131, almost of a third, of them were missed.

Hot-shot Drake torments Villa

TED DRAKE, the Arsenal centre-forward, led the way in a season that showed the art of scoring goals was far from lost. At Villa Park on December 14, it seemed that everything that Drake touched turned to gold.

Arsenal were without Alex James and Joe Hulme, both of whom were injured, and Drake played with his injured knee heavily strapped. With Arsenal so weakened, Aston Villa dominated the first 15 minutes.

Drake gave Arsenal the lead with his first shot of the match. Then, 10 minutes later, Drake had another shot, and he scored again. And again ... and again ... and again ... and again. Six shots and six goals.

Aston Villa did not know what had hit them. They tried to mark Drake out of the game but it did not make any difference.

Drake's next two efforts did not go in (one hit the crossbar and was cleared, and the other was saved), but he equalled the long-standing record of seven League goals in a match a minute from time.

Drake's injured knee forced him to miss much of the rest of the season. After a long lay-off following a cartilage operation he returned to the Arsenal team for two matches. He scored the only goal of the match both times – to beat Aston Villa in the League and Sheffield United in the Cup final.

Bell strikes nine, Payne hits ten

TED DRAKE was not the only forward with his shooting boots on. Robert "Bunny" Bell raised the League's individual scoring record to nine on Boxing Day when Tranmere demolished Oldham.

The two teams had met in the Third Division North on Christmas Day and Oldham ran out easy 4-1 winners. Perhaps the team celebrated too much that night because they were left punch-drunk when they went to Prenton Park for the return match.

Bell and Tranmere ran riot and rewrote the record books. Bell's nine goals were a record, Tranmere's 13 goals equalled the League record and the final score, 13-4, was a record aggregate for a League match. Not surprisingly, Bell finished the season as the Division's leading scorer, with 33 goals. Despite his efforts, Tranmere missed promotion by five points.

If Bell's performance was outstanding then Joe Payne's was almost unbelievable. Payne had joined Luton as a centre-forward but had failed to make the grade in either the first team or the reserves.

When Luton played Bristol Rovers in the Third Division South on April 13 both of their regular centre-forwards were injured and they were forced to play Payne. He got off to a slow start, needing 20 minutes to score his first goal. From then on it was all one-way traffic.

Payne completed his hat-trick before half-time and claimed his place in the record books with five minutes left in the match, scoring his tenth goal in Luton's 12-0 victory.

Winning habit: Arsenal celebrate their sixth trophy in seven years

Seed sows, Charlton blossom

JIMMY SEED had worked wonders since his arrival at Charlton in 1933. The former Sunderland, Tottenham and Sheffield Wednesday inside-forward had been tempted to manage the club by the big-spending Gliksten brothers, who were determined to take the ailing team out of the shadow of their more illustrious London neighbours.

Despite his relative inexperience as a manager (a brief spell at Clapton Orient) Seed had firm ideas about how a team should be run. Although the Glikstens were prepared to spend whatever was necessary, Seed eschewed the transfer market, concentrating his efforts on scouting, particularly in his native north-east.

Seed unearthed a steady stream of talent and Charlton were promoted to the First Division only a year after winning the Third Division South. The Glikstens were rewarded with average attendances of 30,000 and a profit of £7,000.

The press dismissed Charlton as a flash in the pan, but Seed proved them wrong. Charlton went on to be runners-up in their first season in the First Division, and then finished fourth and third in the next two years.

FOR THE RECORD

■ The Irish League beat the Football League at Blackpool in September, the first time they had won in 37 encounters.

■ A record League crowd of 82,905 saw Chelsea draw with Arsenal at Stamford Bridge on October 12.

■ Swansea travelled a record 400 miles to play two matches in two days. On Good Friday they won at Plymouth and after trekking north they lost at Newcastle the next day.

■ Arsenal, bedevilled by injuries, adopted a policy of using their best players in the Cup but resting them for League matches. The League were not impressed and fined Arsenal £250 for fielding below-strength teams.

■ The Football League, in an attempt to thwart the pools companies in February, tried to keep teams' opponents secret until a day before the kick-off. The pools companies responded by printing coupons listing only the home sides. When clubs complained that their attendances were suffering the idea was dropped within weeks.

■ Rangers won the Scottish Cup for the third year in a row, despite being outplayed by Third Lanark virtually throughout the final. The Rangers hero was their goalkeeper Jerry Dawson. Jerry Denmark, the Third Lanark centre-half, was so impressed by his performance he told Dawson: "They should give you the whole 11 medals."

■ Despite several successful experiments in friendlies and amateur matches, the League rejected a proposal to have two referees controlling a match.

■ Rangers were denied a third successive Double, finishing five points behind Celtic in the League.

THE 1936-37 SEASON

Free-scoring City leave everybody else trailing

AFTER being made to look foolish in the FA Cup against Millwall, Manchester City recovered some face with a barnstorming performance in the League which brought them their first championship.

Their potent team was packed with internationals – Frank Swift in goal, Sam Barkas at full-back, and Eric Brook in attack all played for England, and Brook's striking partner Peter Doherty played for Ireland. With such a galaxy of talent Manchester City were able to sweep all before them.

Liverpool were singled out for particularly fierce treatment. Manchester City won 5-1 at Maine Road and then went to Anfield and scored another five goals in one of the best displays of attacking football seen for years.

The goals kept flowing and City finished the season with 107. Charlton Athletic, the runners-up by three points, finished a staggering 49 goals behind.

Record crowd sees Scotland slam England

HAMPDEN PARK had just opened a new stand, but not even the 4,500 increase in the ground's capacity was enough to cope with the crowd that flocked to see Scotland play England in the Home Internationals.

The official attendance figure on April 17 was 149,547, a world record. But another 10,000 were estimated to have forced their way into the ground by breaking down several sets of gates.

England dominated the first half, and Freddie Steele, the Stoke centre-forward gave them a 1-0 lead. But after the interval Scotland turned on the style so impressively that some commentators compared their performance to that of the Wembley Wizards.

Tommy Walker, the Hearts inside-forward, was Scotland's driving force. His hard work created two goals and also made the space for Jimmy Delaney to run at the English defence.

Delaney set up the equaliser for Frank O'Donnell just after the re-start. Despite all the pressure, Scotland did not make another breakthrough until the last 10 minutes. Then, though, Bob McPhail struck twice to put the game beyond England's reach.

Hampden witnessed another huge crowd a week later. This time 144,303 people saw Celtic beat Aberdeen 2-1 in the Scottish Cup final with goals from Buchan and Crumb. Armstrong scored for Aberdeen. It was the biggest attendance in the world for a football match between two club sides.

Millwall minnows cut giants down to size

End of the line: Sunderland stopped David's goliaths in the semi-final

MILLWALL'S giant-killing feats won Dave Mangnall, their player-manager, the title of "David the Giant Killer". It was easy to see why as a procession of clubs came to the Den and got devoured by the Lions.

After a 6-1 victory at Aldershot, in which Mangnall scored four goals, the Third Division South team were drawn at home in every round of the FA Cup. A 7-0 defeat of Gateshead brought a visit by Fulham. The Second Division club were sent packing 2-0.

Next it was the turn of a First Division club to try their luck. Chelsea went home even more embarrassed, beaten 3-0. But that was nothing compared with what awaited Derby, runners-up in the First Division the previous year. A record 48,672 crowd packed into The Den, and the Rams went like lambs to the slaughter as first Mangnall scored and then his striking partner McCartney got the winner with four minutes left.

Even after all this, nobody gave Millwall a chance against Manchester City in the quarter-finals. They should have known better. That man Mangnall rang rings round City's star-studded team with a goal in each half.

That made Millwall the first Third Division team to reach the semi-finals but their luck ran out when they were forced to leave home to face Sunderland at Huddersfield. Yet again, Mangnall put Millwall ahead, but goals from Gurney and Gallacher in the second half ended their dream.

Sunderland were mightily relieved to escape with their reputation intact and, inspired by Raich Carter, they went on to win the Cup, coming back from a goal down at half-time to beat Preston 3-1.

Runners-up: Charlton had a great debut in the First Division

FOR THE RECORD

■ The first football match to be shown on television was film of Arsenal's match against Everton, broadcast on August 29.

■ The 17-year-old Tommy Lawton moved from Burnley to Everton in December for £6,500.

■ Ambrose Brown of Wrexham was sent off after 20 seconds in the Third Division North match at Hull on Christmas Day. It was the fastest dismissal ever.

■ Dixie Dean passed Steve Bloomer's record of 352 goals in the League, finishing the season with 375.

■ A Private Member's Bill introduced by R J Russell which made a further attempt to ban football pools was defeated by 287 votes to 24 on its second reading.

■ Jimmy McGrory, the Celtic and Clydebank forward, retired. He scored 410 goals in the League at an average of just over one a match.

■ Joe Payne scored 55 goals in the season as Luton won the Third Division South. Ted Harston scored the same number of goals for Mansfield, but they could only finish ninth in the Third Division North.

■ Sir Charles Clegg, the president of the FA, died on June 26, 1937.

THE 1937-38 SEASON

Preston didn't mind Mutch

THE Cup final had been a dour affair. Only seconds remained in extra time when it was won by a controversial penalty.

George Mutch, the Preston inside forward, was tackled by Alf Young, the Huddersfield centre-half, right on the edge of the penalty area. Mutch went down and the referee instantly awarded a penalty. Some observers thought the challenge was not a foul and others believed that the tackle was made just outside the penalty area, which analysis of the newsreel film seemed to confirm.

Mutch could not shed much light on what had happened because he was knocked out when he fell. He said: "When I came round I did not even understand that a penalty had been awarded. They handed me the ball and I placed it automatically. As I took my run I wondered what I was doing and why. I don't remember aiming at the goal."

He was so groggy that he almost missed the penalty. The ball just bounced over the line after crashing down off the crossbar. It was a cruel way for Huddersfield to lose but perhaps some justice had been done. When they beat Preston in the 1922 Cup final it was thanks to a disputed penalty.

England salute Nazis

THE NAZIS had only just annexed Austria when England arrived in Berlin to play Germany at the start of their end-of-season tour of Europe. There was much debate about whether the team should give the Nazi salute when the German national anthem was played.

Some of the players were not keen and Eddie Hapgood, their captain, argued that standing to attention would be sufficient. But the British ambassador said that it would give offence to their hosts not to give the salute. The only concession made was that the Germans agreed not to include any Austrian players in their team in exchange for Aston Villa playing a friendly against a combined German and Austrian team the next day.

So when the anthem was played the team followed orders and gave the Nazi salute. Then, watched by Goebbels, Hess and von Ribbentrop, England took Germany apart. Cliff Bastin quickly put England ahead and by half-time they led 4-2. On a sweltering afternoon England kept up the pressure to win 6-3, and even the German press was forced to admit that their team was clearly second best.

When Aston Villa played, they refused to give the Nazi salute and were jeered by the crowd throughout the game.

Following orders: England's players were told to salute the Germans

Mutch ado: the penalty that cost Huddersfield the FA Cup

The others leave City trailing

THE FINAL weeks of the season produced one the most nail-biting finishes ever seen in the First Division. When Huddersfield went to Wembley for the Cup final they were one of 11 teams still trying to escape relegation. And on the morning of the final Saturday of the season the bottom six clubs all had 36 points.

Stoke, Birmingham, Portsmouth and Grimsby all won to survive, leaving the result of the match between Huddersfield and Manchester City to decide who would go down with West Bromwich Albion, who lost 4-1 at Middlesbrough.

Huddersfield won 1-0 and Manchester City, the champions last season, were doomed. Amazingly, only four points separated the bottom 11 clubs. Even more amazingly, the 80 goals Manchester City scored in the season were more than any other team in the First Division.

The championship also went right to the wire. Wolverhampton went into their final match a point ahead. But they lost to Sunderland and Arsenal put five goals past Bolton to sneak through on the rails.

WORLD CUP 1938
Italy reassert their supremacy

THE shadow of war and the upheavals in Europe loomed over the 1938 World Cup in France. Spain was in the throes of Civil War, Mussolini's Italy had invaded Abyssinia and Hitler's Germany had annexed Austria. No longer an entity, Austria were forced to withdraw from the tournament and Germany promptly annexed their best players as well.

Once again the South American presence was reduced. Uruguay still had not forgiven Fifa for the European "boycott" in 1930 and stayed at home. As did Argentina, who had applied to host the tournament and were insulted when it was awarded to France, believing that World Cups should alternate between Europe and South America.

With the British nations still refusing to play despite desperate pleas from Fifa, and the presence of such unlikely football nations as the Dutch East Indies and Cuba, once again the tournament was not representative of world football. Only three non-European countries competed and perhaps the structure of the finals – still straight knock-out – was also a deterrent, because a team could travel thousands of miles by boat and only play one match.

Still under the guidance of the legendary manager Vittorio Pozzo, Italy, as holders and the winners of the Olympics in Berlin in 1936, were the narrow favourites. But Brazil were a wonderfully talented side, as were Hungary.

Norway, who had almost knocked Italy out in the Olympic semi-final, were also a difficult prospect. Coincidentally, they were drawn against Italy in the first round and again gave the holders a fright. Although a goal down after two minutes Norway rallied brilliantly, hitting the bar and the post three times before equalising in the second half. Norway also had a goal disallowed and the Italian goalkeeper, Olivieri, had to make a spectacular save. Somehow, Italy held on and, in extra time, conjured up the winner. It was probably their hardest match in the tournament.

Some giants did fall at the first hurdle: Germany played atrociously against Switzerland in a replay and lost 4-2; Cuba astounded themselves by beating Romania 2-1 after a 3-3 draw.

But the most extraordinary match of the World Cup – and perhaps any World Cup – was between Poland and Brazil. By half-time, with the score 3-1, Leonidas, Brazil's fabulous centre-forward, had scored a hat-trick. But after the interval Ernst Willimowski, Poland's inside left, turned the match inside out. He scored twice to complete his own hat-trick and level the scores at 4-4 with two minutes to go. In extra time both forwards scored yet again. The deadlock was finally broken by Brazil's inside right, Romeo, and Brazil sneaked through.

In the next round, the quarter-finals, the tournament returned to a semblance of normality as the giantkillers, Cuba and Switzerland, were themselves felled by Sweden and Hungary, and Italy cruised past France, the hosts, in front of 58,000 spectators – not surprisingly the largest crowd of the tournament.

However, the match between Brazil and Czechoslovakia produced real fireworks and was called the Battle of Bordeaux. Shortly after the kick-off Brazil's Zeze callously kicked Nejedly, Czechoslovakia's free-scoring inside forward, and was dismissed. This precipitated mayhem and by the end of a 1-1 draw Nejedly had a broken leg; Planicka, the Czech goalkeeper, a broken arm; another Czech and two Brazilians were injured and three players (two Brazilians and a Czech) had been sent off. By comparison, the replay two days later was a placid affair as 15 team changes were made. But for Czechoslovakia the damage had been done. Unable to field their injured stars, Nejedly and Planicka, they succumbed 2-1.

Brazil had been so confident they would beat Czechoslovakia in the replay in Bordeaux that their main party left for the semi-final against Italy before the match began. Such over-confidence would prove to be their undoing when they decided to rest the Black Diamond, Leonidas their star goalscorer, for the semi-final.

Without Leonidas Brazil were woefully weak in front of goal. And it was Leonidas's replacement, Peracio, who squandered the two real chances they had. Italy were not a team to look a gift horse in the mouth and with Piola, their big centre-forward, continually unsettling the Brazilian defence they easily won 2-1, Brazil only scoring three minutes from time. Italy had reached their second World Cup final.

Their opponents were Hungary who had an easy task in disposing of Sweden 5-1 in the semi-final, even though the Swedes scored in the first 35 seconds. One commentator described the one-sided game as "an excellent training match for the Hungarians." By rights the Swedes should not even have got that far. They were awarded the first round match because Austria had to withdraw after the Anschluss and strolled through the quarter finals by thrashing the hapless Cubans 8-0. By contrast, the Hungarians were regarded as arguably the best footballing side in Europe, their one weakness being a lack of finishing power.

The Italians tackled the World Cup final in a fashion that would be familiar to Italian sides today.

Hot shots: Italy won a one-sided final that produced a feast of goals

Knowing that the Hungarians – and in particular their eminently gifted forward Sarosi – did not relish physical contact, they combined Latin flair with Italian muscle, athleticism, and resolute defence. It was to prove decisive.

By half-time the "modern" Italians had ripped the Hungarians of the 1930s to shreds. In the fifth minute, in a move that swept dazzlingly like lightning from one end of the pitch to the other, they were ahead with a goal from their winger, Colaussi.

The Hungarians equalised within two minutes when an unmarked Titkos was found by Sarosi. But to no avail as Meazza, Italy's captain, took a firm, and unshakeable, grip on the midfield. In the 16th minute he created a goal for Piola, and then the Italians started to motor. Nineteen minutes later Meazza found an unmarked Colaussi and he scored his second goal to give the World Cup holders a virtually unassailable 3-1 lead.

And they knew it. In the second half the Italians simply closed the game down, relying on their defence to contain the Hungarian attacks. Sarosi reduced the lead 20 minutes from time after a mix-up in the Italian penalty area. But then, with eight minutes left, came the coup de grace, and the best goal of the game. Biavati exchanged several passes with Piola as they scythed through the tiring Hungarian defence. His final pass was a cheeky back-heel which Piola smashed into the net.

Italy, with two World Cups and the Olympics to their credit in the space of four years, had proved to be the dominant team of the 1930s and their genius of a manager, Pozzo, one of the all-time greats.

Within 15 months football, and World Cups, would be swept aside as the Second World War first engulfed Europe and then the world. It would be a dozen years before the World Cup was held again. By then there would be a new order as Brazil and Hungary began to fulfil the promise they had displayed in the last World Cup of the first half of the century.

Dashed hopes: Hungary's finishing touch deserted them in the final (top) and the powerful Germans were stunned by Switzerland in the second round (bottom)

FOR THE RECORD

FIRST ROUND
Switzerland 1 Germany 1 aet
HT 1-1 Att. 30,000
Replay: **Switzerland 4 Germany 2**
HT 1-2 Att. 22,000
Cuba 3 Romania 3 aet
HT 1-1 Att. 6,000
Replay: **Cuba 2 Romania 1**
HT 0-1 Att. 5,000
Hungary 6 Dutch East Indies 0
HT 4-0 Att. not recorded
France 3 Belgium 1
HT 2-1 Att. not recorded
Czechoslovakia 3 Holland 0 aet
HT 0-0 Att. not recorded
Brazil 6 Poland 5 aet
HT 3-1 Att. not recorded
Italy 2 Norway 1
HT 1-0 Att. not recorded

SECOND ROUND
Sweden 8 Cuba 0
HT 4-0 Att. not recorded
Hungary 2 Switzerland 0
HT 1-0 Att. not recorded
Italy 3 France 1
HT 1-1 Att. 58,000
Brazil 1 Czechoslovakia 1 aet
HT 1-0 Att. 25,000
Replay: **Brazil 2 Czechoslovakia 1**
HT 0-1 Att. not recorded

SEMI-FINALS
Italy 2 Brazil 1
HT 0-0 Att. 35,000
Hungary 5 Sweden 1
HT 3-1 Att. 17,000

THIRD PLACE PLAY-OFF
Brazil 4 Sweden 2
HT 1-2 Att. not recorded

FINAL
Italy 4 Hungary 2
HT 3-1 Att. 55,000

Teams
Italy Olivieri; Foni, Rava, Serantoni, Andreolo, Locatelli, Biavati, Meazza, Piola, Ferrari, Colaussi
Hungary Szabo; Polgar, Biro, Szalay, Szucs, Lazar, Sas, Vincze, Sarosi, Zsengeller, Titkos

Leading goalscorers 8 da Silva (Brazil); 7 Zsengeller (Hungary); 5 Piola (Italy), 4 Sarosi (Hungary), Colaussi (Italy), Wetterstrom (Sweden), Willimowski (Poland)
Total goals scored 84
Average per game: 4.67
Sendings-off Pesser (Germany) v Switzerland, 1st game; Referee Jean Langenus (Belgium). Procopio (Brazil) v Czechoslovakia, Machado (Brazil) v Czechoslovakia, Riha (Czechoslovakia) v Brazil, all 1st game; Referee: Paul Van Hertzka (Hungary)
Number of players used by finalists 14 Italy, 17 Hungary

THE
1938-39
SEASON

England's handicap

ENGLAND'S first match against Italy since the infamous Battle of Highbury in 1934 took place in a highly charged atmosphere, particularly because the referee was German. War against the fascist powers of Italy and Germany loomed over Europe. Fortunately, the match in Milan on May 13 turned on German myopia and Italian fists, rather than fisticuffs.

The score was 1-1 early in the second half when Piola "scored" a second goal for Italy. The only problem was that he had punched the ball into the net rather than kicked it. The players saw it, the crowd saw it but Dr Bauwens, the German referee didn't. Despite England's protests he allowed the goal to stand.

Stanley Rous, the FA secretary was watching the match with the Crown Prince of Italy. The Prince was so embarrassed by the incident that he offered to escort Rous on to the pitch and explain to the referee that he was wrong. Diplomatically, Rous declined the offer.

Worse, as England poured forward in search of another goal they were thwarted more than once by Italian hands and German refereeing. One shot was blatantly punched clear by an Italian defender, and two other efforts were handled away even after they had crossed the goalline.

The referee didn't seem to notice any of this either. But even he could not fail to miss England's equaliser. The ball was blasted into the net by Willie Hall, who hit his shot so hard that nobody could get a hand to it.

Wolves fall apart

MOST TEAMS had a mascot, but not many clubs had a good-luck charm as strange as that of Portsmouth. Jack Tinn, their manager, was convinced that his white spats were lucky. He even had a ritual about wearing them. Freddie Worrall, the team's right winger, had to d]o them up, and he had to put on the left one first.

But hardly anybody in the country thought that it would be third time lucky for Tinn, who had already lost two Cup finals with Portsmouth. Wolverhampton, who had been challenging for the championship, were 5–1 on to beat Portsmouth, who had spent most of the season fighting to avoid relegation. Wolverhampton were even said to have taken a secret monkey-gland potion to improve their strength, although Stan Cullis, their captain, subsequently admitted that the story was a publicity stunt dreamt up by his manager, Major Frank Buckley.

But Wolverhampton were weak at the knees. When the traditional autograph book, signed by both teams before the kick-off, arrived in the Portsmouth dressing-room, Tinn pointed out that the Wolverhampton players were so nervous that they had hardly been able to sign their names.

In front of the biggest crowd, 99,370, since the White Horse final of 1923, Wolverhampton simply froze. Bert Barlow, who had joined Portsmouth from Wolverhampton only two months before, gave the underdogs the lead after 30 minutes. Two more goals in three minutes either side of half-time, including a second strike from Barlow, finished Wolverhampton off. Portsmouth coasted to a 4-1 triumph and, for once, Tinn's spats had done their job.

Making a monkey of Wolves: Portsmouth with their first FA Cup

Arsenal break transfer record to capture Jones

ARSENAL needed a replacement for Alex James, who had recently retired, and George Allison, their manager, was convinced that Bryn Jones was the man he wanted. So, at the start of the season he broke the transfer record, paying £14,000 in four instalments to Wolverhampton to bring the Welsh inside-forward to Highbury.

The deal was a remarkable indicator of Major Frank Buckley's ability to spot and develop talent. Wolverhampton had discovered Jones playing for the Welsh non-League team Aberaman. His transfer to Arsenal meant that Buckley had collected more than £110,000 in four seasons from the sale of players.

From playing fields to battlefields

LEADING FOOTBALLERS' involvement in the war effort provided a valuable source of propaganda. The importance of their role in maintaining the public's morale was wonderfully illustrated by the Italians.

In 1941, Rome Radio claimed that the Arsenal forward Cliff Bastin was a prisoner of war in Italy. It was an exceedingly optimistic boast given that Bastin had never left England because he had not been passed fit for active service due to his increasing deafness.

Bastin spent the entire war as an ARP warden in London, manning a lookout post on top of the main stand at Highbury and playing for Arsenal in his spare time. Strangely, although he had won 21 England caps between 1932 and 1938, Bastin never appeared in any of the war-time internationals.

While the Italians were claiming to have captured Bastin, British newspapers carried pictures of two great adversaries, Ted Drake, the Arsenal centre-forward, and Sam Bartram, the Charlton goalkeeper, together on guard duty at a depot "somewhere on the East coast".

Bartram went on to become a physical training instructor, as did Tommy Lawton of Everton. Most new recruits to the forces viewed physical training with a great deal of dread, conducted, as it always seemed, by a sergeant-major who bordered on the sadistic. So for volunteers lucky enough to be trained by the men they had idolised from the terraces, physical training was less of an ordeal.

There were some mutterings that footballers had an easy time of it, being given duties that enabled them to continue playing football. But the benefits clearly outweighed the disadvantages. One 17-year-old, who had last played for his local school and choir side, never forgot the day he lined up opposite Stanley Matthews in an inter-services match between his navy unit and an RAF team.

Cliff Bastin: victim of Italian deception

Tommy Lawton: physical training instructor

Ted Drake and Sam Bartram: defensive duties on the east coast

LEAGUE TABLES AND RESULTS 1930 – 1939

	1930-31	1931-32	1932-33	1933-34	1934-35
WORLD CUP				Italy 2 Czechoslovakia 1	
FA CUP	West Bromwich Albion 2 Birmingham 1	Newcastle United 2 Arsenal 1	Everton 3 Manchester City 0	Manchester City 2 Portsmouth 1	Sheffield Wednesday 4 West Bromwich Albion 2

FIRST DIVISION

1930-31
	P	W	D	L	F	A	Pts
Arsenal	42	28	10	4	127	59	66
Aston Villa	42	25	9	8	128	78	59
Sheff Wed	42	22	8	12	102	75	52
Portsmouth	42	18	13	11	84	67	49
Huddersfld	42	18	12	12	81	65	48
Derby	42	18	10	14	94	79	46
Middlesbro	42	19	8	15	98	90	46
Man City	42	18	10	14	75	70	46
Liverpool	42	15	12	15	86	85	42
Blackburn	42	17	8	17	83	84	42
Sunderland	42	16	9	17	89	85	41
Chelsea	42	15	10	17	64	67	40
Grimsby	42	17	5	20	82	87	39
Bolton	42	15	9	18	68	81	39
Sheff Utd	42	14	10	18	78	84	38
Leicester	42	16	6	20	80	95	38
Newcastle	42	15	6	21	78	87	36
West Ham	42	14	8	20	79	94	36
Birmingham	42	13	10	19	55	70	36
Blackpool	42	11	10	21	71	125	32
Leeds	*42*	*12*	*7*	*23*	*68*	*81*	*31*
Man Utd	*42*	*7*	*8*	*27*	*53*	*115*	*22*

1931-32
	P	W	D	L	F	A	Pts
Everton	42	26	4	12	116	64	56
Arsenal	42	22	10	10	90	48	54
Sheff Wed	42	22	6	14	96	82	50
Huddersfld	42	19	10	13	80	63	48
Aston Villa	42	19	8	15	104	72	46
West Brom	42	20	6	16	77	55	46
Sheff Utd	42	20	6	16	80	75	46
Portsmouth	42	19	7	16	62	62	45
Birmingham	42	18	8	16	78	67	44
Liverpool	42	19	6	17	81	93	44
Newcastle	42	18	6	18	80	87	42
Chelsea	42	16	8	18	69	73	40
Sunderland	42	15	10	17	67	73	40
Man City	42	13	12	17	83	73	38
Derby	42	14	10	18	71	75	38
Blackburn	42	16	6	20	89	95	38
Bolton	42	17	4	21	72	80	38
Middlesbro	42	15	8	19	64	89	38
Leicester	42	15	7	20	74	94	37
Blackpool	42	12	9	21	65	102	33
Grimsby	*42*	*13*	*6*	*23*	*67*	*98*	*32*
West Ham	*42*	*12*	*7*	*23*	*62*	*107*	*31*

1932-33
	P	W	D	L	F	A	Pts
Arsenal	42	25	8	9	118	61	58
Aston Villa	42	23	8	11	92	67	54
Sheff Wed	42	21	9	12	80	68	51
West Brom	42	20	9	13	83	70	49
Newcastle	42	22	5	15	71	63	49
Huddersfld	42	18	11	13	66	53	47
Derby	42	15	14	13	76	69	44
Leeds	42	15	14	13	59	62	44
Portsmouth	42	18	7	17	74	76	43
Sheff Utd	42	17	9	16	74	80	43
Everton	42	16	9	17	81	74	41
Sunderland	42	15	10	17	63	80	40
Birmingham	42	14	11	17	57	57	39
Liverpool	42	14	11	17	79	84	39
Blackburn	42	14	10	18	76	102	38
Man City	42	16	5	21	68	71	37
Middlesbro	42	14	9	19	63	73	37
Chelsea	42	14	7	21	63	73	35
Leicester	42	11	13	18	75	89	35
Wolves	42	13	9	20	80	96	35
Bolton	*42*	*12*	*9*	*21*	*78*	*92*	*33*
Blackpool	*42*	*14*	*5*	*23*	*69*	*85*	*33*

1933-34
	P	W	D	L	F	A	Pts
Arsenal	42	25	9	8	75	47	59
Huddersfld	42	23	10	9	90	61	56
Tottenham	42	21	7	14	79	56	49
Derby	42	17	11	14	68	54	45
Man City	42	17	11	14	65	72	45
Sunderland	42	16	12	14	81	56	44
West Brom	42	17	10	15	78	70	44
Blackburn	42	18	7	17	74	81	43
Leeds	42	17	8	17	75	66	42
Portsmouth	42	15	12	15	52	55	42
Sheff Wed	42	16	9	17	62	67	41
Stoke	42	15	11	16	58	71	41
Aston Villa	42	14	12	16	78	75	40
Everton	42	12	16	14	62	63	40
Wolves	42	14	12	16	74	86	40
Middlesbro	42	16	7	19	68	80	39
Leicester	42	14	11	17	59	74	39
Liverpool	42	14	10	18	79	87	38
Chelsea	42	14	8	20	67	69	36
Birmingham	42	12	12	18	54	56	36
Newcastle	*42*	*10*	*14*	*18*	*68*	*77*	*34*
Sheff Utd	*42*	*12*	*7*	*23*	*58*	*101*	*31*

1934-35
	P	W	D	L	F	A	Pts
Arsenal	42	23	12	7	115	46	58
Sunderland	42	19	16	7	90	51	54
Sheff Wed	42	18	13	11	70	64	49
Man City	42	20	8	14	82	67	48
Grimsby	42	17	11	14	78	60	45
Derby	42	18	9	15	81	66	45
Liverpool	42	19	7	16	85	88	45
Everton	42	16	12	14	89	88	44
West Brom	42	17	10	15	83	83	44
Stoke	42	18	6	18	71	70	42
Preston	42	15	12	15	62	67	42
Chelsea	42	16	9	17	73	82	41
Aston Villa	42	14	13	15	74	88	41
Portsmouth	42	15	10	17	71	72	40
Blackburn	42	14	11	17	66	78	39
Huddersfld	42	14	10	18	76	71	38
Wolves	42	15	8	19	88	94	38
Leeds	42	13	12	17	75	92	38
Birmingham	42	13	10	19	63	81	36
Middlesbro	42	10	14	18	70	90	34
Leicester	*42*	*12*	*9*	*21*	*61*	*86*	*33*
Tottenham	*42*	*10*	*10*	*22*	*54*	*93*	*30*

SECOND DIVISION

1930-31
Champions: Everton
Also promoted: West Bromwich Albion
Relegated: Reading, Cardiff City

1931-32
Champions: Wolverhampton Wanderers
Also promoted: Leeds United
Relegated: Barnsley, Bristol City

1932-33
Champions: Stoke City
Also promoted: Tottenham Hotspur
Relegated: Chesterfield, Charlton Athletic

1933-34
Champions: Grimsby Town
Also promoted: Preston North End
Relegated: Millwall, Lincoln City

1934-35
Champions: Brentford
Also promoted: Bolton Wanderers
Relegated: Oldham Athletic, Notts County

THIRD DIVISION SOUTH

1930-31
Champions: Notts County
Runners-up (not promoted): Crystal Palace

1931-32
Champions: Fulham
Runners-up (not promoted): Reading

1932-33
Champions: Brentford
Runners-up (not promoted): Exeter City

1933-34
Champions: Norwich City
Runners-up (not promoted): Coventry City

1934-35
Champions: Charlton Athletic
Runners-up (not promoted): Reading

THIRD DIVISION NORTH

1930-31
Champions: Chesterfield
Runners-up (not promoted): Lincoln City

1931-32
Champions: Lincoln City
Runners-up (not promoted): Gateshead

1932-33
Champions: Hull City
Runners-up (not promoted): Wrexham

1933-34
Champions: Barnsley
Runners-up (not promoted): Chesterfield

1934-35
Champions: Doncaster Rovers
Runners-up (not promoted): Halifax Town

SCOTTISH CUP

1930-31	1931-32	1932-33	1933-34	1934-35
Celtic 4 Motherwell 2, after 2-2	Rangers 3 Kilmarnock 0, after 1-1	Celtic 1 Motherwell 0	Rangers 5 St Mirren 0	Rangers 2 Hamilton Academical 1

SCOTTISH FIRST DIVISION

1930-31
	P	W	D	L	F	A	Pts
Rangers	38	27	6	5	96	29	60
Celtic	38	24	10	4	101	34	58
Motherwell	38	24	8	6	102	42	56
Partick	38	24	5	9	76	44	53
Hearts	38	19	6	13	90	63	44
Aberdeen	38	17	7	14	79	63	41
Cowdenb'th	38	17	7	14	58	65	41
Dundee	38	17	5	16	65	63	39
Airdrie	38	17	5	16	59	66	39
Hamilton	38	16	5	17	59	57	37
Kilmarnock	38	15	5	18	59	60	35
Clyde	38	15	4	19	60	87	34
Queen's P	38	13	7	18	71	72	33
Falkirk	38	14	4	20	77	87	32
St Mirren	38	11	8	19	49	72	30
Morton	38	11	7	20	58	83	29
Leith	38	8	11	19	52	85	27
Ayr	38	8	11	19	53	92	27
Hibernian	*38*	*9*	*7*	*22*	*49*	*81*	*25*
East Fife	*38*	*8*	*4*	*26*	*45*	*113*	*20*

1931-32
	P	W	D	L	F	A	Pts
Motherwell	38	30	6	2	119	31	66
Rangers	38	28	5	5	118	42	61
Celtic	38	20	8	10	94	50	48
T Lanark	38	21	4	13	92	81	46
St Mirren	38	20	4	14	77	56	44
Partick	38	19	4	15	58	59	42
Aberdeen	38	16	9	13	57	49	41
Hearts	38	17	5	16	63	61	39
Kilmarnock	38	16	7	15	68	70	39
Hamilton	38	16	6	16	84	65	38
Dundee	38	14	10	14	61	72	38
Cowdenb'th	38	15	8	15	66	78	38
Clyde	38	13	9	16	58	70	35
Airdrie	38	13	6	19	74	81	32
Morton	38	12	7	19	78	87	31
Queen's P	38	13	5	20	59	79	31
Ayr	38	11	7	20	70	90	29
Falkirk	38	11	5	22	70	76	27
Dundee	*38*	*6*	*7*	*25*	*40*	*118*	*19*
Leith	*38*	*6*	*4*	*28*	*46*	*137*	*16*

1932-33
	P	W	D	L	F	A	Pts
Rangers	38	26	10	2	113	43	62
Motherwell	38	27	5	6	114	53	59
Hearts	38	18	11	9	84	51	50
Celtic	38	20	8	10	75	44	48
St J'stone	38	17	10	11	70	57	44
Aberdeen	38	18	6	14	85	58	42
St Mirren	38	18	6	14	73	60	42
Hamilton	38	18	6	14	92	78	42
Queen's P	38	17	7	14	78	79	41
Partick	38	17	6	15	75	55	40
Falkirk	38	15	6	17	70	70	36
Clyde	38	15	5	18	69	75	35
T Lanark	38	14	7	17	70	80	35
Kilmarnock	38	13	9	16	72	86	35
Dundee	38	12	9	17	58	74	33
Ayr	38	13	4	21	62	96	30
Cowdenb'th	38	10	5	23	65	111	25
Airdrie	38	10	3	25	55	102	23
Morton	*38*	*6*	*9*	*23*	*49*	*97*	*21*
E Stirling	*38*	*7*	*3*	*28*	*55*	*115*	*17*

1933-34
	P	W	D	L	F	A	Pts
Rangers	38	30	6	2	118	41	66
Motherwell	38	29	4	5	97	45	62
Celtic	38	18	11	9	78	53	47
Q of South	38	21	3	14	75	78	45
Aberdeen	38	18	8	12	90	57	44
Hearts	38	17	10	11	86	59	44
Kilmarnock	38	17	9	12	73	64	43
Ayr	38	16	10	12	87	92	42
St J'stone	38	17	6	15	74	53	40
Falkirk	38	16	6	16	73	68	38
Hamilton	38	15	8	15	65	79	38
Dundee	38	15	6	17	68	64	36
Partick	38	14	5	19	73	78	33
Clyde	38	10	11	17	56	70	31
Queen's P	38	13	5	20	65	85	31
Hibernian	38	12	3	23	51	69	27
St Mirren	38	9	9	20	46	75	27
Airdrie	38	10	6	22	59	103	26
T Lanark	*38*	*8*	*9*	*21*	*62*	*103*	*25*
Cowdenb'th	*38*	*5*	*5*	*28*	*58*	*118*	*15*

1934-35
	P	W	D	L	F	A	Pts
Rangers	38	25	5	8	96	46	55
Celtic	38	24	4	10	92	45	52
Hearts	38	20	10	8	87	51	50
Hamilton	38	19	10	9	87	67	48
St J'stone	38	18	10	10	66	46	46
Aberdeen	38	17	10	11	68	54	44
Motherwell	38	15	10	13	83	64	40
Dundee	38	16	8	14	63	63	40
Kilmarnock	38	16	6	16	76	68	38
Clyde	38	14	10	14	71	69	38
Hibernian	38	14	8	16	59	70	36
Queen's P	38	13	10	15	61	80	36
Partick	38	15	5	18	61	68	35
Airdrie	38	13	7	18	64	72	33
Dunfermline	38	13	5	20	56	96	31
Albion	38	10	9	19	62	77	29
Q of South	38	11	7	20	52	72	29
Ayr	38	12	5	21	61	112	29
St Mirren	*38*	*11*	*5*	*22*	*49*	*70*	*27*
Falkirk	*38*	*9*	*6*	*23*	*58*	*82*	*24*

SCOTTISH SECOND DIVISION

1930-31
Champions: Third Lanark
Also promoted: Dundee United

1931-32
Champions: East Stirling
Also promoted: St Johnstone

1932-33
Champions: Hibernian
Also promoted: Queen of the South

1933-34
Champions: Albion Rovers
Also promoted: Dunfermline Athletic

1934-35
Champions: Third Lanark
Also promoted: Arbroath

1935-36 · 1936-37 · 1937-38 · 1938-39

WORLD CUP

1937-38:
Italy 4
Hungary 2

FA CUP

1935-36	1936-37	1937-38	1938-39
Arsenal 1	Sunderland 3	Preston North End 1	Portsmouth 4
Sheffield United 0	Preston North End 1	Huddersfield Town 0	Wolverhampton Wanderers 1

FIRST DIVISION

1935-36

	P	W	D	L	F	A	Pts
Sunderland	42	25	6	11	109	74	56
Derby	42	18	12	12	61	52	48
Huddersfld	42	18	12	12	59	56	48
Stoke	42	20	7	15	57	57	47
Brentford	42	17	12	13	81	60	46
Arsenal	42	15	15	12	78	48	45
Preston	42	18	8	16	67	64	44
Chelsea	42	15	13	14	65	72	43
Man City	42	17	8	17	68	60	42
Portsmouth	42	17	8	17	54	67	42
Leeds	42	15	11	16	66	64	41
Birmingham	42	15	11	16	61	63	41
Bolton	42	14	13	15	67	76	41
Middlesbro	42	15	10	17	84	70	40
Wolves	42	15	10	17	77	76	40
Everton	42	13	13	16	89	89	39
Grimsby	42	17	5	20	65	73	39
West Brom	42	16	6	20	89	88	38
Liverpool	42	13	12	17	60	64	38
Sheff Wed	42	13	12	17	63	77	38
Aston Villa	*42*	*13*	*9*	*20*	*81*	*110*	*35*
Blackburn	*42*	*12*	*9*	*21*	*55*	*96*	*33*

1936-37

	P	W	D	L	F	A	Pts
Man City	42	22	13	7	107	61	57
Charlton	42	21	12	9	58	49	54
Arsenal	42	18	16	8	80	49	52
Derby	42	21	7	14	96	90	49
Wolves	42	21	5	16	84	67	47
Brentford	42	18	10	14	82	78	46
Middlesbro	42	19	8	15	74	71	46
Sunderland	42	19	6	17	89	87	44
Portsmouth	42	17	10	15	62	66	44
Stoke	42	15	12	15	72	57	42
Birmingham	42	13	15	14	64	60	41
Grimsby	42	17	7	18	86	81	41
Chelsea	42	14	13	15	52	55	41
Preston	42	14	13	15	56	67	41
Huddersfld	42	12	15	15	62	64	39
West Brom	42	16	6	20	77	98	38
Everton	42	14	9	19	81	78	37
Liverpool	42	12	11	19	62	84	35
Leeds	42	15	4	23	60	80	34
Bolton	42	10	14	18	43	66	34
Man Utd	*42*	*10*	*12*	*20*	*55*	*78*	*32*
Sheff Wed	*42*	*9*	*12*	*21*	*53*	*69*	*30*

1937-38

	P	W	D	L	F	A	Pts
Arsenal	42	21	10	11	77	44	52
Wolves	42	20	11	11	72	49	51
Preston	42	16	17	9	64	44	49
Charlton	42	16	14	12	65	51	46
Middlesbro	42	19	8	15	72	65	46
Brentford	42	18	9	15	69	59	45
Bolton	42	15	15	12	64	60	45
Sunderland	42	14	16	12	55	57	44
Leeds	42	14	15	13	64	69	43
Chelsea	42	14	13	15	65	65	41
Liverpool	42	15	11	16	65	71	41
Blackpool	42	16	8	18	61	66	40
Derby	42	15	10	17	66	87	40
Everton	42	16	7	19	79	75	39
Huddersfld	42	17	5	20	55	68	39
Leicester	42	14	11	17	54	75	39
Stoke	42	13	12	17	58	59	38
Birmingham	42	10	18	14	58	62	38
Portsmouth	42	13	12	17	62	68	38
Grimsby	42	13	12	17	51	68	38
Man City	*42*	*14*	*8*	*20*	*80*	*77*	*36*
West Brom	*42*	*14*	*8*	*20*	*74*	*91*	*36*

1938-39

	P	W	D	L	F	A	Pts
Everton	42	27	5	10	88	52	59
Wolves	42	22	11	9	88	39	55
Charlton	42	22	6	14	75	59	50
Middlesbro	42	20	9	13	93	74	49
Arsenal	42	19	9	14	55	41	47
Derby	42	19	8	15	66	55	46
Stoke	42	17	12	13	71	68	46
Bolton	42	15	15	12	67	58	45
Preston	42	16	12	14	63	59	44
Grimsby	42	16	11	15	61	69	43
Liverpool	42	14	14	14	62	63	42
Aston Villa	42	16	9	17	71	60	41
Leeds	42	16	9	17	59	67	41
Man Utd	42	11	16	15	57	65	38
Blackpool	42	12	14	16	56	68	38
Sunderland	42	13	12	17	54	67	38
Portsmouth	42	12	13	17	47	70	37
Brentford	42	14	8	20	53	74	36
Huddersfld	42	12	11	19	58	64	35
Chelsea	42	12	9	21	64	80	33
Birmingham	*42*	*12*	*8*	*22*	*62*	*84*	*32*
Leicester	*42*	*9*	*11*	*22*	*48*	*82*	*29*

SECOND DIVISION

1935-36	1936-37	1937-38	1938-39
Champions: Manchester United	Champions: Leicester City	Champions: Aston Villa	Champions: Blackburn Rovers
Also promoted: Charlton Athletic	Also promoted: Blackpool	Also promoted: Manchester United	Also promoted: Sheffield United
Relegated: Port Vale, Hull City	Relegated: Bradford City, Doncaster Rovers	Relegated: Barnsley, Stockport County	Relegated: Norwich City, Tranmere Rovers

THIRD DIVISION SOUTH

1935-36	1936-37	1937-38	1938-39
Champions: Coventry City	Champions: Luton Town	Champions: Millwall	Champions: Newport County
Runners-up (not promoted): Luton Town	Runners-up (not promoted): Notts County	Runners-up (not promoted): Bristol City	Runners-up (not promoted): Crystal Palace

THIRD DIVISION NORTH

1935-36	1936-37	1937-38	1938-39
Champions: Chesterfield	Champions: Stockport County	Champions: Tranmere Rovers	Champions: Barnsley
Runners-up (not promoted): Chester	Runners-up (not promoted): Lincoln City	Runners-up (not promoted): Doncaster Rovers	Runners-up (not promoted): Doncaster Rovers

SCOTTISH CUP

1935-36	1936-37	1937-38	1938-39
Rangers 1	Celtic 2	East Fife 4	Clyde 4
Third Lanark 0	Aberdeen 1	Kilmarnock 2, after 1-1	Motherwell 0

SCOTTISH FIRST DIVISION

1935-36

	P	W	D	L	F	A	Pts
Celtic	38	32	2	4	115	33	66
Rangers	38	27	7	4	110	43	61
Aberdeen	38	26	9	3	96	50	61
Motherwell	38	18	12	8	77	58	48
Hearts	38	20	7	11	88	55	47
Hamilton	38	15	7	16	77	74	37
St J'stone	38	15	7	16	70	81	37
Kilmarnock	38	14	7	17	69	64	35
Partick	38	12	10	16	64	72	34
Dunfermline	38	13	8	17	73	92	34
T Lanark	38	14	5	19	63	71	33
Arbroath	38	11	11	16	46	69	33
Dundee	38	11	10	17	67	80	32
Queen's P	38	11	10	17	58	75	32
Q of South	38	11	9	18	54	72	31
Albion	38	13	4	21	69	92	30
Hibernian	38	11	7	20	56	82	29
Clyde	38	10	8	20	63	84	28
Airdrie	*38*	*9*	*9*	*20*	*68*	*91*	*27*
Ayr	*38*	*11*	*3*	*24*	*53*	*98*	*25*

1936-37

	P	W	D	L	F	A	Pts
Rangers	38	26	9	3	88	32	61
Aberdeen	38	23	8	7	89	44	54
Celtic	38	22	8	8	89	58	52
Motherwell	38	22	7	9	96	54	51
Hearts	38	24	3	11	99	60	51
T Lanark	38	20	6	12	79	61	46
Hamilton	38	18	5	15	91	96	41
Dundee	38	12	15	11	58	69	39
Clyde	38	16	6	16	59	70	38
Kilmarnock	38	14	9	15	60	70	37
St J'stone	38	14	8	16	74	68	36
Partick	38	11	12	15	73	68	34
Arbroath	38	13	5	20	57	84	31
Queen's P	38	9	12	17	51	77	30
St Mirren	38	11	7	20	68	81	29
Hibernian	38	6	13	19	54	83	25
Q of South	38	8	8	22	49	95	24
Dunfermline	*38*	*5*	*11*	*22*	*65*	*98*	*21*
Albion	*38*	*5*	*6*	*27*	*53*	*116*	*16*

1937-38

	P	W	D	L	F	A	Pts
Celtic	38	27	7	4	114	42	61
Hearts	38	26	6	6	90	50	58
Rangers	38	18	13	7	75	49	49
Falkirk	38	19	9	10	82	52	47
Motherwell	38	17	10	11	78	69	44
Aberdeen	38	15	9	14	74	59	39
Partick	38	15	9	14	68	70	39
St J'stone	38	16	7	15	78	81	39
T Lanark	38	11	13	14	68	73	35
Hibernian	38	11	13	14	57	65	35
Arbroath	38	11	13	14	58	79	35
Queen's P	38	11	12	15	59	74	34
Hamilton	38	13	7	18	81	76	33
St Mirren	38	14	5	19	58	66	33
Clyde	38	10	13	15	68	78	33
Q of South	38	11	11	16	58	71	33
Ayr	38	9	15	14	66	85	33
Kilmarnock	38	12	9	17	65	91	33
Dundee	*38*	*13*	*6*	*19*	*70*	*74*	*32*
Morton	*38*	*6*	*3*	*29*	*64*	*127*	*15*

1938-39

	P	W	D	L	F	A	Pts
Rangers	38	25	9	4	112	55	59
Celtic	38	20	8	10	99	53	48
Aberdeen	38	20	6	12	91	61	46
Hearts	38	20	5	13	98	70	45
Falkirk	38	19	7	12	73	63	45
Q of South	38	17	9	12	69	64	43
Hamilton	38	18	5	15	67	71	41
St J'stone	38	17	6	15	85	82	40
Clyde	38	17	5	16	78	70	39
Kilmarnock	38	15	9	14	73	86	39
Partick	38	17	4	17	74	87	38
Motherwell	38	16	5	17	82	86	37
Hibernian	38	14	7	17	68	69	35
Ayr	38	13	9	16	76	83	35
T Lanark	38	12	8	18	80	96	32
Albion	38	12	6	20	65	90	30
Arbroath	38	11	8	19	54	75	30
St Mirren	38	11	7	20	57	80	29
Queen's P	*38*	*11*	*5*	*22*	*57*	*83*	*27*
Raith	*38*	*10*	*2*	*26*	*65*	*99*	*22*

SCOTTISH SECOND DIVISION

1935-36	1936-37	1937-38	1938-39
Champions: Falkirk	Champions: Ayr United	Champions: Raith Rovers	Champions: Cowdenbeath
Also promoted: St Mirren	Also promoted: Morton	Also promoted: Albion Rovers	Also promoted: Alloa

Bert's our man

BERT TRAUTMANN was captured in Belgium in 1945 and passed through a series of prisoner-of-war camps before ending up in Lancashire, in June.

Trautmann was a keen sportsman who had represented Bremen, at football and athletics. So he played football at the camp. His regular position was at centre-half, but when he was injured he played in goal.

He soon discovered he was a better goalkeeper than halfback and his performances against local teams attracted the attention of St Helens Town. Trautmann chose to stay in England rather than be repatriated and joined the semi-pro club.

Into battle – but only with a ball

WITH many footballers as physical training instructors it was hardly surprising that wherever the British armed forces went football was played. Before the retreat from Dunkirk, an Army XI, captained by Stan Cullis and with Denis Compton, Wilf Copping, Tommy Lawton, Joe Mercer and Bert Sproston in the team, played three matches against a French international team. Even during the height of the D-Day landings a group of soldiers found time for an impromptu match on the beach they had just captured. The game did not last long – it was hastily abandoned when one of the goals exploded. Another squad parachuted into Holland and played in full battledress in case of a sudden counter-attack. They beat the local team 5-2 while waiting for reinforcements to arrive.

In Cairo, the nerve-centre of the north African campaign there were so many players that a full-blown League was organ-

Flying start: Ted Ditchburn's debut in a 6-2 victory over Scotland

ised. Each team represented an Army or Air force unit, and adopted the name of a famous English club. Morale was all important. When a group of Yugoslav partisans started winning matches against the Allies, the Army assembled a special team, who were ordered to beat the locals to put them in their place. Nowhere was morale more important than in prisoner-of-war camps. The Geneva convention said that prisoners should be allowed to play sport, so the Red Cross sent thousands of parcels of equipment.

Football was so popular at Stalag Luft I that there were 60 teams organised into five Leagues. The only problem was that the pitch was surrounded by barbed wire, which was continually puncturing the ball. Stalag Luft VIIB boasted 50 teams and a Cup competition with the winners receiving two barrels of beer as their prize.

War-time winners

1939-40
East Midland League: Chesterfield
Midland League: Wolverhampton Wanderers
North-east League: Huddersfield Town
North-west League: Bury
South A League: Arsenal
South B League: Queen's Park Rangers
South C League: Tottenham Hotspur
South D League: Crystal Palace
South-west League: Plymouth Argyle
West League: Stoke City
League Cup: West Ham United
Scottish West and South League: Rangers
Scottish East and North League: Falkirk
Scottish emergency Cup: Rangers

1940-41
Football League South: Watford
Northern Regional League: Preston North End
Southern Regional League: Crystal Palace
League Cup: Preston North End
Combined Cities Cup: Middlesbrough
Lancashire Cup: Manchester United
London Cup: Reading
Midland Cup: Leicester City
Western Cup: Bristol City
Scottish Southern League: Rangers
Scottish Southern League Cup: Rangers
Scottish Summer Cup: Hibernian
South American championship: Argentina

■ Albert Stubbins, with 226 goals, was the leading scorer during the period from 1939 to 1946. He was followed by Jock Dodds (221) and Tommy Lawton (212)

1941-42
London League: Arsenal
North League: Blackpool
South League: Leicester City
League Cup: Wolverhampton Wanderers
London Cup: Brentford
Scottish North-east League: Rangers (first competition), Aberdeen (second competition)
Scottish Southern League: Rangers
Scottish Southern League Cup: Rangers
Scottish Summer Cup: Rangers
South American championship: Uraguay

1942-43
North League: Blackpool
South League: Arsenal
West League: Lovells Athletic
North League Cup: Blackpool
South League Cup: Arsenal
West League Cup: Swansea Town
Scottish North-east League: Aberdeen (both competitions)
Scottish Southern League: Rangers
Scottish Southern League Cup: Rangers
Scottish Summer Cup: St Mirren

1943-44
North League: Blackpool
South League: Tottenham Hotspur
West League: Lovells Athletic
North League Cup: Aston Villa
South League Cup: Charlton Athletic
West League Cup: Bath City
Scottish North-east League: Raith Rovers (first

competition), Aberdeen (second competition)
Scottish Southern League: Rangers
Scottish Southern League Cup: Hibernian
Scottish Summer Cup: Motherwell

1944-45
North League: Huddersfield Town
South League: Tottenham, Hotspur
West League: Cardiff City
North League Cup: Bolton Wanderers
South League Cup: Chelsea
West League Cup: Bath City
Scottish North-east League: Dundee (first competition), Aberdeen (second competition)
Scottish Southern League: Rangers
Scottish Southern League Cup: Rangers
Scottish Summer Cup: Partick Thistle
South American championship: Argentina

1945-46
FA Cup Derby County 4 Charton Athletic 1
North League: Sheffield United
South League: Birmingham City
Third Division North-west: Accrington Stanley
Third Division North-east: Rotherham United
Third Division South (northern section) Queen's Park Rangers
Third Division South (southern section): Crystal Palace
Third Division North Cup: Rotherham United
Third Division South Cup: Bournemouth
Scottish Southern A League: Rangers
Scottish Southern B League: Dundee
Scottish Southern League Cup: Aberdeen
Scottish Victory Cup: Rangers

Players keep the home flags flying

WHEN Britain declared war on Germany the football season had just started and Blackpool topped the First Division with three wins from three matches. All sport in the country stopped, because emergency regulations forbade the assembly of large crowds.

A joint emergency meeting of the League and the FA decided to halt play for the moment, and suspend players' contracts. But within weeks, permission had been given for matches to resume, subject to the approval of the local police and strict crowd limits, providing that they did not hamper the war effort. Clubs were restricted to paying a maximum match fee of 30 shillings per player and were allowed to use guests to replace men on National Service. Many clubs had already volunteered en bloc and some teams decided to close down for the duration of the war.

The others were organised into 10 regional Leagues because travelling to away matches was restricted to journeys that could be completed on the day of the game. A Cup competition was also staged, with no guest players allowed, and was completed in under two months at the end of the season. West Ham beat Blackburn Rovers 1-0 in the final, watched by survivors of the Dunkirk evacuation.

International matches were also continued (75,000 people saw England draw 1-1 with Scotland at Hampden Park in May 1940) and representative matches were also staged to raise money for the Red Cross. The pools companies, faced with Post Office's refusal to deliver coupons because they were not essential mail, combined forces to produce joint coupons, with a share of the stakes in the Unity Pool going to charity. By 1943 the Red Cross had raised more than £1m, and football was one of the leading sports contributors with just over £70,000.

Not surprisingly, the standard of football was extremely variable with clubs always struggling to raise a team and not having time to train. Halifax's match against Leeds was described as of "a level usually associated with the village green", while there were goals aplenty in other matches. Brighton lost 18-0 at Norwich but that was hardly surprising. Their goalkeeper arrived late and missed the kick-off, despite being given a lift to the ground by a passing fire engine. Half of the team never even made it to the match and Brighton had to borrow players from the Norwich reserves and even the crowd.

Players earned their money wherever they could. Tommy Lawton appeared for Morton while he was on his honeymoon in Scotland and played twice on Christmas Day – for Everton in the morning and then scoring twice for Tranmere in their 2-2 draw at Crewe in the afternoon. Len Shackleton also managed two games on Christmas Day, for Bradford City and Bradford Park Avenue.

One Bradford City player said that he played for eight different clubs in nine weeks, and Notts County used 132 players in a season. Bath, assisted by Stan Mortensen, won the Western Cup twice. Mortensen was the England substitute at Wembley in September 1943 but he finished the match in the Welsh team, who did not have a replacement when one of their players was injured. Even more amazingly, Lovells Athletic, a team fielded by a toffee factory, won the Western League two years in a row.

With so much disruption, the League's and FA's rules were in a state of flux. Since it was almost impossible for clubs to complete all their fixtures it was suggested that the Leagues should be decided solely on goal average, with no points awarded for wins and draws. That idea was rejected, although the Southern League was decided by taking the average number of points per game won by each club and using that figure to calculate how many points the club would, in theory, have gained if they had played 18 matches. Football had learnt the lesson of the First World War, when an initial decision to carry on as normal was widely criticised. There were mutterings of dissent when, in 1942, Sir Stafford Cripps told parliament: "Our motto can neither be business as usual nor pleasure as usual."

But Winston Churchill was strongly in favour of sport continuing. Football received an official seal of approval when Winston Churchill was introduced to the players before England played Scotland in 1941. Seven Cabinet ministers also attended the match. The game between the two countries in 1944 was watched by the King and Field-Marshal Montgomery, a keen patron of Portsmouth's team.

Football, like everybody else, had paid a terrible price by the time the war ended. Nearly a hundred professionals were killed, and others were so badly injured that they never played again.

Churchill: hands across the field

Tonic for the troops: soldiers enjoy a brief respite from battle and flock to a match at Stamford Bridge

Nippy Carter unzips Charlton

WHEN the war ended the game faced enormous problems. Many players were still engaged on national service, grounds were bomb-damaged and petrol rationing restricted transport. So the League was divided into regional sections to reduce travel; promotion and relegation were suspended; the FA Cup was played on a two-leg home and away basis; and clubs were allowed to continue using guest players.

None of that stopped the crowds flocking back, and with the Leagues having an unreal feel to them most interest was concentrated on the FA Cup. The public were rewarded with a classic encounter between Derby and Charlton in the final.

For the first time in a Cup final, the ball burst minutes before the end of normal time when Jack Stamps, Derby's centre-forward, unleashed a fierce shot. There was another entry in the record books when Bert Turner of Charlton became the first man to score for both sides. He put Derby ahead when he deflected a shot into his own net, and seconds later he had a shot of his own deflected to give Charlton the equaliser.

In extra time Raich Carter showed that his skills were still as great as in the 1930s. Derby had shrewdly bought him from Sunderland for £6,000 in December and he had established a telling inside-forward partnership with Peter Doherty.

Doherty and the silver-haired Carter produced a quicksilver display which left the tiring Charlton defence floundering. Stamps scored twice and Doherty once as Derby's 4-1 victory convinced the crowd that football was back to its pre-war best.

Russians quit unbeaten

DYNAMO MOSCOW'S tour of Britain produced one of the strangest series of matches that anybody could recall. The Russians demanded that they should eat all their meals at the Soviet Embassy, and provide their own referee for at least one match. Then, in their first match against Chelsea, they presented each of their opponents with a bunch of flowers.

The press had written the visitors off as a group of pedestrian amateurs, but in front of 82,000 people their quick, precise football brought them back from 2-0 down against the run of play to a 3-3 draw.

Cardiff were destroyed 10-1 before a match with Arsenal, who played Stanley Matthews and Stan Mortensen as guests. The fog over White Hart Lane (Highbury was being rebuilt) was so thick that the Russian referee chose to patrol one touchline, with two English linesmen on the other sideline.

Both sides claimed that it was the other's fault that the game was not cancelled, and with nobody able to see more than five yards it was little wonder that hardly anybody knew exactly how the Russians came back from 3-1 down to win 4-3.

Moscow then played an ill-tempered 2-2 draw with Rangers, and were due to meet an FA XI at Villa Park. But just before that game was to be held they vanished, flying home without giving any reason.

Bert Turner, who scored for both teams, wins a corner for Charlton

Flower power: Chelsea were presented with bouquets by Dynamo Moscow

33 crushed to death at Bolton

THE second round FA Cup match between Bolton and Stoke on March 9 made it tragically apparent that war-scarred grounds could not cope with the crowds that were now flocking to matches. The official attendance at Burnden Park was put at 65,419, but it was estimated that nearer 85,000 people came to see whether Stoke could overcome a 2-0 deficit from the first leg.

With rationing still in force, a considerable number of policemen were guarding food in one of the stands. This was regarded as a more important duty than dealing with the gatecrashers who started climbing over the turnstiles in one corner of the ground.

■ Struggling Manchester United, £15,000 in debt and forced to share Maine Road with Manchester City, appointed Matt Busby their manager in February.

■ The FA Cup semi-final replay between Derby and Birmingham at Maine Road attracted a crowd of 80,407, a record for a midweek match between two clubs outside of Wembley. This caused the government to become so concerned about the effect of absenteeism on the efforts to rebuild the country that it soon banned midweek afternoon matches.

■ With huge crowds flocking to grounds, football clubs were making a fortune at the turnstiles. Players complained that they were not sharing in the bonanza, and threatened to go on strike unless their pre-war wages of £8 a week were raised. They won an increase to £9.

■ Aberdeen beat Rangers 3-2 in the final of the Scottish Southern League Cup. The following season the competition became the Scottish League Cup.

■ The FA persuaded all the British associations to rejoin FIFA.

As a result, part of the terracing became so overcrowded that the crush barriers collapsed. In the space of a few yards 33 people died and more than 500 were injured in the worst disaster in British football. The Home Office conducted an inquiry, which called for stricter safety standards at grounds but the recommendations were largely ignored.

League back with a storm

EVEN THE heavy rain on August 31 could not dampen the enthusiasm for the resumption of the League. Nearly a million people flocked to the 43 matches that day, which were identical fixtures to the first day of the short-lived 1939 season.

But the season was to become the longest on record as a bitter winter played havoc with fixtures. By January, so many pitches were white with snow and ice that the lines had to be marked out using red paint. More than 140 matches were postponed in three months but the fans were still keen to watch football. When Portsmouth used jets of steam to clear their pitch they were rewarded with a crowd of more than 10,000 for a reserve team game.

In the end, everything hinged on two matches. Wolves, who had been 11 points clear at one stage, needed to win their last match against Liverpool to secure the title. But they lost 2-1 at Molineux, which gave the leadership of the First Division to Liverpool, a solid team built around Albert Stubbins, Billy Liddell and Bob Paisley.

Liverpool, though, had to wait a fortnight until June 14 when the final game of the season was Stoke's visit to Sheffield United. If Stoke had won they would have taken the title on goal average. But United's 2-1 victory gave the championship to Liverpool and left Stoke in fourth place.

Old salts bale out sinking Arsenal

AFTER a third of the season the only thing that kept Arsenal off the bottom of the table was goal average. They lost nine of their first 14 matches and were heading for an unimaginable drop into the Second Division.

Up and coming young players were almost impossible to find, so Arsenal turned to a pair of old hands. Joe Mercer, 31 and suffering with a dodgy knee, was said to be contemplating retirement. But Arsenal persuaded him to play on for a little longer and paid £7,000 to Everton for their stalwart left half. Ronnie Rooke, at 35, was also said to be past it and could not command a place in the Fulham team. But Arsenal signed the veteran centre-forward in exchange for £1,000 and two of their reserve team players.

The rest of the country scoffed. Arsenal were clearly getting desperate. In fact, Arsenal were getting two bargains. Mercer, immediately made captain, brought authority to the side's play and Rooke showed that he had not lost his touch, scoring 21 goals in 24 matches. Arsenal only lost one of their next nine games as they hauled themselves clear of relegation.

Magical Mercer: the Arsenal captain steps out in style at Highbury

FOR THE RECORD

■ Len Shackleton scored six goals for Newcastle on his debut against Newport County in the Second Division after his £13,000 transfer from Bradford.

■ Sam Bartram, the Charlton goalkeeper, played with a hot poultice on his stomach to counter food poisoning in the FA Cup semi-final against Newcastle. Charlton went on to win the FA Cup and, amazingly, the ball burst for the second successive year during the final.

■ Neil McBain, New Brighton's 52-year-old manager, had to play in goal when the club's only regular keeper was injured. McBain became the oldest man ever to play in the League in a 3-0 loss to Hartlepools in the Third Division North.

■ Derby broke the British transfer record when they paid £15,500 for Billy Steel of Morton, the Scottish international inside-forward.

■ Stanley Matthews was controversially transferred from Stoke to Blackpool for £11,500.

■ Doncaster Rovers set four records in the Third Division North: total points (72), away points (37), total wins (33) and away wins (18). They also equalled the division's record of only three defeats.

England favour Winterbottom

ENGLAND resumed playing internationals in September with a 7-2 victory in Belfast and life was looking good for the national side when they blasted eight goals past Holland.

But then England suffered an embarrassing 1-0 defeat by Switzerland in Zurich on May 18. That was enough to prompt Stanley Rous, the FA secretary, to have Walter Winterbottom, who had been appointed chief coach in 1946, made the first England team manager.

England bounced back by thrashing Portugal 10-0 in Lisbon on May 27. Stan Mortensen, nicknamed "the electric eel" for his ability to wriggle through defences, celebrated his debut with four goals.

The other great international of the season was played by Great Britain and the Rest of Europe at Hampden Park in May to celebrate the home nations rejoining Fifa. Mannion and Lawton both scored twice in the 6-1 victory over a scratch side led by Johnny Carey of Manchester United and Ireland that included players from 10 countries.

Strong stuff: Duffy rockets the ball past Strong to win the Cup for Charlton

Busby steadies United nerves

MATT BUSBY had learnt the manager's art during the war as a company sergeant-major in the army working with Tommy Lawton, Joe Mercer and Arthur Rowe.

With little money to spend at Manchester United, Busby invested his time in cultivating the latent talent at the club. His tactical vision and readiness to experiment produced a transformation.

The Irish international Johnny Carey was moved to right back from inside right, where the mercurial Johnny Morris took over. John Aston, the inside left, became the left back, making room for Stan Pearson to become the brains of the attack. With Jimmy Delaney, Jack Rowley and Charlie Mitten completing the forward line, United had a scintillating strike force.

Busby predicted that United would win the FA Cup, but they had to play a First Division team in every round. In the third round they were involved in an amazing match at Aston Villa – they conceded a goal straight from the kick-off, were ahead 5-1 at half-time, had their lead cut to 5-4 and finally prevailed 6-4.

At Wembley, United faced a resurgent Blackpool, who had reached the final for the first time. With Stanley Matthews and Stan Mortensen in tandem, Blackpool were 2-1 ahead with 20 minutes left. Blackpool were playing superbly, and any other team would have succumbed.

Not United. At half-time Busby and Carey had told the team not to panic and their riposte was sublime. Three goals came in 16 minutes and the crowd was left thrilled by a match that had been all-out attack from start to finish. The sergeant-major's team were truly on the march.

Arsenal do the business

TOM WHITTAKER the newly-appointed Arsenal manager, had his faith in Joe Mercer rewarded. Arsenal only dropped two points in their first 13 games and did not lose in the League until their 18th match.

The game was becoming more defensively minded and Arsenal were stuck with the label "lucky", because many people thought they played boring football and did not deserve to win.

But there was nothing lucky about their fine start, which was made without the Compton brothers, Denis and Leslie, who were helping Middlesex win cricket's County Championship. Nor did Arsenal fans care if their club was supposedly boring. The match at Chelsea brought traffic to a standstill for miles and touts were offering five-shilling tickets at 10 times the price; the meeting with Manchester United broke the League attendance record when 83,260 packed into Maine Road.

Arsenal had a solid, settled side and coasted to their sixth title with almost a month to spare. Mercer, again contemplating retirement, was persuaded to play on for another year.

Third Division go first class

A PAIR of audacious transfers created enormous interest in the Third Division. Tommy Lawton was determined to leave Chelsea, but they had rejected several offers before Notts County, a moderate Third Division North side, persuaded them to sell in November.

Meadow Lane was electrified by Britain's first £20,000 transfer. Lawton's debut was a sell-out, County's attendance record was broken within a few weeks and Lawton became the first Third Division player to appear for England.

Hull, too, wanted to improve themselves. In March they persuaded Derby to sell Raich Carter for a nominal fee. As well as playing, Carter would also be Hull's assistant manager. But when Major Frank Buckley resigned as manager within weeks to go to Leeds, Carter was given complete charge and Hull's attendances boomed.

Investment rewarded: Notts County fans flocked to watch Lawton

Keeping his head: Jack Rowley rises above the Blackpool defence

FOR THE RECORD

■ Jack Fairbrother moved from Preston to Newcastle for £7,000, a record fee for a goalkeeper. The feeling that the transfer market was getting out of hand was increased when Charlton paid £6,000 for two non-League players from Dartford.

■ Millwall's ground was closed for seven days after crowd trouble.

■ Newcastle, with an average home crowd of more than 56,000, gained promotion to the First Division despite selling Len Shackelton to Sunderland in February. The deal raised the transfer record again, to £20,500.

■ Hibernian won the Scottish League title for the first time. Willie McCartney, who had assembled the side, died in January before he could enjoy the club's finest moment.

■ The total attendance for the season rose again, topping 40 million for the first time. In Scotland, 143,750 people saw Rangers beat Hibs in the Cup semi-final. And 133,570 attended the Scottish Cup final replay, a record for a midweek match.

■ The BBC claimed that 1 million people watched the Cup final on television.

■ Southern League Colchester reached the last 16 of the FA Cup. Then their M-plan for stopping Stanley Matthews backfired as Blackpool won 5-0. All of the goals were scored by players whose surname started with M.

THE 1948-49 SEASON

Hull on top as Carter pulls it off

AS FAR as the people of Hull were concerned, Raich Carter became an instant hero in his first full season in charge. Patrolling the left wing, his skills were still, at 35, far superior to any other player's in the Third Division North.

Carter's emphasis on high-class football gave Hull a start of nine successive victories in the League, and after 13 away matches they had not been been beaten either. They also reached the quarter-finals of the Cup, where they were unlucky to lose 1-0 to Manchester United because their goalkeeper played most of the match with concussion.

It was little wonder that average attendances at Boothferry Park virtually doubled as Hull made their long-awaited return to the Second Division.

Carter: wily grey fox

Sunderland fall off Yeovil's cliff-hanger

ALEC STOCK, Yeovil's player-manager, ran the lowly Southern League club virtually single-handed – including cutting the grass of the soon to be famous pitch.

The press only started to pay attention to his team of part-timers when they reached the third round of the FA Cup and faced Second Division Bury. The media gave Stock a useful weapon; he talked up the 8ft slope on his pitch until, as he put it: "By the time Bury arrived the entire country thought we played on the side of a house."

Bury must have felt that way too as they fell 3-1. They probably did not know about Stock's other secret weapon either. His players were on a special diet – glucose, eggs and sherry – to give them strength.

Yeovil hit the jackpot when they were then drawn at home to mighty Sunderland. The First Division giants were out-run and out-fought as Stock put Yeovil ahead after 30 minutes. Sunderland managed to equalise and force extra time but it merely postponed the inevitable. Bryant put Yeovil ahead again, Stock's diet gave his team the strength to survive the last 15 minutes and Yeovil were on their way to Manchester United.

It was the greatest day out Somerset had ever had and although Yeovil were crushed 8-0 Stock was pragmatic: "We just felt numb. But then we heard that our share of the gate (over £7,000) was more than our entire receipts for the previous season. Suddenly, what had happened on the field was of no significance."

Stock: crafty schemer

Pompey's senior service sail serenely to the title

SO MANY servicemen had been stationed on the south coast during the war that Portsmouth had been able to recruit the pick of the crop. But because their entire team had only cost a few thousand pounds they were not rated by the pundits.

However, it was Portsmouth's golden jubilee year and they wanted to celebrate the anniversary with a trophy. They also had a president who did not like losing, Field Marshal Montgomery. He was forever urging his players on in the way that he used to inspire his troops in battle. The Portsmouth captain received a missive from Montgomery suggesting it would be a good idea to hit Chelsea for six.

Portsmouth, not a team to disobey orders, obliged.

Portsmouth had their best ever start to the season and were on course for the Double but they were caught napping by Leicester in the FA Cup semi-final and the Second Division team, inspired by Don Revie, won 3-1. As often happens, being knocked out of the Cup concentrated the team's minds on the League.

The match that ultimately decided the League was at St James's Park in April, where Portsmouth's half-backs utterly stifled Newcastle to set up a 5-0 win. The title was theirs and Montgomery proudly received the trophy at Fratton Park.

Rangers grab their first treble chance

RANGERS made such a habit of winning the Scottish League and Cup that their fans expected nothing less. So they went one better and completed the first treble. Surprisingly, their rivals Celtic did not bother them in any of the competitions: Rangers won the League by one point from Dundee; beat Clyde 4-1 in the Cup final; and had a 2-0 victory over Raith in the League Cup final.

The Rangers team was built around the "Iron Curtain" defence. At its heart was the formidable George Young, who made more than 50 appearances for Scotland. He was ably supported by the hard tackling Willie Woodburn, Sammy Cox and Jock Shaw. But Rangers were not a purely defensive side, with the two Willies, Waddell and Thornton, keeping up a steady flow of goals.

Scotland put pride before World finals

SCOTTISH supporters, still revelling in their 3-1 victory over England at Wembley last season, paid dearly for the arrogant attitude towards Fifa displayed by their FA.

Fifa were prepared to give the United Kingdom two places in the 1950 World Cup finals, with the winners and runners-up in the Home International championship qualifying. But the proud Scots insisted that they would only go to Brazil if they were actually to win the domestic tournament.

Both England and Scotland easily beat Wales and Northern Ireland, setting up a showdown at Hampden. England won 1-0 although Scotland were unlucky when Willie Bauld's shot bounced off the bar and hit the goal line but did not go in. A draw would have meant that Scotland, the previous year's champions, would have retained the trophy and gone to the World Cup.

Bauld: unlucky miss

Compton brothers saving double-act

Capital conquest: Arsenal won the FA Cup without leaving London

ARSENAL'S ageing stars proved they still had some life left in their legs with a resounding 2-0 victory over Liverpool in the FA Cup final. It was a fitting finale for Denis Compton, who was forced to stop playing at the end of the season by his knee injury.

Arsenal had Denis and his brother Leslie to thank for their appearance in the final. They were 2-1 down to Chelsea with seconds to go when Denis took a corner. Leslie ignored Joe Mercer's order not to join the attack and, as a result, was in just the right spot to score the equaliser.

The final was played in pouring rain on a strength-sapping pitch and at the interval Denis was exhausted. But revived by a large brandy he was able to set up the second goal that enabled Arsenal to withstand Liverpool's late rally.

While Arsenal were winning the Cup without ever having to play a game outside of London, their neighbours Tottenham were also attracting interest.

The Tottenham board were unhappy about their team never quite being good enough to get out of the Second Division, so they had recently appointed Arthur Rowe. The new manager told his team: "Make it simple, make it quick."

They did so with a vengeance, going 23 matches without defeat, topping the table throughout the season, and running away with the division by nine points. The team was talked about as the best side the club had ever produced, but Rowe disagreed – he knew they were capable of better things yet.

Championship just chimes again for Portsmouth

PORTSMOUTH won the League for the second year running, but this time the race was much closer, with several teams in the hunt and the title undecided until the end of the season.

Wolves, with their young team, made the early pace, not losing until their 13th match. They were overhauled by Liverpool, who went 19 matches before being beaten. Manchester United, who had just returned to Old Trafford, were as strong as ever and Portsmouth, Blackpool and Sunderland were not far behind.

Manchester United caught up with Liverpool in the spring and then faded, leaving Sunderland to edge in front at Easter. The international between England and Scotland was played on a Saturday, depriving several clubs of key players and giving Portsmouth a chance to go top for the first time.

Even then, only one point separated the top four clubs. And that was the way it stayed to the final Saturday, May 6. Portsmouth led Wolves on goal average and Sunderland were one point behind.

All three teams had emphatic wins: Portsmouth 5-1, Wolves 6-1 and Sunderland 4-1. It was enough to give Portsmouth the title by 0.4 goals, the first time the championship had been decided on goal average for a quarter of a century.

LEGEND TABLES AND RESULTS 1945–1950

	1945-46	1946-47	1947-48	1948-49	1949-50
WORLD CUP					Uruguay 2 Brazil 1
FA CUP	Derby County 4 Charlton Athletic 1	Charlton Athletic 1 Burnley 0	Manchester United 4 Blackpool 2	Wolverhampton Wanderers 3 Leicester City 1	Arsenal 2 Liverpool 0

FIRST DIVISION

1946-47
	P	W	D	L	F	A	Pts
Liverpool	42	25	7	10	84	52	57
Man Utd	42	22	12	8	95	54	56
Wolves	42	25	6	11	98	56	56
Stoke	42	24	7	11	90	53	55
Blackpool	42	22	6	14	71	70	50
Sheff Utd	42	21	7	14	89	75	49
Preston	42	18	11	13	76	74	47
Aston Villa	42	18	9	15	67	53	45
Sunderland	42	18	8	16	65	66	44
Everton	42	17	9	16	62	67	43
Middlesbro	42	17	8	17	73	68	42
Portsmouth	42	16	9	17	66	60	41
Arsenal	42	16	9	17	72	70	41
Derby	42	18	5	19	73	79	41
Chelsea	42	16	7	19	69	84	39
Grimsby	42	13	12	17	61	82	38
Blackburn	42	14	8	20	45	53	36
Bolton	42	13	8	21	57	69	34
Charlton	42	11	12	19	57	71	34
Huddersfld	42	13	7	22	53	79	33
Brentford	42	9	7	26	45	88	25
Leeds	42	6	6	30	45	90	18

1947-48
	P	W	D	L	F	A	Pts
Arsenal	42	23	13	6	81	32	59
Man Utd	42	19	14	9	81	48	52
Burnley	42	20	12	10	56	43	52
Derby	42	19	12	11	77	57	50
Wolves	42	19	9	14	83	70	47
Aston Villa	42	19	9	14	65	57	47
Preston	42	20	7	15	67	68	47
Portsmouth	42	19	7	16	68	50	45
Blackpool	42	17	10	15	57	41	44
Man City	42	15	12	15	52	47	42
Liverpool	42	16	10	16	65	61	42
Sheff Utd	42	16	10	16	65	70	42
Charlton	42	17	6	19	57	66	40
Everton	42	17	6	19	52	66	40
Stoke	42	14	10	18	41	55	38
Middlesbro	42	14	9	19	71	73	37
Bolton	42	16	5	21	46	58	37
Chelsea	42	14	9	19	53	71	37
Huddersfld	42	12	12	18	51	60	36
Sunderland	42	13	10	19	56	67	36
Blackburn	42	11	10	21	54	72	32
Grimsby	42	8	6	28	45	111	22

1948-49
	P	W	D	L	F	A	Pts
Portsmouth	42	25	8	9	84	42	58
Man Utd	42	21	11	10	77	44	53
Derby	42	22	9	11	74	55	53
Newcastle	42	20	12	10	70	56	52
Arsenal	42	18	13	11	74	44	49
Wolves	42	17	12	13	79	66	46
Man City	42	15	15	12	47	51	45
Sunderland	42	13	17	12	49	58	43
Charlton	42	15	12	15	63	67	42
Aston Villa	42	16	10	16	60	76	42
Stoke	42	16	9	17	66	68	41
Liverpool	42	13	14	15	53	43	40
Chelsea	42	12	14	16	69	68	38
Bolton	42	14	10	18	59	68	38
Burnley	42	12	14	16	43	50	38
Blackpool	42	11	16	15	54	67	38
Birmingham	42	11	15	16	36	38	37
Everton	42	13	11	18	41	63	37
Middlesbro	42	11	12	19	46	57	34
Huddersfld	42	12	10	20	40	69	34
Preston	42	11	11	20	62	75	33
Sheff Utd	42	11	11	20	57	78	33

1949-50
	P	W	D	L	F	A	Pts
Portsmouth	42	22	9	11	74	38	53
Wolves	42	20	13	9	76	49	53
Sunderland	42	21	10	11	83	62	52
Man Utd	42	18	14	10	69	44	50
Newcastle	42	19	12	11	77	55	50
Arsenal	42	19	11	12	79	55	49
Blackpool	42	17	15	10	46	35	49
Liverpool	42	17	14	11	64	54	48
Middlesbro	42	20	7	15	59	48	47
Burnley	42	16	13	13	40	40	45
Derby	42	17	10	15	69	61	44
Aston Villa	42	15	12	15	61	61	42
Chelsea	42	12	16	14	58	65	40
West Brom	42	14	12	16	47	53	40
Huddersfld	42	14	9	19	52	73	37
Bolton	42	10	14	18	45	59	34
Fulham	42	10	14	18	41	54	34
Everton	42	10	14	18	42	66	34
Stoke	42	11	12	19	45	75	34
Charlton	42	13	6	23	53	65	32
Man City	42	8	13	21	36	68	29
Birmingham	42	7	14	21	31	67	28

SECOND DIVISION

1946-47	1947-48	1948-49	1949-50
Champions: Manchester City Also promoted: Burnley Relegated: Swansea Town, Newport County	Champions: Birmingham City Also promoted: Newcastle United Relegated: Doncaster Rovers, Millwall	Champions: Fulham Also promoted: West Bromwich Albion Relegated: Nottingham Forest, Lincoln City	Champions: Tottenham Hotspur Also promoted: Sheffield Wednesday Relegated: Plymouth Argyle, Bradford Park Avenue

THIRD DIVISION SOUTH

1946-47	1947-48	1948-49	1949-50
Champions: Cardiff City Runners-up (not promoted): Queen's Park Rangers	Champions: Queen's Park Rangers Runners-up (not promoted): Bournemouth	Champions: Swansea Town Runners-up (not promoted): Reading	Champions: Notts County Runners-up (not promoted): Northampton Town

THIRD DIVISION NORTH

1946-47	1947-48	1948-49	1949-50
Champions: Doncaster Rovers Runners-up (not promoted): Rotherham United	Champions: Lincoln City Runners-up (not promoted): Rotherham United	Champions: Hull City Runners-up (not promoted): Rotherham United	Champions: Doncaster Rovers Runners-up (not promoted): Gateshead

SCOTTISH CUP

1946-47	1947-48	1948-49	1949-50
Aberdeen 2 Hibernian 1	Rangers 1 Morton 0, after 1-1	Rangers 4 Clyde 1	Rangers 3 East Fife 0

SCOTTISH FIRST DIVISION

1946-47
	P	W	D	L	F	A	Pts
Rangers	30	21	4	5	76	26	46
Hibernian	30	19	6	5	69	33	44
Aberdeen	30	16	7	7	58	41	39
Hearts	30	16	6	8	52	43	38
Partick	30	16	3	11	74	59	35
Morton	30	12	10	8	58	45	34
Celtic	30	13	6	11	53	55	32
Motherwell	30	12	5	13	58	54	29
T Lanark	30	11	6	13	56	64	28
Clyde	30	9	9	12	55	65	27
Falkirk	30	8	10	12	62	61	26
Q of South	30	9	8	13	44	69	26
Queen's P	30	8	6	16	47	60	22
St Mirren	30	9	4	17	47	65	22
Kilmarnock	30	6	9	15	44	66	21
Hamilton	30	2	7	21	38	85	11

1947-48
	P	W	D	L	F	A	Pts
Hibernian	30	22	4	4	86	27	48
Rangers	30	21	4	5	64	28	46
Partick	30	16	4	10	61	42	36
Dundee	30	15	3	12	67	51	33
St Mirren	30	13	5	12	54	58	31
Clyde	30	12	7	11	52	57	31
Falkirk	30	10	10	10	55	48	30
Motherwell	30	13	3	14	45	47	29
Hearts	30	10	8	12	37	42	28
Aberdeen	30	10	7	13	45	45	27
T Lanark	30	10	6	14	56	73	26
Celtic	30	10	5	15	41	56	25
Q of South	30	10	5	15	49	74	25
Morton	30	9	6	15	47	43	24
Airdrie	30	7	7	16	40	78	21
Queen's P	30	9	2	19	45	75	20

1948-49
	P	W	D	L	F	A	Pts
Rangers	30	20	6	4	63	32	46
Dundee	30	20	5	5	71	48	45
Hibernian	30	17	5	8	75	52	39
East Fife	30	16	3	11	64	46	35
Falkirk	30	12	8	10	70	54	32
Celtic	30	12	7	11	48	40	31
T Lanark	30	13	5	12	56	52	31
Hearts	30	12	6	12	64	54	30
St Mirren	30	13	4	13	51	47	30
Q of South	30	11	8	11	47	53	30
Partick	30	9	9	12	50	63	27
Motherwell	30	10	5	15	44	49	25
Aberdeen	30	7	11	12	39	48	25
Clyde	30	9	6	15	50	67	24
Morton	30	7	8	15	39	51	22
Albion	30	3	2	25	30	105	8

1949-50
	P	W	D	L	F	A	Pts
Rangers	30	22	6	2	58	26	50
Hibernian	30	22	5	3	86	34	49
Hearts	30	20	3	7	86	40	43
East Fife	30	15	7	8	58	43	37
Celtic	30	14	7	9	51	50	35
Dundee	30	12	7	11	49	46	31
Partick	30	13	3	14	55	45	29
Aberdeen	30	11	4	15	48	56	26
Raith	30	9	8	13	45	54	26
Motherwell	30	10	5	15	53	58	25
St Mirren	30	8	9	13	42	49	25
T Lanark	30	11	3	16	44	62	25
Clyde	30	10	4	16	56	73	24
Falkirk	30	7	10	13	48	72	24
Q of South	30	5	6	19	31	63	16
Stirling	30	6	3	21	38	77	15

SCOTTISH SECOND DIVISION

1946-47	1947-48	1948-49	1949-50
Champions: Dundee Also promoted: Airdrie	Champions: East Fife Also promoted: Albion Rovers	Champions: Raith Rovers Also promoted: Stirling Albion	Champions: Morton Also promoted: Airdrie

SCOTTISH LEAGUE CUP

1946-47	1947-48	1948-49	1949-50
Rangers 4 Aberdeen 0	East Fife 4 Falkirk 1, after 1-1	Rangers 2 Raith 0	East Fife 3 Dunfermline 0

THE WORLD CUP in Brazil was the most chaotic, disorganised and ramshackle tournament in the event's history. It was marked by mass withdrawals, teams having to travel thousands of miles to fulfil fixtures in their own group, a structure that meant there was no official World Cup final and a showpiece stadium that was unfinished – even by the concluding match. But most of all it will be remembered for two of the most stunning upsets in World Cup history: England's defeat at the hands of the United States and Brazil's loss of the Jules Rimet Trophy when all they needed was a draw.

Because of the ravages of the Second World War there had not been a World Cup for 12 years (although the South Americans carried on with their own championships largely unaffected by outside events). Everything had augured well for the 1950 World Cup: the four British associations had finally rejoined Fifa in 1946 and would compete for the first time; the hosts were to build the biggest and greatest stadium the world had ever seen – the three-tiered, 200,000 capacity Maracana; and to celebrate the survival of the event the World Cup was renamed the Jules Rimet Trophy, after one of the initiators of the championship who had kept the trophy under his bed in France during the war lest the invading Germans found it and melted it down.

Almost immediately things started to go wrong. Czechoslovakia would not enter, nor would Hungary or the Soviet Union. So there were only 32 entries for the qualifying tournament. Then Argentina, Austria, Belgium, Burma, Ecuador, India, and Peru withdrew without playing a single match. Turkey pulled out after qualifying, as did Scotland.

The decision by the Scots was a classic example of cutting off your nose to spite your face. Fifa, delighted to have the four British associations back in the world family, had generously designated the home championships as a World Cup qualifying group, with two teams qualifying. Scotland arrogantly declared that they would only go to Brazil as British champions. England narrowly beat them 1-0 at Hampden, leaving the Scots in second place. Despite the protestations of the English and Scottish players, the Scottish Football Association stubbornly stayed at home.

It got worse. After Turkey, having qualified, withdrew Fifa invited France (who had been knocked out by Yugoslavia) to take their place. France accepted and then saw their itinerary, which involved thousands of miles criss-crossing Brazil. Their appeals against the schedule were rejected so they, too, withdrew. Portugal, also eliminated in the qualifying rounds, were offered Scotland's place – and they refused.

By the time the tournament got underway there was only a rump of 13 teams left, which were absurdly disorganised into two groups of four, one of three and one of two, these two being Uruguay and Bolivia, both of whom had qualified without playing a

match. Uruguay had thrashed Bolivia five times out of six and scored 27 goals. In Brazil they added another eight without reply. No other team would ever get such an easy ride to the final round.

The catalogue of fiascos was compounded by the well-meaning replacement of the simplistic knock-out structure of the previous three World Cups with leagues only, including the final round. But, amazingly, the organisers had omitted to schedule an actual World Cup final. Fortuitously, the gods rescued them when the concluding match of the tournament did decide the winners of the trophy (historians now refer to this match as a World Cup final).

Also, nobody had realised that groups should be centred on one, or

at most two, cities (only the Brazilians were to enjoy such an advantage) so that teams should not have to traipse all over the place playing matches hither and thither, often within days of each other. And this in a country as vast as Brazil, the fourth largest in the world covering nearly half the area of the whole of South America.

But out of this chaos came one of the most extraordinary tournaments. As Brazil were sweeping all before them with the sublime football that has made them world renowned, England, the nation that gave the game to the world, were to suffer the most humiliating result in their history in Belo Horizonte.

There was little indication that England were to fall flat on their faces. For the first time they had a full-time manager, Walter Winterbottom, and a team bristling with talent: Bert Williams in goal; Billy Wright and Alf Ramsey in defence; and an incomparable forward line of Tom Finney, Stan Mortensen, Wilf Mannion and Stanley Matthews. They were undoubtedly one of the favourites for the tournament, and some thought them the best side in the world.

England had won their first game unimpressively against Chile, and against the American minnows decided to stick with the same team – without Matthews – and treat it as practice match. And for the first half-hour that was what it appeared to be as England played virtually in the American half, shooting almost

Travelling hopefully: England arrived in Brazil full of confidence only to be sent packing by the Americans

at will, hitting the bar, and shooting over the bar. It seemed only time before the deluge came.

Then the unthinkable happened eight minutes before half-time. A shot from the left seemed well covered by the England goalkeeper when it was suddenly deflected by the head of the Haitian-born Larry Gaetjens. Nobody was sure whether he had hit it, or it hit him. Whatever, England were 1-0 down. And try as they might – including a dubiously disallowed goal from a Ramsey free-kick – the famous English forwards could not score.

When the result came over the wires in Britain some newspapers thought it a typing error and changed it 10-1. In Belo Horizonte the 10,000 crowd built bonfires on the terraces in celebration and carried the victorious Americans off shoulder high. "Bloody ridiculous," Mannion said. "Can't we play them again tomorrow?" England lost their next game, to Spain, and were on the boat home in ignominy.

In the final round Brazil had coasted through to the last match having scored 13 goals and conceded a mere two to amass four points. Uruguay, their opponents, had struggled to gain three. Brazil, therefore, only needed a draw to take the World Cup.

A world record crowd of 199,854 arrived at the Maracana to watch the inevitable. Before the match the Rio state governor proclaimed Brazil as champions. For the first half it looked that way as the Brazilians mounted wave after wave of attacks, and it seemed only time before their opponents would be overrun. But the first half was goalless and Brazil only scored, through Friaça, three minutes after the interval. Yet this did not break the Uruguayans' resolve. The now familiar trait of Brazilian over-confidence took over and, instead of falling back into defence, they continued to pour forward.

In the 66th minute Uruguay fashioned the equaliser when Schiaffino scored from a pass from Ghiaggia on the right wing. At this point Brazil were still winning the tournament but it seemed the strut had gone from their game. Sixteen minutes from time Ghiaggia again turned them on the wing, this time to score himself with a wonderful individual goal. The unimaginable had happened and the World Cup had returned to Montevideo.

Losing out: England (top) only won one match, against Chile; Billy Wright's men were to be shocked by defeat by the USA; the final attracted almost 200,000 spectators but they saw the hosts Brazil surprisingly beaten

Rowe pushed slick Spurs to run rings round First Division

ARTHUR ROWE had spent time coaching in Europe and he brought the best of continental thinking to a Tottenham team that was just reaching maturity. Many of the players were the products of the Northfleet nursery, the Kent club that Spurs sent their young prospects to to finish their football education. All Rowe had to do was teach them to play his way.

He had a novel way of explaining what he wanted. Returning from one away match he used sugar cubes on the table of the train's dining car to illustrate why Tottenham's last-minute winning goal had been so brilliant.

"I spread the sugar out to map the moves," he said. "There were seven passes starting from our penalty area. I argued that if we could play like that, instead of just hoping for something to happen, we would score more often."

Rowe's theory was based on short passes and three-man triangles. It was dubbed "push and run", although Rowe did not like the term. But whatever it was called, his players relished following the Rowe style.

There was a great deal of speculation about how the First Division's upstarts would fare against more established sides. The answer was not long in coming. Five goals went past Portsmouth and, in November, Newcastle came to White Hart Lane and conceded seven, four of them before half-time.

A report of the Newcastle match said: "It is hard to imagine a more brilliant exposition of the game. This was vintage champagne, something to savour and remember. When the mechanism clicks at speed, with every pass placed to the last refined inch, there is simply no defence against it."

Tottenham won eight games in a row in the autumn and kept the momentum going just as spectacularly as they had done in the Second Division the previous season. They made sure of the title, the first in the club's history, in April – with a match still in hand.

Transfer fee ceiling spurned as clubs throw money around

PLAYERS finally won an improvement in their conditions with the establishment of a provident fund and an increase in their wages by a Labour Ministry tribunal, but elsewhere there was a feeling that the game had gone money mad.

The tribunal suggested limiting transfer fees to a maximum of £15,000 but the clubs swiftly rejected the idea. That was hardly surprising when Sunderland were prepared to spend a record £30,000 on Trevor Ford, the Aston Villa centre-forward. But despite having three forwards who cost a total of £70,000 Sunderland failed to score in nearly a third of their League matches.

The record did not last long. Minutes before the March transfer deadline Sheffield Wednesday paid Notts County £34,000 for Jackie Sewell, making the forward worth his weight in gold. Not that it did Wednesday any good – they were relegated on goal difference.

It was not only the big spending clubs that suffered. Brentford, despite an average home gate of 19,000, were losing money and forced to sell two of their best players, Jimmy Hill to Fulham and Ron Greenwood to Chelsea.

Making ends meet: Brentford were compelled to realise two of their key assets, Jimmy Hill (left) to Fulham and Ron Greenwood to Chelsea

Milburn rediscovers his lethal touch as Newcastle conquer Cup jitters

NEWCASTLE had gone from strength to strength since winning promotion and their fanatical supporters, remembering the club's great tradition, were keen for another trophy to come to St James's Park. Their wish was granted in the FA Cup, but not before Newcastle had had some scares on the way to Wembley.

In the fourth round they trailed Bolton 2-1 before scraping through 3-2, and then they had to ride out a series of storming attacks from Stoke to win 4-2. Their biggest fright came in the sixth round against the minnows of Bristol Rovers.

The entire Bristol Rovers side had cost £350 but they held Newcastle's £60,000 team to a 0-0 draw at St James's Park. Then Bristol Rovers had the temerity to take the lead in the replay before Newcastle won 3-1.

Newcastle also needed a replay to beat Wolves in the semi-final and then faced a nervous seven-week wait before the final. During this time their form deserted them.

They won only one League match out of 11, and "Wor" Jackie Milburn, their star striker, was dropped for one League game because he was suffering "a bad attack of

Wembley jitters". But Milburn rediscovered his composure in time for the final against Blackpool.

It was not a classic match because Blackpool, inexplicably, chose to play the offside trap.

They had had several close calls before Milburn started a run from the halfway line, with the Blackpool players appealing for offside again. But Milburn had timed his break to perfec-

Milburn: beat offside trap

tion and, unchallenged, he ran half the length of the pitch to slide the ball under the advancing goalkeeper George Farm.

There was no doubting his second goal four minutes later. He worked a quick one-two with Ernie Taylor and unhesitatingly hit the backheeled return pass. Farm had barely moved by the time the 25-yard angled shot went into the top corner of the net.

Little respite as England slip further

ENGLAND returned from the World Cup in Brazil painfully aware that they were no longer the pre-eminent football nation. And there were soon plenty of signs that British football was slipping behind the rest of the world.

England chopped and changed their side and gave away a 2-0 lead against Yugoslavia, who became the first continental team to draw a full international in England. Then England lost the decisive home international match against Scotland 3-2, and had to come from behind to beat Argentina.

England's only excuse was in the match against Scotland in April. Wilf Mannion was carried off with a suspected fractured skull after a terrible collision with Billy Liddell. Despite being reduced to 10 men for most of the match, England, for once, played with great resolve, even briefly taking the lead against the run of play.

Scotland also had their problems. They lost their first ever home match against a foreign team when Austria won 1-0 in December. The return fixture was even worse. Scotland lost 4-0 in Vienna in May, when Billy Steel became the first Scottish international to be sent off.

Master blaster: Milburn's second goal left the goalkeeper stranded

Hot-shot United the top guns

AN early glut of goals restored the public's faith in the quality of the English game and set the scene for an exciting season in which six different teams led the First Division.

Jackie Milburn set the ball rolling on the first Saturday with a hat-trick in Newcastle's six goal demolition of Stoke. His striking partner George Robledo was not to be outdone and hit a hat-trick in the first week of September when Newcastle humbled Tottenham, the stylish champions of the previous season, 7-2 at St James's Park. Robledo then added another four as Newcastle put seven goals past Burnley.

But the real hat-trick king was Jack Rowley of Manchester United, who had scored three hat-tricks by the first week of September, the fastest this had ever been accomplished in the First Division.

Nat Lofthouse was also among the goals for Bolton, Portsmouth with their all-international half-back line of Scoular, Froggatt and Dickinson were going well and Arsenal were as consistent as ever, especially at home.

After the Christmas holidays the top three teams in the First Division – Arsenal, Manchester United and Portsmouth – were all level on points. Arsenal were still disliked. People claimed they played negative football but this may have been prompted by jealousy at their continuing success – they were not beaten until the end of April.

Manchester United stayed in touch with them though. And when his team showed signs of going off the boil Matt Busby made a series of tactical switches. The two most important were moving John Aston from full-back to centre-forward and installing Roger Byrne on the left wing, where he scored seven goals in the last six matches.

With two matches to go Arsenal and Manchester United were level on points, with the mouth-watering prospect of the two clubs meeting in the final game of the season. But an ever-increasing injury list took its toll on Arsenal and, forced to play six reserves, they lost 3-1 to West Bromwich.

That left Arsenal needing to win 7-0 at Old Trafford to take the League on goal difference and keep their hopes of the Double alive. The task was clearly beyond them, and Manchester United celebrated their first title in more than 40 years with a 6-1 victory, Jack Rowley scoring yet another hat-trick.

Lionhearted Lofthouse waltzes around Vienna

AUSTRIA were widely regarded as the best team in Europe, so it was hardly surprising that their game against England was dubbed the "match of the century".

The match also provided a fascinating contrast in styles. Austria relied on a slow, measured build-up and their centre-half Ernst Ocwirk had a wide-ranging role as the team's playmaker. England still played the "old-fashioned" way with a traditional formation and the emphasis on speed and quick passing.

England took the match very seriously and, for the first time, arranged a full-scale practice session at Maine Road. But the contest at Wembley lost some of its edge when several leading players were injured in League matches the Saturday before forcing England to field a scratch side.

Austria struck first when Ocwirk set up Melchior with a long pass. But Alf Ramsey kept England in the game with a penalty and was instrumental in giving them the lead seven minutes from time when his free kick was headed in by Nat Lofthouse. Two minutes later though Austria equalised when Stojaspal scored a penalty awarded for handball.

The draw raised the expectations for the return match even higher and the game in Vienna six months later was labelled "the unofficial championship of Europe".

Nat Lofthouse gave England the lead after 20 minutes with a well-taken volley but Austria

Lofthouse: merry dance

were level almost immediately when Froggatt brought down Dienst and Huber scored the penalty.

Jackie Sewell quickly restored England's advantage but Dienst equalised again before the interval. The second half brought wave after wave of attacks from Austria and England only stayed on terms thanks to some excellent saves from Gil Merrick.

But Austria had left themselves open to counter-attacks and with less than 10 minutes left Lofthouse set off on a 50-yard solo run. The Austrian goalkeeper rushed off his line and Lofthouse shot just before the two players collided.

Lofthouse was knocked out by the impact and was lying unconscious on the ground as the ball crossed the goal line. He had to be carried off and was so dazed he could not play in the remainder of the match, but his brave-hearted effort earned him the title "The Lion of Vienna".

Hat-trick hero: Rowley shrugs off Ramsey's challenge

Adventure of the famous five

THE root of Hibernian's post-war triumphs could be traced back to one man, the incomparable Matt Busby. He had been stationed in Scotland during the hostilities and had played for Hibs as a guest, captaining a team of raw teenagers.

Managed by the late Willie McCartney and now by Hugh Shaw, Hibs had become the most powerful team in Scotland. They won the League for the third time in five years, and the second year running.

The key to their success was the "Famous Five" forward line of Eddie Turnbull, Bobby Johnstone, Gordon Smith, Lawrie Reilly and Willie Ormond, players whose skills complemented

each other perfectly. The versatile Bobby Coombe played in five different positions and Tommy Young kept goal despite having to do his national service. Hibs regarded Young as so valuable that they persuaded his regiment to let him fly home from Germany each weekend.

The season was also notable for being the first time since 1895 that neither Rangers nor Celtic won a trophy. Celtic's shock defeat by Third Lanark in the first round of the Cup was to have far-reaching consequences. Desperate to shore up their defence they turned to Llanelli, a far-flung outpost of the Welsh League, to sign the centre-half Jock Stein.

Dooley: inspired switch

Double blow for battling Arsenal

ARSENAL'S valiant attempt to do the Double ended with a second disappointment when Newcastle United became the first club to retain the FA Cup since 1891. But although Newcastle took the honours Arsenal won all the praise for their incredible spirit.

Arsenal's team was wracked by injuries; Ray Daniel played with his broken wrist in plaster, Doug Lishman had a cut that had turned septic and Jimmy Logie was suffering internal bleeding in a thigh injury.

To add to their misery, Wally Barnes, the right back, limped

off after a few minutes with torn ligaments when he twisted his right knee trying to make a quick turn on the lush turf. He returned with his knee heavily bandaged but could not continue, so Arsenal were forced to play most of the match with 10 men.

They mounted a brave rearguard action, with Don Roper holding his own as a makeshift defender and the indefatigable Joe Mercer appearing to be everywhere at once. As the minutes passed and Newcastle were kept at bay, the crowd warmed to Arsenal's heroic efforts.

They had even created the best chance of the match when Lishman hit the bar with an overhead kick.

But with less than 10 minutes to go Roper went down injured allowing Bobby Mitchell to cross to George Robledo, who headed the ball against the post and into the goal.

Newcastle's celebrations were muted because they appreciated the courage that Arsenal had shown. Tom Whittaker, the Arsenal manager, summed up the match when he said: "I have never been prouder of Arsenal than today."

Walking wounded: Lishman, playing with a septic cut, bravely attempts a shot at Newcastle's goal

THE
1952-53
SEASON

Tragic end cuts short blossoming of Dooley

DEREK DOOLEY'S uncompromising play at centre-forward had worked wonders for Sheffield Wednesday as they won promotion but it was less well received in the First Division.

After three matches Wednesday left him out of the team "to emphasise our protest against the rough treatment he was getting from defences and for the marked-man attention from referees". Liverpool, the last team to play Wednesday, were incensed by the suggestion and retorted: "Dooley got no more than he gave."

There was no doubting, though, that Dooley's direct and unorthodox style was highly effective. He continued to pulverise opposing defences and had scored 16 goals in 29 games before his career was ended by a terrible accident.

Dooley was being touted as a prospect for England when Wednesday played at Preston in February. But he broke his right leg in the match when he challenged the goalkeeper for a 50-50 ball.

At first it seemed to be a straightforward injury, but Dooley had suffered a cut on the leg earlier. Just as he was about to leave hospital the cut became infected and then gangrene set in.

Doctors had no option but to amputate most of his leg and Dooley's career, which had seen him score 64 goals in 63 League matches, was over at the young age of 23.

Matthews casts a magic spell

WHEN Blackpool reached the Cup final again everybody in the country, apart from the residents of Bolton, were hoping that they would win. Stanley Matthews, at 38, was playing at Wembley for the third time and everybody believed that this was his last chance to collect a winner's medal.

Blackpool had enjoyed mixed fortunes on the way to Wembley. They had lost Allan Brown, who broke his leg as he scored the winner against Arsenal in the quarter-finals. Then they were lucky to beat Tottenham against the run of play in the semi-final when Alf Ramsey's terrible back pass let Jackie Mudie score with seconds remaining.

It looked as if Blackpool had used up all their luck as Bolton scored a soft goal in the second minute and led 3-1 after an hour. But Matthews was never a player to stop chasing lost causes. With 22 minutes left he made yet another run down the right wing, looped in a cross that Stan Hanson, the Bolton goalkeeper, fumbled and Stan Mortensen made it 3-2.

Blackpool played like a team possessed and the 100,000 crowd began to sense that the miracle might happen. But time was fast running out as Blackpool searched for the elusive equaliser.

There were only three minutes left when Mudie was fouled just outside the box. Mortensen, with one of the hardest shots in the game, studied the defensive wall, spotted the smallest of gaps and crashed the ball just inside the post to complete his hat-trick.

Now there was only going to be one outcome. As the players lined up for the kick-off Matthews looked at his team and clapped his hands three times. The ball was played out to Matthews and the maestro set off towards the goal, jinking this way and that.

Three Bolton defenders were left standing utterly confused by Matthews' trickery. And although he slipped slightly as he made his final pass into the penalty area the ball was still placed inch-perfect for Bill Perry to score the winning goal from 10 yards.

So dreams could come true after all. And although Mortensen had scored a hat-trick to go with the goals he had got in all the other rounds the final would always be remembered as "the Matthews final".

Crowning glory: Johnston holds the FA Cup aloft but the day belonged to the old maestro Matthews

Finishing touch: Perry latches on to an inch-perfect pass from Matthews for Blackpool's winning goal

Crowds flock to amazing amateur theatricals

THE LITTLE clubs enjoyed another good year in the FA Cup and their standard-bearer was Walthamstow Avenue, who became the first amateur side since Corinthians to reach the fourth round.

Their reward was a trip to Manchester United and thanks to some inspired goalkeeping they only trailed by one goal in the last 15 minutes. Then Trevor Bailey, the England cricketer, was fouled and Walthamstow scored an unexpected equaliser from the free kick. They lost the replay at Highbury 5-2 but the total crowd for the two matches was more than 85,000, earning the club £4,000.

The amateurs of Finchley were also involved in a replay, but in stranger circumstances. Thick fog blanketed their second round match and Crystal Palace had to field two youth

Howzat: Bailey, the Old Trafford hero, was caught out at Highbury

players when two of the first team could not reach the ground because of the weather.

Finchley were leading 3-1

when the match was abandoned after an hour. To prove that was not a fluke they won the replay by exactly the same score.

Busby's babes born in a baptism of fire

MANCHESTER UNITED, like Arsenal, were an ageing team. They started their campaign with the same side that had won the championship, but Matt Busby knew something had to be done.

When United slipped into the First Division basement in October Busby decided the time was right to start blooding his next crop of talent. Duncan Edwards was 15 when he made his debut, David Pegg was 17, Dennis Viollet was 19, Billy

Foulkes was 20. Tommy Taylor, bought from Barnsley for £30,000, was a comparatively "old" 21 but was picked by England within five weeks.

The combination of youth playing alongside experienced men served United well and they recovered to finish in eighth place. The rest of the country could only marvel at how Busby produced such great players, universally known as the Busby Babes before the season was out.

Busby: still ahead

Arsenal sneak home in tight finish

ARSENAL'S final match in the League on the Friday before the Cup final was every bit as dramatic as the events that unfolded at Wembley the next day.

For the second year in a row the First Division was a close-run thing which, in the final months, had four contestants – Arsenal, Burnley, Preston and Wolves. First Burnley then Wolves faded, reducing the field to a two-horse race.

When Preston beat Arsenal the Saturday before and con-

demned Derby to relegation on Wednesday they led the table by two points, with all their matches completed. Arsenal had to beat Burnley in their last match and then goal average would come into play.

Burnley were no pushovers and, in heavy rain, they took the lead at Highbury after eight minutes. Alec Forbes chose the perfect moment to score his first goal of the season for Arsenal and then Doug Lishman and Jimmy Logie put them firmly

on course with a 3-1 lead at half-time.

Arsenal then became complacent and allowed Burnley to cut the deficit. It needed all of Joe Mercer's experience to keep his side calm and stop them conceding another goal.

Arsenal and Preston finished with identical records (21 wins, 12 draws, nine defeats). But Arsenal won the title for a record seventh time by a tenth of a goal – their goal average was 1.51 to Preston's 1.41.

It was an emotional occasion at Highbury when Mercer came out to meet the joyous crowd massed outside the East stand. The man who was always going to play for "just one more season" said that he had finally decided to retire.

SIR STANLEY MATTHEWS
Wondrous winger
with the quicksilver touch

David Hunn

STANLEY MATTHEWS and I were at Blackpool together, both claiming space along that right touchline. He was on one side of it in a tangerine shirt, I was on the other in Air Force blue. Every fortnight he seemed to have much less trouble securing his area than I did mine. He played at two speeds, an amble and a flash. The ball was always passed straight to him, and hard. He never wanted to run into space, somebody else might get there first. He wanted the ball at his feet. That way he knew he would beat one man, draw another, leave him and pop the ball over straight on to Stan Mortensen's head.

Matthews was the fastest man in football over 10 yards and those are the yards that matter. But the memory of him is of a meandering man, shorts a bit long and baggy, leaning over the ball as he caressed it up the touchline. The elbows were loose and the feet were pure magic.

Full-backs never knew what to do. Lunge in and you were done for. Matthews was away with the ball, and you never touched him. They would back off and back off, mesmerised, until they had to make a stand. He would show them the ball with one foot and take it away with the other. That body, which had seemed so idle, would shimmy to the left and ghost to the right, leaning so far over he should surely have fallen.

But it was the poor defender who bit the grass, heaving in frustration at a ball that was not there, at feet that had twinkled like stardust down the line. How the crowd loved it and loved Matthews, the greatest pure winger the game has ever seen. When we met for the first time, 46 years later, he was unmistakeable, the frame as spare as ever, his legs still threatening to deceive even as he crossed the road towards me. The same good old Stan, but white-haired now.

Even though he is, and has been for nearly 30 years, Sir Stanley Matthews, CBE, he is still Stan to the man in the street at Stoke. Twice he helped them to the Second Division championship and promotion – twice, 30 years apart. In the end they made him their president and erected a statue to him at Hanley, where he was born over a barber's shop. The statue showed him dribbling – what else – and recently the football was cut off it and stolen. At the Victoria Ground they would tell you that was the only time anybody got the ball off Stanley Matthews.

It takes dedication to be a successful genius.

Running rings round defenders: Matthews skips past Norman, the Tottenham centre-half

STANLEY MATTHEWS

Born February 1, 1915, Hanley, Staffordshire

PLAYING CAREER
Stoke City 1930-47, 1961-65
1930-47 203 pre-war appearances
Guested for Morton, Blackpool and others during the war
23 post-war appearances, 4 goals
1961-65 59 appearances, 3 goals
Played his last game against Fulham on February 6, 1965 and was the oldest player in the First Division at 50 years and 5 days
Honours Second Division: Winners 1933, 1963
Blackpool 1947-1961
379 appearances, 17 goals
Matthews was never booked throughout his entire career
Honours FA Cup: Winners 1953, Finalists 1948, 1951
League Championship: Runners-up 1956
Internationals England debut v Wales 1934
84 appearances (including twice for Great Britain), 11 goals (including goal on debut)

MANAGEMENT CAREER
Port Vale Manager 1965-68
Hibernian Manager 1970

Other career honours Knighted 1965. CBE 1957. European Footballer of the Year 1956. Footballer of the Year 1948, 1963. International Fair Play Committee award for services to sport 1987

Matthews never smoked, never drank, ate salads and fruit, starved on Mondays and still gets up before six every morning to exercise: "It somehow doesn't feel right later than that." At 50 he was as fit as a flea, and there was nothing fitter than his feet. "The Co-Op used to pay me £20 a week to wear their boots, and pretty early on I realised I didn't need these great stiff things with their rigid toecaps. So I went to the factory and got them to take the sole plate out and the toecap off and make me a really soft pair. It was the first time anybody had done that, and they were beautiful. I could fold them up and put them in my pocket. I got them to make me a white pair once, but I never wore them. Too embarrassed."

However many times you read the Matthews record, there seems little possibility that it can be true. He joined the Stoke ground staff at 15 on £1 a week, played his first Football League match for them six weeks after his seventeenth birthday and his last five days after his fiftieth. When he was 32 he began his 14 years with Blackpool, during which they reached three FA Cup finals. They won the last, in 1953 against Bolton, the match that the British football world will ever remember as the "Stanley Matthews Cup Final".

Blackpool were 3-1 down with 20 minutes to play; 3-2 down with three minutes left (a Matthews centre to Mortensen); and 3-3 (Mortensen's third) with less than one minute of injury time to the whistle. The ball went to Matthews on the wing. He beat the full-back and raced for the goalline. The Bolton centre-half abandoned his hope of halting him to cover Mortensen in the centre. Stan pulled the ball back behind Mort towards the penalty spot. Perry, the left wing, was there: 4-3 and delirium.

For England there were 84 internationals between 1934, when he was 19, and 1957, when

Still going strong: Matthews at 48

he was 42. You might think he was way past his best by then, but when he was two months short of his fortieth birthday West Germany came to Wembley and Matthews destroyed the left-back. Of that match the Daily Telegraph reporter wrote: "Through the changing scenes of international football, the genius of Stanley Matthews remains a radiant beacon. He won this match for England just as nearly 20 years ago he inspired the 3-0 defeat of Germany at Tottenham."

In the Mirror, Matthews was "immense, indescribable"; and in The Times "… a tour de force by the greatest player in football". Three months later he set up (according to Nat Lofthouse, the centre-forward) all seven goals that England scored against Scotland. The left-back that day, poor man, was Harry Haddock, aged 25. In David Miller's biography of Matthews, Haddock

vividly recreated the humiliations of that and many another day.

"He'd walk towards you with the ball on his right foot, feint to his left, and you'd go with him to your right. He'd touch the ball the other way, and be gone. You'd see it, and could do nothing. I knew that's what he'd do, and I wanted him to do it, because I thought I had the speed to stay with him. But he lost me."

Losing left-backs was Stanley's favourite pastime. He did it for 30 years on just about every ground he played. Football fans knew he was going to do it, and wherever he went they went too. In 1934 Stoke drew an average of more than 66,000 to six consecutive matches. It was small wonder that even at the age of 46, when he was slowing down a bit too much for First Division Blackpool, Stoke were glad to have him back.

In 1961 they had to pay Blackpool £3,500 for the privilege and they offered Matthews the highest wage he had ever known: £50 a week plus a £25 match fee. The week before his return, Stoke's home gate was 8,409. Two weeks later, with Matthews on the wing against Huddersfield (left-back, England's Ray Wilson) it was 35,288. "People told me I should have asked for £100," Matthews said. "But the money doesn't make you play better, does it? I was happy there. They were nice people. I had a lot of friends, thousands of them, on the other side of the touchline." In 1963 Stoke clinched promotion to the First Division once more. Matthews had played in 35 of their 42 matches, and he was 48 years old.

He never read the biography quoted above, excellent though it was. "I read the first page and to tell you the truth, David, I was embarrassed. I can't take people going on about how good I was. You just do your best, don't you?"

His genius was a "radiant beacon" for England

Wembley wizard: Matthews crosses for Perry to score the winning goal in the 1953 Cup final

Hungary hit England for six...

Joy at last for Cullis

ALL THE hard work that Stan Cullis had put in at Wolverhampton was repaid when his team won the League championship for the first time. The triumph was especially sweet because Cullis had suffered two great disappointments as a Wolves player – losing the 1939 FA Cup final and missing out on the championship in the 1946-47 season in his last match before he retired.

When Cullis took over as manager he continued the regime introduced by Major Frank Buckley, hard work in training, strict discipline at the club and all-out attack on the field. Wolves's critics argued that their reliance on long passes was no more than a glorified form of kick and rush. But Cullis argued that he was using basically the same approach as the mighty Hungarians, and the quicker and more often the ball was in the opponents' penalty area the more likely his team was to score.

Cullis used scientific research by Wing-commander Charles Reep to support his theory, and he silenced his critics when Wolves won the title by four points from West Bromwich, scoring 96 goals in the process.

Cullis: hard work pays off

Taken apart 1: Grosics saves from Mortensen as the Mighty Magyars demolish England

IT HAD to happen sooner or later, but nobody could ever have been prepared for the scale of England's first home defeat by continental opposition. There had been enough warning signs in the past few years but hardly anybody was prepared to accept that England no longer ruled the world.

Until, that is, the fateful November afternoon when the Hungarian team, the 1952 Olympic champions and unbeaten in more than 20 matches, came to Wembley. It was not a case of England playing badly – by their standards they performed well. Ferenc Puskas and his Mighty Magyars were simply in a different class.

Hungary needed a mere 60 seconds to take the lead. Nandor Hidegkuti drew the defence out of position with a body swerve and swept a 20-yard shot through the gap and past the bewitched Gil Merrick.

The rest of the match followed the same pattern. England were out-played, out-passed and out-thought by a heady mixture of individual flair and clever teamwork. Hungary simply ran rings round a flat-footed and bemused England team.

> *Yesterday the inevitable happened. England at last were beaten by the foreign invader*
>
> THE TIMES

England were given a faint glimmer of hope when Jackie Sewell scored an equaliser after 15 minutes, but then they were destroyed in a breathtaking seven-minute spell. Hidegkuti scored again from close range, Puskas breezed past Billy Wright with brilliant trickery for the third goal and also scored the fourth from a free-kick.

Stan Mortensen brought the score back to 4-2 at half-time, but for every goal England got the Hungarians created two. First Bozsik struck, then Hidegkuti completed his hat-trick. Mercifully, the Hungarians eased up towards the end of the match and England added a third goal with a penalty from Alf Ramsey.

The headlines the next day said it all: "The New Wembley Wizards"; "Now It's Back To School For England – With Hungary The Soccer Masters" and "Make 'em Run – We Couldn't".

Worlds apart: Hungary ran England ragged at Wembley

... and then give them another painful lesson

ENGLAND had six months to reflect on the lessons they had been taught at Wembley before they went to Budapest to play Hungary again. At least, given the partisan attitudes displayed by some commentators, nobody tried to claim that the Wembley result was a fluke. The debate was whether English football had gone backwards or European football had progressed.

The England selectors had no real answer to the question other than to make seven changes to the team. They admitted that it was an experimental side, chosen to see if there was a better way of countering the Hungarians.

The answer, emphatically, was no. It soon became clear that nobody in England was a match for the Hungarians, and England were not going span the gulf in skills in such a short time.

This time they went down 7-1 in the People's Stadium, England's heaviest defeat ever. Hungary fielded 10 of the 11 players that had tormented England at Wembley and this time the torture was even worse. The Hungarians did not ease up late in the match and Puskas and company showed that they could turn on the style at will and there was nothing England could do about it.

Taken apart 2: England had no answers in Budapest

- Alf Ramsey scored a penalty in the last minute to spare England's blushes as they came back from 3-1 down to salvage a 4-4 draw with the Rest of Europe in a match at Wembley as part of the FA's 90th anniversary celebrations.

- Arsenal, despite saving a penalty in the second minute and then taking the lead, were beaten 2-1 at Highbury by Third Division Norwich in the fourth round of the FA Cup.

- Arsenal signed the 34-year-old Tommy Lawton from Brentford to bolster their team and to coach their younger players.

- Sam Bartram set a League record when he made his 500th appearance for Charlton on March 6.

- Wolves beat Racing Club of Buenos Aires 3-1 in a friendly at Molineux in March.

- Jimmy Delaney collected his third Cup-winners' medal in different countries with Derry City. He had already won the Scottish Cup with Celtic in 1937 and the FA Cup with Manchester United in 1948.

- Uefa was formed at a meeting during the World Cup finals in Switzerland.

- Scot Symon, the former East Fife manager who had guided Preston to the FA Cup final, took over as the manager of Rangers from Bill Struth in June. Symon, who had represented Scotland at football and cricket, was brought in to rebuild the club.

Unstoppable Port Vale take the League and Cup by storm

FORGET the wonderful Wolves, the team of the Midlands was surely Port Vale. They reached the semi-finals of the FA Cup, where they lost to West Bromwich Albion the eventual winners, and won the Third Division North championship by a street. Their Cup exploits meant they were the first Third Division side since the war to reach the semi-finals.

But in the League they were virtually unstoppable. They were the only team in all four divisions to be unbeaten at home; they lost a mere three matches away; they conceded a record low of only 21 goals in their 46 League matches while putting 74 past their opponents, and romped away with the championship 11 points clear of their nearest rivals.

Stein comes from nowhere to work wonders

CELTIC, who had not won the championship since 1938 and had won the Scottish Cup only once since that, ended their barren period by walking off with the Double. Even more remarkable was that the architect of their triumph was a veteran has-been, Jock Stein.

Stein, who had been the captain of Albion Rovers during their brief foray in the First Division in 1948-49, had been plucked from the obscurity of the Welsh non-League club Llanelli in December 1951 as a 29-year-old veteran. Celtic had recruited the solid, but slow centre-half simply to bolster the

reserve team and steady Celtic's youngsters. However a string of injuries accidentally propelled the bulky defender into the first team within two months.

Stein soon made the centre-half's position his own. Then when Sean Fallon, the captain, broke his arm Stein took his place. The promotion transformed Celtic. Stein was a born leader and his acute footballing brain soon became apparent both on and off the field. Celtic, who had finished eighth the previous season, made a dramatic charge on the championship and won 20 of their 30 League fixtures to capture the title, five

points clear of Hearts.

In the Scottish Cup Stein's rejuvenated side won a series of away ties, overcame Motherwell in the semi-final after a replay and faced Aberdeen, who had narrowly lost the Cup to Rangers the year before, in the final. Aberdeen gave away an unfortunate own goal shortly after the interval but equalised within a minute.

However, in the 63rd minute, Willie Fernie, one of Scotland's trickiest ball-players, set off on a mazy run that mesmerised the Aberdeen defence. So much so that Fallon, centre-forward for the day, was left unmarked.

Fernie slipped him the ball and Stein's miraculous rise from the depths of the Welsh valleys to the heights of the Double was complete.

Stein: born leader

THAT HUNGARY, unquestionably the greatest team in the world, lost the 1954 World Cup final was an even greater shock than Brazil losing to Uruguay four years earlier. Hungary, with Ferenc Puskas, Nandor Hidegkuti, Josef Bozsik, Sandor Kocsis and Zoltan Czibor, were a blend of artistry, intelligence and athleticism that neither Europe nor the world had ever seen. "The Magnificent Magyars" – as the British press dubbed them after their 6-3 and 7-1 drubbings of England in 1953 and 1954 – lost only one match between 1950 and 1956: the World Cup final in Switzerland. How they lost could be put down to two factors: the loopholes in the new structure that was introduced for the finals, and the utter cynicism of the West Germans who were eventually to triumph in the final.

The structures of the final stages of the past four World Cups had been deeply flawed (from straight knock-out to a simple League system without a designated final). On the face of it, the formula for the 1954 tournament ironed out many of the problems. Sixteen teams would qualify for the finals, they would be divided into four groups of four out of which eight teams would qualify for a straight knock-out tournament. This would be the structure for the next four World Cups.

However, in Switzerland, there was a bizarre bias added. In each group two teams would be seeded, and they would only play the unseeded teams. So each team only played two games not three, and the strongest only played the weakest. The formula was open to wicked exploitation.

West Germany were drawn against Hungary, Turkey and South Korea in group two with Hungary and, strangely, Turkey – who surprisingly had eliminated Spain in the qualifiers – as the the two seeds. West Germany's first match was against Turkey, a simple 4-1 runout. Their second was against Hungary. And now the devilry began.

The West Germans calculated that by losing to Hungary and then beating Turkey in the resultant play-off they could then avoid Brazil, one of the favourites, in the quarter-finals. They duly subsided 8-3 with virtually a reserve side. But worse than that, Puskas, Hungary's star player, was crocked in the process when he was deliberately

WORLD CUP 1954

Hungary fail the final test

Battered into submission: Hungary's Magnificent Magyars (top) suffered at the hands of a cynical West German team

kicked on the ankle by the West German centre-half Werner Liebrich, and did not play again until the World Cup final. For the play-off against Turkey, the Germans made seven team changes and won 7-1.

But before the Germans and the Hungarians could meet in the final there were several strong, and talented teams, to overcome. Not least Uruguay, the holders and a country that had never lost a game in the World Cup. They had reached the quarter-finals by humiliating Scotland 7-0 and then completed a British double by knocking out England 4-2. Gil Merrick, England's goalkeeper, should have saved at least two of the the Uruguayan goals but despite the skills in defence of Billy Wright, and in attack of Stanley Matthews, the Uruguayans prevailed to meet Hungary in the semi-finals. But only after Hungary had won the brutal "Battle of Berne" against Brazil.

That it became a match largely remembered for its physical side was a terrible indictment of two sides more renowned for their skills on the ball than their fouls off it. History has laid the principal blame at Brazil's door, not that the Hungarians – nor indeed Puskas, who wasn't even playing – were exactly innocent parties.

Hungary had begun in their usual madcap way and were two goals up in seven minutes. But a series of niggling fouls from the Hungarians disturbed the volatile South Americans and the rot began to set in. Then two penalties, the first for Brazil in the 18th minute, then one for Hungary in the 54th made the score 3-1.

With 24 minutes left Brazil made it 3-2 and were in the hunt. Within minutes, Bozsik and Nilton Santos were at each other's throats and both were sent off. Vicious tackling became the hallmark of the match. By the end, Hungary had a fourth goal in the 89th minute and another player was sent off, Humbert Tozzi of Brazil. There was an after-match brawl in which it was alleged that Puskas, only a spectator, had struck Pinheiro, the Brazilian centre-half, in the face with a bottle after the Brazilians had invaded the Hungarian dressing-room. Whatever the truth, Pinheiro left the ground with a bandaged five-inch head wound.

The quarter-final between Austria and Switzerland, the hosts, was just as extraordinary – but this time for the right reasons. It had been an extremely high-scoring tournament (by the finish 140 goals would have been scored in a mere 26 games) but the match in Lausanne took the biscuit. Austria were losing 3-0 after 23 minutes. Ten minutes later they were up 5-3. By half-time they were 5-4 in the lead, having missed a penalty. They were eventually 7-5 winners, with all 12 goals coming in the space of only 49 minutes of playing time.

Then in the semi-finals Austria, who were playing a West Germany that had out-muscled a delightful Yugoslavian side 2-0 in the quarter-final, simply collapsed. The Austrians were one of the most sublimely equipped teams in Europe and should, on paper, have beaten the nation that had so rudely taken them over in the Anschluss, yet they were swept aside 6-1 with their goalkeeper, Walter Zeman, making a string of disastrous errors. Zeman, who had been dropped because he was out of form, had been restored to the team only for this match.

By contrast the other semi-final, Hungary v Uruguay, was one of the most keenly contested matches ever witnessed in the World Cup finals, and some people have called it the finest game of football ever played. It pitted the best in the world (Hungary) against the twice world champions (Uruguay). Both sides were at their brilliant, mercurial best and the match swung like a pendulum.

Hungary went 2-0 up, but by full-time Uruguay, with Juan Schiaffino in scintillating form, had levelled the scores. But then a tiring Uruguay fell to the genius of Kocsis, who scored twice, and were eliminated 4-2. "We beat the best team we have ever met," Gyula Mandi, the Hungarian manager, said.

Now they were to be beaten by an inferior side, West Germany. But for the first 10 minutes of the World Cup final no bookmaker in the world would have thought it. In their inimitable fashion the Hungarians were 2-0 up within eight minutes despite the pouring rain. A predictable rout was on the cards.

But Hungary were vulnerable. Puskas, still suffering from the ankle injury he had received against the Germans in the early matches, had insisted on playing. Sadly the great player, despite scoring the opening goal, inevitably turned out to be a liability. Within eight minutes the West Germans had equalised and, with Puskas unbalancing the side, they scented an unprecedented triumph despite the Hungarians relentlessly attacking their goal.

Helmut Rahn and Toni Turek, the goalkeeper, were the West German heroes on the day. Turek, and the post, made save after save as the Hungarian forward line pounded them. Rahn, who had scored the equaliser in the 16th minute, then found himself in front of four defenders with seven minutes remaining. He went straight for goal and shot perfectly past Grosics into the corner for the winning goal.

Two minutes later Puskas thought he had equalised but the goal was dubiously ruled offside. Then Czibor fired a brilliant shot that Turek miraculously leaped to punch away. It was over, and the best team in the world had lost.

Hard times: England suffered from poor goalkeeping against Uruguay in the quarter-finals: Puskas suffered in the first round and was a shadow of his normal self in the final, allowing Walter, the West German captain, to collect the trophy

THE
1954-55
SEASON

Reshuffled Celtic let lucky Clyde off the hook

CLYDE'S first triumph in the Scottish Cup final since 1939 was somewhat fortuitous. Trailing 1-0 to Celtic, to a goal scored by Walsh in the 38th minute, the little team from the East End of Glasgow squeezed an equaliser from Robertson with three minutes remaining. Thus, despite being outplayed by their illustrious rivals, Clyde had narrowly forced a replay.

The Celtic directors did not see it that way and foolishly decided to reshape the team, dropping the bustling Collins and disorientating the forward line by playing Fallon, a full back, at centre-forward. Wisely, Clyde stuck to the same 11 players.

Celtic's makeshift attack hardly bothered the Clyde defence, enabling Clyde to push men forward in numbers. The winning goal came in the 52nd minute from Clyde's left winger, Ring, and the team that had swept to the Double so brilliantly the previous season never looked like scoring an equaliser, and finished the season empty-handed.

With Aberdeen winning the championship and Hearts the Scottish League Cup, the two Old Firm clubs were left with nothing to show for their efforts. The best they could manage were the minor places in the League, Celtic finishing second, three points behind Aberdeen, and Rangers third, a further five points adrift. This was only the second season in history (the other was 1951-52) that neither Rangers nor Celtic had won a major trophy.

Whirlwind Wolves

World beater: Hancocks scored against Spartak and Honved

WOLVERHAMPTON proved that they had become a formidable team with two remarkable results against top European sides. Their series of friendlies against foreign opposition started in October, when First Vienna were lucky to get a draw at Molineux. A fortnight later Maccabi Tel Aviv found themselves thumped 10-0.

Floodlit matches against foreign teams were becoming the vogue and no game was more eagerly anticipated than the visit of Moscow Spartak in November. Spartak had already scored five goals against Arsenal in Moscow, and had just won the return fixture 2-1 at Highbury.

With fog swirling around a ground packed to the rafters there was no score for nearly an hour until Dennis Wilshaw gave Wolves the lead. But the final minutes of the match were electrifying. Johnny Hancocks put Wolves further ahead then, straight from the kick-off, Roy Swinbourne weaved through the entire Spartak team to score Wolves's third.

No sooner had the match restarted then the ball was in the net again, but Hancocks's effort was disallowed. Not to be deterred, he got Wolves's fourth goal less than a minute later. In little more than three minutes

Spartak had been torn apart in what one commentator described as "our greatest post-war victory."

But there was better still to come. A month later Wolves took on Honved, who had the incomparable Ferenc Puskas and several other members of the Hungarian national side in their ranks. Wolves trailed 2-0 at half-time and it looked as if the "Mighty Magyars" were about to teach English football another lesson.

Wolves were transformed by a stern lecture by Stan Cullis, their manager, at half-time and a switch in tactics. Cullis had noticed that the Hungarian team had a very square defence so he instructed his players to hit their long passes even longer.

With their wingers getting behind the Honved defence Wolves came storming back with a penalty from Hancocks and two goals in two minutes from Swinbourne. "Wolves the great!" the newspaper headline said the next day, and all the writers agreed that their victory was even better than the demolition of Spartak.

For Cullis, it was a vindication of his methods and he proudly boasted that Wolves were now the unofficial champions of the world, a claim that was to have far-reaching consequences.

Revie and Matthews rout Scots

SCOTLAND thought that they were the best team in Britain because they had only lost 4-2 to Hungary. Compared with England's suffering the previous season they regarded that as a moral victory. But when they came to Wembley for the Home international championships they received a rude awakening.

Duncan Edwards became the youngest player to represent England, making his debut at the age of 18, but the star of the show was the old man of the England team, Stanley Matthews.

Matthews was 40, but age had not blunted his skills. In tandem with Don Revie he simply shredded Scotland. England scored twice in under 10 minutes and the final tally was four goals for Dennis Wilshaw, two for Nat Lofthouse and one for Revie. Scotland were lucky that the 7-2 score did not reach double figures, because several other chances were missed.

Matthews left the pitch with the crowd's cheers ringing in his ears while Scotland slunk away knowing that they had suffered their worst ever defeat in the Home internationals. So much for them thinking that they were the best in Britain.

Matthews: still going strong

Newcastle's record run

Winning habit: Newcastle rewrote the FA Cup record books

NEWCASTLE blazed into the record books when they beat Manchester City 3-1 in the FA Cup final. They became the first team to win the Cup three times in five seasons; their sixth victory meant they equalled the Cup-winning records of Blackburn Rovers and Aston Villa and they were the first club to compete in 10 Cup finals. To cap it all their first goal, scored by Jackie Milburn in 45 seconds, was the fastest at Wembley.

Unfortunately their victory was soured by an injury to Manchester City's right-back Jimmy Meadows, who had to be taken off with badly wrenched ligaments of the knee and lower leg in the 18th minute leaving City with only 10 men. Ironically Meadows, injured himself yards from where Arsenal's Wally Barnes had suffered the same fate – in the same minute – in Newcastle's last Cup triumph, the 1952 final. And who were they both trying to tackle? The elusive Bobby Mitchell.

Mitchell proceeded to torment Billy Spurdle, who had been moved from the right wing into Meadows's position. In the second half – Bobby Johnstone having headed an equaliser a minute before the interval – Mitchell wrapped up the match for Newcastle.

In the 53rd minute, he latched on to a pass from White, left Spurdle for dead and virtually on the byeline, just as Traut-mann was expecting a cross, the left-winger slotted the ball between the goalkeeper and the post. Seven minutes later Jimmy Scoular found Mitchell with a long pass over Spurdle's head. The left-winger placed the ball perfectly for George Hannah to give Trautmann no chance from 12 yards.

The advantage of playing against 10 men had virtually been cancelled out in the second half as both Milburn and Len White were clearly injured and continued only half-fit. Nonetheless, Newcastle were convincing winners, particularly given the battles they had endured getting to Wembley.

In the fifth round it had taken two replays to overcome Nottingham Forest; in the sixth round, a replay was required to dispatch Huddersfield and in the semi-final they came close to being embarrassed by York City. The Third Division club had been the revelation of the season, eliminating Blackpool and Spurs.

In the semi-final at Hillsborough they had the gall to go 1-0 up with a goal from Arthur Bottom until Vic Keeble forced another replay. Even then, at Roker Park, York battled away and Newcastle were mightily relieved not to go down in history as the side that allowed the first Third Division side to reach a Cup final. That was one record they didn't want.

Keeping it in the family: Len and Ivor Allchurch

Double act: John and Mel Charles also played for Wales

Brazil dazzled by Matthews

THERE WAS no stopping Stanley Matthews. He was the creator of almost all of England's attacks as Brazil were outshone under the Wembley floodlights.

Matthews's talents were more than a match for the Brazilians' skills and England led 2-0 after five minutes. But any ideas of a rout were dispelled when Brazil equalised in the second half. England finally ran out 4-2 winners, with Matthews creating three of the goals, but, amazingly they failed to score two penalties.

One produced a comic interlude. A Brazilian player, unhappy at the referee's decision, picked up the ball and marched off. He was chased by the referee who, in turn, was pursued by several other members of the Brazilian team, with Billy Wright, the England captain, following along behind. The crowd thought the game of "follow the leader" was hilarious.

One England player who followed Matthews's footsteps was Duncan Edwards. The youngster, fresh from Manchester United's triumph in the championship, gave a stirring performance during England's summer tour.

England were being run ragged by West Germany at the start of their match in Berlin. Edwards collected the ball in the heart of defence and set off on a storming run upfield. He swept imperiously past tackle after tackle before scoring with a thunderous 25-yard drive. The power of the shot so amazed the spectators that they started calling Edwards "Boom Boom".

The goal turned the tide in the match. Goals from Colin Grainger and Johnny Haynes gave England a 3-1 victory.

Heroic Trautmann wins the Cup despite a broken neck

Walking wounded: Trautmann (right) did not discover his neck was broken until three days later

ALTHOUGH it was Don Revie's scheming brilliance that brought the FA Cup to Manchester City the year after their disappointment against Newcastle, the hero of the match was surely Bert Trautmann, City's blond German goalkeeper, and Footballer of the Year.

Twice Trautmann dived at the feet of onrushing forwards and twice he was injured. When he flung himself at Peter Murphy he received terrible blows on his head and neck and was knocked cold. Somehow he instinctively stopped the ball. Five minutes later he was in another collision, but he still got up to soldier on for the last 15 minutes of the match. The full extent of the former PoW's bravery was not known until three days later when, after complaining of recurring headaches, a second set of X-rays revealed that he had played on with a broken neck. Amazingly, the injury did not end Trautmann's career, and he returned to the team just before Christmas.

But if Trautmann should have sensibly left the field, half of Manchester believed Revie, who was playing only his second Cup game, should never have been on it at all. Revie had been in dispute with the club for much of the season and was only brought into the side on the eve of the match as City's manager, Les McDowall, reshuffled his forward line.

Revie had perfected the art of the deep-lying centre-forward, a strategy he had adopted from Ferenc Puskas, and it proved to be the undoing of Birmingham City, red-hot favourites to win the Cup. His impact was immediate. After three minutes

Revie passed the ball from the half-way line to Roy Clarke on the left wing, raced to meet the return and cheekily back-heeled the ball for Joe Hayes to score.

Birmingham's equaliser, after 15 minutes from Noel Kinsey, was never going to stop Revie's men. In five minutes in the second half they waltzed off with the Cup. Now the architect was the Scottish international Bobby Johnstone, another controversial selection because he was carrying an injury and playing out of position.

He started the move that led to Ken Dyson's 65th minute goal and, five minutes later, Johnstone raced from the wing to collect Dyson's through ball and fire the ball past Gil Merrick, to become the first man to score in successive Cup finals.

Chelsea denied a place in Europe

THE IDEA of staging a European Cup had been doing the rounds since the mid-1920s but the proposals had always received short shrift until Stan Cullis's boast that his Wolverhampton team were the best in the world stung the rest of Europe into action.

L'Equipe, the French sports newspaper, responded by inviting what they regarded as the top 18 clubs in Europe to a meeting in Paris. Sixteen teams attended, including Chelsea, the English League champions, and Hibs, who were regarded as having a better record in the past few season than Aberdeen, the Scottish champions.

The 16 readily agreed to a European Cup played on a home and away basis, and the tournament was sanctioned by Fifa on May 8, 1955, the tenth anniversary of VE Day. Fifa only imposed one restriction on the tournament, that all the entrants had to be approved by their national associations.

That ruling cost Chelsea their place. Although Chelsea were drawn against Djurgaarden of Stockholm they needed permission to play from the Football League. English football still had a very insular attitude to Europe, and the League's man-

Start of an era: Real Madrid win the first European Cup in Paris

agement committee decided to ask Chelsea to "reconsider" because the extra fixtures might be difficult to fulfil. Chelsea took the far from subtle hint and withdrew.

The Scottish authorities, with much more vision, allowed Hibs to take part. They beat Rot Weiss Essen 5-1 on aggregate in the first round, Djurgaarden 3-1 and 1-0 in the second round, but lost 3-0 overall to Rheims in the semi-final. The "extra" matches did not create any fixture congestion and left Hibs with a £25,000 profit.

The final, in Paris, was a sellout and the crowd got their money's worth. Rheims were two goals up against Real Madrid in little more than 10 minutes. But Real Madrid, for whom Alfredo di Stefano seemed to be able elude defenders at will, equalised after half an hour.

Rheims led again in the second half but Real Madrid were back on terms within five minutes. With di Stefano seemingly everywhere they scored the decisive goal in the 79th minute. Di Stefano had engineered all four goals in what was a great finish to what was going to turn out to be Europe's most prestigious competition.

FOR THE RECORD

■ **Harold Bell (above)**, the Tranmere centre-half, finally missed a League match in September after playing a record 401 consecutive matches since the start of the 1946-47 season.

■ **Uefa** started the Inter-Cities Fairs Cup, for teams from cities that staged industrial fairs and trade shows. The idea was that the football matches would complement the exhibitions. The first tournament took three years to complete.

■ **Accrington Stanley** fielded a team of 11 Scotsmen in the Third Division North several times during the season. All but four of their squad of 19 players were born in Scotland.

■ **Floodlights**, pioneered by several clubs in friendly matches, were first used in the FA Cup on November 28, for a second round replay between Carlisle and Darlington at Newcastle. The first League match to be played under lights was between Portsmouth and Newcastle on February 22. The game was held up for 30 minutes when the fuses failed. The first floodlit League match in Scotland was on March 7 at Ibrox, when Rangers beat Queen of the South 8-0.

■ **Derby**, who had slumped into the Third Division North after winning the first post-war FA Cup final, were beaten 6-1 at home by non-League Boston United in the second round of the FA Cup.

■ **The Home** international championship finished in a four-way tie for the first time, all the teams having three points.

■ **Hearts** beat Celtic 3-1 in the Scottish Cup final to win their first trophy for 50 years.

Busby's Babes quickly come of age

MANCHESTER UNITED'S fourth League championship began with a stuttering start but was eventually won at a canter. By November, United had lost four games, largely because of the absence of a settled side, but once Matt Busby found the right balance the side clicked into title form. They lost only three more League matches and were unbeaten at home with 18 wins and three draws to take the title by 11 points from Blackpool.

Ominously for the rest of the First Division – propitiously for United – the average age of the side was 23, one of the most youthful championship-winning sides in League history. Although United had last won

One of the secrets of Manchester United's success is that nearly all of us grew up together as boy footballers. The Manchester United way is the only way we know

ROGER BYRNE

the title four years earlier, only two players, Roger Byrne and Johnny Berry, survived from that side. The rest, apart from three who were purchased from other clubs, were home-grown talent. Busby's Babes had quickly grown into a team to be reckoned with.

Byrne: second championship

93

THE
1956-57
SEASON

Busby defies the League to enjoy a European adventure

Facing the challenge: Byrne and Busby with a memento from their match in Madrid

Falkirk spoil the party for Kilmarnock

FALKIRK, who had spent all season battling against relegation, stunned all of Scotland when they won the Scottish Cup for the second time in their history. Indeed, on the eve of the final it was still touch and go whether they would end up in the Second Division.

Managed by Reggie Smith, a Londoner who had played for Millwall, Falkirk were a bunch of misfits he had to knock into shape. While he was moderately successful in the League, inexplicably Falkirk were unstoppable in the Cup, knocking out Aberdeen, Clyde who were in blistering form in the Second Division, and Raith Rovers who finished fourth in the First Division, en route to Hampden.

Kilmarnock, their opponents in the final, were overwhelming favourites and had already laid on the civic reception to celebrate their triumph but, on the day, they seemed to panic. Toner, their centre-half, gave away a penalty in the 32nd minute and Prentice, the Falkirk captain, converted. Seconds before the interval Kilmarnock equalised with Curtlett heading in from a free kick. The second half was a goalless, mundane affair and Kilmarnock's celebrations were put on ice.

By contrast the replay was full of flowing football. Falkirk scored first in the 24th minute with Merchant heading in Murray's cross, but after fierce pressure in the second half Curtlett levelled the scores. In extra time, the favourites finally fell when Moran flicked a bouncing ball into the Kilmarnock goal.

MANCHESTER UNITED as the League champions, were entitled to enter the fledgling European Cup and the club's board of directors unanimously accepted the FA's invitation to take part.

Matt Busby, the United manager, was keen to test his team. He thought that his young players would benefit from the experience, and that England had a lot to learn from Europe.

The Football League thought otherwise. As they had done with Chelsea last season, they tried to dissuade United. "United's participation was not in the best interests of the League," they wrote. But United refused to be bullied and Busby said: "Prestige alone demanded that the Continental challenge should be met, not avoided."

After winning 2-0 in Belgium, United had to play the return leg against Anderlecht at Maine Road because Old Trafford did not yet have floodlights. Manchester City scoffed and said

Some people called me a visionary, others a reactionary, while a few called me awkward or stubborn

MATT BUSBY

they did not expect more than 10,000 people to attend.

In fact, the crowd was more than 40,000 and they saw United record their biggest ever victory. United led 5-0 at half-time and kept going; Dennis Viollet scored four goals, Tommy Taylor got a hat-trick, Billy Whelan two and Johnny Berry one. When the score reached 10-0 United spent the rest of the match trying and failing to engineer a goal for David Pegg, who had created five chances for his colleagues and was the only United forward not to score.

After beating Borussia Dortmund 3-2 on aggregate in the next round, all the goals coming at Maine Road, United had a

real adventure in the quarter-finals.

Their flight to Bilbao was plagued by heavy snow and the plane had to land in a deserted field. Then, after losing 5-3, the United players had to help shovel the snow off the runway before the plane could return home. Undeterred, United made up the deficit at Maine Road and won 6-5 on aggregate.

Their reward was yet another trip to Spain in the semi-final. Again they returned home two goals adrift. But this time, with the prospect of an unbelievable treble on the horizon, they could only draw 2-2 with Alfredo di Stefano's Real Madrid at Old Trafford, where the floodlights had finally been installed, and were eliminated 5-3 on aggregate.

Busby was honest enough to admit that: "A great experienced side will always triumph over a great inexperienced side." But there was no doubt that United's exploits had captured the public's imagination.

Jinx dashes United's Double hopes

THE WEMBLEY jinx struck again, but this time not only did it deprive Manchester United of the FA Cup it also destroyed their ambitions of being the first club this century to win the Double. For the third time in five years a serious injury to a player had effectively reduced one team to 10 men and turned English football's most prestigious occasion into a farce.

This time it was Manchester United's goalkeeper, Ray Wood, who was laid low six minutes after the final had started by a foul challenge by Peter McParland. Four yards from the goal, Aston Villa's Irish international winger crashed into a stationary Wood, who had just collected McParland's header. Wood was taken off with a fractured cheek-bone, though he did return in the 33rd minute to limp along the right wing.

Jackie Blanchflower replaced him in goal with Duncan Edwards moving to centre-half and Frank Whelan, United's leading goalscorer, to left half. But although this makeshift United held out for nearly an hour, McParland was the man who once again did the damage scoring twice, in the 65th and 71st minutes.

When Tommy Taylor headed home Edwards's corner with seven minutes remaining, Roger Byrne, the United skipper, gambled everything on forcing a replay and Wood returned to play in goal. Now every Villa player was behind the ball, but United just could not find the crucial equaliser.

So Villa preserved their record as being the last club to win the Double, in 1897, and

Wood: fractured cheek-bone

broke another by winning the FA Cup for the seventh time. However it was a hollow victory and a hollow record. Amazingly the FA had discussed the use of substitutes 24 hours before the final and rejected the idea.

Charles seeks his fortune in Italy

Record-breaker: Juventus doubled the British transfer record to sign Charles from Leeds

SHOCK WAVES went through English football in April when Juventus, the extremely wealthy Italian club, purchased John Charles from Leeds United for £70,000, more than doubling the British transfer record. Charles was paid a £10,000 signing-on fee and £60 a week basic wages, four times the maximum permitted in England. Did this mean that there would be an exodus of stars to the Continent, or would players' wage demands in the Football League spiral out of hand?

Charles, a Welsh international, was an extremely popular and successful centre-forward with Leeds, where he had scored 151 goals in 297 games. In Italy he was equally successful and won three championships and two Italian Cups with Juventus. Charles, dubbed the Gentle Giant by his adoring Italian fans, was also versatile: during his career in Italy he showed he could equally well play as a centre-half.

95

WOLVES IN THE 1950s
The team that dominated a decade

James Wilson

SENTIMENT, 40 years on, should not blind one to how completely Wolves dominated their era and what a consistently great side they were. Three times within the decade they won the League, three times they were runners-up, and twice they won the FA Cup.

They had strong opposition as well: Manchester United, Manchester City, Arsenal, Chelsea, Tottenham, Blackpool and Burnley all had simultaneously memorable teams. So, too, in those days when the maximum wage still ruled, did Bolton and Wolves's local rivals West Bromwich Albion. If Everton and Liverpool were below their subsequent standards, Portsmouth and Newcastle United, three times the FA Cup winners in five seasons, more than made up for any temporary deficiencies on Merseyside. It was a period when the available talent was widely spread, which makes the Wolverhampton dominance even more remarkable.

The seeds of this greatness were sown in the late 1930s under a strong manager, Frank Buckley, who, skilfully trading in the transfer market, developed a homespun side at Molineux which, but for the war, might have become as dominant as the Wolves of the 1950s. Buckley was one of the first managers to appreciate the value of publicity. When he introduced injections for the Molineux playing staff the press maintained that this was "monkey gland" treatment, calculated to make Wolves, already well known as one of the fastest teams in the League, even quicker to the ball and in the way their movements developed. It was all nonsense of course. The injections were merely the primitive anti-flu affairs of those days and, in any event, the ploy sadly miscarried when Wolves, in 1939 the hottest favourites to win the Cup anybody can remember, went down 4-1 to Jack Tinn's spats and his unfancied but workmanlike Portsmouth.

Buckley's chief contribution to the subsequent Wolves success lay in his selection of Stan Cullis as captain of the club. Cullis, a natural leader of the old school, already believed in hierarchy and discipline, a faith further developed by his wartime service in the Army, first in the South Staffords and later as a formidable sergeant-major in the Army Physical Training Corps. When, in 1947, Cullis retired from active football he was the obvious choice to become the manager at Molineux. His were the standards and tactical concepts which underlaid the years of subsequent triumph.

If Cullis was a disciplinarian and determined to have his own way in football matters at Wolverhampton, he was also thoughtful and capable of a level of football analysis well ahead of his time. Characteristically, though he was as tough an individual as one could meet, he disliked bad language and never used it himself. His "tellings off" were legendary, but always couched in plain, correct terms – a technique he had doubtless mastered in the army.

Though there were many gifted individuals on the Wolves staff, the strength of Cullis's teams was always much greater than the mere sum of his chosen 11. The tactics were simple, so much so that those who did not understand their basis sometimes, mistakenly, dismissed them as "kick and rush". It was all based on pressure through teamwork, each player working to make the task of his colleagues as simple and easy as possible. Wolves were extremely fit, moved the ball quickly and ran brilliantly to support the player in possession. Cullis liked the ball moved quickly out of defence. Upfield players such as Swinbourne, the centre-forward, or those talented wingers Hancocks and Mullen were good enough to hold the ball until help arrived from behind, often in the shape of Broadbent, a wonderfully mobile inside-forward and instinctive reader of the game. The first support player to arrive always moved to help the player in possession, who, by using the easy option thus provided, retained possession for his own side.

The ultimate aim was to get a player to the byline; as a defender himself, Cullis realised how much more threatening a cross pulled back can prove than something directed vaguely forward from a midfield position. Wolves specialised in crosses – either delicate chips, a Hancocks speciality, or fast low ones, often converted at the far post by the timely arrival of whoever could get there first from midfield. The concept sounds, and was, simple. To execute it well, as Wolves did consistently, required great dedication and concentration, and especially an ability to control the ball quickly.

The real strength of the Wolves side lay in their half-backs, Wright, Flowers, Slater and Clamp to name four of the most distinguished. Wright, Cullis's choice of captain, played at No 5 for all of his later career. He had begun, however, as a wing-half, where he learnt to tackle and use the ball intelligently.

The half-backs were expected to win the ball in midfield; once they had done so they were able to exert the pressure on opponents which so often, especially in the second half, caused their downfall. Pressure exerted from midfield was, in fact, the main factor in Wolves's astonishing success. Their half-backs were skilful and adaptable. Slater, before coming to Wolverhampton, had played as an inside-forward for Blackpool, sometimes partnering Stanley Matthews. Later, his knowledge of the game and innate intelligence – he was a professor of physical education at Birmingham University – made him the obvious choice to succeed Wright when the latter retired as captain and wearer of the No 5 shirt. Flowers and Clamp were equally fine performers; all were expected to get forward whenever they saw a chance of doing so, and each reckoned to score a dozen or so goals in an average season.

Though Wolves were essentially an attacking side they were also solid at the back. In Bert Williams they had an outstanding goalkeeper; he won 24 caps for England and was unlucky not to have received more. Agility and athleticism (he

Molineux stretch: Booth missed but the ball went in off Bolton's Hennin in a 1959 Cup-tie

neither smoked nor drank) were his chief attributes, making up for his relative lack of height, only 5ft 10in. His successor, Finlayson, a Scot signed from Millwall, was also a sound goalkeeper even if he lacked Williams's personality and special abilities.

Wolves also had good full-backs such as Showell, Pritchard and Springthorpe, but Cullis did not like them to be spectacular. Overlapping was the province of the wing-halves, and Wright in the centre was the defender who mostly caught the eye.

It will be hard to overestimate Wright's contribution to Wolves, though this tends to be overshadowed by his 105 caps for England. He was an outstanding captain leading by example. He did not believe in shouting if things went wrong on the field, preferring to concentrate on rectifying matters by restoring Wolves's pressure, which so often won them matches which otherwise, and with a lesser team spirit, would have been lost.

And one should not forget the Wolves crowd. Seldom less than 30,000, and for important games 40,000 or more, the sheer volume of noise they created was an important part of the pressure Wolves aimed to exert. The supporters were fine people, too, and knew their football; they were good to talk to before or after the match and one seldom left Wolverhampton without deepening one's knowledge of the game.

Could the Wolves style work successfully nowadays? Sadly, my conclusion is that it would be impossible, not least because modern players would never tolerate for long the Cullis code of discipline, or be able to generate the Molineux team spirit of the 1950s.

Though some of the Wolves players came from outside the Midlands they were essentially a Black Country team. There were few transfers over the period; as Broadbent said: "There was little point in leaving." When, unusually, Cullis attempted to strengthen his team by expensive imports from outside the newcomers often failed to settle. Henderson, from Portsmouth, and Hooper, from West Ham, both good players, were instances. Nor would the Wolves playing

style be effective against the present system of flat defences pressing forward to deny space to opponents. Goals were easier to score in the 1950s. There was more room and long balls into space were sensible tactics and unable to be dismissed as a last refuge of the incompetent. It was a different football world then; looking at things through the wrong end of a telescope is seldom profitable, and to attempt now to play like the Wolves of the 1950s would be a mistake.

Let nobody doubt that Wolves in those days were a great team, epitomising the additional strengths of the English game. Their famous victory over Honved, the Hungarian club side which included most of the players who so humiliated England at Wembley in 1953, went far towards restoring confidence in our style. Those like me who were privileged to have watched Wolves in their great days can, perhaps, be forgiven a grateful and nostalgic tear for the passing of the Molineux legend.

Wright: cool head in defence

Hancocks: delicate chips from the wing

Cullis's all-conquering team: Wolves won the FA Cup but the Double just eluded them

Pioneers: Broadbent scores against Vorwaerts

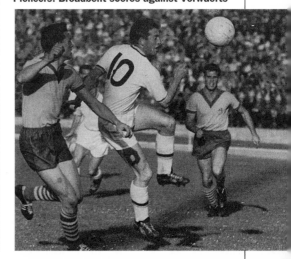

STAN CULLIS

Born October 25, 1915, Ellesmere Port

PLAYING CAREER
Wolverhampton Wanderers 1934-47
Honours FA Cup: Finalist 1939
League Championship: Runners-up 1938, 1939
Internationals England debut 1937
12 appearances. Also played in 20 war-time internationals

MANAGEMENT CAREER
Wolverhampton Wanderers Assistant Manager 1947-48; Manager 1948-64
Honours FA Cup: Winners 1949, 1960
League Championship: Winners 1954, 1958, 1959; Runners-up 1950, 1955, 1960

Fiery Fernie runs rings round Rangers

WILLIE FERNIE was one of those absolutely infuriating players: when he was brilliant he was the greatest player on earth, and when he wasn't he was an utter liability. On October 19 Fernie woke up and he decided he was the former. Unfortunately for Rangers they were playing Celtic in the League Cup final that day.

Twisting, turning, spraying the ball about, there was nothing that Fernie touched that didn't turn to gold from his pivotal right-half position. At half-time the score was only 2-0, with goals from Sammy Wilson and Neil Mochan, but Celtic had hit the woodwork three times.

In the second half the floodgates opened and Celtic ran in another five goals. No matter how hard Rangers tackled Fernie, and some of the challenges were verging on the brutal, he was irrepressible. Mochan, on the left wing, and Charles Tully, on the right, ran the Rangers defence ragged creating the space for Fernie to exploit.

Billy McPhail was on the receiving end of many of Fernie's raking passes and he helped himself to a hat-trick in the second half, seemingly able to score at will. Mochan got another goal and it was Fernie himself who completed the rout, converting a penalty.

The 7-1 thrashing was the largest score in any British final. Heads had to roll. Poor Johnny Valentine, the centre-half who had been bought from Queen's Park at the beginning of the season, was made the chief scapegoat. It was his ninth and last game for the Rangers first team.

Munich air crash tragedy devastates Busby's Babes

Terrible toll: Back row: Tom Curry, Duncan Edwards and Mark Jones died; Ray Wood, Bobby Charlton, Bill Foulkes and Matt Busby survived. Front: John Berry survived; Bill Whelan, Roger Byrne, David Pegg and Eddie Colman died.

THE HEART was ripped out of English football in the snow at Munich airport on February 6. The aeroplane carrying the Manchester United team, attempting to take off for a third time, was unable to get enough height and hit a house at the end of a runway and crashed. Twenty-three of the passengers, including eight of the legendary "Busby Babes", died.

Manchester United were returning home from Yugoslavia where a 3-3 draw with Red Star Belgrade had qualified them for the semi-finals of the European Cup, and their plane had touched down to refuel. In appalling conditions the pilots attempted to get the plane home rather than stop over for a night.

Seven players, Geoff Bent, Roger Byrne, Eddie Colman, Mark Jones, David Pegg, Tommy Taylor and Billy Whelan died that night. Duncan Edwards, one of the most talented English footballers of the century, was in a coma for a fortnight until he, too, passed away.

Matt Busby, whose chances were estimated at 50-50, managed to pull through. Two other "Babes", Jackie Blanchflower and Johnny Berry never played again. United's trainer, coach and secretary also perished, as did eight journalists, among them Frank Swift, the former Manchester City goalkeeper.

The whole country went into deep mourning at this sad loss of so many young lives. What was lost that fateful day was to be forever etched into the memories of all those that loved football. Except the Football League. When Wolves were crowned champions, Uefa – as a gesture of respect for their sorrow – invited Manchester United to enter the 1958-59 European Cup alongside Wolves.

The League, however, had never forgiven Busby for entering the competition against their express instructions in 1956 and so they refused to allow United's participation. The reason they gave was that it would be breaking Uefa's own rules, conveniently ignoring the fact that Uefa had already decided to waive its own rules.

Edwards: great talent lost

Lofthouse sinks makeshift United to dash the dream of a fairytale final

THE FA Cup final was always going to be a Manchester United fairytale ending, or the match Manchester United lost. Bolton couldn't win, even though they did, with two goals from England's lion-hearted centre-forward, Nat Lofthouse.

After the Munich aircrash, United had struggled to finish their season, slumping to ninth in the League, but in the Cup a tidal wave of emotion had carried them to the final. Matt Busby had somehow managed to survive, and was just passed fit to attend the final.

The mantle had passed to his assistant, Jimmy Murphy, who had managed to put together a scratch side made up of four of the "Busby Babes" that had survived, Bobby Charlton, Dennis Viollet, Harry Gregg and Billy Foulkes, first-team reserves and experienced players bought in.

Despite the weight of emotion hanging over the final, United were never really in it, espe-

Unhappy ending: Lofthouse, who scored both goals, challenges Gregg

cially after Lofthouse scored his first goal in the third minute. His second, in the 55th minute, was highly controversial as Loft-house bundled goalkeeper Gregg over the line. The referee awarded a goal and there was no fairytale ending.

Terrible trio blast Hearts to title

HEARTS' first championship this century was one of the most convincing ever witnessed in the British Isles. They lost only one of their 34 League matches, winning 29, scored a record 132 goals conceding a mere 29, leaving them with the staggering goal difference of 103. Rangers trailed in a sad second, 13 points behind.

The secret behind the Edinburgh club's success was their dynamic trio of Willie Bauld, Alfie Conn and Jimmy Wardhaugh in attack, and their human dynamo in midfield, Dave Mackay. With Mackay making the bullets the terrible trio could certainly fire them. Bauld was a tower in the air, Conn an industrious provider

and Wardhaugh the fastest thing on two legs.

Sadly for Hearts, in their annus mirabilis, the Double eluded them when their Edinburgh rivals, Hibernian, had the better of a seven goal thriller at Tynecastle in the third round of the Scottish Cup. Hearts had the last laugh though, Hibs lost 1-0 in the final to Clyde.

Quick-fire Summers revives Charlton

JOHNNY SUMMERS was a journeyman forward and Charlton were his fourth club. Aged 30, he was entering the twilight of his career, and on December 21 it became apparent that he was saving his best until the last.

Not that spectators at The Valley for the Second Division match against Huddersfield had any clue about what was coming. In fact, the only thing that

seemed to be coming was a whitewash.

Charlton lost Derek Ufton after 15 minutes when he broke his collar bone. They were only 2-0 down at half-time, but seven minutes after the interval they were 5-1 behind.

Then Summers, who was wearing a new pair of boots that he had not even broken in, went to work. He scored a hat-trick in

six minutes and then hit another two goals, all with his weaker right foot, to give Charlton a 6-5 lead.

Even then the drama was not over. Huddersfield equalised with two minutes left but Summers was not going to beaten. With the last move of the game he set John Ryan up for the winner in an almost unbelievable 7-6 match.

WORLD CUP 1958

Pele the master of the universe

EDSON Arantes do Nascimento was just 17 when he played for Brazil in the 1958 World Cup finals in Sweden, the youngest player ever to play in the final stages. Pele, as he was now called, made his World Cup debut in Brazil's final game of the first round against the Soviet Union. Three matches and six goals later Brazil were the world champions and Pele was a household name worldwide.

The lithe, black teenager from impoverished Tres Corações had captured the hearts of everybody in the first World Cup to enjoy television coverage. Pele was blessed with everything: agility, athleticism, improbable ball skills, a powerful shot, unsurpassable heading skills, and – perhaps most importantly – the ability to read a game while in the thick of the action. Nobody had ever seen anything like it.

His first goal in the final best expressed his genius: 11 minutes after half-time, with Brazil only 2-1 ahead, Pele, in the midst of a melee in the Swedish penalty area and with his back to goal, trapped a high ball on his chest, lobbed it over his own head, spun round the defender and volleyed into the net. Any team would have been finished after a goal like that, and so it proved with the Swedes.

Not that the World Cup winners were a one-man show. Pele's divine talents were superbly complemented by an extraordinary Brazilian side, which, if it had not been for the emergence of Pele, could themselves have become as big superstars as the great man: Garrincha, Didi, Nilton Santos, Zito or Vava. Also Brazil played 4-2-4, then a revolutionary formation, that neatly expounded the artistry of their players while confounding their opponents. Yet strangely their team was only forged in the crucible of the final stages in Sweden. Indeed they almost did not qualify, only scraping through against Peru thanks to a Didi free-kick.

Brazil were not the only strong side to encounter problems in the qualifying rounds. Uruguay and Italy, both of whom had won the World Cup twice, fell to unfancied opposition, Paraguay and Northern Ireland respectively. Amazingly Spain, with Alfredo di Stefano and a clutch of the almighty Real Madrid team in their side, were eliminated by Scotland. Thus, by the time the World Cup began in

Sweden on June 8, the 16 teams were an odd mix indeed.

Argentina, who had surprisingly lost the first World Cup final in 1930, had finally deigned to enter again and, despite the Italians poaching all their best players, had managed to qualify. But they were a debilitated side and probably wished they had not taken part, for when they returned home having won only one game they were pelted with rubbish. Hungary were no longer the force they had been in the previous World Cup after the Soviet invasion during the 1956 "revolution", and many of their key players, including Ferenc Puskas, Zoltan Czibor and Sandor Kocsis, defected to the West. Unsurprisingly, Hungary also failed to reach the quarter-finals.

Oddest of all were Wales, who had come second to Czechoslovakia in their qualifying group, yet still managed a back door entry to the finals thanks to Fifa's inexplicable political naivety. Despite the fact that Israel and Egypt had been at war in 1955, Israel were put into the African-Asian group. Inevitably Egypt, Indonesia, Sudan and Turkey withdrew one after the other, leaving Israel as qualifiers without having played a single game. As this was against Fifa rules they decided to draw lots among the teams that had finished second in their groups with the winner playing off against Israel. Wales won and promptly beat Israel home and away. With England also qualifying, all four home nations had reached the finals for the first time.

England were in disarray after the Munich air crash of February 1958 that had killed eight Manchester United players and ripped the heart out of both teams. The loss of the incomparable Duncan Edwards, Tommy Taylor and Roger Byrne was a blow from which England never recovered. Yet they compounded their problems by leaving out Stanley Matthews and Nat Lofthouse and bringing only 20 players, although they were permitted 22. Bobby Charlton was one of the 20, but was never selected.

Despite these setbacks they performed creditably: drawing 2-2 with the Soviet Union (but losing Tom Finney to injury in the process), 0-0 with Brazil and 2-2 with Austria in the strongest group in the tournament. They were the only team to stop Brazil scoring, and England

World class: John Charles inspired Wales to reach the finals for the first time and Juste Fontaine of France was the tournament's leading scorer

should probably have been awarded a penalty. However they finished level with the Soviet Union and lost in the play-off for a place in the quarter-finals against Sweden.

Of the four home nations Scotland fared the worst, finishing bottom of their group with a solitary point. Northern Ireland and Wales proved to be the unlikely stars, both reaching the quarter-finals after play-offs.

Northern Ireland, under the inspirational managership of Peter Doherty, had been turned into more of a club side and with brilliant outfield players such as Danny Blanchflower, Billy Bingham and Jimmy McIlroy, and with Harry Gregg in goal, they ensured that they were never going to be pushovers – as the multi-talented Italy had learnt to their cost in the qualifiers.

Wales were of a similar ilk: an ebullient manager in Jimmy Murphy, a solid keeper in Jack Kelsey, Ivor Allchurch at inside-forward and the impressive John Charles at centre-forward. But in the quarter-finals both sides met formidable opposition. Wales, unfortunately without the injured Charles, only went down to Brazil when a 73rd minute goal from Pele ended their brave and resolute defence. Kelsey played magnificently in goal yet was eventually beaten by a deflection from one of his own defenders. Northern Ireland, ravaged by injuries, succumbed to France who scored four goals in a blistering 24 minutes, two of them from Juste Fontaine.

Fontaine, alongside Pele, was the other revelation of the tournament. He had come expecting only to be the reserve centre-forward, but after a training injury to the No1 choice he struck up a seemingly psychic understanding with the midfield impresario Raymond Kopa of Real Madrid and scored 13 goals in six matches, a World Cup record.

France, not particularly highly regarded before the tournament, went on to play attractive and entertaining football. However, in the semi-final, even a Fontaine goal after eight minutes was not going to upstage Brazil and Pele. A second-half hat-trick in 23 minutes from the 17-year-old maestro destroyed the French and set up the final against Sweden.

The Swedes had been lacklustre hosts and their attendances were

No stopping Brazil: even an injury to one of their players did not stop the flow of goals; Pele scored his second and Brazil's fifth as Sweden were swept aside in the final

pitiful. The highest, 51,000, was in Gothenburg for Brazil's first round match against the Soviet Union. For their semi-final against West Germany, however, they suddenly discovered their nationalism in Gothenburg, whipped up by the presence of cheerleaders on the pitch, and roared on their team, particularly after they fell behind.

A dubious equaliser, a German sent off, one injured and two goals

in the last nine minutes and the hosts faced the exhilarating Brazilians in the final in Stockholm. But without the cheerleaders on the pitch, now banned, the crowd was strangely hushed. Sweden took the early lead they wanted, after four minutes. To no avail. Vava, Garrincha, Zagalo and, of course, Pele ran them ragged with a scintillating display. The best had proved they were the best.

Wright rewrites the records

Quixall deal breaks bank

JOHN CHARLES'S record move to Juventus fuelled speculation about what would happen in the domestic market, and the answer was not long in coming. His brother Mel moved from Swansea to Arsenal for £40,000 and two players, but even that deal was nothing compared with the transfer of Albert Quixall.

Matt Busby knew that he had to reinforce his squad in the wake of the Munich disaster. The only answer was to make a rare foray into the transfer market. But other clubs, knowing his plight, and knowing that United had plenty of money, were asking ridiculous prices for moderate players. Busby was determined to spend his money wisely and in September he pounced, spending £45,000, a record deal between two British clubs, to buy Quixall, who was an England schoolboy and full international, from Sheffield Wednesday.

Both clubs were happy with the deal. It was the third time in under 10 years that Wednesday had sold a player for a record amount, and they still won the Second Division without Quixall. And United, with their new signing, finished a creditable second in the First Division.

Quixall: £45,000 transfer

Ton up: Wright leads the team out in his 100th match for England

BILLY WRIGHT became the first man in the world to play 100 times for his country when England beat Scotland 1-0 at Wembley on April 11.

It was a remarkable achievement by the Wolves centre-half, who had only missed three of England's 103 matches after the end of the Second World War. He had captained his country 85 times and the match at Wembley was a record 65th consecutive appearance for England.

Wright joined Wolves at the age of 14 and made his first-team debut in October 1939, at 15. Manager Major Frank Buckley was not over-impressed with his apprentice and threatened to send him home because he was too small at 5ft 3in. Fortunately for Wolves, Buckley relented.

Wright played alongside Stan Cullis and inherited the captaincy from him. By the age of 24, Wright had also been chosen to captain England for the first time, for the match against Ireland. Wright only heard the news when he was shown the stop press column in the local paper by a bus conductor.

With Cullis continuing the traditions established by Buckley at the club and Wright a model professional on the field, Wolves flourished and, after a shaky start, Wright had an unequalled record for England – 59 wins and 22 draws in the 100 matches that he played in.

After Buckley tried Wright in various positions in his early days (Wright thought his natural place was on the right wing) he established him as a wing-half. But it was Cullis who made the transformation that was to enable Wright to enjoy such a long career.

Cullis, probably the finest centre-half to play for Wolves, realised that, at 30, Wright was losing some of his pace. So he convinced Wright to switch to centre-half. Despite his lack of height Wright soon adapted to the position, advised by Cullis on how to out-think the opposing centre-forward.

The change gave Wright a new lease of life as the linchpin of the defence and playmaker, and he went on to complete 105 matches for England, retiring on May 8 after the 8-1 victory over the United States. To add to his achievements, Wolves won the League championship again, scoring 110 goals.

Forest overcome final adversity

Breaking the jinx: Dwight gives Forest the lead before they were reduced to 10 men

ONCE AGAIN the FA Cup final was marred by an injury which reduced one team to 10 men – this phenomenon seems to be a hallmark of the 1950s – but for once the 11-man side didn't triumph. In the 32nd minute Roy Dwight, Nottingham Forest's right-winger, broke his right shin bone in a seemingly innocuous challenge with Luton's Brendan McNally. Dwight was carried off and watched the rest of the match on television from a hospital bed.

Fortunately for Forest they were 2-0 up at the time, Dwight having scored the first goal in the tenth minute when he hit Stewart Imlach's centre perfectly past Ron Baynham. Playing scintillating football, Forest added a second four minutes later when Imlach, from the left-back position, hit a glorious long pass to Billy Gray, whose diagonal ball to the far post was headed home by Tom Wilson. For the next 18 minutes Forest played Luton off the park. Then came the Dwight injury.

Luton now faced a team imbued with the Dunkirk spirit and despite the fillip of playing against 10 men could not even force a Forest save until six min-

utes into the second half. However, in the 62nd minute, Luton got the goal they needed when Billy Bingham played a short corner to Ken Hawkes whose cross sailed past the Forest defence to give David Pacey a simple opportunity on the far post.

Still Forest hung on. Their worst moment came four minutes from time when Bingham swung in a cross from the right corner flag that Allan Brown, racing in with all the desperation of a man trying to catch a train, headed just past the post. The jinx was beaten.

Goals galore as Greaves starts with a bang and Clough keeps up his phenomenal strike rate

TWO HOTSHOTS were breaking all scoring records in the League, Jimmy Greaves and Brian Clough. Jimmy Greaves, who scored on his debut for Chelsea against Spurs in August 1957 when just 17, just kept rattling them into the back of the net.

A month later he scored on his debut for the England U-23 side against Bulgaria. In August he scored five for Chelsea against Wolves, the League champions, to become at 18 the youngest ever player to score five in a First Division match. Then, proving he was no flash in the

pan, Greaves scored on his full England debut against Peru in Lima in May. Unsurprisingly, Greaves finished as the leading First Division scorer with 33 goals.

Brian Clough, five years older than Greaves, was also knocking the goals in for Middlesbrough in the Second Division. For the second consecutive year Clough was the division's leading scorer, with 42 goals. This was the third season Clough had averaged a goal a game, and he reached 100 League goals in fewer games than any previous player.

Greaves: debut goal

Clough: leading scorer

Big clubs snub League Cup

THE FOOTBALL LEAGUE, who had opposed Chelsea's participation in the first European Cup in 1955 because of fixture congestion, performed a remarkable U-turn in June and launched a new domestic competition, the League Cup. Within days the leading clubs condemned it as an unnecessary burden on the players.

Wolves, Tottenham, West Brom, Arsenal and Sheffield Wednesday (four of which had finished in the top five that season) refused to take part. Bill Nicholson, the Spurs manager, was especially vociferous. He called for a smaller First Division with fewer games and condemned the League for demanding too much from the players.

England quick to drop Clough

BRIAN CLOUGH's scoring feats for Middlesbrough had not gone unnoticed and he was picked for the Football League against the Irish League.

He wasted no time in making his mark and scored all the goals in the 5-0 victory in Belfast on September 23. That performance undoubtedly helped him earn his first full England cap, against Wales. But a draw in Wrexham, and a defeat by Sweden at Wembley 11 days later, were enough to convince the selectors that Clough was not going to strike up a fruitful partnership with Jimmy Greaves.

Clough was dropped, and never played for England again. Undeterred, though, he kept on scoring goals for Middlesbrough. He finished the season with 39 League goals.

Real Madrid turn on the style

THE European Cup final between Real Madrid and Eintracht Frankfurt at Hampden Park in May has gone down in history not only as one of the greatest club games ever played, but also the match that forever changed British attitudes to Continental football. Its impact was as great as Hungary's rout of England at Wembley seven years earlier. And at the centre of the whirlwind, again, was Ferenc Puskas.

Puskas was now working in tandem with Alfredo di Stefano, the Argentinian maestro, and the pair, both 33, scored seven goals between them to dazzle the 127,000 spectators and millions more watching on television. Real's reputation was well known, they had won the European Cup every year since it started in 1955-56, but the performance they put on in Glasgow reached new heights.

Eintracht were no pushovers – they had annihilated Rangers 12-4 in the semi-final – and they showed as much by taking the lead in the 19th minute. That however simply set off the Madrid goal machine. Within 11 minutes di Stefano had put the European champions 2-1 up, then Puskas added one before the interval, and two shortly afterwards.

The match reached its breathtaking climax in the 70th minute. Puskas scored, Eintracht got another one back, di Stefano scored immediately after the re-start to complete his hattrick before Eintracht scored their third. Four goals in four minutes. Little wonder the awestruck Scottish crowd gave both teams an ovation when the referee blew the final whistle.

Opening the floodgates: di Stefano scores Real Madrid's first goal in their 7-3 victory

Burnley steal Wolves's thunder

IN A DRAMATIC finish to the season Burnley beat Manchester City 2-1 at Maine Road on the last day of the season to sneak past Wolves and snatch the League championship by a single point. It was the first time all season Burnley had led the table. If Burnley had drawn at Maine Road Wolves would have been the champions on goal difference.

Thus, by a whisker, Wolves were deprived not only of a League title, but of a memorable record that would have established them as the greatest, and most successful, club side in English football. The 1959-60 championship would have completed a hat-trick of successive League titles – to emulate Herbert Chapman's Huddersfield and Arsenal teams – and would have left them poised to achieve the elusive Double. Five days after losing the League title they were due to meet Blackburn in the FA Cup final and were widely expected to win (which they did).

However, the team that brought about Wolves' downfall was not Burnley but Tottenham, who went to Molineux in the penultimate match of the season. Danny Blanchflower, and Spurs, had their sights set on the Double as well – but for next season. Stopping Wolves would leave the way open for Spurs to grab the glory of being the first club this century to win the Cup and the League in a season.

Blanchflower held his team talk on the pitch, fired up his team and they beat Wolves 3-1. Burnley did their part by picking up maximum points in their last two matches and Wolves's extraordinary place in history slipped from their grasp. Sadly Wolves have not won the League or FA Cup since.

Angry fans pelt referee after 'Dustbin final'

Jeered off: Wolves's fierce tackles angered the crowd

AN INJURY turned the course of the Cup final once again and resulted in scenes the like of which had never been seen at Wembley. Blackburn Rovers had already been rocked by Derek Dougan demanding a transfer an hour before the kick-off and they were a goal down to Wolverhampton after 30 minutes when their full-back David Whelan broke his leg trying to tackle Norman Deeley.

A player short, Blackburn lost 3-0 as Deeley scored twice in the second half in a very poor match. The crowd were already incensed by Wolves's fierce tackling and the way Kevin Howley, the youngest person to referee a Cup final, had handled the match, and were booing long before the end of the game.

When Wolves tried to make their traditional lap of honour the spectators' anger boiled over and they pelted the players and the referee with orange peel, apple cores and rubbish. The press said that what should have been the season's show-piece match was so badly tarnished that it should have been called the "Dustbin final".

Cup exploits rewarded at last as the Posh step up in class

PETERBOROUGH were finally elected to the League on May 28 at the 21st attempt. There was no doubt that their exploits in the FA Cup in recent years helped their cause. In the past seven seasons they had reached the third round twice and the fourth round on two other occasions.

This season they had beaten Second Division Ipswich in the third round before going out to Sheffield Wednesday from the First Division. The other time they reached the fourth round,

they also beat another Second Division side, Lincoln, before losing to Huddersfield.

Another reason for Peterborough's being chosen to replace Gateshead was their determined approach. The Midland League team had been founded in 1923 and had been fully professional since the early 1930s. The club's 30,000 capacity stadium at London Road was the envy of many League clubs, and its facilities were so grand that the club were nicknamed "The Posh".

Fond farewell: Finney joins in the singing of Auld Lang Syne

LEAGUE TABLES AND RESULTS 1950 – 1960

	1950-51	1951-52	1952-53	1953-54	1954-55

WORLD CUP

| | | | | West Germany 3 Hungary 2 | |

FA CUP

1950-51	1951-52	1952-53	1953-54	1954-55
Newcastle United 2 Blackpool 0	Newcastle United 1 Arsenal 0	Blackpool 4 Bolton Wanderers 3	West Bromwich Albion 3 Preston North End 2	Newcastle United 3 Manchester City 1

FIRST DIVISION

1950-51

	P	W	D	L	F	A	Pts
Tottenham	42	25	10	7	82	44	60
Man Utd	42	24	8	10	74	40	56
Blackpool	42	20	10	12	79	53	50
Newcastle	42	18	13	11	62	53	49
Arsenal	42	19	9	14	73	56	47
Middlesbro	42	18	11	13	76	65	47
Portsmouth	42	16	15	11	71	68	47
Bolton	42	19	7	16	64	61	45
Liverpool	42	16	11	15	53	59	43
Burnley	42	14	14	14	48	43	42
Derby	42	16	8	18	81	75	40
Sunderland	42	12	16	14	63	73	40
Stoke	42	13	14	15	50	59	40
Wolves	42	15	8	19	74	61	38
Aston Villa	42	12	13	17	66	68	37
West Brom	42	13	11	18	53	61	37
Charlton	42	14	9	19	63	80	37
Fulham	42	13	11	18	52	68	37
Huddersfld	42	15	6	21	64	92	36
Chelsea	42	12	8	22	53	65	32
Sheff Wed	*42*	*12*	*8*	*22*	*64*	*83*	*32*
Everton	*42*	*12*	*8*	*22*	*48*	*86*	*32*

1951-52

	P	W	D	L	F	A	Pts
Man Utd	42	23	11	8	95	52	57
Tottenham	42	22	9	11	76	51	53
Arsenal	42	21	11	10	80	61	53
Portsmouth	42	20	8	14	68	58	48
Bolton	42	19	10	13	65	61	48
Aston Villa	42	19	9	14	79	70	47
Preston	42	17	12	13	74	54	46
Newcastle	42	18	9	15	98	73	45
Blackpool	42	18	9	15	64	64	45
Charlton	42	17	10	15	68	63	44
Liverpool	42	12	19	11	57	61	43
Sunderland	42	15	12	15	70	61	42
West Brom	42	14	13	15	74	77	41
Burnley	42	15	10	17	56	63	40
Man City	42	13	13	16	58	61	39
Wolves	42	12	14	16	73	73	38
Derby	42	15	7	20	63	80	37
Middlesbro	42	15	6	21	64	88	36
Chelsea	42	14	8	20	52	72	36
Stoke	42	12	7	23	49	88	31
Huddersfld	*42*	*10*	*8*	*24*	*49*	*82*	*28*
Fulham	*42*	*8*	*11*	*23*	*58*	*77*	*27*

1952-53

	P	W	D	L	F	A	Pts
Arsenal	42	21	12	9	97	64	54
Preston	42	21	12	9	85	60	54
Wolves	42	19	13	10	86	63	51
West Brom	42	21	8	13	66	60	50
Charlton	42	19	11	12	77	63	49
Burnley	42	18	12	12	67	52	48
Blackpool	42	19	9	14	71	70	47
Man Utd	42	18	10	14	69	72	46
Sunderland	42	15	13	14	68	82	43
Tottenham	42	15	11	16	78	69	41
Aston Villa	42	14	13	15	63	61	41
Cardiff	42	14	12	16	54	46	40
Middlesbro	42	14	11	17	70	77	39
Bolton	42	15	9	18	61	69	39
Portsmouth	42	14	10	18	74	83	38
Newcastle	42	14	9	19	59	70	37
Liverpool	42	14	8	20	61	82	36
Sheff Wed	42	12	11	19	62	72	35
Chelsea	42	12	11	19	56	66	35
Man City	42	14	7	21	72	87	35
Stoke	*42*	*12*	*10*	*20*	*53*	*66*	*34*
Derby	*42*	*11*	*10*	*21*	*59*	*74*	*32*

1953-54

	P	W	D	L	F	A	Pts
Wolves	42	25	7	10	96	56	57
West Brom	42	22	9	11	86	63	53
Huddersfld	42	20	11	11	78	61	51
Man Utd	42	18	12	12	73	58	48
Bolton	42	18	12	12	75	60	48
Blackpool	42	19	10	13	80	69	48
Burnley	42	21	4	17	78	67	46
Chelsea	42	16	12	14	74	68	44
Charlton	42	19	6	17	75	77	44
Cardiff	42	18	8	16	51	71	44
Preston	42	19	5	18	87	58	43
Arsenal	42	15	13	14	75	73	43
Aston Villa	42	16	9	17	70	68	41
Portsmouth	42	14	11	17	81	89	39
Newcastle	42	14	10	18	72	77	38
Tottenham	42	16	5	21	65	76	37
Man City	42	14	9	19	62	77	37
Sunderland	42	14	8	20	81	89	36
Sheff Wed	42	15	6	21	70	91	36
Sheff Utd	42	11	11	20	69	90	33
Middlesbro	*42*	*10*	*10*	*22*	*60*	*91*	*30*
Liverpool	*42*	*9*	*10*	*23*	*68*	*97*	*28*

1954-55

	P	W	D	L	F	A	Pts
Chelsea	42	20	12	10	81	57	52
Wolves	42	19	10	13	89	70	48
Portsmouth	42	18	12	12	74	62	48
Sunderland	42	15	18	9	64	54	48
Man Utd	42	20	7	15	84	74	47
Aston Villa	42	20	7	15	72	73	47
Man City	42	18	10	14	76	69	46
Newcastle	42	17	9	16	89	77	43
Arsenal	42	17	9	16	69	63	43
Burnley	42	17	9	16	51	48	43
Everton	42	16	10	16	62	68	42
Huddersfld	42	14	13	15	63	68	41
Sheff Utd	42	17	7	18	70	86	41
Preston	42	16	8	18	83	64	40
Charlton	42	15	10	17	76	75	40
Tottenham	42	16	8	18	72	73	40
West Brom	42	16	8	18	76	96	40
Bolton	42	13	13	16	62	69	39
Blackpool	42	14	10	18	60	64	38
Cardiff	42	13	11	18	62	76	37
Leicester	*42*	*12*	*11*	*19*	*74*	*86*	*35*
Sheff Wed	*42*	*8*	*10*	*24*	*63*	*100*	*26*

SECOND DIVISION

1950-51	1951-52	1952-53	1953-54	1954-55
Champions: Preston North End Also promoted: Manchester City Relegated: Chesterfield, Grimsby Town	Champions: Sheffield Wednesday Also promoted: Cardiff City Relegated: Coventry City, Queen's Park Rangers	Champions: Sheffield United Also promoted: Huddersfield Town Relegated: Southampton, Barnsley	Champions: Leicester City Also promoted: Everton Relegated: Brentford, Oldham Athletic	Champions: Birmingham City Also promoted: Luton Town Relegated: Ipswich Town, Derby County

THIRD DIVISION SOUTH

1950-51	1951-52	1952-53	1953-54	1954-55
Champions: Nottingham Forest Runners-up (not promoted): Norwich City	Champions: Plymouth Argyle Runners-up (not promoted): Reading	Champions: Bristol Rovers Runners-up (not promoted): Millwall	Champions: Ipswich Town Runners-up (not promoted): Brighton & Hove Albion	Champions: Bristol City Runners-up (not promoted): Leyton Orient

THIRD DIVISION NORTH

1950-51	1951-52	1952-53	1953-54	1954-55
Champions: Rotherham United Runners-up (not promoted): Mansfield Town	Champions: Lincoln City Runners-up (not promoted): Grimsby Town	Champions: Oldham Athletic Runners-up (not promoted): Port Vale	Champions: Port Vale Runners-up (not promoted): Barnsley	Champions: Barnsley Runners-up (not promoted): Accrington Stanley

SCOTTISH CUP

1950-51	1951-52	1952-53	1953-54	1954-55
Celtic 1 Motherwell 0	Motherwell 4 Dundee 0	Rangers 1 Aberdeen 0, after 1-1	Celtic 2 Aberdeen 1	Clyde 1 Celtic 0, after 1-1

SCOTTISH FIRST DIVISION

1950-51

	P	W	D	L	F	A	Pts
Hibernian	30	22	4	4	78	26	48
Rangers	30	17	4	9	64	37	38
Dundee	30	15	8	7	47	30	38
Hearts	30	16	5	9	72	45	37
Aberdeen	30	15	5	10	61	50	35
Partick	30	13	7	10	57	48	33
Celtic	30	12	5	13	48	46	29
Raith	30	13	2	15	52	52	28
Motherwell	30	11	6	13	58	65	28
East Fife	30	10	8	12	48	66	28
St Mirren	30	9	7	14	35	51	25
Morton	30	10	4	16	47	59	24
T Lanark	30	11	2	17	40	51	24
Airdrie	30	10	4	16	52	67	24
Clyde	*30*	*8*	*7*	*15*	*37*	*57*	*23*
Falkirk	*30*	*7*	*4*	*19*	*35*	*81*	*18*

1951-52

	P	W	D	L	F	A	Pts
Hibernian	30	20	5	5	92	36	45
Rangers	30	16	9	5	61	31	41
East Fife	30	17	3	10	71	49	37
Hearts	30	14	7	9	69	53	35
Raith	30	14	5	11	43	42	33
Partick	30	12	7	11	48	51	31
Motherwell	30	12	7	11	51	57	31
Dundee	30	11	6	13	53	52	28
Celtic	30	10	8	12	52	55	28
Q of South	30	10	8	12	50	60	28
Aberdeen	30	10	7	13	65	58	27
T Lanark	30	9	8	13	51	62	26
Airdrie	30	11	4	15	54	69	26
St Mirren	30	10	5	15	43	58	25
Morton	*30*	*9*	*6*	*15*	*49*	*56*	*24*
Stirling A	*30*	*5*	*5*	*20*	*36*	*99*	*15*

1952-53

	P	W	D	L	F	A	Pts
Rangers	30	18	7	5	80	39	43
Hibernian	30	19	5	6	93	51	43
East Fife	30	16	7	7	72	48	39
Hearts	30	12	6	12	59	50	30
Clyde	30	13	4	13	78	78	30
St Mirren	30	11	8	11	52	58	30
Dundee	30	9	11	10	44	37	29
Celtic	30	11	7	12	51	54	29
Partick	30	10	9	11	55	63	29
Q of South	30	10	8	12	43	61	28
Aberdeen	30	11	5	14	64	68	27
Raith	30	9	8	13	47	53	26
Falkirk	30	11	4	15	53	63	26
Airdrie	30	10	6	14	53	75	26
Motherwell	*30*	*10*	*5*	*15*	*57*	*80*	*25*
T Lanark	*30*	*8*	*4*	*18*	*52*	*75*	*20*

1953-54

	P	W	D	L	F	A	Pts
Celtic	30	20	3	7	72	29	43
Hearts	30	16	6	8	70	45	38
Partick	30	17	1	12	76	54	35
Rangers	30	13	8	9	56	35	34
Hibernian	30	15	4	11	72	51	34
East Fife	30	13	8	9	55	45	34
Dundee	30	14	6	10	46	47	34
Clyde	30	15	4	11	64	67	34
Aberdeen	30	15	3	12	66	51	33
Q of South	30	14	4	12	72	58	32
St Mirren	30	12	4	14	44	54	28
Raith	30	10	6	14	56	60	26
Falkirk	30	9	7	14	47	61	25
Stirling A	30	10	4	16	39	62	24
Airdrie	*30*	*5*	*5*	*20*	*41*	*92*	*15*
Hamilton	*30*	*4*	*3*	*23*	*29*	*94*	*11*

1954-55

	P	W	D	L	F	A	Pts
Aberdeen	30	24	1	5	73	26	49
Celtic	30	19	8	3	76	37	46
Rangers	30	19	3	8	67	33	41
Hearts	30	16	7	7	74	45	39
Hibernian	30	15	4	11	64	54	34
St Mirren	30	12	8	10	55	54	32
Clyde	30	11	9	10	59	50	31
Dundee	30	13	4	13	48	48	30
Partick	30	11	7	12	49	61	29
Kilmarnock	30	10	6	14	46	58	26
East Fife	30	9	6	15	51	62	24
Falkirk	30	8	8	14	42	54	24
Q of South	30	9	6	15	38	56	24
Raith	30	10	3	17	49	57	23
Motherwell	*30*	*9*	*4*	*17*	*42*	*62*	*22*
Stirling A	*30*	*2*	*2*	*26*	*29*	*105*	*6*

SCOTTISH SECOND DIV

1950-51	1951-52	1952-53	1953-54	1954-55
Champions: Queen of the South Also promoted: Stirling Albion	Champions: Clyde Also promoted: Falkirk	Champions: Stirling Albion Also promoted: Hamilton Academical	Champions: Motherwell Also promoted: Kilmarnock	Champions: Airdrie Also promoted: Dunfermline Athletic

SCOTTISH LEAGUE CUP

1950-51	1951-52	1952-53	1953-54	1954-55
Motherwell 3 Hibernian 0	Dundee 3 Rangers 2	Dundee 2 Kilmarnock 0	East Fife 3 Partick 2	Hearts 4 Motherwell 2

1955-56

WORLD CUP

EUROPEAN CHAMPIONSHIP

EUROPEAN CUP: Real Madrid 4, Reims 3

FAIRS CUP

FA CUP: Manchester City 3, Birmingham City 1

FIRST DIVISION

	P	W	D	L	F	A	Pts
Man Utd	42	25	10	7	83	51	60
Blackpool	42	20	9	13	86	62	49
Wolves	42	20	9	13	89	65	49
Man City	42	18	10	14	82	69	46
Arsenal	42	18	10	14	60	61	46
Birmingham	42	18	9	15	75	57	45
Burnley	42	18	8	16	64	54	44
Bolton	42	18	7	17	71	58	43
Sunderland	42	17	9	16	80	95	43
Luton	42	17	8	17	66	64	42
Newcastle	42	17	7	18	85	70	41
Portsmouth	42	16	9	17	78	85	41
West Brom	42	18	5	19	58	70	41
Charlton	42	17	6	19	75	81	40
Everton	42	15	10	17	55	69	40
Chelsea	42	14	11	17	64	77	39
Cardiff	42	15	9	18	55	69	39
Tottenham	42	15	7	20	61	71	37
Preston	42	14	8	20	73	72	36
Aston Villa	42	11	13	18	52	69	35
Huddersfld	42	14	7	21	54	83	35
Sheff Utd	42	12	9	21	63	77	33

SECOND DIVISION
Champions: Sheffield Wednesday
Also promoted: Leeds United
Relegated: Plymouth Argyle, Hull City

THIRD DIVISION SOUTH
Champions: Leyton Orient
Runners-up (not promoted): Brighton & Hove Albion

THIRD DIVISION NORTH
Champions: Grimsby Town
Runners-up (not promoted): Derby County

SCOTTISH CUP: Hearts 3, Celtic 1

SCOTTISH FIRST DIVISION

	P	W	D	L	F	A	Pts
Rangers	34	22	8	4	85	27	52
Aberdeen	34	18	10	6	87	50	46
Hearts	34	19	7	8	99	47	45
Hibernian	34	19	7	8	86	50	45
Celtic	34	16	9	9	55	39	41
Q of South	34	16	5	13	69	73	37
Airdrie	34	14	8	12	85	96	36
Kilmarnock	34	12	10	12	52	45	34
Partick	34	13	7	14	62	60	33
Motherwell	34	11	11	12	53	59	33
Raith	34	12	9	13	58	75	33
East Fife	34	13	5	16	61	69	31
Dundee	34	12	6	16	56	65	30
Falkirk	34	11	6	17	58	75	28
St Mirren	34	10	7	17	57	70	27
Dunfermline	34	10	6	18	42	82	26
Clyde	34	8	6	20	50	74	22
Stirling A	34	4	5	25	23	82	13

SCOTTISH SECOND DIV
Champions: Queen's Park
Also promoted: Ayr United

SCOTTISH LEAGUE CUP: Aberdeen 2, St Mirren 1

1956-57

EUROPEAN CUP: Real Madrid 2, Fiorentina 0

FA CUP: Aston Villa 2, Manchester United 1

FIRST DIVISION

	P	W	D	L	F	A	Pts
Man Utd	42	28	8	6	103	54	64
Tottenham	42	22	12	8	104	56	56
Preston	42	23	10	9	84	56	56
Blackpool	42	22	9	11	93	65	53
Arsenal	42	21	8	13	85	69	50
Wolves	42	20	8	14	94	70	48
Burnley	42	18	10	14	56	50	46
Leeds	42	15	14	13	72	63	44
Bolton	42	16	12	14	65	65	44
Aston Villa	42	14	15	13	65	55	43
West Brom	42	14	14	14	59	61	42
Birmingham	42	15	9	18	69	69	39
Chelsea	42	13	13	16	73	73	39
Sheff Wed	42	16	6	20	82	88	38
Everton	42	14	10	18	61	79	38
Luton	42	14	9	19	58	76	37
Newcastle	42	14	8	20	67	87	36
Man City	42	13	9	20	78	88	35
Portsmouth	42	10	13	19	62	92	33
Sunderland	42	12	8	22	67	88	32
Cardiff	42	10	9	23	53	88	29
Charlton	42	9	4	29	62	120	22

SECOND DIVISION
Champions: Leicester City
Also promoted: Nottingham Forest
Relegated: Bury, Port Vale

THIRD DIVISION SOUTH
Champions: Ipswich Town
Runners-up (not promoted): Torquay United

THIRD DIVISION NORTH
Champions: Derby County
Runners-up (not promoted): Hartlepools United

SCOTTISH CUP: Falkirk 2, Kilmarnock 1, after 1-1

SCOTTISH FIRST DIVISION

	P	W	D	L	F	A	Pts
Rangers	34	26	3	5	96	48	55
Hearts	34	24	5	5	81	48	53
Kilmarnock	34	16	10	8	57	39	42
Raith	34	16	7	11	84	58	39
Celtic	34	15	8	11	58	43	38
Aberdeen	34	18	2	14	79	59	38
Motherwell	34	16	5	13	72	66	37
Partick	34	13	8	13	53	51	34
Hibernian	34	12	9	13	69	56	33
Dundee	34	13	6	15	55	61	32
Airdrie	34	13	4	17	77	89	30
St Mirren	34	12	6	16	58	72	30
Queen's P	34	11	7	16	55	59	29
Falkirk	34	10	8	16	51	70	28
East Fife	34	10	6	18	59	82	26
Q of South	34	10	5	19	54	96	25
Dunfermline	34	9	6	19	54	74	24
Ayr	34	7	5	22	48	89	19

SCOTTISH SECOND DIV
Champions: Clyde
Also promoted: Third Lanark

SCOTTISH LEAGUE CUP: Celtic 3, Partick 0, after 0-0

1957-58

WORLD CUP: Brazil 5, Sweden 2

EUROPEAN CUP: Real Madrid 3, AC Milan 2

FAIRS CUP: Barcelona beat London 2-2 6-0

FA CUP: Bolton Wanderers 2, Manchester United 0

FIRST DIVISION

	P	W	D	L	F	A	Pts
Wolves	42	28	8	6	103	47	64
Preston	42	26	7	9	100	51	59
Tottenham	42	21	9	12	93	77	51
West Brom	42	18	14	10	92	70	50
Man City	42	22	5	15	104	100	49
Burnley	42	21	5	16	80	74	47
Blackpool	42	19	6	17	80	67	44
Luton	42	19	6	17	69	63	44
Man Utd	42	16	11	15	85	75	43
Nottm F	42	16	10	16	69	63	42
Chelsea	42	15	12	15	83	79	42
Arsenal	42	16	7	19	73	85	39
Birmingham	42	14	11	17	76	89	39
Aston Villa	42	16	7	19	73	86	39
Bolton	42	14	10	18	65	87	38
Everton	42	13	11	18	65	75	37
Leeds	42	14	9	19	51	63	37
Leicester	42	14	5	23	91	112	33
Newcastle	42	12	8	22	73	81	32
Portsmouth	42	12	8	22	73	88	32
Sunderland	42	10	12	20	54	97	32
Sheff Wed	42	12	7	23	69	92	31

SECOND DIVISION
Champions: West Ham United
Also promoted: Blackburn Rovers
Relegated: Notts County, Doncaster Rovers

THIRD DIVISION SOUTH
Champions: Brighton & Hove Albion
Runners-up (not promoted): Brentford

THIRD DIVISION NORTH
Champions: Scunthorpe United
Runners-up (not promoted): Accrington Stanley

SCOTTISH CUP: Clyde 1, Hibernian 0

SCOTTISH FIRST DIVISION

	P	W	D	L	F	A	Pts
Hearts	34	29	4	1	132	29	62
Rangers	34	22	5	7	89	49	49
Celtic	34	19	8	7	84	47	46
Clyde	34	18	6	10	84	61	42
Kilmarnock	34	14	9	11	60	55	37
Partick	34	17	3	14	69	71	37
Raith	34	14	7	13	66	56	35
Motherwell	34	12	8	14	68	67	32
Hibernian	34	13	5	16	59	60	31
Falkirk	34	11	9	14	64	82	31
Dundee	34	13	5	16	49	65	31
Aberdeen	34	14	2	18	68	76	30
St Mirren	34	11	8	15	59	66	30
Third Lanark	34	13	4	17	69	88	30
Q of South	34	12	5	17	61	72	29
Airdrie	34	13	2	19	71	92	28
East Fife	34	10	3	21	45	88	23
Queen's P	34	4	1	29	41	114	9

SCOTTISH SECOND DIV
Champions: Stirling Albion
Also promoted: Dunfermline Athletic

SCOTTISH LEAGUE CUP: Celtic 7, Rangers 1

1958-59

EUROPEAN CUP: Real Madrid 2, Reims 0

FA CUP: Nottingham Forest 2, Luton Town 1

FIRST DIVISION

	P	W	D	L	F	A	Pts
Wolves	42	28	5	9	110	49	61
Man Utd	42	24	7	11	103	66	55
Arsenal	42	21	8	13	88	68	50
Bolton	42	20	10	12	79	66	50
West Brom	42	18	13	11	88	68	49
West Ham	42	21	6	15	85	70	48
Burnley	42	19	10	13	81	70	48
Blackpool	42	18	11	13	66	49	47
Birmingham	42	20	6	16	84	68	46
Blackburn	42	17	10	15	76	70	44
Newcastle	42	17	7	18	80	80	41
Preston	42	17	7	18	70	77	41
Nottm F	42	17	6	19	71	74	40
Chelsea	42	18	4	20	77	98	40
Leeds	42	15	9	18	57	74	39
Everton	42	17	4	21	71	87	38
Luton	42	12	13	17	68	71	37
Tottenham	42	13	10	19	85	95	36
Leicester	42	11	10	21	67	98	32
Man City	42	11	9	22	64	95	31
Aston Villa	42	11	8	23	58	87	30
Portsmouth	42	6	9	27	64	112	21

SECOND DIVISION
Champions: Sheffield Wednesday
Also promoted: Fulham
Relegated: Grimsby Town, Barnsley

THIRD DIVISION
Champions: Plymouth Argyle
Also promoted: Hull City
Relegated: Stockport, Doncaster Rovers, Notts County, Rochdale

FOURTH DIVISION
Champions: Port Vale
Also promoted: Coventry City, York City, Shrewsbury Town

SCOTTISH CUP: St Mirren 3, Aberdeen 1

SCOTTISH FIRST DIVISION

	P	W	D	L	F	A	Pts
Rangers	34	21	8	5	92	51	50
Hearts	34	21	6	7	92	51	48
Motherwell	34	18	8	8	83	50	44
Dundee	34	16	9	9	61	51	41
Airdrie	34	15	7	12	64	62	37
Celtic	34	14	8	12	70	53	36
St Mirren	34	14	7	13	71	74	35
Kilmarnock	34	13	8	13	58	51	34
Partick	34	14	6	14	59	66	34
Hibernian	34	13	6	15	68	70	32
Third Lanark	34	11	10	13	74	83	32
Stirling A	34	11	8	15	54	64	30
Aberdeen	34	12	5	17	63	66	29
Raith	34	10	9	15	60	70	29
Clyde	34	12	4	18	62	66	28
Dunfermline	34	10	8	16	68	87	28
Falkirk	34	10	7	17	58	79	27
Q of South	34	6	6	22	38	101	18

SCOTTISH SECOND DIV
Champions: Ayr United
Also promoted: Arbroath

SCOTTISH LEAGUE CUP: Hearts 5, Partick 1

1959-60

EUROPEAN CHAMPIONSHIP: USSR 2, Yugoslavia 1

EUROPEAN CUP: Real Madrid 7, Eintracht Frankfurt 3

FAIRS CUP: Barcelona beat Birmingham City 0-0 4-1

FA CUP: Wolverhampton Wanderers 3, Blackburn Rovers 0

FIRST DIVISION

	P	W	D	L	F	A	Pts
Burnley	42	24	7	11	85	61	55
Wolves	42	24	6	12	106	67	54
Tottenham	42	21	11	10	86	50	53
West Brom	42	19	11	12	83	57	49
Sheff Wed	42	19	11	12	80	59	49
Bolton	42	20	8	14	59	51	48
Man Utd	42	19	7	16	102	80	45
Newcastle	42	18	8	16	82	78	44
Preston	42	16	12	14	79	76	44
Fulham	42	17	10	15	73	80	44
Blackpool	42	15	10	17	59	71	40
Leicester	42	13	13	16	66	75	39
Arsenal	42	15	9	18	68	80	39
West Ham	42	16	6	20	75	91	38
Man City	42	17	3	22	78	84	37
Everton	42	13	11	18	73	78	37
Blackburn	42	16	5	21	60	70	37
Chelsea	42	14	9	19	76	91	37
Birmingham	42	13	10	19	63	80	36
Nottm F	42	13	9	20	50	74	35
Leeds	42	12	10	20	65	92	34
Luton	42	9	12	21	50	73	30

SECOND DIVISION
Champions: Aston Villa
Also promoted: Cardiff City
Relegated: Hull City, Bristol City

THIRD DIVISION
Champions: Southampton
Also promoted: Norwich City
Relegated: York City, Mansfield Town, Wrexham, Accrington Stanley

FOURTH DIVISION
Champions: Walsall
Also promoted: Notts County, Torquay United, Watford

SCOTTISH CUP: Rangers 2, Kilmarnock 0

SCOTTISH FIRST DIVISION

	P	W	D	L	F	A	Pts
Hearts	34	23	8	3	102	51	54
Kilmarnock	34	24	2	8	67	45	50
Rangers	34	17	8	9	72	38	42
Dundee	34	16	10	8	70	49	42
Motherwell	34	16	8	10	71	61	40
Clyde	34	15	9	10	77	69	39
Hibernian	34	14	7	13	106	85	35
Ayr	34	14	6	14	65	73	34
Celtic	34	12	9	13	73	59	33
Partick	34	14	4	16	54	78	32
Raith	34	14	3	17	64	62	31
Third Lanark	34	13	4	17	75	83	30
Dunfermline	34	10	9	15	72	80	29
St Mirren	34	11	6	17	78	86	28
Aberdeen	34	11	6	17	54	72	28
Airdrie	34	11	6	17	56	80	28
Stirling A	34	7	8	19	55	72	22
Arbroath	34	4	7	23	38	106	15

SCOTTISH SECOND DIV
Champions: St Johnstone
Also promoted: Dundee United

SCOTTISH LEAGUE CUP: Hearts 2, Third Lanark 1

Player power forces League to abolish slavery contracts

Italy spends a fortune to buy Britain's best

THE moment that the maximum wage was abolished Tommy Trinder, the Fulham chairman, made Johnny Haynes the first £100 a week footballer in England.

That persuaded the England international not to seek his fortune abroad. But the debilitating effect of the maximum wage and restrictive contracts in Britain became clear when four more leading players followed John Charles's lead and were tempted by the lure of lira.

Joe Baker started the season by scoring nine times for Hibs in their 15-1 victory over Peebles Rovers in the first round of the Scottish Cup. But he soon went to Turin for £73,000.

Money was no object to foreign clubs determined to satisfy their fanatical supporters with the best players in the world, and Baker was joined in Italy by Denis Law of Manchester City, who also went to Turin for £100,000; Jimmy Greaves, who moved from Chelsea to AC Milan for £80,000 and Gerry Hitchens, who was transferred to their rivals Inter Milan for £80,000.

Greaves was in two minds but Milan made an unrefusable offer: £15,000 immediately and £40,000 over three years.

ENGLISH football was only days away from its first national strike when the Football League backed down in its long-running dispute with the PFA.

The arguments over players' wages and the terms of their contracts had dragged on for years. Professionals were restricted to a earning a maximum of £20 a week during the season and £17 in the summer. Although not a pittance by the standards of the wages paid in the early days of the League, it was far short of the money that players could make by moving abroad.

The players, led by Jimmy Hill, the PFA chairman, won their first breakthrough on January 9, when the maximum wage was abolished. But the League refused to budge on the contracts issue.

Players were not allowed to move to a club of their choosing when their contract expired, something that Hill described as a "slave contract". George Eastham, who wanted to move from Newcastle to Arsenal, was challenging his contract in court, arguing that it was a restraint of trade.

The PFA said it would call a strike, starting with the matches due to be played on Saturday, January 21. The League responded by ordering clubs to play their matches the day before to beat the strike. That ruling was greeted with derision —the Daily Mirror, in an editorial headlined "What a way to run a sport!", accused the League of being "idiotic".

It was apparent that most people supported the players' stance, and the League had to make a humiliating climbdown. After five hours of last-ditch talks at the Ministry of Labour on January 18, the League finally agreed to abandon the regulations that effectively tied a player to one club for life.

The players' victory was finally confirmed when Eastham's case reached the High Court, which ruled in his favour. At long last, football had been dragged, kicking and screaming all the way, out of the dark ages and into the modern era.

Fame and fortune: Baker is mobbed when he arrives in Rome

Demands met: Hill leaves the crisis talks at Ministry of Labour

England humiliate hapless Haffey

Unstoppable: England parade the Home International trophy after annihilating Scotland

APRIL 15 was the worst day in Frank Haffey's life as his golden opportunity to shine for his country turned into a day of humiliation. Nothing could have prepared him for the 9-3 slaughter that England inflicted on their bitterest international rivals that day at Wembley. In his only other appearance for Scotland, the previous April, Haffey had played creditably and the only goal he conceded was a Bobby Charlton penalty as England scraped a 1-1 draw at Hampden.

Poor Haffey was not even Scotland's first-choice goalkeeper for the England match. Injuries to Bill Brown and Leslie had pushed the Celtic keeper into the team at the last minute, but it still was not a weak side that Scotland fielded that fateful afternoon. The line-up included such leading players as Denis Law, Dave Mackay, Billy McNeill and Ian St John. However England were on a roll: they had scored 23 goals in their previous four fixtures. Then against Scotland, England's attack moved up a gear.

Bobby Robson opened the scoring and by half-time England were 3-0 up. However, within six minutes of the second half Scotland had rallied and were only 3-2 down. Then the roof fell in. Jimmy Greaves helped himself to a hat-trick, Bobby Smith bagged a pair, as did Johnny Haynes, and one from Bryan Douglas completed the hammering. The English press were ecstatic, hailing England's forward line as their best ever and comparing them to Real Madrid, the kings of Europe.

Poor Haffey trudged off the field, head bowed, destined never to be picked to play for his country again. In England the match so captured the popular imagination that a long-playing record of the match commentary was released and endlessly played to taunt the hapless Scots. And, as if to prove it was no fluke, the next month England – without Greaves – trounced Mexico 8-0.

Revie sweet-talks Collins into saving Leeds

SOON AFTER he took charge of Leeds United, Don Revie made a secret visit to Old Trafford to seek Matt Busby's advice on how to be a good manager. The Manchester United manager's words almost certainly helped to keep Leeds out of the Third Division. "All you have to do is treat your players well. Be honest with them and never lie to them. In return they'll doing anything for you."

Leeds were staring relegation in the face in March when Revie bought Bobby Collins from Everton for £25,000, just days before the transfer deadline. But within days of arriving at Elland Road, Collins said that he wanted to leave.

But, recalling Busby's words, Revie persuaded the little inside-forward to withdraw his transfer request. Collins responded by guiding Leeds to safety. The team did not lose any of their last 10 League matches and when the chips were down in the final match of the season they won 3-0 at Newcastle to guarantee their survival.

Rain robs Law of Cup record

DENIS LAW was left cursing the heavy rain that cost him a place in the record books.

Manchester City's fourth-round FA Cup tie against Luton should not have gone ahead because heavy storms had turned Luton's ground into a quagmire. In almost impossible conditions, the Second Division team took a 2-0 lead in the first 20 minutes.

The huge pools of water on the pitch did not hamper Law in the slightest and, despite the ball being almost unplayable, he hit six goals in succession to equal the FA Cup record.

Much to his chagrin though, the referee abandoned the match with just over 30 minutes remaining. Then, to make matters worse, Luton won the replay 3-1 with Law scoring City's consolation goal.

Glorious Double for Spurs

Double sealed: Gordon Banks dives in vain and Spurs' Double is nearly complete

Football is not really about winning, or goals, or saves, or supporters – it's about glory. It's about doing things in style, doing them with a flourish; it's about going out to beat the other lot, not waiting for them to die of boredom; it's about dreaming of the glory that the Double brought

DANNY BLANCHFLOWER

Blanchflower: dream fulfilled

EVERYBODY believed that the modern-day Double could not be done – apart from one man. So many teams had gone heartbreakingly close but failed at the final hurdle that it was almost established as a "fact" that the Double was a physical impossibility.

Danny Blanchflower, though, believed otherwise. As far back as 1958 he had said as much. On the flight home from the World Cup finals he had lectured Stan Cullis and Joe Mercer on the subject. "It is going to be done," Blanchflower said. "And Spurs will be the team to do it."

Quietly, and with very little fuss, Bill Nicholson had been staging a revolution at White Hart Lane. Just as Arthur Rowe had assembled the famous push-and-run team seemingly out of nowhere, Nicholson had built a formidable team around Blanchflower.

Just how all-powerful that team was was soon revealed.

Tottenham had a record-breaking start to the season, winning their first 11 League matches. They only dropped one point in their first 16 matches (a draw at home to Manchester City) and were so far ahead by Christmas that bookmakers refused to take any more bets on their winning the title.

By the turn of the year Spurs had 46 points from 25 matches and the only other blots on their copybook form were a defeat at Sheffield Wednesday, their nearest rivals, and a 4-4 draw at home to Burnley in a match which they had led 4-0. Only 27 goals were conceded while an enormous 82 were scored.

But still people thought that Tottenham, like the teams before them would crack. Some chance. The second half of the season was as much a procession as the first. Record after record tumbled as Tottenham marched to the title on April 17 with three games in hand when they beat Sheffield Wednesday in front of a rapturous crowd at White Hart Lane. Amazingly, Tottenham only had one player booked and only conceded one penalty all season.

Although Blanchflower's performances were crucial, Tottenham were far from a one-man band. Bobby Smith and Les Allen scored 51 goals between them; Cliff Jones and Terry Dyson dominated the wings; Dave Mackay was redoubtable in midfield and Bobby Brown was a safe pair of hands in goal

behind the defending of Peter Baker, Ron Henry and Maurice Norman.

Blanchflower was quick to acknowledge the importance of his team-mates, who gave him the time and the space needed to spur Tottenham's devastating attacks. As he said: "I could change the rhythm and change the pace, slow it down if necessary or speed it up when we needed to. I had the ball much more often than anybody else, so I should have done something with it, shouldn't I?"

By the standards of the rest of the season, Tottenham did not do a great deal in the FA Cup final. The burden of having everybody wanting them to win, but people still thinking that the Double could not be done, seemed to weigh heavily on Spurs.

Leicester dominated the early exchanges and created three good chances. But they were knocked out of their stride when Len Chalmers wrenched his right knee in a collision with Les Allen. The Leicester right-back limped on out on the wing, but was forced to come off just after Smith gave Tottenham the lead in the 69th minute.

With Leicester's defence in disarray Dyson added a second goal shortly afterwards. It was the seventh time in nine years that the Cup final had been affected by an injury, but not even that could take the gloss off Tottenham's "impossible" achievement.

How the double eluded clubs before Spurs in 1961		
1904	Manchester City	League runners-up and FA Cup winners
1905	Newcastle United	League champions and FA Cup finalists
1913	Sunderland	League champions and FA Cup finalists
1913	Aston Villa	League runners-up and FA Cup winners
1928	Huddersfield	League runners-up and FA Cup finalists
1932	Arsenal	League runners-up and FA Cup finalists
1939	Wolves	League runners-up and FA Cup finalists
1948	Manchester United	League runners-up and FA Cup winners
1954	West Bromwich Albion	League runners-up and FA Cup winners
1957	Manchester United	League champions and FA Cup finalists
1960	Wolves	League runners-up and FA Cup winners

Treble eludes Rangers as sucker punches fell them at the final hurdle

RANGERS improved on their European performance of the previous season – a heavy defeat in the semi-finals of the Champions Cup – by reaching the final of the newly created European Cup Winners Cup.

It was the third of the European competitions to be launched and initially was seen very much as the poor relations to the Champions' Cup. Unlike Britain, where the domestic Cup competition predates the Leagues, many European countries did not have their own Cup and, if they did, its significance was not great. Thus only 10 clubs entered the inaugural European Cup-Winners' Cup.

After a shaky start against Ferencvaros in the preliminary round, Rangers scraped through 5-4 on aggregate, they strolled into the semi-finals by trouncing Borussia Moenchengladbach 11-0. There they met the once mighty Wolves who were now sadly entering a period of decline. A 2-0 victory at Ibrox proved too much for the English Cup winners to overhaul. They could only manage a 1-1 draw in the second leg at Molineux and Rangers became the first Scottish club to reach a European final.

A glittering treble was now possible as Rangers had won the Scottish championship by a point from Kilmarnock and beaten the same team 2-0 to capture the Scottish League Cup. However Italy's Fiorentina were too much for Rangers who, having acquired Jim Baxter from Raith Rovers, had developed into a highly skilled and attractive side.

The vagaries of European football were still new to the Scottish side and despite their constant raids on the the Italian goal they were unable to score at Ibrox. Instead Fiorentina's Milani caught them with two sucker punches, in the 12th and 88th minutes. In Florence Rangers again conceded a 12th minute goal to Milani but, despite an equaliser from Scott on the hour, Fiorentina were never going to surrender their aggregate lead. Four minutes from time Hamrin wrapped it up for the Italians.

Foreign fields: Greaves leaves London airport for Italy

■ Peterborough, in only their first season in the League, raced through the Fourth Division and were promoted as champions, having scored a record 134 goals. Terry Bly was their leading marksman with 52 goals in the League, which was a post-war record.

■ Ipswich, managed by Alf Ramsey, also scored 100 goals as they won the Second Division title. Ray Crawford's 39 goals made him the division's leading scorer.

■ Jimmy Greaves left England for Italy as the First Division's leading scorer, with 41 goals in the League.

■ Several famous clubs of the past fell on hard times. Preston were relegated to the Second Division after 10 seasons in the top flight, Newcastle went down after 13 seasons in the First Division, and Blackpool only escaped relegation by one point. Portsmouth also went down to the Third Division for the first time since the 1920s.

Stein works another miracle as Dunfermline hit the heights

JOCK STEIN was earning himself a reputation as a miracle worker in Scotland. Having amazingly saved Dunfermline from certain relegation the season before, he had now, in his first full season as the manager, guided the club to mid-table safety and their first major trophy, the Scottish Cup. To complete the fairy-tale their defeated opponents in the final had been Celtic, Stein's former club.

Bolstered by some astute purchases from England, Dunfermline breezed through the early rounds of the Cup, sweeping away Berwick and Stranraer. Then stunned all of Scotland by beating Aberdeen 6-3 at Pittodrie in the third round. Alloa were brushed aside 4-0 in the next round, and in the semi-final – the furthest Dunfermline had ever gone in the Cup – St Mirren were eventually beaten 1-0 after a replay.

The final was where the bubble should have burst as Celtic mounted attack after attack. But even a late injury that saw them reduced to 10 men did not deter Dunfermline and they hung on to force a replay. Once again Dunfermline had to fight a rearguard action, but two breakaway goals from Thomson and Dickson gave the Fife club victory and the Cup. Was there any end to the miracles that Stein could work?

Stein: beat his old club in the Scottish Cup final

Ramsey's yeomen march past the First Division aristocrats

IPSWICH, a team largely composed of non-entities and whom everybody outside of East Anglia had tipped for relegation, rocked the aristocrats of the First Division by winning the championship in their first ever season in the top flight. Alf Ramsey, a right back for Tottenham and England in the 1950s and now the Ipswich manager, was the guiding force behind this mind-boggling triumph.

Ramsey had taken the helm in 1955 when the club had just been relegated to the Third Division South. Their foray in the Second Division had been brief, just one season, but it had been the most the club had ever achieved. Ramsey, who had always been a thoughtful and deliberate footballer, got Ipswich back into the Second Division in 1957 and then spent the next three years assembling a close-knit squad of players loyal to him. Ramsey blended astute bargain basement purchases with younger players.

It was this squad that won Ipswich the Second Division championship in 1961 and, apart from the acquisition of Doug Moran from Falkirk for £12,000, it was the same squad that won the First Division championship. Ipswich thus emulated the Tottenham side of 1950 and 1951 who were the first club to win the Second and First Division championships in consecutive seasons. Ironically Ramsey had been a crucial member of those Tottenham teams.

Ipswich had achieved their extraordinary success because of Ramsey's tactical nous. He had two free-scoring strikers in Ray Crawford and Ted Phillips, and two wingers in Jimmy Leadbetter and Ray Stephenson. However Ramsey innovatively used his two wingers in midfield – a crude form of the 4-4-2 system that was to dominate English football by the end of the decade.

Ipswich had begun the season badly, taking only one point from their first three matches, but Ramsey stuck to his tactical guns and the results started coming. With Tottenham distracted by their European and FA Cup exploits and Burnley blowing up over the last seven League games, Ipswich stole home to take the title with a mere 56 points.

Stoke make a fortune from Matthews mania

Generation gap: Gerry Bridgwood, 17, welcomes Matthews

STOKE gave £3,500 to Blackpool to bring Stanley Matthews home, and paid the 46-year-old winger £50 a week, plus a £25 appearance fee. It was the best money the struggling Second Division club ever spent.

The match before Matthews arrived only drew just over 8,000 people to the Victoria Ground. The crowd attracted by his first home game was a staggering 35,288. The club was delighted and Matthews's teammates were equally happy – every week the attendance exceeded 12,000 they all received a bonus of £1 per thousand people.

Matthews made his debut against Huddersfield, who had the England international Ray Wilson at full-back. Stoke won 3-0 and Matthews was involved in all the goals, albeit with a little help from the referee who seemed to have been swayed by the occasion.

Wilson said: "Whenever the ball came to Matthews the crowd erupted. Once, I slid in quickly, got the ball from his foot and never touched him. But the whistle went. A foul!"

The fans flocked in week after week (the police had to impose a crowd limit of 50,000 for the FA Cup fourth round against Blackburn) and the money they spent enabled Stoke to strengthen their squad and finish the season in eighth place. There seemed to be no end to the magic that Matthews could work.

Unstoppable: Ray Crawford tormented First Division defences

European agony for Tottenham

Off target: Mackay heads the ball against the crossbar in the last minute

TOTTENHAM'S European Cup semi-final against the holders Benfica produced two of the most pulsating, dramatic, and ultimately heart-wrenching matches of the decade. The contest was given further edge as both managers believed the tie would provide the eventual winners with Real Madrid, the likely other finalists, clearly a waning force.

In the first leg, in Lisbon, Tottenham were in trouble after 20 minutes, Benfica having taken a 2-0 lead with goals from Aguas and Augusto. Bobby Smith reduced the arrears but Augusto restored their two-goal cushion for the return at White Hart Lane with a header. Tottenham had hauled back such a deficit before, notably in the preliminary round match against Gornik, but what really rankled was that the team believed that two good goals – one from Jimmy Greaves, the other from Smith – had been disallowed for offside.

Aguas made matters worse in the second leg improving Benfica's aggregate lead to 4-1 after 15 minutes. Then another Greaves goal was dubiously disallowed for offside. With three decisions going against him in the two legs it seemed as if Greaves's speed on the ball was just too fast for the officials to follow. Seven minutes before the interval Smith reduced the arrears and, four minutes into the second half Danny Blanchflower coolly stroked home a penalty. Spurs were now one goal behind on aggregate with 40 minutes left to play.

With the 65,000 crowd roaring them on and Dave Mackay playing like a man possessed, Tottenham threw everything at the Benfica goal. But it was not to be. Spurs hit both posts and, just before the final whistle, Mackay cracked one off the crossbar. It was a sad end to a glorious European campaign. Greaves also thought it was desperately unfair. Referring to the first leg in Lisbon, he said: "To this day I reckon the Swiss referee, Muellet, refereed us out of the final."

Nicholson saves a pound and spends a fortune on Greaves

TOTTENHAM strengthened their already formidable side when they brought Jimmy Greaves back from Italy in December for £99,999. The fee was deliberately £1 short of six figures because Bill Nicholson, the Spurs manager, did not want the England striker burdened with the label of Britain's first £100,000 footballer.

Greaves, who at 21 had been the youngest player to score 100 League goals, had been transferred from Chelsea to AC Milan in June for £80,000. Although he had settled well into his new team – scoring on his debut and amassing nine goals in 14 games – he had never settled into the Italian way of doing things. He resented the authoritarian style of management, bucked against their disciplinarian methods, and detested the negative tactics characteristic of Italian football.

Unfortunately for Spurs, because of the timing of his transfer, Greaves was not eligible to play in the European Cup for his new club until the semi-finals. Typically Greaves achieved what he always did when he arrived at a new club, scored in his first match.

Man apart: Greaves (back, second left) and ten others

Greaves's opening shots

1957	August 23	Tottenham v CHELSEA	Scored
1957	September 25	ENGLAND U-23 v Bulgaria	Scored twice
1959	May 17	Peru v ENGLAND	Scored
1961	June 7	MILAN v Botafogo	Scored
1961	December 16	TOTTENHAM v Blackpool	Scored hat-trick
1962	May 4	First Cup final. TOTTENHAM v Burnley	Scored
1970	March 20	Manchester City v WEST HAM	Scored twice

FOR THE RECORD

■ Last season's League Cup final was played at the start of this season. Aston Villa lost the first leg 2-0 to Rotherham on August 25, but won the Cup 3-0 in extra time on September 5. It was the first time that the final of a major domestic season had been held over from one season to the next.

■ Brian Clough, who had scored 197 goals in 213 games for Middlesbrough, moved to Sunderland for £45,000 at the start of the season.

■ Eintracht Frankfurt's 3-2 victory over Rangers on October 17 attracted 104,493 people to Hampden Park, the record attendance for a friendly.

■ Three exiles, Denis Law, John Charles and Gerry Hitchens, helped the Italian League beat the Scottish League 2-0 at Hampden Park in November.

Cup scant reward for Spurs

Finishing touch: Blanchflower's penalty made sure Spurs retained the Cup

Oxford step up as Accrington admit defeat

ACCRINGTON STANLEY finally admitted defeat in their fight for financial survival and resigned from the Football League on March 6. They had played 33 matches in the Fourth Division, but all their results were expunged.

Accrington's finances had declined along with their form. In 1955 they had attracted a crowd of more than 15,000 to one match as they just missed promotion to the Second Division. Now, struggling in the Fourth Division, their attendances were a fraction of that.

Matters were not helped by the club spending £14,000 to improve their ground by buying the grandstand used for the Aldershot military tattoo and erecting it as a new stand. Accrington's last League match was a 1-0 defeat at Crewe on March 2, and the club was wound up by the High Court.

Strangely, the little clubs who had complained so often about being kept out of the League by the end of season re-elections did not rush to take Accrington's place.

The League's annual meeting on June 2 only received two applications, from Oxford United and Wigan Athletic. Curiously, Oxford had enjoyed a huge improvement in their fortunes since the club was renamed from Headington United in 1960. After the change they won the Southern League two years in a row and that form, combined with a reasonable record in the FA Cup, was enough to win them a place in the Fourth Division by 39 votes to five.

TOTTENHAM'S season, which had looked so promising in March when they had the triple targets of the League title, FA Cup and European Cup in their sights, at last yielded one trophy: the FA Cup when they beat Burnley, the League runners-up, 3-1 in the final. Tottenham became only the second club this century to win the FA Cup in successive years, emulating Newcastle's achievement exactly a decade earlier.

Burnley, whose form deserted them in the closing stages of the title race, were never really a match for a Spurs team now becoming past masters of Cup competitions. Jimmy Greaves, their expensive signing from Milan, had Burnley on the rack as early as the third minute when he scored a stupendous goal.

Smith had headed the ball down perfectly to Greaves who ran straight at the heart of Burnley defence. Just as he seemed to be surrounded by a posse of defenders Greaves stopped dead, wrong-footing all of them. He turned on the ball and slid a left-footed ground shot past the outstretched Adam Blacklaw.

Five minutes into the second half Jimmy Robson put Burnley briefly back into the game when he met Harris's deadly centre

Return trip: Spurs bring the Cup back again

with his shins. But within a minute Spurs had struck again. This time it was Smith who bamboozled the Burnley defence when, having trapped John White's cross, he turned and whacked the ball into the net. Ten minutes from time Danny Blanchflower delivered the coup de grace with a penalty after Tom Cummings had handled Terry Medwin's shot on the goal-line.

Tottenham's joy at retaining the Cup was muted. They had entertained high hopes of winning all three honours. Indeed they can trace their loss of the League championship to one

fateful match. On March 14, Spurs were at home to Ipswich and Bill Nicholson, the Spurs manager, raised with his players a change of tactics to counter Jimmy Leadbetter, Ipswich's deep-lying left-winger. However the players dissented and Nicholson, reluctantly, gave way. Spurs lost the match 3-1. If that result had been reversed Spurs would have won the Double again.

Nicholson proved his point in the Charity Shield at Portman Road in August. He insisted the players use the tactics they had spurned in March and Tottenham duly ran out 5-1 winners.

'The ball kept on hitting the net'

THE arrival of Jim Baxter in 1960 had galvanised Rangers. The team that had missed out on the treble last season showed every sign of being able to win all three honours this time, particularly with Davie Wilson in such prolific goalscoring form.

Wilson used to have a bet with his fellow forwards Jimmy Millar and Ralph Brand as to who would score first in each match. But Millar was not on hand to see one of Wilson's most spectacular performances.

Millar was injured so Rangers moved Wilson from the wing to replace him against Falkirk on March 17. The switch in position did not unsettle him and he scored six times - including three goals in eight minutes - in a 7-1 rout at Brockville. "The ball just kept on hitting the net," Wilson said modestly when asked about his feat.

Despite Wilson's goals – 28 in total – the Treble eluded Rangers once again. They retained the League Cup, although they were taken to a replay in the final by Hearts. The Scottish Cup, which had proved their downfall last season, was won at a canter.

Arbroath were hit for six in the second round, Aberdeen conceded five goals in the third round replay, Kilmarnock were brushed aside 4-2 and Motherwell, their conquerors in the Cup last season were dispatched 3-1 in the semi-final. The final was not particularly taxing either – Brand and Wilson shared the spoils in a 2-0 defeat of St Mirren.

Scot Symon's team, though could not retain the League title. Rangers lost the same number of matches as Dundee (five), but they drew three more games to hand Dundee their first championship.

Benfica's Eusebio upstages Puskas

BELA GUTTMANN was one of football's great nomads. He had played for Hungary in the 1924 Olympics, left home to coach in America and Holland, survived a Second World War concentration camp and returned to Hungary to take Ujpest to the national championship.

But his travels were far from over. He moved to Italy and guided AC Milan to the title, but was then sacked while his team were leading the League once again. Then he went to Brazil, where he took Sao Paulo to the top in 1958 and was credited with pioneering the 4-2-4 system that Brazil unveiled at the 1958 World Cup finals.

While Guttmann was working in Brazil he learnt to speak Portuguese, which explained why his next port of call was Benfica. And, as he had done everywhere else in the world, he had a winning team.

Benfica won the European Cup for the second year running and the final, in Amsterdam on May 2, showed that the balance of power in Europe was shifting. Bill Nicholson had watched Real Madrid during Tottenham's European campaign and was of the opinion that Real "were not the side they had been". Guttmann agreed with him.

It was hard to believe that Real were in decline when Fer-

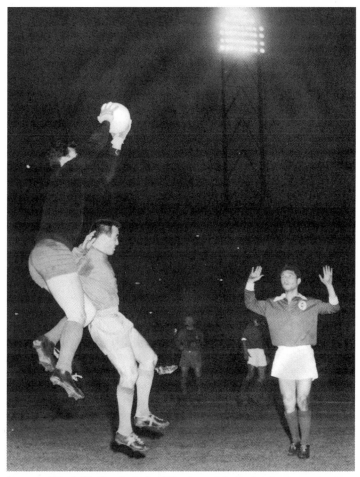

Keeper of the faith: Pereira helped Benfica retain the trophy

enc Puskas scored a hat-trick in the first 38 minutes. But Benfica had pegged them back to 2-2 and equalised again early in the second half.

With Puskas's age and weight starting to take their toll it was time for him to make way for the next great player. Guttmann's wealth of experience enabled him to make the tactical changes that enabled the 20-year-old Eusebio to wrap up the game 5-3 with two goals in three minutes.

WORLD CUP 1962

Irresistible Brazil retain their trophy

THE SEVENTH World Cup, although full of drama, incident and surprises, is mostly remembered for what did not happen. Three of the world's greatest players were set to grace the world's greatest stage, and somehow didn't.

Pele, after one outstanding match in which he made one goal and scored the other having beaten four defenders, limped off in the second with a torn thigh muscle and was out of the tournament. At least he played; Alfredo di Stefano didn't. The world's most versatile forward used the excuse of a pulled muscle before the tournament began to fuel his personal row with Helenio Herrera, Spain's manager, and sullenly refused to kick a ball.

Lev Yashin, the world's No1 goalkeeper did play – after a fashion. His errors were so disastrous that the Soviet Union qualified for the quarter-finals despite him but then promptly lost 2-1 to unfancied Chile after Yashin inexplicably failed to save two speculative long shots. For Chile, the host nation, it was their finest hour. Because of Yashin's mishaps they had reached a semi-final against Brazil, the holders and the overwhelming favourites to retain their trophy.

That Chile even hosted the tournament in the first place was a minor miracle. They beat out bids from Argentina and West Germany, despite not having the stadiums nor the footballing tradition of either of the other candidates. Then there had been a devastating earthquake in 1960. But the zeal of the Chileans was not to be denied.

Carlos Dittborn, the president of the Chilean football federation, exemplified this when Fifa proposed to re-allocate the event. "We have nothing, that is why we must have the World Cup," he said. His cri de coeur spoke volumes and won the day. Two splendid stadiums were constructed and the tournament went off successfully. Sadly Dittborn, who had been the driving force behind the venture, died a month before the finals began.

However as some of the brightest stars faded, others shone. With Pele out injured, Brazil pulled another wonder out of their pocket: the 24-year-old "White Pele" Amarildo, another athletic genius who knew precisely where the goal was. As did Garrincha who blossomed into a truly world-class player in Pele's absence. Garrincha's sinuous runs and deadly crosses were now complemented by powerful shooting and strength in the air. He was certainly the man of the tournament as England found out to their cost.

England were the only home nation to qualify – Scotland were knocked out in a play-off match with Czechoslovakia and Wales were eliminated by Spain. Although England's approach to the finals was more organised than before (Walter Winterbottom had Jimmy Adamson, the Burnley captain, as his assistant) their build-up was far from perfect; a middle-aged Australian millionaire played in one practice match.

The team was built round its captain Johnny Haynes at inside-left, and the emphasis on one player was to prove England's undoing. The Yugoslav manager summed it up neatly: "Number 10 takes the corners. Number 10 takes the throw-ins. So what do we do? We put a man on number 10. Goodbye England."

And so it proved in the first match. Hungary's defence stifled Haynes and England were beaten 2-1 with Haynes complaining to a journalist: "You want us to lose." Alan Peacock replaced Gerry Hitchens at centre-forward for the next match and the switch helped England's forwards temporarily rediscover their touch as Argentine were easily beaten 3-1. But a poor performance against Bulgaria, and a 0-0 draw, left England second in their group and having to face Brazil in the quarter-finals.

Garrincha simply took England apart. The English defence had no answer to his penetrating runs and he gave Brazil the lead after half an hour with a soaring leap and header. Hitchens quickly equalised but Garrincha finished England off in the second half with a thunderous free-kick. The ball bounced off Ron Springett's chest and fell to Vava, who tucked away the easiest of chances. Six minutes later Garrincha hit a wicked, swerving long-range shot and Springett, whose eyesight was thought to be suspect, was completely wrong-footed.

Chile, Brazil's next opponents, were involved in one of the most disgraceful games ever seen at a World Cup finals. Their first round match with Italy was dubbed the "Battle of Santiago" after 90 minutes of brawling that the English referee Ken Aston could do little to prevent. He described the match as "uncontrollable". The tension was created by Italy's habit of poaching South American players and two intemperate articles written by Italian journalists claiming that Chile was a dreadful country.

Right from the kick-off the players were at each others' throats. Aston did not see the worst incident, which took place behind his back, but television viewers saw Leonel Sanchez, the son of a professional boxer, break Humberto Maschio's nose with a left hook. Amazingly neither linesman drew Aston's attention to what had happened.

Giorgio Ferrini, who seemed to be conducting a private war with Sanchez, was sent off for kicking Landa but refused to go. The match was stopped for 10 minutes, Italian officials were summoned on to the pitch, and Ferrini was finally marched away by a group of policemen. Then Mario David was dismissed for trying to kick Sanchez in the head and Italy, reduced to nine men, lost 2-0. Ferrini was banned for one match but, amazingly, David and Sanchez were let off by Fifa, who merely gave them "severe admonishment". The managers of all 16 countries were called to a meeting by the organising committee and warned about their teams' conduct.

After their victory over the Soviet Union, Chile were brought down to earth by Brazil in the semi-final. The Brazilians, with Garrincha rampant once again, played as if they were in a different class. Garrincha and Vava both bagged a pair as Chile were swept aside 4-2. Garrincha was sent off for retaliation late in the match, and was struck by a bottle thrown from the crowd as he left. Brazil feared that he would not be eligible for the final, but he was not suspended because he had been badly provoked throughout the match.

Brazil's opponents in the final, Czechoslovakia, had surprised

White Pele: Amarildo successfully stepped into the injured star's boots

everybody, including themselves, by progressing so far. That they did was due to the sublime goalkeeping of Wilhelm Schroiff. As Yashin waned, Schroiff waxed. His saves against the more fancied Hungary (in the quarter-final) and Yugoslavia (in the semi-final) were the stuff of legend. It seemed as if he was unbeatable no matter what was thrown at him. Schroiff's virtuosity was as vital to Czechoslovakia as was Garrincha's to Brazil. The Czechs were slow, precise and defensive minded, although in Josef Masopust they possessed a very inventive and cunning left-half.

Unfortunately for Czechoslova-kia and Schroiff, his form inexplica-bly deserted him in the final. The Czechs had taken a shock lead in the 16th minute when Masopust bisected the Brazilian defence and calmly slotted the ball home. But within two minutes Amarildo out-foxed Schroiff for the equaliser. As he cut in from the left, Schroiff guarded the near post only to watch helplessly as Amarildo's shot sailed in at the other end of the goal. In the second half Zito headed Amar-ildo's stunning cross into an open goal and Schroiff dropped Djalma Santos's lob into the path of the onrushing Vava for the brave Czechs to go down 3-1.

First blood: Chile strike first in the Battle of Santiago

Oops: Schroiff's gaffe allowed Vava to score Brazil's third goal

Twice winners: Brazil came from behind to retain the Jules Rimet trophy

FOR THE RECORD

FIRST ROUND

GROUP 1	P	W	D	L	F	A	Pts
Soviet Union	3	2	1	0	8	5	5
Yugoslavia	3	2	0	1	8	3	4
Uruguay	3	1	0	2	4	6	2
Colombia	3	0	1	2	5	11	1

GROUP 2	P	W	D	L	F	A	Pts
W. Germany	3	2	1	0	4	1	5
Chile	3	2	0	1	5	3	4
Italy	3	1	1	1	3	2	3
Switzerland	3	0	0	3	2	8	0

GROUP 3	P	W	D	L	F	A	Pts
Brazil	3	2	1	0	4	1	5
Czech	3	1	1	1	2	3	3
Mexico	3	1	0	2	3	4	2
Spain	3	1	0	2	2	3	2

GROUP 4	P	W	D	L	F	A	Pts
Hungary	3	2	1	0	8	2	5
England	3	1	1	1	4	3	3
Argentina	3	1	1	1	2	3	3
Bulgaria	3	0	1	2	1	7	1

QUARTER-FINALS

Chile 2   Soviet Union 1
HT 2-1 Att. 17,268

Yugoslavia 1   West Germany 0
HT 0-0 Att. 63,264

Brazil 3   England 1
HT 1-1 Att. 17,736

Czechoslovakia 1   Hungary 0
HT 1-0 Att. 11,690

SEMI-FINALS

Brazil 4   Chile 2
HT 2-1 Att. 76,594

Czechoslovakia 3   Yugoslavia 1
HT 0-0 Att. 5,890

THIRD PLACE PLAY-OFF

Chile 1   Yugoslavia 0
HT 0-0 Att. 66,697

FINAL

Brazil 3   Czochoslovakia 1
HT 1-1 Att. 68,679

Teams
Brazil Gilmar; D Santos, Oliveira, Zozimo, N Santos, Zito, Didi, Garrincha, Vava, Amarildo, Zagalo
Czechoslovakia Schroiff; Tichy, Pluskal, Popluhar, Novak, Kvasnak, Masopust, Popsichal, Scherer, Kadraba, Jelinek

Leading goalscorers 4 Valentin Ivanov (Soviet Union), Leonel Sanchez (Chile), Garrincha (Brazil), Vava (Brazil), Florian Albert (Hungary), Drazan Jerkovic (Yugoslavia); 3 Amarildo Tavares de Silveira (Brazil), Adolf Scherer (Czechoslovakia), Lajos Tichy (Hungary), Milan Galic (Yugoslavia)
Total goals scored 89
Average per game: 2.78
Sendings-off Vladimir Popovic (Yugoslavia) v Uruguay; Ruben Cabrera (Uruguay) v Yugoslavia; Referee: Karol Galba (Czechoslovakia). Giorgio Ferrini (Italy) v Chile; Mario David (Italy) v Chile; Referee: Ken Aston (England). Garrincha (Brazil) v Chile; Honorino Landa (Chile) v Brazil; Referee: Arturo Maldonado Yamasaki (Peru).
Number of players used by finalists
12 Brazil; 15 Czechoslovakia

● Four players have appeared for two nations in the World Cup final stages: Jose Altafini (then known as Mazzola) for Brazil in 1958 and Italy in 1962; Luis Monti Argentina 1930 and Italy 1962; Ferenc Puskas Hungary 1954 and Spain 1962; and Jose Santamaria Uruguay 1954 and Spain 1962.
● Vaclav Masek's goal for Czechoslovakia against Mexico was scored in 15 seconds, the fastest ever at the World Cup finals. However, his team lost the first round match 3-1 but still went on to the final.

Ramsey vows: 'England will win the World Cup in 1966'

Genius Baxter and Rangers unstoppable

WITH Jim Baxter at his mercurial best, slicing defences open from midfield, the Rangers forwards were able to enjoy a field day. Ralph Brand, Jimmy Millar and Davie Wilson scored 105 goals between them, with the partnership of Millar and Brand doing most of the damage.

"We were just right for each other," Millar said. "Ralph was ahead of his time — always wanting to try out something new."

Millar was plagued by a bad back, and many people thought he was too small to play at centre-forward. But his timing was so good that he had no difficulty in out-jumping defenders and heading the ball on to Brand, who was no giant either.

Millar said that the Rangers team was "just about unbeatable in Scotland". There was no disputing his assessment as Rangers raced away with the League title, only losing two matches. Rangers finished nine points clear of Kilmarnock, and Millar was the division's leading scorer with 27 goals.

The Millar and Butler double act, known throughout Scotland as "a dose of M&B", was also the undoing Celtic in the Scottish Cup final replay.

Baxter, who took even more delight in running rings round Celtic than he did in tormenting other teams, produced a sublime display of skills.

Celtic were so bedazzled that Miller and Brand had no difficulty in applying the coup de grace — Brand scoring two goals and Millar one as Rangers collected the trophy for the third time in four years.

Three wise men: Ramsey with Denis Follows and Joe Richards at an FA committee meeting

THE FA and England entered a new era when Alf Ramsey was appointed to replace Walter Winterbottom as the manager of the national side. It was a critical appointment as England were the hosts for the 1966 World Cup and a repeat of their moderate performances in the previous four tournaments would be a public embarrassment. The post would now be full-time and Ramsey would decide all team selections. Under Winterbottom the team had been selected by an FA committee.

Ramsey had not been the obvious, or even first, choice. At Winterbottom's suggestion Jimmy Adamson, the Burnley manager, was offered the job but declined because he was reluctant to move South. Strangely the FA then turned to Ramsey rather than club managers with a more sustained run of success such as Bill Nicholson, of Spurs, or Stan Cullis, of Wolves. Ramsey was, after all, nothing more than a one-hit wonder and his championship-winning Ipswich were struggling to survive in the First Division.

Ramsey's first match in charge was an abject failure and England were eliminated from the European Nations Cup in the first round. In Paris in February England went 3-0 down to France, rallied with goals from Bobby Smith and Bobby Tampling but eventually succumbed 5-2, the first time England had conceded five goals for five years.

Ramsey's next two matches, against Scotland and Brazil, were little better but then, suddenly in the summer his team caught fire. Czechoslovakia were beaten 4-2 in Bratislava, East Germany 2-1 in Leipzig and Switzerland hammered 8-1 in Basle, Bobby Charlton scoring a hat-trick.

The press were effusive in their praise of the new regime and even Ramsey, normally dour, uncommunicative and deeply cautious, got carried away. "England will win the World Cup in 1966," he said. "We have the ability, strength, character and players with the right temperament." Brave words.

Winterbottom: replaced

Pools companies use experts to make up results and beat freeze

THE BIG FREEZE that gripped the country played havoc with football for months and forced the season to be extended by several weeks. On January 5, only three of 32 FA Cup third round matches and a handful of League games could be played. The following week was even worse, and only eight matches were played on January 19.

Clubs tried everything to beat the freeze – Blackpool used a flame-thrower on their ground and Leicester put a tent over their pitch – but to no avail. Nearly half of the Cup matches were postponed at least 10 times, and Lincoln only played Coventry at the 16th attempt.

The pools companies were forced to declare three successive coupons void, with the money carried forward to make the jackpot ever larger. Then, to keep the interest going, they hit on the idea of using a panel of experts to forecast the results. Four former players, Ted

Five wise men: the panel picked seven draws

Drake, Tom Finney. Tommy Lawton and George Young, and a former referee, Arthur Ellis, chose seven draws, eight away wins and 23 homes on January 26.

The results were announced on television and, not surprisingly, some punters who did not agree with the selections called

the process a farce. But the pools panel was here to stay.

The bad weather dragged on into February when, on the 9th, only seven out of 64 matches were played, a record low. The worst hit club of the lot, though, was Bolton who went a record time without a match, from December 8 to February 16.

Dundee and Dunfermline come through their European baptism of fire in a blaze of glory

DUNDEE and Dunfermline, two of Scotland's less fashionable clubs, made successful forays into European competition. Indeed, the progress of both clubs was only halted when they were up against the eventual winners of their respective competitions.

In the European Cup, Dundee, the surprise champions of Scotland the season before, majestically reached the semi-finals, even sweeping away Anderlecht 4-1 in Belgium. But, as Ipswich had discovered in the second round, AC Milan were virtually unstoppable in their San Siro stadium.

Dundee's European hopes went crashing as they were trounced 5-1 in the first leg with four of Milan's goals coming in the second half. Dundee's lame excuse was that their goalkeeper, Bert Slater, had been unable to see the crosses from

Milan's sprightly wingers because he was dazzled by the flash bulbs of the photographers. In the return leg at Dens Park, Alan Gilzean scored the only goal of the game and then managed to get himself sent off for retaliation.

Milan went on to win the European Cup beating Benfica, the holders, at Wembley despite conceding a 19th minute goal to Eusebio. Two goals from Altafini in the second half were sufficient to give Italy its first European Cup.

In the Fairs Cup, Dunfermline drew Everton, who went on to win the League title, in the first round and a canny, tactical performance from Jock Stein's team at Goodison left Everton with only a slender 1-0 lead to defend in the second leg. A bravura performance in Scotland saw Dunfermline conquer Everton 2-0. It seemed that

Stein had grasped the knack of European competition.

Then Dunfermline faced Valencia, who had disposed of Celtic in the first round, and were shredded 4-0 in Spain. Somehow Stein inspired his players to reach unbelievable heights and at East End Park Valencia incredibly lost 6-2 to leave the tie level at 6-6. However in the replay, in Portugal, Valencia just managed to scrape a 1-0 victory.

The Spanish club then crushed Hibs in the quarter final and waltzed off with the trophy, even winning both legs of the final against Dynamo Zagreb. So there was some consolation for Stein: Dunfermline had been the only side to interrupt Valencia's steady progress to the Fairs Cup and two other Scottish clubs had proved to be mere cannon fodder for the Spaniards.

Eusebio: first blood

Matthews the miracle worker

STANLEY MATTHEWS chose the perfect moment to score his first goal of the season for Stoke. They were leading 1-0 at home to Luton in their last match of the season, and Matthews's goal made sure of victory and the Second Division championship.

Although Matthews took a long time to get on the scoresheet he was a vital member of Stoke's side. Even though he was 48, he played in 35 League matches and his stylish performances created countless goals for the rest of the team.

Stoke's return to the First Division after a decade was a close thing, with Chelsea and Sunderland also vying for the two promotion places. The issue was not settled until the final matches of the season. When Stoke beat Chelsea in their penultimate match it appeared that they had done Sunderland a favour.

But Chelsea went to Sunderland and won 1-0, which left them needing to win their last match to overtake Sunderland on goal average. Chelsea made absolutely sure of promotion by thumping Portsmouth 7-0, their biggest win since the 1910-11 season.

Matthews: vital goal

Blanchflower talks Dyson into playing the game of his life

TOTTENHAM'S record-breaking start to the 1960s continued in Rotterdam on May 15 when they imperiously dismissed Atletico Madrid 5-1 to capture the European Cup Winners Cup and become the first British team to win a European trophy. It was a magnificent achievement. Atletico, the runners-up in the Spanish League, were the holders and Spurs were without their midfield dynamo Dave Mackay, who was unable to play because of a severe stomach upset.

Even Danny Blanchflower, their inspirational captain, was only partially fit and only played with the aid of a pain-killing injection. In a previous round against Rangers, Blanchflower had been sandwiched by two defenders seriously damaging his knee. The injury kept him out for 22 matches and he effectively had to play on one leg in Rotterdam. However, his influence on the field proved decisive, as did his dressing-room speech before the match.

The loss of Mackay seemed to have unnerved Bill Nicholson, the Spurs manager, and instead of a rabble-rousing team talk he spoke only of the quality of the opposition. After Nicholson had left Blanchflower took centre-stage and went through the Spurs team player by player. He convinced them that they were all world beaters, especially Terry Dyson, a winger not noted for his match-winning abilities.

Spurs had taken a 2-0 half-

Blanchflower's triumph: the first European trophy for a British club

time lead with goals from Jimmy Greaves and John White, but two minutes after the restart Ron Henry conceded a penalty and Atletico were back in the match battling for the equaliser. The next 20 minutes were frantic as Spurs desperately fought to preserve their lead. Then, in the 67th minute, out of the blue Dyson turned the match around.

The left winger hit a high cross into the Spanish penalty area that floated close to the keeper. Somehow he misread the flight of the ball and it sailed over his head and into the net. A fluke? Maybe, though Dyson claimed

he had spotted the keeper off his line. Whatever, it galvanised Dyson to play the game of his life.

Thirteen minutes later Dyson crossed for Greaves to add a fourth, and with five minutes left Dyson scored a virtuoso goal, running 30 yards with the ball, outwitting defender after defender, before slamming a 25-yard shot into the goal. It certainly was the perfect game for the diminutive left winger. As Spurs left the field Bobby Smith advised Dyson to retire on the spot. Why? "Because you'll never play a better game," the centre-forward told him.

Everton go shopping and buy championship

DESPITE the weather, Everton cruised to their first League title since the war. But their success was not universally acclaimed. The club were labelled the "cheque book champions" because of the number of players their manager had bought.

Harry Catterick had spent £175,000 on five players last season and he added to his squad during Everton's enforced idle

spell in the depths of the big freeze by buying Tony Kay from Sheffield Wednesday for £60,000 and the Scottish international winger Alex Scott from Rangers for £40,000.

Everton's strength in depth enabled them to see off the challenge of Tottenham, Burnley and Leicester with games to spare. Everton regained the leadership of the First Division

in April when they beat Tottenham, and made sure of the title when they beat Fulham in their last game of the season.

The 4-1 victory meant that Tottenham, who lost to Manchester City that day, could not overhaul them, even though they had two more games to play. Tottenham only collected one point from those matches and finished a distant second.

Busby's swoops turn United around

Match winner: Denis Law (No 10) scored the first goal and sealed United's victory

MANCHESTER UNITED were a team still in transition after the Munich disaster. With no home-grown talent coming through the ranks Matt Busby was forced to continue buying players to keep his team afloat. Despite spending a small fortune, his team, which had cost close to a third of a million pounds, came very close to sinking into the Second division.

Before the season began Busby decided that he needed another goalscorer to sharpen his team's attack. He always wanted the best players, regardless of the cost, so he brought Denis Law back from Italy for £115,000. Law had walked out on Torino during an Italian Cup match when the team's coach forbade him from taking a corner.

After Law arrived at Old Trafford Busby decided that his forward was not getting enough chances created for him. So Busby plunged into the transfer market again to buy Pat Crerand from Celtic.

Despite the signings, United struggled terribly in the League. Their final match of the season, at Maine Road, would decide whether they, or Manchester City, were relegated. City

Match winner: Law's goal put Manchester United in the final

needed to win while a draw would suffice for United.

City led 1-0 in the second half until Law was brought down in the penalty area. Albert Quixall converted the penalty and the match finished 1-1. So, ironically, Law had played a large part in condemning his former club to the Second Division.

While his team had been struggling in the League Busby kept their spirits up by telling them that United were going to win the FA Cup. Because of fixture congestion United had to play three matches in 15 days.

Home wins against Huddersfield, Aston Villa and Chelsea took United to the quarter-finals.

United eased into the final by beating Third Division Coventry and Second Division Southampton. Their opponents at Wembley, Leicester, were the favourites because they had displayed much more consistent form in the League.

United had an early scare when their captain Noel Cantwell nearly headed a harmless cross into his own goal, but from that point on Law started to

repay a large slice of his record transfer fee.

Law produced a virtuoso performance. He scored the first goal after half an hour and his incessant attacking unsettled the Leicester defence enough for David Herd to add two more in the second half. The 3-1 victory was an emotional moment for Busby, who saw his team collect their first trophy since their blackest hour in 1958.

121

Gentleman Jim a gent to end

Ten players in betting coup

FOOTBALL was rocked to its foundations on the morning of Sunday April 12 when a newspaper revealed that three Sheffield Wednesday players, two of them England internationals had fixed a match to stage a betting coup.

The People revealed that Peter Swan, the England centre-half, Tony Kay, who had also played for England after being transferred to Everton, and David Layne made sure Sheffield Wednesday were beaten 2-0 by Ipswich in December 1962. Each of them won £100 by betting on their team to lose.

Rumours had abounded for some time about matches being fixed, and the disclosures were just the tip of the iceberg. Jimmy Gauld, the former Everton and Charlton forward who was at the heart of the bribery scandal, revealed that two other matches, between Lincoln and Brentford in the Third Division and York and Oldham in the Fourth Division, had been fixed on the same day.

Within weeks, the number of players implicated in the affair had more than trebled. Dick Beattie, who had played in goal for the Scottish Under-23 and Scottish League teams, was accused of being involved as were Walter Bingley (Halifax), Jackie Fountain (York), Harry Harris (Portsmouth), Ron Howells (Walsall), Bert Linnecor (Lincoln) and Peter Wraggs (Bradford).

The League suspended most of the players for life and 10 of them were convicted at Nottingham Assizes on January 26, 1965. Gauld received the heaviest sentence, four years in jail plus £5,000 costs. The other nine were also jailed for between four and 15 months.

Swan: bet on his team to lose

Little Luxembourg rock European big shots

JIMMY DICKINSON finally retired at the age of 39, having made a record 764 League appearances for Portsmouth, his only club.

Dickinson was recruited during the war and turned professional while he was still serving in the Royal Navy. He was a key member of the team that won the championship in the 1948-49 season, Portsmouth's golden jubilee year, and retained it the following year.

Dickinson's cultured play for an unfashionable club brought him recognition by England, and he made 48 appearances at left-half for his country over nine years. He only lost his place in the national side after the emergence of Duncan Edwards and Portsmouth switched him to centre-half.

The finest achievement in Dickinson's career was to never fall foul of authority. In a career that spanned almost 20 years he was never spoken to by a referee, let alone booked, earning him the distinction of being known as "Gentleman Jim".

THE Grand Duchy of Luxembourg (population 300,000) pulled off one of the greatest feats of giant-killing when they astounded Holland (population 12m) by knocking them out of the European championships in October. And it was no fluke – both legs were in Holland.

Normally Holland would field only a 'B' team against Luxembourg, but because of the importance of the tie they put out a full-strength side for the first game in Amsterdam in September. Everything seemed to be going to plan when Nuninga put Holland ahead after five minutes. However the expected flurry of goals never materialised and May levelled the scores in the 35th minute. Despite constant Dutch pressure there were no more goals.

In the second leg, in Rotterdam, the Dutch made wholesale changes bringing in the bulk of the Feyenoord side to avoid any further embarrassment. But to no avail. Dimmer gave Luxembourg the lead in the 20th minute, Kruiver equalised 10 minutes before half-time, and the Dutch play became frantic.

The Luxembourg goal was under constant barrage but it seemed that nothing could get past Nico Schmitt, the Duchy's goalkeeper. Dimmer provided the coup de grace with his second goal to put his country into a quarter-final tie against Denmark (population 4.7m).

Surely Luxembourg couldn't do it again? This time they played the first leg at home and, in the very first minute, Pilot shot them into the lead. Denmark, fearful of making the same mistake as Holland, piled on the pressure. The match see-sawed back and forth to end 3-3, with Ole Madsen getting a hat-trick for Denmark.

If Denmark thought the second leg was going to be a doddle, Luxembourg soon shook them out of their complacency when Leonard gave them an early lead. Madsen, though, rose to the occasion, to equalise and then score again. But still Luxembourg would not lie down and Schmidt took the tie into a third match with an equaliser six minutes from time.

Sadly for Luxembourg the bubble burst in the play-off in December in Amsterdam when Madsen scored his sixth goal against the Grand Duchy a minute before half-time. It was the only score of the match and the heroics of the Luxembourg national side were over.

But meanwhile Jeunesse Esch, their League champions, were upsetting the odds in the European Cup. In the first round the eight-times champions came back from a 4-1 defeat in Finland by Valkeakosken to register a thrilling 4-0 home victory that put them through to the second round – the first and only time a Luxembourg club had progressed that far.

They did not disgrace themselves either, astonishingly beating Partisan Belgrade 2-1 at home before losing 6-2 in Yugoslavia (population 18,500,000). To tiny Luxembourg it was their annus mirabilis: the year they tweaked the noses of the European big boys.

Heart and soul ripped out of Spurs

SADLY, Tottenham's fabulous Double side was disintegrating in front of Bill Nicholson's eyes. Terry Medwin, 30, had been injured on their summer tour to South Africa and missed the entire season. Nicholson also lost Dave Mackay, 29, in December when a broken leg kept him out for the rest of the season. Then Danny Blanchflower, 37, whose damaged knee had never fully recovered from the injury he had picked up against Rangers the previous season, announced his retirement. Bobby Smith, 31, was transferred to Brighton in May.

But the saddest blow of all came in July when John White, 27, was killed by lightning on a golf course while sheltering from a thunderstorm under a tree. Suddenly Spurs were deprived of one of the greatest midfield line-ups to grace an English pitch: Mackay, Blanchflower and White.

Blanchflower, whom Nicholson had inherited when he became the Spurs manager in October 1958, had joined the club in 1954, a £30,000 signing from Aston Villa. Mackay had been Nicholson's first major signing for the club when he snapped up the captain of Hearts and Scotland for £32,000 in March 1959. White followed in November of the same year, bought from Falkirk for £20,000. They were three of the most astute purchases Tottenham ever made.

As a threesome they could hardly be more different. Yet on the field they complemented each other wonderfully. Blanchflower was the most cultured, cerebral and elegant wing-half of the era. Mackay was tigerish, in the tackle and in the flesh. Nicholson called him the heartbeat of the team.

White, although slight in his frame, had been a cross-country champion and was a strong runner who had a knack of finding defence-splitting passes and also possessed a venomous shot. His ability to appear from nowhere earned him the nickname of "The Ghost".

It was surely the magic in midfield that these three players conjured up that was the key to Tottenham's winning the "impossible' Double in 1960-61. They were all irreplaceable.

Mackay: always the boss on the field for Tottenham

White: the ghost

When Bill Nicholson started to talk about identifying John White's body he broke down and had to go into the toilet. He never broke down like that

DAVE MACKAY
on how Nicholson broke the news of White's death to the Spurs players

United win the domestic battle but then lose the European war

TOTTENHAM'S defence of the European Cup Winners Cup did not last very long. After a bye in the first round, they were drawn against Manchester United in the second. Spurs won 2-0 at White Hart Lane on December 3 with goals from Dave Mackay and Terry Dyson. A week later they travelled to Old Trafford and walked into a double disaster.

Bobby Smith seemed to have got Tottenham off to the perfect start when he connected with Mackay's cross, but his header went directly to the keeper. Then Tottenham's night turned to dust. In the sixth minute David Herd met David Sadler's cross with a diving header to reduce the aggregate arrears. Seconds later, the heart was ripped out of Tottenham in the 20th minute when Mackay was carried off to hospital with a broken leg after a clash with Noel Cantwell. Mackay was out for the rest of the season.

Tottenham, with only 10 men, battled on and somehow managed to prevent United scoring again the first half. However, Herd scored a second early in the second half to level the scores. But still the Cup-holders refused to give in and a minute later they suddenly found themselves in the lead when Jimmy Greaves headed home a John White cross.

The fairytale ending was not to be. Bobby Charlton volleyed home the equaliser in the 78th minute and, with two minutes on the clock, he found the net again to knock Spurs out of Europe, and put his team into the quarter finals. There United met Sporting Club of Portugal, the eventual winners, who thrashed them 5-0 in Portugal and went through 6-4.

Capital's clubs turn the tide		
From 1900 to 1960, the FA Cup was only won six times by clubs from London. But then the balance tipped firmly back in their favour.		
Winners		
1961 Tottenham	1970 Chelsea	1980 West Ham
1962 Tottenham	1971 Arsenal	1981 Tottenham
1964 West Ham	1975 West Ham	1982 Tottenham
1967 Tottenham	1979 Arsenal	

"I have never been as nervy during a match – even after I scored the first equaliser"

JOHN SISSONS

Sneaky Boyce breaks Preston's heart

ON PAPER, the Cup final was going to be one-sided. On the pitch it was anything but.

West Ham had reached Wembley the hard way, beating two other First Division teams, Burnley and Manchester United, in the quarter-finals and semi-finals. Second Division Preston North End, meanwhile, had beaten Fourth Division Oxford and Second Division Swansea.

The underdogs, though, took the lead after 10 minutes when Jim Standen could only parry Alec Dawson's shot and Doug Holden followed up. West Ham equalised within a minute with a goal from the 18-year-old John Sissons, who made a fine solo run past two defenders.

Preston played the far better football in the first half and Howard Kendall, the youngest player to appear in a Cup final, (aged 17 years and 345 days) dominated midfield. Deservedly, Preston regained the lead five minutes before the interval. Standen slipped as he came out for a corner and Dawson was left unmarked for an easy header.

Bobby Moore, the Footballer of the Year, had been so ineffectual that Ron Greenwood, the West Ham manager, was forced to change his tactics to counter the threat posed by Kendall and Nobby Lawton. Their distribution was inch-perfect while West Ham's moves were breaking down too often as passes went astray.

West Ham began to get a grip on the midfield after the interval and Geoff Hurst just managed to score another equaliser.

His header hit the bar and Alan Kelly, the Preston goalkeeper, managed to get a hand to the rebound. The ball dropped behind Kelly and as he turned it trickled, agonisingly slowly, over the line.

There was further agony for Preston two minutes into injury time. Hurst made one last surging run and slipped the ball to Peter Brabrook. His cross sailed over the defence and Ron Boyce sneaked in unmarked on the blind side to head the winner.

It was a heartbreaking finish for Preston whose cultured play made a mockery of their underdogs label. Their contribution to the match had been so great, that the game was hailed by the press as being almost as exciting as the famous Matthews Cup final.

Moment of joy: Boyce scores the winning goal in the dying seconds

Rangers' greatest team rewarded with the Treble

THE TREBLE in Scotland (League, Scottish Cup and Scottish League Cup) was seen as an accomplishment as difficult as the Double in England. And since the inception of the Scottish League Cup in 1946-47 only one club had achieved it, Rangers in 1949. Then, gloriously, they did it again, with one of the greatest Ibrox teams ever to pull on the famous blue jerseys.

In Jimmy Millar, Ralph Brand and, occasionally Jim Forrest (who scored four goals in the Scottish League Cup final) they had a strike force second to none. To bolster their attack, Rangers also had Willie Henderson and Davie Wilson as marauding wingers. The midfield was also incomparable with the elegant Jim Baxter and his perfect foil, Ian McMillan. And all this in front of an unflappable defence composed of Bobby Shearer, David Provan, John Greig and Ron McKinnon. Little wonder that Scot Symon's team swept all before them.

Rangers demolished Morton 5-0 in the Scottish League Cup final, won the League in a canter, six points clear of Kilmarnock, and then Millar and Brand scored two goals in the last minute to win the Scottish Cup final against Dundee.

South Americans frighten Ramsey

Pick of the crop: di Stefano, Law and Lev Yashin turned out against England

ALF RAMSEY'S glorious summer extended into winter and then spring as England continued to rack up impressive victories. Wales were dispatched 4-0 in Cardiff, the Rest of the World – a team including fabulous players such as Alfredo di Stefano, Ferenc Puskas, Eusebio, Denis Law and Jim Baxter – 2-1 at Wembley, and then Northern Ireland were thrashed 8-3 with Jimmy Greaves scoring four times and Terry Paine helping himself to a hattrick.

There was a minor hiccup in Glasgow when Ramsey dropped Greaves for Roger Hunt and England lost 1-0 to Scotland, but once Greaves was restored to the side the victories continued. By the time England faced Brazil in Rio de Janeiro on May 30 in the four-country "Little World Cup" they had beaten Uruguay (2-1), Portugal (4-3 in Lisbon), the Republic of Ireland (3-1 in Dublin) and the USA (10-0 in New York). Confidence was sky high.

The Brazilians shattered England's aura of invincibility with scintillating football. England were outclassed in every department as Pele tore Ramsey's carefully selected side to shreds. The 5-1 scoreline could easily have been more. Shell-shocked, Ramsey dropped five players for the match against Portugal five days later in Sao Paulo and scraped a 1-1 draw.

If the Brazil match had shaken Ramsey's self-belief, then Brazil's subsequent 3-0 defeat at the hands of Argentina must have had him reaching for the cyanide. Merciless in their cynical and negative tactics, Argentina nullified Pele and reduced the apparently brilliant Brazilians to non-entities. England fared a little better when they met Argentina in Rio, only losing 1-0, but Ramsey's South American experience was a devastating blow to England's hopes for the World Cup in two years' time.

Shankly's silver tongue licks Liverpool into shape

BILL SHANKLY had played a canny game last season. He had used Liverpool's first year back at the top to convince his players that they were every bit as good as anybody else in the Division. "He's past it," Shankly would say. "He's nursing an injury. He's over-rated."

His players listened and learnt. Then they went out and put the lessons into practice. After an indifferent start, Liverpool took the First Division by the scruff of the neck. They beat Everton, the champions, 2-1 at Anfield in the tenth game of the season and never looked back.

The crowds flocked to Anfield to see teams taken apart. Ipswich were hit for six, as were Sheffield United, Stoke and Wolves. Aston Villa and Arsenal fared little better, both conceding five goals.

Roger Hunt was the club's leading scorer with 31 goals, many of which were created from the left wing by Peter Thompson, signed from Preston in August for a club record £40,000. Liverpool's strike rate was prodigious, particularly at home where they scored 60 goals.

Three straight wins over Easter virtually guaranteed Liverpool the title, which they won by four points from Manchester United. The Anfield faithful, who had started to doubt Shankly's ability in the Second Division were utterly convinced – Liverpool's average crowd for home games was only just short of 50,000.

Shankly: wise words

Thompson: shrewd purchase

TOTTENHAM IN THE 1960s
And the Spurs went marching on

Nick Pitt

THE GREAT teams have a life beyond their days on the field. Their innovations become the norm. The cheers that greeted them echo down the years. Their achievements inspire generations unborn.

But their legacy can also be curiously negative, and none has made life more difficult for their successors than the team that has come to be known as the Spurs Double team.

Since the early 1960s, when that team reigned supreme, there have been several worthy, even brilliant, Tottenham teams, many trophies won and a host of great individual players, including Osvaldo Ardiles and Glenn Hoddle. But each team has found itself compared to the Double team and has inevitably been found wanting.

At the time, the Double of the League and the FA Cup was a kind of holy grail. It had not been achieved in the 20th century, and although both Wolverhampton Wanderers and Manchester United had narrowly missed out on it in the late 1950s, many believed the Double to be impossible in modern times.

The man who built the Double team was Bill Nicholson. He had been a solid wing-half for Spurs, and had won one England cap. In October 1958 he was promoted from coach and assistant manager to manager. Nicholson was a dour, practical Yorkshireman, but he built a team in

the best Tottenham traditions of stylish, attacking football. He was fortunate that several of the components of the team were already in place when his appointment was celebrated with a remarkable 10-4 win against Everton.

Already present were Bobby Smith, the burly, fearless centre-forward with a ferocious shot and surprising touch; Maurice Norman, a rock at centre-half; Cliff Jones, the brilliant Welsh winger noted for his greyhound speed and flying headers (though he had not yet been accepted by the ever-critical Spurs fans); and Danny Blanchflower, that most cultivated and original of winghalves and, importantly, perhaps the greatest of all penalty-takers.

Nicholson entered the transfer market, and secured a series of bargains. From Hearts he bought the lion-hearted Dave Mackay; from Dundee the invariably secure goalkeeper Bill Brown; from Falkirk he bought the gifted John White, whose ability to create chances through stealth led him to be called The Ghost.

Rarely has a team achieved such balance. There was a spine of three uncompromisingly tough players: Smith, Mackay, Norman. There were two players with remarkable creative gifts: Blanchflower and White. The right flank was as strong as the left. The defence, typified by the full-backs, Peter Baker and Ron Henry, was

strong but not showy; the attack scintillating.

It is hard to be sure exactly why a certain collection of individuals should function as a team, while another might not. But Spurs gloriously achieved the collective ideal, thanks to the team's balance and the influence of Blanchflower on the field and Nicholson off it. "I tried to keep our football as simple as possible," Nicholson recalled in the club's official history. "We had good players [a typical Nicholson understatement] but I didn't want them to indulge themselves too much as individuals. I used to tell them they had to be effective, not exhibition players."

In the summer of 1958 Blanchflower returned from playing for Northern Ireland in the World Cup, convinced that Spurs had a team that could achieve the elusive Double. In the 1959-60 League season Tottenham might have won but came third. In the Cup they had a remarkable tie against Crewe Alexandra, drawing 2-2 away before winning the replay 13-2. That match gave some idea of the attacking force Spurs would become. They led Crewe 10-1 at half-time and coasted the second half. But in the next round they were knocked out by Blackburn Rovers.

The following season, 1960-61, Spurs swept all before them. They opened their League campaign with a record: 11 consecutive victories, 36 goals for and 11 against. Such a run could not last forever. Spurs were held in their 12th game by Manchester City and were to lose seven times in their 42-match campaign. But their superiority to every other club was obvious and they won the championship by eight points from Sheffield Wednesday.

In the FA Cup, Tottenham defeated Charlton, Crewe, Aston Villa, Sunderland and Burnley to reach the final against Leicester. They were expected to win in style, but the final was a disappointment. Two late goals enabled Blanchflower, who 48 hours before had received the Footballer of the Year award, to climb the stairs of the Royal Box to claim the trophy and to fulfil the promise he had made to the Spurs chairman at the start of the season: the League and Cup double. The glory days, and nights, were just beginning. The following season Jimmy Greaves, English football's greatest goalscorer, was bought from AC Milan for £99,999. His impact was immediate, not least in the Cup, which was retained with a 3-1 win against Burnley, Greaves scoring in the third minute.

But it was in the European arena that the Spurs Double side was to find its finest expression. European ties on Wednesday nights at White Hart Lane under the floodlights, with the

The Spurs go marching on: the team celebrates retaining the FA Cup in 1962

THE NICHOLSON YEARS

Born July 26, 1919, Scarborough

PLAYING CAREER

Tottenham 1936-55

He signed professional forms at 18 and made his League debut in 1938 as a full-back. After the war he became Tottenham's first choice centre-half, and moved to right-half in 1947, where he was an essential part of the team that won the League championship in 1951

Internationals One England cap v Portugal May 19, 1951

One goal (scored with his first touch after 19 seconds)

COACHING AND MANAGEMENT CAREER

First team coach 1955-58

Manager 1958-74

Honours European Cup: Semi-final 1962

European Cup Winners Cup: Winners 1963; Semi-final 1968; First round 1964

Uefa Cup: Winners 1972; Runners-up 1974; Semi-final 1973

League Championship: Winners 1961; Runners-up 1963; Third 1960, 1962, 1967, 1971; Fourth 1964

FA Cup: Winners 1961, 1962, 1967

League Cup: Winners 1971, 1973; Semi-final 1969, 1972

Other honours PFA Merit Award 1984

Hot shot: Greaves's arrival from AC Milan increased Tottenham's already formidable firepower

crowd singing "Glory, Glory, Hallelujah, the Spurs go marching on", became legendary. There always seemed a deficit to make up, and Spurs always seemed to make it up in style.

In their first European Cup match, against Gornik, the Polish champions, Tottenham trailed 4-2 after the first leg, but won 8-1 at home. Against Dukla Prague, the Czech champions, Spurs lost 1-0 away and won the second leg 4-2.

In the semi-final they faced Benfica of Portugal, having lost the first leg 3-1 with two goals disallowed. Benfica scored first but Tottenham attacked relentlessly, pulling back with a goal by Smith and a penalty by Blanchflower four min-

utes after the interval. The final 40 minutes were frenzied. Spurs hit the woodwork three times but could not score the vital goal.

There was real consolation the following season, when Spurs won the European Cup Winners' Cup to become the first English team to win a European competition. On the way to the final they had lost their first-leg match against Slovan Bratislava 2-0 but won the second leg 6-0. In the final they defeated Atletico Madrid 5-1, belatedly proving themselves as good as any team in Europe in the early 1960s.

That was the Double team's glorious signing-off. Within a year the team's heart, its midfield,

had been destroyed. Blanchflower, who had been suffering from injury, retired; White, a quiet player but considered by many to be the finest of them all, was killed by lightning while sheltering on a golf course; Mackay broke a leg in a match at Old Trafford.

Greaves and the others remained, soon to be joined by the wonderful Alan Gilzean. Over the next 30 years and more, Spurs would win many more cups, but never the League championship. And never again could they consistently achieve the sublime combination of breathtaking attack and certain defence that characterised the finest English club of them all.

Keeping it simple: Nicholson and Blanchflower emphasised attacking play

Smith: fearless forward with a fearsome shot

Liverpool gain as Byrne defies pain

Using his head: Ian St John's flying header past Gary Sprake in extra time crushes Leeds

Heartbreak for Leeds as United sneak home

FOR only the fourth time the League championship was decided on goal average, Manchester United pipping Leeds by 0.686 of a goal. Heart-breakingly, Leeds also lost the FA Cup final in extra time. So, by the slenderest of margins, the Double had slipped through their fingers.

Leeds had arrived in the First Division with a reputation as a hard and ruthless team and their performances did nothing to dispel this image. They won their first three League matches and by January were two points clear. By the spring the race was effectively between United and Leeds, who also met in the FA Cup semi-final.

The first match was an ugly goalless confrontation, and the replay, which Leeds won 1-0, was not much better. A fortnight later Manchester exacted their revenge in the League with a 1-0 victory at Elland Road. This result was the beginning of a marvellous run as United won six of their seven League matches after the semi-final. Their 3-1 defeat of Arsenal five days before the Cup final clinched their first title since 1957.

After Leeds lost the Cup final someone asked Bill Shankly, the Liverpool manager, if Don Revie's Leeds had failed. "Failed?" Shankly said. "Second in the championship. Cup finalists. Ninety per cent of managers would pray for 'failures' like that."

Red machine: Liverpool won the FA Cup for the first time after two disappointments

ONE TROPHY had always eluded Liverpool, the FA Cup. They had been to the final twice before and lost on both occasions so against Leeds it was a case of third time lucky.

Liverpool were inspired by display of a raw courage by Gerry Byrne, who broke his collarbone after five minutes when he collided with Bobby Collins. With no substitutes allowed, Byrne insisted that he wanted to play on so that Leeds would not gain an advantage. Leeds never knew how badly he was hurt until after the match because, despite the pain, Byrne showed all his usual determination.

The final pitted two of the best defences in the country against each other so it was hardly surprising that the first 90 minutes were dour and goalless.

Byrne even created Liverpool's first goal in extra time. He resisted the temptation to try a shot from a narrow angle, instead slipping the ball across to give Roger Hunt the easiest of chances.

Leeds equalised two minutes later when Billy Bremner crashed a volley into the roof of the net. Liverpool, though, drew strength from Byrne's example. Ian St John glanced a header past Gary Sprake with nine minutes remaining and this time Liverpool were not going to be denied.

Matthews hits a half-century before bowing out a knight

STANLEY MATTHEWS finally retired at the end of the season, bringing to a close a wonderful career that had spanned more than 30 years.

His final game for Stoke was on February 6, when he created one of their goals in the 3-1 victory over Fulham. Matthews had just celebrated his birthday and the match made him the oldest player to appear in the First Division at the age of 50 years and five days.

Matthews had always placed great store by his fitness and he was asked what it was like to play when he was so old. "In my own mind I never had any doubts about my fitness," he said. "Stamina never worried me. I would never have played had I not felt 100 per cent fit."

Many of his greatest adversaries from his days as an England player – Josef Masopust, Ferenc Puskas, Alfredo di Stefano and Lev Yashin – played for an International XI against Stoke in a special benefit match on April 28.

Yashin and Puskas carried him from the pitch on their shoulders in tribute, but by then Matthews had already received an even greater honour. Already a CBE, he was knighted in the New Year's honours list, the first footballer ever to receive this distinction.

> *Stanley Matthews knew exactly when, and where, to go. People could never tackle him, and nobody could touch him for speed over 10 yards. Even when he was nearing 50, he still had his magic*
>
> BOBBY CHARLTON

■ When Jim Standen (above), the West Ham goalkeeper, reported for duty at the start of the season he had just topped the first-class bowling averages. He took 64 wickets for Worcestershire, who won the county championship for the first time.

■ Derek Forster, the Sunderland goalkeeper, was the youngest person to play in the First Division. He faced Leicester in August at the age of 15 years and 185 days.

■ Arthur Rowley, the Shrewsbury player-manager retired in February, having scored a record 434 goals in the League.

■ Gillingham's 1-0 defeat by Exeter on April 10 was the first time they had been beaten at home in 52 matches stretching back to April 1963.

Mackay's second leg injury adds to Spurs' woe

DAVE MACKAY'S and Tottenham's agony knew no bounds. Nine months after the ferocious midfielder broke his leg at Old Trafford in a European Cup-winners' Cup match, the old warhorse returned for his first match, and broke the same left leg again.

Playing for the reserves against Shrewsbury in September at White Hart Lane he suddenly fell to the ground clutching his leg and clearly in severe pain.

It was typical of Mackay's indomitable spirit that his first thoughts were not whether his career was over, but of Bill Nicholson, his beleaguered manager, for whom nothing seemed to be going right.

Nicholson was experiencing major problems re-building his Spurs team as, one by one, the stars of the Double team were fading away. "Don't let Bill Nicholson know," Mackay said to those carrying him off the pitch, "not yet."

Past glories: Mackay's playing career seemed to be over

Sinking Celtic turn to Stein, the man with the Midas touch

JOCK STEIN, who had left Dunfermline to revitalise Hibs a year ago, was lured by ailing Celtic to revive their fortunes in February. Stein's magic touch had transformed Dunfermline and even in the short time Stein had been with Hibs he had turned the club around.

Celtic had not won a major trophy since 1958 – and that was only the Scottish League Cup – and were completely overshadowed by Rangers who had silverware galore in their trophy cabinet. Stein, who had captained Celtic to the Double in 1954, and seemed to have the Midas touch when it came to winning trophies, was regarded as the perfect choice.

Curiously, the Scottish Cup semi-finals pitted Dunfermline against Hibs and Celtic v Motherwell. Celtic reached the final beating Motherwell 3-0, after a replay. Of his two former clubs, Dunfermline prevailed over Hibs 2-0.

In the final Stein's luck held good and Celtic were 3-2 winners at Hampden. Stein the miracle worker had done it again, within three months of taking over at Parkhead he had captured a major trophy.

Limp England a sorry sight

ENGLAND'S torrid time in South America – where they were outclassed by Brazil and out-thought by Argentina – last summer seemed to have cast a cloud over Alf Ramsey's preparations for the World Cup next year. Although England were undefeated in their next nine internationals the opposition was generally modest, and four of the matches were unsatisfactory draws.

Narrow wins over Northern Ireland (4-3 in Belfast), Wales (2-1), Hungary (1-0) and Sweden (2-1 in Gothenburg) interspersed with scrappy draws with Belgium (2-2), Holland (1-1 in Amsterdam), Scotland (2-2) and Yugoslavia (1-1 in Belgrade) was hardly the form of world beaters. The very critics that had heaped such lavish praise on Ramsey a year earlier now claimed that England no longer had a realistic chance of winning the World Cup.

The one bright spot in all this gloom was the match between England and West Germany in Nuremberg in May. The Germans were considered one of the stronger sides in Europe and a Terry Paine goal gave England a much needed fillip as they won 1-0.

Paine: upstaged West Germany

Sheer perfection from Moore

Wembley wizards: West Ham return to collect another Cup

WEST HAM returned to Wembley for the second year running, for the final of the European Cup Winners Cup, and this time they showed none of the hesitation they had suffered in the FA Cup final against Preston last season.

They had made steady, if unspectacular progress in their first campaign in Europe. Most of their matches were won by the odd goal – Ghent were beaten 2-1 on aggregate in the first round, Sparta Prague 3-2 in the second round and Lausanne 6-4 in the quarter-finals.

In the semi-finals West Ham met Real Zaragoza, who had already eliminated Britain's two other representatives in the competition, Dundee in the second round and Cardiff in the quarter-finals. Once again, West Ham prevailed by a single goal, winning 2-1 at Upton Park then drawing 1-1 in Spain.

Bobby Moore, the West Ham captain, knew what had given his team the edge in all the matches – the presence of Martin Peters, who had just established himself in the side. "In Europe you need more skill," Moore said. "And Martin added an extra quality to our game."

West Ham had to reshuffle their team on May 19 because their two experienced forwards Peter Brabrook and Johnny Byrne were both injured. Ron Greenwood was forced to play the untested Alan Sealey, but he need not have worried about the winger's lack of experience.

Munich 1860 tried to match West Ham by playing attacking football themselves, and the entertaining game swung back and forth. Sealey decided the match with two goals in two minutes and Bobby Moore was able to lead his team up the steps once again to collect another trophy.

Moore thought it had been West Ham's best ever team effort. "There was a lot of good

Sealey: double strike

football and we played really well against a good side." Greenwood was much more succinct: "This was Bobby Moore's greatest game. Technical perfection."

Shankly fumes at daylight robbery

BILL SHANKLY was looking forward to pitting his wits against the best continental clubs in the European Cup, but the way that Liverpool were eliminated from the competition left him with a distrust of all things foreign.

Liverpool were only the second English team to reach the semi-finals and they had to face Inter Milan, the holders of the European Cup, days after winning the FA Cup. Their victory at Wembley enabled Shankly to employ a clever piece of gamesmanship.

Hours before the kick-off Anfield was packed solid, and everybody in the ground wanted to see the FA Cup. Shankly waited until Inter had gone out on to the pitch and told his team to wait in the dressing room. He then ordered two of his injured players to slowly parade the FA Cup around the touchline.

When Gerry Byrne and Gordon Milne lapped the ground Anfield erupted. The Inter players had to stand and fret in the middle of the pitch while the Liverpool fans went wild. The ploy worked and, with their nerves stretched to breaking point, Inter lost 3-1.

But Inter Milan's coach, the legendary Helenio Herrera, replayed the compliment in spades. The San Siro was a cauldron for the second leg; Liverpool were greeted by firecrackers, sirens, rockets, smoke bombs and a hail of bottles.

Worse, they were robbed by a series of dubious decisions by the referee. Inter led 3-0 after 20 minutes, but one of the goals appeared to have been scored straight from an indirect free kick. Another was allowed even though Tommy Lawrence, the Liverpool goalkeeper, was charged by an Inter player and had the ball kicked out of his hands.

Liverpool had a goal disallowed, at which point Tommy Smith threatened to punch the referee, and they were beaten 4-3 on aggregate. Shankly told his players that they were still the greatest team in the world. But he also believed that the referee had been bribed and the bitter experience meant that he never trusted a European team again.

■ Stan Lynn (above), the Birmingham full-back, was his club's leading scorer with 10 goals, eight of them penalties. It was only the second time that a full-back had scored most goals in a season for his team.

■ Wolves sacked Stan Cullis on August 24 and were relegated to the Second Division for the first time since 1932.

■ Northampton were promoted to the First Division, having climbed up from the Fourth Division in the space of five seasons.

Hearts lose out in numbers game

THE final day of the League season had dramatic consequences not just because one match would settle the outcome of the championship but also because it would lead to a fundamental change in the rules.

Kilmarnock went to Tynecastle needing to beat Hearts by two clear goals to pip them for the title on goal average. When the Ayrshire club duly won 2-0 and collected the championship, Hearts were understandably upset. The two clubs had exactly the same record (22 wins, 6 draws and 6 losses), but Hearts had scored 90 goals, conceding 49, whereas Kilmarnock had scored 62, conceding 33.

This gave Hearts a goal average of 1.837, and Kilmarnock a superior average of 1.879. However if goal difference had been used Hearts, with plus 41, would have been the champions instead because Kilmarnock's goal difference was only 29. Hearts' manifest disappointment at losing the title because of mathematical vagaries prompted them to propose to the Scottish Football League that goal difference, rather than average, should be used to separate teams on the same number of points, and this was adopted.

Fate however decided to be cruel to the Edinburgh club. The next time they came close to lifting the title – 21 years after Kilmarnock deprived them – Celtic pipped Hearts to the championship on the final day of the season . . . on goal difference. Ironically, if goal average had been used instead Hearts would have been the 1986 champions.

Ferencvaros finally prevail as the Fairs Cup becomes a farce

THIS SEASON'S Fairs Cup was probably the most chaotic and farcical competition Uefa had ever organised, even surpassing the inaugural tournament of 1955 which took three years to play 23 games.

Uefa's problems began when they accepted 48 entries and decided not to have any byes in the first round. If they had given 16 byes and played 16 ties they would have had a straightforward competition. Instead they ended up with six teams in the quarter finals and had to give two of them byes into the semi-finals.

To muddy the waters further Uefa had not devised a satisfactory way of deciding ties that finished all square. No fewer than nine ties went to a third match, and one had to be decided by the toss of a coin.

In the midst of all this confusion Manchester United and Everton, the two English representatives, progressed easily until they met each other in the third round where, in a tightly contested tie, United prevailed 3-2 on aggregate. In the six-team quarter-finals, however, United were unfortunately one of the teams not given a bye and had to play RC Strasbourg, who had eliminated Barcelona on the toss of a coin in the previous round.

A 5-0 thrashing at Old Trafford and a goalless draw in France pitted United against Ferencvaros in the semi-finals. Despite a battling performance by Matt Busby's team — the first two matches finished all square — they went out in the replay to the Hungarian club.

But Uefa still had one more idiosyncrasy to come before the competition was concluded. Instead of playing the one-match final on a neutral ground as they had the previous year, they elected to stage it in the Stadio Comunale in Turin, the home ground of the other finalist, Juventus. Ferencvaros had the last laugh though: Fenyvesi scored the only goal in the 74th minute and the Hungarians became the first club from the Eastern bloc to capture a European trophy.

131

No chance for Stein in selection nightmare

SCOTLAND'S determination to reach the World Cup finals in England had been demonstrated at the end of the previous season when the SFA had begged Celtic to allow Jock Stein to act as the caretaker manager of the national side. Their faith in the big man had soon been born out when Scotland drew 1-1 with Poland in Chorzow on May 23 and four days later beat Finland 2-1 in Helsinki.

However Scotland's hopes received a serious setback in October at Hampden when, without the brilliant Jim Baxter but leading 1-0 with a goal from Billy McNeill, they were beaten by Poland's two late goals which stole victory. Stein now had a formidable task on his hands: to beat Italy home and away. Scotland achieved the first objective with a John Greig goal in November, this left a tricky task in Naples – the graveyard of many visiting international sides – in December.

Stein's task was made virtually impossible by losing almost half his squad beforehand. Some were missing because their English clubs refused to release them; some were injured and some were not picked by the SFA. The list of the absent read like a who's who of Scottish talent: Baxter, Pat Crerand, Alan Gilzean, Denis Law and Dave Mackay. Conceding that his novice side would never beat a full-strength Italy, Stein aimed for a draw – gambling on a

Benfica led a merry dance by El Beatle's one-man band

BENFICA were undoubtedly the leading side in Europe. They had reached the final of the European Cup four times in the past five seasons, and had won the tournament twice. With Eusebio at the peak of his career they were content to leave Old Trafford 3-2 down after the first leg of their European Cup quarter-final against Manchester United.

The Portuguese team were convinced that they could easily make up the deficit at home. Matt Busby, the United manager, also knew that his team would face one of their toughest challenges ever. He ordered his players to contain Benfica for the first quarter of the match and then go in search of goals.

As Busby said afterwards, the precocious George Best "must have had cotton wool in his ears" during the team talk. The teenager was not going to hang around doing nothing for 20 minutes, he wanted to score goals.

Within 12 minutes he had put United 2-0 up. His first goal silenced the crowd, the second, a brilliant solo run, sent them into raptures. The rest of the team took their cue from Best and Busby's orders were ignored as United blitzed Benfica 5-1.

The Stadium of Light was dazzled by United, and particularly by Best. Every time Best touched the ball the crowd shouted "El Beatle" in unison. And, just like the pop stars, Best was mobbed at the end of the match. Busby was horrified when one Portuguese fan chased Best across the pitch, brandishing a knife. He needn't have worried – all that the man wanted was a lock of Best's hair.

A star is born: Best disobeyed orders and dazzled Benfica

Unfortunately for United, the happy ending did not last. Making their first appearance in the European Cup since the Munich disaster, they could not lay the ghosts of 1958 and were beaten by Partizan Belgrade in the semi-finals.

replay. Unfortunately it failed miserably, Italy hammered the Scots 3-0, and Stein's reign ended with him bitterly complaining of the lamentable national set-up.

None of the other Home countries managed to qualify either. Northern Ireland were only narrowly edged out by Switzerland, both sides beating each other at home, but Northern Ireland's two draws with Holland and Albania – giving the Eastern bloc country their only point – cost them a place in the finals. Wales won all three of their home matches, but also lost all three of their away games and the Soviet Union coasted to the finals.

Catterick buys the winning ticket

EVERTON had not conceded a goal on the way to Wembley, so they were doubly shocked to trail Sheffield Wednesday 2-0 in the FA Cup final. To add to their problems, they had hardly staged any penetrating attacks in the first half and their fans were getting restless, doubting the wisdom of dropping the experienced Fred Pickering for the young Mike Trebilcock.

Harry Catterick, the Everton manager, had come in for some stick from the club's supporters earlier in the season when he bought the little-known Trebilcock from Plymouth for £18,000. But even after Wednesday had scored their second goal in the 57th minute he said that he was not panicking.

Mike Trebilcock, too, had remained calm when it seemed that the unfancied Wednesday were going to run rings round Everton. A minute after David Ford had scored he crashed in a half-volley to give Everton hope. Five minutes later, with a tiring Wednesday starting to feel the effects of their exertions, he took advantage of a weak clearance by Sam Ellis to score another unstoppable goal.

Everton's decisive goal, in the 80th minute, was heartbreaking for Wednesday, and particularly Gerry Young. A long punt by the Everton goalkeeper should not have caused Young any problems. But, inexplicably, the left half let the ball run away from him. Quick as flash, Derek Temple whipped past him and ran on to score the winning goal.

Young was mortified by his mistake and slumped to the ground in despair. "I am inconsolable," he said. "Ninety-nine times out of a hundred I would have tamed that ball, but the hundredth time had to be in the Cup final."

Bringing home the bacon: Trebilcock rewarded Catterick's faith with the vital equaliser

Pickles finds World Cup to dig FA out of hole

THE FA were severely embarrassed when they lost the World Cup months before the finals were due to start.

Some time during the afternoon of Sunday March 20, a thief broke into Central Hall, Westminster, where the Jules Rimet trophy was on display at a stamp exhibition. He ignored all the rare stamps, with a value of at least £3m, and only took the trophy, worth £3,000 at most.

A £15,000 ransom demand was made but when the police arrested the culprit he turned out to be a hoaxer. Nobody knew what had happened to the Cup until a week after it had vanished, when David Corbett took his dog for a walk in Norwood, south London.

Pickles, a black and white mongrel, disappeared into some bushes and started digging furiously. He unearthed a brown paper parcel that contained the 12-inch high trophy.

Pickles had got the FA out of a pickle (they had started making emergency plans in case the trophy was not recovered) and was handsomely rewarded. When England won the World Cup Pickles was invited to the celebration banquet and allowed to lick the plates clean. His owner collected a £6,000 reward but the thief was never caught.

Pickles: celebration dinner

THE
1965-66
SEASON

Gento guides Madrid back to the heights

ONLY Francisco Gento, now 32 years old, remained of the fabulous Real Madrid side of the 1950s when they won five European Cups in succession with breathtaking football. The rebuilt Madrid team were criticised for being a shadow of their predecessors but then they would be: how can you replace a Puskas or a Di Stefano?

However their younger and more athletic successors took the famous club back to the top of the European summit when they beat Partizan Belgrade 2-1 in the European Cup final in Brussels.

Real's new stars were Amancio, Pirri and Velasquez. And it was Amancio who equalised after Vasovic had headed the Yugoslavs into the lead early in the second half. Serena, the right winger, thundered the winner from outside the penalty area six minutes from time.

For Gento, now Real's captain, it was a memorable occasion. It was his eighth European Cup final and the sixth time he was on the winning side, a record unlikely to be surpassed.

As a left-winger Gento was a wonder to behold. Jimmy Greaves held him in awe: "He was one of the fastest players I have ever seen. He streaked down the left wing like an Olympic sprinter, and even when at full pace managed to retain control of the ball. A small compact man with powerful thighs, Gento packed a thundering left-foot shot and his passes were always pin-pointed."

Gento retired in 1971 having played 761 matches and scored 253 goals for his club and helping them to 12 championships.

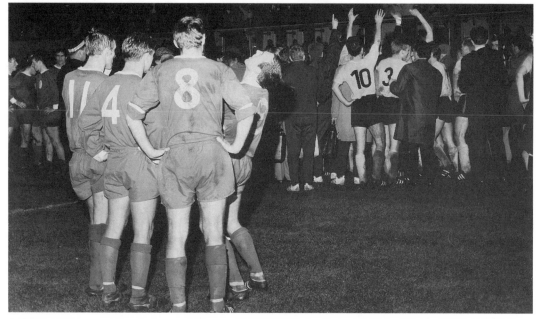

Bad times 1: Liverpool were left disconsolate at Hampden Park

THE MANNER in which Liverpool dismissed the opposition to land their seventh League title had all the hallmarks of an emerging dynasty. Bill Shankly's team had assumed the leadership of the First Division at the end of November and simply raced away with the title, finishing six points clear of Leeds. It was their third major title in three seasons, and it equalled Arsenal's record of seven League championships.

Shankly had built a super-fit team that never seemed to suffer from injuries, indeed he had only used 14 players throughout the season and one of those made his one appearance in the final League game when the title was already secure. Shankly's defence, built around Ron Yeats and Tommy Smith, was resolute; his strike-force of Ian St John and Roger Hunt was prolific as they fed off the eager service of Liverpool's two wingers, Ian Callaghan and Peter Thompson.

Apart from their unexpected elimination in the third round of the FA Cup by Chelsea at Anfield, the only real disappointment in Liverpool's season was their failure to be the first British club to have completed a League and European double.

Liverpool's progress in the European Cup Winners Cup

Bad times 2: Held opens the scoring for Borussia Dortmund

had been impressive. They had disposed of Juventus, Standard Liege and Honved in successive rounds before meeting Celtic in the semi-final. In the first leg at Parkhead, Liverpool, without Hunt their leading scorer, struggled to withstand Celtic's attacking momentum and were fortunate to escape with a single goal defeat.

At Anfield the roles were reversed and by half-time Liverpool were still trailing to that single goal. A venomous free-kick from Smith levelled the scores. Geoff Strong, who had spent much of the half limping because of an injury, managed to find some extra spring in his legs and rose above the Celtic defence to score. With a minute left it appeared Bobby Lennox had equalised, but the referee blew for offside.

Liverpool's opponents in the final at Hampden were Borussia Dortmund who had beaten West Ham, the holders, in the other semi-final. Siggy Held gave the West German club the lead just after the interval, Hunt equalised but then, with seconds left, failed with a simple chance and the match went into extra time. Liverpool were now faltering and in the 17th minute goalkeeper Tommy Lawrence, under pressure from Held, was forced to punch a ball from the edge of his area. Libuda pounced on the clearance and blasted the ball 40 yards past the stranded keeper.

Ramsey hones his grand plan to win World Cup

ENGLAND began their vital build-up to the summer's World Cup finals as badly as they had ended the previous season with a disappointing 3-2 defeat by nondescript Austria at Wembley in October. It later transpired that Jimmy Greaves, who had been out of sorts in the match, was suffering from jaundice and he did not return to the side until May.

With Greaves absent, Ramsey began to experiment with a 4-3-3 formation and, in December, England beat Spain 2-0 in Madrid, an extremely encouraging result. Although other results were patchy – notably a 1-1 draw with Poland at Goodison – there were more encouraging signs, including a 1-0 defeat of West Germany at Wembley in February with Geoff Hurst making a satisfactory debut. In April Hurst retained his place, and scored the first goal in a 4-3 defeat of Scotland at Hampden, England's first victory over the Scots in five years.

Ramsey now embarked on a wholesale series of changes in personnel and formations, searching not just for the right blend, but to create a squad flexible enough to cope with whatever problems other countries might create in the finals. He had not forgotten the harsh lessons the Argentinians had dished out in the "Little World Cup" in the summer of 1964.

Ramsey and his squad then retreated to Lilleshall, where he subjected them to a military-style regime designed to foster camaraderie and mould them into a team rather than a collection of gifted individuals. Fifteen days before the finals began, Ramsey and his team went on a whirlwind European tour. They played four matches in nine days, winning all of them with, once again, more team changes and experimentation. By the opening match, against Uruguay on July 11. Ramsey and England were now ready to face the best the world could throw at them.

Heading for the heights? Ramsey warms up for the World Cup finals

Wright: left Arsenal

- Both Chester full-backs were carried off with broken legs during the Fourth Division match against Aldershot on January 1. Despite the setback, Chester still won 3-2.

- Arsenal parted company with Billy Wright, their manager, at the end of the season.

- Bradford Park Avenue were the second-highest scorers in the League with 102 goals. But they only finished 11th in the Fourth Division because they lost 20 matches and allowed their opponents to score 92 times.

- Malcolm Allison teamed up with Joe Mercer at Manchester City and they guided the club back to the First Division.

- Northampton, newly promoted to the First Division, went straight back down to the Second Division.

Dynamic duo: Mercer and Allison revived Manchester City

Stein takes charge and widens Celtic's horizons

BOLSTERED by his success in the Scottish Cup the previous season, Jock Stein set about realising his expansive ambitions for Celtic. First he refused to countenance a joint managership with Sean Fallon, and then he persuaded the club's board of directors that he would have a completely free hand in team selection. This was unheard of, but Stein got his way, the first Celtic manager to enjoy such power.

Although Stein, as the caretaker manager of the Scottish national side, was encumbered until December when they were eliminated from the World Cup finals, he soon had Celtic mounting a strong challenge for the championship. In January

Celtic whipped Rangers 5-1 and, despite their Ibrox rivals chasing them for the rest of the season, that result was decisive. Celtic won the title two points ahead of Rangers, having scored a phenomenal 106 goals.

Celtic had also captured the Scottish League Cup beating Rangers 2-1. However Rangers denied Stein the satisfaction of a treble in his first full season in charge when, after a 0-0 draw, they took the Scottish Cup 1-0 in the replay. Stein's horizons were now wider than simply being the top dogs in Scotland. Perhaps foolishly, the Celtic boss announced that next season's priority was to win the European Cup, which no British club had ever come near winning.

WORLD CUP 1966

Wingless Wonders give England home win

ENGLAND's victory in the World Cup final in 1966 will forever be remembered for two things: Kenneth Wolstenholme's immortal words at the end of extra time, and Geoff Hurst's controversial second goal that effectively won the trophy. In the dying seconds of the final, with England clinging on to a slender 3-2 lead against West Germany, Bobby Moore, instead of wildly clearing the ball, hit a precision pass to Hurst who raced upfield and unleashed a ferocious shot. The crowd, in anticipation of the final whistle, had begun to come on to the Wembley pitch. Wolstenholme remarked: "They think it's all over," just as Hurst's left-footed shot flew into the roof of the West German net. With the briefest pauses, Wolstenholme added: "It is now".

While those words have been fondly remembered ever since, England's third goal has been hotly debated ever since. Even today Germans will swear blind it was not a goal and film and photographic evidence have never given a conclusive answer. At the time two people were equally certain it was a goal: Roger Hunt and Backhramov, the Russian linesman.

Alan Ball had, somehow finding extra pace from his weary legs, latched on to Nobby Stiles's pass, raced past Karl-Heinz Schnellinger and crossed the ball to Hurst who was standing with his back to the goal. The West Ham striker controlled the ball, instantly turned and crashed it against the underside of the bar. The ball bounced on to the line and was cleared. Hunt, following up in the goalmouth, turned away, arms raised in celebration. But did the ball cross the line? The Germans thought not. Dienst, the Swiss referee, consulted his linesman and awarded the most controversial goal in the history of the World Cup.

It is a pity that the 1966 final will not properly be remembered for thrilling game it truly was. West Germany had taken an early lead in the 12th minute when a poor clearance from Ray Wilson was punished by Helmut Haller. Six minutes later a quickly-taken free-kick from Moore was headed in by Hurst.

England finally took the lead with 12 minutes remaining when Martin Peters scored from the rebound after Hurst's shot had

been blocked. Seconds before the final whistle, West Germany conjured up a heart-breaking equaliser. From a dubious free-kick awarded against Jackie Charlton, Lothar Emmerich blasted the ball into the penalty area, it hit Schnellinger's back, fell to Held whose cross ricocheted off George Cohen's knee. Weber poked the ball in at the far post.

England's manager, Alf Ramsey, gave what was probably his most informal team talk ever during the break before extra time. "You've beaten them once," he told his weary men as they sprawled on the grass, "now you've got to do it again. Look at them. They're finished!"

Ramsey's speech was inspirational, even though most people perceived him as a man of few words. Ramsey was a first-rate motivator whose only problem was that he found it difficult to deal with the press. But out of the spotlight, working with players who always seemed to raise their game for him, he was a master tactician.

Ramsey had been appointed in 1962, and was the first England manager to have total control of team selection. And he made it very clear what his project was: to win the World Cup and win it his way. To this end Ramsey had worked unceasingly for the 1966 World Cup.

His way meant that for four years Ramsey experimented with formations and players to such an extent that players, press and public were bewildered. Ramsey also put a high premium on hard work and hard running, disposing of the wingers who historically had been the cornerstone of English football. This

infuriated his critics, and few believed that England really could capture the ultimate prize.

However Ramsey knew exactly what he was doing: producing a world-beating team for the modern era. Although Ramsey's Wingless Wonders were vilified for their lack of flair and their emphasis on work-rate there was probably more talent in that England team than at any time since.

Ramsey was the most misunderstood of managers. Because of his dismissive, aloof personality he seemed to be a fish out water in the Swinging Sixties, but in reality he was a successful revolutionary. He was also his own man, something else that did not endear him to the public or FA officials. After the match against France in the first round Stiles perpetrated an horrendous tackle right in front of the Royal Box. Two FA bigwigs instructed Ramsey to drop Stiles for the next match. Ramsey refused and said that if Stiles did not play, he would resign. Such player loyalty was his hallmark and at Wembley on July 30 they repaid him handsomely.

England made an unconvincing start, but as their group was probably the weakest they easily qualified to meet Argentina in the quarter-finals. The South Americans were formidable opponents, but their undoubted skills were marred by a vicious streak of cynicism. Antonio Rattin, their captain, seemed to think he was above the rules of the game and beyond the referee's authority. While Kreitlein, the West German referee, was booking several of Rattin's teammates, Rattin was fouling with impunity. Eventually the referee could

stand it no more and sent him off. But Rattin refused to go and the referee was surrounded by the entire Argentine team, who threatened to walk off en masse. The game was delayed for 11 minutes before Rattin reluctantly left.

Ramsey was offended by the Argentinians' conduct and after England won 1-0 he raced on to the pitch to stop his players exchanging shirts with their opponents. Ramsey branded Argentina "animals", although he did apologise later for the remark.

Pele, too, was a victim of a series of harsh tackles. He was injured by a Bulgarian defender in the first round and missed the next match against Hungary. Then he was repeatedly scythed down as Portugal beat Brazil 3-1 to put them out of the competition. Pele returned to Brazil threatening never to play in the World Cup again.

Amid all the bitterness, the unlikely minnows from North Korea captured many hearts. Their team of tiny players had precious little international experience, but a goal from Pak Doo-ik, an army dentist, against Italy took North Korea into the quarter-finals at Italy's expense. The Italian team returned home in disgrace and were pelted with rotten fruit at Genoa airport.

North Korea almost pulled off another upset when they led Portugal 3-0 after 22 minutes. But their chances of reaching the semi-finals were undone by their lack of experience of how to shut a game down. Eusebio rallied Portugal with four goals in 32 minutes and although North Korea finally succumbed 5-3 their brave performances won them many friends.

However all of Eusebio's brilliance could not save Portugal in the semi-final against England and his penalty eight minutes from time was too late to overhaul Bobby Charlton's two brilliant goals. It was undoubtedly the match of the tournament ... until the final and the intervention of a Russian linesman.

High drama 1: Perfumo of Argentina and Haller of West Germany engage in aerial combat; North Korea gave several teams the fright of their lives; and Weber snatches a last-gasp equaliser in the final

FIRST ROUND

GROUP 1	P	W	D	L	F	A	Pts
England	3	2	1	0	4	0	5
Uruguay	3	1	2	0	2	1	4
Mexico	3	0	2	1	1	3	2
France	3	0	1	2	2	5	1

GROUP 2	P	W	D	L	F	A	Pts
W. Germany	3	2	1	0	7	1	5
Argentina	3	2	1	0	4	1	5
Spain	3	1	0	2	4	5	2
Switzerland	3	0	0	3	1	9	0

GROUP 3	P	W	D	L	F	A	Pts
Portugal	3	3	0	0	9	2	6
Hungary	3	2	0	1	7	5	4
Brazil	3	1	0	2	4	6	2
Bulgaria	3	0	0	3	1	8	0

GROUP 4	P	W	D	L	F	A	Pts
Soviet Union	3	3	0	0	6	1	6
North Korea	3	1	1	1	2	4	3
Italy	3	0	1	2	2	5	1
Chile	3	0	1	2	2	5	1

QUARTER-FINALS

England 1 Argentina 0
HT 0-0 Att. 90,584
West Germany 4 Uruguay 0
HT 1-0 Att. 33,751
Portugal 5 North Korea 3
HT 2-3 Att. 51,780
Soviet Union 2 Hungary 1
HT 1-0 Att. 26,844

SEMI-FINALS

West Germany 2 Soviet Union 1
HT 1-0 Att. 43,921
England 2 Portugal 1
HT 1-0 Att. 94,493

THIRD PLACE PLAY-OFF
Portugal 2 Soviet Union 1
HT 1-1 Att. 87,696

FINAL
England 4 West Germany 2 aet
HT 1-1 Att. 96,924

Teams
England Banks; Cohen, J Charlton, Moore, Wilson, Stiles, B Charlton, Ball, Hunt, Hurst, Peters
West Germany Tilkowski; Hottges, Schulz, Weber, Schnellinger, Haller, Beckenbauer, Seeler, Held, Overath, Emmerich

Leading goalscorers 9 Eusebio Ferriera da Silva (Portugal); 5 Helmut Haller (West Germany); 4 Geoff Hurst (England), Franz Beckenbauer (West Germany), Valeri Porkujan (Soviet Union), Ferenc Bene (Hungary)
Total goals scored 80
Average per game: 2.78
Sendings-off Jorge Albrecht (Argentina) v West Germany; Referee: Konstantin Zecevic (Yugoslavia). Horacio Troche (Uruguay) v West Germany; Hector Silva (Uruguay) v West Germany; Referee: Jim Finney (England). Antonio Rattin (Argentina) v England; Referee: Rudolf Kreitlein (West Germany). Igor Chislenko (Soviet Union) v West Germany; Referee: Conceto Lo Bello (Italy).
Number of players used by finalists 14 West Germany; 15 England

● Over 40 nations have withdrawn from the World Cup for one reason or another. Egypt (1938, 1958, 1962 and 1966) have withdrawn the most often.

High drama 2: Hurst's second goal was surrounded by controversy

Moore the merrier: England's captain leads the celebrations

Dynamic duo join Derby

SECOND DIVISION Derby County plucked the Hartlepools United managerial duo of Brian Clough and Peter Taylor out of the doldrums of the Fourth Division in the hope that the pair would soon restore them to the First Division. Clough, a prolific striker whose promising England career had been curtailed because of injury, had caused something of a stir when he took over at Hartlepools as the youngest manager in the League.

Sam Longson, Derby's chairman, had decided to gamble on the inexperienced Clough and Taylor, having been tipped off by Len Shackleton, the former England centre-forward turned journalist, that they were capable of rescuing a club who had finished 17th that season. Longson promised that £70,000 would be available to buy new players.

Clough: youngest manager

Taylor: valuable sidekick

Berwick make Rangers suffer the worst day of their lives

Worlds apart: Celtic were League champions again and Rangers finished nowhere

BERWICK 1 RANGERS 0 was the most sensational result in Scottish football history. Berwick, who had never finished higher than eighth in the Second Division, had bundled mighty Rangers, who had won the Scottish Cup four times in the previous five seasons, out of the Cup in the first round on January 28. The result sent shock waves through Scotland and rocked Ibrox to its foundations.

The hero of the day was Jock Wallace who combined the job of manager with that of goalkeeper. After Sammy Reid had put Berwick (whose ground is actually just in Northumberland) ahead in the 32nd minute Wallace pulled off save after save to the consternation of the Rangers players and fans. The repercussions from the match were extraordinary.

Jim Forrest and George McLean, the two strikers, were held entirely responsible for the debacle and never played for Rangers again. Forrest (145 goals in 164 games) was transferred in March to Preston for £38,000 and McLean (82 goals in 116 games) went to Dundee a month later in exchange for Andy Penman.

Scot Symon, the manager, did not fare much better. His 13-year reign – which included six Scottish championships, five Scottish Cups, four Scottish League Cups and two European Cup Winners Cup finals – came to an inglorious end in November when the Rangers chairman, John Lawrence, sent an intermediary to break the extraordinary news that he was sacked. Rangers were leading the table at time, having won six and

drawn two of their eight fixtures.

However between the end of January and the beginning of November Celtic had also rocked Scottish football. To their European Cup triumph, Rangers' bitter rivals had added the League, the Cup, the League Cup and the Glasgow Cup. An unbelievable year for Parkhead, a desperately embarrassing year for Ibrox, and so Symon was made the scapegoat.

David White replaced Symon but his two-year stint never put a dent in Celtic's stranglehold, and he had to give way to Willie Waddell who had achieved wonderful things with Kilmarnock. As he was to do with Rangers, especially the appointment in June 1970 of a coach who had come a long way in a short time: Jock Wallace, formerly of Berwick Rangers.

Manchester United's winning ways put the smile back on Busby's face

ENGLAND'S triumph in the World Cup final brought a renewed sense of optimism to the game. The Daily Telegraph said: "England are now acknowledged as the leaders of world soccer. It is essential that we exploit a spirit of adventure and resist in the months ahead a temptation to resort to tactics of dreary defence."

Matt Busby, the Manchester United manager, needed no urging to play attractive football. But at the start of the season he was in despair. "We'll never win the European Cup now," Busby told Pat Crerand, reflecting on United's defeat in the semi-finals last season.

Then Denis Law demanded a big increase in his wages and a signing-on fee to renew his contract. Busby retaliated by putting his international striker on the transfer list.

But the crises passed. Law made his peace with the club and Busby set about taking United back into Europe. United were not beaten in the League after December 16 and, apart from being beaten at Old Trafford by Norwich in the fourth round of the FA Cup, were almost invincible at home.

They made sure of the title in convincing style, hammering the West Ham of Bobby Moore, Geoff Hurst and Martin Peters 6-1 at Upton Park in May. Bobby Charlton, Crerand and Bill Foulkes put United three up after 10 minutes and George Best added a fourth after 25 minutes. Law completed the rout with two goals in the second half.

One reporter wrote: "This was a triumph for that ever-diminishing school of managers who believe soccer is primarily an entertainment. Manchester United believe their customers should not only be granted the satisfaction of another victory, but should be delighted by the performance that earns it."

For Busby, who had even contemplated retirement at the start of the season, the European dream was alive once again.

FOR THE RECORD

■ Figures released by the Television Audience Measurement Society showed that England's triumph in the World Cup final had been the most widely watched programme of the month, seen by 10.5 million households. However, the two semi-finals were less popular. England's defeat of Portugal shared second place with No Hiding Place while the Soviet Union v West Germany matched ranked lower than Juke Box Jury and The Dickie Valentine Show.

■ Everton bought Alan Ball from Blackpool in August in the first six-figure transfer between English clubs.

■ Workington increased their board of directors to 13 in October, more than their full-time playing staff. Not surprisingly, with more chiefs than Indians they were relegated to the Fourth Division.

■ Alf Ramsey was knighted in the New Year's honours list.

Dazzling Baxter inspires Scotland to defeat the Auld Enemy and claim they are world champions

FOR SCOTLAND the "real" World Cup final was played on April 15, 1967 at Wembley, not July 30, 1966 – and they won it. England's victory the summer before rankled north of the border like no other result, especially as Scotland failed even to reach the finals. So to take on

> *If anybody had asked me who, out of all the teams in the world will come to Wembley and beat you, I would have said the Scots. It meant more for the Scots to beat the English than it did for the English to beat the Scots*
>
> BOBBY CHARLTON
> on England's defeat

Crowning glory: Jim McCalliog scores Scotland's winning goal at Wembley

the world champions on their own pitch and beat them was pure heaven.

Although Scotland's margin of victory was slender, 3-2, it was the style of it that enraptured Scottish fans. Jim Baxter was at his mercurial best, waltzing through an England team which, apart from Jimmy Greaves in for Roger Hunt, was the same one that had defeated West Germany nine months earlier.

Baxter's dazzling cheek of taunting the England players and defying them to win possession of the ball was emulated by his teammates Denis Law, Billy Bremner and Tommy Gemmell.

It was sweet revenge as Scotland embarrassed the Auld Enemy and wiped out the bitter memory of their 9-3 humiliation six years ago to the day.

Mee rings the changes at Arsenal

THE WINDS of a quiet revolution seemed to be blowing through the marble corridors of Highbury. The sacking of Billy Wright in the summer of 1966 after four years as their manager was not really a surprise. After all Arsenal had not won anything since their championship victory in 1953 and in the meantime their deadly rivals, Spurs, had enjoyed spectacular success both at home and in Europe. But the appointment of Bertie Mee was.

Mee, the club's unassuming 46-year-old physiotherapist, was hardly the big-name appointment expected of a club as big as Arsenal. It even stunned Mee. "It was a surprise, but a very pleasant one," he said. "I had not planned to become a football manager."

Undeterred, Mee, with his coach Dave Sexton whom he had lured from Fulham, set about the job with gusto. By October he had sold the crowd-pleasing, but erratic, George Eastham to Stoke; exchanged Tommy Baldwin plus £50,000 for Chelsea's George Graham and bought Bob McNab from Huddersfield for £50,000 – a record for a full back.

Of course Mee was uniquely placed to put his finger on the pulse of the problem at Highbury. The Arsenal dressing-room had been his domain for the past six years as he worked to get the players fit. Known as a no-nonsense physio, he began the task of restoring Arsenal to their former glories with the advantage that the players respected him and knew that he was no pushover.

Stein and Celtic bring home the greatest prize in Europe

BY ALL footballing standards Celtic stood absolutely no chance of beating Inter Milan in the European Cup final. Inter, a collection of glittering internationals managed by the arch strategist of the era Helenio Herrera, had won the competition twice, in 1964 and 1965, and were the most sophisticated side in the world at gaining a 1-0 lead and then utterly closing the game down.

By contrast Celtic were an all-Scottish side unsophisticated in Continental ways, incapable of any master strategy and whose only tactic was out and out attack. Their domestic success was simply a product of the paucity of Scottish football. The Italian maestros would easily put the upstarts in their place. Anyway, that was the script.

Stein, of course, had other ideas. He knew that much of such criticism was valid but, if he could get his players to play above themselves and to play to their traditional strengths with marauding wingers providing the bullets for his front men to fire, then the Italians might well wilt under the barrage. He also had a few of his own tricks up his sleeve, if not on the field of play then away from it.

Typically, the Italian players were holed up in their camp and kept away from the press and hangers-on. Stein decided to build on the camaraderie his players shared by virtually running an open house at the team hotel, and kept his players in a permanently relaxed atmosphere. When the Celtic players went out on to the pitch they were noisily singing the Celtic song to the amazement of their Italian rivals. Stein even upstaged the great Herrera by stealing the bench he had earmarked for himself. Herrera was furious, but Stein would not give way. His players thought it was wonderful, knockabout stuff.

You'll be an immortal
BILL SHANKLY to JOCK STEIN
after the European Cup final

The first half followed the Herrera script. In the seventh minute Inter were awarded a penalty, Mazzola scored and, as expected, they promptly shut up shop. That, Herrera thought, was that. Stein was unfazed by the containing, counter-attacking game Herrera employed and the Celtic manager stuck to his guns. At half-time Stein exhorted his players to continue with their game-plan: to fire in accurate shot after accurate shot until the Italians cracked.

Luck seemed against them when Bertie Auld and Tommy Gemmell hit the bar, but the constant bombardment on the Inter goal never wavered. In the 63rd minute Celtic got their reward. Bobby Murdoch picked up Gemmell's pass, switched to Jim Craig on the right wing who found Gemmell with enough space in the middle to thunder the ball past the Italian keeper from 20 yards. With five minutes to go, and extra time on the cards, Gemmell was involved again, his left-wing pass to Murdoch was driven into the area and cannoned off Steve Chalmers for the winner.

Celtic had simply ripped the script into shreds. Jock Stein, manager for a little over two seasons, had taken Celtic to the pinnacle of club success, the European Cup, the first British side to mount the summit.

Gemmell: the match-winner

Against the odds: Celtic celebrate the winning goal in the European Cup final in Lisbon

West Brom caught napping by QPR

THE League Cup, once labelled "Hardaker's Folly", finally came of age thanks to two inspired changes to the competition. The final was made a single match and moved to Wembley, instead of being played over two legs home and away. And the winners would qualify for Europe, getting an automatic place in the Fairs Cup provided that they were a First Division team.

The incentive of European football persuaded several clubs that had spurned the competition previously to take part. Only Liverpool, the League champions, and Everton, the FA Cup holders, did not enter.

But things did not go quite to plan when First Division West Bromwich Albion succumbed to Third Division Queen's Park Rangers in the final. West Brom raced into a 2-0 lead before half-time with both goals scored by Clive Clark, a former QPR player.

But after the break West Brom's dominance evaporated. They played as if they were already day-dreaming about Europe and were comprehensively caught napping.

First Roger Morgan scored then, with 15 minutes remaining, Rodney Marsh equalised with a solo run and a shot that went in off the post. Still West Brom did not wake up and Mark Lazarus scored the winner for QPR late in the game.

QPR were denied a place in Europe but they had further cause for celebration when they ran away with the Third Division title by 12 points.

Chelsea outflanked by Tottenham

Capital punishment: Bonetti is beaten for the second time in the all-London Cup final

TOTTENHAM and Chelsea provided the first all-London FA Cup final this century, but that was all they had in common.

The contrast in styles between the two clubs was enormous. Tottenham had Bill Nicholson, one of the, if not the best, managers of the decade. Chelsea had the upstart Tommy Docherty in charge. Tottenham were a team with a common purpose. Chelsea were riven by internal disputes all season, and the wrangling over bonuses continued long into the night after the Cup final had ended. Tottenham had rebuilt their Double team. Chelsea were dependent on individual skills.

Before the match, Docherty said that Tottenham would only play as well as Chelsea allowed them to. But it was Docherty's decision to pack his midfield and employ a 4-4-2 formation that effectively handed the game to Tottenham.

Nothing epitomised Tottenham's spirit more than Dave Mackay, still soldiering on after injuries that would have finished the career of lesser men. What he lacked in pace he made up for in determination. And Mackay had, weeks before the match, pointed out the virtues of using wingers.

Tottenham, playing a classical 4-2-4 line-up had all the space they wanted to run at Chelsea. Jimmy Robertson made one wing his own and put Tottenham ahead on the stroke of half-time. Frank Saul, abetted by overlapping runs from the full-back Joe Kinnear, prowled the other flank and added a second goal with a stunning shot hit on the turn. Jimmy Greaves (with Mackay the only man to have played in Tottenham's last Cup-winning side) and Alan Gilzean tormented the heart of the Chelsea defence.

Against such an onslaught, Charlie Cooke's runs from midfield and Tony Hateley's efforts in attack were largely ineffectual. Bobby Tambling scored a consolation goal four minutes from time, but by then Tottenham's domination was such that they had been able to slow the game to almost walking pace.

The 2-1 scoreline hardly reflected Tottenham's superior tactics. But perhaps the greatest insight into the gulf between the two teams came at the post-match banquets.

One Chelsea player, complaining about his £50 loser's bonus said: "We are not money-grabbers. We are professionals and we believe that, for getting to Wembley, we deserve more."

Nicholson, meanwhile, was happy to do his job without so much as a contract. "I have all I want. What is the use of a contract? Your only security is your ability." The Double, two more FA Cups, and the European Cup Winners Cup said it all.

JOCK STEIN
A legend in his own lifetime

Roddy Mackenzie

The Big Man: Stein was a colossus in Scotland

FOR MANY Scots it was the day that football died. On the morning of September 11, 1985, Scotland should have been nursing a massive hangover after a 1-1 draw with Wales in Cardiff had secured qualification for the country's fourth successive World Cup finals. Instead, the nation shuffled to work gloomily.

Jock Stein, "The Big Man" of Scottish football, had died of a heart attack in the bowels of Ninian Park just minutes after masterminding another triumph the previous night. It was the way Stein would have wished to depart – in his working clothes and with football people watching over him.

Recalling that night, Roy Aitken, who played under Stein for Celtic and Scotland, was to recount: "In the dressing-room we should have been in celebratory mood at the end of the match. Scotland had made it to Mexico. But there was near silence as we changed and waited for more news. It must have been 20 minutes later that we were told. I looked at the physio Jim Steel's face and knew without any words that the worst had happened."

For a country which prides itself on its football, Stein had become a national hero. If it is said that most people can remember where they were when they heard of President Kennedy's assassination, then most Scots can tell you what they were doing when news of Stein's death came

Simply the best: Gemmell and Johnstone

through. It was felt that deeply. Ten thousand people lined the streets of Glasgow to pay their last respects as the funeral cortege made its way to Linn crematorium.

Scottish football had lost its leader, its ambassador and its keeper of dreams. Nobody has commanded the same respect since and the Scottish game is still coming to terms with the loss. "John, you're immortal," Bill Shankly told Stein after he had guided Celtic to the European Cup in 1967 and, in terms of Scottish football, it was no hyperbole.

Stein, from humble origins, was a man of the people who never lost the common touch. Raised in the Lanarkshire mining community of Burnbank, on the outskirts of Hamilton, it was obvious from an early stage of his football involvement that he would transcend barriers. Burnbank has yielded such football talent as Bobby Shearer, Jim Bett and Davie Cooper over the years. As Protestants, all took the natural path to Ibrox and Rangers. Stein, of the same faith, found his way to Celtic, a club with Roman Catholic roots.

He found his way to the club he was to make his name with as a player and a manager via the unglamorous route of Albion Rovers and the Welsh non-league side Llanelli. At Celtic Park he formed a formidable half-back line with Bobby Evans and Bertie Peacock and, as captain, led the club to a League and Scottish Cup double in 1954. He never pulled on the dark blue shirt of Scotland and an ankle injury led to his premature retirement from playing.

But it was to be on the coaching side of the game that Stein was to work his alchemy. Stein was one of the new breed of tracksuit managers in the British game and left no doubt that his place was on the shop floor with his workers.

Pat Stanton played under Stein at Hibernian and at Celtic. He remembers: "Stein had this knack of getting the best out of players, whatever their ability. He had some difficult players to deal with like Willie Hamilton at Hibs and Jimmy Johnstone at Celtic but he had his own methods. He was very much a man of the people and left you in no doubt that you were privileged to be a football player." I remember on one occasion the trainer at Hibs asked a couple of the players to help carry the kit hamper from the team bus. They thought this was beneath their dignity. But Stein intervened and reminded them that, had it not been for football, they could have been carrying bricks around for a living."

Stanton admits that he had one or two arguments with the manager in his time and points out: "He could be quite ruthless. Some of the players were frightened of him but they all respected him and his great knowledge of the game, and of human nature. Stein was not a man to hold grudges. Once he had made his point and told you what he felt, it was forgotten about." It is said that he would go to the extent of slapping his own face to make it red before he went into a dressing-room before a game to give the players the impression that he was in a rage, and that he would not tolerate a sub-standard performance. It is an example of the psychology and attention to fine detail that Stein employed to get a response from his players.

Stein was also one of the first managers to manipulate the media to his advantage. If one of the clubs he managed had played poorly on the Saturday, Stein would invariably stage a hastily-arranged press conference on the Sunday morning where he would "absent-mindedly" drop into conversation the fact that he was interested in signing such and such a player. The Monday newspapers would not be filled with an analysis of Celtic's defeat on the Saturday but with a positive Celtic story.

One of his typical coups came in the 10-month period he managed Hibernian in 1964-65. Hibernian's city rivals, Hearts, had qualified for the Fairs Cup so Stein, not to be outdone, arranged a challenge match for Hibs in Edinburgh – against Real Madrid, who had played in the European Cup final in seven out of the previous nine seasons.

Hibs drew 30,000 to the match, Hearts's European tie was eclipsed and, to top it all, Real Madrid were beaten 2-0. One local journalist had predicted a 7-0 win for the Spanish side and Stein, never one to miss a chance to make his point, dragged the sportswriter into the Hibs dressing-room afterwards to explain himself to the exuberant players.

Stein's first managerial charge was at Dunfermline between 1960 and 1964, where he helped the club win the Scottish Cup in 1961 and left a side which was still challenging for honours later in the decade. His sojourn with Hibs was followed by the inevitable return to Celtic Park

Crowning glory: Celtic celebrate the defeat of Inter Milan in the European Cup final

in 1965; to a club which had not won the league title since Stein's captaincy 11 years previously.

Stein's renewed liaison with the club was to bring 10 league titles (including a world record nine in succession between 1966 and 1974), eight Scottish Cups and six League Cups. The crowning glory was the European Cup when Celtic, competing in the event for the first time, beat Inter Milan 2-1 in the final in Lisbon in May 1967. In one fell swoop, Stein dismantled the Italian defensive system of cattenaccio, created by Inter's coach Helenio Herrerra, and the result was to change the face of the European game.

Stein also took Celtic to another European Cup final in 1970 but, on that occasion, the Scottish champions lost to Feyenoord 2-1, a result which signalled the start of the Dutch domination of the competition.

However, Celtic and Stein were to part company in 1978. Stein had almost lost his life in a car accident and it was taken for granted that when he recovered he would be offered a place on the Celtic board at a time when Billy McNeill, who captained Stein's European Cup winning side, was brought back from Aberdeen to fill the manager's chair. But Celtic had never had a Protestant director and Stein was, instead, offered a commercial position within the club. He regarded the offer as an insult and left to join Leeds United as manager.

That was to last only a matter of months as he was lured back to Scotland to take over as national team manager after the debacle of Argentina in 1978. Stein led Scotland to the 1982 World Cup finals in Spain – where they shared a memorable celebration of football in a match with Brazil in Seville – and then he masterminded the qualifying campaign for 1986 before his untimely death. Many have copied his methods, picked up his habits and employed his tactics since then. But Scottish football will never see his like again.

The team that Jock built: Celtic's squad in 1966. They went on to win the League a record nine years in a row

THE
1967-68
SEASON

Leeds end their trophy famine and then do it again for good measure

Celtic's argy-bargy

Mayhem in Montevideo: riot police had to separate the brawling players

CELTIC'S clash with Racing Club for the world club championship was the unacceptable face of football at its very worst.

Celtic, the European Cup holders, beat the Argentine side in a niggling match at Hampden. But not even that could have prepared them for the reception they got in Buenos Aires on November 1.

As the team were led on to the pitch by a piper their goalkeeper, Ronnie Simpson, was felled by a stone and carried off barely conscious. When Celtic took the lead with a penalty the violence got even worse, with Jimmy Johnstone singled out as a target for particularly brutal treatment.

Half-time took on an air of farce when Celtic discovered that the water had been cut off in their dressing room. The interval lasted for 26 minutes because Celtic refused to resume the match until they had had a shower.

Racing Club put two goals past Celtic's stand-in goalkeeper Sean Fallon and Jock Stein foolishly agreed to a play-off match in Uruguay three days later.

This time both teams plumbed the depths, with the Celtic players determined to get their retribution in before they received any more punishment. Johnstone was sent off for elbowing an opponent, John Hughes was dismissed for kicking the Racing goalkeeper and Bobby Lennox also received his marching orders. Two Racing players were also sent off, and the violence got so bad that armed police had to separate the brawling players.

Towards the end of the match Celtic even had a fourth player dismissed. But amid the confusion nobody seemed to know that they had been ordered off so Celtic played on with eight men when they should have been reduced to seven.

Racing won 1-0 but the result did not matter. The world was horrified by the violence. Despite the fact that they had faced extreme provocation Stein fined all his players and publicly apologised for his team's misbehaviour.

FINALLY Don Revie's Leeds broke their duck and captured a major trophy. Leeds were in danger of forever being known as the nearly men. Since their return to the First Division in 1964 they had twice been runners-up (once on goal average), losing FA Cup finalists and losing Fairs Cup finalists. So when they faced Arsenal at Wembley in March in the revitalised League Cup final, the fear of failure hung over the Leeds players like a shroud.

Revie had considered winding his players up before the match by opening out a barren trophy case, but when he saw the jittery state they were in he hastily abandoned the idea. Not surprisingly football was the loser. Unimaginative Arsenal could find no way to break down the cautious and physical Leeds game plan. Terry Cooper, the Leeds full-back, provided the single bright spot in a dour match when he scored the only goal in the 20th minute, blasting a loose ball into the roof of the net.

In August Leeds, having disposed of three Scottish clubs in successive rounds (Hibs, Rangers and Dundee) found themselves in the Fairs Cup final for the second year in a row. Their opponents were Ferencvaros who came to Elland Road for the first leg with the most extraordinary strategy. They pulled shirts, kicked ankles, made little attempt to attack and always had at least eight men behind the ball.

Mick Jones scored an opportunist goal four minutes before half-time. Yet in the second half the Hungarians persisted with their negative tactics and if anything intensified their cynicism. Johnny Giles had to go off with concussion with Jones following him shortly after having been kicked in the groin. Leeds then went to Budapest in September protecting a 1-0 lead and missing Giles.

The Hungarians fought vainly to break down a determined Leeds defence in front of their fanatical 76,000 fans but Leeds had been battle-hardened in European competition and were able to cling on to their advantage and double the silverware in their trophy room.

Nearly men no more: Bremner brandishes the League Cup

Cardiff's starring role on the European stage

OUTSIDE of Wales, winning the Welsh Cup was seen as a backdoor way into Europe. However, Cardiff City proved that they could do just as well on the international stage as any of the bigger clubs from England and Scotland.

Cardiff had already reached the quarter-finals of the Cup Winners Cup once before, in the 1964-65 season when they had knocked out the holders Sporting Lisbon. This time the struggling Second Division club went one better. It was particularly embarrassing for Aberdeen and Tottenham, both of whom were eliminated in the second round.

The finest performances produced by Jimmy Scoular's team came in the quarter-finals, which they reached by beating Shamrock Rovers and Breda. Thanks to Barrie Jones, Cardiff took a 1-0 lead over Torpedo Moscow to the Soviet Union. They hung on to lose only 1-0 in the depths of winter, necessitating a replay in West Germany.

Cardiff's team was devastated by injuries before the match on April 3. Scoular was forced to play five reserves, with Ritchie Morgan making his first-team debut at centre-half.

The new boys played like old hands and Cardiff won when the teenage John Toshack set up Norman Dean, the reserve centre-forward for the only goal of the match.

After a 1-1 draw in Hamburg Cardiff were only one match away from the final. But their brave run ended with a 3-2 defeat at home. Even so, they could hold their heads high as the most successful Welsh club in Europe of all time.

■ Pat Jennings (above), the Tottenham goalkeeper, scored a goal against Manchester United in the Charity Shield when his long, punted clearance was caught by the wind and bounced over Alex Stepney, the United goalkeeper.

■ Matt Busby was knighted.

■ Goalkeepers were limited to taking four steps with the ball by the International Board.

■ The government commissioned Norman Chester and a group of football experts to produce a report on the future of English football. Not surprisingly, its visionary recommendations were largely ignored by the League and the FA.

■ Arsenal had three players sent off in four days during two bad-tempered matches against Burnley. Bob McNab was dismissed in the League Cup quarter-final and Frank McLintock, the Arsenal captain, and Peter Storey were sent off in a League match.

■ Jimmy Scoular, the Cardiff manager, got a nasty shock when his team's match against Millwall was abandoned after half an hour. A visiting fan demanded a refund of his admission money and when Scoular explained that it was not possible he got punched in the face for his troubles.

White's black day as one slip deprives Rangers of the title

Winners lose: Rangers beat Celtic but lost the championship

DAVIE WHITE, the new man at the helm at Ibrox, soon discovered what an awesome task managing Rangers was. White had replaced Scot Symon in September and had guided the club to the final match of season unbeaten in the League. Unfortunately for White, a last-minute goal from Aberdeen gave them a 3-2 victory at Ibrox and certainly handed the title to Celtic.

The Rangers players left the field to a hail of abuse from their own supporters despite having taken 61 points from 34 games and having been the only team to have beaten Celtic in the League. The Ibrox fans obviously had short memories preferring to forget the glory days of the late 1950s and early 1960s and instead dwell on the current success enjoyed by Jock Stein and Celtic.

Extra special Astle

IT WAS certainly a dreadful FA Cup final, but West Bromwich Albion didn't care. Their 1-0 victory over Everton, the red-hot favourites, more than made amends for their embarrassing defeat the previous season at the hands of Third Division QPR in the League Cup final.

Jeff Astle scored the solitary goal in the third minute of extra time, amazingly with his left foot. As he said himself: "That's the dummy leg – the one that's just for standing on. My mates make a joke of it. Yet that's the third goal in a row it has brought me."

Astle broke the deadlock when his right-footed shot cannoned off Colin Harvey and rebounded to him. Without a single second's hesitation Astle whipped a shot from 20 yards into the far corner of the Everton goal. "You don't stop and think about what you're going to do in moments like that," he said. "You just hit the ball and hope for the best."

If Jimmy Husband had heeded Astle's advice it would have been Everton's name on the Cup, not West Brom's. Five minutes from the end of normal time Howard Kendall's cross was deflected to John Morrissey who brilliantly lobbed the ball into the open goal area. Husband, who was utterly unmarked, had all the time in the world to measure his header. Sadly for Everton he got his calculations wrong and sent it over the bar.

Everton pushed John Hurst up for the last 15 minutes but when he headed past the post it was all over.

On paper Everton had been dead certs for the Cup. Their midfield trio of Kendall, Harvey and Alan Ball was majestic, and with Brian Labone in defence and Joe Royle up front they were everybody's favourites. But Alan Ashman's unfashionable team closed them down, cluttered the midfield and Everton were not allowed to play the football of which they were capable.

Labone did a good job containing Astle. The West Brom striker only had two chances in the entire 120 minutes, but that was enough. Astle went into the final as the country's leading scorer with 34 League and Cup goals and had scored in every round, a record he maintained to blistering effect.

145

Lancashire's two-city dominance in the Swinging Sixties and the Beatles era		
League championship	**FA Cup:**	**In Europe:**
1963 Everton	1963 Manchester Utd	1966 Liverpool finalists Cup Winners Cup
1964 Liverpool	1965 Liverpool	1968 Manchester Utd winners European Cup
1965 Manchester Utd	1966 Everton	1970 Manchester City winners Cup Winners Cup
1966 Liverpool	1968 Everton runners-up	
1967 Manchester Utd	1969 Manchester City	*Of the 16 senior domestic trophies*
1968 Manchester City		*available in those eight years*
1970 Everton		*Lancashire clubs won 11 of them*

City's title tips Lancashire's balance of power

MANCHESTER CITY won the League championship for only the second time in dramatic style as they pipped their illustrious neighbours United on the very last day of the season. City had to win at Newcastle to take the title, a task that seemed awesome when, having taken the lead, City went in at half-time level at two apiece.

Malcolm Allison, the charismatic and visionary coach that the new manager Joe Mercer had hired in 1965 when City were in the doldrums of the Second Division, gave an inspired team talk. He said nothing. The team he had coached to super fitness and explosive speed knew what was expected of them and did it. Playing like men inspired, they stormed to a two-goal lead and a late Newcastle goal made no difference, the title was theirs.

It had been a close run race. Leeds and Liverpool had also been in contention until the final stages and when the dust settled a mere six points spanned the top five clubs. When the season began City had hardly looked contenders, taking only one point from their first three matches. Indeed, at one stage, United were five points clear of the pack.

Mercer and Allison reorganised their team, moving Mike Summerbee from the wing to centre-forward, and added Francis Lee to the forward line, at a cost of £60,000 from Bolton. A stirring derby at Old Trafford closed the gap when City gained a fully merited 3-1 victory. Then as the toll of United's European Cup campaign told, City became the principal beneficiaries.

With United lifting the European Cup, the axis of English football shifted from one part of Lancashire to another. Last year Merseyside had the top dogs with Liverpool as champions and Everton as the FA Cup winners. This year belonged to Manchester.

Mullery makes history as first dismissal puts paid to England's hopes

ENGLAND had mixed fortunes in their European championship campaign. True they finished a consoling third and had qualified by eliminating Scotland, cancelling out their embarrassing defeat at Wembley in 1967, but Alan Mullery's dismissal in the semi-final seriously dented England's international image.

The Home championships for this and the previous season had been designated as a qualifying group for the quarter-finals. Although Scotland had a clear advantage over England from their Wembley victory in 1967, their 1-1 draw with Wales left them needing to beat England at Hampden on February 24 to qualify. The Scots were missing Denis Law and Jim Baxter and, despite a virtuoso performance by Charlie Cooke, were fortunate to escape with a 1-1 draw.

England sailed past Spain to meet Yugoslavia in the semi-final in Florence on June 5. It was a bruising, cynical encounter that culminated in the second half with Mullery being sent off, the first time an England player had been dismissed. Mullery had his excuses – he had just been brought down with a late tackle by Trivic – but his retaliatory kick at the perpetrator, compounded by the forward's thespian display, left the referee with little choice.

Down to 10 men, England struggled to hold the young Yugoslav side and four minutes from time Dragan Dzajic, their outstanding winger, scored the only goal of the match. Three days later, in Rome, goals from Bobby Charlton and Geoff Hurst dispatched the Soviet Union to give England third place. In the final Yugoslavia took Italy, the hosts, to a replay before succumbing 2-0.

Moment of madness: Mullery foolishly retaliated and was sent off

United lay Munich ghosts to rest and make Manchester football's capital

TEN YEARS after the Munich disaster, Manchester United finally won the one trophy that mattered more to the club than any other, the European Cup.

Twice, though, it seemed that Matt Busby's long-held dream would turn into a nightmare once again. In the semi-finals United took a slender 1-0 to Real Madrid and, completely outplayed, were 3-1 down at half-time. Busby then gambled everything on all-out attack and, in a remarkable turn-around, goals from David Sadler and the Munich survivor Bill Foulkes took them through to the final against Benfica.

The match, at Wembley on May 29, was equally nerve-wracking. Bobby Charlton gave United the lead with a rare headed goal but Benfica equalised with 15 minutes to go.

Only seconds remained in the match when Eusebio burst through the United defence and had the goal at his mercy. Busby turned away in despair. All Eusebio had to was place the ball past Alex Stepney. Eusebio had rattled the crossbar with a fierce shot earlier, and once again he chose to hit the ball as hard as possible.

He blasted his shot too close to Stepney instead of tucking it into the corner. That mistake allowed Stepney to somehow get his fingertips to the ball and keep United's hopes alive with a reflex save. "Eusebio went for the glory," Nobby Stiles said. "He tried to break the net."

After 90 minutes, the United team were exhausted but Busby prepared them for extra time with a few simple words: "If you pass the ball to each other you will beat them." Stiles recalled the 1966 World Cup final. "Benfica were like the Germans – knackered."

Just how tired Benfica were became apparent in the third minute of extra time. Stepney's clearance was passed to George Best who, tired or not, took off on a 25-yard run. He beat one player, rounded another, and with the Benfica defence in disarray calmly sidestepped the goalkeeper and guided the ball into the net.

The goal lifted a huge burden from United's shoulders and from then on they were unstoppable. Their weariness was forgotten as Brian Kidd celebrated his 19th birthday by scoring a minute later, and Charlton scored a fourth goal soon afterwards. As Stiles had thought, it was like the World Cup final all over again.

When the final whistle blew Charlton collapsed exhausted and burst into tears. Overcome with emotion, Busby also wept when he joined his players on

---

It was like something from Roy of the Rovers

GEORGE BEST

---

the pitch. His grief over the Munich air crash eased.

"The moment when Bobby took the Cup it cleansed me," Busby said. "It eased the pain of the guilt of going into Europe. It was my justification."

Ten years on: Charlton hoists the European Cup a decade after Munich

Media man: Jimmy Hill joins the communications business

■ After five years as the hugely successful manager of Coventry, Jimmy Hill quit his post to work exclusively for television as a pundit. Hill steered the Midlands club from the Third Division to the First and gave the club a modern, go-ahead image. Noel Cantwell replaced Hill.

■ Port Vale were expelled from the Fourth Division for making improper payments to players. They were promptly re-elected. Peterborough had 19 points deducted for a similar offence, and were relegated from the Third Division as a result.

FOR THE RECORD

■ The British transfer record was broken twice, first when Martin Chivers moved from Southampton to Tottenham for £125,000 and then when Allan Clarke joined Leicester from Fulham for £150,000.

■ No team in the League managed to score 100 or more goals, the first time this had happened since the 1953-54 season.

■ Dave Mackay moved from Tottenham to Derby in July, saying: "I could do nothing more for them, nor they for me."

Mercer and Allison in overdrive as City's bandwagon keeps rolling on

MANCHESTER CITY'S revival under the managerial partnership of Joe Mercer and Malcolm Allison continued when they added the FA Cup to the League trophy they had won the previous season. Not bad for a team which four years earlier had finished 11th in the Second Division. Sadly for Leicester, the Wembley losers, they limped away from their Cup final defeat and failed to secure the seven points they needed from their last five League matches to avoid relegation to the Second Division.

But given the chances they had to win the Cup, it was not surprising they were League flops as well. Allan Clarke, their wonderfully gifted striker, had a magnificent shot pushed away for a corner in the 30th minute. Then Peter Rodrigues, Leicester's right-back, missed the opportunity of the match when he failed to connect feet from the goal.

Leicester's errors in front of goal continued in the second half. Andy Lochhead fluffed a simple chance from Clarke's header and then with 15 minutes remaining Lochhead blew another chance when he was hustled off the ball.

However, Manchester City were worthy winners. The forward line of Colin Bell, Francis Lee and Mike Summerbee in particular were a handful for Leicester throughout the 90 minutes. And Neil Young's goal in the 24th minute was the finest strike of the afternoon. The inside left latched on perfectly to Summerbee's pulled-back pass from the goal line to thump the ball past the hapless Peter Shilton. It was a goal worthy of a winner's medal, and so it proved.

City slickers: Oakes and Bell hoist the FA Cup

Busby bows out with every honour won

WITH HIS 60th birthday on the horizon, Sir Matt Busby announced his retirement on January 14. Manchester United were sixth from bottom of the First Division and Busby said that it was time for a younger man to take charge. In reality, with the European Cup won there was nothing else left for him to achieve.

Busby was the longest-serving manager in the League and,

> *I had never met anyone else like him in the game. The longer you knew him the more you felt for him, which was why he had everybody doing the things they did*
>
> DENIS LAW
> on Matt Busby

since the end of the war, he had overseen a remarkable transformation at Old Trafford. He had taken a club that was deep in debt and, by the sheer force of his personality, turned it around.

His first team was, by force of necessity, built from nothing. But Busby's determination to develop his own players rather than spend money in the transfer market laid the very foundations of the club.

With his post-war players ageing, Busby told his board of directors: "I am going to make the move which will make or break Manchester United." Overnight, half of the team were replaced by young reserves and the Busby Babes were born.

The gamble was the making of United, and also the breaking of the club's heart when so many brilliant careers were cut short one fateful night in Munich. Busby barely survived the plane crash, twice receiving the last rites, and was on the brink of quitting.

But urged on by his devoted wife Jean he fought back and rebuilt United yet again, although this time he was forced into the transfer market to replace his lost young stars.

Once again, Busby contemplated retirement when United were beaten by Partizan Belgrade in the semi-final of the

Midas touch: Busby parades one of the many trophies he won

European Cup. But his life's work was never going to be done until the emotional night that Bobby Charlton held the trophy aloft at Wembley.

Busby said that he would stay with the club as general manager, and there was feverish speculation about who would replace him. Don Revie was the bookmakers' favourite, but the methods he had used at Leeds were anathema to Busby.

Wilf McGuinness the assistant manager was a 6-1 outsider.

But once Busby discovered that Dave Sexton, the Chelsea manager, did not want to move north then McGuinness was his choice. Busby waited nearly three months, until he was sure United were in no danger of relegation, before making the announcement.

The first McGuinness knew about it was the day before, when he was told to wear a tie to work the following morning. He would soon discover that Busby was an impossible act to follow.

Arsenal's guns silenced by Rogers

DON ROGERS did next to nothing for the first 90 minutes of the League Cup final. The pitch was a muddy swamp but the Swindon winger started extra time with barely a mark on his shirt or shorts. Then he burst into life to scupper Arsenal with two goals.

Arsenal had been expected to stroll past Third Division Swindon but they did have their excuses. The pitch had been ruined by the International Horse of the Year show, and most of the team were still recovering from flu.

They hardly had any excuses for the way Swindon took the lead. Ian Ure's feeble back pass left Bob Wilson stranded and Roger Smart scored the easiest of goals. Arsenal then laid siege to the Swindon goal, but they were repeatedly beaten back by Peter Downsborough. During one frantic spell the Swindon goalkeeper faced nine corners in 10 minutes.

Another goalkeeping mistake, this time by Downsborough, let Bobby Gould force in an equaliser with four minutes remaining. But extra time was the last thing Arsenal wanted.

Heavy rain and the after-effects of the flu had sapped their strength while Rogers was still as fresh as a daisy.

He tucked a corner away to give Swindon the lead and then, in the last minute of the match, he made doubly sure. Starting from the half-way line, he ploughed through the mud to score a sparkling solo goal.

Swindon, as a Third Division club, were ineligible to take up a place in the Fairs Cup. But, like QPR, the last Third Division team to take the trophy, they won promotion instead.

White knight: Rogers (centre) did nothing apart from score two goals to capture the League Cup

Muddy heroes: the grimy Swindon players celebrate their dramatic victory in extra time at Wembley

United find Argy-bargy strikes again

DESPITE the assaults Celtic had suffered in the world club championship last season, Matt Busby was determined that Manchester United were going to play in the competition. Like Jock Stein before him, after two maulings he probably wished he hadn't.

United went to Argentina for the first leg. The local press claimed that Nobby Stiles was "The Assassin", and even the match programme said he was a brute and a bad sportsman.

Not surprisingly, Estudiantes went out to get him. Stiles was the victim of a blatant head butt and was then sent off for dissent. Bobby Charlton was in the wars as well, needing several stitches in a deliberately inflicted leg wound.

The return leg, with Estudiantes holding a 1-0 lead, produced slightly better football in the 1-1 draw and even more violence. Denis Law was kicked so badly by the Argentinian goalkeeper that he had to be taken off and George Best was victimised throughout the match. His patience finally snapped and he was sent off with Medina for fighting.

Tostao spoils England's summer trip

FRESH from having retained the Home international championships – beating Northern Ireland, Wales and Scotland in eight days in May – England enjoyed a reasonably successful tour to Latin America. Their first stop was Mexico City where the World Cup final will be next summer.

England found adjusting to the heat, humidity and altitude no easy matter and they laboured to achieve a goalless draw against the national side. Two days later England fared much better in Guadalajara when they beat a Mexican XI 4-0. Guadalajara is 2,000 feet lower than the capital and, fortunately for England, the site of their Group matches in the World Cup finals.

Colin Lee and Geoff Hurst both scored in England's next match in the tour, a satisfying 2-1 defeat of Uruguay in Montevideo. And with 10 minutes remaining of their final match – against Brazil in Rio de Janeiro – they seemed set to pull off a remarkable coup.

Colin Bell had put them ahead in the first half when he pounced on a deflection and their luck held when Gordon Banks saved Carlos Alberto's penalty. But Pele's team were in no mood to surrender meekly and a late rally broke a brave England visibly wilting in the heat.

Tostao equalised and two minutes from the end laid on a perfect pass for Jairzinho to score the winner. It was a cruel finish to the tour but Ramsey's men had held their own against the best in the world for 80 minutes.

Leeds tear up record books in relentless march to title

LEEDS finally clicked into gear and won their first League championship in their 69-year history. It was no more than they had been threatening for the past five seasons, but somehow it had always eluded them. Almost certainly their success in winning the League Cup and the Fairs Cup the previous season had made all the difference. At last the monkey was off their shoulders: they had something to show for all their endeavours.

Don Revie and Leeds executed their championship pursuit in their inimitable, clinical fashion. They did it without breaking sweat and swept all setbacks aside. Even an incredible 5-1 defeat by Burnley was ignored (though they made sure to thump them 6-1 in the return) as Leeds proceeded to reel off 28 matches without defeat.

Their only other defeat in the League was at the hands of Manchester City on September 14, three days after the exertions of winning the Fairs Cup in Budapest. It was the only match that Leeds did not win in their first nine League fixtures. They began in magnificent style and maintained it throughout the season, breaking records galore.

To suffer only two defeats was a record; their final total of 67 points from 42 matches broke Arsenal's record of 1931; and, curiously, their goals tally – a mere 66 – was lower than any championship-winning side since the offside law was altered in 1925. To be fair it was an extremely low-scoring First Division, only two clubs scored more goals than Leeds.

Nor could Revie's team be justifiably criticised for negative play. Indeed he had deliberately set out to be more attack-minded because of the way Manchester City had won the title the previous season. City, he felt, had succeeded by attacking teams home and away and had arguably won the title from United by beating them 3-1 at Old Trafford.

For once bad luck ran Leeds'

Guiding force: Billy Bremner, the Leeds captain, inspired his team to their first League championship in the club's 69-year history

way with early defeats in the League Cup, FA Cup and Fairs Cup. Unlike previous seasons, where an ambitious assault on several fronts had stretched their resources and left them with nothing to show for it, in 1969 they had been left with a single objective: the championship. This time they got it.

QPR kick out Stock to start managerial musical chairs

IN November Jim Gregory, the QPR chairman, sacked Alec Stock, the manager who had just guided them from the Third to the First Division in successive seasons. Incredibly it set off a chain reaction that by the end of the season resulted in 35 managerial changes.

Two days later Tommy Docherty left Rotherham to take over at QPR and Bill Dodgin was demoted to assistant manager. A fortnight later Ronnie Allen quit Wolves and Bill McGarry left Ipswich to replace him. The next day Bobby Robson was sacked at Fulham and Johnny Haynes was appointed player-manager with Dodgin as his assistant.

In December Nottingham Forest got rid of John Carey and installed Matt Gillies, who resigned from Leicester. Then ·Docherty walked out of QPR after a bust-up with Gregory leaving Les Allen as player-manager. Haynes continued the madness by packing in the manager's job after just four games. Dodgin stepped up.

The vacant spot at Leicester was taken by Torquay's Frank O'Farrell. Docherty quickly bounced back and was snapped up by Aston Villa. Stock also gained another job, just six weeks after his sacking at QPR, as Luton's manager. Stock also had the last laugh: QPR finished plumb bottom of the First Division and were relegated.

Newcastle belie their lowly status

NEWCASTLE confounded all the critics by romping away with the Fairs Cup, the fifth English club to win a European trophy since 1963. The criticism of Newcastle was nothing to do with the club, but the absurd way they had qualified for the tournament. Under Uefa's antiquated rules, adopted in 1955, the Fairs Cup was supposed to be for the benefit of European cities that organised trade fairs, and originally was supposed to be contested by a team drawn from all clubs in a city. This had soon fallen by the wayside, and instead a one city, one team policy obtained.

At the end of the 1968 season Newcastle had finished tenth with three London, and two Liverpool, clubs and the FA Cup winners above them. With Manchester City and United (as holders) in the European Cup; Liverpool, Leeds and Chelsea in the Fairs Cup; WBA in the Cup Winners Cup; the fourth Fairs Cup place fell to Newcastle by default.

Notwithstanding the amazing combination of circumstances that allowed Newcastle in through the back door, they grasped their golden opportunity with verve, scything their

Double top: Newcastle beat Ujpest Dozsa home and away

way through impressive European opposition. In successive rounds they eliminated Feyenoord, Sporting Lisbon, Real Zaragoza, Vitoria Setubal and Rangers.

In the final they scaled even higher peaks when they faced Ujpest Dozsa who had beaten Leeds in both legs in the quarter finals. At St James's Park, in the first leg, the Newcastle captain Bobby Moncur virtually won the tie single-handed. Frustrated by his team's inability to score against the Hungarians the defensive midfielder decided to throw himself into the attack, with immediate reward. Moncur scored two goals in the 63rd and 72nd minutes. They were Moncur's first goals in seven years. Jim Scott made it 3-0 seven minutes from time.

Moncur and Newcastle were no less impressive in the return in Budapest a fortnight later. Despite being 2-0 down at half-time, Moncur rallied his troops with a goal a minute after the restart and then Ben Arentfot and Alan Foggon completed a remarkable 3-2 away victory. Chastened critics now claimed that Newcastle's runaway success proved the strength in depth of the Football League.

World Cup sparks war in Honduras

THE semi-final matches between Honduras and El Salvador in the central and north American qualifying group for the World Cup finals were responsible for the start of a full-scale war between the two countries.

The two-legged semi-final went to a play-off after both teams won one match. There was rioting at all three games, which provoked skirmishes along the border between the two countries, which had been at loggerheads for some time. Hondurans claimed that their country was being over-run by migrant farmers from El Salvador, who in turn said that their people were being persecuted.

Soon after El Salvador finally won 3-2 in Mexico the two countries broke off diplomatic relations. A fortnight later, on July 14, El Salvador invaded Honduras, bombing military targets and the capital city's airport. Honduras retaliated with an immediate counter-attack and more than 2,000 people were killed in the fighting.

MATT BUSBY & GEORGE BEST
The dream team that fell to earth

Chris Nawrat

I N ITS own sweet way Matt Busby and George Best was a marriage made in heaven: Busby was the avuncular manager who simply adored footballers and loved it if they could express their skills in his teams. Best was the imp of the Sixties with a talent so outrageous that he captured not only Busby's heart, but the world's too.

Their two trajectories intersected at Wembley on May 29, 1968 when Manchester United gloriously captured the European Cup. For Busby, 59, it was the vindication of more than 20 years of steadfast devotion to United and exorcised the ghosts of the Munich air crash a decade earlier. For Best, 22, it was proof positive that he was the best player in Europe, if not on the earth. He had demonstrated that his talent was not so much errant, but beyond the comprehension of other mortals. It was to be only the beginning of even greater glories to come.

Busby's liaison with Manchester United began in the debris of the Second World War. Working with next to nothing more than the players on United's books he miraculously put together an FA Cup-winning side and a championship-winning side in the late 1940s and early 1950s built around Johnny Carey. Then, within a season, he transformed the club by introducing a host of home-grown teenagers, the Busby Babes, to replace his veteran side, including Carey. It was a bold, but realistic, gamble and it marked out Busby as a manager with the character for the big decisions. His reward was two further League titles and that his "unknowns" became household names, in particular Duncan Edwards.

That team, including Edwards, was cut down in 1958 in Munich when Busby himself was fortunate to escape alive. It was the worst moment in his life, his brilliant young team, his "Babes", destroyed because Busby wanted to pursue the future: success against Continental opposition. Busby dug into his soul, contemplated packing it in and came out fighting. He rebuilt United again, first with the cheque book, and then with what he loved best, Manchester United's own home-grown players.

In 1961, a frail 15-year-old Belfast kid arrived at Old Trafford for a trial. His name was George Best. Within 24 hours he was on the ferry back because he was homesick. Busby gave him another chance and Best returned a fortnight later. Despite the lack of size that had caused other professional clubs to reject him, Busby and United had instantly spotted Best's amazing talents. It is almost certain that if Best had gone to another club those talents would never have blossomed in the way they did. United never trained Best's ball skills out of him, as other clubs would have. Best's hallmarks – nutmegging opponents; shimmying, dazzling runs that left a host of defenders on their backsides; goalkeepers cheekily lobbed at the most ludicrous of angles – would have been consigned to the dustbin of the school playground.

But not at United. Busby allowed Best to indulge in the kind of football only found in kids' comics, and Best revelled in it. As Eamon Dunphy, a contemporary of Best's at Old Trafford, put it: "Footballers as people first, that was Busby's secret. Even the oldest of men were boys to him. His job was to facilitate their development as human beings, their innate talent would then blossom. That was his formula." Best concurred: "We never talked about how we were going to play. We just went out on to the pitch and got on with it. We were audacious and flamboyant, dangerous and unpredictable." None more so than Best.

By the mid-1960s Best was being hailed as the Fifth Beatle and was duly granted rock star status. For a quiet, shy lad from the back streets of Belfast who preferred the snooker hall, the pub and the bowling alley to the discotheque, the nightclub and the limelight it was an overwhelming experience. It had its advantages (Best was adored and chased by myriad women) and its disadvantages (the hangers-on and the demon drink) but it was the Swinging Sixties, so why not

Audacious: Law leads a United attack against Fulham in United's heyday

GEORGE BEST

Born May 22, 1946, Belfast

PLAYING CAREER
Manchester United 1963-73
361 appearances, 137 goals
Honours European Cup: Winners 1968
League Cup: Winners 1965, 1967
Internationals Northern Ireland debut 1964
  (aged 17)
37 appearances, 9 goals
Also played for Bournemouth, Dunstable Town, Fort Lauderdale Strikers, Fulham, Hibernian, Los Angeles Aztecs, Motherwell, Stockport

Other career distinctions Leading scorer in the League (jointly with Ron Davies of Southampton) in 1967-68 with 28 goals. Elected Footballer of the Year and European Footballer of the Year in 1968

let the lad enjoy himself? By and large Busby and United turned a blind eye to Best's excesses and attempts to rein him in usually proved fruitless.

Best, Busby, Manchester United and the Swinging Sixties hit their apogee with the European Cup final. It was the crowning glory, the apex of achievement, like climbing Everest. But it meant different things to different people. Later Best realised that it had signalled the beginning of the end for him and his beloved United: "For Matt and Bobby Charlton, for Bill Foulkes, for Denis Law … they'd done it. And then they sat back and you could almost hear the energy and ambition sighing out of the club. It was like being in at the winding up of a company."

Best was still only 22, the rest of that United team were in the twilight of their careers and there were no more fabulous youngsters coming through on the legendary Old Trafford production line. Nor had Busby gone into the transfer market to strengthen his fading, ageing team. In the four years from 1964 to 1968 he had only bought one player, Alex Stepney, the goalkeeper. This was not the Busby of the 1950s and early 1960s always with an eye on the future, this was Busby sticking to the remnants of the 1958 side hoping against hope they could ease the pain of that horror on a Munich runway. Best understood this, but now that the European Cup had been finally won, he wanted wholesale changes.

Best confronted Busby in his office. He told the boss bluntly that Bobby Charlton (the two had hated each other from day one), Denis Law and Pat Crerand had to go. They were over the hill and holding the side back. The only solution,

Fateful flight: the Munich plane crash tore the heart out of Manchester United

Best told Busby, was to rebuild the side around him and make him the captain. Busby refused point blank, claiming that Best wasn't responsible enough. "Make me the captain and I will be responsible," was Best's retort. That exchange effectively ended the era of Busby and Best and saw Manchester United enter a downward spiral that would take more than a generation to reverse.

Six years later the club were relegated to the Second Division for the first time since 1938. Busby had retired in 1969, giving way to Wilf McGuinness but always leaving him in his shadow. Busby returned in 1970, retired again, this time handing over to Frank O'Farrell, but deposed him in 1972 and brought in Tommy Docherty. Throughout all this managerial mayhem Best had battled to hold a struggling side

together, battled to keep his personal life on an even keel, and battled to beat the bottle. He didn't win one of those contests. By 1973, having walked out and returned on numerous occasions, Best finally quit Old Trafford. The golden dreams that had beckoned so gloriously in 1968 had now turned to dust.

So did Busby fail a most precocious and extraordinary talent at the very zenith of his powers? Or did the boy wonder vaingloriously piss it all away in an orgy of self-indulgence?

Bob Paisley has this observation: "If you look at Matt and ask where he might have failed you immediately think of George Best. But could anybody have handled him? It's a shame that his talent wasn't fully used because after the age of 26 he just played around. But if Matt Busby couldn't handle him, nobody could."

SIR MATT BUSBY

Born May 26, 1909, Bellshill, Lanarkshire

PLAYING CAREER
Manchester City 1928-36
Over 200 appearances
Honours FA Cup: Winners 1934; Finalists 1933
Liverpool 1936-39
Internationals Played one full match for Scotland in 1933 and also captained the Scottish team during the war-time internationals

MANAGEMENT CAREER
Manchester United Manager 1945-69
Retired as team manager in 1969, but took charge temporarily in the 1970-71 season when Wilf McGuinness left the club
Appointed a director of Manchester United in 1971 and subsequently became the club's president
Honours European Cup: Winners 1968
FA Cup: Winners 1948; Finalists 1958
League Cup: Winners 1952, 1956, 1957, 1967

Other honours Knighted 1968. CBE 1958
Football League vice-president 1982

Died January 20, 1994

Happy days: Crerand, Busby and Best

Tragic loss: Edwards died at Munich

Leeds' treble turns to nought

Revie: finished empty-handed

LEEDS, under Don Revie, were without doubt the most unpopular side in the country. Their uncompromising – some would say ruthless – style of play won them few friends but many enemies. However the blows that fate dealt them in April surely melted the hardest of hearts.

On March 28 Leeds had played a total of 52 matches and lost only three. Within five weeks they played a further 10 matches but could only win one. In that terrible spell three prestigious trophies had slipped from their grasp: the League championship, the FA Cup and the European Cup. The impossible Treble had proved just that. Impossible.

First, on April 1, they lost the championship race to Everton, the team that had ended their unbeaten run of 34 League games in August. Leeds had taken over the First Division leadership in January but by mid-March Everton had regained it.

And on the same night Leeds went down 1-0 at Elland Road to Celtic in the European Cup semi-final, George Connelly scoring after 90 seconds. It was Leeds's eighth fixture in 22 days. In the return, a fortnight later, despite a thundering equaliser from Billy Bremner in the first quarter of an hour, the English champions could not

> *There is no doubt in my mind that they would have done that Treble had it been a normal season*
>
> BILL SHANKLY

hold the rampant Scottish champions. Two minutes into the second half John Hughes regained the lead for Celtic and then a dazzling, mazy run from Jimmy Johnstone, their quicksilver winger, set up Bobby Murdoch for the killing goal.

Four days earlier, on April 11, Leeds had met a robust Chelsea side in the FA Cup final and were held to a draw. In the replay at Old Trafford on April 29 once again Chelsea were their match. This time Chelsea prevailed in extra time and Leeds's last chance for honours had evaporated. It was a cruel way for the finest team in England to end the season: empty-handed.

So what went wrong? Two factors probably converged to wreck Leeds's season. First, because the World Cup was to be held in June, the season was foreshortened adding to fixture congestion and fatigue, particularly as Leeds were involved in so many competitions.

And second, the FA Cup semi-final against Manchester United certainly sapped their energy and playing resources. It took Leeds three matches, over 12 days, to shake off their rivals. The last match came two days before Leeds began their hectic Easter programme and the sheer volume of fixtures simply overwhelmed them.

Arsenal's barren years ended by the new kids on the block

ARSENAL produced a remarkable comeback on April 28 to end a long barren spell that had not seen a trophy come to Highbury since the League championship in 1953.

Their progress to the final of the Fairs Cup had been built on a series of resounding wins at home – 3-0 against Glentoran in the first round, a defeat of Sporting Lisbon by the same margin in the second round, a 7-1 thrashing of Dinamo Bacau in the quarter-finals, and yet another 3-0 win, against Ajax in the semi-finals.

But Arsenal's extraordinary defeat of Anderlecht in the final owed much to two of their teenagers, Ray Kennedy and Eddie Kelly.

Kennedy had signed for Arsenal the previous season and had yet to establish himself in the first team – starting only two League games and twice coming on as a substitute.

When he replaced Charlie George in the first leg of the final in Belgium on April 22, Arsenal were 3-0 down and looked to be on their way out. But five minutes from the end he scored with a header to give some hope to the 51,000 fans who packed into Highbury for the second leg.

Kelly, at 19, was just a few months older than Kennedy. He, too, was in his first season in the first team. But the young midfield player showed no signs of nerves when, in the 26th minute, he calmly trapped the ball and drove it into the net.

Arsenal were now only a goal behind and if they could score again they would take the Cup on the away goals rule. Roared on by the crowd they kept pressing forward, but Anderlecht would not succumb.

Finally, with just under 20

Flying high: McLintock launches himself at the Ajax goalkeeper

minutes remaining, Bob McNab looped a cross into the penalty area. John Radford produced a majestic leap to get to the ball and his header delivered the desperately needed goal. Then, a minute later, Jon Sammels clipped in a third goal to give Arsenal the outright victory and put the seal on a perfect night.

England go it alone as British sides join an illustrious list of failures in the World Cup

FROM the British Isles' point of view it was fortunate England had won the World Cup in 1966 because otherwise the home nations would have had no representatives in the 1970 finals in Mexico whatsoever. As holders, of course, England were spared the problems of qualification. It was a different story for Scotland, Wales and the two Irelands.

Scotland had much the best excuse. They had been drawn in the same group as West Germany, the beaten finalists in 1966, and Austria. Scotland's faint hopes disappeared when they drew 1-1 with West Germany at Hampden, lost 3-2 in Germany and 2-0 in Vienna. They did finish runners-up, edging out Austria by a point.

Wales also had a tough task: their opponents were Italy and East Germany. Predictably they lost all four games, conceding 10 goals and only scoring four. The

Finishing touch: Libuda scores for West Germany against Scotland

Republic fared little better as they scraped one point from six matches, and that a 1-1 draw at home to Denmark, as Czechoslovakia and Hungary slugged it out for the plane to Mexico. The Czechs eventually prevailed 4-1 in a play-off in Marseille.

Northern Ireland could not get past the Soviet Union, drawing at home and losing away. So for the third successive World Cup finals England were left to fly the flag on their own.

Not that the home nations were the only European casualties of note. Spain, Portugal and Yugoslavia also joined Hungary on the scrap heap of also-rans. There were upsets too in South America and Africa as Argentina, who had hoped to host the finals, were eliminated by Peru and Morocco, not Ghana, emerged as that continent's representatives. They were the first African side in the finals since 1934.

City capture a majority shareholding in two Cups

MANCHESTER CITY enjoyed their third season of success with a Cup double at home and abroad. And their first triumph, in the League Cup, was particularly sweet because it included a defeat of their illustrious neighbours Manchester United.

After an easy victory over Southport in the second round, City had to work harder in the next two stages, with home matches against First Division opponents each time – Liverpool were edged out 3-2 and Everton were dispatched 2-0.

City's finest victory was undoubtedly in the semi-finals, where they met their old rivals over two legs. The contest was effectively decided in the first match at Maine Road, which City won 2-1 thanks to a penalty scored by Francis Lee. They were able to hold on to their slender advantage at Old Trafford and a 2-2 draw was enough to take them to Wembley. It was

delicious revenge for United's 3-0 defeat of City in the fourth round of the FA Cup.

The final, on March 7, brought two of England's finest forwards, Lee and Jeff Astle, into opposition. Astle struck first, giving West Brom the lead in the first half. Lee, however, was not able to add to his tally and it was Michael Doyle who took the match into extra time and then Glyn Pardoe who scored the winner.

When it came to Cup matches it seemed that City were always saving their best for Maine Road, particularly in the European Cup Winners Cup. They had to play the first leg of every round away from home, and they only managed one win in four matches abroad.

But once they had got their opponents back to Manchester it was a different story, with four victories and 14 goals. City twice hit five goals, the most notable

Up for the Cup: Tony Book brandishes the European Cup Winners Cup

time being their 5-1 victory over Schalke in the semi-finals after a 1-0 setback in West Germany.

With their indifferent away form, the omens might not have appeared to be too good for their trip to Vienna to play the Polish side Gornik in the final.

But Lee, as happened so often, was irrepressible. In tandem with Neil Young he was responsible for both goals. The

first came early in the match when Lee's shot hit a post and Young scored from the rebound. Then, just before half-time, Young was brought down by the Polish goalkeeper and Lee converted the penalty.

Gornik scored a consolation goal in the second half but that was not going to stop City collecting their fourth trophy in the past three years.

Celtic fail Grand Slam test

LEEDS weren't the only British side to see their hopes of a Grand Slam of trophies turn to dust. Much the same thing happened to Celtic, Leeds's conquerors in the European Cup semi-final.

But in Celtic's case they had been chasing four trophies and won two, while Leeds had pursued three and lost the lot. In both cases fixture congestion and fatigue played a vital part in their downfall.

Celtic snapped up their first honour in October when they dispatched little St Johnstone in the Scottish League Cup final despite being without the injured Bobby Lennox, the suspended Willie Wallace and the disgraced Tommy Gemmell, who had been sent off for Scotland playing against West Germany. The 1-0 scoreline flattered St Johnstone.

Celtic's 25th League title was a one-horse race: the Parkhead side eventually finishing 12 points ahead of Rangers, having won 27 of their 34 League matches.

On April 11, Celtic went into the Scottish Cup final against Aberdeen at Hampden seemingly holding all the Grand Slam aces. They held a 1-0 lead against Leeds in the European Cup semi-final with the home leg to come the following Wednesday and were red-hot favourites to swagger past Aberdeen. That was the script, the reality was somewhat different.

Two incidents in the first half-hour probably turned the game Aberdeen's way. First the referee awarded a dubious penalty when Derek McKay's cross hit a defender's hand, Joe Harper converting, and then a Bobby Lennox "goal" was disallowed minutes later.

However, with seven minutes remaining, there had been no further goals until McKay pounced to give Aberdeen a 2-0 lead. Lennox got one back with two minutes to go, only for McKay to dash upfield and seal a famous 3-1 victory.

But there was still the European Cup, although Celtic were extremely fortunate to have reached the semi-final. In the second round in November Celtic had taken an impressive 3-0 lead to Benfica only to concede three goals themselves. With the scores tied at three apiece Celtic went through on the toss of a coin.

Against Leeds the 1-0 cushion

Israel: undid Celtic

they had from Elland Road was always going to be too much for Leeds who, despite levelling the scores after 13 minutes, succumbed 3-1 on aggregate.

Once again Celtic went into a final a shade too confident. This time the opponents were Feyenoord in Milan on May 6 and the Dutch champions proved to be more of a handful that Celtic had anticipated. Although Gemmell had given the Glasgow side the lead after half an hour with a powerful shot reminiscent of the goal in Lisbon that had won the European Cup three years earlier, the Dutch equalised minutes later. The scorer was Rinus Israel, their sweeper.

Israel was to prove the key to Celtic's undoing as Feyenoord were playing a sweeper system with a difference: the sweeper also attacked. Thus Israel stole out of defence to catch the Celtic defence unawares with a deft header.

Celtic, baffled by the Dutch style of play and with Jimmy Johnstone marked out of the game, failed to score and the match went into extra time. Four minutes from the end Billy McNeill handled the ball, the referee waved play on, and Ove Kindvall scored the winner as Feyenoord became the first Dutch club to win the European Cup.

Webb redeems himself

CHELSEA, who had finished third in the League, were probably the last team Leeds wanted to face in the FA Cup final after a long and grinding season. The London club were probably one of the few sides that could counter Leeds's steel with steel of their own. And so it proved.

The teams met at Wembley on April 11 just as the first two legs of Leeds's fabulous Treble, the League championship and the European Cup, were eluding them. It was a typical hard-fought battle with neither side giving any quarter.

A first-half header from Jack Charlton had given Leeds the lead before Peter Houseman levelled the scores. With six minutes remaining Leeds seemed finally to have one hand on the Cup when Mick Jones scored their second. But the fates hadn't finished with Leeds just yet. Two minutes later Ian Hutchinson levelled the scores and took the game into extra time. A barren half-hour necessitated a replay, the first since 1912.

Thus, a fortnight later, both teams travelled to Old Trafford.

The second match was, if anything, more brutal than the first. Peter Bonetti was virtually knocked out by a late charge from Jones and the match was held up for several minutes as the Chelsea goalkeeper received attention. Shortly afterwards a dazed Bonetti was unable to stop a Jones shot and Leeds were ahead for the third time.

But Chelsea just would not give up. Peter Osgood, with a magnificent diving header, put them back into contention with 12 minutes of normal time remaining.

And, one minute after the extra time interval, Chelsea took the lead for the first time after 226 minutes of play when David Webb, at the far post, contrived to bundle Hutchinson's long throw into the net.

Fate had dealt its final card. Webb had been dreadful in the first match – Eddie Gray had run the full back ragged – so much so that Chelsea had moved him into the centre of defence, but here was the Wembley "failure" turned Old Trafford hero. Cruel indeed.

Saved: Chelsea players embrace Osgood after his equaliser in the replay

Moore accused of jewel theft – charges vanish into thin air

DAYS before England were to play Romania in the first match of the World Cup finals in Mexico, Bobby Moore, their captain, was arrested for alleged theft in Bogotá, Colombia.

Moore was accused by a shopgirl, Clara Padilla, who worked in the Green Fire jewellery store in the hotel the England party were staying in, of stealing a £600 emerald and gold bracelet. Moore and Bobby Charlton had visited the shop but when they were asked to explain the disappearance of the bracelet they were astonished. Moore could not even recollect having looked at it. Moore and Charlton made statements to the police and thought nothing of it.

Then the England team, who were in South America to acclimatise for the finals, flew to Ecuador for a friendly match. On their return, en route to Mexico, they stopped over in Bogotá and Moore was put under house arrest. Apparently another "witness" had emerged. The England team were forced to depart without their captain and the incident became an international scandal.

For four days the controversy raged as diplomats were hauled in to clear up the matter. Harold Wilson, the Prime Minister, was in the throes of an election campaign but that did not deter him from applying political pressure on the Colombian authorities.

Gradually the case against Moore began to fall apart, particularly when it was discovered that other visiting celebrities such as bullfighters and singers had been similarly "stung" and had paid up to avoid publicity.

Moore was "bailed" to play in the finals and joined his teammates in Mexico. The case eventually subsided when the mystery witness disappeared and the perpetrators, Padilla and the owner of the shop, were charged with conspiracy in 1972.

Moore leaves court in Bogota after a four-hour investigation

Hundred up: Bobby Charlton and Terry Neill lead the teams out

■ Bobby Charlton captained England and scored a goal when he made his 100th international appearance, against Northern Ireland at Wembley on April 21.

■ England and Scotland's 0-0 draw at Hampden Park on April 25 was only the second time this result had occurred. The first was the inaugural match between the two countries in 1872.

■ Second Division Swindon won the end of season Anglo-Italian Cup. They were leading 3-0 at Napoli when the match was abandoned with 10 minutes still to play because of crowd trouble.

■ The annual meeting of the Football League decided to fix the minimum admission charge at six shillings.

■ Uefa decided to use penalty kicks, rather than the toss of a coin, to decide matches that finished all-square in the three Cup competitions.

■ Ronnie Simpson, the Celtic goalkeeper, retired in May. He had been playing since June 3, 1945, when he made his first appearance for Queen's Park.

Old guard bite the dust

SOME of the biggest names in England ended the season with a brutal reminder that their glory days were long past. Chief among them were Preston, the first ever winners of the Double, and Aston Villa, who occupied the bottom two places in the Second Division and were relegated – the first time that both clubs had ever sunk so low.

Sunderland and Sheffield Wednesday were also in decline, slipping out of the First Division. Sheffield Wednesday only had themselves to blame though. In their last match of the season they needed to beat Manchester City at home to condemn Crystal Palace in their place.

But they lost 2-1 and thus found themselves out of the top flight for the first time since the 1958-59 season. Huddersfield, another historic club, had been out of the First Division even longer.

They bounced back though, running away with the Second Division and finishing seven points clear of another famous club, Blackpool, who also reclaimed their place among the elite.

At the other extreme, the League finally bowed to pressure from non-League clubs, who felt that they were continually being denied a chance to prove themselves. Bradford Park Avenue failed to gain re-election and were replaced by Cambridge United, the Southern League champions. It was the first change that had been made since Oxford had replaced Accrington Stanley in 1962.

LEAGUE TABLES AND RESULTS 1960 – 1970

1960-61

WORLD CUP

EUROPEAN CHAMPIONSHIP

EUROPEAN CUP
Benfica 3
Barcelona 2

EUROPEAN CUP WINNERS CUP
Fiorentina beat Rangers 2-0 2-1

FAIRS CUP
AS Roma beat Birmingham City 2-2 2-0

FA CUP
Tottenham Hotspur 2
Leicester City 0

FIRST DIVISION

	P	W	D	L	F	A	Pts
Tottenham	42	31	4	7	115	55	66
Sheff Wed	42	23	12	7	78	47	58
Wolves	42	25	7	10	103	75	57
Burnley	42	22	7	13	102	77	51
Everton	42	22	6	14	87	69	50
Leicester	42	18	9	15	87	70	45
Man Utd	42	18	9	15	88	76	45
Blackburn	42	15	13	14	77	76	43
Aston Villa	42	17	9	16	78	77	43
West Brom	42	18	5	19	67	71	41
Arsenal	42	15	11	16	77	85	41
Chelsea	42	15	7	20	98	100	37
Man City	42	13	11	18	79	90	37
Nottm F	42	14	9	19	62	78	37
Cardiff	42	13	11	18	60	85	37
West Ham	42	13	10	19	77	88	36
Fulham	42	14	8	20	72	95	36
Bolton	42	12	11	19	58	73	35
Birmingham	42	14	6	22	62	84	34
Blackpool	42	12	9	21	68	73	33
Newcastle	42	11	10	21	86	109	32
Preston	42	10	10	22	43	71	30

SECOND DIVISION
Champions: Ipswich Town
Also promoted: Sheffield United
Relegated: Portsmouth, Lincoln City

THIRD DIVISION
Champions: Bury
Also promoted: Walsall
Relegated: Tranmere Rovers, Bradford City, Colchester United, Chesterfield

FOURTH DIVISION
Champions: Peterborough United
Also promoted: Crystal Palace, Northampton Town, Bradford PA

LEAGUE CUP
Aston Villa beat Rotherham United 0-2 3-0

SCOTTISH CUP
Dunfermline Athletic 2
Celtic 0, after 0-0

SCOTTISH FIRST DIVISION

	P	W	D	L	F	A	Pts
Rangers	34	23	5	6	88	46	51
Kilmarnock	34	21	8	5	77	45	50
T Lanark	34	20	2	12	100	80	42
Celtic	34	15	9	10	64	46	39
Motherwell	34	15	8	11	70	57	38
Aberdeen	34	14	8	12	72	72	36
Hibernian	34	15	4	15	66	69	34
Hearts	34	13	8	13	51	53	34
Dundee	34	13	7	14	60	58	33
Dundee U	34	13	6	15	61	53	32
Partick	34	13	6	15	59	69	32
Dunfermline	34	12	7	15	65	81	31
Airdrie	34	10	10	14	61	71	30
St Mirren	34	11	6	17	53	58	29
St J'stone	34	10	9	15	47	63	29
Raith	34	10	7	17	46	67	27
Clyde	34	6	11	17	55	77	23
Ayr	34	5	12	17	51	81	22

SCOTTISH SECOND DIV
Champions: Stirling Albion
Also promoted: Falkirk

SCOTTISH LEAGUE CUP
Rangers 2
Kilmarnock 0

1961-62

WORLD CUP
Brazil 3
Czechoslovakia 1

EUROPEAN CUP
Benfica 5
Real Madrid 3

EUROPEAN CUP WINNERS CUP
Atletico Madrid 3
Fiorentina 0, after 1-1

FAIRS CUP
Valencia beat Barcelona 6-2 1-1

FA CUP
Tottenham Hotspur 3
Burnley 1

FIRST DIVISION

	P	W	D	L	F	A	Pts
Ipswich	42	24	8	10	93	67	56
Burnley	42	21	11	10	101	67	53
Tottenham	42	21	10	11	88	69	52
Everton	42	20	11	11	88	54	51
Sheff Utd	42	19	9	14	61	69	47
Sheff Wed	42	20	6	16	72	58	46
Aston Villa	42	18	8	16	65	56	44
West Ham	42	17	10	15	76	82	44
West Brom	42	15	13	14	83	67	43
Arsenal	42	16	11	15	71	72	43
Bolton	42	16	10	16	62	66	42
Man City	42	17	7	18	78	81	41
Blackpool	42	15	11	16	70	75	41
Leicester	42	17	6	19	72	71	40
Man Utd	42	15	9	18	72	75	39
Blackburn	42	14	11	17	50	58	39
Birmingham	42	14	10	18	65	81	38
Wolves	42	13	10	19	73	86	36
Nottm F	42	13	10	19	63	79	36
Fulham	42	13	7	22	66	74	33
Cardiff	42	9	14	19	50	81	32
Chelsea	42	9	10	23	63	94	28

SECOND DIVISION
Champions: Liverpool
Also promoted: Leyton Orient
Relegated: Bristol Rovers, Brighton & Hove Albion

THIRD DIVISION
Champions: Portsmouth
Also promoted: Grimsby Town
Relegated: Torquay United, Lincoln City, Brentford, Newport County

FOURTH DIVISION
Champions: Millwall
Also promoted: Colchester United, Wrexham, Carlisle United

LEAGUE CUP
Norwich City beat Rochdale 3-0 1-0

SCOTTISH CUP
Rangers 2
St Mirren 0

SCOTTISH FIRST DIVISION

	P	W	D	L	F	A	Pts
Dundee	34	25	4	5	80	46	54
Rangers	34	22	7	5	84	31	51
Celtic	34	19	7	8	81	37	46
Dunfermline	34	19	5	10	77	46	43
Kilmarnock	34	16	10	8	74	58	42
Hearts	34	16	6	12	54	49	38
Partick	34	16	3	15	60	55	35
Hibernian	34	14	5	15	58	72	33
Motherwell	34	13	6	15	65	62	32
T Lanark	34	13	5	16	59	60	31
Aberdeen	34	10	9	15	60	73	29
Raith	34	10	7	17	51	73	27
Falkirk	34	11	4	19	45	68	26
Airdrie	34	9	7	18	57	78	25
St Mirren	34	10	5	19	52	80	25
St J'stone	34	9	7	18	35	61	25
Stirling A	34	6	6	22	34	76	18

SCOTTISH SECOND DIV
Champions: Clyde
Also promoted: Queen of the South

SCOTTISH LEAGUE CUP
Rangers 3
Hearts 1, after 1-1

1962-63

EUROPEAN CUP
AC Milan 2
Benfica 1

EUROPEAN CUP WINNERS CUP
Tottenham Hotspur 5
Atletico Madrid 1

FAIRS CUP
Valencia beat Dynamo Zagreb 2-1 2-0

FA CUP
Manchester United 3
Leicester City 1

FIRST DIVISION

	P	W	D	L	F	A	Pts
Everton	42	25	11	6	84	42	61
Tottenham	42	23	9	10	111	62	55
Burnley	42	22	10	10	78	57	54
Leicester	42	20	12	10	79	53	52
Wolves	42	20	10	12	93	65	50
Sheff Wed	42	19	10	13	77	63	48
Arsenal	42	18	10	14	86	77	46
Liverpool	42	17	10	15	71	59	44
Nottm F	42	17	10	15	67	69	44
Sheff Utd	42	16	12	14	58	60	44
Blackburn	42	15	12	15	79	71	42
West Ham	42	14	12	16	73	69	40
Blackpool	42	13	14	15	58	64	40
West Brom	42	16	7	19	71	79	39
Aston Villa	42	15	8	19	62	68	38
Fulham	42	14	10	18	50	71	38
Ipswich	42	12	11	19	59	78	35
Bolton	42	15	5	22	55	75	35
Man Utd	42	12	10	20	67	81	34
Birmingham	42	10	13	19	63	90	33
Man City	42	10	11	21	58	102	31
Leyton O	42	6	9	27	37	81	21

SECOND DIVISION
Champions: Stoke City
Also promoted: Chelsea
Relegated: Walsall, Luton Town

THIRD DIVISION
Champions: Northampton Town
Also promoted: Swindon Town
Relegated: Bradford Park Avenue, Brighton & Hove Albion, Carlisle United, Halifax Town

FOURTH DIVISION
Champions: Brentford
Also promoted: Oldham Athletic, Crewe Alexandra, Mansfield Town

LEAGUE CUP
Birmingham City beat Aston Villa 3-1 0-0

SCOTTISH CUP
Rangers 3
Celtic 0, after 1-1

SCOTTISH FIRST DIVISION

	P	W	D	L	F	A	Pts
Rangers	34	25	7	2	94	28	57
Kilmarnock	34	20	8	6	92	40	48
Partick	34	20	6	8	66	44	46
Celtic	34	19	6	9	76	44	44
Hearts	34	17	9	8	85	59	43
Aberdeen	34	17	7	10	70	47	41
Dundee	34	15	8	11	67	52	41
Dunfermline	34	13	8	13	50	47	34
Dundee U	34	12	9	13	60	49	33
Motherwell	34	10	11	13	60	63	31
Airdrie	34	14	2	18	52	76	30
St Mirren	34	10	8	16	52	72	28
Falkirk	34	12	3	19	54	69	27
T Lanark	34	9	8	17	56	68	26
Q of South	34	10	6	18	36	75	26
Hibernian	34	8	9	17	47	67	25
Clyde	34	9	5	20	49	83	23
Raith	34	2	5	27	35	118	9

SCOTTISH SECOND DIV
Champions: St Johnstone
Also promoted: East Stirling

SCOTTISH LEAGUE CUP
Hearts 1
Kilmarnock 0

1963-64

EUROPEAN CHAMPIONSHIP
Spain 2
USSR 1

EUROPEAN CUP
Inter Milan 3
Real Madrid 1

EUROPEAN CUP WINNERS CUP
Sporting Lisbon 1
MTK Budapest 0, after 3-3

FAIRS CUP
Real Zaragoza 2
Valencia 1

FA CUP
West Ham United 3
Preston North End 2

FIRST DIVISION

	P	W	D	L	F	A	Pts
Liverpool	42	26	5	11	92	45	57
Man Utd	42	23	7	12	90	62	53
Everton	42	21	10	11	84	64	52
Tottenham	42	22	7	13	97	81	51
Chelsea	42	20	10	12	72	56	50
Sheff Wed	42	19	11	12	84	67	49
Blackburn	42	18	10	14	89	65	46
Arsenal	42	17	11	14	90	82	45
Burnley	42	17	10	15	71	64	44
West Brom	42	16	11	15	70	61	43
Leicester	42	16	11	15	61	58	43
Sheff Utd	42	16	11	15	61	64	43
Nottm F	42	16	9	17	64	68	41
West Ham	42	14	12	16	69	74	40
Fulham	42	13	13	16	58	65	39
Wolves	42	12	15	15	70	80	39
Stoke	42	14	10	18	77	78	38
Blackpool	42	13	9	20	52	73	35
Aston Villa	42	11	12	19	62	71	34
Birmingham	42	11	7	24	54	92	29
Bolton	42	10	8	24	48	80	28
Ipswich	42	9	7	26	56	121	25

SECOND DIVISION
Champions: Leeds United
Also promoted: Sunderland
Relegated: Grimsby Town, Scunthorpe United

THIRD DIVISION
Champions: Coventry City
Also promoted: Crystal Palace
Relegated: Millwall, Crewe Alexandra, Wrexham, Notts County

FOURTH DIVISION
Champions: Gillingham
Also promoted: Carlisle United, Workington, Exeter City

LEAGUE CUP
Leicester City beat Stoke City 1-1 3-2

SCOTTISH CUP
Rangers 3
Dundee 1

SCOTTISH FIRST DIVISION

	P	W	D	L	F	A	Pts
Rangers	34	25	5	4	85	31	55
Kilmarnock	34	22	5	7	77	40	49
Celtic	34	19	9	6	89	34	47
Hearts	34	19	9	6	74	40	47
Dunfermline	34	18	9	7	64	33	45
Dundee	34	20	5	9	94	50	45
Partick	34	15	5	14	55	54	35
Dundee U	34	13	8	13	65	49	34
Aberdeen	34	12	8	14	53	53	32
Hibernian	34	12	6	16	59	66	30
Motherwell	34	9	11	14	51	62	29
St Mirren	34	12	5	17	44	74	29
St J'stone	34	11	6	17	54	70	28
Falkirk	34	11	4	19	54	84	26
Airdrie	34	11	4	19	52	97	26
T Lanark	34	9	7	18	47	74	25
Q of South	34	5	6	23	40	92	16
E Stirling	34	5	2	27	37	91	12

SCOTTISH SECOND DIV
Champions: Morton
Also promoted: Clyde

SCOTTISH LEAGUE CUP
Rangers 5
Morton 0

1964-65

EUROPEAN CUP
Inter Milan 1
Benfica 0

EUROPEAN CUP WINNERS CUP
West Ham United 2
Munich 1860 0

FAIRS CUP
Ferencvaros 1
Juventus 0

FA CUP
Liverpool 2
Leeds United 1

FIRST DIVISION

	P	W	D	L	F	A	Pts
Man Utd	42	26	9	7	89	39	61
Leeds	42	26	9	7	83	52	61
Chelsea	42	24	8	10	89	54	56
Everton	42	17	15	10	69	60	49
Nottm F	42	17	13	12	71	67	47
Tottenham	42	19	7	16	87	71	45
Liverpool	42	17	10	15	67	73	44
Sheff Wed	42	16	11	15	57	55	43
West Ham	42	19	4	19	82	71	42
Blackburn	42	16	10	16	83	79	42
Stoke	42	16	10	16	67	66	42
Burnley	42	16	10	16	70	70	42
Arsenal	42	17	7	18	69	75	41
West Brom	42	13	13	16	70	65	39
Sunderland	42	14	9	19	64	74	37
Aston Villa	42	16	5	21	57	82	37
Blackpool	42	12	11	19	67	78	35
Leicester	42	11	13	18	69	85	35
Sheff Utd	42	11	12	19	50	64	35
Fulham	42	11	12	19	60	78	34
Wolves	42	13	4	25	59	89	30
Birmingham	42	8	11	23	64	96	27

SECOND DIVISION
Champions: Newcastle United
Also promoted: Northampton Town
Relegated: Swindon Town, Swansea Town

THIRD DIVISION
Champions: Carlisle United
Also promoted: Bristol City
Relegated: Luton Town, Port Vale, Colchester United, Barnsley

FOURTH DIVISION
Champions: Brighton & Hove Albion
Also promoted: Millwall, York City, Oxford United

LEAGUE CUP
Chelsea beat Leicester City 3-2 0-0

SCOTTISH CUP
Celtic 3
Dunfermline Athletic 2

SCOTTISH FIRST DIVISION

	P	W	D	L	F	A	Pts
Kilmarnock	34	22	6	6	62	33	50
Hearts	34	22	6	6	90	49	50
Dunfermline	34	22	5	7	83	36	49
Hibernian	34	21	4	9	75	47	46
Rangers	34	18	8	8	78	35	44
Dundee	34	15	10	9	86	63	40
Clyde	34	17	6	11	64	58	40
Celtic	34	16	5	13	76	57	37
Dundee U	34	15	6	13	59	51	36
Morton	34	13	7	14	54	54	33
Partick	34	11	10	13	57	58	32
Aberdeen	34	12	8	14	59	75	32
St J'stone	34	9	11	14	57	62	29
Motherwell	34	10	8	16	45	54	28
St Mirren	34	9	6	19	38	70	24
Falkirk	34	7	7	20	43	85	21
Airdrie	34	5	4	25	48	110	14
T Lanark	34	3	1	30	22	99	7

SCOTTISH SECOND DIV
Champions: Stirling Albion
Also promoted: Hamilton Academical

SCOTTISH LEAGUE CUP
Rangers 2
Celtic 1

	1965-66	1966-67	1967-68	1968-69	1969-70
WORLD CUP	England 4 West Germany 2				Brazil 4 Italy 1
EUROPEAN CHAMPIONSHIP			Italy 2 Yugoslavia 0, after 1-1		
EUROPEAN CUP	Real Madrid 2 Partizan Belgrade 1	Celtic 2 Inter Milan 1	Manchester United 4 Benfica 1	AC Milan 4 Ajax 1	Feyenoord 2 Celtic 1
EUROPEAN CUP WINNERS CUP	Borussia Dortmund 2 Liverpool 1	Bayern Munich 1 Rangers 0	AC Milan 2 SV Hamburg 0	Slovan Bratislava 3 Barcelona 2	Manchester City 2 Gornik Zabrze 1
FAIRS CUP	Barcelona beat Real Zaragoza 0-1 4-2	Dynamo Zagreb beat Leeds United 2-0 0-0	Leeds United beat Ferencvaros 1-0 0-0	Newcastle United beat Ujpest Dozsa 3-0 2-3	Arsenal beat Anderlecht 1-3, 3-0
FA CUP	Everton 3 Sheffield Wednesday 2	Tottenham Hotspur 2 Chelsea 1	West Bromwich Albion 1 Everton 0	Manchester City 1 Leicester City 0	Chelsea 2 Leeds United 1, after 2-2

FIRST DIVISION

1965-66
	P	W	D	L	F	A	Pts
Liverpool	42	26	9	7	79	34	61
Leeds	42	23	9	10	79	38	55
Burnley	42	24	7	11	79	47	55
Man Utd	42	18	15	9	84	59	51
Chelsea	42	22	7	13	65	53	51
West Brom	42	19	12	11	91	69	50
Leicester	42	21	7	14	80	65	49
Tottenham	42	16	12	14	75	66	44
Sheff Utd	42	16	11	15	56	59	43
Stoke City	42	15	12	15	65	64	42
Everton	42	15	11	16	56	62	41
West Ham	42	15	9	18	70	83	39
Blackpool	42	14	9	19	55	65	37
Arsenal	42	12	13	17	62	75	37
Newcastle	42	14	9	19	50	63	37
Aston Villa	42	15	6	21	69	80	36
Sheff Wed	42	14	8	20	56	66	36
Nottm F	42	14	8	20	56	72	36
Sunderland	42	14	8	20	51	72	36
Fulham	42	14	7	21	67	85	35
Northampton	*42*	*10*	*13*	*19*	*55*	*92*	*33*
Blackburn	*42*	*8*	*4*	*30*	*57*	*88*	*20*

1966-67
	P	W	D	L	F	A	Pts
Man Utd	42	24	12	6	84	45	60
Nottm F	42	23	10	9	64	41	56
Tottenham	42	24	8	10	71	48	56
Leeds	42	22	11	9	62	42	55
Liverpool	42	19	13	10	64	47	51
Everton	42	19	10	13	65	46	48
Arsenal	42	16	14	12	58	47	46
Leicester	42	18	8	16	78	71	44
Chelsea	42	15	14	13	67	62	44
Sheff Utd	42	16	10	16	52	59	42
Sheff Wed	42	14	13	15	56	47	41
Stoke	42	17	7	18	63	58	41
West Brom	42	16	7	19	77	73	39
Burnley	42	15	9	18	66	76	39
Man City	42	12	15	15	43	52	39
West Ham	42	14	8	20	80	84	36
Sunderland	42	14	8	20	58	72	36
Fulham	42	11	12	19	71	83	34
Soton	42	14	6	22	74	92	34
Newcastle	42	12	9	21	39	81	33
Aston Villa	*42*	*11*	*7*	*24*	*54*	*85*	*29*
Blackpool	*42*	*6*	*9*	*27*	*41*	*76*	*21*

1967-68
	P	W	D	L	F	A	Pts
Man City	42	26	6	10	86	43	58
Man Utd	42	24	8	10	89	55	56
Liverpool	42	22	11	9	71	40	55
Leeds	42	22	9	11	71	41	53
Everton	42	23	6	13	67	40	52
Chelsea	42	18	12	12	62	68	48
Tottenham	42	19	9	14	70	59	47
West Brom	42	17	12	13	75	62	46
Arsenal	42	17	10	15	60	56	44
Newcastle	42	13	15	14	54	67	41
Nottm F	42	14	11	17	52	64	39
West Ham	42	14	10	18	73	69	38
Leicester	42	13	12	17	64	69	38
Burnley	42	14	10	18	64	71	38
Sunderland	42	13	11	18	51	61	37
Soton	42	13	11	18	66	83	37
Wolves	42	14	8	20	66	75	36
Stoke	42	14	7	21	50	73	35
Sheff Wed	42	11	12	19	51	63	34
Coventry	42	9	15	18	51	71	33
Sheff Utd	*42*	*11*	*10*	*21*	*49*	*70*	*32*
Fulham	*42*	*10*	*7*	*25*	*56*	*98*	*27*

1968-69
	P	W	D	L	F	A	Pts
Leeds	42	27	13	2	66	26	67
Liverpool	42	25	11	6	63	24	61
Everton	42	21	15	6	77	36	57
Arsenal	42	22	12	8	56	27	56
Chelsea	42	20	10	12	73	53	50
Tottenham	42	14	17	11	61	51	45
Soton	42	16	13	13	57	48	45
West Ham	42	13	18	11	66	50	44
Newcastle	42	15	14	13	61	55	44
West Brom	42	16	11	15	64	67	43
Man Utd	42	15	12	15	57	53	42
Ipswich	42	15	11	16	59	60	41
Man City	42	15	10	17	64	55	40
Burnley	42	15	9	18	55	82	39
Sheff Wed	42	10	16	16	41	54	36
Wolves	42	10	15	17	41	58	35
Sunderland	42	11	12	19	43	67	34
Nottm F	42	10	13	19	45	57	33
Stoke	42	9	15	18	40	63	33
Coventry	42	10	11	21	46	64	31
Leicester	*42*	*9*	*12*	*21*	*39*	*68*	*30*
QPR	*42*	*4*	*10*	*28*	*39*	*95*	*18*

1969-70
	P	W	D	L	F	A	Pts
Everton	42	29	8	5	72	34	66
Leeds	42	21	15	6	84	49	57
Chelsea	42	21	13	8	70	50	55
Derby	42	22	9	11	64	37	53
Liverpool	42	20	11	11	65	42	51
Coventry	42	19	11	12	58	48	49
Newcastle	42	17	13	12	57	35	47
Man Utd	42	14	17	11	66	61	45
Stoke	42	15	15	12	56	52	45
Man City	42	16	11	15	55	48	43
Tottenham	42	17	9	16	54	55	43
Arsenal	42	12	18	12	51	49	42
Wolves	42	12	16	14	55	57	40
Burnley	42	12	12	18	56	61	39
Nottm F	42	10	18	14	50	71	38
West Brom	42	14	9	19	58	66	37
West Ham	42	12	12	18	51	60	36
Ipswich	42	10	11	21	40	63	31
Soton	42	6	17	19	46	67	29
C Palace	42	6	15	21	34	68	27
Sunderland	*42*	*6*	*14*	*22*	*30*	*68*	*26*
Sheff Wed	*42*	*8*	*9*	*25*	*40*	*71*	*25*

SECOND DIVISION

1965-66	1966-67	1967-68	1968-69	1969-70
Champions: Manchester City Also promoted: Southampton Relegated: Middlesbrough, Leyton Orient	Champions: Coventry City Also promoted: Wolverhampton Wanderers Relegated: Northampton Town, Bury	Champions: Ipswich Town Also promoted: Queen's Park Rangers Relegated: Rotherham United, Plymouth Argyle	Champions: Derby County Also promoted: Crystal Palace Relegated: Bury, Fulham	Champions: Huddersfield Town Also promoted: Blackpool Relegated: Aston Villa, Preston North End

THIRD DIVISION

1965-66	1966-67	1967-68	1968-69	1969-70
Champions: Hull City Also promoted: Millwall Relegated: Southend United, Exeter City, Brentford, York City	Champions: Queen's Park Rangers Also promoted: Middlesbrough Relegated: Swansea Town, Darlington, Doncaster Rovers, Workington	Champions: Oxford United Also promoted: Bury Relegated: Grimsby Town, Colchester United, Scunthorpe United, Peterborough United	Champions: Watford Also promoted: Swindon Town Relegated: Northampton Town, Hartlepool, Crewe Alexandra, Oldham Athletic	Champions: Orient Also promoted: Luton Town Relegated: Bournemouth, Southport, Barrow, Stockport County

FOURTH DIVISION

1965-66	1966-67	1967-68	1968-69	1969-70
Champions: Doncaster Rovers Also promoted: Darlington, Torquay United, Colchester United	Champions: Stockport County Also promoted: Southport, Barrow, Tranmere Rovers	Champions: Luton Town Also promoted: Barnsley, Hartlepools United, Crewe Alexandra	Champions: Doncaster Rovers Also promoted: Halifax Town, Rochdale, Bradford City	Champions: Chesterfield Also promoted: Wrexham, Swansea City, Port Vale

LEAGUE CUP

1965-66	1966-67	1967-68	1968-69	1969-70
West Bromwich Albion beat West Ham United 1-2 4-1	Queen's Park Rangers 3 West Bromwich Albion 2	Leeds United 1 Arsenal 0	Swindon Town 3 Arsenal 1	Manchester City 2 West Bromwich Albion 1

SCOTTISH CUP

1965-66	1966-67	1967-68	1968-69	1969-70
Rangers 1 Celtic 0, after 0-0	Celtic 2 Aberdeen 0	Dunfermline Athletic 3 Hearts 1	Celtic 4 Rangers 0	Aberdeen 3 Celtic 1

SCOTTISH FIRST DIVISION

1965-66
	P	W	D	L	F	A	Pts
Celtic	34	27	3	4	106	30	57
Rangers	34	25	5	4	91	29	55
Kilmarnock	34	20	5	9	73	46	45
Dunfermline	34	19	6	9	94	55	44
Dundee	34	19	5	10	79	51	43
Hibernian	34	16	6	12	81	55	38
Hearts	34	13	12	9	56	48	38
Aberdeen	34	15	6	13	61	54	36
Dundee	34	14	6	14	61	61	34
Falkirk	34	15	1	18	48	72	31
Clyde	34	13	4	17	62	64	30
Partick	34	10	10	14	55	64	30
Motherwell	34	12	4	18	52	69	28
St J'stone	34	9	8	17	58	81	26
Stirling A	34	9	8	17	40	68	26
St Mirren	34	9	4	21	44	82	22
Morton	*34*	*8*	*5*	*21*	*42*	*84*	*21*
Hamilton	*34*	*3*	*2*	*29*	*27*	*117*	*8*

1966-67
	P	W	D	L	F	A	Pts
Celtic	34	26	6	2	111	33	58
Rangers	34	24	7	3	92	31	55
Clyde	34	20	6	8	64	48	46
Aberdeen	34	17	8	9	72	38	42
Hibernian	34	19	4	11	72	49	42
Dundee	34	16	9	9	74	51	41
Kilmarnock	34	16	8	10	59	46	40
Dunfermline	34	14	10	10	72	52	38
Dundee	34	16	9	11	68	62	37
Motherwell	34	10	11	13	59	60	31
Hearts	34	11	8	15	39	48	30
Partick	34	9	12	13	49	68	30
Airdrie	34	11	6	17	41	53	28
Falkirk	34	11	4	19	33	70	26
St J'stone	34	10	5	19	53	73	25
Stirling A	34	5	9	20	31	85	19
St Mirren	*34*	*4*	*7*	*23*	*25*	*81*	*15*
Ayr	*34*	*1*	*7*	*26*	*20*	*86*	*9*

1967-68
	P	W	D	L	F	A	Pts
Celtic	34	30	3	1	106	24	63
Rangers	34	28	5	1	93	34	61
Hibernian	34	20	5	9	67	49	45
Dunfermline	34	17	5	12	64	41	39
Aberdeen	34	16	5	13	63	48	37
Morton	34	15	6	13	57	53	36
Kilmarnock	34	13	8	13	59	57	34
Clyde	34	15	4	15	55	55	34
Dundee	34	13	7	14	62	59	33
Partick	34	12	7	15	51	67	31
Dundee	34	10	11	13	53	72	31
Hearts	34	13	4	17	56	61	30
Airdrie	34	10	9	15	45	58	29
St J'stone	34	10	7	17	43	52	27
Falkirk	34	7	12	15	36	50	26
Raiths	34	9	7	18	58	86	25
Motherwell	*34*	*6*	*7*	*21*	*40*	*66*	*19*
Stirling A	*34*	*4*	*4*	*26*	*29*	*105*	*12*

1968-69
	P	W	D	L	F	A	Pts
Celtic	34	23	8	3	89	32	54
Rangers	34	21	7	6	81	32	49
Dunfermline	34	19	7	8	63	45	45
Kilmarnock	34	15	14	5	50	32	44
Dundee	34	17	9	8	61	49	43
St J'stone	34	16	5	13	66	59	37
Airdrie	34	13	11	10	46	44	37
Hearts	34	14	8	12	52	54	36
Dundee	34	10	12	12	47	48	32
Morton	34	12	8	14	58	68	32
St Mirren	34	11	10	13	40	54	32
Hibernian	34	12	7	15	60	59	31
Clyde	34	9	13	12	35	50	31
Partick	34	9	10	15	39	53	28
Aberdeen	34	9	8	17	50	59	26
Raith	34	8	5	21	45	67	21
Falkirk	*34*	*5*	*8*	*21*	*33*	*69*	*18*
Arbroath	*34*	*5*	*6*	*23*	*41*	*82*	*16*

1969-70
	P	W	D	L	F	A	Pts
Celtic	34	27	3	4	96	33	57
Rangers	34	19	7	8	67	40	45
Hibernian	34	19	6	9	65	40	44
Hearts	34	13	12	9	50	36	38
Dundee U	34	16	6	12	62	64	38
Dundee	34	15	6	13	49	44	36
Kilmarnock	34	13	10	11	62	57	36
Aberdeen	34	14	7	13	55	45	35
Dunfermline	34	15	5	14	45	45	35
Morton	34	13	9	12	52	52	35
Motherwell	34	11	10	13	49	51	32
Airdrie	34	12	8	14	59	64	32
St J'stone	34	11	9	14	50	62	31
Ayr	34	12	6	16	37	52	30
St Mirren	34	8	9	17	39	54	25
Clyde	34	9	7	18	34	56	25
Raith	*34*	*5*	*11*	*18*	*32*	*67*	*21*
Partick	*34*	*5*	*7*	*22*	*41*	*82*	*17*

SCOTTISH SECOND DIV

1965-66	1966-67	1967-68	1968-69	1969-70
Champions: Ayr United Also promoted: Airdrie	Champions: Morton Also promoted: Raith Rovers	Champions: St Mirren Also promoted: Arbroath	Champions: Motherwell Also promoted: Ayr United	Champions: Falkirk Also promoted: Cowdenbeath

SCOTTISH LEAGUE CUP

1965-66	1966-67	1967-68	1968-69	1969-70
Celtic 2 Rangers 1	Celtic 1 Rangers 0	Celtic 5 Dundee 3	Celtic 6 Hibernian 2	Celtic 1 St Johnstone 0

WORLD CUP 1970

Brazil keeps Trophy as flair overcomes fear

DESPITE the drawbacks of holding the World Cup finals in Mexico, the 1970 tournament was certainly the finest of the century. Brazil, who were the worthy winners, played fabulous free-flowing attacking football and had assembled probably the greatest side on earth. England, the holders, had strengthened their 1966 team, and their match with Brazil in the early stages, which was billed as the "real" final, lived up to expectations. And although the modern trend of containing, defensive football was prevalent all over the globe, there were a host of thrilling matches and the average number of goals per match actually increased over the previous two World Cups.

Mexico in June was never the ideal location. And when, at the behest of European television, the kick-off times were adjusted to noon when the heat and humidity were at their worst, it was feared that the players would simply wilt in the conditions. Amazingly, they didn't and the football was of the highest standard.

England, the only British team at the finals, still had the core of the side that had triumphed at Wembley. Six of that team played in Guadalajara and there were exciting new faces – Terry Cooper, Alan Mullery and Francis Lee to name but three. Experts were agreed that England's squad was, in fact, stronger than four years previously. Brazil, as well, had unearthed a new crop of talent – Jairzinho, Rivelino and Tostao.

The game was played in 98-degree heat – army training manuals of the day said that it was folly to undertake even the lightest exercise in temperatures above 85°F – and the England players got precious little sleep the night before the match as their hotel was surrounded by thousands of noisy fans all chanting for Brazil.

England were not fazed. Brazil were kept at bay in the first half by a save by Gordon Banks that defied belief. The match was only 10 minutes old when Jairzinho delivered a perfect centre to Pele. Banks was covering his near post when Pele forcefully headed the ball towards the opposite corner. Pele wheeled away convinced that he had scored but, somehow, Banks flung himself the width of the goal and with a breathtaking one-handed save turned the ball away with his fingertips.

But, in the second half Banks was powerless when Tostao swept past three defenders and passed to Pele, who instantly pushed the ball on for Jairzinho to score. Even then England were not finished and for much of the rest of the match it was all Brazil could do hold on to their lead. However, England wasted at least five good chances, the best producing a terrible miss by Jeff Astle.

Even though they lost 1-0 England still reached the quarter-finals. So after the "real" final came a repeat of the 1966 final, a match against West Germany in Leon. This time, Banks could do nothing for England. The night before the match he drank a bottle of beer that left him with such bad food poisoning that Peter Bonetti had to play in his place.

The enforced change did not seem to matter when England were leading 2-0 with 22 minutes remaining, thanks to goals from Mullery and Martin Peters. But Bonetti, diving to stop a drive from Franz Beckenbauer, let the ball under his body when it looked like he had the shot covered.

Helmut Schoen, the West German manager, had already made a substitution. The arrival of Jurgen Grabowski had brought fresh heart, and a fresh pair of legs to Germany. The England team started to flag. As Germany pressed for the equaliser, panic also started to set in on the England bench.

Sir Alf Ramsey was never a man happy with making substitutions. Two players, Cooper and Bobby Charlton, were clearly suffering from exhaustion. To most observers Cooper's problem was the more pressing as Grabowski was taking him apart. Inexplicably Colin Bell replaced Charlton and Ramsey left Cooper on the field. Then, to compound his error, Ramsey replaced Martin Peters with Norman Hunter, and disastrously the whole shape of the England team had been changed.

If the point of bringing on Hunter was to bolster a sagging defence, it backfired. In the 81st minute Uwe Seeler scored an extraordinary header following a defensive lapse by the tired Brian Labone. Psychologically England were now finished. In extra time Gerd Muller administered the coup de grace. The holders were out, and the dream final against Brazil – a mirage.

Few would have expected West Germany's semi-final against Italy to be as drama-laden and thrilling, particularly as the Italians were in the grip of the notoriously defensive catenaccio system. They had, in fact, got through the first stage by winning their opening game 1-0 and the shut up shop for the next two matches, settling for goalless draws against Uruguay and Israel.

They did much the same thing against Germany, sitting on a 1-0 lead they had taken in the seventh minute. Once again they thought they had done just enough, but up popped Karl-Heinz Schnellinger with a last-minute equaliser. Then the game really came to life in the space of 16 minutes in extra time. Muller gave Germany the lead, Italy equalised and then took the lead themselves, Muller levelled the scores again and a minute later Italy's Rivera scored the decisive goal in a 4-3 thriller to reach the final.

There they met Brazil, who had cruised past Uruguay in the other semi-final. It was in a sense the perfect match. As both teams had won the World Cup twice they were battling for outright possession of the Jules Rimet trophy, but more importantly it was viewed as a showdown for the soul of football. Brazil, with their flamboyant style of play, represented Latin flair and all that was good about the game. Italy, with their emphasis on negative thinking, were, despite the undoubted skills their players possessed, the epitome of Latin fear. To add edge to the contest it was the New World versus the Old.

There was only one winner. Italy's man-for-man marking system collapsed in the face of the Brazilian onslaught and a rampant Pele. Brazil took the lead in the 18th minute with a spectacular Pele header. Italy were somewhat fortunate to equalise eight minutes before half-time when a sloppy back-pass let Boninsegna round the keeper. In the second half Gerson's 66th minute goal from outside the penalty are opened the floodgates. Five minutes later, Gerson lifted a free-kick to Pele, who nodded the ball down into the path of the onrushing Jairzinho, who became the first player to have scored in every round of the World Cup.

The match had became a football fiesta. And Pele, the world's greatest player, graced the world final by conjuring up an incomparable goal four minutes from time. Jairzinho had found him with a perfectly weighted through pass, Pele then laid the ball off sublimely for Carlos Alberto to thunder it into the net. It was the result all neutrals had thirsted for: Brazilian brio had vanquished the Italian inquisition.

Brilliant Brazil: Banks with his brilliant save was one of the few people to stop Brazil, for whom Jairzinho scored in every round, Pele was irrepressible and Tostao was his perfect foil

FOR THE RECORD

FIRST ROUND

GROUP 1	P	W	D	L	F	A	Pts
Soviet Union	3	2	1	0	6	1	5
Mexico	3	2	1	0	5	0	3
Belgium	3	1	0	2	4	5	2
El Salvador	3	0	0	3	0	9	0

GROUP 2	P	W	D	L	F	A	Pts
Italy	3	1	2	0	1	0	4
Uruguay	3	1	1	1	2	1	3
Sweden	3	1	1	1	2	2	3
Isreal	3	0	2	1	1	3	2

GROUP 3	P	W	D	L	F	A	Pts
Brazil	3	3	0	0	8	3	6
England	3	2	0	1	2	1	4
Romania	3	1	0	2	4	5	2
Czech	3	0	0	3	2	7	0

GROUP 4	P	W	D	L	F	A	Pts
W. Germany	3	3	0	0	10	4	6
Peru	3	2	0	1	7	5	4
Bulgaria	3	0	1	2	5	9	1
Morocco	3	0	1	2	2	6	1

QUARTER-FINALS

West Germany 3   England 2
HT 0-1 Att. 24,000
Italy 4   Mexico 1
HT 1-1 Att. 24,000
Brazil 4   Peru 2
HT 2-1 Att. 54,000
Uruguay 1   Soviet Union 0 aet
HT 0-0 Att. 45,000

SEMI-FINALS

Italy 4   West Germany 3 aet
HT 1-0 Att. 80,000
Brazil 3   Uruguay 1
HT 1-1 Att. 51,000

THIRD PLACE PLAY-OFF

West Germany 1   Uruguay 0
HT 1-0 Att. 104,000

FINAL

Brazil 4   Italy 1
HT 1-1 Att. 107,000

Teams
Brazil Felix; Carlos Alberto, Brito, Piazza, Everaldo, Clodoaldo, Gerson, Jairzinho, Tostao, Pele, Rivelino
Italy Albertosi; Burgnich, Cera, Rosato, Facchetti, Bertini (sub: Juliano), Mazzola, De Sisti, Domenghini, Boninsegna (sub: Rivera), Riva

Leading goalscorers 10 Gerhard Muller (West Germany); 7 Jair Ventura Filho Jairzinho (Brazil); 5 Teofilo Cubillas (Peru); 4 Pele (Brazil), Anatoliy Bishovets (Soviet Union)
Total goals scored 95
Average per game: 2.97
Sendings-off None
Number of players used by finalists
16 Brazil; 17 Italy

● In the qualifier between the USA and Bermuda in Kansas City on November 3, 1968, both goalkeepers were carried off injured before half time. The first goalkeeper to be substituted in the finals was Steve Adamache of Romania, who came off with an injury after 29 minutes of the game against Brazil on June 10, 1970. He was replaced by Necula Raducanu.
● When Mario Zagalo managed Brazil to their 1970 triumph, he became the first man to play in and then manage a World Cup winning team. He was a member of the Brazilian sides which won the trophy in 1958 and 1962.

Busby legacy breaks his successor

SIR MATT BUSBY'S decision to hand over the reins at Manchester United was finally confirmed on August 10 when Wilf McGuinness was appointed manager. The decision pitched the club into a season of turmoil.

Many of the United team looked on Busby as a father figure. In contrast, they had very little respect for McGuinness. There was talk of a dressing-room revolt and of some of the senior members of the squad not being prepared to play for him.

By the standards expected at Old Trafford, United had a terrible first half of the season, only winning five of their 22 League matches before Christmas. The pressure mounted inexorably on McGuinness until, on December 28, he was demoted to reserve team trainer.

The humiliation was too much for him to take and, on February 27, he resigned, saying: "For 18 years I have been devoted to United. Now I must find a future away from Old Trafford."

Busby took over again temporarily, but he was still determined to retire. He thought he had found the ideal successor when, after a secret meeting at a petrol station in April, Jock Stein agreed to take the job. But Stein, perhaps fearful of having to work in the shadow of Busby, quickly had second thoughts, leaving United in the lurch once again.

It was hardly surprising that the upheavals took their toll on the players. And it was also hardly surprising that the person most affected was George Best. He had been missing training sessions with increasing frequency, and on January 10

McGuinness: no chance

the club suspended him for two weeks. Best was also fined a record £250 by the FA's disciplinary committee when he arrived 90 minutes late for a hearing.

The upheavals continued until well past the end of the season, when Frank O'Farrell was appointed manager and Busy joined the United board. But O'Farrell was soon to discover what Stein had feared – that Busby was an almost impossible act to follow.

Hateley keeps the flag flying

Full circle: the wandering Hateley finally returned home to Notts County

THE TIMES were a-changing for many of the players who had graced football for the last decade. And as the old stars bowed out a new generation came forward to fill their boots.

Sir Alf Ramsey, with one eye on the European championships, decided that it was time to start rebuilding the England team. Bobby Charlton, who made his 500th appearance for Manchester United the day before his 33rd birthday in October, was dropped from the side that beat East Germany in November. The same fate befell his brother, Jack, and England's long-serving goalkeeper Gordon Banks, who made way for Peter Shilton.

Two other England stars decided to retire, the former captain Jimmy Armfield and Jimmy Greaves, who became only the fourth person to score more than 350 goals in the League.

The much-travelled Tony Hateley was also entering the

twilight of his career, back where it first started with Notts County. Hateley returned to the club where he had started out in 1958 in a £20,000 deal with Birmingham in October. In total, Hateley had now been involved in transfers worth £400,000, with his share of the fees being in the region of £20,000. But Hateley showed that there was plenty of life left in his legs when he hit his 200th League goal on May 1.

Ted MacDougall, too, was on target. He scored 49 goals in the season for Bournemouth, 42 in the League and seven in the FA Cup, with six of them coming in the 8-1 demolition of Oxford City in the first round replay.

Trevor Francis, although a good deal younger, was equally prolific. In only his first season he ran up a sequence of 12 goals in eight League matches for Birmingham. They included all four against Bolton, the first time a 16-year-old had achieved this feat.

The impossible double act: George Best and Sir Matt Busby

Arsenal's Double defies critics

North Bank hero: Charlie George delights his fans with the winning goal at Wembley which secured the Double

WINNING the Double is more than extraordinary – after all, only Tottenham in 1961 had achieved it this century – but to win it in the manner Arsenal did was almost to defy belief. In September they had been thrashed by Stoke 5-0; by the end of February they were seven points behind Leeds; and in the FA Cup semi-final against Stoke they were 2-0 down after 30 minutes and only equalised, from a hotly-disputed penalty, in the dying moments of the match.

Yet Arsenal matched all of this adversity with a determination that eventually outlasted all of their opponents. Their 5-0 mauling by Stoke made them a closer-knit side as they closed ranks, particularly against the media who had branded Arsenal as boring and mechanistic.

Their dramatic let-off against Stoke in the FA Cup semi-final on March 27 (they won the replay 2-0 four days later) came in the midst of an awesome run. Between March 2 and May 3 Arsenal played 13 League matches and won 11, drawing one. The only loss was away to Leeds. In that time Arsenal won 1-0 on six occasions. That was the kind of competition they were.

Their final victory in that spectacular 13-match run was probably the sweetest. On May 3 Arsenal travelled to White Hart Lane and only their neighbours, and bitter rivals, Tottenham stood between them and the title. Arsenal either had to win or draw 0-0. (Because of the vagaries of goal average, any score draw would have given Leeds the championship).

With a capacity 50,000 inside, and as many locked out, the match went to the wire. Ray Kennedy headed Arsenal into the lead two minutes from time, but this was largely irrelevant, as a Spurs goal would have given the title to Leeds. Two minutes seemed an age as Spurs desperately attacked the Arsenal goal to deprive their foes of the coveted Double, but keeper Bob Wilson bravely denied Tottenham.

Five days later Liverpool were the obstacles at Wembley. Only four teams this century (Newcastle in 1905, Sunderland in 1913, Manchester United in 1957 and Tottenham in 1961) played in an FA Cup final and were League champions. All, apart from Tottenham, had had their hopes of the elusive Double dashed.

After a scoreless 90 minutes, Arsenal found themselves down 1-0 after two minutes of extra time thanks to Steve Heighway, and with a mountain to climb. Liverpool had one of the meanest defences in the League and had only conceded one goal in the Cup. But then they conceded two: the first a scrambled equaliser from Eddie Kelly and the second a scorching blaster from Charlie George, the darling of the North Bank, eight minutes from the end. Once again Arsenal had come from behind to triumph and their manager had achieved what even the legendary Herbert Chapman hadn't: the fabulous Double.

Chelsea complete London's coup

THE FIRST round of the European Cup Winners' Cup brought a feast of goals, with Cardiff demolishing Larnaca 8-0 at home and Chelsea powering past Aris Salonika 6-2 on aggregate.

Cardiff were the surprise package of the tournament.

They won just as emphatically in the second round, dispatching Nantes 7-2 on aggregate, and were rewarded with a money-spinning quarter-final against Real Madrid. The first match, in Cardiff on March 10, went down in Welsh folklore when Brian Clark scored the only goal of the game for the Second Division side. Cardiff, though, could not hang on to their advantage and lost the second leg 2-0.

Chelsea almost went out in the quarter-finals as well when they fell two goals behind in Bruges. But a resounding 4-0 victory at Stamford Bridge put them through to the last four, where they were drawn against Manchester City, the holders.

City could count themselves lucky to have got that far. They had only squeezed past Linfield on the away goals rule in the first round, and had needed a replay to beat Gornik in the quarter-finals after both matches finished 2-0.

Both Chelsea and Manchester City were depleted by injuries. But the London club, even though they were missing Peter Bonetti, Peter Osgood and Ian Hutchinson, prevailed 1-0 in both legs to avenge their exit from the FA Cup at the hands of City.

Chelsea were back at full strength for the final against Real Madrid in Athens on May 19. Inspired by Charlie Cooke, they took the lead with a goal from Osgood. But a mistake by John Dempsey near the end allowed Real to equalise. Bonetti had to be at his brilliant best in extra time as Chelsea came under increasing pressure, and they were grateful to hang on for the replay two days later.

Dempsey made amends for his error by giving Chelsea the lead once again, rifling a shot in after his header had been parried. Osgood extended Chelsea's advantage, and even though Real scored a consolation goal the third trophy of the season was on its way to London.

Second time around: Chelsea needed a replay to beat Real Madrid

Colchester 3 Leeds 2: 'The most fantastic result you'll ever see'

EVERY YEAR there are headline making upsets in the FA Cup, but the fifth-round result from Layer Road on February 13 will certainly be remembered as one of the all-time shocks. Colchester, of the Fourth Division, with six players over the age of 30, beat mighty Leeds, stuffed with internationals such as Jack Charlton, Norman Hunter and Johnny Giles, 3-2. The result was so incredible that one newspaper called it: "The most fantastic result you'll ever see."

The hero of the afternoon – among an entire team of heroes – was the veteran Ray Crawford, who nine years earlier had spearheaded Ipswich to their only League title. Crawford, who had been in non-League football and on the dole a few months before he was rescued from obscurity by Colchester's manager Dick Graham, rocked Leeds in the 18th minute with a headed goal.

Six minutes later Crawford collided with Gary Sprake, the Leeds goalkeeper, and both men tumbled to the ground. Quick-thinking Crawford showed he had lost none of his predatory skills by hooking the ball into the net with his left foot while still on the ground: 2-0. The half-time scoreline was received with incredulity around the country.

Amazingly, plucky Colchester made no effort to sit on their lead in the second half. Instead they continued to attack and harass their illustrious opponents. Their bravery was rewarded when Dave Simmons headed them into a 3-0 lead in the 54th minute. Ecstatic supporters rushed on to the pitch to congratulate him.

Inevitably, Leeds, the runaway League leaders, rallied and as the Colchester players tired snatched two goals from Hunter and Giles with 15 minutes remaining.

Leeds then threw everybody into attack and relentlessly bombarded the Colchester goal,

Upset of the century: Ray Crawford heads the first goal for Colchester

but Graham Smith, the keeper, rose to the occasion brilliantly and played like an international to frustrate Don Revie's star-studded team and earn a place in the sixth round, and history.

Jubilant fans hoisted Crawford on to their shoulders and paraded him around the ground as the dishevelled Leeds players slunk off in disbelief. The reward for the Colchester players was a tie at Goodison against Everton in the quarter finals, and a free fortnight's holiday with their wives promised to them by Graham if they beat Leeds. At Goodison, inevitably, the bubble burst and they went down 5-0. Still, they had their famous victory to savour as they lazed on a beach in the summer.

Ibrox tragedy leaves 66 dead

The day after: officials inspect the mangled crush barriers of staircase 13 at Ibrox

THE worst sporting disaster in Britain cast a pall over the New Year's celebrations in Scotland. The traditional Old Firm match between Rangers and Celtic drew the usual huge crowd to Ibrox Park on January 2, and with 80,000 people packed into the ground the conditions existed for the third tragedy to hit the stadium.

With a few minutes remaining Celtic led 1-0 and thousands of people were leaving the terraces to make their way home. Then Colin Stein scored a late equaliser and the remaining home supporters roared their approval.

The departing fans, alerted by the noise, turned and tried to rush back to see what the excitement was about. As they forced their way up staircase 13 they collided head-on with people still trying to leave the ground.

Although Ibrox had been designed to handle large crowds, the crush was simply too great. As wide as the staircase was, it could not cope with the sudden pressure and crush barriers started to buckle under the strain.

As the barriers gave way people slipped and fell headlong down the steep staircase. This started a domino effect and soon hundreds of people were swept away in the pandemonium. Panic quickly set in, making matters worse.

For a few brief moments it was thought that the accident was relatively minor. But it did not take long for the full horror to emerge. In all, 66 people died and more than 200 were injured. Many of the victims were suffocated by the sheer weight of other people lying on top of them.

The public was appalled that so many people had been killed and that, once again, their deaths had been caused by crush barriers giving way. Reginald Maudling, the Home Secretary, immediately announced that there would be a formal inquiry. The Wheatley Report called for much stricter crowd control at matches, and for football grounds to be subject to the same stringent safety rules as other places of public entertainment such as cinemas.

But the Safety of Sports Grounds Act was not introduced until 1975, and even then the legislation was not able to save the lives of countless other people who were to die at football matches.

Football ground disasters

1902	Twenty-five people died and more than 500 were injured when a stand collapsed under the weight of people who had come to watch the Scotland v England international at Ibrox Park.
1914	Seventy-five people were injured at Hillsborough when a wall collapsed during an FA Cup replay between Sheffield Wednesday and Wolverhampton.
1946	Thirty-three people died and 400 were injured when crush barriers collapsed at Burnden Park during the match between Bolton and Stoke.
1961	Two people died at Ibrox when crush barriers collapsed during Rangers' match against Celtic.
1964	The world's biggest football disaster. Three hundred people died and more than 500 were injured in a riot after a disputed goal was scored in Lima, Peru.

Dougan: players' choice

165

Fairs Cup Revie's only consolation

LEEDS gained some consolation for their domestic disappointments by becoming the fourth English club in a row to win the Fairs Cup. But, like their campaigns at home, it was a gruelling battle that lasted until the first week of June.

The semi-finals produced an all-English pairing and Leeds played two titantic matches against Liverpool. The first game, at Anfield, was decisive with Billy Bremner, who had been out of action for over a month with an injury, scoring the only goal of the two legs.

Leeds's strength was sapped further in the first leg of the final, against Juventus in Turin. Eddie Gray dislocated his shoulder and then torrential rain forced the match to be abandoned after 55 minutes.

Leeds showed great fortitude two days later when they came back from two down thanks to goals from Paul Madeley and Mick Bates, who came on as a substitute 15 minutes from the end and scored two minutes later.

The return match was just as testing. Allan Clarke gave Leeds an early lead but Juventus struck back with a goal from Anastasi. The Italians knew that they were still behind on the away goals rule and they had to score again.

Leeds started to look wearier and wearier as the game went on, but their defence remained resolute and Juventus were unable to find a way past the determined tackling. Somehow Leeds conjured up the will to survive the 90 minutes and collect some reward for a season of toil that had lasted not far short of a full year.

Winning the marathon: Mick Jones, the Leeds striker, battles with Tancredi of Juventus

The last lap: Allan Clarke celebrates the final goal in a gruelling Cup run that went on until June

Fans riot after ref's blunder

TWO TERRIBLE decisions by match officials and the hot-temperedness of Don Revie's Leeds players sparked off a riot that seriously damaged the sport's reputation and certainly changed the destiny of the League championship. All parties were to blame, but it was Leeds who paid the price.

On April 17, Leeds were two points clear of Arsenal, but had played two games more so they desperately needed to beat lowly West Bromwich Albion at Elland Road. With 28 minutes remaining and Leeds trailing 1-0, WBA's Tony Brown blocked a pass from Norman Hunter and hared after the ball as it rebounded into the Leeds half with Colin Suggett running in support.

The Leeds defence, the arch exponents of the offside trap, stopped and pointed out to the referee, Ray Tinkler, that his linesman had flagged Suggett as yards offside. Even Brown had stopped. Inexplicably Tinkler waved play on, claiming afterwards that Suggett was not interfering with play.

Brown, now in virtually an empty half, passed to Jeff Astle, who also looked clearly offside. Once again the Leeds defence ground to a halt and appealed to the linesman but he resolutely refused to raise his flag. Astle then calmly sidefooted the ball past Gary Sprake. There was instant uproar.

The entire Leeds team encircled Tinkler, pushing, shoving and arguing furiously. But the referee would not bend, whereupon nearly 40 irate Leeds fans invaded the pitch in pursuit of revenge against Tinkler. In the ensuing chaos the Leeds players had to protect Tinkler from the marauding fans, the linesman was hit by a stone, and it took the police nearly five minutes to restore order.

Thirty-two spectators were arrested. The match was resumed and Leeds managed to score, leaving the final result 2-1 to WBA. On the same day, Arsenal beat Newcastle 1-0 to take over the leadership of the First Division on goal difference.

Unsurprisingly, Revie and the

Leeds club chairman, Percy Woodward, condemned the match officials and condoned the fans. To add grist to their mill, Alan Ashman, WBA's manager, also agreed the goal was offside. Television evidence hung both parties. Yes, West Brom's second goal was offside twice, but did that really justify the players' outburst and the consequent riot? The FA soon made their answer clear: Leeds were fined £750 and ordered to play their first four home games of the next season away from Elland Road.

But the cost to Leeds was even greater than the FA's punishment. Sixteen days after the Elland Road fracas, Arsenal stole home in the title race by one point – the point they could have had if referee Tinkler had followed Brian Clough's dictum: "If he's not interfering with play, what is he doing on the field?" Leeds finished the season with 64 points, the highest amount (under the two-points for a win rule) a club had ever accumulated without winning the championship.

Astle: punished

League Cup brings Rangers some cheer at last

Sweet sixteen: Johnstone was the youngest player in a Scottish Cup final

AT LAST Rangers had something to shout about: they had beaten Celtic 1-0 to win the Scottish League Cup. Admittedly it wasn't much to shout about as Celtic once again won the Double of the Scottish League and Cup, but when the silverware cupboard had become as bare as Ibrox's, something was better than nothing. Rangers had not won a major trophy for five years, a Rangers record made all the worse as Celtic in those years had been sweeping all before them, including the European Cup.

The League Cup victory, on October 24, also promised hope for Ibrox's future as the winning goal was scored by 16-year-old Derek Johnstone, the youngest player ever to appear in a Scottish final. But Rangers never capitalised on their early season success and after New Year and the tragedy of the Ibrox disaster

only won a mere six League matches out of 16 to finish a sorry fourth in the First Division. However, in the Scottish Cup final they gave Celtic a real run for their money as another precocious Johnstone goal forced a replay which Celtic only won 2-1 thanks to a Hood penalty.

PELE
Simply the Best

Garth Crooks

THE PELE YEARS

Born October 23, 1940, Tres Coraçes

PLAYING CAREER
Santos 1955-74
Debut v Corinthians 1956 and scored 126
   goals in 1959
Honours World Club Cup 1962, 1963
South American Club Cup 1962, 1963
National champions 1968
State champions 1955, 1956, 1958, 1960,
   1961, 1962, 1964, 1965, 1967, 1968, 1969,
   1973
Brazilian Cup 1961, 1962, 1963, 1964, 1965
Rio-Sao Paulo Tournament 1959, 1963, 1964
Roberto Gomez Pedroza Tournament 1968
New York Cosmos 1975-77
105 appearances, 55 goals
Internationals Debut v Argentina 1957
111 appearances, 97 goals (including 'A'
   internationals)
Honours World Cup: Winners 1958, 1962,
   1970

Other career honours Fifa ambassador. South
American Footballer of the Year 1973. Became
first player to score 1,000 goals (in 909
games) in 1969. He scored 1,283 goals in total
(1,365 games).

I WAS in Spain covering the World Cup campaign as a member of the BBC TV World Cup panel, a genuine thrill for me that helped to take my mind off being dropped from the England squad that was taking part in football's supreme tournament.

Italy had just secured their second triumph against an unpopular German team, and I was sitting in the lounge of the Porto Ramana hotel in Marbella still fantasising about an elusive goal that could have transformed me from a League player to one with full international status.

Suddenly, like a dream sequence in some great Hollywood movie, from the recesses of the hotel lobby emerged the greatest footballer of all time, the one player who had inspired all my dreams and aspirations. And this man walked over to me and said: "Excuse me. I am told you like playing tennis. Would you like to play?" Practically speechless and head spinning, I remember managing to mutter something barely audible and totally unintelligible to the demi-god, Pele.

The moment still ranks as one of the most precious in my life, to be conjured up for endless mental action replays, and crystallises exactly what Pele meant to me, and thousands of youngsters like me all over the world.

It was the perfect set-up. Without the sting. Alan Durban, the former Stoke City manager, had arranged something so special for me that I could never hope to express my gratitude. Durban understood the moment perfectly.

The boy later to be known throughout the world simply as Pele was baptised Edson Arantes do Nascimento in a small town called Tres Coraçes. Legend has it that he learned the fundamentals of the game in the backstreets of Brazil, with balls made of old rags stuffed in socks. But the game was already in his blood; his father Dondinho was a promising player before injury curtailed his career. The son not only had the inspiration in his genes, he was equally blessed with the resilience and resolve of great men. All these attributes would make an indelible mark on the history of the game.

In 1956, a packed Wembley Stadium saw England, inspired by Stanley Matthews, beat Brazil 4-2. It was Matthews' last great international performance, and as night fell on the career of one great player dawn was breaking on that of another. Pele was just 17, but even with his extraordinary talent he could never have envisaged the future ahead.

In 1958 Sweden were the World Cup hosts, determined to emulate Uruguay (1930) and Italy (1934) by becoming the third host nation to win the Jules Rimet Trophy. Pele, meanwhile, scored his first goal in the World Cup, in the quarter-final against Wales. He went on to complete a memorable hat-trick against France in the semi-final. His second goal was struck superbly with the outside of his right foot, flying into the roof of the net. But it was his third goal that was vintage. He caught a through ball on his thigh and before a Frenchman could assess the danger he volleyed an unstoppable shot past the stranded goal-keeper. The boy from Tres Coraçes had arrived.

A wet Rasunda stadium in Stockholm found Pele as precocious in the final against Sweden as in the earlier rounds. Brazil's innovative 4-2-4 formation suited the youngster, and in the 55th minute he flicked the ball over the head of Parling, leaving the embarrassed Swedish left-half swinging wildly at Pele's midriff. Pele not only kept his balance but also his composure, volleying the ball home to give Brazil their third goal. Yet it was Brazil's fifth goal which displayed Pele's athleticism and bravery. He nonchalantly back-heeled the ball to Zagalo and, running for the return pass, leaped above the defender to nod home his second goal of the match.

Tears of joy flowed down the face of the prodigy as Brazil lifted the trophy for the first time. What the world had witnessed was not just a new philosophy of play but a player about to fuel the greatest sporting explosion since Joe Louis.

Brazil retained the trophy in Chile, the first team to do so since Italy before the war. Pele, however, missed much of that tournament, including the final, when he was injured in the early stages of the competition.

By 1964 the Brazilian team was respected worldwide, particularly in Britain. Fifa had decided to stage the 1966 World Cup in England and, somewhat fittingly, the hosts were invited to

Victimised: Pele during the 1966 World Cup

Mesmeric: Brazil bewitched the world

take part in a tournament to mark Brazilian football's 50th anniversary. Brazil, not surprisingly, were in carnival mood with Pele leading the samba. England lost 5-1, leaving Alf Ramsey and the rest of Europe to go away and try to devise sophisticated methods of stopping this South American phenomenon.

A confident Brazilian team arrived in England in 1966 in search of a third consecutive World Cup. By this time Pele was an international superstar and, along with Cassius Clay, had become the most famous sportsman in the world.

Brazil's opening game against Bulgaria was a physical one. Regardless, the defending champions won 3-1 and left Goodison Park to a standing ovation. But what became apparent throughout the game was that Pele was a marked man. Injured in that match, he missed the following game, a classic against Hungary.

Meanwhile, members of the international media were anxious to know whether or not Pele felt he was being deliberately singled out for special treatment. His reply was noble: "We all play hard to win but no player goes out deliberately to hurt another." But the evidence clearly did not support it. The next game, against Portugal, saw Pele choke on those very words. Not only singled out, he was carried off with damaged knee ligaments. Brazil lost and Pele returned to Santos vowing never to return to the game's greatest tournament.

If this inglorious treatment of the sport's greatest hero led to the decision, England's winning performance also helped give the game a different complexion. Alf Ramsey's emphasis on efficiency temporarily rendered the Brazilian philosophy as a style now out of date. Pele, however, continued to add to his already glittering career at home and he scored his 1,000th goal while playing for Santos against Vasco da Gama in that cathedral of Brazilian football the Maracana stadium.

Rejuvenated, and after careful consideration, Pele decided to make himself available for the 1970 World Cup in Mexico, his fourth finals and, at 30, presumably his last chance to show off his skills on the world stage.

What took place in the heat and altitude of Guadalajara ignited the sport with Pele, at the heart of a mesmeric Brazilian side, fulfilling all his promise and inspiring fantasies among professionals and pundits the world over.

Immortalised by colour television, the superb rhythmic play of the South Americans is legendary with Pele providing the most spectacular, memorable moves to the unmistakable backbeat of the Brazilian drum. Five hundred million viewers thrilled to the sheer inventive audacity of Pele lobbing the Czech goalkeeper from the halfway line, only to miss the goal by inches. It was a move revered and since copied, only to remind us of the original genius.

And Britain revels in the memory of the England match. Jairzinho making it to the byline when only he thought it was possible, sending the perfect cross over to the far post for Pele, who seemed to suspend himself in mid-air for what

Finest hour: Brazil won the 1970 World Cup with a series of dazzling performances

appeared to be an eternity before heading the ball downwards, crying, as legend has it, "goal", only for both the move and the execution to be equalled by one of the most astonishing saves of all time from our own national hero Gordon Banks.

Pele scored four goals in the tournament, including the first goal of a victorious final which secured an unprecedented third World Cup, allowing Brazil to keep the Jules Rimet Trophy and inscribing them and Pele in football history.

Acknowledged as the footballing icon of his age, it was Pele who was the main catalyst in the endeavour to make football a truly international sport with his move to New York Cosmos and the instigation of the North America Soccer League. It is testament to his patronage and status within the sport that within a few years of his retirement the NASL died.

I never got to play football against this great ambassador of sport. Indeed, television and video have been my only opportunities to see him play. With one memorable, magical exception in 1969, when Santos played, gratifyingly, my old home team, Stoke City. Standing in the miserable, damp, vile weather with 24,000 other people packed into the Victoria Ground to watch Stoke lose 3-2 (Pele put a thunderous right-footer past Banks) was, however, every bit as thrilling for this 11-year-old kid as playing tennis with the living legend one afternoon in the sunny climes of Marbella.

Icon of his age: Pele's modesty made him football's greatest ambassador

Partick spoil Celtic's party

IN OCTOBER, Partick Thistle, an unfashionable mid-table side, pulled off one of the upsets of the decade when they overwhelmed their all-conquering neighbours Celtic to win the Scottish League Cup 4-1, their first trophy for more than 50 years.

The former European champions were stunned as Partick raced into a 4-0 lead within 37 minutes with goals from Alex Rae, Bobby Lawrie, Denis McQuaide and Jim Bone. When the half-time score was announced at grounds around the country it was greeted by disbelief, then derision before it was confirmed.

Celtic had their excuses: their captain Billy McNeill was out with an injury and their quicksilver winger Jimmy Johnstone was substituted early in the first half, but they could not deny that the ferocity of Partick's attacks in the opening minutes unsettled them, and ultimately cost them the Cup.

Their hopes of a second European Cup vanished at Parkhead in the semi-final. After two goalless draws with Inter Milan and a barren 30 minutes of extra time Celtic fell victim to the lottery of the penalty shoot-out. Dixie Deans missed his spot-kick while Inter scored all theirs and marched on to the final 5-4. Jock Stein, Celtic's manager, was inconsolable: "We don't consider we lost on football," he said, "but to a circus turn."

Their consolation was a League and Cup Double, their second in succession, and Deans made up for his European Cup gaffe in the Scottish Cup final, scoring a hat-trick as Celtic trounced Hibs 6-1.

Derby frolic as Leeds stumble

ON the face it, the title race could be described as a thriller with an unexpected twist on the final page; in reality, it was more like musical chairs. Thus when the music stopped, Derby County, sitting on a beach in Majorca, were, to everybody's surprise, the League champions.

But in the early days of the season all the talk was of newly promoted Sheffield United, who overwhelmed Leeds 3-0, beat Arsenal's Double-winning side at Highbury and were top of the table. Four successive defeats in October ended their fairytale hopes. Manchester United, with George Best in ebullient form, established an eight-point lead before also slipping away.

By Easter the destiny of the title was finely balanced between four contenders: Derby, Leeds, Liverpool and Manchester City. Liverpool had crept into the race with a fabulous late surge, winning 13 and drawing two in a 15-match run between January and May. City were the first to crack, strangely enough after Malcolm Allison had bought the quixotic Rodney Marsh from QPR and unwittingly disrupted his side.

For Leeds there was more at stake than the championship, there was also the little matter of the Double to be won and the pain of the previous season to be erased. With a week to go to the Cup final the top of the First Division looked like this:

	P	Pts
Manchester City	42	57
Liverpool	40	56
Derby	41	56
Leeds	40	55

Only Liverpool, Derby and Leeds could win the title as Derby still had to play Liverpool and therefore it was mathematically impossible for Manchester City, who had played all their games, to become champions.

In midweek Leeds beat Chelsea and Derby seemed to have done them a favour by ending Liverpool's unbeaten run. Leeds were now in the driving seat. To win the Double all they had to do was to beat Arsenal in the final and not lose to Wolves at Molineux.

Their task was inexplicably made much harder by the League's decision that Leeds had to play their final League mixture on the Monday after the Cup final. Despite a personal plea from Don Revie to Alan Hardaker, the League secretary, there was to be no respite, the match would have to be played 48 hours after the final.

On the Saturday a goal from Allan Clarke in a sterile final gave Leeds the first half of the Double. But there were no celebrations. Within an hour of the final whistle the Leeds players were in their coach heading north for their date with destiny.

And once again fate dealt them a sorry blow. Two penalties, both for blatant handball, were rejected and Leeds went down 2-1. Meanwhile, at Highbury, Liverpool, facing a jaded and disappointed Arsenal, had the championship within their grasp. If Leeds lost (and their fans kept shouting to the players, "Leeds are losing") and they won, the title would go to Anfield. But they failed to score and the goalless draw handed the championship to Brian Clough and his Derby holidaymakers.

Leeds could claim that they had in fact lost the title the previous season. Because of the riot provoked by referee Ray Tinkler's controversial offside decision in the match against WBA, Leeds were ordered to play their first four home games away from Elland Road. In those four "home games" they dropped two points – exactly the same number they dropped in their genuine 17 home games.

Although they were the Cup winners for the first time any joy they felt was swept away by the loss of the title. "It was as if we had nothing," Clarke said. "We wanted that League championship so badly." For the second successive season it had escaped them by a single point.

Singular failure: Munro scores for Wolves to dash Leeds's title chances for the second season running

Newcastle, Hereford's stepping stone to big time

Look what we've done: Ron Radford and Ricky George scored the goals that brought down Newcastle, six times winners of the FA Cup

HEREFORD'S exploits in the FA Cup were undoubtedly instrumental in winning them a place in the League at the end of the season, even though they only finished runners-up in the Southern League.

Hereford had only enjoyed limited success in the Cup before, twice reaching the third round in 1958 and 1966. So reaching the third round again (by beating Northampton for the second year in a row), was an achievement in itself. When they were drawn against First Division Newcastle everybody expected their progress would be halted at St James's Park.

The match was postponed because of bad weather and when it was played nine days late Hereford produced the shock of the round by holding Newcastle 2-2. But there was a bigger shock to come.

The replay was also plagued by the weather and was postponed several times. When the match was finally played on February 5, Hereford's pitch resembled a swamp. But Newcastle could not blame the conditions for their defeat – they created enough chances to have easily beaten Hereford.

Fred Potter, the Hereford goalkeeper, had an outstanding game but he could not stop Malcolm Macdonald giving Newcastle the lead 10 minutes from time. Three minutes later though, Ron Radford ploughed his way through the mud to score a scorching equaliser with a shot from 30 yards. Newcastle flagged in extra time allowing Radford to set up Ricky George for an historic winner.

Because the two matches had taken so long to complete, Hereford had to play their fourth round match four days later. There was so much interest in the visit of West Ham to Edgar Street that forged tickets were discovered in the city the day before the match.

Hereford produced another minor miracle when they held the First Division side 0-0. Ron Greenwood, the West Ham manager, admitted: "We are lucky to still be in the Cup."

Hereford succumbed to a Geoff Hurst hat-trick in the replay but their brave efforts did not go unnoticed. At the League's annual meeting in June they received the same numbers of votes as Barrow, who were seeking re-election. But, just as they had done against Newcastle, Hereford triumphed in the replay, winning 29-20 in a second ballot.

FOR THE RECORD

■ Norman Burtenshaw, the referee, reported the entire Benfica team to Uefa when he was attacked after Arsenal won a friendly against the Portuguese side 6-2 at Highbury in August.

■ Crystal Palace's match against Nottingham Forest was delayed for five minutes when the Forest players disputed a goal scored by Palace. Steve Kember of Crystal Palace admitted that the ball had not gone into the net and it was disallowed.

■ Dave Sexton, the Chelsea manager, put Peter Osgood on the transfer list for "lack of effort" but then changed his mind a fortnight later.

■ Aston Villa were fined £3,000 and suspended until the end of the next season by the FA's disciplinary committee.

■ Brian Phillips, the former Mansfield player banned for life after the 1963 bribery scandal, had his sentence lifted under the new rule allowing banned players to appeal after seven years.

■ Tommy Docherty was appointed Scotland manager on September 12.

Osgood: unmovable feast

Docherty: movable feast

Rangers' triumph ends in disaster

POOR old Rangers. Just as they were poised to celebrate winning their first European trophy and lay the ghost of Celtic's 1967 European Cup triumph their victory was besmirched by the behaviour of their fans.

Some 20,000 had travelled to Barcelona for the European Cup Winners Cup final against Moscow Dynamo and were in the mood for a party. Their antics delayed the start of the match as they spilled over on to the field and the players had to leave three times before the match could commence.

Rangers played sweet football and by the 50th minute were 3-0 up with a goal from Colin Stein and two from Willie Johnston. Unfortunately each goal was greeted by a pitch invasion from the jubilant supporters. Rangers eased up in the second half and with three minutes remaining were hanging on at 3-2 to a slender victory. When the final whistle came thousands of relieved Rangers supporters invaded the pitch. Opinions differ as to who was to blame for what happened next.

The Spanish police believed they were confronted by a drunken, riotous mob and acted accordingly. The Scottish supporters believed Franco's fascist police came at them wielding clubs and batons and they were simply defending themselves. Whatever, a pitch battle ensued in which one man died and 150 were injured. Hundreds more were arrested and thrown into jail as the mayhem spread to the streets of Barcelona.

The sourness of Rangers' victory was made even more bitter when Uefa banned them from European competition for two years (subsequently reduced to one year). As Dynamo had demanded the match be replayed Rangers could consider that they got off lightly.

After Rangers' triumph, and disaster, they re-shuffled their management with Willie Waddell moving upstairs and Jock Wallace taking over the running of the team.

Wallace obviously thought that Johnston and Stein were disruptive influences in the Ibrox dressing room and had to be dispatched as soon as possible. Johnston was sold to West Bromwich in September for £135,000, and Stein went to Coventry in October for £90,000 plus another player.

After the pair had gone Wallace said: "We have sold two stars and found a team."

Blond bombshell: Stein, an old-fashioned centre-forward

Johnston: double strike

Keegan quick to make a mark for Liverpool and his country

WITH GEORGE BEST on the wane, have Liverpool unearthed British football's next superstar in Kevin Keegan? Early indications are that their £33,000 close-season signing from Scunthorpe has all the hallmarks of one the greats. Keegan, working in tandem with John Toshack, was one of the crucial elements that propelled Liverpool up the League table after the New Year when they were unbeaten in 15 League matches.

Keegan, another one of Bill Shankly's canny acquisitions, exploded into the First Division when he scored against Nottingham Forest on the opening day of the season. His ability so impressed the normally cautious England manager Sir Alf Ramsey that he quickly recruited him to the England Under-23 team.

Perhaps other First Division managers had overlooked Keegan because of his size. For at 5ft 8in he does not look the part of a striker, but despite his height he is powerful in the air and brave on the ground. And but for their inability to score in the final match of the season, Keegan would have had a championship medal in his first season.

Rising star: Keegan, another nugget unearthed by Bill Shankly

Referees' hard line goes soft

ON THE face of it, football's decision to enforce the laws of the game was eminently sensible. It would, so the pundits said, bring England in line with the rest of the world and herald a return to the age of sportsmanship. But a secret meeting on Sunday August 15 had far-reaching consequences that nobody could have dreamt of when the League and the FA instructed referees to start the crackdown.

Henceforth, tackling from behind was banned and even the most technical of offences would lead to automatic bookings. To remind the players of the rules, lists of all the misdemeanours that were subject to cautions were posted in every dressing-room.

The effect on the game was immediate and dramatic. By the following Saturday four players had been sent off and 120 had been booked. On September 4 alone 50 players were booked, taking the total to 292 after four weeks.

That prompted an immediate reaction from the players. After a seven-hour meeting, Derek Dougan, the PFA chairman, said: "The livelihood of our members has been put in jeopardy. We appreciate that something needed to be done, but we are getting away from commonsense and instead finding chaos and confusion."

The turning point came in October when Dougan successfully appealed against a booking he had received in August. The disciplinary committee decided that the booking would still stand, but it would not count against him.

That decision opened the floodgates. By the start of January, when there had already been more than 1,100 bookings, the FA had been inundated with hundreds of appeals. And it did not take long for the FA's disciplinary committee to be accused of applying double standards.

The problem was that although the referees were properly carrying out their instructions, the disciplinary committee seemed all too willing to let players off on appeal. Bob Lord, the Burnley chairman, said that referees should resign en masse because they were not getting any support from their masters. "Referees are made to look fools in the eyes of players," he said.

It was hardly surprising that the match officials became more and more perplexed and despondent. If they upheld the law they were criticised and, as in the case of John Thacker, who did not book anybody after 20 players were involved in a brawl during the match between Ipswich and Arsenal, they were also condemned for not being strict enough.

As the confusion mounted, the League argued that they should control the disciplinary process because it was their players who were affected. Eldon Griffiths, the Minister for Sport, also became involved because the government said that football was subject to the terms of the Industrial Relations Act.

A measure of compromise was finally reached by the end of the season, with referees applying a greater degree of discretion in the way they interpreted the rules. The League also won the introduction of a totting-up system, with penalty points for offences and an automatic two-match ban for players who collected 12 points.

Tackles from behind, like John Loughlan's challenge on Wyn Davies, became subject to automatic bookings, but many players were let off on appeal

173

Ramsey writes the wrong scripts

Netzer: midfield maestro

Rock bottom: Neill condemns England to their second defeat in a row at Wembley

ENGLAND'S progress to the quarter-finals of the European championships was smooth enough, with five wins and a draw in group three. And when they were drawn against West Germany Sir Alf Ramsey was confident enough to write: "England will not only beat West Germany but will also go on to win the championship."

How wrong he was. The first leg, at Wembley on April 29, brutally exposed how much the two countries' fortunes had changed since they had met in the 1966 World Cup final. West Germany had developed a mighty side – Franz Becken-bauer as sweeper, Gunter Net-zer in midfield and Gerd Muller up front – and they took England apart.

With 10 minutes left the score was 1-1, but that was highly flattering to England. Out-thought and totally out-played they conceded two more goals in the last six minutes. Ramsey was roundly criticised for his team selection and tactics and he compounded matters by picking an equally stolid side for the return leg in Berlin, which was drawn 0-0.

Ramsey's other predictions about the tournament were equally off-target. When he said that England would win he highlighted Italy, Yugoslavia and Hungary as the other likely semi-finalists. Of those three teams, only Hungary made it. Hungary eventually finished in fourth place and West Germany proved how far they had progressed by sweeping past Russia 3-0 in the final.

There was worse to come for Ramsey in the home internationals. He rang the changes for the match against Northern Ireland and the public that had been calling for new faces turned on him when England lost 1-0 to a Terry Neill goal. It was Northern Ireland's first victory against England since 1957 and the first ever occasion that England had lost two matches in a row at Wembley. England's sole consolation was a scrappy victory over Scotland at Hampden Park for a share of the title.

Maverick genius climbs the heights and plumbs the depths

GEORGE BEST'S tempestuous relationship with Manchester United hit rock bottom at the end of a roller-coaster season that had promised much but delivered only disappointment.

Things did not start well when Best was sent off in United's second match of the season, against Chelsea. However, he was cleared by the FA and celebrated in the next match by demolishing West Ham almost single-handed. His hat-trick included a goal that Trevor Brooking was moved to describe as "fantastic" – Best beat three defenders in quick succession and then turned Bobby Moore inside out with an incomparable dummy before hammering in his shot.

Best scored 11 goals in 10 League matches in the autumn and it looked as if he was back to his breathtaking best. The problem was that his off the field antics were taking an ever-increasing toll.

At the turn of the year he admitted: "I'm off form and I'm sick about the way I'm playing." Best promptly vanished and was dropped by Manchester United for missing an entire week's training. United ordered Best to move back into his old digs for the rest of the season, but that hardly curbed his carousing and the flow of goals dried up.

By the end of the season Best had managed to play in 40 of United's 42 League matches, and he was the club's leading scorer. But there was no doubt that he was cracking up fast.

The final straw came in May, when Best was dropped by Northern Ireland for not joining their squad before the home international against Scotland. Best claimed that he was a physical and mental wreck, and admitted that his drinking had become excessive.

He fled to Spain, refusing to talk to anybody. Best said that he was going to retire and, at the age of 26, it looked as if his career was over.

Mullery gets his own back

THE Uefa Cup final between Tottenham and Wolves provided two milestones in the history of English football: it was the first European final to be contested by two English clubs, and when Tottenham proved victorious they became the first British club to have won two different European competitions. Their first success had been in 1963 in the European Cup Winners Cup.

Martin Chivers had virtually engraved Tottenham's name on the new trophy (it replaced the old Fairs Cup) with two classic breakaway goals in the first leg at Molineux, and the 2-1 lead they took back to White Hart Lane left Wolves with a daunting task.

Alan Mullery made it even harder with an extraordinary header from a free kick taken by Martin Peters. Wolves refused to wilt and David Wagstaffe gave them a lifeline shortly before half-time with a thundering 20-yard shot that cannoned

Down but not out: Mullery is injured after scoring against Wolves

off the post. But Tottenham's midfield held and, with Pat Jennings resolute in goal, Spurs made history.

The Spurs players hoisted Mullery on to their shoulders and paraded him around the pitch. It was a fitting tribute to their 30-year-old captain. Two months before, his career seemed to be in tatters as he was banished on loan to Fulham, his former club.

A spate of injuries forced his return and in the semi-final of the Uefa Cup against AC Milan it was Mullery's long-range equaliser in the San Siro stadium that earned Spurs a place in the final. It was Mullery's swansong: in the summer he returned to Fulham permanently.

At long last, a real Cup for Stoke's hand-picked vintage crop

STOKE were one of the oldest teams in the League but in their lengthy history they had never been to Wembley. And it was thanks to two of their oldest players that they collected their first major trophy.

Stoke's appearance in the League Cup final was entirely thanks to the 34-year-old Gordon Banks. The semi-final against West Ham had finished level on aggregate and there were only three minutes left in extra time when Banks saved Geoff Hurst's penalty to keep Stoke's hopes alive.

The first replay ended goalless but there was plenty of drama early in the fourth meeting between the two teams. Bobby Ferguson, the West Ham keeper, was concussed and Bobby Moore had to take over in goal. Moore even managed to parry a penalty but was beaten by the follow-up shot.

Inspired, West Ham took the lead although Stoke were level by half-time. Terry Conroy

Saving grace: Banks keeps out Hurst's penalty with three minutes to go in the semi-final

scored just after the break and Stoke just hung on to win a pulsating match 3-2. Tony Waddington, the Stoke manager, said: "The game was out of this world. After this, Wembley could be something of an anti-climax."

He was almost proved right. Although Conroy scored after five minutes Stoke looked no match for Chelsea. Peter Osgood equalised and Chelsea continued to dominate. It was left to George Eastham, at 35 another of Stoke's veterans, to score his first goal in 18 months and give Stoke something to celebrate at long last.

End of an era as the Charlton brothers retire

AN ERA came to a painful end when both Charlton brothers left the clubs that they had served so loyally and moved into management.

Before the season had even started Leeds announced that Jack was no longer their first-choice centre-half. They wanted him to spend his time watching their upcoming opponents, but Jack refused to accept that his career was over.

Bobby, too, was out of favour. On August 25 Manchester United demoted him to the second team, the first time he had played for the reserves in 10 years. With Old Trafford in turmoil he chose his words carefully: "There are things I could say about the situation here that I would regret later."

The parting of the ways was an emotional occasion. More than 60,000 people attended his testimonial match against Celtic, a record, and another 57,000 came to his last home match at Old Trafford. It was a fitting tribute for a man who had played for the club since 1956 and had won every honour in the game.

Celtic, too, provided the opposition for Jack's testimonial, with nearly 35,000 packing Elland Road. But his career ended on a flatter note as he was forced to limp off with a hamstring injury during Leeds's match at Southampton.

Both men had played more than 600 times for their clubs and their experience was not lost to the game: Bobby took over as manager at Preston North End and Jack took charge at Middlesbrough.

Charltons bow out: Jack (left) and Bobby swapped their boots for a manager's chair

O'Farrell: United's latest whipping boy

Two things brought about Frank O'Farrell's downfall at Manchester United. One – United's terrible form – he had some influence over; the other – George Best – he could do nothing about at all.

Manchester United did not win in the League until their tenth match and spent the first third of the season on or near the bottom of the table. To compound their misery they were knocked out of the League Cup by Bristol Rovers, going down 1-0 at home.

O'Farrell had already spent a fortune bringing players to Old Trafford and his response to the crisis was to lash out another £200,000 on Bournemouth's ace striker Ted MacDougall. The fee was a record for a Third Division player.

Best, meanwhile, had made his peace with the club once again. Having fled to Spain in the summer, saying that his career was over and he intended to retire, he had returned home. But he was as wayward as ever, and when he skipped training at the end of November O'Farrell dropped him. When he left Manchester without permission and was seen in a London nightclub he was put on the transfer list.

But within 10 days Louis Edwards, the United chairman, said that Best would resume training with the club, and everybody assumed that this meant he had been taken off the transfer list. O'Farrell was said to be deeply unhappy at the way Best was being treated and there was widespread specula-

Docherty: big spender

tion that the United manager was about to resign, particularly because United had just suffered their heaviest defeat in four years, 5-0 at Crystal Palace.

But before he got a chance to act United struck first. On December 19 the board announced that O'Farrell, his coach Malcolm Musgrove and the chief scout John Aston had all been fired. When O'Farrell asked why he had been dismissed he was told that it was because United were bottom of the table.

Within three days Tommy Docherty had been appointed on a salary that was said to be in the region of £15,000 a year. Not one for understatement, he said: "Only one word can sum up my feelings – fantastic. My aim has always been to be the best manager in football. At Old Trafford I will get the best chance of proving I have what it takes."

Like O'Farrell, Docherty decided to spend his way out of trouble. He clearly favoured Scottish players, buying George Graham for £120,000, Alex Forsyth for £100,000 and Lou Macari for £200,000.

Even so it took him a while to record his first victory in the League, which did not come until mid-February. United did just enough to drag themselves clear of relegation. And despite the club's dismal performance the Old Trafford faithful did not appear to be disheartened – they attracted more than a million people to their 21 home League matches.

However, Manchester United's problems with Best would not go away. At first, Best, who quit yet again on the day that O'Farrell was sacked, said that he would never play for the club again. But he resumed training in late April, having reached an understanding with Docherty. The club would overlook his off the field antics providing Best made up for any missed training sessions in his own time. But, like everything else at Old Trafford, it would not be long before it all ended in tears.

Allison finds life without Mercer starts badly and gets even worse

MALCOLM ALLISON'S time at Manchester City was every bit as turbulent as the upheavals at Old Trafford. And the drama started even before a ball had been kicked.

Allison's partnership with Joe Mercer came to a bitter end in the summer when Mercer was demoted and Allison was given sole charge of the team. This was more than Mercer could stomach and within days he had left to become the manager of Coventry in place of Gordon Milne.

Allison promised that City would play attractive football and named Leeds as their greatest challengers for the championship. But he was being wildly over-optimistic. City lost seven of their first 10 League matches and slid down the table almost as fast as United.

It was unheard of for both Manchester clubs to be propping up the rest of the division. And, like at United, it was almost impossible to imagine City being put out of the League Cup by a minnow. Worse, the side that claimed their scalp were their near-neighbours Bury.

Allison was soon at loggerheads with his board. Despite his objections, they sold Ian Mellor to Norwich for £65,000. The board said that City needed the cash but Allison, not a man to mince his words, retorted: "My row with the directors has gone right to the heart of football's greatest problem.

"It has been about money – the need for it and the balancing of it against such assets as young players. My directors insisted we sold Mellor. They are responsible for the club and I am not going to resign."

When Mercer returned to Maine Road with Coventry the fans made their feelings about Allison clear. Mercer was cheered before the match and was the model of diplomacy after Coventry won 2-1. "I don't regard it as putting one over on City. How can I when I know these lads so well?" Allison, though, could not resist having a sly dig at his former mentor. "Gordon Milne has done a very good job at Coventry," he said.

Allison certainly had a way with words. Three weeks after saying that he was not going to resign he was catching a train south. The morning's papers were full of reports that Crystal Palace were in no rush to appoint a new manager. But, within an hour of arriving in London, Allison was being presented to the press as the man to save Palace from relegation.

The long-suffering Maine Road faithful had the last laugh though. Manchester City finished the season comfortably in mid-table while Allison's Palace were consigned to the Second Division.

Moore: centurion

Going down: Allison's new club, Crystal Palace, were doomed, while his old club, Manchester City, survived

How could I avoid being Player of the Year playing behind our defence?

PAT JENNINGS
Tottenham's goalkeeper

Jennings: Spurs' saviour

Clemence's homework pays off

In a league of their own: Liverpool parade the championship trophy

THE PUNDITS predicted a two-horse race for the championship: between Leeds and Manchester City. They were right about two clubs dominating the race for the title, but wrong about their identities. Liverpool went top on September 23, were harried all the way by Arsenal, who briefly took the top spot for a fortnight in February when they won 2-0 at Anfield, but in the end comfortably won the League with three points to spare.

Liverpool's foray into Europe was much more nerve-wracking. In the Uefa Cup semi-final in April they faced the holders, Spurs. Liverpool won the first leg at Anfield with an Alec Lindsay goal. At White Hart Lane, in a magnificent match,

Martin Peters scored twice for Spurs but a vital goal from Steve Heighway meant his team went through to the final against Borussia Moenchengladbach on the away goals rule. Both managers praised the quality of play and Bill Shankly promised to go for the Double.

The first leg of the final on May 11 was yet another tremendous match as Liverpool finished 3-0 winners with two goals from Kevin Keegan and one from Larry Lloyd. However, the Germans were unfortunate not to score: they hit the post and both sides missed a penalty.

Shankly, mindful of the semi-final against Spurs, was quick to point out the importance of not conceding a goal. Ray Clemence, who saved the

penalty, justifiably claimed the credit: "I watched Heynckes take a penalty in the semi-final on TV and decided to dive the same way. It was a reward for my homework."

And rewarded it was. Twelve days later Liverpool were thoroughly outplayed in the second leg, losing 2-0, but tenaciously clung on to their slender lead to win their first European trophy and complete a unique Double of League and European trophy in a single season, the first English team to achieve such a feat.

It did not escape Clemence, nor Shankly, that if he had not saved that penalty at Anfield the away goals rule that had favoured Liverpool at Tottenham would have given the Cup to Borussia Moenchengladbach.

Norwich's great escape rounds off a roller-coaster season

NEWLY PROMOTED Norwich found their first ever season in the First Division to be a heady cocktail of dismal failure, partial success and, ultimately, nerve-tingling survival.

Ron Saunders' team were sixth in the table on November 18 and then did not win another League match until they beat Chelsea 1-0

on April 14. Somehow they scuffled into the League Cup final on March 3, having eliminated Arsenal and Chelsea.

There, Tottenham, another London club, awaited the Norfolk club who had actually won the trophy in 1962 when the big boys ignored the fledgling competition. Sadly for Norwich it

was Spurs who became the first club to win the trophy twice. The final was a disappointing affair as the two midfields bogged each other down. Ralph Coates, a 22nd-minute substitute for John Pratt, scored the only goal 18 minutes from time.

Somehow Norwich managed to rescue their season in their

last five League matches, winning three and losing two to finish 20th and two points away from relegation. Crucially, in three days, they beat West Brom 1-0 at the Hawthorns and Crystal Palace 2-1, with a goal from Dave Stringer in injury time, to send both clubs into the Second Division.

Porterfield and Montgomery the two unlikeliest of Cup-winning lads

EACH season the FA Cup keeps true to its romantic image by producing a clutch of upsets as the little clubs tweak the noses of their betters. However, by the time of the final the form book has reasserted its authority and, so the theory goes, "normality" will prevail at Wembley. Unfortunately for Don Revie's mighty Leeds, Second Division Sunderland did not keep to the script.

Leeds, the Cup holders, were the hottest favourites in years. Eleven of their 12-man squad were internationals, they were in the final of the European Cup Winners Cup and had finished third in the First Division.

Sunderland, who had spent much of the season battling to avoid relegation to the Third Division, were a bunch of unknowns and the club had not played in a Cup final since 1937. The nation warmed to this modern-day battle of David and Goliath, not least because Leeds, with their abrasive and cynical methods of play, were the most unpopular side in the country. However, few outside of Wear-side actually believed it was possible.

There had been indications that Sunderland should not be lightly dismissed – they had imperiously dismissed Manchester City and Arsenal to reach the final – and they had some of the most vocal and fanatical fans in the country. Thus, on May 5, Wembley echoed to continuous renditions of "Ha'way the lads" and Leeds had their comeuppance.

The pattern of the match was settled in the first half-hour when Sunderland refused to be cowed by Leeds and even went close to scoring when Michael Horswill's 20-yard shot went narrowly wide. Then, in the 31st minute, Leeds's world turned upside down.

Billy Hughes's corner swung over to the far post – big Dave Watson failing to connect but he distracted two defenders – and Vic Halom's knee knocked it back across goal where it fortuitously fell to Ian Porterfield. The midfielder found the time to control the ball and shoot over David Harvey and score.

The goal seemed to knock the stuffing out of Leeds, but after half-time they attacked with a vengeance throwing both full backs into the attack. In the 65th minute they seemed to have the equaliser. Paul Reaney, the right back, crossed to the far post where Trevor Cherry, the other full back, came with a brilliant blind-side run to head the ball perfectly towards goal.

But Jim Montgomery instinctively dived and parried the ball only for it to fall to Peter Lorimer, five yards in front of an open goal. The man with the hardest shot in football took aim and fired. Incredibly Montgomery had scrambled up. He pushed the ball on to the underside of the bar and the danger was over.

Montgomery's historic double save had won the Cup. When the final whistle blew, Bob Stokoe, the Sunderland manager since December, hared across the pitch to embrace his match-winning goalkeeper amid scenes of uncontrollable joy.

And the FA Cup had added another chapter to its never-ending romantic history.

The moment that finished Leeds: Porterfield (far right) scores the winning goal

Stokoe: Midas touch

179

THE
1972-73
SEASON

Leeds denied European trophy by Greek referee and Italian keeper

DON REVIE may have assembled one of the most gifted and professional club sides in Britain but once again major honours heartbreakingly eluded them. Eleven days after their humbling defeat in the FA Cup final they succumbed to AC Milan 1-0 in the European Cup Winners Cup final in Salonika.

But for once Leeds, notorious for their cynicism, could justly claim to have been robbed. They fell behind to a fourth-minute goal from a free-kick that the Greek referee, Christos Michas, should probably not have given. Chiarugi's free kick from 20 yards was deflected off the Leeds wall. Worse was to come.

Leeds, despite being deprived of Billy Bremner, Allan Clarke, Eddie Gray and Johnny Giles, comprehensively out-played the Italian side but simply could not score. Vecchi, Milan's goalkeeper, played outstandingly to beat out shot after shot. However, his heroics were aided by Michas's inept refereeing.

The catalogue of dubious decisions was extraordinary: Mick Jones was clearly brought down in the penalty area by Anquilletti right in front of the referee; Zignoli handled a cross from Peter Lorimer in the area and Jones was again felled in the box, this time by Zignoli. Even the Greek crowd were incensed by what they were watching and began to chant for the hapless Leeds team.

The game ended in fisticuffs when a frustrated Norman Hunter retaliated after a vicious foul by Rivera and, in the ensuing melee, Hunter and Sogliano were sent off. The crowd shouted: "Shame, shame," when the Italian players attempted to celebrate their victory.

With his season in tatters Revie must have rued the boast he made in March when he committed his team to a Treble: "We shall play our strongest team for everything we are involved in – championship, FA Cup, European Cup Winners Cup."

Victim of injustice: Hunter was sent off when his patience snapped in a terrible final

Nine years of Leeds's fluctuating fortunes

Year	League	FA Cup	League Cup	Europe
1965	2	final	3rd rnd	
1966	2	4th rnd	3rd rnd	Fairs Cup semi-final
1967	4	semi-final	4th rnd	Fairs Cup final
1968	4	semi-final	winners	Fairs Cup winners
1969	winners	3rd rnd	4th rnd	Fairs Cup quarter-final
1970	2	final	3rd rnd	Champions Cup semi-final
1971	2	5th rnd	2nd rnd	Fairs Cup winners
1972	2	winners	3rd rnd	Uefa Cup 1st rnd
1973	3	final	4th rnd	Cup-Winners' Cup final

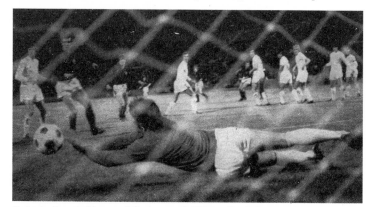

Unlucky break: Harvey fails to reach Chiarugi's deflected free kick

Celtic's title record a close-run thing

CELTIC'S eighth consecutive championship – a record in Scottish League history – was not quite the canter it appeared to be at the start of the season.

For, as Celtic came out of the starting stalls with three consecutive wins, Rangers began with the worst start in their history and by the beginning of October were lying an embarrassing 13th in the table.

Then the Ibrox team mounted a fightback that bordered on the miraculous: winning 24 of their next 28 League matches and losing only one. However the task was always going to be too much and Celtic pipped Rangers to the title by a solitary point – albeit with a far superior goal difference. But Rangers' renaissance was not all in vain.

At Hampden on May 5 Rangers prevented Celtic from achieving the Double in a thrilling see-saw Cup final which they finally won 3-2.

Kenny Dalglish gave Celtic the lead in the 24th minute only for Derek Parlane to equalise 10 minutes later. Rangers then took the lead themselves immediately after the beginning of the second half. Alfie Conn, with a blistering burst of pace, completely bamboozled Billy McNeill and scored a memorable goal only to see it squandered when John Greig handled in the penalty area and George Connelly coolly slotted home the equaliser. In a frantic finish Derek Johnstone's header struck the post, rolled along the goalline and Tommy Forsyth stuck out a foot to score his first goal for Rangers and snatch the Cup.

Despite their League success, Celtic did not have much luck in the League Cup either, losing the final in December for the third consecutive year. This time it was Hibs – still smarting from the 6-1 hammering Celtic had given them in the previous year's Scottish Cup final – who did the damage. Pat Stanton put Hibs ahead on the hour and laid on a second for Jim O'Rourke. Dalglish got one back for Celtic with 20 minutes remaining, but to no avail.

Brave Banks unable to battle his way back after losing an eye in a head-on car crash

Forced to admit defeat: Banks's retirement was announced on the BBC

EVEN THOUGH he was 35, Gordon Banks was still regarded as the best goalkeeper in the country, and many people thought he was the best keeper of all time. He had just signed a long contract with Stoke and was still a key member of Sir Alf Ramsey's squad for the 1974 World Cup.

But his career was brought to an untimely end in October when his car collided head-on with a van and shards of glass from the shattered windscreen badly damaged his right eye. It seemed almost inconceivable that two sportsmen could be cut down in their prime by the same freak injury – it was only a few years since the celebrated England and Northamptonshire cricketer Colin Milburn had lost the sight in one eye in a car crash.

Banks refused to be beaten and said that he hoped to resume training in the New Year and continue playing by wearing contact lenses. He was picked for a representative match, but playing on the right wing. Stoke said that he would return to action in their summer tour of Australia and New Zealand, and Ramsey chose him for an FA XI to play in Gibraltar.

Sadly, all the optimism was in vain and Banks was forced to admit in August that he would never play again.

Spot on: Pele scores against Fulham at Craven Cottage

BOBBY MOORE
The perfect Englishman respected throughout the world

Steve Hutchings

BOBBY MOORE was the quintessential Englishman. While the rest of the team celebrated winning the World Cup in 1966 their captain could only think of one thing – collecting the trophy from the Queen. It wasn't the glory and drama of the moment that was on his mind. No, Moore was worried that his muddy hands would spoil the Queen's white gloves when he shook hands with her. So before stepping forward to receive the trophy Moore carefully wiped his hands clean on the velvet drapes lining the approach to the Royal Box. But that was Moore all over – quiet and unassuming even at the pinnacle of his career.

Moore was arguably the best defender of his generation, only rivalled by the subsequent emergence of Franz Beckenbauer. Yet, for such a great defender, he was always lacking in pace. He knew it was a failing and compensated for it with outstanding vision and forethought. Moore was hardly ever caught out because he always seemed to be in the right place at the right time.

He owed that knack to the two men who were most influential on his early days at West Ham – Malcolm Allison, who coached the young players, and Noel Cantwell, another of the senior pros. Moore asked Cantwell whether it was possible to be a great player if you were not quick enough. Cantwell, picking his words carefully to avoid damaging Moore's confidence, explained what it was that made Johnny Haynes such a respected striker. Haynes, he said, lacked pace. But even before he received the ball he knew where everybody was on the pitch. He knew instantly what he was going to do.

Starting out: began his career at West Ham

Moore heeded the advice, and England's final goal against West Germany in the World Cup final was a case in point. With seconds remaining, Moore had possession of the ball. Jack Charlton and Nobby Stiles screamed at him to blast it high into the crowd, safely out of reach of the Germans. But that was not Moore's style; not the way he thought the game should be played. In his mind's eye he knew where Geoff Hurst, his West Ham teammate would be. Quick as a flash he placed his clearance into space for Hurst to run on to and complete his hat-trick. Speed of thought was, truly, every bit as important as speed of action. It was the perfect vindication of everything he had learnt from Cantwell and Allison.

Moore virtually idolised both of them when he joined the Upton Park ground staff. Like a puppy, he followed them around everywhere, wanting to talk football all the time. They spent so much time talking in a cafe near the ground that the owner banished them to an upstairs room to make room for his other customers. And on his honeymoon in Majorca, Moore discovered that Allison and Cantwell were on holiday on the same island. He promptly decamped to their villa and spent the night talking football, leaving his wife far from delighted.

Moore's willingness to learn his trade enabled him to rise through the ranks at West Ham after arriving as just another youngster with puppy fat and no more than ordinary ability. Allison was so impressed by Moore's determination that he persuaded Ted Fenton, the West Ham manager, that he had the makings of a great player. Ironically, it was Allison who was not picked when Moore, on Cantwell's recommendation, made his first-team debut at 17.

Moore had already progressed to the England Youth team, coached by Ron Greenwood, who replaced Fenton at West Ham in 1961. Moore was a willing disciple of Greenwood's ideas of how football should be played, and he was soon promoted to captain. But off the field the two men's relationship was not quite so smooth.

Moore nearly missed the 1966 World Cup finals because he was arguing with Greenwood over a transfer and how much he was paid. Days before the tournament was due to start, Moore had still not signed a contract with West Ham so, according to FA rules, he was ineligible to play. Greenwood was summoned to the England team's hotel and the problem was circumvented by Moore signing a temporary contract.

Ramsey also had his run-ins with Moore. Despite his diffident, gentlemanly image, Bobby was one of the lads. A terrible insomniac, Moore often found it difficult to relax. A few beers in the evening helped him to unwind. Ramsey, with his old-fashioned notions of discipline, was not pleased to discover that Moore was one of a group of players to have broken a curfew, albeit by a matter of minutes. And Greenwood was incandescent with rage when Moore went out for a few drinks the night before West Ham were

---

BOBBY MOORE

Born April 12, 1941, Barking

PLAYING CAREER

West Ham United 1958-74

Joined the West Ham ground staff, and signed as a professional in 1958

Made his debut against West Ham United against Manchester United on September 8, 1958

Played 642 times (544 in the League) and scored 22 League goals

1964: Won the FA Cup. Elected Footballer of the Year, the youngest player to win the honour

1965: Won the European Cup Winners Cup

Fulham

Signed for Fulham on March 14, 1974. Played 150 matches (124 in the League) and scored one League goal

1975: FA Cup beaten finalist

Retired: May 14, 1977

Internationals Played for the England Youth (18 times) and Under-23 teams (eight times). Made his full international debut against Peru in May 1962. Appointed England captain May 20, 1963

Played a record 108 matches for England, captaining his country 90 times and scoring two goals

1966: Won the World Cup

1970: World Cup quarter-finals

Also played for San Antonio Thunder, Seattle Sounders and Team America

MANAGEMENT CAREER

Oxford City Manager 1979-81

Coached Eastern Athletic (Hong Kong) in 1983

Southend United Manager 1984-86

1967: Awarded an OBE

Died February 24, 1993

First honour: Moore captained West Ham to victory in the 1964 Cup final

Ultimate honour: the World Cup at Wembley

embarrassed by Blackpool in the FA Cup.

Unlike George Best and Jimmy Greaves, who revelled in the liberal 1960s, Moore knew how to conduct himself in a proper fashion. So he enjoyed a couple of lagers from time to time? But he never allowed a night out to affect his game and he never gave less than 100%. Ramsey knew that players had to left off steam from time to time and he was never going to let the rare minor indiscretions cloud his belief that Moore was the cornerstone of the England team.

After his first match in charge, a 5-2 defeat in France, Ramsey spent most of the journey home deep in discussion with Moore about what they were going to do next. Moore was appointed the captain of England in 1963, in only his 12th international. With Moore his loyal lieutenant, Ramsey was free to experiment with the rest of the team in his unceasing search for the right combination to win the World Cup.

A measure of Moore's importance to England can be gleaned by comparing him with Billy Wright, England's other great leader. Both men captained the team 90 times. Under Wright, England won 49 matches and conceded 135 goals. Under Moore, there were 57 victories and only 75 goals against.

Ever dependable: Moore won 108 caps

Perhaps the only mistake that Ramsey made was persevering with Moore a little bit too long. But who could blame him. Moore was seemingly unflappable, and at a time when football was becoming ever more defensively minded he still believed that there was more to defending than just stopping your opponent by any means. The bone-crunching tackle was not for him; rather the surgical strike that left Moore on his feet with the ball under control, ready to be stroked upfield to start the counter-attack.

Moore's determination to play the ball cleanly was, sadly, his and England's undoing in Katowice in a qualifying match for the 1974 World Cup. England trailed 1-0 (under pressure, Moore had deflected a free kick into his own net) when Moore, for once, was caught in possession and Poland scored again. The 2-0 defeat was the beginning of the end for both Ramsey and Moore.

Three more internationals took Moore past Bobby Charlton's record 106 caps, and Greenwood (having vetoed moves to Tottenham and Brian Clough's Derby) finally allowed him to leave West Ham. Moore wanted to go to Crystal Palace, to team up with his old mentor Allison. Instead, he was transferred to Fulham. There was one more trip to Wembley, for an FA Cup final – lost to his old club West Ham – before Moore retired in 1977.

Unsuccessful spells in management with Oxford City and Southend, and failed business ventures did nothing to diminish Moore's reputation. The global superstar from working-class east London never forgot the debt he owed football. He played again for England, against West Germany, to raise funds for the victims of the Bradford fire. And he returned to Wembley, his home from home, in 1986 to team up with Best in a match for Sports Aid.

His sudden death, from cancer, at 51, shocked everybody. Ken Bates, the outspoken Chelsea chairman, spoke for the country when he said: "He will never grow old in people's minds, in the same way that President Kennedy won't." Allison, for all his flamboyance, cried his heart out. Cantwell was inconsolable.

Pele, undoubtedly the world's greatest player, had no doubts about Moore's greatness. After Brazil had beaten England 1-0 in the 1970 World Cup finals Pele and Moore exchanged shirts as a mark of the respect that each man had for the other. When Pele heard of Moore's death he said: "Words cannot sum up the grief I feel for my great friend. He was one of the world's finest defenders and a great sportsman."

That was the key to Moore. Never mind that his critics said that he was one-paced. Never mind that Beckenbauer might have been a more accomplished player. At a time when so many idols had turned out to have feet of clay Moore will always be remembered for being the perfect gentleman.

As Reg Burr, the Millwall chairman, said: "Bobby's type of Englishness drew on the better side of our national character, on our sense of fair play and of dignity. People of all ages feel we have lost a link to a better, more decent time."

Bowing out: Moore ended his career in America

Clown makes fools of England

DESPITE a 90-minute onslaught by England in front of a packed Wembley crowd, their failure to do better than a 1-1 draw against Poland condemned them to World Cup oblivion. The hero of the night was Jan Tomaszewski, the Polish goalkeeper. He had been dubbed a "clown" by Brian Clough, TV pundit and Derby manager, before the match. However, his antics on October 17 made fools of England instead.

Tomaszewski was simply unbeatable: he used every single part of his body – fist, fingertip, leg, hand, torso and foot – to thwart England. The only thing that got past him all night was a penalty. Tomaszewski's inspired performance, part brilliance, part sheer luck, was compounded by England's misfortune – they hit every part of the woodwork – and the ability of defenders to miraculously clear off the line whenever the occasion demanded.

Domarski of Poland scored first, in the 57th minute, when Norman Hunter, picked instead of Bobby Moore, was caught in possession. Allan Clarke levelled the scores six minutes later from a generously awarded penalty. The Polish goal now came under permanent bombardment and Moore, on the bench, exhorted Sir Alf Ramsey to use one of his substitutes.

With five minutes remaining, Ramsey, who had never been comfortable with substitutions, relented. "Kevin, get stripped," he ordered. Kevin Keegan duly took off his tracksuit. "Not that Kevin, the other one." With 100 seconds left Kevin Hector made his England debut. And he still had the best chance of the match, but his header was inches wide.

So Poland would go to the World Cup finals in West Germany, and England had, for the first time, failed to qualify. It was a chastening experience for the nation and on a par with the humiliating defeat by Hungary in the same stadium 20 years earlier. Ramsey, who had played his last international in that match, understood the pain of such public failure only too well.

However, England had only themselves to blame for their misery. In their three-team group they had failed to beat Wales at Wembley in March, and had given a spineless performance in Chorzow in June, where Moore made an uncharacteristic blunder and they lost 2-0.

> *It would have changed the course of English football history if Hector's header had gone into the net*
>
> JIMMY GREAVES

Ramsey's 11-year record as England manager						
P	W	D	L	F	A
113	69	27	17	224	99

Clough deserts Derby

Clough: war of words

BRIAN CLOUGH'S big mouth and his battles with the Derby board produced an explosive showdown and one that, for once, he did not win.

Clough brought the behind the scenes warfare out into the open by making two blistering attacks. The first was on the FA, whom he condemned for their handling of Leeds's disciplinary record. In a newspaper article he said that Leeds should have been demoted and "the men who run soccer missed the most marvellous chance of cleaning up the game in one swoop".

Then, days before England's crucial World Cup qualifying game against Poland he accused some of his own players of being cheats. He claimed they were not giving 100 per cent for the club because they were more concerned with the international match.

Sam Longston, the Derby chairman, was horrified. He feared that his club would receive heavy punishment and could even be expelled from the League. So he told Clough to shut up and stop writing for newspapers and appearing on television.

Clough was having none of it and thought he could call the club's bluff by resigning. But Derby stood firm and on October 17 Clough and his assistant Peter Taylor left. Derby appointed Dave Mackay, and the former player had a torrid time for the rest of the season, having to deal with revolts by the fans and his players – all of whom were intensely loyal to Clough.

Clough and Taylor soon agreed to take charge at Brighton, and their arrival trebled the attendance for the Third Division club's next home match. But it was not long before Clough was up to his old tricks.

Brighton were bundled out of the Cup 4-0 by Walton and Hersham and were then thrashed 8-2 by Bristol Rovers. Clough said that he was ashamed by the performances and accused his players of not knowing their own trade, lacking heart and shirking their moral responsibilities.

Then he fell foul of the Brighton board as well. Clough admitted that he was interested in a £400 a week offer from the Shah of Iran to take charge of his country's national side.

The Brighton board vetoed the move and said that Clough and Taylor had to honour their contracts. Clough's response was grudging: "Of course I wanted to go to Iran, but I'm staying at Brighton to do a job. I'm not saying I'm happy here."

And just how unhappy matters had become would soon become apparent.

> *Britain, an island of 55 million Poms, will be green with envy when Australia compete in the World Cup finals*
>
> Melbourne Newspaper

End of the road: Tomaszewski foils yet another England attack

The violent and ugly side of the beautiful game

England's worst export: Tottenham fans go on the rampage in Rotterdam

■ After a season of wrangling, the chairmen of the League clubs finally accepted a three-year deal with television on July 17.

■ Joao Havelange replaced Sir Stanley Rous as president of Fifa.

■ Chris Balderstone was stripped of the Carlisle captaincy in August when he decided to continue playing county cricket until the end of the season, and thus missed his football team's opening matches.

■ Mainz, the German professional club, thought they were playing Wolverhampton Wanderers in a friendly on Aug 15. In fact their opponents were a Sunday amateur side who, not surprisingly, lost 21-0.

■ Ted Croker replaced Denis Follows as secretary of the FA on September 6.

■ Trevor Hockey became the first Welsh international to be sent off when Wales lost 3-0 in Poland on September 26.

■ Birmingham paid a record fee for a goalkeeper, £100,000, when they bought Gary Sprake from Leeds.

■ Cardiff beat Orient on December 1 to record their first away win in more than two years.

■ Ray Cashley, the Bristol City goalkeeper, scored against Hull when his clearance bounced straight past Jeff Weelands, the Hull goalkeeper.

Spurs shamed

The second leg of Tottenham's Uefa Cup final against Feyenoord in Rotterdam was overshadowed by rioting Spurs fans. Seventy people were arrested and more than 200 were injured in the disturbances.

Sydney Wale, the Tottenham chairman, made an impassioned plea to the crowd at half-time: "You hooligans are a disgrace to Tottenham and England. This is a football game, not a war."

It was to no avail and the Spurs board wrote to Feyenoord and the Rotterdam police apologising for the shameful behaviour. Spurs lost the final 4-2 on aggregate.

Cup disgrace

Three Atletico Madrid players were sent off in the first leg of the European Cup semi-final against Celtic. Four Atletico players and two Celtic players were also booked.

Atletico, managed by Juan Carlos Lorenzo, the man in charge of the 1966 Argentina World Cup side branded "animals" by Alf Ramsey, had six of their players banned for the return leg. They were also fined £14,000 by Uefa. Celtic lost the semi-final 2-0 on aggregate.

Birch thugs

In a sign of what was to come, hundreds of arrests were made at pre-season friendlies. Len Shipman, the League president, said the government should bring back the birch. "Ruthless action is imperative. Fines will not stop violence."

Players blamed

The Police Federation said that players' behaviour was also to blame for the troubles dogging the game. "When an England player in an international match is seen by millions of TV viewers getting himself sent off after attacking an opponent, what happens? He is picked again and only prevented from playing by a higher authority. Can we wonder at the behaviour of young hooligans?"

Referee ignored

Mike Doyle and Lou Macari refused to leave the pitch when they were both sent off after a fracas during Manchester United's ill-tempered match with Manchester City at Old Trafford on March 13.

Clive Thomas, the referee, took both teams off the pitch until his instruction was obeyed, and also booked four more players. The match was a 0-0 draw.

No nonsense: Clive Thomas stood his ground

Sir Alf made the scapegoat

SIX MONTHS after England's dismal elimination from the World Cup finals at the hands of Poland, the FA summarily dismissed Sir Alf Ramsey, the manager who had won them the World Cup in England eight years previously.

However, the failure in the 1970 World Cup in Mexico when England lost to West Germany 3-2 in extra time, with Ramsey being blamed for bringing on two substitutes, and the Poland debacle, where he was blamed for bringing on a substitute too late, made his sacking inevitable.

Ramsey, the first of the "modern" England managers, was never popular with the press or the FA mandarins. Indeed the two forces virtually colluded in his downfall. Fleet Street knives were out for him immediately after England's elimination and Sir Harold Thompson, the FA's vice-chairman, made sure they hit their mark.

Ramsey was given his marching orders on April 21 but the decision was not announced until 10 days later once they had found a suitable stand-in. Up stepped genial Joe Mercer, Coventry's general manager and the former manager of Manchester City, who was appointed to hold the fort as a caretaker manager.

"I do not want the job on a permanent basis," the smiling 59-year-old said. "I'll just hold the reins for a few weeks. I'll tell the players to go out and enjoy themselves." Mercer was in complete contrast to the diffident and stand-offish Ramsey, and, during his short tenure, it worked. England lost only one of seven matches.

By July the FA reverted to type and appointed Don Revie, of Leeds, and the outstanding English manager of the decade. The fun period was over and dour professionalism was once again the order of the day, of which Revie was the arch exponent.

Alan Hardaker, the secretary of the Football League and never one to mince his words, told the FA secretary: "You must be off your heads." He later amplified this comment: "Revie as England manager was a classic case of poacher turning gamekeeper."

England's greatest manager

Born: January 22, 1920 in Dagenham, Essex.

Signed for Southampton in April 1944 and made his first-team debut in October 1946. Played 90 matches and scored eight goals.

Joined Tottenham in May 1949 and played for them until 1954, scoring 24 goals in 226 matches. Second Division champions in 1950, First Division champions in 1951, and First Division runners-up in 1952.

Made his debut for England on December 1, 1948, against Switzerland at Highbury. Won 32 caps, including 29 consecutively. Scored three goals, all of them penalties.

Appointed the manager of Ipswich in 1955. Third Division South champions in 1957, Second Division champions in 1961 and First Division champions in 1962. Thus, he achieved the feat of winning the Second and First Divisions as both a player and a manager.

Became the manager of England in May 1963 and was dismissed in April 1974. Was the most successful England manager ever, only losing 17 matches out of 113 (with 69 wins and 27 draws).

Won the World Cup in 1966 and was knighted for services to football in January 1967.

Briefly managed Birmingham in the 1977-78 season.

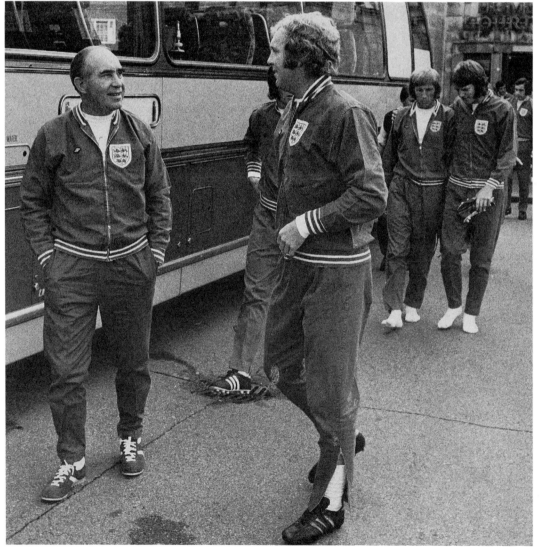

Mentor and maestro: Ramsey and Moore discuss tactics in one their last matches together

Mercer: caretaker

Big-spending Docherty hits rock bottom at Manchester United after Best storms out and City condemn them to relegation

TOMMY DOCHERTY'S attempts to spend his way out of trouble and tame George Best both ended in disaster as Manchester United were relegated to the Second Division for the first time in 36 years.

Once again, their form in the League was abysmal and at Christmas their goalkeeper, Alex Stepney, was their joint leading goalscorer with two penalties. Then, in the New Year, the club finally parted company with George Best.

At first it seemed that Docherty had reached an understanding with his wayward genius and Best returned to the first team in October. However, their relationship reached breaking point just before United's third round FA Cup match against Plymouth.

Best missed a training session but thought he had kept his side of the bargain by making up the work in his own time. However, Docherty dropped him and Best's retort was: "If I can't get into a struggling team like Manchester United then it's time to quit." This time it really was the end of the line.

In the end, United were undone by one of their former

Getting his own back: Law's goal doomed United

stalwarts Denis Law, who had joined Manchester City after being released by Docherty during the close season. United needed to win both of their final two games of the season to stand any chance of staying up

They came unstuck in their penultimate match, at Maine Road. Francis Lee's run towards the penalty area appeared to be covered by the United defence but he threaded the ball into the six-yard box, where Law hit a cheeky back-heel into the corner of the net.

Ironically, Law, at the start of his career with United, had won a penalty against City in the 1962-3 season in a game that relegated City and kept United in the First Division.

Eight minutes from the end of the match the United fans went wild and invaded the pitch, forcing the referee to abandon the match. The League decided to let the score stand.

Revie's record run speaks for itself

AFTER the heartbreak of last season, when Don Revie speculated about going for an historic Treble and ended up with nothing, Leeds were not going to make any more rash promises. Instead, they let their football do the talking for them.

They won their first seven matches, swept past Sheffield United's record of 23 matches without defeat from the start of a season, and were within an ace of passing Burnley's all-time unbeaten record when they lost their 30th League match, 3-2 at Stoke on February 23.

That was one of only four defeats in the League that Leeds suffered all season and the other three came in consecutive matches in March. They lost to Liverpool, their closest rivals, went down 4-1 to struggling Burnley, their worst home defeat since Don Revie had taken charge, and were then beaten 3-1 by West Ham. People started to wonder whether

Revie: kept quiet

Leeds's nerve was going to crack once again – particularly as Liverpool had closed the gap to four points with three games in hand.

But Leeds, free to concentrate on the League after their shock exit from the FA Cup at the hands of Bristol City in the fifth round, kept their resolve. It was Liverpool, still busy in the FA Cup, who slipped and handed the title to Leeds when they lost at home to Arsenal with two matches still to go.

With Leeds in the spotlight, Bristol Rovers' performance in the Third Division went virtually unnoticed. They almost matched Leeds's unbeaten run, not losing until their 27th match, at Wrexham on February 2.

Shankly bows out on a high note with yet another trophy

BILL SHANKLY crowned his glittering career with yet another trophy, the FA Cup, and then announced that he was bowing out at the summit because of the continual strain of being involved in top-flight football. There was a smooth handover of power as Liverpool promoted his assistant Bob Paisley, who had been with the club since 1939.

Liverpool's 3-0 victory over Newcastle in the FA Cup final was a wonderful demonstration of all that Shankly held dear. Although there was no score at half-time Liverpool smoothly moved up through the gears in the second half and were soon cruising to victory.

Tommy Smith's pinpoint cross picked out Kevin Keegan, who deftly controlled the ball and dispatched it with brio. Then John Toshack sliced the Newcastle defence open, Steve Heighway produced a clever change of direction and that was goal number two.

It was not Liverpool's style to ease up when they had the game under control. Their hallmark was precise passing, and Keegan's second, two minutes from time, was a wonderful culmination of a flowing move. It was a crushing end for Newcastle who had undergone an ordeal even to reach Wembley.

They were 2-1 down at home to Nottingham Forest in the sixth round when the visitors were awarded, and scored, a penalty in the second half. Pat Howard was sent off for arguing with the referee over the penalty and Newcastle fans invaded the pitch, stopping the game for nearly 10 minutes.

Despite being reduced to 10 men, Newcastle recovered to win 4-3 when play resumed. But Nottingham Forest successfully appealed against the result and the FA said that the match had to be replayed at a neutral venue. Malcolm Macdonald, the Newcastle striker, said: "My reaction is one of disgust but not surprise. I half expected a ridiculous solution and they came up with one."

It needed another 210 minutes of football in four days at Goodison Park before Newcastle finally prevailed, thanks to a single goal from Macdonald.

Shankly's achievements

Born: September 2, 1913 in Glenbuck, Ayrshire

Played for Carlisle United and Preston North End. Won the FA Cup with Preston in 1938.

Won five Scottish caps in the 1938-39 season.

Appointed the manager of Carlisle in 1949. Moved to Grimsby in 1951, Workington in 1953 and Huddersfield in 1956.

Became the manager of Liverpool in December 1959.

1962   Second Division champions.

1964   First Division champions.

1965   FA Cup winners.

1966   First Division champions, European Cup Winners Cup beaten finalists.

1969   First Division runners-up.

1971   FA Cup beaten finalists.

1973   First Division champions, Uefa Cup winners.

1974   FA Cup winners, First Division runners-up.

Shankly retired at the end of the 1973-74 season and was awarded the OBE.

Died: September 28, 1981 in Liverpool.

Bill Shankly was one of five brothers who played professional football. Bob Shankly was also a successful manager, taking Dundee to the Scottish championship for the first time in 1962.

The last hurrah: Shankly retired on a winning note

One way street: Keegan and Liverpool dominated Newcastle

Docherty's boys do the business

Leading light: the predatory Jordan was always Scotland's spearhead

TOMMY DOCHERTY may not have rescued Manchester United from relegation, but the two precious wins Scotland secured against Denmark under his stewardship the previous year virtually clinched Scotland's place in the World Cup finals in West Germany. By September all Willie Ormond's team had to do was beat Czechoslovakia once, either home or away.

But in the first match, at Hampden on the 26th, the Czechs drew first blood when, in the 33rd minute, Nehoda broke clear on the right and his speculative cross skated under the goalkeeper. Within seven minutes a Docherty stalwart, Jim Holton, the imposing Manchester United centre-half, had equalised, nodding in Tommy Hutchison's corner.

In the second half Scotland threw everything into attack. In the 70th minute, with the Czech defence under fearful pressure, a Billy Bremner free kick struck a post and it seemed the Czechs had survived yet another onslaught. But the ball broke to Willie Morgan (another Docherty player at United) and Joe Jordan, brought on to replace Kenny Dalglish six minutes earlier, became Scotland's hero as he met Morgan's centre to head home the winner.

It was the fourth time Scotland had qualified for the World Cup finals (though in 1950 in a fit of pique they refused to take up the invitation). The return match in Bratislava in October was irrelevant, although any disappointment they may have had by going down to a Nehoda first-half penalty was tempered by the news that England had been eliminated by Poland.

FOR THE RECORD

■ Bob Latchford joined Everton from Birmingham in exchange for Howard Kendall and Arthur Styles and £80,000. The total value of the deal was put at £350,000, a record.

■ Exeter defied a League instruction to play their match against Scunthorpe because they only had nine fit players. Scunthorpe were awarded the points and Exeter were fined £5,000 and ordered to pay £1,000 compensation to Scunthorpe.

■ Celtic won the Scottish League for the ninth year running to equal the world record for successive championships. They also completed the Double with a 3-0 victory over Dundee United in the Scottish Cup.

■ Jack Charlton, in his first season as a manager, guided Middlesbrough to the Second Division championship. They won the title by a record 15 points.

■ Bishop's Stortford beat Ilford 4-1 in the last Amateur Cup final.

■ Denis Law made a record 54th appearance for Scotland on May 11 in the 1-0 defeat by Northern Ireland.

■ Lord Westwood became president of the League in June after Len Shipman resigned because off ill-health.

Stand-in keeps City at bay as Wolves find the right formula

WOLVERHAMPTON won the League Cup, their first major honour since they took the FA Cup in 1960, thanks in no small part to their reserve goalkeeper Gary Pierce.

Pierce had been deputising for Phil Parkes for several weeks and he produced a series of good saves in the second half just when the match was threatening to swing Manchester City's way.

Wolves dominated the first half and took the lead just before the interval when Kenny Hibbitt mis-hit a shot but still scored. But Manchester City came back strongly and Colin Bell's fierce shot gave Pierce no chance. Bell hit the woodwork again and that was the best chance Manchester City had.

From then on, Pierce kept them at bay and Wolverhampton's confidence slowly returned. In a match that got more exciting the longer it went on, John Richards scored the winner for Wolves with only six minutes remaining.

The post-match celebrations were spoiled by an act of petulance by Rodney Marsh. The moment the final whistle blew the Manchester City forward headed straight for the dressing-room, refusing to applaud the winning team or to go to collect his loser's souvenir tankard.

Golden reserve: Pierce makes another save to deny Lee

WORLD CUP 1974
Europeans dominate as West Germany triumph

TOTAL FOOTBALL swept the tenth World Cup off its feet. With Pele gone and Brazil reneging on their birthright, the stage was set for Holland's Johann Cruyff and West Germany's Franz Beckenbauer to battle for the accolade of the world's greatest footballer. But for the billions watching around the globe the tournament was more than a titanic struggle between two individuals, it was the revelation of a whole new team game: Total Football.

However for West Germany and Holland, the two exponents of this method, it meant two different things. For Holland, blessed with remarkable talent, it meant that forwards were also defenders, and defenders forwards, with Cruyff the puppet-master pulling all the strings. Each member of the team had to be prepared to function as a multi-purpose player instead of being tied to their traditional role. The world gasped at this innovation. Others pointed out that at last they were doing their job: they were footballers.

West Germany's version was something entirely different. Their system had evolved out of catenaccio, the Italians' use of a sweeper behind the defensive back line to negate attacking moves. However this stiflingly defensive tactic was turned on its head by West Germany, who used their sweeper, the incomparable Beckenbauer, to explode out of his lair to launch devastating attacks. Paul Breitner, too, was nominally a defender but he was equally dangerous going forward, particularly in support of their two genuine wingers, Jurgen Grabowski and Uli Hoeness.

Little wonder then, in the Olympic stadium in Munich on July 7, these two great, revolutionary sides clashed in the World Cup final. If it wasn't the most amazing final of all time, it began with the most extraordinary piece of drama. Straight from the kick-off, Cruyff set off on another of his scintillating runs. His pace and ball control took him sweeping and twisting past the entire German team. Only Hoeness, frantically racing back to try to cover the danger, got anywhere near him. But Hoeness's last-ditch tackle was ill-timed and brought Cruyff down just inside the penalty area. Jack Taylor, the English referee unflinching under the

pressure of the home crowd, had no hesitation in awarding a penalty. Johann Neeskens duly scored from the spot. It was the fastest goal in a World Cup final and West Germany were behind without having touched the ball.

West Germany hardly got a look in for the next 20 minutes as well. The Dutch domination was total, and the German crowd gasped at the ease with which Cryuff's side strung together a host of pretty passes. But perhaps they thought it was going to be all too easy, because they failed to convert their arrogant superiority into more goals. West Germany clung on to Holland's coat tails and were rewarded for their perseverance after 25 minutes

when Taylor awarded another penalty when Jansen tripped Holzenbein. Germans in the crowd thought that justice had been done, although the decision was far less clear-cut.

Breitner scored from the spot and then Gerd Muller gave Germany the lead two minutes before half-time. He was a classic striker, and his goal proved the point. The pass from Bonhof was not quite on target and as Muller controlled the ball it ran away from him slightly. But, in a flash, he dragged it back and hit his shot past Jan Jongbloed.

And just to prove that the match was not entirely about outfield players, Sepp Maier gave a virtuoso performance in the second half. He

made one particularly good save from Johann Neeskens, after which Holland's momentum finally ebbed away. And Germany recaptured the World Cup they had first won in 1954. Coincidentally, having been the first team to win the World Cup after losing a match in the finals, 20 years later they repeated the "feat".

So in the end, football reigned supreme. But it was a close-run thing. The tenth World Cup was beset with problems. Fifa had unveiled a widely criticised new-look second phase that abolished the quarter-finals and semi-finals. They were replaced by two groups of four qualifiers from the first round, the winners of each group to contest the final. This was done to allow another eight revenue-generating matches to be staged. Not surprisingly there were fears that commercialism was ruining the game with off-the-field financial deals apparently more important that what took place on the pitch.

Concerns about security in West Germany in the wake of the 1972 Olympic massacre in Munich did not help matters, nor did Brazil – forsaking their adventurous style in favour of defensive European play. To boot, it seemed to rain all the time.

England and Sir Alf Ramsey, of course, were not present – thanks to a Polish goalkeeper. But Scotland's pride in being the only British representatives, the first time they had qualified since 1958 – was ultimately dented by their own naivety.

Their first match of the tournament, when they beat Zaire by only 2-0, was their downfall. A brave 0-0 draw with Brazil, a shadow of their former selves, followed. Billy Bremner was inspirational and was unlucky not to score, as were Joe Jordan and Peter Lorimer. In the meantime, though, Yugoslavia had demolished Zaire 9-0, a scoreline that hardly reflected their total domination of the match.

With the Yugoslavs holding such a huge goals advantage Scotland had to beat them. But Scotland slipped behind eight minutes from time and a late equaliser from Jordan was not enough to save them as Brazil beat Zaire 3-0 to edge Scotland out by a single goal, the first time the World Cup finals had used goal difference to separate teams.

Despite drawing with Brazil, Scotland were eliminated on goal difference

Strangely, Scotland were the only team in the tournament not to have lost a match, as West Germany lost to East Germany 1-0 in their first meeting since the countries had been divided after the Second World War.

England did gain some solace from the tournament. Poland, who as supposed minnows had eliminated them at Wembley from the finals, were the surprise package of the tournament, finishing in third overall place when they beat Brazil 1-0 in a bitter and bruising game.

Their match against West Germany, to decide which team would qualify the final, was played on a quagmire. They lost 2-1, but many believe the result would have been reversed had the playing surface been better. In Kazmiercz Deyna,

Bang on target: Lato of Poland was the tournament's leading scorer, Neeskins's penalty gave Holland an early lead but Muller's goal won the final for West Germany

Gadocha and Grzegorz Lato, Poland had three of the world's best players and Lato finished as the tournament's leading scorer.

However West Germany were worthy finalists (despite their slip-up against their comrades from across the Iron Curtain). And against Holland West Germany had faced the other team of the tournament. It was the final the whole world wanted to see, much as in the 1970 World Cup finals the mouth-watering confrontation was between England and Brazil. But was the triumph of Total Football truly going to herald a new dawn?

It would fanciful to think that many other countries could copy the strategy of Total Football. As Rinus Michels, the Dutch team manager, pointed out: you need at least seven world-class players – one fewer and you are in trouble. And who, apart from Holland and West Germany, could boast seven world-class players? The next World Cup would give us a clue.

Keegan and Bremner shamed

THE Charity Shield was supposed to provide a showpiece start to the season but the conduct of Billy Bremner and Kevin Keegan at Wembley on August 10 reduced the event to an all-time low.

The match was shown live on television for the first time and viewers saw an ill-tempered match between Leeds and Liverpool boil over after an hour when Bremner and Keegan traded punches. There was no doubt that they both deserved to be sent off but as they left the pitch they both petulantly tore off their shirts and threw them away.

The match finished 1-1 and Liverpool won the penalty shoot-out when the Leeds goalkeeper David Harvey took Leeds's sixth kick and lofted it over the bar. But everybody was more interested in what action the authorities would take rather than the result.

A disgusted spectator tried to have Bremner and Keegan charged with a breach of the peace, but a magistrate refused to issue a summons. The FA were nowhere near as lenient. Bremner and Keegan were each fined £500 and banned until the end of September, which meant that they would miss 11 matches.

Vernon Stokes, the chairman of the disciplinary committee, admitted that the punishment might not have been so severe if the match had not been played at Wembley and shown on television. This did not impress either club and Bob Paisley, the Liverpool manager, said: "People who don't know how to run the country are trying to run football, which they know even less about."

But Ted Croker was adamant that the right decision had been taken. "We are trying to make football more acceptable to a wider range of people. Players must learn that they cannot throw punches at each other."

Bremner: petty gesture

Keegan: petty gesture

Leeds banned for four years after disallowed goal sparks riot

NOTHING, it appeared, was going right for Leeds. After a series of gruelling battles to reach the final of the European Cup their potential day of glory turned into a night of shame in Paris.

Leeds's uncompromising style had won them few friends on the continent. Both Leeds and Ujpest Dozsa were reduced to 10 men when Leeds won 2-1 in Hungary and Duncan McKenzie, who was sent off for retaliation, was banned for three matches by Uefa. Then, in the second leg of the semifinal, with Leeds trying to protect a one-goal advantage in Barcelona, Gordon McQueen was sent off for hitting a Spanish player.

Leeds, only the second English club to reach the final, had high hopes of beating Bayern Munich, the European Cup holders, on May 28. The final was also a physical match – Andersson was carried off after four minutes after a clash with Terry Yorath and Hoeness also limped off before half-time.

With Bayern forced to reshuffle their formation Leeds dominated most of the match. Their

Last tango in Paris: French riot police survey the wrecked Parc de Princes after the European Cup final

fans believed that two penalties should have been awarded against Beckenbauer, and when Lorimer had a goal disallowed for offside in the 66th minute a mob ran wild.

While French riot police tried to quell the unrest on the terraces first Roth and then Muller put the trophy beyond Leeds. Each goal was the signal for a further outbreak of fighting.

The disturbances continued throughout the night after the match and Uefa, thoroughly sick of the conduct of English hooligans, banned Leeds from Europe for four years.

All change at the top in Scotland

THE WINDS of change were sweeping through Scottish football, and Celtic fans were none too happy about it. First, the entire structure of the League format had been rewritten for the start of the next season. Second, their glorious run of nine successive League titles was brought to an end by their bitter rivals, Rangers.

After years of heated and lengthy argument the 37 clubs at last agreed on much-needed change. From next season there would be a three-division League. The first tier, the Premier Division, would comprise 10 clubs, the other two tiers, to be called the First and Second Divisions, would have 14 clubs in each

(Meadowbank were admitted to the League to balance the numbers). Promotion and relegation would be two up and two down.

The new format meant that the Premier Division clubs would play each other four times in the League. It was hoped that this would make the top division, in particular, more competitive and therefore more attractive. However, Celtic fans – with a whiff of paranoia – suspected the changes were introduced to hinder the continuance of their utter domination of trophies in the last decade.

Their fears probably had more to do with the swagger with which Rangers carried off the championship: seven points

clear of Hibs, the runners-up, and 11 points ahead of Celtic in third place.

Under the authoritarian and fitness-obsessed regime of Jock Wallace, their manager, and the cool elegance of Sandy Jardine, Rangers were worthy champions. They beat Celtic in both League matches, the second on January 4 taking them to the top of the table, whereupon Celtic seemed to have lost heart.

Still, by the standards of any other club, Celtic had a successful season winning both Cups. The Scottish Cup victory, 3-1 against Airdrie, was their 24th success and it also marked the retirement of their captain, Billy McNeill.

Chester's Cup run helps lift their League burden

At last: Ray Graydon broke Ron Saunders' duck

THE League Cup certainly lived up to its reputation as the second-best Cup in England as Second Division clubs blasted their betters from the First and managed to provide three of the four semi-finalists alongside Fourth Division Chester.

While the Second Division was to yield the eventual winner, little Chester's amazing run defied all logic. Alone of the 92 League clubs, Chester had never been promoted and when they began their campaign by beating Walsall 2-1 in the first round nobody could have dreamed of how far they were going to go. Second Division Blackpool and Third Division Preston also succumbed to give the men from Cheshire a home fourth-round tie against star-studded Leeds.

Two goals from John James and one from defender Trevor Storton rocked the Yorkshire side and gave Chester a thoroughly deserved victory. A goalless draw at St James's Park and another James goal at Sealand Road saw off Newcastle.

The semi-final, over two legs against Aston Villa, saw two dramatic matches. In the first, Chester, at home, were twice behind but snatched a 2-2 draw. In the second, Chester again fell behind, this time 2-0. The

Fourth Division side rallied to level the scores, but a Brian Little goal ended the fairytale.

Chester did get one consolation from their record-breaking run: when Lincoln lost at Southport on the last Tuesday of the season Chester took the fourth promotion place by four-hundredths of a goal and the burden of being the only club not to have won promotion was finally lifted.

Villa, their semi-final conquerors, went on to beat Norwich 1-0 in a dour final. The deadlock was finally broken 10 minutes from time when Ray Graydon successfully followed through after Kevin Keelan had parried his penalty.

Ron Saunders, Villa's manager, probably did not care too much about the quality of the football. It was the third successive year he had led a side to the League Cup final (Norwich in 1973, Manchester City in 1974) but the first he'd actually won.

Wimbledon the pick of the pack in a season when the underdogs savaged their masters

Leeds dismiss Clough after 44 stormy days

Clough: stormy reign

BRIAN CLOUGH'S brief sojourn at Brighton ended in acrimony in July when he left the Third Division club to become manager of Leeds. Mike Bamber, the Brighton chairman, accused Leeds of going back on a compensation agreement and issued a writ against Clough, alleging breach of contract.

But that was nothing compared with the storm that engulfed Clough when he arrived at Leeds. Clough plunged into the transfer market, put established players on the transfer list and imposed authoritarian discipline at the club. When Leeds won only one of their first six League matches and slipped to 19th in the table Clough was continually barracked by the Leeds fans.

A newspaper claimed that there had been a dressing-room revolt and the players had passed a vote of no confidence in Clough. At first, Manny Cussins, the Leeds chairman, denied the report. But hours later Clough and his solicitor were summoned to a meeting at which Clough was sacked. He received a £44,000 pay-off on his five-year contract.

Clough's reign had lasted just 44 days. Cussins, who had described Clough as "the ideal manager" when he appointed him, said: "What has been done is for the good of the club. The club and the happiness of the players must come first."

Although the players claimed that they had had no part in Clough's dismissal, he was bitterly disappointed: "I think it is a very sad day for Leeds and for football." For once, the press agreed with him. Headlines accused Leeds of cowardice and one respected commentator said: "This disgraceful affair now more than ever raises the question: who is running professional football – the managers or the players?"

Jimmy Armfield, after much deliberation, agreed to take charge at Leeds. Clough returned to the game in January when he was appointed manager of Nottingham Forest. Yet again, he was quick to make his mark.

His first match in charge was the FA Cup third round replay against Tottenham. Despite being a struggling Second Division side, Forest produced one of the shocks of the round when Neil Martin's solitary goal brought them victory at White Hart Lane.

THE bizarre trail of upsets that had characterised the League Cup somehow spilled over into the FA Cup, making it most certainly the season of the underdogs. Pride of place went to Southern League Wimbledon who lost in a fourth round replay, but non-League Altrincham, Leatherhead, Stafford Rangers and Wycombe Wanderers also seriously embarrassed supposedly superior opposition.

All five survived the first matches in the third round and went into the draw for the fourth round. Wimbledon beat First Division Burnley 1-0 at Turf Moor (the first time a First Division club had been beaten at home by a non-League club since the formation of the Third Division in the 1920s); Altrincham drew with Everton 1-1 at Goodison having led, but a nine-man Everton rallied to equalise with a penalty; Leatherhead stunned Brighton 1-0 at the Goldstone ground; Stafford drew 0-0 with Rotherham; and Wycombe also held Middlesbrough in a goalless draw.

Although Altrincham and Wycombe narrowly lost the replays, Stafford convincingly beat Rotherham away 2-0 and three non-League clubs had made it to the next round – an unheard of feat.

Wimbledon faced mighty Leeds at Elland Road, a daunting task for any side. To everybody's surprise they were equal to the occasion with Dickie Guy, their part-time goalkeeper and full-time clerk, the hero. Guy pulled off a succession of extraordinary saves – including a Peter Lorimer penalty – to deny Leeds in a thrilling goalless draw.

Wimbledon's luck did not hold in the replay – played at Selhurst Park to accommodate the huge number of fans fascinated by the little club's exploits – when a wayward Johnny Giles shot was deflected off Dave Bassett for the only goal.

Leatherhead had their heroics, too, at Filbert Street where they actually led 2-0 before Leicester decided enough was enough and dispatched the upstarts 3-2. Stafford also went down, 2-1 away to Peterborough, and the non-League challenge was extinguished. But not the challenge of the underdogs.

Seemingly encouraged by this orgy of giant-killing, League clubs in the lower divisions took up the mantle. First Division Spurs and Sheffield United were knocked out by Second Division Nottingham Forest and Aston Villa, and Third Division Walsall demolished Manchester United and Newcastle. Amid all this carnage, Second Division Fulham were quietly making progress towards their first FA Cup final.

Clever Dick: Guy's saves were the inspiration for Wimbledon's FA Cup run

Disillusioned Nicholson quits over players' greedy demands

End of the road: "Players have become impossible. There is no longer respect."

BILL NICHOLSON resigned as the Tottenham manager in August, exasperated at the way money had come to control the game he loved. Spurs had equalled their worst ever start to a season by losing their first four League matches but that was not what persuaded Nicholson the time had come to go.

The problem was the increasing demands that players were making. Nicholson had been involved in an acrimonious contract dispute with Martin Chivers, who, had publicly described the club's offer as "rubbish". Chivers was put on the transfer list and Nicholson's attempts to sign a replacement were thwarted by several players' demands for under-the-counter payments.

When Tottenham lost the fourth match, 2-1 at home to Manchester City with Chivers restored to the side, Nicholson had finally had enough after 38 years with the club as a player and manager.

He emphasised that Tottenham's poor start had nothing to do with his decision to leave – he would have gone at the end of last season had Tottenham won the Uefa Cup. Nicholson left nobody in any doubt what the problem was.

"Players have become impossible. They talk all the time about security but they are not prepared to work for it. I am abused by players. There is no longer respect," he said.

Both Nicholson and his chairman, Sidney Wale, confirmed that Tottenham had faced unwarranted demands in the past few seasons. They said that the "going rate" for players to join a London club was at least £7,000 and often a five-figure sum.

Both the board and a deputation of senior players, led by the captain Martin Peters, tried to convince Nicholson to stay, but he could not be talked round. Nicholson tried to persuade Johnny Giles to apply for the job, and then favoured the former Spurs hero Danny Blanchflower.

The Spurs fans were far from impressed when, of all people, the board appointed a former Arsenal captain. Nicholson was scathing about the Hull City and Northern Ireland manager: "I thought they'd appoint Danny," he said. "I don't even know Terry Neill."

Neill: surprise choice

195

Precocious Taylor runs rings round Fulham's wise old heads

FULHAM'S path to only the second all-London Cup final with West Ham had been less than smooth. The Second Division side had needed seven games to eliminate Hull and Nottingham Forest to reach the fifth round, and pipped Birmingham in the semi-final replay with just nine seconds remaining. By contrast West Ham swept to Wembley in a run reminiscent of their successful 1964 campaign.

Then their captain had been Bobby Moore, but this time Moore was on the opposite side and partnered by another veteran, and former England captain, Alan Mullery. But it was a youngster, 21-year-old Alan Taylor, who captured the headlines. The centre forward, who had been playing for Fourth Division Rochdale before Christmas and had cost a mere £40,000, burst Fulham's bubble with two devastating goals in the space of five minutes.

On the hour, Pat Holland set up Billy Jennings whose far-post shot was only pushed away by Peter Mellor, the Fulham goalkeeper. Taylor pounced and cracked the ball into the opposite side of the goal.

Minutes later, Holland was again in the thick of things. He struck a beautifully weighted pass to Graham Paddon who unleashed a ferocious shot. Once again the hapless Mellor was unable to hold the ball and, falling backwards, dropped it in front of the predatory Taylor.

Goal maker: Jennings's pressure on the Fulham defence created the opportunity for Taylor

Now we are going into Europe and I have only ever been abroad twice. And that was to Spain on my holidays

ALAN TAYLOR
West Ham's FA Cup
final hero

When the dust settled only Derby were standing

DAVE MACKAY put the tensions created by Brian Clough's departure from Derby behind him as he guided the club to their second championship in four years. And, as had happened previously, they won the title thanks to other teams' results.

Derby did not go to the top of the table until early April and the race was so close that five teams were still in contention. Stoke's defeat on April 12 ruled them out. A week later, even though Derby only drew, Everton's and Liverpool's losses ruled them out. Then, four days later, Ipswich could only draw at Manchester City. Thus, Derby became the First Division champions before they played their last match.

It was a fascinating climax to a title race that had been remarkably close all season and had witnessed some amazing fluctuations in fortunes. Newly-promoted Carlisle were one of the early pace-setters but nosedived straight back into the Second Division. Ipswich, the other front-runners in the autumn, failed to score in five consecutive League matches but only slipped from first place to third. Stoke signed Peter Shilton, went top, but then lost three matches in a row over Christmas. Everton had their turn in front, as did Liverpool . . . and so it went on.

Six different teams had topped the table by December and, in all, the lead changed hands a record 21 times. The only thing that was certain was that London's best were having one of their worst years ever. At one stage Chelsea, Arsenal, Tottenham and QPR filled four of the bottom five places. In the end only Chelsea went down, although Tottenham only escaped by beating Leeds on the last day of the season.

Macdonald head of the class

MALCOLM MACDONALD, restored to Don Revie's England side, wrote his name into the history books and lifted England's hopes of reaching the quarter-finals of the European championships when he scored all five goals when the national side demolished Cyprus at Wembley. Macdonald became the first player to score five goals in a Wembley international.

Revie, who in two previous internationals ignored the Newcastle centre forward, had been reluctant to pick him. Despite this, Macdonald rose to the occasion in his typical bulldog manner. Macdonald had got his name on the score sheet as early as the second minute when he headed in Alan Hudson's free kick, but by half-time the score was only 2-0, against the weakest team in the group.

Macdonald turned the match into a rout in the second half with three headed goals and emulated Willie Hall's feat against Ireland in 1938. This gave England a healthier goal difference in a group that had become a two-horse race with Czechoslovakia.

England, however, could well rue their goalless draw with Portugal at Wembley in November, particularly as Czechoslovakia thumped five past them in Prague and England could only muster a 1-0 win in the return with Cyprus in Limassol.

Bang on target: Macdonald scores against West Germany

Still going strong: A month later he grabbed all five against Cyprus

Quitting while he was ahead: Law retired rather than play in the reserves

■ Denis Law retired rather than play reserve team football for Manchester City. He said: "I always wanted to call it a day while I am still on the top."

■ The FA rejected a proposal to show instant action replays on giant screens during England's 100th international at Wembley, against West Germany, on March 12. They said it would undermine the referee's authority.

■ Notts County became the first team to play 3,000 matches in the League. They drew 2-2 with their local rivals Nottingham Forest on March 25.

■ Stan Bowles had to retake a penalty for QPR when a spectator threw a second ball on to the pitch at Luton. He scored both times.

■ Sir Stanley Rous was the first winner of the Sports Writers Association annual award for services to sport.

■ Jimmy Hill became the unpaid managing director of Coventry in April.

■ Wales's 3-1 victory in Luxembourg on May 1 was the first time they had ever won four European championship matches in a row.

■ Orient finished 12th in the Second Division despite having scored only 28 goals. They drew 20 of their 42 matches and finished with 42 points.

United back at first attempt

MANCHESTER UNITED bounced back into the First Division without too much difficulty a year after they had been relegated. Although they had established a five-point lead before the end of September, and were not beaten at home until February 1, they were never able to run away with the title.

Sunderland and Norwich kept up the pressure and Aston Villa came with a late charge. In the end, Norwich, like Manchester United, went straight back to the Division and Villa finished runners-up by three points.

The return to winning ways brought the fans flocking back to Old Trafford. More than 60,000 came to the match against Sunderland in November, the biggest attendance anywhere in the League since 1973. The only problem was that Manchester United suffered as much as anybody else from hooligans. The FA and League jointly agreed in December that all United's away matches should be all-ticket in an effort to combat the problem.

After their recent upheavals United enjoyed the period of calm, with a settled side and tranquillity behind the scenes. Frank Blunstone turned down the opportunity to become the manager of Chelsea because he wanted to stay at Old Trafford "for job satisfaction and loyalty".

DON REVIE
The ultimate pro who lost his way

Martin Searby

Master tactician: Revie planned exhaustively

NOBODY could have envisaged what a glittering future was in store for Leeds United when Don Revie was appointed player-manager in March 1961. They were a struggling Second Division club, £100,000 in debt with a decrepit ground, and the new boy won only once in the remaining nine games of the season.

He was lucky to get the job when Jack Taylor was sacked. Harry Reynolds, a director who was later to become chairman, wrote a letter recommending his ageing midfield star as the manager of Bournemouth, before realising that Revie might be as effective as anybody else available at the time. At the end of the season Reynolds must have been wondering if he had picked the right man for the job as Leeds barely escaped relegation to the Third Division.

But Revie was a shrewd footballer who first saw the way ahead when the Hungarians came to England in 1953 and were the first overseas team to win at Wembley, 6-3. When they followed that with a 7-1 annihilation in Budapest Revie quickly adapted the deep-lying centre-forward role of Nandor Hidegkuti, who scored a hat-trick in the first match. Revie played the role with such distinction at Manchester City that he was the Footballer of the Year in 1955.

Not the easiest of men to manage because of his own ideas, Revie started playing at Leicester City and went on to Hull, Manchester City and Sunderland before arriving at Leeds in November 1958. The four transfers amounted to £80,000, a record for those days, and made it clear that his talent was apparent to many, even if the underlying defects, which were to surface after his Elland Road days, were not.

Revie's first, and some might argue most crucial, move into the transfer market did not look all that sound when he paid £25,000 for a 5ft 4in 31-year-old midfield player from Everton. Within days of arriving, Bobby Collins wanted to leave. But Revie persuaded him to stay at Leeds, and Collins became the cornerstone of Revie's first team, leading them to promotion in 1964.

Collins collected the Footballer of the Year award the next season when Leeds came close to the League and Cup double, though ultimately missing both trophies, and Revie was rewarded with a then unheard of seven-year contract.

Billy Bremner, Jack Charlton, Willie Bell and Albert Johanneson were already in the team when Revie took over. But not the least of Revie's talents was the ability to plan ahead, appoint talented staff and delegate authority. While he was making the League side a force to be reckoned with Syd Owen, the coach, Maurice Lindley, Revie's assistant, and Les Cocker, the trainer, were inculcating Revie's ideas into young players who would become world names.

Norman Hunter, Paul Reaney, Paul Madeley, Peter Lorimer, Eddie Gray, Terry Cooper and the much, and often wrongly, maligned Gary Sprake started as juniors before becoming an inherent part of the club's history as, in the next 10 years, they won two League titles, the FA Cup, the League Cup, and the Fairs Cup twice.

It was on their first foray into Europe that fate dealt Leeds a blow which, at the time, looked crippling but, in the event, led to one of the most outstanding midfield duos of all time, the pairing of Johnny Giles and Bremner. In the first round of the Fairs Cup in Turin, Collins broke his thigh bone and Giles, the extraordinary Irishman who was the youngest person ever to play for the Republic, came in off the wing, where he had played since his move from Manchester United for a bargain £35,000 two years earlier.

Giles, who was capped 60 times, was a hugely gifted player with the ability to pass long and short, bend the ball, and unleash a tremendous shot. He was also no shrinking violet and players who tried to kick him often received more than they had bargained for in return. He was an extension of Revie's tactical acumen on the field and intuitively altered the course of events as if he was radio controlled.

Revie searched for discipline on the field, and he made sure his players knew how to negate opposition strengths. But Leeds were getting a reputation as "the nearly men": runners-up twice and fourth twice in the championship, and losing semi-finalists twice and runners-up in the FA Cup in the four years since their promotion.

But a goal from Cooper in the League Cup final against Arsenal, and one from Mick Jones in the Fairs Cup final against Ferencvaros put some silver on the sideboard.

The 1968-69 season was to prove a memorable nine months for Revie as only Manchester City and Burnley managed to beat his team, who swept to their first League title with six points to spare over Liverpool. Ironically, it was Leeds's

Strike force: Clarke struck up a telling partnership with Jones, Revie's first £100,000 signing

very success that alienated many football followers outside the Yorkshire city. Revie's insistence on rigorous defence meant Sprake kept 24 clean sheets and only 26 goals were conceded.

Leeds were perceived as a negative side, far removed from their great rivals on Merseyside and 16 of their matches contained only a solitary goal. The soccer public of that era expected more and it gave rise to all sorts of fanciful talk about "total football"; 25 years later Revie's tactics would have been widely applauded.

Revie's first £100,000 signing was Jones, the Sheffield United centre-forward who had already won two England caps. A bull of a striker, he did not really come into his own until Allan Clarke arrived from Leicester City two years later. The pair struck up a partnership which brought Leeds 188 goals in five seasons as they remained one of the top sides in the championship, in both domestic cups and in Europe. The "nearly" tag returned in 1970 when they lost to Celtic in the European Cup semi-final, conceded the League by fielding a reserve team against Derby County (for which they were fined £5,000), and lost the FA Cup final in a replay with Chelsea after the first draw in 42 years of Wembley finals.

Magic moment: Bremner and Charlton are introduced to Prince Philip at the 1977 Cup final

Two seasons later they beat Arsenal in the Centenary final, but 48 hours after Clarke headed the winner at Wembley they failed to beat Wolves and were again runners-up in the League as Derby took the title by one point.

With so many fine players now highly experienced after growing up in the Revie family, Leeds gained a wider acceptance with more outgoing, confident play. Most of the time the players didn't see "the boss" except on match days, when he would give his usual profound analysis of the opposition, and the team was on automatic pilot during the latter part of Revie's reign.

There were still huge disappointments: Sunderland beat them in the 1973 FA Cup final, and they lost of the European Cup Winners' Cup to AC Milan, which ended with the referee, Michas, banned for cheating, but Revie's last season proved to be his greatest triumph.

Leeds started the 1973-74 season with seven straight wins and did not lose a game until they went down at Stoke on February 23, eventually taking the title by five points from a tremendous Liverpool side.

In 1974 Revie left to take over the England team. Although there was a European Cup final under his ultimate successor, Jimmy Armfield, the glory days were over, and as the aging team broke up unthinkable relegation was only six seasons ahead.

Perhaps Revie's greatest achievement was to reciprocate the fierce loyalty of his players who were constantly united under his banner for 13 years. On his death from motor neurone disease in 1989 to a man they paid tribute to the person they always saw as a father figure.

His tactics and strategy did not always win friends but who could doubt the efficacy of them? He had a shrewd eye for a player but was more interested in the character and ability to comply with his overall plan. That may have made Leeds negative in the early years but maturity brought the ability to perform within his basic structure.

He cast such a long shadow over Elland Road that one of the first things Howard Wilkinson did when he arrived 14 years later was to take down the blown-up pictures of Revie's men which still adorned the foyer. "That's all history," he said. But what a history.

Runaway champions: Leeds were not beaten until February on their way to the 1973-74 League title

THE REVIE YEARS

Born July 10, 1927, Middlesbrough

PLAYING CAREER
In his teens he played for Middlesbrough Swifts where Bill Sanderson, the manager, collected huge dossiers on the opposition

Leicester City 1946-49
Made his debut for Leicester City in war-time football aged 16

Hull City 1949-51

Manchester City 1951-56
Honours Footballer of the Year 1955

Sunderland 1956-58

Leeds United 1958-61

Internationals Six England caps, 1955-57 (4 goals)

MANAGEMENT CAREER
Leeds United Manager 1961-74
Honours European Cup: Semi-final 1970
European Cup Winners Cup: Runners-up 1973
Fairs/Uefa Cup: Winners 1968, 1971; Runners-up 1967; Semi-finalists 1966; Fourth round 1969; Third round 1974
FA Cup: Winners 1972; Runners-up 1965, 1970 (after a replay), 1973; Semi-final 1967, 1968; Fifth round 1963, 1971, 1974; Fourth round 1964, 1966; Third round 1962, 1969
Second Division: Winners 1964
League Championship: Winners 1969, 1974; Runners-up 1965, 1966, 1970, 1971, 1972; Third 1973; Fourth 1967, 1968
League Cup: Winners 1968; Fourth round 1962, 1964, 1967, 1969, 1973; Third round 1963, 1965, 1966, 1970, 1972; Second round 1971, 1974

England Manager 1974-77

THE 1975-76 SEASON

Crackpot ideas wheeled out to crack down on hooliganism

ONE thing was getting to be certain. When the season kicked off the thugs on the terraces would be back, kicking each other and anybody else who got in their way.

But within weeks the violence took a frightening turn for the worse. So-called Chelsea fans, having failed to get their match with Luton abandoned by staging a pitch invasion when they were losing 3-0 and attacking the Luton goalkeeper, rampaged through the town and destroyed a train on the way back to London. On the same day, another train was halted at Crewe when hooligans set it on fire.

British Rail promptly stopped running football specials for the rest of the season and refused to sell cheap tickets until after 3pm on Saturdays. If fans wanted to travel, their club would have to charter a special train and be responsible for the damage.

Elsewhere, the reactions to violence were remarkably predictable. Don Revie, the England manager, called for the return of the birch, saying: "We have tried everything else, we might as well try this drastic deterrent." Eric Reed, the referee of the match between Chelsea and Luton agreed with him.

With a growing clamour for the introduction of identity cards, some people had more novel solutions. Dan Tana, the Brentford chairman, made a citizen's arrest of a troublemaker at one of his team's home matches. "Some louts used bad language," he said. "I was embarrassed so I nabbed the worst offender and handed him over to a policeman."

The Police Superintendents' Association even suggested that matches should be classified in the same way as films with fans under the age of 16 banned from "X-rated" games unless they were accompanied by an adult. Chelsea, with some of the worst problems, were not impressed with this bizarre proposal. "Who would decide which matches were selected?" Brian Mears, their chairman, asked.

West Ham attempt one escape act too many

Shell-shocked: Day conceded a hotly-disputed goal

WEST HAM made up for their indifferent domestic form by producing a series of inspired performances in the European Cup Winners Cup. But their travels were not without some strange moments.

In the second round they travelled to Armenia to play Ararat Erevan and were leading 1-0. Mervyn Day, their goalkeeper had hold of the ball and was about to throw it upfield when an Ararat player dived in and headed the ball out of his hands. Both men went down in a heap

and the ball trickled over the line. West Ham expected to be awarded a free kick for the foul on the goalkeeper but the West German referee allowed the equaliser to stand. That night West Ham's interpreter stunned his hosts at the post-match dinner by lecturing them on the importance of sportsmanship.

West Ham's finest performances came in the quarter-finals. Trailing 4-0 at half-time to Den Haag, they battled back to 4-2. Then, at Upton Park, they turned the tables, won 3-1 and went through on the way goals rule.

But West Ham could not pull off another great escape in the final, against Anderlecht in Belgium. Despite equalising twice they went down 4-2 to a vastly experienced side. Ironically, when West Ham had won the Cup Winners Cup in 1965 they had done it at "home" at Wembley. This time, too, the winners played in their own country.

> *Some of the players picked are donkeys. Give them a lump of sugar and they run all day and play bingo all night*
>
> ALAN BALL
> attacking Don Revie's choice of players for the England squad

Unimpressed: Mears scoffed at the police's ideas

Poor Newcastle founder on rock-solid Doyle

Opening shot: Barnes gives Manchester City the lead at Wembley in the League Cup final

BOTH Manchester City and Newcastle were back at Wembley for the second time in three years after having suffered setbacks there, and it was Newcastle who were to go home disappointed again.

The 30-year-old Mike Doyle was the cornerstone of Manchester City's 2-1 victory in the League Cup final. The veteran who had been to Wembley three times before was the backbone of City's defence and also created their first goal. At a well-rehearsed set piece he headed the ball down for Peter Barnes to score in the 12th minute.

Doyle looked to have City's defence well organised, but one moment of inattention allowed Alan Gowling in for a sweetly-taken equaliser. Dennis Tueart restored City's lead just after the interval with a spectacular overhead kick and that was the game all but over. Newcastle tried hard to get back on terms but Doyle's composure kept them at bay.

- The League decided to switch from goal average to goal difference at the start of next season. But they rejected an idea to award bonus points depending on the number of goals a team scored.

- Bobby Charlton resigned as the manager of Preston in August after a dispute with his board about transfers. Charlton said: "I refuse to have players at the club that I don't want."

- Numbered boards to signal substitutions were used in England for the first time at the Charity Shield, when Derby beat West Ham 2-0.

- Pat Jennings broke Tottenham's appearance record on October 4 when he played his 419th League game for the club. Later in the season, Jennings also broke the Northern Ireland record with 61 caps. Another goalkeeper, Peter Bonetti, also passed a milestone when he made his 500th appearance for Chelsea in November.

- Fifa's ban on George Best playing anywhere in the world was lifted when Manchester United released him and allowed him to join Stockport.

- Three players were sent off in the space of four minutes in the match between Brentford and Rochdale on December 5.

Bremner's shenanigans put him out in the cold

BILLY BREMNER, the captain of Scotland and Leeds, had his international career curtailed on September 8 when the Scottish selectors banned him and four other internationals from playing for their country for life. Bremner and the four players (Arthur Graham, Joe Harper, Pat McCluskey and Willie Young) were accused of incidents in a nightclub and then in the team's hotel in Copenhagen after Scotland's European championship qualifier against Denmark on September 3, which the Scots won with a Harper goal.

When the allegations occurred in the press, Bremner said: "I have heard about these rumours. They are nonsense. There was no row in the club, no fight, and no trouble about the bill. Anyway, what we do in our spare time is nothing to do with anybody else."

Despite his protestations, the Scottish selectors' committee relied on reports from officials and took their decision without calling on any of the five players to defend themselves. "I am staggered," Bremner said after the ban was announced, "I don't know if I shall be allowed to appeal."

Leeds also reprimanded Bremner, and warned him about his future conduct. For Bremner, 32 and capped 54 times for his country, his career in the top flight was effectively over and a year later he was transferred to Hull City in the Second Division.

Astounded: Bremner was banned for life by Scotland

Bayern's third European title

BAYERN MUNICH confirmed their status as the No1 team in Europe when they beat St Etienne 1-0 in the European Cup final at Hampden in May. It was their third consecutive success and emulated Ajax's hat-trick of 1971-73.

St Etienne, the French champions, were formidable opponents although their classy international right-winger, Dominique Rocheteau, was recovering from a leg injury and only played as a substitute for the last eight minutes. But in midfielder Dominique Bathenay, the Argentinian centre-half Osvaldo Piazza and the centre-forward Herve Revelli they had the resources to pose a serious threat.

Not that Bayern were a bunch of nonentities with Franz Beckenbauer at sweeper, Gerd Muller in attack and Karl-Heinz Rummenigge on the wing. The German champions had shown impressive form in reaching the final: Benfica were trounced 5-1 in Munich and Real Madrid 2-0.

The final lived up to expectations – St Etienne hit the bar twice in the first half – and was only settled by a single goal from Franz Roth in the 57th minute. From a free kick just outside the penalty area Roth pounced on the ball and blasted it past Ivan Curkovic, St Etienne's Yugoslav goalkeeper.

Bayern could have scored more than once, but Curkovic pulled off some remarkable saves – as did Sepp Maier at the other end. Rocheteau weaved his magic for the last few minutes but Maier was not going to allow the historic achievement to slip through Bayern's fingers.

Stokes sends Saints to heaven

Second best: Southampton emulate Sunderland's feat by overturning Manchester United

"SUNDERLAND" was the entire content of Tommy Docherty's team talk to his young Manchester United team before their FA Cup final against Second Division Southampton. Docherty's concern was self-explanatory: if Sunderland could pull off the Cup final shock of the century by beating Leeds in 1973, anything was possible. "It is the perfect warning to my lads," Docherty said. "To take nothing for granted."

Manchester United were in much the same predicament as Leeds had been three years previously: overwhelming First Division favourites against Second Division underdogs. There was more fearful symmetry: Leeds and Manchester United had finished third in the First Division with Sunderland and Southampton sixth in the Second Division. Unfortunately for Docherty and his tyros, the warning failed and symmetry triumphed, as Manchester United went down by exactly the same score – 1-0.

Bobby Stokes scored the all-important goal seven minutes from time, just as both leg-weary teams were mentally preparing themselves for the ordeal of extra time. Jim McCalliog, a former Manchester United player, executed a perfect through pass for Stokes, who despite thinking he might be offside, ran on with ball waiting for the whistle. The United defence froze. Alex Stepney, the goalkeeper, now the last line of hope, came out to cut off the angle, but Stokes nervelessly pushed the ball to the left past the diving Stepney.

United really had only themselves to blame, although if Sammy McIlroy's header in the 59th minute had gone in instead of hitting the top of bar it might well have been a different story. But for the team that had played such scintillating football throughout the season, and, just 10 days before this May Day confrontation, still had hopes of a League and Cup Double, it was a miserable performance.

The hallmarks of their football: pace and flair just were not there. Gordon Hill, one of their two orthodox wingers, played so badly he had to be taken off in the 66th minute. Lou Macari was similarly ineffectual. By contrast, Mike Channon and

Stokes: nerveless

Peter Osgood easily outshone their younger, and more illustrious, opponents. For the Southampton manager, Lawrie McMenemy, it was a moment to savour as his fans gave him an ovation. "It's not so long ago they were throwing things at me," he said.

Not even Celtic can halt Rangers

THE FIRST season of the revolutionary 10-club Premier Division in Scotland – initiated to make the League more competitive – resulted in a two-horse race for the championship: between Rangers and Celtic. After an initial burst by Rangers, Celtic led the table for much of the season until a dramatic collapse in April and May handed their rivals the title on plate.

Celtic had their problems with Jock Stein out of the manager's chair after his car crash in July and his assistant Sean Fallon having to deputise. But to win only one of the final seven League matches (losing four) with Rangers breathing down your neck is carelessness in the extreme.

Rangers, under the dictatorial control of Jock Wallace, went about the task of being the first Premier Division champions with military precision. Wallace took the view that a winning settled side – whoever was in it – was the formula. So, once Wallace had found the winning formation he stuck to it. If that meant leaving Derek Parlane and Sandy Jardine on the bench, so be it.

Celtic's eclipse by Rangers had begun back in October when they lost the Scottish League Cup final to a second-half header from Alex MacDonald. By the end of the season the misery was piling on: they had failed to beat Rangers all season, losing two of their Premier matches by a single goal and drawing the other two. Then in May Rangers completed the Treble. And in style.

Derek Johnstone put Rangers ahead against Hearts after only 41 seconds. Johnstone had even made the chance by getting a free-kick from a Jim Jeffries foul. Johnstone soared above the Hearts defence to head

Johnstone: match winner

home. From then on it was one-way traffic. MacDonald extended the lead just before the interval and Johnstone secured the victory nine minutes from time. A Graham Shaw tap-in kept the score to 3-1.

Heavyweight clubs upstaged by lightweight rivals

THE FA Cup was obviously fated to be an upset year the moment the results of the first round came through: six League clubs had been beaten by non-League opposition and another four could only muster draws. Then, in the third round in January, the previous year's finalists, West Ham and Fulham, also fell by the wayside.

Meanwhile the heavyweight opposition were knocking each other out. Derby disposed of Liverpool, Everton and Newcastle before themselves succumbing to Manchester United in the semi-final. Wolves flattened Arsenal and Ipswich before Manchester United laid them low in a sixth round replay. And Stoke toppled Tottenham Hotspur and Manchester City, until they ran into Second Division Sunderland.

The carnage was such that the last 16 in the competition were seven clubs from the First Division, seven from the Second Division, one from the Third and one from the Fourth. And

Capital punishment: Crystal Palace beat Chelsea 3-2 en route to the semi-final

on it went. Bradford knocked out Norwich 2-1 with an 87th minute goal to become only the third Fourth Division club to reach the sixth round. Crystal Palace went one better and progressed to the semi-finals and became the fourth Third Division club since the war to do so.

Their semi-final against Second Division Southampton at Stamford Bridge was disparaged by Manchester United's manager Tommy Docherty, whose team were facing Derby in the other semi-final. "This is the first time that the Cup final will be played at Hillsborough," he said. "The other semi-final is a bit of a joke, really." For all the little clubs who had battled so hard on the road to Wembley, Southampton gave them the last laugh.

Taylor and Lincoln fit like two peas in a pod

GRAHAM TAYLOR repaid his chairman's faith as Lincoln produced a record-breaking season to race away with the Fourth Division title. When Taylor's playing career was cut short by a hip injury in 1972 the Lincoln chairman appointed Taylor the manager of the club. Half of the board opposed the move, because of Taylor's lack of experience – at 28 he was the youngest manager in the League.

The journeyman defender took to management like a duck to water and fostered a remarkable spirit at the club. His insistence on developing links with the local community brought the crowds flocking back to Sin- cil Bank, and the supporters were rewarded by greatly improved performances.

"We concentrate on doing the simple things well," Taylor said. And Lincoln played remarkably well. They were unbeaten at home, only lost four games away, scored 111 goals and finished with a record 74 points.

Pressure increases on dithering Revie

THE FACT that Czechoslovakia, who qualified for the European championship quarter-finals instead of England, eventually triumphed in the final against West Germany, the world champions, was scant consolation to England and Don Revie. His failure, hard on the heels of Sir Alf Ramsey's failure to make it to the World Cup finals in 1974, meant that press and public were baying for his blood.

Revie's tenure, in place of the disgraced Ramsey, had begun brightly enough. England had beaten Czechoslovakia 3-0 at Wembley, West Germany 2-0, hammered Cyprus 5-0, and had won the Home international championship by demolishing Scotland 5-1. At the end of his first season, Revie's record was: P8, W5, D3, L0. So far, so good.

But was it? Along the way England drew 0-0 with Portugal at Wembley in a pitiful display against a packed Portuguese defensive midfield. Czechoslovakia thundered five past the hapless Portuguese. Moreover, it was clear that Revie was prone to dithering. In the eight matches only Dave Watson was an ever-present as Revie anxiously rotated 27 other players, unsettling the squad.

In Bratislava, England went ahead courtesy of Mick Channon, but still lost 2-1 to the Czechs. A handsome win in Lisbon was essential – the significance of the goalless draw at Wembley against Portugal finally sinking in – but in the end England were fortunate to scrape a 1-1 draw. Czechoslovakia completed the formalities by winning in Cyprus 3-0.

Flashpoint: Brian Flynn restrains a fan after Toshack's goal was disallowed at Ninian Park

To rub matters in, Wales – the only British country to do so – comfortably qualified for the quarter-finals, beating Hungary home and away in the process. Their opponents in the quarter- finals were Yugoslavia.

Wales lost the first leg 2-0 away and faced a stern task in the return leg at Ninian Park, made worse when Yugoslavia took the lead from a penalty. Ian Evans equalised just before half-time. Then 20 minutes into the second half the East Ger- man referee disallowed a Welsh goal, spectators invaded the pitch, beer cans were thrown and play was suspended for five minutes. When play was resumed, another Welsh goal was disallowed and a Terry Yorath penalty was saved. Four players were booked, the police had to escort the referee from the field, and Wales were igno- miniously dumped out of the semi-finals.

The semi-finals, both played in Yugoslavia, threw up the intriguing possibility of a repeat of the 1974 World Cup final: Holland v West Germany. In the event Czechoslovakia easily dis- posed of Holland 3-1 after extra time (the Dutch goal coming from a fortuitous deflection) and West Germany somehow scrambled past Yugoslavia.

Spurred on by their partisan crowd, the hosts annihilated the normally rock-solid defence to hold an easy 2-0 lead at half- time. But complacency set in and, with two astute substitu- tions, the West Germans had levelled by full-time. In the extra period, Yugoslav despair at having squandered such an advantage set in and West Ger- many ran in another two goals.

In the final, Czechoslovakia, now clearly on a roll, rattled in two goals and once again the West Germans were on the rack. Gerd Muller managed to pull one back before half-time. It was enough to put the world champions back into the game as the Czechs visibly tired. A dubious equaliser (it appeared the Czech keeper was fouled) forced yet another match into extra time, and, despite another Czech onslaught, there were no more goals.

In the penalty shoot-out, seven shots went in, then Uli Hoeness blazed his shot over the bar. Panenka, of Czechoslo- vakia, stepped up to take the kick that would win the trophy. The West German goalkeeper went the right way, but Panenka coolly lofted the ball over him.

Paisley gets it right as Liverpool thrive on their never-say-die spirit

BOB PAISLEY, in his second season in charge, collected his second trophy when Liverpool completed the double of the League and the Uefa Cup for the second time. And, as had happened in the League, Liverpool were taken right to the wire.

Liverpool's spirits were lifted in the semi-final when they went to the formidable Nou Camp and beat the Barcelona of Johann Cryuff and Johann Neeskens 1-0. A 1-1 draw at Anfield was enough to take them to the final against Bruges.

Everything looked lost when Bruges raced into a 2-0 lead at Anfield after just 12 minutes. Liverpool, though, came storming back in the second half with three goals in five minutes, a long-range effort from Ray Kennedy, a close-in shot from Case and finally a penalty from Keegan.

The second leg was every bit as gripping. Bruges took another early lead, which meant that although the scores were level they had the advantage on the away goals rule. Keegan quickly scored yet again, bending a shot past the goalkeeper from a free kick, and the battle was really on.

Bruges were relentless in their pursuit of the winning goal

Clemence: vital save

Case: vital goal

and Liverpool were forced to pull almost everybody apart from Keegan back into defence. Somehow Liverpool always seemed to be able to block the ball at the vital moment although there was one last scare to come when Clemence was forced to make a great save with just a few minutes to go.

So Paisley had silenced the

doubters who thought he would not be able to fill Bill Shankly's shoes. However, it was not a vintage season for Liverpool. Too often they were dependent on Keegan and John Toshack – or even David Fairclough, who seemed to work miracles every time he came off the bench. So much so that he earned himself the title "Super Sub".

QPR's run fizzles out short of the winning post

QPR's home victory over Liverpool on the first Saturday of the season was widely thought to be a flash in the pan; most commentators regarded it as two points dropped by Bob Paisley's Liverpool rather than a good result by Rangers.

How wrong they were. QPR were unbeaten in their first 10 matches and led the First Division at the end of September. Everybody seemed surprised by the unfashionable club's start, but it was not as unexpected as it appeared.

Dave Sexton had a formidable array of talent at his disposal: Phil Parkes, Frank McLintock, David Webb, Don Masson, Gerry Francis, John Hollins, David Thomas, Don Givens and Stan Bowles. The majority were international players, and Francis had just been appointed the England captain.

But Sexton also had two problems. Stan Bowles was unsettled – constantly asking for a transfer because his wife was homesick for the north – and his team did not have the experience of having been involved in a close title race before.

A bad patch either side of

Christmas saw them slip to fifth in the table and it began to look as if they were going to be a flash in the pan after all. But Sexton steadied the ship and QPR had a remarkable second half of the season, winning 13 of their last 15 matches. The game that would come back to haunt them was a 3-2 defeat at Norwich in April.

Liverpool, though, were past masters of the close finish and they were never more than a point or two behind. QPR finished their programme 10 days before Liverpool and held a one point advantage which meant

that everything depended on Liverpool's final game, at Wolverhampton.

When Wolves took an early lead and were still ahead with 15 minutes left there were echoes of 1972, when Leeds had lost the title at Molineux. Liverpool, though, drew on all their reserves of experience and three late goals brought them a record ninth championship. QPR, despite their great finish, were left to reflect on what might have been had they not lost to Norwich, although second place was their highest ever finish.

Wayward Macari accidentally changes course of history

LIVERPOOL could point to end of season fixture congestion for their downfall in the FA Cup final on May 21, but there was no denying that Manchester United were determined to lay

Aerial combat: Pearson and Case battle for supremacy

the ghost of their defeat by Southampton the year before.

Liverpool had had an easy passage to the final and were clear favourites to complete the second leg of their Treble. But Tommy Docherty's Manchester United, despite a slightly suspect defence, were capable of playing top-quality football.

With both sides equally matched the game was finely balanced for the first half. Although Liverpool appeared to have an advantage in midfield they went behind in the 50th minute when Stuart Pearson scored a somewhat fortunate goal.

His low shot should not have posed too many problems for a goalkeeper of Ray Clemence's calibre, but somehow Clemence let the ball slip under his body. The goal brought the game to life and within two minutes Liverpool had equalised when

Jimmy Case crashed a shot into the top corner.

If Manchester United's first goal was slightly lucky there was no doubt that their second, three minutes later, was a fluke. Even Jimmy Greenhoff, the scorer, admitted as much. His shot rebounded off a defender into the path of Lou Macari. With Macari having a clear chance of scoring, Greenhoff decided to get out of his way. But Macari mis-hit his shot, which was going well wide until it cannoned off the retreating Greenhoff and ballooned over Clemence's head.

For once, Liverpool's control of midfield could not bring them another goal. As Manchester United celebrated at the final whistle, Bob Paisley was left to console his players and try to lift their spirits at a moment when it seemed that their dream was about to turn into a nightmare.

One certainty for managers – getting the sack

IT WAS a bad time for managers. Among the most notable names to vacate the hot seat were Tony Waddington, who had been Stoke's manager since 1960; Bob Stokoe, who had guided Sunderland to their 1973 FA Cup triumph and promotion to the First Division last season; and Fulham's legendary Alec Stock.

As Johnny Giles pointed out when he quit West Bromwich Albion in April: "In the last 10 months 33 League clubs have changed managers. The directors have power without responsibility. The government should issue a health warning to managers: the only certain thing is the sack."

His former teammate at Leeds, Jack Charlton, who quit Middlesbrough the day after Giles at WBA, was also disenchanted with the game. But his discontent was aimed at Middlesbrough's lukewarm fans rather than his directors. Hav-

Giles: health warning

ing guided the North East club to the First Division in his first season in charge in 1974 and to the top of the table in October, he had seen attendances slump from around 25,000 to 14,000 in weeks as Middlesbrough gravitated to a comfortable mid-table position.

Early casualty: Stokoe and Sunderland part company

Hearts hit the self-destruct button

FOR the first time in their 103-year history proud Hearts were relegated. Yet inexplicably they reached the semi-finals of both the Scottish Cup and League Cup. Quite how their Cup form deserted them in the League is a mystery that Willie Ormond, their new manager having retired from his post as the national manager, will have to solve if Hearts are to immediately bounce back into the Premier Division.

Their start in the League, although indifferent – they drew seven, and won one of their first 10 matches – did not presage the horror that was to come by the season's end. In the next 21 matches Hearts effectively cut their own throats losing on 14 occasions. Although they won two and drew three of their last five games it was all too late, and they went down with Kilmarnock. Ayr United, the other candidates for relegation, had effectively rescued themselves with a dramatic burst of form in March and April.

At the other end of the table it was business as usual with Celtic crowned as champions, and Rangers occupying the runners-up spot. Celtic were runaway champions and it was obvious by the beginning of the year that nobody could realistically overhaul them. They eventually finished eight points ahead of Rangers, who had mounted a thrilling late run of six consecutive victories to steal second place.

They were less fortunate in the Scottish Cup final where they succumbed 1-0 to Celtic, allowing their rivals to complete the Double. Celtic's goal came as early as the 20th minute, when Derek Johnstone handled Kenny Dalglish's chip and Andy Lynch converted the penalty. The Rangers strike force was muted in the rain-sodden conditions, although Chris Robertson, who came on as a substitute, twice went close to scoring the equaliser.

It was a poor final though memorable for two historic footnotes. It was live on television, which many blamed for the poor attendance of 54,000 – the worst for over 50 years; and Alfie Conn, playing for Celtic, became the first player to win the Cup with both Old Firm sides. He had been on Rangers' Cup-winning side in 1973 when they beat Celtic 3-2. Two Old Firm Cup finals and each time on a different winning team!

Celtic also made another piece of history when they reached the League Cup final for the 13th consecutive year. Aberdeen spoiled the celebrations by winning the trophy 3-2 in extra time with a goal from David Robb. It was their first League Cup triumph since the season of 1955-56.

Villa's Little finally ends 330-minute stalemate

WEMBLEY was starting to feel like home from home for Ron Saunders. For the fourth time in five years he was back there for a League Cup final. His record so far was two losses (with Norwich in 1973 and Manchester City in 1974) and one win (with Aston Villa in 1975).

This time he left with a draw as Aston Villa were held 0-0 by Everton. The replay, four days later, also ended all square although Everton scored both goals – Roger Kenyon's own goal being cancelled out by Bob Latchford's scrambled effort in the 90th minute.

The second replay provided more excitement than both the previous games put together. Everton led with 10 minutes to go; Aston Villa equalised then took the lead a minute later; then two minutes after that Everton forced the game into extra time once again. Matters were finally resolved when Brian Little scored his second goal to give Saunders his second trophy after 330 minutes of largely unimpressive toil.

Evasive action: John Burridge ducks under Duncan McKenzie

We couldn't have beaten 11 dustbins

TERRY NEILL
after Arsenal lost 3-0 at Middlesbrough

207

Liverpool rise to the occasion

BOB PAISLEY had assembled a settled side at Liverpool, and his team appeared to be making serene progress towards a fabulous Treble of the League, the FA Cup and the European Cup.

Apart from one brief spell around Christmas, Liverpool were hardly troubled in the League. They only lost two of their first 16 games, and although they could never totally shake off the pursuing Ipswich and Manchester City, they took the title with a game to spare, thanks to a sequence that saw them only lose two matches from the start of February to the end of the season.

Bob Paisley, who had been given a job for life, faced his toughest challenge in lifting the team's morale after Liverpool were beaten by Manchester United in the FA Cup final. His players responded magnificently.

The European Cup final against Borussia Moenchengladbach in Rome on May 25, a mere four days after the FA Cup final, was widely acclaimed as the greatest game in recent history. Liverpool's performance was regarded as even more phenomenal than their victory over St Etienne in the quarter-final.

Liverpool trailed 1-0 to the French club after the first leg, and the return match was one of the most electrifying ever seen at Anfield. Kevin Keegan's lob after two minutes levelled the aggregate score, but St Etienne, roared on by their supporters' chants of "Allez les Verts", pounded the Liverpool goal. Both teams left the pitch to a standing ovation at half-time.

Bathenay scored for St Etienne and Ray Kennedy struck back, but Liverpool were facing elimination on the away goals rule. With the Kop mimicking the French fans by shouting "Allez les Reds" the stage was set for David Fairclough. With eight minutes to go, Liverpool's Super Sub ran half the length of the pitch, waltzed past two defenders and scored one of the best individual goals seen at Anfield.

Emlyn Hughes described the match as the most exciting he had ever played in, but it was nothing compared with the final. Liverpool played sublime football and took the lead with a goal from Terry McDermott. But Allan Simonsen equalised for Borussia early in the second half and then it was the Germans' turn to dominate.

It looked to be only a matter of time before the Liverpool defence gave way but the turning point was yet another brilliant save by Ray Clemence. The Germans started to lose heart and Liverpool came storming back. Steve Heighway's corner eluded the flailing Borussia goalkeeper and up popped Tommy Smith of all people to head a vital goal.

Liverpool were now rampant and Borussia were totally unable to contain Keegan. When he was chopped down by Berti Vogts in the 83rd minute, Phil Neal's penalty put the result beyond doubt. The disappointments of Wembley were forgotten as the Liverpool fans painted the town red. The celebrations lasted long into the night and nobody was complaining when the Liverpool fans found the team's hideaway and joyously threw several Liverpool players into the hotel swimming pool.

Mighty atom: Keegan gives Vogts the slip again

You'll never walk alone: the Kop moved lock, stock and barrel to Rome

Scots wreck Wembley

Tartan terrors: rampaging Scots tear down the goal

THE biennial invasion of Wembley by Scotland's travelling army of fans truly was an invasion. After the 2-1 defeat of England, hordes of drunken Scottish fans, bedecked in tartan scarves and caps, charged across the pitch to fete their victorious players

Then they turned their attention to the goalposts (tearing them down and ripping out the nets) and the Wembley turf (carving pieces out of it to take home as souvenirs). During the weekend of June 4, 132 Scots were arrested and some £18,000 of damage caused at Wembley with both goals broken, goalmouths bereft of turf, and terraces littered with thousands of broken bottles and discarded beer cans.

Although the victory was only their fifth on English soil since 1938 and meant that Scotland had retained the Home championship, it was hard to understand what had so excited the Scottish fans, aside from large amounts of alcohol.

It was not a memorable match as England were missing two key players, Kevin Keegan and Trevor Brooking. The Scots were deserving winners, with Danny McGrain, Kenny Dalglish and Lou Macari the outstanding players. Gordon McQueen had given them the lead three minutes before half-time when he headed home Don Masson's free-kick, Dalglish made it 2-0 in the 60th minute, and Mick Channon scored an 87th minute penalty to make the score somewhat more respectable.

Immediate calls were made to ban travelling Scottish fans from all England-Scotland matches at Wembley. Ted Croker, the FA secretary, went further and said: "The ground will be fenced in by November for the Italy match." Quite why he thought that the Scots would come to Wembley to see England v Italy in a World Cup qualifier was perplexing. Or was he just intending to punish English fans for Scottish transgressions?

Treble chancers: Macdonald and Francis were hat-trick heroes

Wimbledon reap benefit of heroic Cup exploits

WIMBLEDON were finally granted their just reward when they won election to the League at Workington's expense on June 17. The Southern League champions proved their credentials with another stirring performance in the FA Cup, which convinced the delegates at the League's annual meeting that their performances against Burnley and Leeds in 1975 were not a flash in the pan.

Once again Wimbledon showed that they were a match for anybody in the country. Although they reached the third round by beating two other non-League sides, they more than held their own against First Division Middlesbrough. After being restricted to a 0-0 draw at Plough Lane, the best that the

Middlesbrough manager Jack Charlton could do was blame the playing surface. Charlton accused Wimbledon of deliberately neglecting their pitch and said: "We couldn't play football today. The replay will show whether Wimbledon are able to play – little or not."

The replay showed that Wimbledon could, indeed, play. Three days later they went down by a single goal at Ayresome Park, and that was a penalty.

Wimbledon were not going to let their new-found status go to their heads, though. The club had been run on a shoestring for a long time and Dickie Guy, their goalkeeper and the hero against Leeds, said that the players were still prepared to play as part-timers.

Bowles blazes dazzling trail across Europe

QPR's first foray into Europe, although it did not provide a trophy, was a more than a creditable success. Indeed Stan Bowles' scoring wizardry proved so bewitching that he finished, with 11 goals, as the Uefa Cup's leading scorer and broke the British record for a European tournament.

Bowles got off to a cracking start against Brann Bergen scoring a hat-trick in both legs of the first-round tie as QPR thrashed the Norwegian side 11-0 on aggregate. Bowles continued in cracking form knocking in another three goals against Slovan Bratislava in the next round.

With Derby and Manchester United knocked out of the Uefa Cup by AEK Athens and Juventus, QPR were the sole British representatives left in the competition and their third round opponents, Cologne, were no pushovers. But once again Bowles inspired the west London club and his brilliant final goal gave them a 3-0 lead to take to West Germany.

And they needed that extra cushion. At half-time QPR were 3-1 adrift and down to 10 men after Dave Clement's dismissal. Yet they held on to squeak through 4-4 on the away goals rule. Their luck ran out against AEK Athens.

A pair of 3-0 results, with Gerry Francis scoring two penalties in his first European match and Bowles his 11th goal, meant a penalty shoot-out. Both sides scored with four of their first five penalties but in the sudden-death stage David Webb's attempt was saved and QPR's adventure was over.

Traitor Revie deserts England

UNLIKE his predecessor, Sir Alf Ramsey, Don Revie didn't wait to be pushed out of his job as the England manager – he jumped. However the manner of his departure shocked the nation and the FA when they learnt from a newspaper that Revie had secretly, and deceptively, found himself another job before quitting his England post.

Ostensibly Revie had gone to Helsinki to watch Italy – England's opponents in a crucial World Cup qualifying match in November – play Finland while his England squad were enjoying a successful summer tour in South America. In reality Revie had gone to Dubai and negotiated a £340,000 tax free four-year contract to manage the United Arab Emirates. Revie's deception did not stop there.

Before he formally resigned, Revie privately approached the FA and, because of the "heartache" the job was causing him and his wife, offered "to save trouble and go" if they paid up the rest of his contract (£50,000) and gave him a £50,000 golden handshake. Because Manchester United had suddenly sacked Tommy Docherty and there was speculation that Revie might be offered the post, they asked Revie directly if he had another job lined up. Revie denied that he had, but the FA still spurned his offer.

Then on July 13, the day after the Daily Mail had exclusively revealed Revie's sudden decision to quit, the same paper revealed his deal with the UAE. The FA were outraged and charged Revie with acting deceitfully and damaging the image of football. Revie refused to attend the subsequent FA hearing and they promptly suspended him from any involvement with football under the FA's jurisdiction until he did so.

Revie was then given a 10-year ban for "bringing the game into disrepute", but in 1979 he successfully overturned this in the High Court because of the probable bias of Sir Harold Thompson, the FA chairman,

Take the money and run: Revie fled to the Middle East

during Revie's disciplinary hearing.

Although the whole affair stunned and dismayed the nation, Revie's decision to pack in the England job after three years was, in itself, no surprise. In that time he had managed England for 29 internationals, winning 14 and losing seven; failed to take them past the European championship qualifying stages and was, barring miracles, poised to see them fail to reach the World Cup finals in Argentina.

Revie, although an extremely successful manager with Leeds – winning two League titles, the FA Cup, the Fairs Cup and reaching the European Cup final – had painfully discovered the huge chasm between international and club management.

Brian Clough was immediately installed as the people's choice to replace him. But Clough, controversial, single-minded and outspoken was not exactly the FA's cup of tea. Diplomatically, they did decide to interview him and were taken aback with his performance – he almost convinced them to give him the job. Caution prevailed however and Ron Greenwood, the avuncular manager of West Ham, who had taken over as a caretaker manager after Revie's sudden departure, was confirmed as national manager in December.

Adulterous Docherty gets the sack

THE colourful and controversial career of Tommy Docherty took another bizarre twist when Manchester United sacked him as their manager on July 4, six weeks after he had led them to triumph in the FA Cup final. Docherty's fault lay not in what he had done on the pitch, but in his behaviour off it. Ten days earlier Docherty had publicly announced that he was leaving his wife and four children to live with Mary Brown, the wife of the United physiotherapist, Laurie Brown. It was a bombshell for a club renowned for its links with Catholicism.

Docherty had explained that this decision had been a difficult and painful one and that his relationship with Mrs Brown was not a casual one – their affair had been going on for some three years. If Docherty had hoped that by bringing his situation into the open he would kill press interest in his personal

> *I have been punished for falling in love. What I have done has got nothing at all to do with my track record as a manager*
>
> TOMMY DOCHERTY

life, he was very much mistaken. If anything it fanned the flames.

The popular press besieged Old Trafford and Docherty's home and the details of his love affair were all over the news pages. As the story raged on the support Docherty had received from the club ebbed away until Louis Edwards, the Manchester United chairman – 24 hours after he had said that Docherty's departure was nonsense – finally bowed to the inevitable.

Docherty was officially dismissed for transgressing the club's "moral code", but one

newspaper claimed that club wives had been instrumental in the sacking. Dave Sexton (who had been released by QPR at his own request) was a quiet, dependable and uncontroversial replacement.

Docherty, who had been the first manager since Sir Matt Busby to bring success to the club, had, in a way, brought this debacle on himself. If he hadn't, because of his outrageous quips and larger-than-life persona not been a household name, it is unlikely that the press would have taken such a passionate interest in something that is, after all, commonplace.

He soon bounced back and the man who had managed Chelsea, Rotherham, Aston Villa, Porto and Scotland, took over the reins at Derby County. The irrepressible Scot was once again confirming one of his one-liners: "I've had more clubs than Jack Nicklaus."

Dalglish steps into Keegan's boots

Smooth succession: Dalglish was Keegan's perfect replacement

NOBODY could understand it when Bob Paisley signed David Johnson from Ipswich just before the start of the season. Why, they wondered, did Liverpool need yet another player when they already had an abundance of riches?

The answer was quite simple, although for most of the season it was a well-guarded secret. Kevin Keegan wanted to move to Europe and one leading club, Real Madrid, had already approached Liverpool with a sizeable offer. Paisley, though, struck a bargain with Keegan: if Keegan stopped at Liverpool for one more season then the club would not stand in the way of him going abroad. As a result, Johnson was being bought as a potential replacement.

Liverpool kept their end of the bargain and the European Cup final was Keegan's swansong before he moved to SV Hamburg for a record £500,000. The deal made Keegan the highest paid English footballer of all time, but Paisley still had his

doubts: He said: "I wouldn't play a man for England if he is with a foreign club. We have to fight against this trend of losing our best players."

Paisley also had his doubts about Johnson. To allay his fans' fears about the loss of Keegan he spent the bulk of the money, £440,000 to buy Kenny Dalglish from Celtic days before the Charity Shield. The deal broke the transfer record between British clubs and as one star had been gone out another was about to be born.

JOHANN CRUYFF
Dutch conquistador still to vanquish the world

Steve Coppell

I REMEMBER the evening well, December 7 1966, huddled around a crackling radio with fading batteries. I was with a group of fellow Liverpool fans when the result came through from Holland: Ajax 5 Liverpool 1. Surely not. It must have been a mistake. Liverpool never lost 5-1 to anybody. What would Shankly say?

The next morning the newspapers revealed the thoughts of the great man. Liverpool were not beaten 5-1 by Ajax, they were beaten 5-1 by the fog! Shankly had been told that because Holland was flat the Dutch were used to playing in the fog and that explained the result. The return leg a week later would be a different story.

That game was the first time I saw Johann Cruyff, one of the best players I have ever seen. Right from the first whistle, I was transfixed by the way the 19 year old glided around the pitch and even at this early stage he was always pointing the way for others.

"Where did 'e come from?" was the most commonly used expression from the Anfield crowd that night. The final score was 2-2 (7-3 on aggregate) and without doubt I had witnessed not only the early days of a great footballing career, but also the embryo of an orchestrated, yet utterly fluid style of play which would make a significant impact on world football for the next two generations.

The zenith of Cruyff's playing career was a prolonged four-year spell in the early 1970s when he could apparently do no wrong. Domestic success was followed by three successive European Cup triumphs with Ajax. In 1974 he moved to Barcelona, who at that time were in lower mid-table. A few months later, after a 20-game unbeaten run, they were the Spanish champions. A couple of months after this, Cruyff was leading his country out in the World Cup final against West Germany.

Although Holland lost that final, at 27 Johann Cruyff had achieved more on the football field than he ever could have imagined. At this point in his career it seems financial reward, rather than success on the football pitch, took over. Cruyff had come from a modest background, so his concern over financial insecurity was understandable.

But his priorities were regrettable. Barcelona reportedly paid a £400,000 signing-on fee to bring him to Spain and every season after his transfer he was campaigning, striving and cajoling to win new contracts and a higher salary. Cruyff's brilliance captivated the huge Barça faithful, but unfortunately it was chimerical. Real Madrid, Barcelona's arch rivals, walked away with the subsequent two League titles.

Cruyff, the maestro of the Total Football strategy by which Holland had enthralled the world in 1974, also became a control freak. He became embroiled in the delirious politics of hiring and firing. Coaches and players fought, and lost, verbal wars with Cruyff until he surrounded himself with a coterie he could manipulate. Unfortunately, total control did not bring success, and a temperamental star who does not deliver the silverware has a short shelf-life, especially in Spain.

Having alienated the Catalan public, Cruyff then enraged the Dutch nation by refusing to play in the 1978 World Cup finals in Argentina. The man in control wanted to finish his career at the top and did not wish to risk his lofty position by going to South America. Many Dutch still feel today that Cruyff would have made all the difference. Without him Holland still reached the World Cup final for the second tournament in succession, and lost in extra time. If their greatest

Tactical genius: Cruyff was the maestro of Holland's total football strategy in the 1970s

---

JOHANN CRUYFF

Born April 25, 1947, Amsterdam

PLAYING CAREER

Ajax Amsterdam 1964-73
Joined Ajax in 1957 as a 10-year-old, and made his debut in 1964; played for Ajax until 1973, winning six League titles, four Cups, three European Cups

Barcelona 1973-78
Honours One League title and one Cup

LA Aztecs 1978-79

Washington Diplomats 1979-80

Levante 1981

Ajax Amsterdam 1982-83
Honours Two League titles, one Cup

Internationals Made his debut for Holland on September 7, 1966 v Hungary and scored once in a 2-2 draw in Rotterdam. Played for Holland until 1978, collecting 48 caps, and scoring 33 goals. Runner-up at the 1974 World Cup

Other honours European Footballer of the Year in 1971, 1973 and 1974

MANAGEMENT CAREER

Feyenoord Player-manager 1983-84
Honours One League title and one Cup

Ajax Amsterdam Manager 1986-88
Honours One European Cup Winners Cup and two Cups

Barcelona Manager 1988-
Honours One European Cup, one European Cup Winners Cup, four League titles and one Cup

player had deigned to grace the occasion, surely they would have won? Instead Holland are forever burdened with being known as the best team never to have won the World Cup.

The Indian sunset of his playing career took place at home in Holland where he won League championships first with Ajax and then Feyenoord. Inevitably a contract dispute brought about his unthinkable transfer from Ajax to rivals Feyenoord.

I was fortunate enough to be living in Holland during this period and I could savour his performances on a regular basis. He was brilliant and transformed an average Feyenoord side into champions. Incidentally, a young player in the side at this time was Ruud Gullit who, according to Cruyff's whims, alternated from sweeper to the right wing.

It would be easy to conclude that Cruyff was a brilliant footballer who was a mercenary megalomaniac. His decision to move into coaching proved that he was also a missionary of sorts. I have always felt that Dutch football was technically and tactically the most advanced in the world, but particularly suited to the Dutch mentality. Cruyff's teams took this distinction to another level again, and he had the will and the coaching ability to have this style adopted successfully by the very different mentality of the Catalan.

It is difficult to describe playing styles on paper but simply I would say English teams play structured, formal football almost rectangular, brick-wall style. German and Italian teams – with obvious character differences – are strong and difficult to beat. Their emphasis is on defence so both can be likened to a triangle with a very solid foundation.

Cruyff's teams defy description. They are rotational, flowing and changing, but the emphasis is on attack. Only two players have strict

Seeking his fortune: Cruyff was a cultivated, and inspirational, player for Barcelona

defensive responsibilities, everybody else is encouraged to attack. Yet he rarely uses a conventional centre-forward. Hence the controversy with first Lineker and more recently Stoichkov, both natural goal-scoring centre-forwards who, in the Cruyff style, had to attack from wide positions. In Cruyff's teams the players conform to the style, and the style wins.

He has coached both Ajax and Barcelona to European Cup Winners Cup triumphs. Last year's Spanish League title completed a hat-trick of successive championships and in 1992 he captured the much sought after European Cup, a trophy that Barcelona had never won. Indeed it was only their third European Cup final. To the Catalans, Cruyff had delivered the Holy Grail, the trophy that Real Madrid from 1956 to 1960 had made their own personal property. At a stroke, Cruyff the coach had erased all his failings as a Barcelona player.

Now, he only has one thing left to win and that is the prize that eluded him as a player, the World Cup. It not surprising that once again money has thwarted his highest achievement. Once Holland had qualified for the World Cup finals in America the plan was for Cruyff to take over the national side from Dick Advocaat. But squabbles over his remuneration with the Dutch FA quickly scuppered that notion.

Given the quality of players at his disposal, now including Gullit, and their already well-voiced support of him, Holland would have been among the favourites to win the trophy and finally lose that unwelcome tag of being the Nearly Men. But once again rows over money,

an issue that seems to have split Dutch teams time and again, resurfaced.

As a player, and as a coach, certainly at club level, Johann Cruyff has had the biggest influence over European football for the last 25 years. It will be interesting to see if he finds it in himself to conquer that last horizon: the World Cup.

Crowning glory: the European Cup in 1992

In the hot seat: Barcelona's manager

Chairmen call players' bluff in strike threat

MANY PLAYERS were still deeply unhappy about their lot, and days before the season started more than 100 of them in the Midlands voted in favour of industrial action over their dispute about freedom of contract. Within days, the PFA had received further support from other areas of the country.

Lawrie McMenemy, the Southampton manager, was dismissive of the threat. "The players will never go on strike," he said. "They are too apathetic." Other clubs were more alert to the danger and an extraordinary meeting of the League was called to try to prevent a showdown.

Prompted by Jimmy Hill, the clubs agreed a compromise although the players were not convinced because the League said it would not announce the details until later in the season. When the details finally emerged in April, players discovered that they were free to choose between clubs, providing the clubs involved agreed a transfer fee. If the clubs could not agree then the case would go to an independent tribunal.

The PFA were far from impressed. Cliff Lloyd, their secretary, said: "This is a long way from what we wanted. The position remains unchanged. Players are completely in the hands of the clubs."

John Lacy became one of the first players to put the new process to the test when he moved from Fulham to Tottenham in July. The tribunal ruled that the fee should be £200,000, £50,000 less than the sum Fulham had demanded.

Scotland's World Cup dream turns into a Welsh nightmare

SCOTLAND were the only country from the British Isles to qualify for the World Cup finals in Argentina, and they booked their tickets to South America at the expense of Wales. England predictably were edged out by Italy on goal difference, but that outcome was virtually certain before Don Revie's infamous desertion to the Middle East in July 1977.

Although Czechoslovakia were the other team in the Scotland-Wales group, it always looked as qualification was between the British pair after Wales had beaten Czechoslovakia 3-0 in March 1977. Then, when Scotland also beat the Czechs, 3-1, in September, they were in the driving seat. If they beat Wales away in October they were through, a draw would mean Wales would have to win in Prague in November to displace them from the finals, while a defeat would require Wales to draw against the Czechs.

The crucial match was played at Anfield because none of the Welsh stadiums met the requisite safety standards, but despite the disadvantage of playing a "home" game away, the Welsh were much the better side and looked the more likely to score. However with 12 minutes remaining the French referee awarded a penalty for a disputed handball. Don Masson converted and Scottish fans in the capacity crowd went delirious. Television replays however showed that the referee had got it wrong. Three minutes from time, a scintillating header from Kenny Dalglish put the result beyond doubt.

Mike Smith, the Wales manager, was crestfallen: "None of my players handled the ball. Words cannot describe how we feel losing a match after putting up such an historic fight."

On the same night England's slender hopes evaporated when they could only beat Luxembourg 2-0 away. Qualification now rested on beating Italy at

Man on the spot: Masson sealed Wales's fate

Wembley in November and praying Luxembourg could sneak a draw in Italy in December. Otherwise Italy would go through on goal difference, and so it proved. England won 2-0, but Italy trounced Luxembourg by 3-0.

England's failure rested not on the two matches with Italy, the two countries exchanged 2-0 victories, but their inability to run up big scores against the minnows of Luxembourg and Finland. The result that certainly damned them was the

woeful 2-1 victory over Finland at Wembley in October 1976. Italy, a year later, hammered the Scandinavians 6-1 and took control of their destiny.

Italy's results will be more crucial than the number of goals England score

RON GREENWOOD
the England manager, two months before Italy qualified on goal difference

United kick off with an own goal

French fracas: United's fans shamed the club in Europe and incurred Uefa's wrath

MANCHESTER UNITED'S foray into Europe brought shame on the club before their first match had started on September 14. The Cup Winners Cup first round match against St Etienne had not kicked off when fighting erupted at the French ground. Riot police stormed the terrace and it was nearly half an hour before the unrest was quelled, although there were further skirmishes all night after the match had been drawn 1-1.

Uefa expelled Manchester United from the competition but the club argued that they were not to blame. They claimed that rival supporters had not been properly segregated, French fans had started the fighting and the riot police had over-reacted and made matters worse.

Manchester United were reinstated on appeal but ordered to play the second leg at least 300km from Old Trafford. Alan Hardaker, aware of the reputation of United's fans, said that the match could not be played in London, so it was switched to Plymouth.

The game passed off without incident and United won 2-0. Their Cup run was ended, though, by Porto in the next round. At least this time all the drama was on the field rather than off it.

Porto won the first leg 4-0. For a while it seemed that United might be able to climb a mountain at Old Trafford when they led 4-1 in the second leg. Needing another two goals they pressed forward, exposing their defence and letting Porto score again. The task was now beyond them and they went out 6-5 on aggregate.

Elton John forms harmonious duet with Taylor

ELTON JOHN was determined to put Watford on the map. Bobby Moore was said to be a candidate to manage his Fourth Division team, but the rock star turned to Graham Taylor instead.

The transformation that Taylor had worked at Lincoln had not gone un-noticed. Big-name teams were eyeing-up Taylor, and Elton John had to work hard to persuade Taylor to join the club.

But once he was installed at Vicarge Road, having told his multi-millionaire chairman that it would cost a mere £1m to get the team into the First Division, Taylor relished getting his teeth into the task.

His impact was immediate. He brought in Bertie Mee, who had led Arsenal to the Double in 1971, and set about turning the club upside down.

Watford adopted the long-ball game, with Luther Blissett as their target man, to deadly effect. Watford romped away with the Fourth Division title by 11 points and the combination of Elton John's money and Taylor's determination were obviously going to be a powerful force.

Villa's European odyssey runs aground in Spain

WHILE Liverpool were taking over Ajax's and Bayern Munich's mantle as the kings of Europe in the Champions Cup, English clubs were finding the Uefa Cup a harder nut to crack. This year it was Aston Villa's turn to fly the flag.

By the time the Birmingham club had reached the quarter-finals they had disposed of Fenerbace (6-0), Gornik Zabrze (3-1) and last year's runners-up, Athletic Bilbao (3-1). But then they ran into Barcelona who had knocked out Ipswich in the previous round on penalties.

A 2-2 draw at Villa Park left the Midlands side a mountain to climb at Nou Camp and despite a valiant rearguard battle the Catalan side won 2-1 to reach the semi-finals.

Forest go right to the top and never look back

NEWLY-PROMOTED Nottingham Forest wasted no time in making their mark in the First Division. Three wins in a row took them straight to the top of the table, a place that they occupied for almost all of the rest of the season.

The arrival of Peter Shilton from Stoke in September for £250,000 added extra strength to an already formidable defence. Forest were unbeaten at home in the League and only conceded a total of 24 goals.

By December the championship was already looking like a two-horse race, with Forest and Everton comfortably clear of the rest. And the title was effectively decided in the space of 48 hours – Everton were hammered 6-2 at home by Manchester United on Boxing Day and then lost 3-1 at Leeds the next day.

Forest finished the holiday programme five points clear and Brian Clough, their manager, was moved to quip: "The last time Nottingham were five ahead of anybody was in a cricket match." Everton did close the gap to a single point at one stage, but there was no stopping Nottingham Forest. They were unbeaten from mid-November to the end of the season and made sure of the club's first championship on April 18, with an incredible five matches still to play.

Clough became the first manager since the legendary Herbert Chapman to win the title with two different clubs. Clough and his assistant Peter Taylor were rewarded with a testimonial match against Derby. While Clough was his usual ebullient self Taylor was more modest, saying: "Our aim was to qualify for Europe but when we signed Shilton I knew we had a great chance of winning the title."

Shilton, however, was not involved in Forest's other triumph, in the League Cup final. Shilton was Cup-tied and Forest had sold their other first choice goalkeeper so Chris Woods, an 18-year-old reserve with no League experience, had to step into the breach against Liver-

Instant success: Forest won the title first time out

pool at Wembley. Woods's goal was peppered by the Liverpool forwards but he showed every bit as much composure as Shilton to keep the game scoreless after extra time.

Woods was equally unflappable in the replay but Forest owed their 1-0 victory to a poor decision by the referee Pat Partridge. There was no doubt that Phil Thompson brought down John O'Hare with a profes-

sional foul, but television replays showed that the incident took place outside the area and a penalty should not have been awarded.

After the match, Taylor was asked whether Forest deserved to have won given that the penalty should not have been given. "Who's got the Cup then?" he asked, quick as a flash, before striding away with the trophy in his arms.

Blyth Spartans the pathfinders in the year of the minnows

RIGHT FROM the start, everybody was calling the FA Cup the "Year of the Minnows". That was hardly surprising when six non-League clubs reached the third round for the first time since 1919.

All the minnows bar one fell by the wayside, leaving Blyth Spartans to carry the standard. Even their flag seemed to be about to be lowered in the fourth round at Stoke when they trailed 2-1 with less than 15 minutes to go, despite having taken the lead early in the game.

But helped by the woodwork they drew level. A free kick hit the post, a follow-up header hit the other post and the rebound was nudged in by Steve Carney. Then, from another free kick, Terry Johnston's volley made sure that they were the first non-League club to reach the fifth round since Yeovil in 1949.

Blyth were drawn against Third Division Wrexham, who had taken two First Division scalps – Bristol City 3-0 after a pulsating 4-4 draw, and Newcastle 4-1 in a replay. This time it

was Wrexham's turn to come back from the dead, snatching an equaliser in the 88th minute and winning the replay 2-1. The second match attracted so much interest that Blyth switched the game to Newcastle's ground to accommodate a 42,000 crowd.

With so many of the big teams knocking each other out, the quarter-finals had a strange look to them with Second Division Millwall and Orient also in contention.

Wrexham went down 3-2 to Arsenal, Millwall were swept

aside 6-1 by Ipswich and the underdogs' baton passed to Orient. They held Middlesbrough to a goalless draw at Ayresome Park and then Peter Kitchen continued his run of scoring in every round as they won the replay 2-1.

Kitchen, though was powerless against Arsenal in the semi-final and Orient bowed out 3-0. Even so, the succession of shocks went to show that it had not been hyperbole to call the season the "Year of the Minnows".

Robson masterminds Ipswich coup

Comeuppance: Osborne's goal taught Arsenal a lesson

IF Arsenal thought all they had to do was turn up at Wembley and their fifth FA Cup would be simply handed over to them, then they hadn't been following the knocks fate had been dishing out to favourites throughout the campaign. The "Year of Minnows" reached its logical conclusion when Ipswich duly lifted the FA Cup for the first time.

Although the final score was 1-0, it did not accurately represent Ipswich's domination. The country cousins from Suffolk out-played, out-thought and out-smarted the pride of London. Indeed they could easily have won by a hatful. Paul Mariner hit the bar, John Wark found the same post twice and Pat Jennings had to make a brilliant save to deny George Burley's header. It was, in fact, a 1-0 rout.

Apparently, Arsenal's humiliation had been hatched by the Ipswich backroom boys who had watched Arsenal three times before the final and deduced that the vast majority of Arsenal's attacks were initiated by Sammy Nelson at left-back. "Stop Nelson and you stop Arsenal," Bobby Robson, the

Smiles all round: Ipswich celebrate their first FA Cup

Ipswich manager, said to his players. Thus David Geddis was pulled out of midfield and instructed to close down the full-back. It worked like a dream.

However with 14 minutes remaining, Ipswich had not converted their tactical superiority into goals. Then Geddis swept past Nelson on the right wing and squared the ball low across the goal, Willie Young attempted to clear but put the ball straight to Roger Osborne who slammed it just inside the upright. It was a vital strike.

The excitement of scoring the winning goal was too much for Osborne and he was taken off to thunderous applause. "I was physically and mentally drained," Osborne said. "I think the sun had got to me. I felt faint and asked to come off."

The Arsenal manager, Terry Neill, conceded that Ipswich deserved their victory but, ominously, went on to say: "We have learnt from this defeat and we will be back next season more determined than ever."

Rangers reverse their fortunes to leave Aberdeen in their slipstream

AFTER their humiliation the previous season when Celtic won the Double and Rangers nothing, the men from Ibrox enjoyed sweet revenge by going one better and captured all three trophies. Surprisingly,

Swansong: Greig stepped up from captain to manager

Celtic were not their main rivals – they never came to terms with the loss of Kenny Dalglish to Liverpool, and finished fifth and out of Europe. Instead it fell to the North East and Billy McNeill's Aberdeen, in his first season in charge, to give Rangers a run for their money.

But as the season began, Rangers looked anything but runaway winners. After two games they were propping up the table! Then Jock Wallace's team embarked on a breathtaking sequence of seven wins, one draw and no losses to march to the top of the Premier Division. Yet, just as Rangers seemed to be comfortably in charge of the title race, Aberdeen began to creep up on them. Their 4-0 defeat of Rangers at Pittodrie on Christmas Eve signalled the beginning of a charge that was

to take the title race to the wire.

Aberdeen did not lose any of their remaining 17 matches (drawing five) and by April had overhauled Rangers to go top themselves, albeit briefly. It eventually all depended on the final games of the season, Rangers beat Motherwell 2-0 while Aberdeen could only draw at Hibernian, and Rangers had taken the title by two points.

The two leading clubs clashed yet again in the Scottish Cup final at Hampden on May 6 where Rangers confirmed their supremacy with a 2-1 victory that flattered McNeill's side, Aberdeen's goal coming four minutes from time. It was a wonderful end to the playing career of the Rangers' captain, John Greig, who three weeks later was installed as their new manager after Wallace had departed to take over at Leicester City.

Spurs scoop world to snatch Ardiles and Villa for £700,000

TWO WEEKS after Argentina had won the World Cup, Keith Burkinshaw, Tottenham's unassuming manager, announced to the press that he had signed two of their squad, Osvaldo Ardiles and Ricardo Villa. The hard-bitten newspapermen were stunned. Ardiles, probably the greatest midfielder in the world, had been the principal architect of Argentina's triumph, and Villa, who twice played as a substitute during the campaign, was a skilled, but tough, midfielder who also scored goals. For £700,000 it was a steal, and perhaps the transfer coup of the century.

After the World Cup everybody expected Argentina's squad to be snapped up by the top European countries, but that usually meant the free-spending Spaniards and Italians, not the English who had no real history of overseas players in their domestic game. Somehow Burkinshaw scooped the world. Even more surprisingly it had all been so easy.

Harry Haslam, the manager

Latin American connection: Villa, Burkinshaw and Ardiles transformed Tottenham's fortunes

of Sheffield United, had direct links with Argentina and alerted Spurs to the possibility of snapping up Ardiles cheaply – Sheffield United could not afford him – and he and Burkinshaw flew to Argentina. When Burkinshaw met Ardiles and his wife, Ardiles was more interested in the weather and the European sights than his salary. Within 20 minutes Ardiles had signed. Then, almost as an afterthought, Ardiles asked Burkinshaw if he liked Villa, because if

he did, he would come to England as well.

Burkinshaw was flabbergasted. He rang the Spurs chairman to get permission to sign a second Argentinian, Villa came to see him the next day and in five minutes he had signed up as well. In all the double transfer negotiations had taken just 25 minutes and transformed Tottenham's prospects for the season.

They had just returned to the First Division after a season in

the Second, but only by the narrowest of margins, on goal difference. Their modest squad had not looked likely to make an impact on the likes of Liverpool, Forest and Everton.

The press reaction spelled out their wonderment at Burkinshaw's audacity. It was described as "shattering new ground in the game", and The Guardian said: "It was as if the janitor had gone to buy a tin of paint and had come back with a Velasquez."

European campaign salvages Liverpool home-front losses

LIVERPOOL, by their standards, had a remarkably listless domestic season. Even though Kenny Dalglish had an immediate impact, and Alan Hansen had also arrived, they could only finish seven points adrift of Nottingham Forest in the League. The FA Cup was even worse. Liverpool went out 4-2 to Chelsea in the third round, prompting Bob Paisley to say: "My players had sawdust in their heads today." And reaching the final of the League Cup for the first time was scant consolation when they were beaten by Nottingham Forest.

But in Europe it was a completely different story – Liverpool still reigned supreme. Dynamo Dresden posed no threat, going down 6-3 on aggregate and Benfica held no terrors either in the quarter-finals. The Portuguese side had not been beaten in 46 matches and took an early lead in Lisbon. Despite torrential rain that threatened to turn the match into a lottery Liverpool stuck to their task. First Jimmy Case, then Emlyn Hughes brought Benfica's sequence to an end. Unhampered by the rain, Liverpool ran away with the second leg 4-1.

The semi-finals pitted Liverpool against their old adversaries Borussia Moenchengladbach. The two sides had met twice before in European finals and Liverpool had won on both occasions. Borussia sensed that, at last, their luck was changing when they won 2-1 at home, their second goal coming in the final minute. Just as Benfica had discovered though, Anfield was a different proposition. The match was one-way traffic with Liverpool scoring three times without reply.

Wembley had been chosen to stage the final, which gave Liverpool an enormous psychological advantage. And their opponents, Bruges, could still recall losing to Liverpool in the Uefa Cup final two years before.

Bruges, in awe of Liverpool and of the crowd, opted to play an ultra defensive game. They barely mounted an attack worthy of the name, just sitting back and absorbing the pressure. That was hardly the way to beat Liverpool, masters of biding their time and waiting for the right moment. It duly arrived in the 66th minute when Dalglish was given far too much space to run at the Bruges defence. As Jensen advanced Dalglish paused for an instant before chipping over the goalkeeper from close range.

Even then, Bruges showed little inclination to go on the attack and Liverpool were content to protect their lead. It was hardly the best of games but that did not matter to Liverpool. They were, after all, the first English club to retain the European Cup.

Magic moment: Dalglish watches his chip beat Jensen to retain the European Cup at Wembley

219

ARGENTINA's eventual triumph in the World Cup final after extra time at home in their capital city of Buenos Aires before their exultant and ecstatic fans on June 25 laid to rest 58 years of disappointment, betrayal, failure, slurs, and theft on the world stage. Argentina had always seen itself, not Brazil, as the home of South American football. So in 1930 the country was mortified when they blew the very first World Cup final to their bitter rivals Uruguay, in Montevideo. That was just the beginning of their World Cup travails.

First Italy began poaching their best players and making them Italian internationals (this went on until the 1960s). Three times they were rejected as the hosts, although Uruguay, Brazil, Chile and Mexico had got the nod. The first time they were snubbed they boycotted the tournament for 24 years. When they did return, their best result was to reach the quarter-finals against England in 1966, when their captain, Antonio Rattin, and his team were branded as "animals". Meanwhile Argentina were a dominant force in their continent, winning 13 of 31 South American championships.

Even when Argentina were finally allowed to host a World Cup it was far from certain that they would actually stage the competition. The country was wracked by unrest as left-wing guerillas fought the an oppressive military dictatorship, the national economy was a shambles and thought unlikely to be able to afford the event and there were repeated calls for the finals to be moved elsewhere, with Holland and Belgium the favourites to take over. But the rebels and the government agreed a truce (national pride on the football field being more important than who ran the country), stadiums were rebuilt and the tournament passed off smoothly.

More importantly, Argentina had, by beating Holland – runners-up in West Germany four years earlier – proved they were world masters. The pain of over a half-century of humiliation was erased in 120 minutes of vibrant football and on that hot June evening the populace went into night-long raptures.

The match had been thrilling, if badly refereed. Mario Kempes, playing the game of his life, gave

WORLD CUP 1978
On home soil Argentina come good

Argentina the lead in the 38th minute when he astutely touched home Leopoldo Luque's pass. Despite numerous Dutch attacks and missed chances – with both defences showing all the signs of the pressure created by the fervent crowd – Argentina clung on to their lead as the game entered its final phase.

In the 81st minute, Arie Haan sprung their offside trap with a through ball to Rene van de Kerkhof. His cross was headed in by the substitute, Dirk Nanninga. With seconds remaining, it appeared that Holland had stolen the game when Rob Rensenbrink's powerful and accurate long-range shot beat the goalkeeper only to rebound of the base of the left-hand post.

That was the last effective chance Holland had. In extra time Kempes popped up again with a powerful run from outside the penalty area to score a wonderful solo goal by beating three players, including Jan Jongbloed the goalkeeper. Ten minutes later Kempes, the leading scorer of the tournament, delivered the killing blow when, after another powerful run, he exchanged a one-two with Daniel Bertoni, who slotted the ball home. Holland had now joined Czechoslovakia and Hungary in a select club: two World Cup finals, no World Cup.

They had their excuses. There was no Johann Cruyff or Rinus Michels, and, as seems commonplace in the Dutch household, bickering was rife. Argentina, too, had their problems for, as usual, many of their stars were playing in Europe. Cesar Menotti, their chain-smoking national coach, wisely decided to focus his squad on home-based players such as Osvaldo

Ardiles, who was the midfield player of the tournament. In fact Kempes was the only overseas player in the winning team.

There were some in South America however that believed that Argentina should not even have been allowed to play in the final. The circumstances surrounding their victory over Peru were engulfed in controversy. After two matches in the second round group, Brazil and Argentina had the same number of points. Everything rested on the last two games, Brazil versus Poland and Argentina against Peru.

Inexplicably, Fifa did not insist that the two games were played simultaneously. So after Brazil had beaten Poland 3-1, Argentina kicked off knowing that they had to win by four goals to reach the final. Peru started well enough but caved in 6-0. The finger of suspicion was pointed firmly at the Peruvian goalkeeper Quiroga, who had been born in Argentina.

There were allegations that the Peruvian team had been bribed by the ruling Argentinian junta, and counter claims that Brazil had offered the Peruvians money to play well. For the Brazilians it was the last straw. They felt they had already been victimised in their first round match against Sweden. With the match level at 1-1, Zico drove a free kick into the net. But Clive Thomas blew for time while the ball was in mid-air and refused to allow the goal, condemning Brazil to face Argentina and Peru in the second round. To this day, the controversial Welsh referee still claims that his action was perfectly justified, as the rules are the rules.

Quite what justification Scotland

could conjure up for their abject performance in Argentina was difficult to fathom. Ally MacLeod's team arrived on a wave of Tartan sentiment and expectation. It was hailed as the greatest team to compete in the World Cup, and once again Scotland were the only British country to qualify – England being edged out on goal difference by Italy.

With players like Martin Buchan, Kenny Dalglish, Archie Gemmill, Joe Jordan, Lou Macari, Don Masson and Bruce Rioch in their squad, the Scots seemed to have good grounds for optimism. Moreover their group, with the exception of Holland, looked easy enough with Iran, playing in their first ever World Cup, and unfancied Peru in their third. Such complacency was to prove Scotland's undoing.

In their match against Peru, Jordan gave them the lead after 14 minutes, yet amazingly Scotland went to pieces and the veteran Teofilo Cubillas ran riot. He created the equaliser two minutes from half-time and scored two high quality goals in the space of seven minutes in the second half as Peru won 3-1.

If that wasn't bad enough, Scotland had to experience the shame of Willie Johnstone being sent home, and banned for a year from international football, for failing a random drugs test after the match. Johnstone protested his innocence, claiming the drugs were for hay fever but subsequently admitted they were stimulants that he also used in domestic, club football.

Scotland's nightmare was only beginning. Now they had to face the novices, Iran. Scotland's performance was utterly inept in the 1-1 draw. They could even count themselves lucky to have got on the scoresheet. Iran gifted Scotland an undeserved half-time lead when one of their players collided with his goalkeeper and the ball ended up in the net. It was the most bizarre, and softest of goals.

This left MacLeod's demoralised and vilified team with a mountain to climb: beat Holland by three goals or get on the plane home. When Holland took the lead with a Rob Rensenbrink penalty, the mountain had become even higher. This time Scotland rose to the challenge. Dalglish equalised just before half-time, Gemmill's penalty put them ahead and, with

Scottish tails up, Gemmill scored the goal of the tournament. He started his run outside the penalty area, beat three Dutch defenders and then confounded the keeper by chipping in under pressure. Was a miracle on the cards?

No, because four minutes later Johnny Rep soon stopped all this Scottish bravado and heroism with a thunderous 25-yard shot to leave the score 3-2 and secure Holland's place in the next round. So once again Scotland had their World Cup glory. As in 1974, when they were the only unbeaten team in the tournament, they comforted themselves with one thought. Forget Peru and Iran, they had beaten the team that had been the thickness of a post from being world champions.

Cubillas: destroyed Scotland **Bettega: beat Argentina**

Fever pitch: the home fans

Goal of the tournament: Gemmill's dribble stunned Holland

FOR THE RECORD

FIRST ROUND

GROUP 1	P	W	D	L	F	A	Pts
Italy	3	3	0	0	6	2	6
Argentina	3	2	0	1	4	3	4
France	3	1	0	3	5	5	2
Hungary	3	0	0	3	3	8	0

GROUP 2	P	W	D	L	F	A	Pts
Poland	3	2	1	0	4	1	5
W. Germany	3	1	2	0	6	0	4
Tunisia	3	1	1	1	3	2	3
Mexico	3	0	0	3	2	12	0

GROUP 3	P	W	D	L	F	A	Pts
Austria	3	2	0	1	3	2	4
Brazil	3	1	2	1	2	3	4
Spain	3	1	1	1	2	2	3
Sweden	3	0	1	2	1	3	1

GROUP 4	P	W	D	L	F	A	Pts
Peru	3	2	1	0	7	2	5
Holland	3	1	1	1	5	3	3
Scotland	3	1	1	1	5	6	3
Iran	3	0	1	2	2	8	1

SECOND ROUND

GROUP A	P	W	D	L	F	A	Pts
Holland	3	2	1	0	9	4	5
Italy	3	1	1	1	2	2	3
W. Germany	3	0	2	1	4	5	2
Austria	3	1	0	2	4	8	2

GROUP B	P	W	D	L	F	A	Pts
Argentina	3	2	1	0	8	0	5
Brazil	3	2	1	0	6	1	5
Poland	3	1	0	2	2	5	2
Peru	3	0	0	3	0	10	0

THIRD PLACE PLAY-OFF
Brazil 2 Italy 1
HT 0-1 Att. 76,609

FINAL
Argentina 3 Holland 1 aet
HT 1-0 Att. 77,260

Teams
Argentina Fillol; Olguin, Galvan, Passarella, Tarantini, Ardiles (sub: Larrosa), Gallego, Kempes, Bertoni, Luque, Ortiz (sub: Houseman)
Holland Jongbloed; Krol, Poortvliet, Brandts, Jansen (sub: Suurbier), W Van de Kerkhof, Neeskens, Haan, Rep (sub: Nanninga), Rensenbrink, R Van de Kerkhof

Leading Goalscorers 6 Mario Kempes (Argentina); 5 Teofilo Cubillas (Peru), Rob Rensenbrink (Holland); 4 Leopoldo Luque (Argentina), Hans Krankl (Austria).
Total goals scored 102.
Average per game: 2.68
Sendings-off Andras Torocsik (Hungary) v Argentina; Tibor Nyilasi (Hungary) v Argentina; Referee: Antonio Garrido (Portugal).
Dirk Nanninga (Holland) v West Germany); Referee: Ramon Barreto Ruiz (Uruguay).
Number of players used by finalists 17 Argentina; 19 Holland.

Local heroes: Luque, Kempes (two goals) and Bertoni (one goal) over-ran the Dutch in extra time

Rejuvenated Toshack calls up old guard

SWANSEA continued their march up the League, winning promotion to the Second Division a year after coming up from the Fourth Division. To add to the delight for John Toshack, their player-manager, he was also recalled to the Welsh team. He celebrated by scoring a hat-trick as Scotland were beaten 3-0 in the Home championships.

Toshack, while developing young players at the club, also turned to two of his former Liverpool teammates to bring experience to the side. Phil Boersma was signed from Luton for £35,000 and Ian Callaghan joined from Liverpool.

They bolstered a team that had already tasted success in the League Cup, beating Tottenham 3-1 at White Hart Lane to win the match 5-3 on aggregate.

Apart from one spell in February, when they went five matches without a win, Swansea were hardly ever out of the promotion race. Fittingly, they made sure of a place in the Second Division when Toshack scored the winning goal against Chester-field in the final match of the season.

Toshack: recalled

Latchford and Greenwood lead England out of the wilderness

Sterling effort: Keegan helps England get a 1-1 draw in Dublin

RON GREENWOOD'S prospects of his tenure as England manager being extended to include the 1982 World Cup finals in Spain clearly depended on England qualifying for the 1980 European championships, particularly as they had not qualified for the previous two World Cup finals. England's group was an intriguing one as it included the two Irelands, Bulgaria and Denmark, with the winner going through to the quarter-finals in Italy.

With so much pressure on him, Greenwood must have had near-apoplexy in their opening game against Denmark in Copenhagen in September. By the 23rd minute two headers from Kevin Keegan had put England 2-0 up. Then, in a three-minute spell, the Danes levelled the scores, their first goal coming from a penalty.

Shortly after the interval Bob Latchford restored the lead and Phil Neal made it 4-2 with five minutes left, only for the Danes to pull another goal back.

Despite frantic efforts by the home team, England clung on. A relieved Greenwood said: "I'm an advocate of attacking football – but that was carrying it to extremes."

A month later England had a creditable 1-1 draw with Eire in Dublin, and then in February they ran riot against Northern Ireland at a packed Wembley with a resounding 4-0 victory, Latchford scoring twice. And to cap Greenwood's first full season officially in charge, Bulgaria were given similar treatment in Sofia in June as England returned 3-0 victors.

Meanwhile the other countries were cutting each other's throats with Northern Ireland beating Bulgaria, but losing to Denmark, and Eire beating Denmark, but losing to Bulgaria. Thus, with half their qualifying games played, England were sitting comfortably at the top of their group, having won three, and drawn one of their four matches with an extremely healthy goal difference.

Latchford: hotshot

I've served more time than Ronnie Biggs did for the Great Train Robbery

MALCOLM ALLISON
appealing against his lifetime ban
from the touchline

Stein puts patriotism before pounds

JOCK STEIN's rich and rewarding managerial partnership with Celtic spanning 13 glorious years was brought to an inglorious end. After the disappointments of the previous season when Celtic finished fifth in the Premier Division, failed to win a trophy or even qualify for Europe while Rangers waltzed to the Treble, Celtic's directors wanted a younger man.

Stein, 56, had agreed in May to hand over the reins to Billy McNeill, his captain when Celtic had won the European Cup in 1967, and who had, in his first season in charge of Aberdeen, run Rangers close in the League and Scottish Cup.

Stein had been given to understand that the club he had served so well (one European Cup, 10 championships, eight Scottish Cups, six Scottish League Cups) would grant him a

McNeill: chosen man

directorship. Instead Celtic offered him the post of commercial director.

He saw it as an insult: that he would be effectively a glorified pools vendor. Consequently, on August 21 he went to England, to manage Leeds United who had never really recovered from

Brian Clough's disastrous 44-day reign in 1974.

Coincidentally, Stein lasted exactly the same number of days at Elland Road. But, unlike Clough, he did not leave under a cloud. Indeed Manny Cussins, the Leeds chairman implored him to stay and offered financial incentives to do so. However a bigger, and more patriotic carrot had been dangled in front of the Big Man: managing his country, something he had briefly done as a caretaker in 1965.

After the debacle of the national side in Argentina, Ally McLeod had resigned on September 26 and the Scottish Football Association, desperate to recover lost pride, naturally turned to their greatest-ever club manager and appointed him on October 4. He had much to do.

Shrewsbury flirt with the big time

GRAHAM TURNER, the newly arrived player-manager of Shrewsbury, certainly brought a breath of fresh air to the club. At the end of his first full season in charge the team had produced their best-ever performances in the League and in the FA Cup.

A 4-1 victory over Exeter in the final game of the season secured the Third Division championship, and promotion to the Second Division for the first time in the club's history, but most of the excitement in the town revolved around the

team's performances in the FA Cup.

Victories over Mansfield, Doncaster and Cambridge earned them a plum tie in the fourth round, at home to Manchester City. The First Division strugglers were swept aside 2-0 but Shrewsbury were left cursing the luck of the draw for the next round.

Instead of being paired with another of the glamour clubs they were presented with a trip to Aldershot. The Fourth Division team were clearly no

slouches either, having beaten Sheffield United in a replay.

Shrewsbury appeared to be down and out when they trailed 2-1 with less than a minute left to play until they snatched a very late equaliser and won the replay 3-1 in extra time.

That put Shrewsbury in the sixth round for the first time and they gave another First Division side, Wolverhampton a run for their money. Shrewsbury drew 1-1 at Molineux thanks to an Atkins penalty, before bowing at 3-1 at Gay Meadow.

Docherty: courting disaster

How television's Snatch of the Day became Swap of the Day

ITV SHOCKED everybody when they announced in November that they would be showing football on Saturday nights next season rather than the BBC. Match of the Day was established as a national tradition, while the ITV companies had to make do with highlights on Sunday afternoons. Everybody, the BBC included, assumed that the established order was not going to change.

So news of ITV's three-year deal with the Football League was greeted with incredulity. Not even all the clubs could believe that the "Snatch of the Day" had happened. Jimmy Hill, the Coventry managing director who was also a Match of the Day presenter, said: "It wasn't an honourable deal, it was railroaded through. The clubs didn't even know whose bid they were accepting."

The BBC had no intention of relinquishing the jewel in their sporting crown and so court action became inevitable. The BBC won a respite when the Office of Fair Trading banned the agreement because it broke the rules regarding restrictive practices.

A £10m four-year compromise, dubbed "Swap of the Day", was reached with the two networks sharing coverage – the

BBC would have Saturday football next season, and then the coverage would alternate.

This offer was thrown out by club chairman because they did not want to commit themselves to such a long-term deal. But, warned by Alan Hardaker that they faced the prospect of no coverage at all with the consequent loss of money, the clubs finally backed down at the League's annual meeting in June.

THE
1978-79
SEASON

Daiglish: top man

Liverpool's mean machine rolls on

RECORDS came thick and fast as three clubs, Liverpool, Nottingham Forest and Everton, vied for the top spot in the First Division, all of them seemingly unbeatable.

Nottingham Forest surpassed Leeds's record of 34 consecutive matches without defeat in the League in October and did not have their run halted until December 9, when they went down at Liverpool. That ended a sequence of 42 League matches (21 wins and 21 draws) stretching back to November 1977.

Everton did not lose until their 20th League match of the season, at Coventry on December 23. But neither side could keep pace with Liverpool, even though Liverpool lost their first game relatively early in the season on October 28. Their 1-0 reverse at Everton was their first defeat in a local derby since 1971.

The thing that kept Liverpool in front was their incredible start to the season. They won six games in a row at the start, scoring 20 goals and conceding one, including a 7-0 destruction of Tottenham, the London club's

Happy anniversary: Paisley celebrated 40 years at Liverpool

record defeat in the League.

When Liverpool lost for the fourth and final time on April 16, Bob Paisley said: "We were absolute rubbish. The League is still wide open." Some chance. Liverpool coasted to the title with a record 68 points and a record low of 16 goals conceded, with Ray Clemence keeping 27 clean sheets. All of this was done by just 15 players, two of whom only made four appearances between them.

It was a breathtaking performance to mark Paisley's 40th year with the club. And when Liverpool made sure of a record

11th title on May 8 the ever-modest Paisley was more concerned for his players than himself. "The atmosphere was overpowering," he said. "I was worried that all the publicity about my anniversary might upset the players' concentration."

The tributes began to flock in. Kenny Dalglish, Liverpool's leading scorer, was voted Player of the Year; the club collected a £50,000 prize from The Sun for beating a target of 84 goals and Paisley, to nobody's surprise, was chosen as Manager of the Year.

Birtles scuppers Southampton after Clough reads the riot act

THE EARLY stages of the League Cup took their usual toll on the big clubs with no less that six First Division clubs going out to lesser opposition in the second round alone.

Liverpool, despite their rampant form in the League, were victims of the biggest upset, losing to Third Division Sheffield United. The "Liverpool old guard" at Swansea brought down Tottenham in a replay, and Arsenal were beaten by yet another Third Division side, Rotherham.

With so many of the big guns gone so quickly things were made considerably easier for the surviving big names. Nottingham Forest, after needing a replay to overcome Oldham, breezed past Oxford, Brighton

and Watford. Their only hard game was a 3-2 win at Everton in the fourth round.

Southampton's route to the final was considerably more difficult – Birmingham, Derby, a replay against Reading, Manchester City and a one-goal aggregate against Leeds in the semi-final.

Nottingham Forest looked remarkably shaky in the first half of the final and they trailed to a goal from David Peach. Brian Clough did not mince his words during the interval and Forest were transformed after the break.

Garry Birtles, a bargain buy from a local non-League side, quickly got the equaliser and Southampton did well not to concede another goal until the

Turning point: Birtles scores the equaliser for Forest

78th minute, when Birtles struck again. Birtles had two other efforts disallowed, both for offside, and a part in Forest's third goal, scored by Tony Woodcock.

Nick Holmes got a late conso-

lation but Southampton never looked like coming back. Winning the trophy for the second year running gave Forest the perfect fillip for the later stages of their other Cup campaign, in Europe.

Francis breaks £1m barrier

WHEN, in 1905, Alf Common was transferred from Sunderland to Middlesbrough for £1,000, there was a hue and cry about the sum of money Middlesbrough had forked out for one player. Seventy-four years later, the Nottingham Forest manager, Brian Clough, born in Middlesbrough, for whom he played before being transferred to Sunderland, provoked similar outrage when he paid £1m for Trevor Francis. Little wonder that the North East is regarded as the hotbed of English football.

Francis, like Common, was one of the most gifted players of his era. He had made his First Division debut for Birmingham when only 16, and in the subsequent eight years had scored 118 goals in 278 appearances, and played for England 12 times. Clough, having led Nottingham Forest out of the depths of the Second Division to the heights of the First Division championship, was ambitious that this success would endure. Hence the absurd outlay on Francis.

The transfer on February 9 doubled the previous record between British clubs, £500,000 paid by West Bromwich Albion for Middlesbrough's David Mills only the month before. To be fair to Clough the £1m price was set by Birmingham themselves. Firmly rooted to the bottom of the First Division table, they stared relegation in the face and knew they could not realistically hang on to their ambitious superstar.

Clough had to outbid Jimmy Hill's Coventry to get his man, and the Forest manager sweetened the deal with Francis by agreeing that he could spend his summers playing for Detroit Express in America.

The striking disadvantage of the deal from Forest's point of view was that it had come so late in the season that Francis would only be eligible for one match in the European Cup – the final. Clough's outrageous gamble would pay off, with Forest making the final, and Francis scoring the only goal.

Spiralling transfer fees in the domestic market

£1,000 Alf Common 1905
(Sunderland to Middlesbrough)

£5,000 Syd Puddefoot 1922
(West Ham to Falkirk)

£10,890 David Jack 1928
(Bolton Wanderers to Arsenal)

£20,000 Tommy Lawton 1947
(Chelsea to Notts County)

£50,000 Denis Law 1960
(Huddersfield to Man City)

£110,000 Alan Ball 1966
(Blackpool to Everton)

£500,000 David Mills 1979
(Middlesbrough to West Brom)

£1,150,000 Trevor Francis 1979
(Birmingham to Nottm Forest)

Smiling all the way to bank: Francis and his wife celebrate the monumental deal with Clough

FOR THE RECORD

■ The FA banned Don Revie for 10 years for signing a secret deal with the United Arab Emirates while still the England manager, and trying to persuade England to pay him £50,000 compensation if he resigned. Revie decided to sue the FA because the sentence was "savage and out of all proportion".

■ Sammy Chapman, the former Nottingham Forest captain, won a test case in court which established that players received money from testimonial games free of tax.

■ The Charlton forwards Mick Flanagan and Derek Hales were sent off for fighting during their team's draw with Maidstone in the FA Cup.

■ Uefa said that England would only be allowed to enter three teams in the 1980-81 Uefa Cup.

English clubs maintain the pressure on European rivals

WHILE winning the European Cup was becoming something of an English habit as Nottingham Forest added to Liverpool's triumphs in the previous two years, the Uefa Cup and the Cup Winners Cup were still proving elusive.

The English contingent went into the Uefa Cup with high hopes and these were duly rewarded in the first round as Arsenal thumped Locomotive Leipzig 7-1, with Frank Stapleton scoring five goals – including one for the opposition, West Bromwich Albion raced past Galatasaray 6-2 and Everton trounced Finn Harps 10-0. Manchester City had a fright against Twente Enschede: only qualifying because of an own goal.

Then luck went against Everton as they fell victims to the away goal rule while Arsenal benefited from it before being out-thought by the classy Red Star Belgrade in the third round. Meanwhile West Brom and Manchester City coasted serenely to the quarter-finals. Indeed City hammered the crack Italian side AC Milan 5-1.

However both were undone in the quarter-finals. Their only consolation was that they were both beaten by the eventual finalists. WBA lost to Red Star Belgrade 2-1 and City succumbed to Borussia Moenchengladbach 4-2. The German side eventually went on to beat Red Star 2-1 in the two-legged final.

It was much the same story for Ipswich Town in the European Cup Winners Cup, where Bobby Robson's team comfortably reached the quarter-finals before their European naivety was exposed. Holding a 2-1 lead from the first leg at Portman Road thanks to Eric Gates, Ipswich conceded a goal to Barcelona's Migueli at Nou Camp and were knocked out on the away goals rule.

When they pulled level, I was dreading extra time because I was knackered and our substitute was already on

LIAM BRADY

Brady: seized the time

United's amazing revival buried by Brady's desperate last-gasp effort

AN UNNECESSARY blunder by Terry Neill, the Arsenal manager, five minutes from time turned a prosaic FA Cup final into one of the most explosive finishes seen at Wembley since Stanley Matthews' heroics in 1953. With five minutes remaining Arsenal were 2-0 ahead and coasting to their fifth FA Cup trophy when Neill pulled off David Price and put on Steve Walford. It utterly disrupted the Arsenal defence and, with a minute to go, Gordon McQueen and Sammy McIlroy had put Manchester United level. Extra time loomed.

But not for Liam Brady, the architect of Arsenal's two first-half goals. Now it was United's turn to fall victim to complacency, and then panic. Brady picked up the ball in his half and ran straight at the heart of the United midfield as they backed off, hoping to deny him space rather than commit themselves to the tackle.

Brady swung his sweet left foot one more time to find Graham Rix clear on the left wing. Meanwhile Alan Sunderland had made a blindside run on the right and arrived perfectly at the far post to connect with Rix's cross and snatch an unbeliev-

Nodding home: Stapleton scores Arsenal's second goal

able winner. United could barely draw breath before the referee blew the final whistle.

For Arsenal, it was the end of a long and arduous FA Cup campaign. Their third round struggle with Jack Charlton's Third Division Sheffield Wednesday had been little short of titanic. It took five matches (three of them at neutral Filbert Street in the course of seven days), involving 16 goals and 540 minutes of play before they could finally meet Notts County in the fourth round. So, what began as a marathon in Sheffield in January, ended as a sprint in London in May.

Manchester United surely had believed the omens were on their side when extra time was imminent. Their road to Wembley had already been paved with London clubs – Chelsea, Fulham and Tottenham falling to Dave Sexton's glittering array of stars. Then they had done the difficult bit: knock out the eventual League champions, Liverpool, after a replay in the semi-final.

Sexton described it as a cruel result: "When we got the two goals back we were thinking of the breather before extra time and lost concentration for a few vital seconds."

Fixture log-jam proves no obstacle to Celtic's dramatic charge

IT WAS a remarkable season by any standards. First, the leading three clubs, Celtic, Rangers and Aberdeen, all had new managers in Billy McNeill, John Greig and Alex Ferguson respectively. Second, the winter was so dire that not only did it play havoc with the early rounds of the Scottish Cup, it made interpreting the League tables with so many games in hand an impossible task. Never more so than at the final run-in.

Dundee United, under Jim McLean, took full advantage of this and led the Premier Division for much of the season, but how false was their position? On April 25 Dundee United had two League matches left,

against Celtic and Aberdeen, with 43 points accumulated. Celtic had seven games to play, two of them against Rangers, and had 36 points. Rangers had 35 points with seven games remaining, but also the Scottish Cup final against Hibs to play. Aberdeen also had 35 points but only five games left, one of them against Rangers. To the winner the spoils, but which was better: points in the bag or games in hand? And who would be the first to lose their nerve?

Dundee United cracked straightaway, losing to Celtic and drawing with Aberdeen, who too then caved in, losing to Rangers and only amassing five points from their five remaining

matches. Meanwhile Rangers were making heavy weather of disposing of Hibs in the Cup, the final going to a second replay. As the others faltered, Celtic had grasped the nettle.

Apart from losing to Rangers at Ibrox 1-0, they won all their remaining fixtures, but none more important than their final match of the season at Parkhead. Rangers, who still had two games in hand, needed at least a draw to prevent Celtic from taking the championship.

With just over 20 minutes remaining Celtic were in trouble, trailing to an Alex MacDonald goal and reduced to 10 men after John Doyle had been sent off. Then they mounted a cham-

pionship-winning recovery as Roy Aitken equalised and George McCluskey gave them the lead. Still Rangers weren't dead: Rob Russell levelled the scores to leave the title tilting Rangers' way.

In the last five minutes Rangers wilted under the green and white onslaught, and MacLeod put Celtic ahead for the second time. To make matters worse poor Colin Jackson put through his own goal to give Celtic a 4-2 victory and the Premier title.

Rangers' sole consolation was that, after two drab 0-0 draws with Hibs, they eventually prevailed 3-2 in the second replay of the Scottish Cup final.

Francis uses his head to give Clough Europe's major prize

Rare occurrence: Francis scored with a header the first time he played in Europe

■ Sammy Nelson (above) of Arsenal was fined £750 and banned for two games for dropping his shorts in front of spectators at the match against Coventry on April 3.

■ Bill McCracken, the Newcastle defender who contributed to a change in the offside rules in 1925 died on January 20, aged 95. During his days as a scout he discovered Pat Jennings.

■ The match between Inverness Thistle and Falkirk in the Scottish Cup was postponed a record 29 times before Falkirk won on February 22. the game should originally have been played on January 6.

■ Alan Ball's match for Southampton on April 21 made him the first player to make 100 League appearances for four different clubs. The other three were Blackpool, Everton and Arsenal.

■ Norwich drew a record 23 League matches during the season.

■ Wimbledon won promotion to the Third Division in only their second season in the League.

NOTTINGHAM FOREST and Liverpool were undoubtedly two of the finest sides in Europe. Liverpool, the European Cup holders, were seeded in the competition but Forest, making their European debut were not. The draw that everybody feared and nobody wanted duly happened and the two teams were paired in the first round.

Both matches were thrilling, and either would have graced the final, so it was a shame that one team had to lose. Forest took a 2-0 lead at the City Ground when Liverpool, pushing forward to try to cancel out Garry Birtles' goal, let Colin Barrett finish off a slick counter-attack near the end.

Liverpool had come back from worse before as Brian Clough knew: "Two goals might not be enough at Anfield," he said. But this time Liverpool's touch deserted them. The woodwork was rattled several times but Liverpool were never going to pull off a miracle and the game finished 0-0.

Forest's semi-final against Cologne, the conquerors of Rangers, was every bit as enthralling as their contest with Liverpool. At home, Forest came back from two goals down after 20 minutes to lead 3-2 only to concede an equaliser to the Japanese substitute Yashiko Okudera, who scored within seconds of coming on.

Although Clough blamed Peter Shilton for two of the goals he was certain that Forest could still reach the final. "Only a fool would write us off," he said. He was right. Ian Bowyer's header in Germany capped a game that Clough described as his "finest hour".

The final, against Malmo was an even finer 90 minutes. Forest were without Archie Gemmill and Martin O'Neill, but Trevor Francis was eligible to play in the European Cup for the first time. And it was Forest's record signing who turned the match. He timed a long run from midfield to arrive at the far post at just the same moment as John Robertson's cross. The crowd were treated to something of a rarity, a headed goal from Francis.

Robertson, Francis and John McGovern dominated the second half and Forest, although not the equal of Liverpool in the League, showed that they were every bit as good in Europe.

Toast of England: Forest won the European Cup for the first time

Transfer fees out of control as the market goes haywire

TREVOR FRANCIS'S £1m move to Forest last season opened the floodgates and big-money transfers became so common-place that everybody thought that football had money to burn.

In August, Bob Paisley, the Liverpool manager, voiced many people's fears when he said: "There is a danger of the whole set-up going berserk and the game being ruined. People who sign contracts should honour them." The very next day, Ray Wilkins became the second most expensive footballer in Britain when he moved from Chelsea to Manchester United for £825,000.

A very few people did show the restraint that Paisley called for. Bob Stokoe resigned as the Blackpool manager because he did not think the club should have bought Brian Smith from Bolton. And Ron Harris, the veteran Chelsea player rejected a move to Luton, even though it would have earned him £15,000. "There are some things money can't buy," he said. "I have spent 19 years with Chelsea, the good times and the bad. There isn't a price on that."

Just about everybody else did have their price. The Francis record was broken on September 5 when Steve Daley joined Manchester City from Wolverhampton. The basic fee was £1,150,000, and the extra costs raised the final bill to £1,437,500. Manchester City had spent more than £5m so far in the season, which had still hardly begun.

Worse, the Daley record only lasted three days. Andy Gray's move from Aston Villa to Wolverhampton upped the ante to £1,469,000. And it was not only the established stars who were commanding million-pound fees. In August Norwich rejected a £1m offer for the still unproven Kevin Reeves. By March the club, suffering from low attendances and declining income succumbed and Reeves joined Manchester City for £1m.

The madness was not only confined to the Football League. The transfer of Ian Redford from Dundee to Rangers broke the Scottish record. And Weymouth collected a non-League record £35,000 when they sold Graham Roberts to Tottenham. Even America got in on the act. The Tampa Bay Rowdies were said to have offered £1m for three Millwall players, although nothing ever came of the rumours.

Amid all the mayhem, one deal shone out. Lawrie McMenemy's luring of Kevin Keegan to Southampton for a mere £420,000 was definitely the bargain of the season.

Small fortune: Daley took Manchester City's spending to more than £5m

Where the money went – Deals in excess of £500,000		
Player	**Teams**	**Value***
Andy Gray	Aston Villa to Wolverhampton	£1,469,000
Steve Daley	Wolverhampton to Manchester City	£1,437,500
Kevin Reeves	Norwich to Manchester City	£1,250,000
Steve Archibald	Aberdeen to Tottenham	£900,000
Ray Wilkins	Chelsea to Manchester United	£825,000
Tony Woodcock	Nottingham Forest to Cologne	£650,000
John Gidman	Aston Villa to Everton	£650,000
Mike Flanagan	Charlton to Crystal Palace	£650,000
Peter Withe	Newcastle to Aston Villa	£500,000

*prices are based on press estimates

Going one better: Wolves spent £1.5m on Andy Gray

How McMenemy captured Keegan

ON FEBRUARY 11 Southampton manager Lawrie McMenemy pulled off a secret transfer coup to rival Keith Burkinshaw's capture of Osvaldo Ardiles and Ricky Villa 18 months earlier. McMenemy's star signing was Kevin Keegan. In both instances the tabloid press – who normally live off such stories – only discovered what was going on when it was formally announced.

In Keegan's case McMenemy had lured football reporters to a country hotel in Hampshire "to meet somebody who will play a big part in Southampton's future." Then he produced, like a rabbit out of a hat, Kevin Keegan. There were gasps of astonishment at McMenemy's conjuring trick.

Keegan, who had left Liverpool three years previously to ply his skills on the Continental stage with Hamburg, had twice been voted European footballer of the year (only the second player to have achieved this) and was one of the hottest properties around. When he had announced that he intended leaving Hamburg at the end of the season, it was assumed that a big Italian, or Spanish, club would lash out a fortune for his services and therefore no English club could compete. And,

This way forward: Keegan comes back to England from Germany

anyway, Liverpool had first refusal on his signature.

McMenemy saw it differently. He knew that transfers between EEC countries were restricted to £500,000 and therefore Keegan was affordable. He also believed that Keegan probably would not want to risk being overshadowed by Kenny Dalglish, his replacement at Anfield and who was now the current darling of the Kop, by returning to Anfield. So McMenemy set to work.

He checked that Keegan would prefer a move to England, particularly as he wished to be part of the England set-up before the 1982 World Cup. Trusting his instincts, McMenemy waylaid Keegan before

England's European championship qualifier against Eire on February 6. After a three-hour discussion, where McMenemy laid out Southampton's plans and ambitions, Keegan was convinced. Especially as he would be teaming up with his best friend in football, Mick Channon. Once it was clear he had Keegan in place Liverpool waived their option and Hamburg, resigned to losing him, settled for £420,000.

The significance of Keegan's decision to return home rather than stay abroad was not lost on Ron Greenwood, the England manager. "Kevin's availability is of the utmost importance to England," he said on hearing the news.

Shilton's blunder ends Forest's reign

NOTTINGHAM FOREST were starting to develop an Indian sign over Liverpool in Cup competitions as, once again, Forest brought about Liverpool's downfall in the League Cup.

Liverpool only had themselves to blame in both legs of the semi-final. In the first, at the City Ground, Ray Clemence brought down Garry Birtles in the last minute and John Robertson converted the penalty kick. Then, at Anfield, Liverpool conceded another penalty which was scored by Robertson. Despite David Fairclough's late goal, Forest reached the final for the third year running.

Their opponents at Wembley were Wolverhampton, who had to overcome two of the surprise teams in the competition. In the fifth round Wolves needed two replays to beat the Third Division highfliers Grimsby, who had already accounted for Second Division Notts County and First Division Everton.

Then they lost the first leg of the semi-final to Swindon before a 3-1 win at Molineux just gave them the verdict 4-3 on aggregate. Swindon themselves had taken two First Division scalps, Stoke and Arsenal after extra time in a replay.

Forest's hopes of winning the League Cup for the third time in

a row were dashed by a terrible blunder by the usually dependable Peter Shilton.

Peter Daniel lofted the ball into the Forest penalty area. David Needham appeared to have the cross covered but Shilton raced off his line and ran straight into his defender. Andy Gray was able to take advantage of the confusion and slip his shot between the two stranded Forest players.

Shilton claimed that he had called for the ball, but said that Needham probably had not heard him above the noise of the crowd. He admitted that the only goal of an otherwise sterile match was his fault.

Needham: defensive mix-up

Harlow's bark was nearly as good as their bite

EVERY DOG, it is said, has its day and this year it was Harlow Town's turn to wag their tail in the FA Cup. The Isthmian League team had to come through five qualifying games, but once they reached the competition proper they really had the bit between their teeth.

The Essex team specialised in containing League opponents in the first match and then surprising them in the replay. In the second round Harlow drew at Southend and then beat them 1-0 three days later. In the third round, once again they came from behind to draw at Leicester and then prevailed 1-0 in the replay at Harlow Sports Centre.

Harlow were finally collared at Watford in the fourth round but not before they almost snatched another draw. Harlow led 1-0 at the interval but Watford bit back with four goals early in the second half. Harlow rallied with two more goals but this time the equaliser was beyond them.

Brooking profits from Arsenal's labours

WHEN Trevor Brooking won the FA Cup for West Ham with only the third headed goal of his career, Arsenal must have wondered if it had been worth all the blood, sweat and tears they had had to endure to reach the final for the third consecutive time, the first club this century to do so. After all, to lose to a 13th minute goal from a Stuart Pearson mis-hit shot that was deflected off Brooking's forehead was scant reward for the heroics Arsenal performed against Liverpool in the semi-final.

It was the most protracted semi-final in the history of the Cup, stretching over four games and 420 minutes of football, and was supposed to produce the eventual Cup winners.

Liverpool and Arsenal began with a 0-0 draw at Hillsborough on April 12, moved on to Villa Park and a pair of 1-1 draws before a change of venue, Highfield Road, Coventry, settled the tie with a Brian Talbot goal. It was May 1, nine days before the final and Arsenal still had two League games to play.

On the day, Arsenal were clearly suffering from their earlier labours and, of course, West Ham had had ample opportunity to analyse their Cup style during the semi-final replays. They took full advantage and, having gone ahead, simply closed them down, and became the third Second Division club in eight years to win the FA Cup. Their margin of victory would probably have been greater if Willie Young had not cynically brought down Paul Allen – the youngest player ever to appear in a final – just outside the area when he was clear.

Stoops to conquer: Brooking's header turned out to be Arsenal's undoing

230

Ferguson and Aberdeen finally end Old Firm's monopoly of the title

ALEX FERGUSON, in only his second season in charge of Aberdeen, pulled off the impossible. He broke the Old Firm duopoly of the League championship for the first time since Kilmarnock in 1965, and gave Pittodrie only their second championship in their 77-year history. But Ferguson's miracle was a damned close-run thing.

For nearly all of the season Celtic had led the table, and at one point had been 10 points clear of Aberdeen, although because of the weather and their League Cup run, they did have three games in hand. But come March Aberdeen mounted a relentless challenge, made all the more interesting because postponed fixtures meant they had to play Celtic twice in the League, away. Could Aberdeen steal the championship from Celtic at Parkhead? Unthinkable.

In the first match, on April 5, Drew Jarvie and Mark McGhee provided the goals to defeat Celtic 2-1. Now the jitters were beginning to show as Celtic

went down 3-0 to Dundee United, although with six games to play Aberdeen still trailed by three points. Celtic then spectacularly crashed 5-1 at Dundee, who were already doomed to relegation, while Aberdeen beat Kilmarnock 3-1.

The crunch match – the game that would almost certainly determine the title – was on April 23 at Parkhead. A George McCluskey penalty gave Celtic the lead, but Steve Archibald, McGhee and Gordon Strachan silenced the Glasgow crowd to rack up a 3-1 win, taking Aberdeen to the top of the Premier Division for the first time that season.

On May 3, Aberdeen, in their penultimate fixture, travelled to Easter Road to play Hibs, while Celtic were playing their final fixture at Love Street against St Mirren. If Aberdeen won and Celtic drew then the championship would – barring mathematical miracles – belong to Aberdeen. Ferguson's team turned on the style and Hibs were duly routed 5-0.

Strachan: turning point

Meanwhile the visiting fans waited for news from Love Street where the match was running late. With minutes remaining, the game was still scoreless when the news went round that Celtic were being awarded a penalty. The referee consulted his linesman, awarded a free-kick outside the box and, shortly afterwards, blew the whistle. Instant jubilation. Aberdeen, providing they didn't lose by 10 goals at Partick Thistle on the following Tuesday (they drew 1-1) were the champions for the first time in 25 years.

Penalty misses in European final deepen Arsenal's season of gloom

"LUCKY old Arsenal," has been the taunt down the decades, and if ever that taunt was going to be forgotten, then May 1980 was the month that should have done it. Four days after losing the FA Cup final Arsenal travelled to the Heysel stadium in Brussels to meet Valencia in the European Cup Winners Cup final. It was Arsenal's 16th match in 46 days.

Valencia were formidable opponents: they were managed by Alfredo di Stefano and had Argentina's World Cup striker, Mario Kempes, and West Germany's Rainer Bonhof, in their team. Yet true to the modern tradition it was a final that both teams refused to either lose or win. After 120 minutes of counter-play, the winner would

be decided by the lottery of a penalty shoot-out. It was the first time a European final would be settled this way.

Kempes took the first penalty and missed. Liam Brady then stepped up. If he scored then Arsenal would have the clear advantage and the pressure would be on the Spanish team. Brady, of all people, fluffed the opportunity. Now the pressure fluctuated back and forth. After eight successful penalties, the contest entered sudden death. Arias put Valencia 5-4 ahead. Graham Rix, 22, had to level the scores or Arsenal had lost. Pereira, the Valencia goalkeeper, moved as Rix shot, but the keeper had guessed right and saved the penalty.

Arsenal's misery was not

over. There was still a Uefa Cup place up for grabs if they won both of their remaining League matches. Two days after the Heysel final they scrambled a 2-1 win at Wolves, but 48 hours after that match their last glimmering hope of rescuing something disappeared. They collapsed 5-0 at Middlesbrough.

Luck just had not rubbed Arsenal's way, despite all their efforts, bravery and determination. As a footnote to a season of failure, they set two incredible records: they were the first English side to play 70 competitive matches in a single season, and they were the first club – who had not lost a game in the competition – to fail to win a European trophy having reached the final.

Rix: heartbroken

Victory for Revie does him no good

DON REVIE's courtroom battle against the FA in December did little to enhance the image of English football.

Revie, banned for 10 years for walking out of the England manager's job to take a highly-paid post in the United Arab Emirates, won the argument that the penalty that had been imposed was an unfair restraint of trade. But during the two-week court case he hardly enhanced his reputation.

Revie's barrister grilled Sir Harold Thompson, the chairman of the FA, about the way Revie had been found guilty of bringing the game into disrepute. But Revie fared little better when he was cross-examined about his motives.

The court found in Revie's favour, with Mr Justice Cantley saying that Thompson had shown a "likelihood of bias" when he was the chairman of the FA inquiry into Revie's conduct. As a result, the 10-year ban had to be overturned.

But Mr Justice Cantley said that he made the ruling "with great regret". He said: "The way Mr Revie resigned presented a sensational and outrageous example of disloyalty, breach of duty, discourtesy and selfishness."

Ted Croker, the FA secretary, said that the judge's ruling had shown that the FA were justified in charging Revie with bringing the game into disrepute. Although, technically, there was nothing to stop the FA taking further action they were not going to pursue the case because they did not want to appear to be vindictive.

England's honour in tatters

ENGLAND, who had comfortably qualified for the European championships in Italy, had high hopes. Kevin Keegan had even said when he signed for Southampton in February that they would win the competition. By the end of a tedious tournament – bar the final – England's reputation was in tatters, both on the field and, more importantly off it.

It might all have been so different if Belgium had not equalised in England's opening match in Turin on June 12. Ray Wilkins had sprung Belgium's offside trap in the 32nd minute, but then Ceulemans equalised six minutes later and fighting broke out on the terraces between Italian and English fans.

The crowd was some 15,000, of which a large number were England supporters somewhat the worse for drink. When the Italians began taunting them about the equaliser, scuffles broke out, seats were torn up and serious fighting ensued behind the England goal. The Italian police stepped in smartly and dispersed the fracas with batons and tear gas.

Unfortunately the gas spread to the pitch and play was held up for five minutes as the players, eyes streaming, fought to regain their breath. Although Tony Woodcock seemed to have grabbed the winner in the 73rd minute – it was ruled offside – the match had effectively been ended by the crowd trouble. More than 70 fans were taken to hospital, and the next day Uefa fined the FA £8,000.

A dark cloud now hung over the event. Italy, their players and officials still reeling from the scandal of bribery allegations against AC Milan and other clubs, did not help matters by playing the most sterile football ever seen at a major tournament.

Their single goal in three matches – against England – was a result of a lacklustre tackle by Phil Neal on Graziani. Fortunately the host nation's spinelessness cost them a place in the final when Belgium outdid them at their own craven game,

Star turn: Schuster brightened the tournament

Flashpoint: England fans rioted after Belgium's goal

secured a 0-0 draw and eliminated them having scored more goals.

The one bright spot in the entire event was Belgium's match with West Germany, who had introduced the youngsters Bernd Schuster, 20, the revelation of the tournament, and

Hans Peter Briegel, 24, into an already impressive side. West Germany's 2-1 victory confirmed them as the pre-eminent European side, but it took a goal three minutes from time headed home by Horst Hrubesch – his second in the match – to shake off the Belgian challenge.

Canny Paisley looks to the future

EMLYN HUGHES had left Liverpool before the season started, and some of the other players were starting to show their age. That apart, nothing much had changed at Liverpool.

After a couple of early setbacks they did the one thing that they were best at – not lose. Sixteen games without defeat took them to the top of the table, and once they had got there in December they were not going to be dislodged. Liverpool's progress was not quite as smooth as last season but they still won the title with a game in hand.

Paisley, meanwhile had his eye on the future. During the summer he heeded the advice of one of his scouts and spent £300,000 on a striker who had only played 33 times in the Fourth Division for Chester – Ian Rush.

Plucked from obscurity: Rush had only played 33 matches

Forest overcome every obstacle to stay on top of Europe's summit

BRIAN CLOUGH was far from happy with some of his players' efforts in the League. After a defeat by Bolton he fulminated: "I know what their approach is to their wages, cars, houses, agents and newspaper columns. I want to know what their attitude to football is, because that's where everything else stems from."

But Clough could have no complaints about his players' attitude in the European Cup. Each round set them a harder task and each time his team responded with more determination.

At least this time the draw kept Nottingham Forest and Liverpool apart in the first round. But Liverpool surprisingly fell at the first hurdle for the second successive year when they badly underestimated the threat posed by Dynamo Tbilisi, losing 3-0 in Russia.

Forest had few problems, apart from the distances they had to travel, against Oester Vaxjo of Sweden and Arges

Pitesti of Romania in the first two rounds. The hard work really started in the quarter-finals.

Dynamo Berlin left the City Ground with a 1-0 advantage but Forest were quick to wipe that out in East Berlin, scoring three goals in the first half with Trevor Francis scoring twice and John Robertson adding a penalty.

With Ajax, Real Madrid and Hamburg the other semi-finalists there were not going to be any easy games. This time Forest did not falter at home and the Francis and Robertson (with yet another penalty) double act was in fine form. Their two goals enabled Forest to withstand a 1-0 defeat at Ajax.

In the final, against Hamburg, Forest were severely hampered. Francis had torn an Achilles tendon and could not play, Peter Shilton limped through the game with a pain-killing injection in his pulled calf muscle, and Stan Bowles had walked out on the club.

With the disruption of his team, Clough, not surprisingly, decided a cautious approach was needed on May 28. He packed the Forest midfield to counter the threat posed by Kevin Keegan and chose to play on the break.

The tactics worked to perfection in the 20th minute when Robertson finished a quick counter-attack with a thunderous shot from outside the area that went in off the post. Forest then shut up shop with Shilton, despite his injury, determined not to make another mistake as he had done in the League Cup final.

So the European Cup returned to England for the fourth year in succession and Forest became only the second English club after Liverpool to retain the trophy. Clough, after his earlier complaints about his players, was delighted: "The odds were stacked against us but it was the best 90 minutes we ever had. It was absolutely marvellous."

Robertson: broke deadlock

233

LEAGUE TABLES AND RESULTS 1970–1980

	1970-71	1971-72	1972-73	1973-74	1974-75
WORLD CUP				West Germany 2 Holland 1	
EUROPEAN CHAMPIONSHIP		West Germany 3 USSR 0			
EUROPEAN CUP	Ajax 2 Panathinaikos 0	Ajax 2 Inter Milan 0	Ajax 1 Juventus 0	Bayern Munich 4 Atletico Madrid 0, after 1-1	Bayern Munich 2 Leeds United 0
EUROPEAN CUP WINNERS CUP	Chelsea 2 Real Madrid 1, after 1-1	Rangers 3 Dynamo Moscow 2	AC Milan 1 Leeds United 0	Magdeburg 2 AC Milan 0	Dynamo Kiev 3 Ferencvaros 0
FAIRS CUP – UEFA CUP (1971)	Leeds United beat Juventus 2-2 1-1 on away goals	Tottenham Hotspur beat Wolverhampton Wanderers 2-1 1-1	Liverpool beat Borussia Moenchengladbach 3-0 0-2	Feyenoord beat Tottenham Hotspur 2-2 2-0	Borussia Moenchengladbach beat Twente Enschede 0-0 5-1
FA CUP	Arsenal 2 Liverpool 1	Leeds United 1 Arsenal 0	Sunderland 1 Leeds United 0	Liverpool 3 Newcastle United 0	West Ham United 2 Fulham 0

FIRST DIVISION

1970-71
	P	W	D	L	F	A	Pts
Arsenal	42	29	7	6	71	29	65
Leeds	42	27	10	5	72	30	64
Tottenham	42	19	14	9	54	33	52
Wolves	42	22	8	12	64	54	52
Liverpool	42	17	17	8	42	24	51
Chelsea	42	18	15	9	52	42	51
Soton	42	17	12	13	56	44	46
Man Utd	42	16	11	15	65	66	43
Derby	42	16	10	16	56	54	42
Coventry	42	16	10	16	37	38	42
Man City	42	12	17	13	47	42	41
Newcastle	42	14	13	15	44	46	41
Stoke	42	12	13	17	44	48	37
Everton	42	12	13	17	54	60	37
Huddersf'd	42	11	14	17	40	49	36
Nottm F	42	14	8	20	42	61	36
West Brom	42	10	15	17	58	75	35
C Palace	42	12	11	19	39	57	35
Ipswich	42	12	10	20	42	48	34
West Ham	42	10	14	18	47	60	34
Burnley	*42*	*7*	*13*	*22*	*29*	*63*	*27*
Blackpool	*42*	*4*	*15*	*23*	*34*	*66*	*23*

1971-72
	P	W	D	L	F	A	Pts
Derby	42	24	10	8	69	33	58
Leeds	42	24	9	9	73	31	57
Liverpool	42	24	9	9	64	30	57
Man City	42	23	11	8	77	45	57
Arsenal	42	22	8	12	58	40	52
Tottenham	42	19	13	10	63	42	51
Chelsea	42	18	12	12	58	49	48
Man Utd	42	19	10	13	69	61	48
Wolves	42	18	11	13	65	57	47
Sheff Utd	42	17	12	13	61	60	46
Newcastle	42	15	11	16	49	52	41
Leicester	42	13	13	16	41	46	39
Ipswich	42	11	16	15	39	53	38
West Ham	42	12	12	18	47	51	36
Everton	42	9	18	15	37	48	36
West Brom	42	12	11	19	42	54	35
Stoke	42	10	15	17	39	56	35
Coventry	42	9	15	18	44	67	33
Soton	42	12	7	23	52	80	31
C Palace	42	8	13	21	39	65	29
Nottm F	*42*	*8*	*9*	*25*	*47*	*81*	*25*
Huddersf'd	*42*	*6*	*13*	*23*	*27*	*59*	*25*

1972-73
	P	W	D	L	F	A	Pts
Liverpool	42	25	10	7	72	42	60
Arsenal	42	23	11	8	57	43	57
Leeds	42	21	11	10	71	45	53
Ipswich	42	17	14	11	55	45	48
Wolves	42	18	11	13	66	54	47
West Ham	42	17	12	13	67	53	46
Derby	42	19	8	15	56	54	46
Tottenham	42	16	13	13	58	48	45
Newcastle	42	16	13	13	60	51	45
Birmingham	42	15	12	15	53	54	42
Man City	42	15	11	16	57	60	41
Chelsea	42	13	14	15	49	51	40
Soton	42	11	18	13	47	52	40
Sheff Utd	42	15	10	17	51	59	40
Stoke	42	14	10	18	61	56	38
Leicester	42	10	17	15	40	46	37
Everton	42	13	11	18	41	49	37
Man Utd	42	12	13	17	44	60	37
Coventry	42	13	9	20	40	55	35
Norwich	42	11	10	21	36	63	32
C Palace	*42*	*9*	*12*	*21*	*41*	*58*	*30*
West Brom	*42*	*9*	*10*	*23*	*38*	*62*	*28*

1973-74
	P	W	D	L	F	A	Pts
Leeds	42	24	14	4	66	31	62
Liverpool	42	22	13	7	52	31	57
Derby	42	17	14	11	52	42	48
Ipswich	42	18	11	13	67	58	47
Stoke	42	15	16	11	54	42	46
Burnley	42	16	14	12	56	53	46
Everton	42	16	12	14	50	48	44
QPR	42	13	17	12	56	52	43
Leicester	42	13	16	13	51	41	42
Arsenal	42	14	14	14	49	51	42
Tottenham	42	14	14	14	45	50	42
Wolves	42	13	15	14	49	49	41
Sheff Utd	42	14	12	16	44	49	40
Man City	42	14	12	16	39	46	40
Newcastle	42	13	12	17	49	48	38
Coventry	42	14	10	18	43	54	38
Chelsea	42	12	13	17	56	60	37
West Ham	42	11	15	16	55	60	37
Birmingham	42	12	13	17	52	64	37
Soton	*42*	*11*	*14*	*17*	*47*	*68*	*36*
Man Utd	*42*	*10*	*12*	*20*	*38*	*48*	*32*
Norwich	*42*	*7*	*15*	*20*	*37*	*62*	*29*

1974-75
	P	W	D	L	F	A	Pts
Derby	42	21	11	10	67	49	53
Liverpool	42	20	11	11	60	39	51
Ipswich	42	23	5	14	66	44	51
Everton	42	16	18	8	56	42	50
Stoke	42	17	15	10	64	48	49
Sheff Utd	42	18	13	11	58	51	49
Middlesbro	42	18	12	12	54	40	48
Manchester	42	18	10	14	54	54	46
Leeds	42	16	13	13	57	49	45
Burnley	42	17	11	14	68	67	45
QPR	42	16	10	16	54	54	42
Wolves	42	14	11	17	57	54	39
West Ham	42	13	13	16	58	59	39
Coventry	42	12	15	15	51	62	39
Newcastle	42	15	9	18	59	72	39
Arsenal	42	13	11	18	47	49	37
Birmingham	42	14	9	19	53	61	37
Leicester	42	12	12	18	46	60	36
Tottenham	42	13	8	21	52	63	34
Luton	42	11	11	20	47	65	33
Chelsea	*42*	*9*	*15*	*18*	*42*	*72*	*33*
Carlisle	*42*	*12*	*5*	*25*	*43*	*59*	*29*

SECOND DIVISION

1970-71	1971-72	1972-73	1973-74	1974-75
Champions: Leicester City Also promoted: Sheffield United Relegated: Blackburn Rovers, Bolton Wanderers	Champions: Norwich City Also promoted: Birmingham City Relegated: Charlton Athletic, Watford	Champions: Burnley Also promoted: Queen's Park Rangers Relegated: Huddersfield Town, Brighton & Hove Albion	Champions: Middlesbrough Also promoted: Luton Town, Carlisle United Relegated: Crystal Palace, Preston North End, Swindon Town	Champions: Manchester United Also promoted: Aston Villa, Norwich City Relegated: Millwall, Cardiff City, Sheffield Wednesday

THIRD DIVISION

1970-71	1971-72	1972-73	1973-74	1974-75
Champions: Preston North End Also promoted: Fulham Relegated: Reading, Bury, Doncaster Rovers, Gillingham	Champions: Aston Villa Also promoted: Brighton & Hove Albion Relegated: Mansfield Town, Barnsley, Torquay United, Bradford City	Champions: Bolton Wanderers Also promoted: Notts County Relegated: Rotherham United, Brentford, Swansea City, Scunthorpe United	Champions: Oldham Athletic Also promoted: Bristol Rovers, York Relegated: Cambridge United, Shrewsbury Town, Southport, Rochdale	Champions: Blackburn Rovers Also promoted: Plymouth Argyle, Charlton Athletic Relegated: Bournemouth, Tranmere Rovers, Watford, Huddersfield Town

FOURTH DIVISION

1970-71	1971-72	1972-73	1973-74	1974-75
Champions: Notts County Also promoted: Bournemouth, Oldham Athletic, York City	Champions: Grimsby Town Also promoted: Southend United, Brentford, Scunthorpe United	Champions: Southport Also promoted: Hereford United, Cambridge United, Aldershot	Champions: Peterborough United Also promoted: Gillingham, Colchester United, Bury	Champions: Mansfield Town Also promoted: Shrewsbury Town, Rotherham United, Chester

LEAGUE CUP

1970-71	1971-72	1972-73	1973-74	1974-75
Tottenham Hotspur 2 Aston Villa 0	Stoke City 2 Chelsea 1	Tottenham Hotspur 1 Norwich City 0	Wolverhampton Wanderers 2 Manchester City 1	Aston Villa 1 Norwich City 0

SCOTTISH CUP

1970-71	1971-72	1972-73	1973-74	1974-75
Celtic 2 Rangers 1, after 1-1	Celtic 6 Hibernian 1	Rangers 3 Celtic 2	Celtic 3 Dundee United 0	Celtic 3 Airdrie 1

SCOTTISH FIRST DIVISION

1970-71
	P	W	D	L	F	A	Pts
Celtic	34	25	6	3	89	23	56
Aberdeen	34	24	6	4	68	18	54
St J'stone	34	19	6	9	59	44	44
Rangers	34	16	9	9	58	34	41
Dundee	34	14	10	10	53	45	38
Dundee	34	14	8	12	53	54	36
Falkirk	34	13	9	12	46	53	35
Morton	34	13	8	13	44	44	34
Motherwell	34	13	8	13	43	47	34
Airdrie	34	13	8	13	60	65	34
Hearts	34	13	7	14	41	40	33
Hibernian	34	10	10	14	47	53	30
Kilmarnock	34	10	8	16	43	67	28
Ayr	34	9	8	17	37	54	26
Clyde	34	8	10	16	33	59	26
Dunfermline	34	6	11	17	44	56	23
St Mirren	*34*	*7*	*9*	*18*	*38*	*56*	*23*
Cowdenb'th	*34*	*7*	*3*	*24*	*33*	*77*	*17*

1971-72
	P	W	D	L	F	A	Pts
Celtic	34	28	4	2	96	28	60
Aberdeen	34	21	8	5	80	26	50
Rangers	34	21	2	11	71	38	44
Hibernian	34	19	6	9	62	34	44
Dundee	34	14	13	7	59	38	41
Hearts	34	13	13	8	53	49	39
Partick	34	12	10	12	53	54	34
St J'stone	34	12	8	14	52	58	32
Dundee	34	12	7	15	55	70	31
Motherwell	34	11	7	16	49	69	29
Kilmarnock	34	11	6	17	49	64	28
Ayr	34	9	10	15	40	58	28
Morton	34	10	7	17	46	52	27
Falkirk	34	10	7	17	44	60	27
Airdrie	34	7	12	15	44	76	26
East Fife	34	5	15	14	34	61	25
Clyde	*34*	*7*	*10*	*17*	*33*	*66*	*24*
Dunfermline	*34*	*7*	*9*	*18*	*31*	*50*	*23*

1972-73
	P	W	D	L	F	A	Pts
Celtic	34	26	5	3	93	28	57
Rangers	34	26	4	4	74	30	56
Hibernian	34	19	7	8	74	33	45
Aberdeen	34	16	11	7	61	34	43
Dundee	34	17	9	8	68	43	43
Ayr	34	16	8	10	50	51	40
Dundee	34	17	5	12	56	51	39
Motherwell	34	11	9	14	38	48	31
East Fife	34	11	8	15	46	54	30
Hearts	34	12	6	16	39	50	30
St J'stone	34	10	9	15	52	67	29
Morton	34	10	8	16	47	53	28
Partick	34	10	8	16	40	53	28
Falkirk	34	7	12	15	38	56	26
Arbroath	34	9	8	17	39	63	26
Dumbarton	34	6	11	17	43	72	23
Kilmarnock	*34*	*7*	*8*	*19*	*40*	*71*	*22*
Airdrie	*34*	*4*	*8*	*22*	*34*	*75*	*16*

1973-74
	P	W	D	L	F	A	Pts
Celtic	34	23	7	4	82	27	53
Hibernian	34	20	9	5	75	42	49
Rangers	34	21	6	7	67	34	48
Aberdeen	34	13	13	6	46	26	42
Dundee	34	16	7	11	67	48	39
Hearts	34	14	10	10	54	43	38
Ayr	34	15	8	11	44	40	38
Dundee	34	16	4	14	53	51	36
Motherwell	34	14	7	13	45	40	35
Dumbarton	34	11	7	16	43	58	29
Partick	34	9	10	15	33	46	28
St J'stone	34	9	10	15	41	60	28
Arbroath	34	10	7	17	52	69	27
Morton	34	8	10	16	37	49	26
Clyde	34	8	9	17	29	65	25
Dunfermline	34	8	8	18	43	65	24
East Fife	*34*	*9*	*6*	*19*	*26*	*51*	*24*
Falkirk	*34*	*4*	*14*	*16*	*33*	*58*	*22*

1974-75
	P	W	D	L	F	A	Pts
Rangers	34	25	6	3	86	33	56
Hibernian	34	20	9	5	69	37	49
Celtic	34	20	5	9	81	41	45
Dundee	34	19	7	8	72	43	45
Aberdeen	34	16	9	9	66	43	41
Dundee	34	16	6	12	48	42	38
Ayr	34	14	8	12	50	61	36
Hearts	34	11	13	11	47	52	35
St J'stone	34	11	12	11	41	44	34
Motherwell	34	14	5	15	52	57	33
Airdrie	34	11	9	14	43	55	31
Kilmarnock	34	8	15	11	52	68	31
Partick	34	10	10	14	48	62	30
Dumbarton	34	7	10	17	44	55	24
Dunfermline	34	7	9	18	46	66	23
Clyde	34	6	10	18	40	63	22
Morton	*34*	*6*	*10*	*18*	*31*	*62*	*22*
Arbroath	*34*	*5*	*7*	*22*	*34*	*66*	*17*

SCOTTISH SECOND DIV

1970-71	1971-72	1972-73	1973-74	1974-75
Champions: Partick Thistle Also promoted: East Fife	Champions: Dumbarton Also promoted: Arbroath	Champions: Clyde Also promoted: Dunfermline Athletic	Champions: Airdrie Also promoted: Kilmarnock	Champions: Falkirk Runners-up: Queen of the South

SCOTTISH LEAGUE CUP

1970-71	1971-72	1972-73	1973-74	1974-75
Rangers 1 Celtic 0	Partick 4 Celtic 1	Hibernian 2 Celtic 1	Dundee United 1 Celtic 0	Celtic 6 Hibernian 3

	1975-76	1976-77	1977-78	1978-79	1979-80
WORLD CUP			Argentina 3 Holland 1		
EUROPEAN CHAMPIONSHIP	Czechoslovakia 2 West Germany 2; Czechoslovakia won 5-3 on penalties				West Germany 2 Belgium 1
EUROPEAN CUP	Bayern Munich 1 St Etienne 0	Liverpool 3 Borussia Moenchengladbach 1	Liverpool 1 FC Bruges 0	Nottingham Forest 1 Malmo 0	Nottingham Forest 1 SV Hamburg 0
EUROPEAN CUP WINNERS CUP	Anderlecht 4 West Ham United 2	SV Hamburg 2 Anderlecht 0	Anderlecht 4 FK Austria 0	Barcelona 4 Fortuna Dusseldorf 3	Valencia 0 Arsenal 0; Valencia won 5-4 on penalties
UEFA CUP	Liverpool beat FC Bruges 3-2 1-1	Juventus beat Athletic Bilbao 1-0 1-2 on away goals	PSV Eindhoven beat Bastia 0-0 3-0	Borussia Moenchengladbach beat Red Star Belgrade 1-1 1-0	Eintracht Frankfurt beat Borussia M'gladbach 2-3 1-0 on away goals
FA CUP	Southampton 1 Manchester United 0	Manchester United 2 Liverpool 1	Ipswich Town 1 Arsenal 0	Arsenal 3 Manchester United 2	West Ham United 1 Arsenal 0

FIRST DIVISION

1975-76		1976-77		1977-78		1978-79		1979-80	
	P W D L F A Pts		P W D L F A Pts		P W D L F A Pts		P W D L F A Pts		P W D L F A Pts
Liverpool	42 23 14 5 66 31 60	Liverpool	42 23 11 8 62 33 57	Nottm F	42 25 14 3 69 24 64	Liverpool	42 30 8 4 85 16 68	Liverpool	42 25 10 7 81 30 60
QPR	42 24 11 7 67 33 59	Man City	42 21 14 7 60 34 56	Liverpool	42 24 9 9 65 34 57	Nottm F	42 21 18 3 61 26 60	Man Utd	42 24 10 8 65 35 58
Man Utd	42 23 10 9 68 42 56	Ipswich	42 22 8 12 66 39 52	Everton	42 22 11 9 76 45 55	West Brom	42 24 11 7 72 35 59	Ipswich	42 22 9 11 68 39 53
Derby	42 21 11 10 75 58 53	Aston Villa	42 22 7 13 76 50 51	Man City	42 20 12 10 74 51 52	Everton	42 17 17 8 52 40 51	Arsenal	42 18 16 8 52 36 52
Leeds	42 21 9 12 65 46 51	Newcastle	42 18 13 11 64 49 49	Arsenal	42 21 10 11 60 37 52	Leeds	42 18 14 10 70 52 50	Nottm F	42 20 8 14 63 43 48
Ipswich	42 16 14 12 54 48 46	Man Utd	42 18 11 13 71 62 47	West Brom	42 18 14 10 62 53 50	Ipswich	42 20 9 13 63 49 49	Wolves	42 19 9 14 58 47 47
Leicester	42 13 19 10 48 51 45	West Brom	42 16 13 13 62 56 45	Coventry	42 18 12 12 75 62 48	Arsenal	42 17 14 11 61 48 48	Aston Villa	42 16 14 12 51 50 46
Man City	42 16 11 15 64 46 43	Arsenal	42 16 11 15 64 59 43	Aston Villa	42 18 10 14 57 42 46	Aston Villa	42 15 16 11 59 49 46	Soton	42 18 9 15 65 53 45
Tottenham	42 14 15 13 63 63 43	Everton	42 14 14 14 62 64 42	Leeds	42 18 10 14 63 53 46	Man Utd	42 15 15 12 60 63 45	Middlesbro	42 16 12 14 50 44 44
Norwich	42 16 10 16 58 58 42	Leeds	42 15 12 15 48 51 42	Man Utd	42 16 10 16 67 63 42	Coventry	42 14 16 12 58 68 44	West Brom	42 11 19 12 54 50 41
Everton	42 15 12 15 60 66 42	Leicester	42 12 18 12 47 60 42	Birmingham	42 16 9 17 55 60 41	Tottenham	42 13 15 14 48 61 41	Leeds	42 13 14 15 46 50 40
Stoke	42 15 11 16 48 50 41	Middlesbro	42 14 13 15 40 45 41	Derby	42 14 13 15 54 59 41	Middlesbro	42 15 10 17 57 50 40	Norwich	42 13 14 15 58 66 40
Middlesbro	42 15 10 17 46 45 40	Birmingham	42 13 12 17 63 61 38	Norwich	42 11 18 13 52 66 40	Bristol C	42 15 10 17 47 51 40	C Palace	42 12 16 14 41 50 40
Coventry	42 13 14 15 47 57 40	QPR	42 13 12 17 47 52 38	Middlesbro	42 12 15 15 42 54 39	Soton	42 12 16 14 47 53 40	Tottenham	42 15 10 17 52 62 40
Newcastle	42 15 9 18 71 62 39	Derby	42 9 19 14 50 55 37	Wolves	42 12 12 18 51 64 36	Manchester	42 13 13 16 58 56 39	Coventry	42 16 7 19 56 66 39
Aston Villa	42 11 17 14 51 59 39	Norwich	42 14 9 19 47 64 37	Chelsea	42 11 14 17 46 69 36	Norwich	42 7 23 12 51 57 37	Brighton	42 11 15 16 47 57 37
Arsenal	42 13 10 19 47 53 36	West Ham	42 11 14 17 46 65 36	Bristol C	42 11 13 18 49 53 35	Bolton	42 12 11 19 54 75 35	Man City	42 12 13 17 43 66 37
West Ham	42 13 10 19 48 71 36	Bristol C	42 11 13 18 38 48 35	Ipswich	42 11 13 18 47 61 35	Wolves	42 13 8 21 44 68 34	Stoke	42 13 10 19 44 58 36
Birmingham	42 13 7 22 57 75 33	Coventry	42 10 15 17 48 59 35	QPR	42 9 15 18 47 64 33	Derby	42 10 11 21 44 71 31	Everton	42 9 17 16 43 51 35
Wolves	*42 10 10 22 51 68 30*	*Sunderland*	*42 11 12 19 46 54 34*	*West Ham*	*42 12 8 22 52 69 32*	*QPR*	*42 6 13 23 45 73 25*	*Bristol C*	*42 9 13 20 37 66 31*
Burnley	*42 9 10 23 43 66 28*	*Stoke*	*42 10 14 18 28 51 34*	*Newcastle*	*42 6 10 26 42 78 22*	*Birmingham*	*42 6 10 26 37 64 22*	*Derby*	*42 11 8 23 47 67 30*
Sheff Utd	*42 6 10 26 33 82 22*	*Tottenham*	*42 12 9 21 48 72 33*	*Leicester*	*42 5 12 25 26 70 22*	*Chelsea*	*42 5 10 27 44 92 20*	*Bolton*	*42 5 15 22 38 73 25*

	1975-76	1976-77	1977-78	1978-79	1979-80
SECOND DIVISION	Champions: Sunderland Also promoted: Bristol City, West Bromwich Albion Relegated: Oxford United, York City, Portsmouth	Champions: Wolverhampton Wanderers Also promoted: Chelsea, Nottm F Relegated: Carlisle United, Plymouth Argyle, Hereford United	Champions: Bolton Wanderers Also promoted: Southampton, Tottenham Hotspur Relegated: Blackpool, Mansfield Town, Hull City	Champions: Crystal Palace Also promoted: Brighton & Hove Albion, Stoke City Relegated: Sheffield United, Millwall, Blackburn Rovers	Champions: Leicester City Also promoted: Sunderland, Birmingham City Relegated: Fulham, Burnley, Charlton Athletic
THIRD DIVISION	Champions: Hereford United Also promoted: Cardiff City, Millwall Relegated: Aldershot, Colchester United, Southend United, Halifax Town	Champions: Mansfield Town Also promoted: Brighton & Hove Albion, Crystal Palace Relegated: Reading, Northampton Town, Grimsby Town, York City	Champions: Wrexham Also promoted: Cambridge United, Preston North End Relegated: Port Vale, Bradford City, Hereford United, Portsmouth	Champions: Shrewsbury Town Also promoted: Watford, Swansea City Relegated: Peterborough United, Walsall, Tranmere Rovers, Lincoln City	Champions: Grimsby Town Also promoted: Blackburn Rovers, Sheffield Wednesday Relegated: Bury, Southend United, Mansfield Town, Wimbledon
FOURTH DIVISION	Champions: Lincoln City Also promoted: Northampton Town, Reading, Tranmere Rovers	Champions: Cambridge United Also promoted: Exeter City, Colchester United, Bradford City	Champions: Watford Also promoted: Southend United, Swansea City, Brentford	Champions: Reading Also promoted: Grimsby Town, Wimbledon, Barnsley	Champions: Huddersfield Town Also promoted: Walsall, Newport County, Portsmouth
LEAGUE CUP	Manchester City 2 Newcastle United 1	Aston Villa 3 Everton 2, after 0-0 and 1-1	Nottingham Forest 1 Liverpool 0, after 0-0	Nottingham Forest 3 Southampton 2	Wolverhampton Wanderers 1 Nottingham Forest 0
SCOTTISH CUP	Rangers 3 Hearts 1	Celtic 1 Rangers 0	Rangers 2 Aberdeen 1	Rangers 3 Hibernian 2, after 0-0 0-0	Celtic 1 Rangers 0

SCOTTISH PREMIER DIVISION

1975-76		1976-77		1977-78		1978-79		1979-80	
	P W D L F A Pts		P W D L F A Pts		P W D L F A Pts		P W D L F A Pts		P W D L F A Pts
Rangers	36 23 8 5 60 24 54	Celtic	36 23 9 4 79 39 55	Rangers	36 24 7 5 76 39 55	Celtic	36 21 6 9 61 37 48	Aberdeen	36 19 10 7 68 36 48
Celtic	36 21 6 9 71 42 48	Rangers	36 18 10 8 62 37 46	Aberdeen	36 22 9 5 68 29 53	Rangers	36 18 9 9 52 35 45	Celtic	36 18 11 7 61 38 47
Hibernian	36 18 7 11 55 43 43	Aberdeen	36 16 11 9 56 42 43	Dundee	36 16 8 12 42 32 40	Dundee	36 18 8 10 56 37 44	St Mirren	36 15 12 9 56 49 42
Motherwell	36 16 8 12 57 48 40	Dundee	36 16 9 11 54 45 41	Hibernian	36 15 7 14 51 43 37	Aberdeen	36 13 14 9 59 36 40	Dundee	36 12 13 11 43 30 37
Hearts	36 13 9 14 39 45 35	Partick	36 11 13 12 40 44 35	Celtic	36 15 6 15 63 54 36	Hibernian	36 12 13 11 44 48 37	Rangers	36 15 7 14 50 46 37
Ayr	36 14 5 17 46 59 33	Hibernian	36 8 18 10 34 35 34	Motherwell	36 13 7 16 45 52 33	St Mirren	36 15 6 15 45 41 36	Morton	36 14 8 14 51 46 36
Aberdeen	36 11 10 15 49 50 32	Motherwell	36 10 12 14 57 60 32	Partick	36 14 5 17 52 64 33	Morton	36 12 12 12 52 53 36	Partick	36 11 14 11 43 47 36
Dundee	36 12 8 16 46 48 32	Ayr	36 11 8 17 44 68 30	St Mirren	36 11 8 17 52 63 30	Partick	36 13 8 15 42 39 34	Kilmarnock	36 11 11 14 36 52 33
Dundee	*36 11 10 15 49 62 32*	*Hearts*	*36 7 13 16 49 66 27*	*Ayr*	*36 9 6 21 36 68 24*	*Hearts*	*36 8 7 21 39 71 23*	*Dundee*	*36 10 6 20 47 73 26*
St J'stone	*36 3 5 28 28 79 11*	*Kilmarnock*	*36 4 9 23 32 71 17*	*Clydebank*	*36 6 7 23 23 64 19*	*Motherwell*	*36 5 7 24 33 86 17*	*Hibernian*	*36 6 6 24 29 67 18*

	1975-76	1976-77	1977-78	1978-79	1979-80
SCOTTISH FIRST DIVISION	Champions: Partick Thistle Also promoted: Kilmarnock Relegated: Dunfermline Athletic, Clyde	Champions: St Mirren Also promoted: Clydebank Relegated: Raith Rovers, Falkirk	Champions: Morton Also promoted: Hearts Relegated: Alloa, East Fife	Champions: Dundee Also promoted: Kilmarnock Relegated: Montrose, Queen of the South	Champions: Hearts Also promoted: Airdrie Relegated: Arbroath, Clyde
SCOTTISH SECOND DIV	Champions: Clydebank Also promoted: Raith Rovers	Champions: Stirling Albion Also promoted: Alloa	Champions: Clyde Also promoted: Raith Rovers	Champions: Berwick Rangers Also promoted: Dunfermline Athletic	Champions: Falkirk Also promoted: East Stirling
SCOTTISH LEAGUE CUP	Rangers 1 Celtic 0	Aberdeen 2 Celtic 1	Rangers 2 Celtic 1	Rangers 2 Aberdeen 1	Dundee United 3 Aberdeen 0, after 0-0

End of home championship

As an international tournament the home championships had been in the doldrums for years. In the first half of the century, before the four home nations embraced Fifa and entered the World Cup, there was a degree of validity in the importance of the event. Indeed in the 1950 and 1954 World Cups it was designated as a qualifying tournament in its own right with the top two countries qualifying for the finals. But by the 1980s the international fixture list both for club and country was extremely crowded what with European competitions, European championships and World Cup qualifying tournaments. As a consequence the gloss had gone off the championship and only the fixture between Scotland and England attracted sizeable crowds.

And that was another problem. The biennial invasion of the rowdy Scots to Wembley had become more than an irritant – particularly when the Tartan army invaded the pitch at Wembley and demolished the goalposts in 1977. Thus in September the FA announced that there would be no tickets available for spectators from Scotland for the 1981 match in England. The Scottish Supporters' Club unsuccessfully challenged this in the courts citing the Race Relations Act. Then the riots during the Maze hunger strike caused both England and Wales to refuse to play in Belfast. The championship was abandoned despite Scotland having fulfilled all their fixtures. It was the death-knell and the championship was finally killed off in 1984, its centenary year.

236

Wind of change needed

As THE decade started Britain was deep in the grip of recession – inflation was still high and unemployment had passed 2m and was still rising – and football was not immune to the country's financial woes. Attendances were declining and there was a growing number of people within the game who realised that football needed to act before the rot really set in.

So on August 11, just before the season started, the Secretaries, Coaches and Managers Association published their detailed analysis of the problem: "Soccer – the fight for survival. A blueprint for the future." It was a wide-ranging review that combined the best of thinking from the elder statesmen and the brightest young minds – the members of the study group were Alan Dicks, Ken Friar, Harry Haslam, Bill Nicholson, Ron Saunders, Graham Taylor and Terry Venables.

Many of their proposals went to the heart of issues that were to dog football for the next decade. But, as always, chairmen seemed to be more concerned with the interests of their of own club rather than the overall good of the game.

Two days of talks were held in October and an extraordinary general meeting was called on February 9. By then many of the proposals had been rejected (reducing the number of clubs in the top two divisions and regionalising the Third and Fourth Divisions; cutting the size of the majority needed to get decisions taken) and others had been deferred for further discussion (appointing one person to have overall charge of the running of football; introducing professional referees).

Football hooligans? Well there are 92 club chairmen for a start

BRIAN CLOUGH

But some progress was made. At the least the clubs managed to agree to award three points for a win next season, increase the voting power of Third and Fourth Division clubs, and limit the number of matches played on Friday and Sunday.

The issue of Sunday football was the perfect illustration of why somebody was needed to settle disputes between the Football League and the Football Association. Because of the three-day week, the Football League decided to allow games to be played on a Sunday for the first time since 1974. But when Port Vale sought permission from the FA to stage a Cup match on a Sunday they were refused, with the FA re-stating its opposition to Sunday play.

And it wasn't only off the field that football had its troubles. Violence at grounds was also becoming commonplace. When Terry Curran of Sheffield Wednesday was sent off at Oldham on September 6 visiting fans ran amok. The match was held up for half an hour and the incident reduced Jack Charlton, the Wednesday manager, to tears. On the same day, a young Middlesbrough fan died when his head was smashed in outside Ayresome Park after the match with Nottingham Forest. And West Ham were forced to play the second leg of their European Cup Winners' Cup match against Castilla behind closed doors because of the outrageous behaviour of their so-called fans in Madrid.

With spectators increasingly unable to afford to go to watch matches, and ever more worried for their safety if they did, it was little wonder that the wise men's fears were justified. By the end of the season attendances had slumped by 2.7m to 21.9m, costing about £6m in lost gate receipts. The transfer market slumped and many clubs were forced to sell star players at a loss to raise money.

The unacceptable face of football: one of 13 arrests which marred Sheffield Wednesday's match at Oldham

Allison's habits cost City dear

Champagne Charlies: John Bond and Malcolm Allison, two managers who squandered Manchester City's millions

THE BIG-SPENDING, high-living Malcolm Allison duly got his comeuppance the second time around at Maine Road when he was sacked as manager in December by Manchester City yet again. But this time he left the club in a financially parlous state having spent over £4m on players, some of them non-descripts.

Allison had formed a flamboyant managerial partnership with Joe Mercer in the late 1960s and the pair put City – always in the shadow of their more illustrious neighbours, United – firmly on the Manchester map when they won the League championship, the FA Cup, the European Cup Winners' Cup and the League Cup. When Mercer left to be the general manager of Coventry City in 1973, Allison had taken sole charge but the golden era quickly came to a sudden end and he left after eight months.

But by January 1979 the cigar-smoking, champagne Charlie was back in favour at Manchester City and he went on a spending spree that was to leave

English football gasping. In came little known "stars" such as Steve Daley for £1.5m from Wolves, Mick Robinson for £750,000 from Preston North End, Kevin Reeves for £1m from Norwich. And with Brian Clough emulating him at Nottingham Forest the transfer market went haywire. In just over a year Allison had bought 10 players for more than £4m and sold nine – nearly all established stars – for £2.5m. And it did not work. By October and after 12 games of the season City had a paltry four points and a huge overdraft. Exit Allison, enter John Bond of Norwich.

Amazingly the whole process started again as Bond sold seven players (including Daley at a loss of £1m) and lashed out £1.2m for Trevor Francis from Forest. But even Francis did not stay long and was soon off to Italy for £1m, another loss. But as Bond wheeled and dealed in the market that Clough and Allison had inflated, it collapsed on him and City were the losers as Bond spent £3m, only recouping £1.8m. In his first

season Bond had lifted City from the foot of the First Division into a comfortable mid-table place and to the FA Cup final. Yet, inexplicably, the former manager of fiscally responsible Norwich had caught the Allison bug in Manchester and City were never quite the same.

Steve Daley: £1m loss

Kevin Reeves: £1m purchase

Dundee Utd's Cup heroics

ALTHOUGH Alex Ferguson's Aberdeen started the season like a runaway train (only losing one League match in their first 22) before grinding to a halt, the team that stood out was Jim McLean's Dundee United. Under their perfectionist, long-serving manager they reached two Cup finals, winning one. The one they captured, the League Cup in December, was particularly sweet. For a start it was their neighbours and fierce rivals, Dundee of the First Division, that were the victims in the first all-Dundee final. And even better it was played at Dens Park, their rivals' ground and, of course, by retaining the trophy at their expense they proved that last year's victory over Aberdeen had not been a flash in the pan.

Dundee United came close to making it a double five months later in the Scottish Cup final against Rangers. McLean's team, one of the most attractive in the Scottish League, were not overawed by the big boys from Glasgow. After all they had dispensed with Celtic, easy Premier Division champions, 3-2 in the semi-final replay. They knew they could hold their own, and so it proved with Rangers outplayed in a 0-0 draw. Though to be fair, Rangers did miss a last-minute penalty. Last-minute Cup dramatics were nothing new to Rangers. They had flirted with elimination in the fourth round against lowly St Johnstone of the First Division and only a last-gasp goal enabled them to escape with a 3-3 draw. However in the Cup final replay they rediscovered their swagger and cruised through 4-1.

Villa finally the right one

WHAT a difference a few days makes. On Saturday May 9, Ricardo Villa, who had spent much of his time in the shadow of Osvaldo Ardiles, had played one of his most inconspicuous games for Tottenham. The entire Spurs team had been ineffective and, a goal down with only 10 minutes to go, the FA Cup was inexorably slipping away from them.

Keith Burkinshaw, the Tottenham manager, took Villa off and the midfield player tearfully trudged towards the sidelines aware that all of Argentina was watching his humiliation. He was so disconsolate that he wanted nothing more to do with the match. But as he reached the mouth of the tunnel he stopped for one last look back at Wembley.

Tottenham had been awarded a free kick just outside Manchester City's penalty area and Glenn Hoddle was standing over the ball. Tommy Hutchison, who had given City the lead in the first half, knew that Hoddle could bend free kicks so he pulled out of the wall to cover the danger.

Even though he should have stayed put, Hutchison had guessed correctly. Hoddle curled the free kick and Hutchison was in just the right place – if you were a Tottenham fan. Hoddle's shot ricocheted off Hutchison's shoulder past a diving Joe Corrigan, who almost certainly would have saved it otherwise.

Villa, still spurning the bench, headed for the dressing room. But if he was upset then Hutchison, only the second man to score for both sides in an FA Cup final, was mortified. Burkinshaw could have disciplined Villa for his display of petulance, but the Tottenham manager had no hesitation in naming an unchanged side for the replay on the following Thursday. Villa repaid his faith by giving Tottenham an early lead, but City struck back with a stunning volley from Steve Mackenzie and a penalty from Kevin Reeves. Garth Crooks slid a rebound past Corrigan and at long last a final that had started so woefully the Saturday before was coming to life. There were still almost 15 minutes left, and the Cup final's first penalty shoot-out was looking a distinct prospect, when Villa received the ball in midfield.

Spurning the safe, simple square pass, Villa headed towards the penalty area. At first, he did not appear to pose any great threat to City as he moved that way, then this. But Villa was blessed with great strength and he repeatedly rode the defence's challenges, leaving Tommy Caton, Ray Ranson and Nicky Reid flat-footed. As Villa weaved his magic Corrigan was alive to the danger. Corrigan raced off his line but Villa kept his balance, slipped the ball through the goalkeeper's legs and scored an outstanding solo goal.

As the crowd roared its approval Villa's joy knew no bounds. He wheeled away in triumph, the previous disappointment forgotten in the euphoria. "It's great after last Saturday," he said. "I don't know how many players I beat but the thrill was terrific when the ball went into the net. I say thank you to the manager."

Burkinshaw repaid the compliment. "He was pleased that I had so much faith in him. But how can you leave out a player of his quality." That quality won the match single-handed and once again it was the year of the one – the year of destiny that Tottenham fans and the club so faithfully believe in. They were rewarded with a trophy in 1901, 1921, 1951, 1961, 1971, and now in 1981.

Year of destiny: Garth Crooks and Ricardo Villa parade the FA Cup, yet another trophy won in a year of One

Hero and villain: Tommy Hutchison scores for the "right" team to give Manchester City the lead in the Cup final

Saving his best until last: Ricardo Villa scores his breathtaking goal in the replay four days later

Crystal Palace's latest craze: musical chairs with their never-ending hot-seat shuffles

CRYSTAL PALACE, who had been hailed under the managership of Terry Venables as the "Team of the Eighties," had the most disastrous of seasons. They were relegated from the First Division having accumulated a bare 19 points from 42 matches; the ownership of the club changed hands in farcical fashion and they changed managers so frequently it appeared that there was a revolving door to the hot seat at Selhurst Park.

First Venables quit in October to take over Tommy Docherty's job at QPR and was replaced by Ernie Walley on a temporary basis. Within two months Walley was given permanent status and installed with Malcolm Allison, who had been sacked by Manchester City, as

joint managers. It did not last long, and Allison was soon made the sole manager. But meanwhile there was another farce being enacted in the boardroom. In December it emerged that Ernie Clay, the Fulham chairman, was negotiating to take over the shares held by Raymond Bloye, the Palace chairman. There was speculation that Ron Noades, the Wimbledon chairman, was one of many other interested parties. Noades denied this and called the rumours "a joke." By the end of January Noades and his partners had bought 75% of the holding in Palace but Noades still continued to run Wimbledon. In February the League chairmen passed a resolution that no club official could be

involved in the affairs of another club. So Noades announced he was going to sell his shares in Wimbledon, only to change his mind the next day but claim that he would have no say in the affairs of Wimbledon.

With Noades in charge of Palace the managerial hot-seat shuffle re-started as Dario Gradi, the Wimbledon manager, replaced Allison. However Gradi could not stop the inevitable slide into the Second Division, and even there Palace continued their downward spiral with seven losses and a draw in their first 13 League matches. Gradi was promptly sacked in November and Steve Kember was back in charge, the fifth manager Crystal Palace had had in the space of 13 months.

Noades: the Palace Don

239

THE 1980-81 SEASON

European success Ipswich's only consolation as Villa snatch title

IPSWICH TOWN, under the shrewd management of Bobby Robson, were chasing a treble of League championship, FA Cup and Uefa Cup before they fell victim to fixture congestion. Never out of the top three in the First Division they led from August through to the middle of October, regained top spot in January and then faltered in the final eight games. They only won two of their games in that sequence, including beating Aston Villa, the eventual champions 2-1 at Villa Park, and they lost in the FA Cup semi-final to Manchester City.

But in the Uefa Cup they did achieve some consolation, knocking out Cologne and St Etienne before beating AZ 67 Alkmaar 5-4 on aggregate in the final. Robson had put together a wonderfully skilful passing side that he built around the two Dutchmen, Frans Thijssen and Arnold Muhren. And with the goalscoring capacity of Paul Mariner, Alan Brazil, Eric Gates and John Wark – all of whom reached double figures and scored 59 goals between them – only the burden of expectation and the weight of matches stopped Robson's team sweeping all before them.

By contrast, Villa, under Ron Saunders, had a much easier ride. Surprisingly they were beaten three times by Ipswich, yet perhaps their defeat by Ipswich in the third round of the FA Cup was a blessing in disguise. With only the championship to play for, and miraculously avoiding a spate of injuries or suspensions (they only used 14 players in the entire campaign) they carried off their first League title for 71 years.

The road to the championship: Peter Withe scores for Villa against Middlesbrough

Something to shout about: 50,000 fans applaud Bobby Robson's team outside Ipswich town hall

Muhren congratulates Wark

Liverpool prove masters of foreign fields yet again

Still going strong: Souness, Daglish and Hansen hold the European Cup aloft in Paris

I've always said there's a place for the press but they haven't dug it yet

TOMMY DOCHERTY

FOR A WHILE, it looked as if the start of the 1980s was going to mark the beginning of the decline of Liverpool from the great heights of the previous decade. They lost 1-0 to Fourth Division Bradford in the second round of the League Cup before going through on aggregate, went out of the FA Cup in the fourth round at Everton, and drew far too many matches in the League, particularly away.

Liverpool's indifferent performances in the League meant that they only finished fifth, their worst placing in 16 years. And they needed two attempts to beat West Ham and collect the League Cup that had always eluded them in the past.

But Liverpool had not lost their touch entirely, and it seemed that they were saving their best performances for the European Cup, and particularly the home legs. Oulu of Finland were swept aside 10-1 with Graeme Souness and Terry McDermott both scoring hat-tricks, Aberdeen were beaten 4-0 and CSKA Sofia, who had put out Nottingham Forest, the holders, conceded five goals with Souness getting another hat-trick. But Bayern Munich were among those who thought that Liverpool were not the side that they were before. When they drew the first leg of the semi-final 0-0 at Anfield they wrote Liverpool off as an unimaginative side and confidently predicted that they would reach the final.

Bayern, though, had overlooked Liverpool's trademark; their strength in depth. Injuries forced Liverpool to start two reserves, Richard Money and Colin Irwin, in the return match. And when an unfit Kenny Dalglish limped off early in the match he was replaced by another understudy, Howard Gayle.

The Germans had not planned on facing players they had not heard of and this, combined with their over-confidence, was their undoing. They were run ragged and the veteran Ray Kennedy tucked away the decisive goal seven minutes from time. Bayern equalised in the dying seconds, but Liverpool went through on the away goals rule.

The final in Paris on May 27 was widely expected to be a scintillating match with Liverpool facing Real Madrid, six times winners of the competition. But the game did not live up to the anticipation, and the first half was a scrappy, niggling affair. The second half was little better, although it gradually became apparent that the remorseless play of Liverpool was grinding Real down.

With eight minutes remaining it was Ray Kennedy who, once again, proved to be decisive. His throw in released Alan Kennedy, whose powerful run took him past a feeble tackle from Cortes, the Real right back. Alan Kennedy had been forced wide and Agustin, the goalkeeper, was quick off his line to close down the angle. But Kennedy kept his cool and forced the ball through the narrowest of gaps between Agustin and the near post.

Although it was not the best of games it confirmed Liverpool's and Bob Paisley's greatness. Liverpool became only the fourth team to win the European Cup three times, and Paisley was the first ever manager to do the hat-trick.

241

He was dynamic. If you lost a game you lost to rubbish. If you won, you had beaten a great team

ROGER HUNT
on Bill Shankly

Shankly: his deep-rooted affection for the game was infectious and it rubbed off on players and public alike

Shankly, the darling of the Kop, dies

BILL SHANKLY died on September 28 in a Liverpool hospital after a heart attack two days earlier from which the doctors had confidently predicted he would recover. He was the darling of the Kop, the man who had dragged Liverpool out of the Second Division and turned them into one of the greatest clubs in the country. His legacy would mean they would go on to be one of greatest clubs in the world.

His lifelong love affair with football had begun 67 years earlier when he had been born into a footballing family in a mining village in Ayrshire. Two of his uncles and all four of his brothers were, or became, professional footballers. Bill would be a Scottish international and win the FA Cup with Preston. The second world war would interrupt his career just, at 25, when he was at his peak. After the war he returned to Preston and played with Tom Finney, whom he idolised. Soon he turned to management with clubs in the lower divisions before Second Division Liverpool appointed him their manager in 1959.

Liverpool had been relegated in 1954 and although they were always narrowly missing out on promotion the board seemed content to jolly along as a successful Second Division club. Shankly did not see it that way but his ambitions were con-

stantly thwarted by the refusal of the directors to spend money on new players. The arrival of an equally ambitious director changed all that and in 1961 Shankly promptly went out and bought Ian St John and Ron Yeats. The next year they were promoted. By 1964 Liverpool were League champions.

Over the next 10 years Shankly's Liverpool would win the championship twice more, the FA Cup twice and the Uefa Cup. He rebuilt his team twice, often unearthing staggering talent such as Emlyn Hughes, Ray Clemence, John Toshack, Steve Heighway and the apple of his eye – Kevin Keegan. The odd blunder was made in the transfer market, often due to his stubborn refusal to admit his mistakes, but by and large he made several spectacular raids.

Europe seemed to have been his Achilles heel. He was naturally xenophobic, hated flying and travelling in general, and was distrustful of most things foreign – in particular their football and their footballers. The European Cup semi-final against Inter Milan in 1965, his first foray into continental competition, confirmed all his worst fears, and certainly embittered him. In the San Siro, with Liverpool holding a comfortable 3-1 lead, the Italian fans jeered his team on to the field and pelted them with bottles and smoke

bombs. The Spanish referee then allowed two Inter goals – one from a blatant foul on the goalkeeper and one from an indirect free-kick – and disallowed a perfectly good Liverpool one. The tie was lost and so were any lingering doubts about foreigners in Shankly's mind.

And yet Shankly bestrode the 1960s. His deep-rooted affection for the game was infectious and it rubbed off on his players and public alike. An eccentric, he became legendary for his wit and instant quips to ingenuous interviewers in that inimitable rasping voice. The most famous of course was: "Football is not a matter of life and death – it's

much more important than that."

His retirement in 1974 immediately after winning the FA Cup came as surprise to everybody. He was 60 and going out at the top, but football was Shankly's life. He had no outside interests, and when Liverpool failed to offer him a directorship or a clear role in the club he felt let down. So much so he would travel to other clubs, other matches where his wit and knowledge were greeted with open arms. His memorial service was attended by tens of thousands as Liverpool flocked to mark the passing of a man who transformed their lives.

Shankly leads out the Preston team in his final season as a player

Toshack the miracle worker rewarded as Swansea take the First Division by storm

SWANSEA CITY'S meteoric rise continued apace as they shot to the top of the First Division only four seasons after playing in the Fourth. Under the inspired managership of John Toshack they took 22 points from their first 10 matches to lead the title race on October 17.

But as the season continued Toshack could not match the consistency of his former club Liverpool, and Swansea soon slipped back. However, they twice regained first place, first over Christmas and then, after a run of seven wins and two draws, again briefly in March. They faded to finish sixth but that, though, was their lowest placing of the season. It was a remarkable performance by a team that had been put together relatively cheaply.

But, among the smaller clubs, what goes up will sooner or later come down again. The bubble burst very quickly and by the start of the 1986 season Swansea were back in the Fourth Division, the heady days of 1981 but a brief memory.

QPR discover it's not so fantastic on plastic

QUEEN'S PARK RANGERS spent the summer tearing up their pitch and replacing it with artificial turf. They saw it as a shrewd investment that would enable Loftus Road to stage other events during the week and bring in more money to the Second Division club.

Their first home match against Luton, themselves soon to experiment with an artificial pitch, created much interest. The press seemed to agree that the new surface was a good idea, with the *Daily Star* saying "it's fantastic on plastic."

But it did not take long for the novelty to wear off. Players were soon moaning about the pace and bounce of the pitch, and there were fears that it was causing more injuries. And after Blackburn lost 2-0 on October 3 they complained to the Football League: "We felt the surface was not suited to good football." Three weeks later, Leicester also complained about the pitch after losing 2-0.

The FA, who were ambivalent about the idea, also had a confrontation with QPR. In November the club said they would withdraw from the FA Cup because they were only going to be allowed to use the pitch on a one-year trial. But the FA made concessions and QPR withdrew the threat.

Although Luton, Oldham and Preston went on to try artificial pitches and various efforts were made to curb the excessive bounce the experiment that the *Daily Star* dubbed "the most important this century" soon fizzled out and before the end of the decade grass was once again growing at Loftus Road.

■ The Football League introduced three points for a win, a decision that was criticised by Alan Durban, the Sunderland manager, on the opening day of the season. After his side had drawn 3-3 at Ipswich he said: "It is outrageous that clubs should lose two points each for drawing after giving a superb exhibition like that."

■ The British transfer record was broken when Bryan Robson (below) moved from West Bromwich to Manchester United for £1.5m on

October 1. The West Brom manager had said "he leaves over my dead body," and the chairman had said he was not for sale "at any price."

■ Bob Lord, the Burnley chairman for 26 years and a former leading light of the Football League, died on December 8, aged 73.

■ Chelsea's fans caused such a disturbance at Derby on November 28 that the FA ordered all their away matches from January 1 to the end of the season to be all-ticket. The ban was lifted in February, just before Chelsea challenged it in the High Court.

■ Sepp Blatter, a former amateur footballer and general secretary of the Swiss Ice Hockey Federation, was elected general secretary of Fifa on January 15.

■ Bad weather during December and January created a backlog of fixtures. The postponed fixtures did not help many clubs facing cashflow problems, and the Fulham manager Malcolm Macdonald suggested that matches should be played during the summer.

■ The Football League management committee proposed to do away with the Fourth Division and replace it with three regional sections of the Third Division. The plan was rejected by Third and Fourth Division clubs in October.

■ The Football League ordered referees to send players off for committing professional fouls next season.

■ Bristol Rovers, in dispute with their landlords, announced plans to share Bristol City's ground in November. But their fans objected so strongly that they resolved the dispute over their rent and stayed at Eastville.

Novelty turn: QPR's artificial surface made its debut against Luton Town on September 1, 1981

THE 1981-82 SEASON

Jimmy Hill leads rebel tour to South Africa

SOUTH AFRICA were desperate to bring high-class sport to their shores and encouraged by a tour of rebel English cricketers they planned a visit by a group of British footballers.

Mindful of international sanctions, Ted Croker, the secretary of the FA, warned that any players who got involved could be putting their career at risk, and Tottenham refused to let Osvaldo Ardiles join the party for fear of prejudicing his transfer to Paris St Germain.

Croker was furious when he discovered that one of the organisers of the trip was Jimmy Hill, the Coventry chairman. "Hill is acting irresponsibly," he said. "It is not South Africa's interest he has at heart." But the tour went ahead in July, with the rebels drawing two matches and winning one. The FA set up a special investigation but took no further action.

England qualify despite Norway debacle

THE radio commentator could not contain himself. "We are the best in the world. We have beaten England. Lord Nelson, Lord Beaverbrook, Sir Winston Churchill, Sir Anthony Eden, Clement Attlee, Henry Cooper, Lady Diana. We have beaten them all. Maggie Thatcher can you hear me? Maggie Thatcher, your boys took a hell of a beating. Norway have beaten England at football."

It was little wonder he was so excited. Norway, everybody's perennial underdogs, had just beaten England 2-1 in Oslo in a Group Four qualifying match for the World Cup. Ron Greenwood, the England manager, said: "We let them play for five minutes and they scored two goals."

It looked as if the defeat on September 9 could cost England their place in the finals. England had already dropped three points to Romania and lost to the equally unfancied Switzerland. They still led the group but only had one match left. Romania, one point behind with two matches in hand, and Hungary, three points behind with three matches in hand, looked set to take the two places on offer in Spain. And Norway and Switzerland were still in with chances.

Fortunately for England every one of the remaining results went in their favour. Romania drew with Hungary and then lost at home to Switzerland. Hungary brushed aside Switzerland and Norway to make sure of their place. Then Romania were held to a goalless draw in Switzerland, which almost put paid to their chances. Thanks in no small part

to their 4-0 drubbing of Norway in the very first match of the group, England knew that a draw with Hungary at Wembley on November 18 would suffice. Hungary, because they had already qualified, looked as if they did not care too much about the result and the only goal of the match from Paul Mariner was enough for England to sneak through to Spain. They were joined by Scotland and Northern Ireland, who both eased their way past Sweden, Portugal and Israel in Group Six. It was the first time since 1958 that Britain had had more than one representative in the finals and it was only goal difference that stopped the home nations making a clean sweep.

The Republic of Ireland finished their campaign with a stirring 3-2 home victory over France on October 14. But they could only sit and watch as France won their last two

Norwegian nightmare: Hallvar Thoresen scores the winning goal in the World Cup qualifying match in Oslo

Sneaking home: Mariner scored the vital goal against Hungary at Wembley

matches to take the second qualifying place in Group Two and eliminate Holland, the beaten finalists in 1978, in the process.

Wales could claim to be even unluckier in Group Three. The match that proved to be their undoing was also on October 14, at Swansea. The floodlights failed, temporarily stopping the match and unsettling Wales, who dropped a crucial point to Iceland in a 2-2 draw.

Aberdeen and Forfar surprise everybody to give Old Firm a close run for their money

BILLY MCNEILL'S Celtic began the season extraordinarily. In the Scottish League Cup in August they faltered alarmingly against St Mirren, losing on the opening day, and then slipped against St Johnstone as well to miss the final stages.

Yet in the League they were in scintillating form: winning their first seven games. In fact they led the table from start to finish. So dominant was their lead that when they met Aberdeen on January 30 everybody assumed it would be the championship decider, and with Celtic triumphant, were already writing their name on the roll of honour. As it turned out, it was the championship decider, but not in the way anybody would have guessed.

It was now Aberdeen's turn to

McNeill: close shave

hit top form and brush aside all opposition. From February 20 to May 15 they won 16 League matches, losing one and drawing one. By the final weekend Celtic's massive lead had been whittled down so much that they were mightily relieved to win

their final match against St Mirren, particularly as Aberdeen had enjoyed a 4-0 goal spree against Rangers at Pittodrie. Aberdeen's consolation was 4-1 victory over Rangers in the Scottish Cup final.

Not all the drama was confined to the Premier Division clubs. Little Forfar Athletic, of the Second Division, were the Cup kings of the season. They reached the quarter-finals of the Scottish League Cup and the semi-finals of the Scottish Cup, having disposed of Hearts, Hamilton and Queen's Park – all of the First Division – en route to a tilt at mighty Rangers. Unfazed by the Ibrox club, Forfar almost pulled off the impossible and Rangers were grateful to escape to a replay in which their class inevitably told.

Liverpool easily run away with the League

BOB PAISLEY started the season by continuing to rebuild Liverpool. Ray Clemence, one of the last players left from the Shankly era was transferred to Tottenham, and Jimmy Case and Ray Kennedy were soon to leave Anfield.

The new-look team took a while to settle and as the New Year started Liverpool were in an unfamiliar position, a lowly 12th in the First Division. But unlike other clubs, they did not suffer too badly from fixture congestion caused by the bad weather in December and January because they went out of the FA Cup in the fifth round and the European Cup in the quarter-finals.

That freed Liverpool to concentrate on the League and by the beginning of March they had climbed to sixth place. After a defeat by Brighton on March 6 they won 11 League matches in a row and did not lose any of their final 16 games.

It was their 13th championship (with a record 87 points, thanks to the introduction of three points for a win) and Paisley said: "I'm proudest of this one because there was so much

to do." An indication of the shrewdness of his rebuilding was that Liverpool only used 16 players in the League throughout the season.

The League Cup final on March 13 was a battle between Liverpool past and Liverpool present. Tottenham led in the

11th minute and their breakaways continually tested Bruce Grobbelaar. But Clemence was finally beaten in the last minutes of the match. Clemence conceded two more goals in extra time and the League Cup was back at Anfield for the second year running.

FOR THE RECORD

■ John Pelosi, the St Johnstone winger, was banned for six months on November 25. He had been sent off for a tackle that broke the leg of Jim Brown of Dunfermline. Brown subsequently decided to sue after being told he was unlikely to play again. Gregor Stevens was also banned for six months in March for breaking a Kilmarnock player's leg. Since he joined Rangers in 1979 Stevens had been sent off five times and booked 19 times.

■ John Hewitt scored in 9.6sec for Aberdeen against Motherwell in the Scottish Cup on January 23. It was the fastest goal in the competition since 1929.

■ Robert Maxwell became the chairman of Oxford United and saved the club by injecting £120,000.

■ Football had its first streaker a week after Erika Roe hit the headlines at Twickenham. Variania Scotney, a 17-year-old waitress from south London, ran topless across the pitch at Highbury as Arsenal were losing 3-1 to Tottenham. Her performance won her an appearance as a page three girl in the Daily Mirror.

■ The League signed a £2m deal with the National Dairy Board on March 1 which led to the League Cup being renamed the Milk Cup.

■ Malcolm Macdonald, the Fulham manager, became the first paid director in England on November 19. The Welsh FA had allowed paid directors earlier in the season.

Extra special: Liverpool snatched an amazing victory in extra time in the League Cup final against Tottenham

Bristol City, Wolves go bust

FOOTBALL reaped the whirlwind of its financial foolishness as the money ran out with a vengeance. The first club to feel the pinch were Bristol City, who had overstretched themselves in the First Division and could not afford their wage bill as the team slid back down the League.

City had lost almost £500,000 the previous season when they were relegated from the Second Division, and by the end of October they were £700,000 in debt (with £120,000 tax outstanding) and losing £3,000 a week. In the week before Christmas two of their directors resigned in order to make way for two local businessmen who promised to raise £500,000 to save the club. But with City wallowing at the foot of the Third Division it was still not enough.

Early in the New Year Bob Houghton resigned as manager and said: "There is nothing more I can do." With losses

reaching more than £4,000 a week accountants were called in to try to save the club.

Their solution was drastic; give eight players, whose wages were costing a staggering £250,000 a year, immediate free transfers. The players used the PFA to try to improve City's offer of compensation but the writing was on the wall on January 26 when the club's chairman said Bristol City would go out of business in a fortnight if agreement was not reached.

Finally, on February 3, the "Ashton Gate Eight" bowed to the inevitable and allowed their contracts to be cancelled clearing the way for the Robins to be reborn from the ashes, although too late to prevent relegation to the Fourth Division.

Wolves, who were relegated from the First Division, went even closer to the brink. Rash spending on players and a £10m bill for the new stand at Molineux left them more than

£2.5m in debt at the end of the season. Then, in early June, Chesterfield issued a writ for an outstanding instalment of a transfer fee. Within a fortnight the Wolves chairman had resigned because "it was impossible for the present board to continue to run the club."

Doug Ellis took over and claimed that the club had been saved with 24 hours to spare, but the problems would not go away and the Official Receiver was called in early in July. Both the League and the Receiver set a deadline for rescue attempts and five consortia battled to raise the money before the end of the month.

In the end Wolves were saved with just three minutes to spare by a group led by Derek Dougan, their former star player. With attendances continuing to fall these were not isolated incidents and many other clubs were forced to make drastic economies just to stay afloat.

Dougan: Wolves' saviour

Aston Villa's novices land the European Cup

ASTON VILLA, the European novices with a novice manager, astounded the continent and probably themselves when they lifted the European Cup. Everybody was especially surprised as they beat the West German champions Bayern Munich, who could boast Paul Breitner in midfield and Karl-Heinz Rummenigge in attack. The European Cup had now been won for six years in succession by an English club.

But who would have thought it would have been Villa? Liverpool, who had won the trophy three times in the previous five seasons, were defending the Cup and Aston Villa's European experience was confined to two Uefa Cup campaigns in 1975-6 and 1977-8. In the first they could not get past the first round, in the second they reached the quarter-finals. And Ron Saunders, the manager who had guided them to their first League title since 1910, walked out in February over a

contractual disagreement leaving Tony Barton, his assistant, in his first managerial post. Although the League champions, Villa were hardly a side composed of household names: Jimmy Rimmer was in goal, Allan Evans in defence, Gordon Cowans, Des Bremner and Dennis Mortimer in midfield, Tony Morley on the left wing, Gary Shaw and Peter Withe in attack. Fortunately their path to the final had not been stuffed with star sides either: Valur Reykjavik of Iceland; Dynamo Berlin of East Germany, whom they beat on away goals; Dynamo Kiev and then Anderlecht of Belgium, who had succumbed by a single goal.

The final in Rotterdam on May 26 should have been a one-sided affair particularly when Rimmer had to go off injured after only eight minutes. The replacement keeper, Nigel Spink, 23, had only played one first team game for Villa. He will never forget his second as

Super sub: Spink comes off the bench to inspire Aston Villa

he played out of his skin and muzzled the predatory Rummenigge. In the 67th minute Morley created a goal of delightful virtuosity from the left wing. He bamboozled the

German right-back, took the ball to the byline and crossed to Withe who scored off the post. It was the only goal, and Villa had proved that inexperience can win the day.

FA Cup scant reward for Tottenham

TOTTENHAM'S centenary year looked to be an *annus mirabilis*. By March they were in the semi-finals of the FA Cup, the final of the League Cup, the semi-finals of the European Cup Winners' Cup and had enough games in hand to capture the League championship.

Then virtually everything went wrong. They lost the League Cup final after extra time (their first defeat in 16 Cup finals, including replays) to Liverpool having led for 87 minutes. A bruising encounter with Barcelona was lost over two legs by a single goal. And a stunning late run of unstoppable form by Liverpool, coupled with a ridiculous fixture backlog – in April and May Tottenham had a colossal 18 fixtures to complete – extinguished their championship aspirations. Worse, on the eve of the FA Cup semi-final against Leicester, Argentina invaded the Falkland Islands and war with Britain looked virtually certain. This placed a great strain on Osvaldo Ardiles and Ricardo Villa, Tottenham's two Argentine aces.

During the semi-final Ardiles was continually booed by the Leicester fans and he left Britain the next day to join Cesar Menotti's defending World Cup side with his future at Spurs in grave doubt. Yet despite the intolerable pressure he was under he made certain that Tottenham would reach their second successive FA Cup final by engineering a magnificent goal. In the 56th minute he received Glenn Hoddle's short corner, eluded a defender and drove a low centre into the penalty area for Garth Crooks to crash home. A spectacular own goal completed Leicester's misery. Tottenham's opponents were to be Second Division QPR, managed by the former Spurs player Terry Venables.

Then, on the eve of the final, history once again conspired to deal Tottenham another blow as the British Task Force approached the Falklands. Diplomatically it didn't seem possible that an Argentinian could take part in one of Britain's great sporting occasions when at any moment there could be news of British fatalities. So Keith Burkinshaw, the manager, and Ricky Villa, the hero of the 1981 final, conceded that he should not play. Villa watched the final on TV at home.

Not that there was much to watch. A long season had taken its toll, the disappointments and the tense political situation only made matters worse. A deflection from Hoddle put Tottenham ahead, but then a Terry Fenwick set-piece goal meant a replay. So five days later they met again at Wembley. Spurs were unchanged, but QPR were now without their captain Glenn Roeder, suspended for a League infringement, and their striker, Clive Allen, who had been injured in the first match. A sixth penalty from Hoddle won a lacklustre final.

So Spurs had won their seventh FA Cup, emulating Aston Villa's record, and repeating their feat of exactly 20 years ago. But the celebrations were short-lived: Ardiles did not return to Britain after the World Cup, signing instead for Paris St Germain on July 5.

FOR THE RECORD

■ **Bobby Robson (above), who had worked wonders at unfashionable Ipswich, was appointed England manager on July 7.**

■ **Diego Maradona joined Barcelona on May 28. They paid a world record £4.2m to Boca Juniors and Argentinos Juniors.**

■ **A fan was stabbed to death after Arsenal's match with West Ham on May 1. The game was held up for more than 10 minutes because of crowd trouble and Terry Neill, the Arsenal manager, said: "It makes you wonder what sort of parents produce mindless morons like this." It was the second football fatality of the season – a fan had also been killed after Tottenham's match against Manchester United on November 21.**

■ **Kevin Keegan was made an OBE in June.**

■ **Alan Mullery resigned as Charlton's manager on June 1 and became Crystal Palace's sixth manager in 20 months three weeks later.**

■ **Jimmy Frizzell, the Oldham manager, was sacked in June after spending 23 years at the club as a player and manager.**

■ **Hereford had a bad season. The directors' wives offered to take over the cleaning duties to save money for the struggling club. And the team was hit so badly by a flu bug that they banned all their players from coming to Edgar Street in late September.**

■ **Wolverhampton finally cancelled the contract of Peter Knowles on June 5. He had walked out of the club in 1969 to become a Jehovah's Witness.**

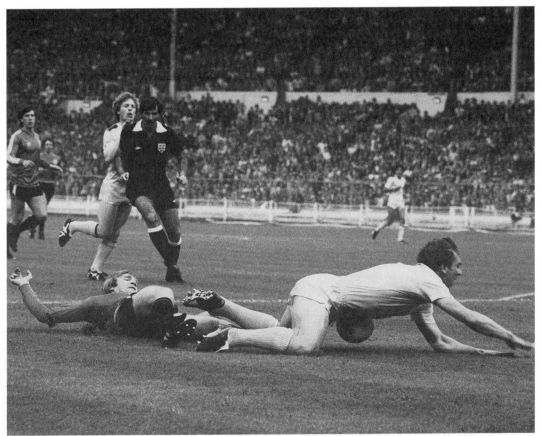

Penalty: Tony Currie brings down Graham Roberts and Glen Hoddle converts the winning spot kick in the replay

247

WORLD CUP 1982

Cynical Italy turn out to be genuine heroes

IT WAS as if there were two Italys playing in the 1982 World Cup finals in Spain. The first cynically chiselled out three draws to qualify for the second phase by the slenderest of margins. The second gloriously exploded on to the world stage and captured the World Cup for the third time.

Italy Mk I began cautiously, with a goalless draw with Poland and a fortunate 1-1 draw against Peru. Their third match against Cameroon, who had refused to be cannon fodder for the rest of the group, would decide who accompanied Poland into the next phase. Cameroon's lack of sophistication and inability to translate possession into goals left them needing to win, despite having drawn their first two matches. The Italians, much more experienced at this level, duly eked out another draw, 1-1, and qualified by virtue of having scored one more goal than their African rivals.

Although Italy Mk I cannot be forgiven for the sterility of their first three games, the tactic of playing not to lose (something they are supposed to be past masters at) was foisted upon the first phase by the political decision of Joao Havelange, the Fifa president, to increase the number of participants. He had done this to reward the Third World countries that had voted him into power by expanding the number of finalists from a sensible and manageable 16 to an overblown and unwieldy 24. Thus, the first phase comprised six groups of four, with the top two in each group qualifying for the next phase i.e. 36 matches were needed to eliminate 12 teams.

With the phoney war over, Enzo Bearzot, their manager, unleashed Italy Mk II and Paolo Rossi with a vengeance. One after another the world's big guns were silenced. Italy's transformation in the second round was a sight to be seen. They were in the same group as Diego Maradona's Argentina and Brazil – who with Eder, Falcao, Junior, Socrates and Zico playing dream football – had rediscovered all the joyous flair that had endeared them to the world in the era of Pele. Against all odds, Italy beat them both.

The match against Brazil was extraordinary. Rossi put Italy ahead in the fifth minute, Socrates equalised seven minutes later only to see Rossi restore Italy's lead in the 25th minute. Brazil, pushing forward exuberantly, levelled the scores again when Falcao dribbled across the penalty area, spotted a gap, and beat Dino Zoff with a stupendous shot. If the score had remained 2-2 then Brazil would have reached the semi-finals but, characteristically, they eschewed any thought of closing the game down. To their cost. Six minutes after the equaliser Rossi completed his hat-trick to the dismay of

Strike force: Armstrong's goal (top) took Northern Ireland into the second round for the first time and Robson was quick off the mark against France

neutral fans all over the world.

Poland, Italy's opponents in the semi-final, were without their key player, Zbigniew Boniek, and succumbed 2-0, both goals coming from Rossi who had clearly discovered a rich vein of form. In the final, in Madrid on July 11, Italy met West Germany and many people thought that their bubble would burst.

In fact, it was the Germans who came down to earth. Even though Antonio Cabrini missed a penalty in the first half there was no stopping Rossi. He put Italy ahead in the 56th minute with a diving header, which established him as the tournament's leading scorer with six goals, and created a goal for Marco Tardelli 13 minutes later. Alessandro Altobelli added a third in the 80th minute and the best that West Germany could muster was a consolation goal from Paul Breitner two minutes later.

Although Italy had begun the tournament in such a craven way, their triumph was well deserved. In successive matches they had beaten Argentina (the world champions), Brazil (the favourites), Poland (who finished third) and West Germany (the European champions). Never mind that these were the only four matches they won in the whole of 1982 – when it mattered Italy beat the best the world could offer.

In the cynicism stakes, West Germany were the real champions. After an amazing 2-1 reverse at the hands of Algeria, everything hinged on West Germany's final game in the first phase. Because Algeria had played the day before, both West Germany and Austria knew that if West Germany won 1-0 both countries would qualify at Algeria's expense. West Germany duly scored early in the game, and for the rest of the match neither team made any effort whatsoever. It was one of the most blatant examples of cheating that anybody had ever encountered. Algeria complained long and loud about the "Great Gijon swindle" but Fifa ignored their protests.

Then, in the semi-final against France, West Germany behaved equally badly. Harald Schumacher, the West German goalkeeper, felled Patrick Battiston with an evil challenge and the French defender was carried off unconscious. Schumacher escaped unpunished and West Germany were even awarded a goal kick. From that moment, everybody wanted West Germany to lose. They appeared to have got their comeuppance when they trailed 3-1 in extra time but the loss of Battiston was a mortal blow to the French. They conceded two goals in five minutes and West Germany won the first ever penalty shoot-out in the finals 5-4. West Germany's qualification for the semi-final had not exactly been impressive either. They engineered a stultifying 0-0 draw against England and beat Spain 2-1. This left Spain with only honour to play for in the final match of their second-phase group against England. For the hosts a draw would be a moral victory, England needed to win by two goals to edge out West Germany.

Ron Greenwood, the England manager, had problems with his squad. Two key players, Kevin Keegan and Trevor Brooking, had been injured and not yet played in the tournament, but both were potential match-winners. It was thought that both players could probably last about 30 minutes, so Greenwood had a choice: play them from the start, or have the option of bringing them on as a double substitution. To the chagrin of the English press, he chose the latter.

Thus it was that, after 60 minutes, with the match scoreless, Keegan and Brooking arrived on the pitch. Within minutes both of them had missed good chances. But the damage had been done in the first hour. England's inability to pierce the Spanish defence had given the host country heart and, as the minutes

ticked away, they became more confident. Greenwood's caution meant that England were eliminated unbeaten, having conceded only one goal in the tournament, but had thrown away a semi-final place.

It had all looked so different in the opening game against France on June 16. Bryan Robson's 27-second goal in their 3-1 defeat of France was the springboard for England's untroubled qualification for the second phase. Only Brazil progressed with a better record.

England could blame Northern Ireland and Gerry Armstrong for having to face Spain at all. Armstrong's second-half goal, an instinctive strike after Luis Arconada, the Spanish goalkeeper, could only push away Billy Hamilton's cross, gave Northern Ireland an upset 1-0 victory against the host country. The no-hopers surprisingly topped the group and joined France and Austria in their second phase group instead of Spain.

Although Northern Ireland did not win a game in the second phase they at least progressed further than Scotland, who were in their third successive World Cup finals. Drawn in a difficult group with Brazil and the Soviet Union, the Scots put on a brave show, drawing with the Soviet Union and briefly leading against Brazil before being routed 4-1. Scotland went out on goal difference and maintained their unenviable record of never having gone beyond the first round of a World Cup finals despite having qualified five times.

FOR THE RECORD

FIRST ROUND

GROUP 1	P	W	D	L	F	A	Pts
Poland	3	1	2	0	5	1	4
Italy	3	0	3	0	2	2	3
Cameroon	3	0	3	0	1	1	3
Peru	3	0	2	1	2	6	2

GROUP 2	P	W	D	L	F	A	Pts
W. Germany	3	2	0	1	6	3	4
Austria	3	2	0	1	3	1	4
Algeria	3	2	0	1	5	5	4
Chile	3	0	0	3	3	8	0

GROUP 3	P	W	D	L	F	A	Pts
Belgium	3	2	1	0	3	1	5
Argentina	3	2	0	1	6	2	4
Hungary	3	1	1	1	12	6	3
El Salvador	3	0	0	3	1	13	0

GROUP 4	P	W	D	L	F	A	Pts
England	3	3	0	0	6	1	6
France	3	1	1	1	6	5	3
Czech	3	0	2	1	2	4	2
Kuwait	3	0	1	2	2	6	1

GROUP 5	P	W	D	L	F	A	Pts
N. Ireland	3	0	2	0	2	1	4
Spain	3	1	1	0	3	3	3
Yugoslavia	3	1	1	1	2	2	3
Honduras	3	0	2	1	2	3	2

GROUP 6	P	W	D	L	F	A	Pts
Brazil	3	3	0	0	10	2	6
Soviet Union	3	1	1	1	6	4	3
Scotland	3	1	1	1	8	8	3
New Zealand	3	0	0	3	2	12	0

SECOND ROUND

GROUP A	P	W	D	L	F	A	Pts
Poland	2	1	1	0	3	0	3
Soviet Union	2	1	1	0	1	0	3
Belgium	2	0	0	2	0	4	0

GROUP B	P	W	D	L	F	A	Pts
W. Germany	2	1	1	0	2	1	3
England	2	0	2	0	0	0	2
Spain	2	0	1	1	1	2	1

GROUP C	P	W	D	L	F	A	Pts
Italy	2	2	0	0	5	3	4
Brazil	2	1	0	1	5	4	2
Argentina	2	0	0	2	2	5	0

GROUP D	P	W	D	L	F	A	Pts
France	2	2	0	0	5	1	4
Austria	2	0	1	1	2	3	1
N. Ireland	2	0	1	1	3	6	1

SEMI-FINALS
Italy 2   Poland 0
HT 1-0 Att. 50,000
West Germany 3   France 3
West Germany won 5-4 on penalties
HT 1-1 Att. 63,000

THIRD PLACE PLAY-OFF
Poland 3   France 2
HT 2-1 Att. 28,000

FINAL
Italy 3   West Germany 1
HT 0-0 Att. 90,000

Teams
Italy Zoff, Cabrini, Scirea, Gentile, Collovati, Oriali, Bergomi, Tardelli, Conti, Rossi, Graziani (sub: Altobelli)
West Germany Schumacher; Kaltz, Stielike, K-H Forster, B Forster, Breitner, Breigel, Dremmler (sub: Hrubesch), Rummenigge (sub: H Muller), Littbarski, Fischer

Leading goalscorers 6 Paolo Rossi (Italy); 5 Karl-Heinz Rummenigge (West Germany); 4 Zbigniew Boniek (Poland); Zico (Brazil)

Total goals scored 146
Average per game: 2.81

Sendings-off Lasislav Vizek (Czechoslovakia) v France; Referee: Paolo Casarin (Italy).
Gilberto Yearwood (Honduras) v Yugoslavia; Referee: Gaston Castro (Chile).
Mal Donaghy (Northern Ireland) v Spain; Referee: Hector Ortiz (Paraguay).
Americo Gallego (Argentina) v Italy; Referee: Nicolae Rainea (Romania).
Diego Maradona (Argentina) v Brazil; Referee: Mario Rubio Vazquez (Mexico).

Number of players used by finalists
15 Italy; 16 West Germany

Contrasting fortunes: Battiston is scythed down by Schumacher (left) and Rossi scores Italy's first goal in the final

Paisley quits on highest note

Paisley: promising wing-half

ON March 26 Bob Paisley climbed the 39 steps at Wembley and held the League Cup aloft. It was a fitting finale for one of the most successful managers Europe has ever seen. In his nine-year reign at Anfield the former Durham miner and bricklayer had won 13 trophies, and this was his third consecutive League Cup.

His track record was mind-boggling. Within weeks Paisley was celebrating another League title, his sixth, comfortably achieved. At one point Liverpool were 16 points ahead of second-placed Watford and they simply strolled home, eventually finishing 11 points clear. Paisley had announced in August that he would be retiring at the end of the season and he kept his word on May 14. Nine days later Joe Fagan, another stalwart of the famous Anfield Boot Room, was appointed as his successor.

Fagan was 62, the oldest manager to make his debut in the history of the Football League. But then smooth succession from within was the Liverpool way. When Bill Shankly retired in 1974 Paisley had been rustled up from the Boot Room as his successor. And like Fagan he, too, had been coerced into the job.

Paisley was born on January 23, 1919 in a Durham mining village. He enjoyed phenomenal success as a schoolboy footballer and as an amateur with Bishop Auckland. By 1939 he was a professional with Liverpool where he fell under the spell of Matt Busby, who became his mentor.

The second world war interrupted the career of this highly promising wing-half, though he did win a League championship with Liverpool in 1947 and only missed the 1950 FA Cup final because of injury. He retired as a player in 1954 but, amazingly in those days, had taken a course in physiotherapy and had a keen interest in training techniques. By 1959 he was appointed Liverpool's full-time trainer. It was a decision that would change his life and transform Liverpool FC.

With the arrival of Shankly later the same year the pair were about to launch Liverpool on an odyssey of success that nobody could ever have dared script. Paisley became Shankly's right-hand man, his hatchet man and his miracle worker.

Paisley was a genius at diagnosing the seriousness of an injury, how to treat it and how long to allow before the player was brought back. These skills were to prove invaluable as Liverpool were honed into the fittest squad in the land and other managers would marvel at how few injuries their players received.

As a manager, Paisley soon showed his astuteness did not stop with the magic sponge. Ray Kennedy, the Arsenal striker Shankly had purchased just before he resigned, had not fitted in at Anfield until Paisley converted him into a midfield player. It was Paisley who broke transfer records when he brought Kenny Dalglish down from Scotland to replace Kevin Keegan and lured Graeme Souness from Middlesbrough.

It was Shankly who transformed Liverpool from a semi-successful Second Division side into a European power-house, but it was his sidekick, Paisley, who ensured that all of the promise of the 1960s and 1970s was fulfilled and that the Anfield legacy would be successfully passed on to future generations of Liverpool managers.

Paisley's nine great seasons

1975	First Division runners-up
1976	Uefa Cup winners; League champions
1977	European Cup winners; League champions; FA Cup finalists
1978	European Cup winners; First Division runners-up; League Cup finalists
1979	League champions
1980	League champions
1981	European Cup winners; League Cup winners
1982	League champions; League Cup winners
1983	League champions; League Cup winners

Continuing the tradition: Paisley hands over the reins to Fagan, another product of the famous Boot Room

Crazy days at Charlton

WHEN Mark Hulyer took control of Charlton the fans hoped that it would mark the start of a revival for the Second Division side. Instead, they saw their club reduced to a laughing stock by a season of off-the-field farce.

Hulyer was a street-wise young businessman who had purchased Charlton from the Gliksten family, who had run the club for half a century. Within months of becoming chairman Hulyer set The Valley buzzing by offering Barcelona £250,000 for Allan Simonsen.

The delighted fans could hardly believe it – Charlton were buying the Danish international forward who was a former European Footballer of the Year and paying him £82,000 a year for two years. The problem was that nobody else could believe it either, least of all Barcelona.

Officially, the deal was done on October 8. But a week later Barcelona, wanting to make sure that they got paid, said that they would not release Simonsen until they received a bank guarantee for £100,000. Almost daily it seemed that the deal was off, then it was back on again,

then it was in yet further doubt.

Simonsen finally made his League debut for Charlton on November 13, scoring a goal in the 3-2 defeat by Middlesbrough. But that was far from the end of the mess. Charlton were struggling near the bottom of the division and on November 22 their manager, Ken Craggs, said that he had been assured by Hulyer that his job was safe. The very next day he was promptly sacked.

It was not long before Charlton realised that they could barely afford the wages they had offered Simonsen. In February they admitted that the entire affair had been a costly mistake. Within weeks Simonsen had made the last of his 16 appearances for the club and had returned to Denmark.

There was worse still to come. In June, Leeds United issued a winding-up notice because they were owed £35,150 by Charlton. It was also revealed that the club had tax debts of £145,000. The High Court told Charlton to pay the money or close, and the club was only allowed to continue when Hulyer reached an agreement with the Inland Revenue.

Great Dane: Ken Craggs welcomes Allan Simonsen to The Valley

Maxwell's madness thwarted

Chairman curbed: Maxwell was shown the door by two sets of fans

ROBERT MAXWELL had been hailed as a hero for saving Oxford United from the brink of bankruptcy. But when he bought a controlling interest in Reading on April 16 he was reviled.

Maxwell caused uproar when he unveiled his grand plan – merge the two clubs into a single team, the Thames Valley Royals. Although the Oxford board unanimously approved the proposal both sets of supporters were not prepared to see their team die. The Oxford fans staged a sit-in on the pitch and a black coffin was paraded around Reading. Maxwell, for once, did not get his way. The Reading chairman and two other directors resigned on May 13 which allowed Roger Smee, who had previously tried to take over the club, to become chairman. With Smee, a former Reading centre-forward, in charge Maxwell was thwarted. He finally lost the battle on June 22 when he was out-voted at an extraordinary general meeting.

*Alcoholism v
Communism*

Banner at Scotland v Soviet Union
game

Military-style thugs destroy little northern club's big day

FOR little Ilkeston Town of the Northern Counties East League, the FA Trophy third round match against Enfield on February 27 should have been the greatest day in the club's history. They had fought their way through three qualifying rounds and had then beaten two Alliance Premier League teams to set up a third round match at home to Enfield, one of the strongest sides in non-League football.

With 15 minutes remaining Enfield had an unassailable 5-1 lead. Then, in what resembled a carefully-planned military operation, hundreds of young hooligans wearing matching green berets invaded the pitch.

The referee was forced to abandon the game, which was awarded to Enfield. There had also been crowd trouble when Ilkeston had won at Barnet in the previous round and the FA ordered an immediate inquiry.

The investigation lasted almost a month and Ilkeston were cleared of any responsibility for the incidents on March 23. In a worrying sign of how far hooliganism was spreading its tentacles throughout the country it was discovered that the gang had nothing to do with the town and had deliberately travelled from Derby just to make trouble.

Scholar takes over at Spurs

A STUNNING COUP by Irving Scholar, a multi-millionaire tax exile resident in Monte Carlo, saw the old, patrician board of directors of Tottenham Hotspur swept away in December and a bustling group of young Turks installed in their place. Scholar and his allies were able to take control of Spurs for little more than £500,000 because of grave doubts about the club's financial viability. Despite having played at Wembley four times in the year and generating a turnover in excess of £3m, profit was a paltry £200,000. Worse, the new West Stand looked like costing nearly twice its original estimate of £3.5m.

Such mismanagement by the old board, led by chairman Arthur Richardson, led to much grumbling among the shareholders but nobody thought that Tottenham were vulnerable to a takeover from outside the board. But political ineptitude and sheer complacency led to their downfall. Richardson had become the Tottenham chairman in 1980, ousting the long-serving Sydney Wale, after a bitter battle in the boardroom. Wale, a significant shareholder, never forgave him.

Richardson believed he was impregnable. Under Tottenham's articles of association all share transfers had to be accepted by the board. So, while Richardson knew that Scholar was buying up shares, he simply refused to register them. What he had not realised was that Scholar was also buying up proxies with the shares. By the beginning of December Wale decided to throw in his lot with the new guard and sold his shares to Scholar, giving him and his allies a majority. Scholar promptly called an extraordinary general meeting and Richardson and his fellow directors resigned. The way was now clear for a new team to take charge at Tottenham. Scholar promised modern management, diversification and a financially secure club.

Scholar: outfoxed old guard

England reject a smash hit at Newcastle

KEVIN KEEGAN'S illustrious career seemed to be in decline after the World Cup. Age was taking its toll on his bad back and before the start of the season Southampton sold him to Second Division Newcastle.

Then Bobby Robson, in his first match in charge, dropped the England captain for the European championship qualifying match against Denmark in Copenhagen. Keegan was deeply hurt that Robson did not tell him before the squad was announced and he said that he never wanted to play for his country again. When England only drew 2-2 on September 22 Robson was roundly condemned. The England manager was spat at when he went to Newcastle to watch a League match; the St James's Park faithful could not understand why their new-found idol had been overlooked.

Ron Greenwood had once described Keegan as the "most modern of modern footballers".

And although Robson thought Keegan was past his best there were many people who thought that, even at 31, he was still the leading forward in England. Keegan scored on his debut for Newcastle and in each of the next two League matches. He hit a rich vein of form and when he hammered four goals past Rotherham on October 2 speculation mounted about him being recalled by England.

But Keegan was adamant that his international career was over. Instead he would devote his energies to helping Newcastle back into the big time.

Keegan: successfully returned to the north-east

Aberdeen and Dundee United upstage Old Firm

GLASGOW's traditional hold on the honours in Scotland was rudely shattered by two clubs from the north east: Aberdeen and Dundee United. Alex Ferguson's Aberdeen captured the Scottish Cup and the European Cup Winners' Cup, while Jim McLean's Dundee United snatched the League championship by a solitary point. Only the League Cup went to Glasgow when Celtic beat Rangers 2-1.

Aberdeen's triumph in Europe was only the third time a Scottish club had won a European trophy and they did it with a swagger – losing only once in any leg of the competition. To get to the final in Gothenburg Aberdeen had to overcome the formidable Bayern Munich in the quarter finals. An impressive defensive display in Germany ended in a 0-0 draw, but with 15 minutes remaining at Pittodrie the Germans were leading 2-1 and seemed certain to go through. Alex McLeish's headed equaliser put Aberdeen back in the match, but unless they scored the winner Bayern would still qualify by virtue of away goals. The improbable was about to happen. Just after the restart up popped John Hewitt, the 20-year-old substitute, to make the score 3-2. Pandemonium. The semi-final was less dramatic. Aberdeen trounced Waterschei of Belgium 5-1 at home making the 1-0 away defeat irrelevant.

The conditions in Sweden on May 11 were atrocious, heavy rain and wind making the pitch virtually unplayable and only 17,804 spectators braved the elements for the final against Real Madrid. Aberdeen led after seven minutes with a thunderous goal from Eric Black.

But the heavy ground conspired against them. McLeish's attempted back pass stopped in the water and a desperate Jim Leighton conceded a penalty when he brought down Santillana, who had pounced on the loose ball. Juanito duly converted to level the scores. The Spanish club were somewhat lucky to have gone into extra time, but then with eight minutes left justice was done when up popped substitute Hewitt – yet again – to head the precious winner.

The Scottish Cup final against Rangers 10 days later was a dour affair, Aberdeen once again winning in extra time with Eric Black scoring the only goal four minutes from time.

Dundee United's first ever League title was the stuff of fiction. It was the classic tale of the tortoise and hare. Celtic led the table until the last month of the season, then Dundee United, with six consecutive victories, stole through to pip Celtic by one point.

Eric Black gives Aberdeen the lead against Real Madrid with an unstoppable shot

Smiling heroes: Black, Hewitt and Cooper happy to have won the European Cup Winners' Cup in Gothenburg

FOR THE RECORD

■ The rule requiring players to be sent off for committing a professional foul meant that 120 players were dismissed by November 28. However, the attempt to eliminate cheating was weakened when the FA referees' committee rescinded the rule in July.

■ Police in south Yorkshire were told to arrest players whose behaviour on the pitch was likely to incite crowd trouble.

■ George Graham was appointed manager of Millwall on December 6. Three months later he was imposing his authority, ordering six players to report for extra training because he thought that anybody who had lost their first-team place should work twice as hard to get it back.

■ Osvaldo Ardiles returned to Tottenham from Paris St Germain on December 29.

■ Celtic's 2-1 win at Rangers on January 1 was their first victory away from home on New Year's Day for 62 years.

■ Malcolm Struel, the Swansea chairman, was rebuked in February for calling the Welsh FA "bumbling amateurs".

He's not only a good player, but he's spiteful in the nicest sense of the word

Manchester United manager
RON ATKINSON
on Norman Whiteside

Another Chester report simply gathers dust

THE favourite response to a problem was to spend a lot of time talking about it and then do very little. So it was hardly surprising that Sir Norman Chester's report, The State of Football, soon sunk without a trace.

Football had plenty of problems and Sir Norman was the ideal choice to come up with some answers because he had conducted a similar investigation in 1968. That report had been well received but its recommendations were largely ignored. Fifteen years later, with football facing a crisis, his second attempt to bring about reform fared little better.

Clubs knew they had to do something to reverse the decline in attendances and cut their ever-increasing losses, but they could not agree on anything.

John Smith, the Liverpool chairman, wanted to create a Super League and, backed by Arsenal and Tottenham, wanted it limited to just 16 teams. But other clubs feared that the few would get richer at the expense of everybody else. Football wanted more money from television, who were not prepared to pay, and neither side could agree on shirt advertising which meant that sponsorship deals were at risk.

Sir Norman must have won-

dered why he bothered publishing his report on March 28. Although its suggestions were, once again, eminently sensible (reducing the size of the First Division; splitting the Third and Fourth Divisions into four regions; allowing home clubs to keep the gate money and changing the League's constitution to make it easier to reach decisions) they were, once again, rejected out of hand.

Within a month most clubs had made it clear that they did not support his proposals. As the bickering went on it was clear that everybody was prepared to put their own interests above the good of the game as a whole.

Watford's glittering first prize: second place

Going straight for goal: Gerry Armstrong tries to reach a long ball lofted into the box, Watford's trademark

ALTHOUGH Liverpool had sewn up the championship in April, Watford were having their title race with Manchester United. First prize: second place. And on May 14 Watford triumphed with the sweetest of 2-1 victories over Liverpool at Vicarage Road. Watford were runners-up, one point ahead of Manchester United.

It was a truly remarkable achievement. Seven years earlier Watford were a modest mid-table Fourth Division club with no history and little ambition. Then Elton John took over the club, injected his own money and appointed Graham Taylor as the manager with Bertie Mee as his assistant. Within two years Watford had escaped the clutches of the Fourth Division and they were on their way.

Over the next five years Taylor, with Elton John's enthusiastic support, assiduously worked his way towards the First Division, discovering such talented players as John Barnes and Luther Blissett. But not without controversy. Using the techniques of "match analysis" pioneered by Wing Commander Charles Reep at Wolves in the 1950s, Taylor perfected a "direct" method of play that was criticised by purists as simply "long ball," i.e. hoofing the ball up in the air, harrying the defence and profiting from any errors. It certainly wasn't pretty, but it did get results.

Brighton rock the big boys

FIVE DAYS before their fourth round FA Cup-tie against Manchester City, Brighton's chairman, Mike Bamber, predicted his club would go all the way in the competition. Bravado it may have been, but come May 21 when Brighton marched out on to the Wembley turf to face Manchester United in the final who would have argued against his prophecy? Certainly not Liverpool. The team who would go on to be the runaway League champions and League Cup winners were widely touted for the treble. And in the fifth round they were hosting lowly Brighton who were sliding inexorably into the Second Division and had never progressed beyond this round.

No problem surely? But Liverpool and the pundits had reckoned without Jimmy Case, still smarting after being sold while still in his prime. Brighton, under the management of the flamboyant Jimmy Melia, led at half-time, Liverpool equalised but then a late goal from Case finished off his former teammates. To add insult to injury, Phil Neal then missed a penalty.

Norwich and Sheffield Wednesday were duly disposed of in the next rounds and the

Melia: always a showman

Brighton chairman's boast did not seem so fanciful after all. However, Brighton had to play the final against Manchester United without Steve Foster, their inspirational captain and centre-half. He was suspended because of a booking in a League match, and despite taking his case all the way to the High Court was forced to sit on the sidelines as Brighton enjoyed the biggest day in their history.

And enjoy it they did. As the underdogs, and already rele-gated from the First Division, they had nothing to lose. So for much of the first half they played composed and relaxed football and put United out of their stride. Brighton's lead at the interval, courtesy of Gordon Smith's 14th-minute header, was well deserved. However, Manchester United soon got a grip on their game and with 17 minutes left, goals from Frank Stapleton and Ray Wilkins appeared to have sealed Brighton's fate as the natural order re-asserted itself. But then that man Case intervened again. His corner, three minutes from time, was pulled back to Tony Grealish who stabbed the ball into the path of Gary Stevens and the final was all square.

In extra time Brighton should have won the Cup just before the end when Mick Robinson set up Smith with a great chance. But just as the nation thought Brighton had pulled off a miracle Smith hesitated and Gary Bailey saved the day. The bubble had burst. In the replay, five days later, and despite the return of Foster, Brighton were swept away 4-0 by an imperious United who were in no mood to flirt with humiliation again.

FOR THE RECORD

■ On February 22 Brian Clough suggested that no football should be shown on television for three years.

■ Pat Jennings (above) became the first person in England to appear in 1,000 senior matches when he kept a clean sheet for Tottenham against Norwich on February 26.

■ The Football League's proposal to allow two substitutes was rejected by clubs on March 27. They claimed it would be too expensive.

■ England were unbeaten as they won the semi-professional tournament in Scarborough on June 4.

■ The International FA Board changed the rules on July 9. Goalkeepers were required to release the ball after taking four steps.

■ Hungary suspended 185 players on July 21. They were accused of fixing matches on the pools coupons. Bradford City, who owed the Inland Revenue £173,000, were wound up in the High Court on July 29. The official receiver formed a new club, Bradford City (1983), to enable the team to continue playing.

■ Four players, two from each side, were sent off as Altrincham beat Rochdale in the FA Cup first round.

■ Richard Bradford, a reserve team player, scored twice as Bishop's Stortford came back from 2-0 down to draw at Middlesbrough in the third round of the FA Cup. The Isthmian League team led in the replay but were beaten 2-1.

■ England beat West Germany 3-2 in Bremen to win the European under-21 championship 5-4 on aggregate. It was the first time England had won the competition.

Brighton lapped: after a shock in the first match Manchester United trounced them in the replay

KEVIN KEEGAN
Heart of oak with a touch of steel

Deryk Brown

H E WAS a natural finisher. He had pace, and could run almost as fast with the ball as without it. He more than jumped his height. He could use his low centre of gravity to ferret into space when none seemed to exist. And he was tough. Kevin Keegan's most notorious sending-off was with Billy Bremner in the Charity Shield. His most costly sending-off came early in his time in West Germany, when he flattened an opponent and was banned for two months. That nearly wrecked his German adventure as soon as it had begun.

But Keegan's charisma and skills were such that he could break the rules – more significantly, teams were ready to play for him and around him. Perhaps at Liverpool this would mean a nod-down from Toshack, or one of those low diagonal forward balls that Keegan so loved to run on to.

And seldom has there been a more intelligent footballer. Overall, it showed in the fact that

Keegan always made the right decision. He joined Liverpool just as they were replacing Leeds United as Britain's best. Liverpool's team-play in the 1970s was superb, and Keegan needed a team, not a collection of ball-jugglers.

On leaving Liverpool he chose not Italy, where he would surely have burnt himself out, but West Germany. He retired as a player at the right time, the biggest name in Geordieland since Jack Milburn. Then, instead of trying to manage Barnsley or Bradford City, he went into exile, De Gaulle like, as though he knew that one day the call to greatness would come.

The call came in February 1992. Keegan returned to manage Newcastle, standing 23rd in the Second Division. They beat Bristol City 3-0 the next Saturday, the gate of 29,263 being almost double that of the previous match. One remembers Keegan's press conference afterwards. Failure had never occurred to him.

Keegan had seen enough failure around him.

He was a man of the 1970s, that era when players wore their hair long. Sometimes they even permed it. They grew bushy sideburns and sported kipper ties and outrageous flared trousers. They were a chirpy, jack-the-lad lot. But they could not build on the World Cup win of 1966. Too many players under-achieved. For instance, Worthington, Currie, Bowles, Beattie and Hudson. Keegan was in a Doncaster pub-disco that dreadful June day in 1970 when England collapsed out of the World Cup to West Germany. He was on the substitutes' bench at Wembley in October 1973 when a Polish goalkeeper called Tomaszewski somehow held England to a 1-1 draw that meant elimination from the finals of 1974. And although England beat Italy 2-0 at Wembley in November 1977, with Keegan scoring, it was not enough to stop the Italians going to Argentina the next year at our expense.

When England did reach the World Cup finals in Spain in 1982, Keegan had back trouble. His tournament lasted 27 minutes as a substitute as England limply drew 0-0 with Spain and were eliminated. It was his last cap. Keegan had worshipped Shankly and liked and respected Don Revie, but there was to be no marriage with Bobby Robson. He dropped Keegan from his squad. Keegan responded in his next match for Newcastle, scoring four goals for the only time in his career.

Soon Keegan retired to the Costa del Sol, where he never went on the beach and never drank champagne (he doesn't like the stuff). He

Little man who made the big time: Keegan scores for Liverpool against Derby

KEVIN KEEGAN

Born February 14, 1951, Armthorpe, South Yorkshire

PLAYING CAREER
Scunthorpe 1967-71
120 League appearances, 18 goals
Liverpool 1971-77
230 League appearances, 68 goals
Honours European Cup: Winners 1977
Uefa Cup: Winners 1973, 1976
FA Cup: Winners 1974; Finalists 1971, 1977
League Championship: Winners 1973, 1976, 1977; Runners-up 1974, 1975
Footballer of the Year 1976
SV Hamburg 1977-80
Honours European Cup: Finalist 1980
West German championship 1979
European Footballer of the Year 1978, 1979
West German Footballer of the Year 1978
Southampton 1980-82
68 League appearances, 37 goals
Newcastle United 1982-84
78 League appearances, 48 goals
Internationals England debut 1972
63 appearances, 21 goals
Captain 29 times

MANAGEMENT CAREER
Newcastle United Manager 1992 to present
Honours First Division: Winners 1993

played golf, he followed the turf. When Tyneside telephoned, the Messiah was ready.

Those 1970s frizzy perms made Keegan and his contemporaries look more like poodles than bulldogs. But Keegan was an English bulldog. Proud to follow the flag. Heart of oak. Never say die. That is why we have always admired him so much.

Keegan travelled to Liverpool one Monday in May 1971. With him was Ron Ashman, his manager at Scunthorpe, the clubs having agreed a transfer fee of £33,000. Ashman was keen to tie up this small fortune for Scunthorpe; Keegan had been told by his father, a miner, not to sell himself cheaply.

Keegan was down-page news at Liverpool, who were five days away from an FA Cup final against Arsenal. The offices at Anfield were temporarily in a hut at the end of a car park. Keegan sat on a dustbin for half an hour before meeting the manager, Bill Shankly.

Keegan's spirits lifted as soon as he heard Shankly talk. This strange Scotsman entranced him. And Shankly was impressed when the 5ft 8in youngster stripped for his medical. "Aye, son, have you ever thought of being a boxer?" purred Shanks. "What a physique son. Have you ever done weights?" Incidentally, Shankly's instincts were right. Keegan had tried boxing in his youth in Doncaster.

Shankly offered Keegan £45 a week. Keegan, remembering his father's orders, looked unimpressed, while Ashman, seeing his £33,000 recede, turned white. Keegan said he earned £35

Making his mark: Keegan at Newcastle

Keegan, scoring against Scotland, had his international career cut short by Bobby Robson

at Scunthorpe plus a £10 win bonus, whereupon Shankly clinched the deal by offering him £50 a week.

On the drive home Ashman reproached Keegan, whose wage was only £30. Keegan, defensively, said that at least he had told the truth about the £10 bonus. "Yes," retorted Ashman, "but whenever did you get a win bonus at Scunthorpe?" And they burst out laughing.

Thus began the rise and rise of Kevin Keegan, the little man who made the big-time. He was not as gifted as some of his contemporaries. But he could move a mountain or two.

Keegan was born in Doncaster on St Valentine's Day 1951. During his six years at Liverpool they won the European Cup once, the Uefa Cup twice, the League championship three times, and the FA Cup once, and Keegan was Footballer of the Year in 1976. He moved to SV Hamburg in June 1977. In his second season he was their top scorer as they won the Bundesliga for the first time in 19 years. He was European Footballer of the Year in 1978 and 1979. He signed for Southampton in July 1980, then played his last two seasons for Newcastle, retiring in May 1984 after leading them to promotion to the First Division. Years later, of course, he returned to Gallowgate as manager to have an even more inspirational effect. He won 63 England caps, scoring 21 goals and captaining the side 29 times. At first, England was different. "When I ran nobody moved out of the way. It was not like Liverpool at all," Keegan said after his international debut in Cardiff in November 1972.

It is quite a record for a little lad once turned away by Coventry City. Why is it so good? Some would say that Keegan was lucky, and Jack Charlton once observed that if Keegan fell into the River Tyne he would surface with a salmon in his mouth. Some would say that he had a genius for PR, and the Southampton players used to say that when Keegan was late for the team bus he was walking the town looking for somebody who did not have his autograph.

Luck and PR, certainly. But much more.

Although Keegan was not as talented as, say, Kenny Dalglish, the man who took his No7 shirt at Liverpool (who was?), he had many virtues. For a start, his self-belief was a mile high. A more enthusiastic, committed footballer you could not find. Shankly inspired in the dressing room, Keegan did so on the field.

Excelling in exile: Keegan led Hamburg's revival

Charlton reprieved

NOTHING seemed to be going right for Charlton. No sooner had they survived one winding-up petition for tax debts at the end of last season than they were back in court again.

The problem was that when Mark Hulyer, the chairman, bought the club from Michael Gliksten, ownership of The Valley remained with one of Gliksten's companies. And Charlton could no longer afford the rent.

Gliksten went to court on October 17, claiming that he was owed more than £500,000. Other creditors, fearful that the edifice would come tumbling down, persuaded the court to postpone a final decision.

The lawyers had a field day as the case dragged on, but it looked as if the game was finally up in February 13. Apart from Gliksten, the Inland Revenue and the Customs and Excise were owed money and Charlton's debts exceeded £1m.

They managed to win another reprieve because Chief Francis Nzeribe, a Nigerian arms dealer, was said to be about to buy the club. That deal came to nothing and a fortnight later a winding-up order was duly issued, Hulyer resigned and Charlton's match with Blackburn was postponed.

On March 8, though, Charlton became the latest in an ever-growing list of clubs to cheat death. The local council offered £250,000 sponsorship, a consortium put up the rest of the money and the court approved the formation of a new company just 25 minutes before Charlton were due to lose their League status.

Fagan's triumphant debut

ANY DOUBTS there were about Joe Fagan stepping into Bob Paisley's shoes were soon dispelled. Liverpool lost the Charity Shield 2-0 to Manchester United, but after that they just marched serenely on.

By the start of November they were top of the First Division and apart from one very brief period in March they stayed there for the rest of the season. Liverpool thus became only the third club after Huddersfield and Arsenal to win the League three years in a row.

They owed much of their success to the goalscoring abilities of Ian Rush. He scored five against Luton, four against Coventry and a hat-trick against Aston Villa as he hit 32 goals in the League and 45 in all. Liverpool's progress in the League Cup was far less assured. They needed three matches to beat Fulham and were held 2-2 at Anfield by Walsall in the semi-final. The final was the first time Liverpool had met Everton at Wembley and everybody in the city was captivated by the occasion.

Heavy rain took the edge off the occasion and the two teams ground out a 0-0 draw. But it did not dampen the crowd's enthusiasm and as the players made their lap of honour after extra time the stadium resounded to chants of: "Merseyside, Merseyside!" A 1-0 victory in the replay at Maine Road left Liverpool on target for a treble of trophies in the European Cup. And the harder the challenge the better Liverpool responded. Some of Liverpool's finest performances of the season came away from home in second leg matches in the European Cup. Athletic Bilbao were beaten 1-0 in the second round, Benfica 4-1 in the quarter-final and Dynamo Bucharest 2-1 in the semi-final, with Rush getting both goals.

But the final, on May 30, was Liverpool's toughest of all. They had to face Roma in the cauldron of the Olympic stadium in Rome. Liverpool showed no signs of nerves and Phil Neal gave them the lead after 15 minutes, albeit somewhat luckily.

On song: Rush becomes Liverpool's highest scorer in a season

Winning ways: Liverpool captured the European Cup for the fourth time

> *Our methods are so easy, sometimes players don't understand them at first*
>
> JOE FAGAN
> Liverpool manager

Pruzzo equalised just before half-time and Roma piled on the pressure. Liverpool did not crack but nor could they score, even in extra time. The penalty shoot-out, at the Italian fans' end of the ground, raised the game to fever pitch.

Neal would normally have led off for Liverpool. But at the last moment Steve Nicol stepped forward and blazed the ball over the bar. Di Bartolomei gave Roma the lead, gently placing the ball in the centre of the goal as Grobbelaar guessed wrongly and dived. The Liverpool fans were subdued.

Neal kept Liverpool in the hunt and then the match was level again as Conti, too, fired over the top. Souness and Righetti traded goals and the ever-dependable Rush was also on target. Graziani hammered his attempt but the ball clipped the crossbar and flew over the top. It was now the Roma fans' turn to fall silent.

Everything depended on Alan Kennedy. He coolly placed the ball just inside the post and Liverpool had won the European Cup again. "I was really confident," he said. "I took a penalty in training and put it in the same spot. Just like that."

Hooliganism unchecked on the domestic front and English fans also wreak havoc throughout Europe

NO SOONER had football resumed than its biggest enemy – the hooligans – renewed their offensive. The second Saturday of the season, September 3, brought trouble at both ends of the country, with disturbances at Ayresome Park during Middlesbrough's match with Leeds and seven policemen injured in running battles with Chelsea fans in Brighton.

Official inquiries cleared all four clubs of any blame and it appeared that the authorities were powerless as more clashes were reported almost every week. Worryingly, it soon became apparent that hooliganism was no longer a purely domestic issue. When Tottenham beat Feyenoord 2-0 in the second round, second leg of the Uefa Cup on November 2 more than 30 people were injured in Rotterdam and Spurs were fined nearly £8,000 by Uefa. And little Luxembourg were left wishing that they had not been drawn in the same European championship qualifying group as England on the night of November 16. Luxembourg had unpleasant memories of England's last visit in 1977 and they had made elaborate plans involving the police forces of four countries.

But the disappointment of failing to reach the finals drove the England fans wild. They ran riot in the city centre and caused thousands of pounds of damage. Only 13 arrests were made, but nine of the offenders were fined and sentenced to up to four months in jail.

And the so-called fans were not content to fight each other either. When Notts County beat Bristol City in the FA Cup on January 10 the referee was hit by a missile during a pitch invasion and complained about the lack of protection he had received from the police.

Pitch invasions were a popular tactic and more than a hundred people were injured when fans of West Ham, who lost 3-0, made two attempts to get their FA Cup match against Birming-

Disgraceful aftermath: thousands of pounds of damage was caused to shops in Luxembourg

Massed ranks: the security forces could not keep England fans under control

ham abandoned on February 18. West Ham were threatened with a two-year ban from the competition, but had the decision reversed on appeal.

All this trouble had been noted with growing concern by Uefa, whose general secretary, Hans Bangerter, threatened to ban British clubs from Europe unless the government stopped hooligans travelling abroad. Little did he know that the apocalypse was soon to come.

Aberdeen double up again

ABERDEEN continued to be the dominant team in Scotland. Having achieved a Double of European Cup Winners' Cup and Scottish Cup the previous season, they proceeded to achieve the "real" Double of League championship and Scottish Cup. Their inspiration was Willie Miller, aided by the likes of Gordon Strachan, Doug Rougvie and Alex McLeish, and guided by the wily management of Alex Ferguson.

The League championship really was a procession. By mid-October they were top and by the end of the season they were seven points clear of Celtic, having won 25 and lost four of their League matches. In the Scottish Cup final on May 19 Celtic were the obstacle to Aberdeen gaining their first "real" Double. Eric Black put Aberdeen ahead in the first half before an ugly incident changed the course of the match. Celtic's Roy Aitken lunged at Mark McGhee and was sent off. Aitken was the first player to be sent off in a Scottish Cup final since 1929.

Having been largely outplayed in the first half, now 10 Celtic players were determined to battle till they dropped. With four minutes to go Paul McStay scored the equaliser and the game went into extra time. Here the advantage of 11 fit men over 10 tired ones told and McGhee scored a cracking winner. And another piece of history was enacted: Aberdeen became only the second club this century to

Miller: inspirational

McGhee: winning goal

lift the Scottish Cup in three successive years.

The one real blot on their season was in the defence of their European Cup Winners' Cup. Having sailed into a semi-final against Porto all they needed to do at Pittodrie was overturn a Portuguese 1-0 lead from the first leg. But Aberdeen were too blasé and lost 1-0 instead.

Goicoechea scythes down Maradona

DIEGO MARADONA had his season cut short by a terrible tackle by Andoni Goicoechea. The Barcelona forward's ankle was shattered by the Bilbao fullback on September 26, and it was immediately predicted that Maradona would be out of action for at least three months.

Barcelona fans, furious at the way their star had been scythed down, tried to storm the Bilbao players' hotel. The Spanish FA were not happy about the incident either, and three days later they acted to ban Goicoechea, dubbed "the Butcher of Bilbao", for 18 matches.

Home nations miss their cue on the European stage

NONE of the Home Nations qualified for the finals of the European championships in France in June, although England, Northern Ireland and Wales came exceedingly close. Scotland were never in the hunt. For Bobby Robson in his first campaign as England manager it was bitterly disappointing as they failed by a single point.

Two results in their five-team group (with only one country to qualify) were England's undoing. They failed to beat Greece at Wembley and then lost at home to Denmark. Both were remarkable results as earlier they had thrashed Greece 3-0 away and taken a point in Denmark, the eventual qualifiers.

The home match against Denmark, on September 21, was the key game in the group as the Danes knew defeat would almost certainly end their hopes of qualifying. However, instead of playing for the draw as expected, they clearly set out to win, playing composed possession football with Michael Laudrup and Allan Simonsen the dominant players. A 39th minute penalty, conceded by Phil Neal when he handled a Laudrup cross and converted by Simonsen, settled the match and Denmark topped the group for the first time. And, apart from a 1-0 defeat by Hungary, they never looked back.

Northern Ireland were the surprise packet of the qualifying stages. Their five-team group was supposed to be a pushover for West Germany, the World Cup runners-up and reigning European champions. But Northern Ireland inflicted two 1-0 victories, home and away, upon West Germany to throw the group wide open. It went down to the wire with the Germans needing to beat Albania at home in their last game on November 20 to qualify, which they did with only 10 minutes to spare, and got through only on goal difference.

Wales, too, did themselves proud, and a victory against Yugoslavia in Cardiff on December 14 would have sent them on their way to France. Instead a 1-1 draw meant that everything hinged on the final match between Yugoslavia and Bulgaria in Split on December 12. A draw would have put Wales through, any victory would do for the Yugoslavs, but a win by Bulgaria could have been sufficient for them to leapfrog into first place. In a dramatic match Bulgaria led after 28 minutes, Yugoslavia equalised two minutes later and then took the lead in the 52nd minute.

The match then swung Bulgaria's way as they grabbed an equaliser on the hour and pressed for the winner. With seconds remaining the scores were tied and it looked as if Wales were through. Then the Yugoslav defender Radanovic headed a winning goal and suddenly they were out.

Britain left holding two winning tickets in penalty lottery

BRITISH CLUBS had their finest night in European competition on March 21. All six clubs involved in the three competitions reached the semi-finals. In the Champions' Cup: Liverpool and Dundee United; in the Cup Winners' Cup: Manchester United and Aberdeen; and in the Uefa Cup: Spurs and Nottingham Forest. And when the draws kept all six apart there was the prospect of three all-British finals.

Unfortunately only Liverpool and Tottenham made it to their respective finals, where Liverpool won in a penalty shoot-out. Amazingly so did Spurs in the two-legged final against Anderlecht. At White Hart Lane, Tottenham's goalkeeper, Tony Parks produced two scintillating saves to give Spurs their third European trophy.

Fame is the spur: Steve Archibald shoots against Hadjuk Split in the Uefa Cup semi-final

Maxwell covets United

THE ABORTIVE attempt to merge Oxford and Reading into the Thames Valley Royals did nothing to dampen Robert Maxwell's desire to own more football clubs. Even though Maxwell owned Oxford and was thus prevented by the League's rules from involvement in any other club he wanted to be bigger and better than everybody else. So less than two months after Oxford had knocked Manchester United out of the League Cup Maxwell turned his greedy eye towards Old Trafford. Maxwell used his newspaper, the *Daily Mirror*, to unveil a £10m bid for Manchester United on February 3.

One of the headlines on the report claimed that the deal would be completed in a week. Although Manchester United fans were incredulous, a deal very nearly was done. Martin Edwards, the chairman, and his brother owned the bulk of the club between them and they were tempted by the offer.

They indicated that if Maxwell raised his bid to £15 a share then they would sell. But Maxwell was not prepared to pay any more and the nego-

tiations ended on February 13. Not to be out-done, Maxwell switched his attention to Derby on March 1. The struggling Second Division club lacked the glamour and status of Manchester United but they were desperately in need of money.

Derby were £1.5m in debt, banned from the transfer market because they still had not paid for players they had bought, and facing a winding-up petition from the Inland Revenue. A judge refused a petition to allow Maxwell to take over the club, but not even that could stop him. By the end of the summer Peter Taylor, the Derby manager, had been sacked and Maxwell had leased the Baseball ground from the local council and installed his son Ian as the Derby chairman.

Just because I'm a professional it doesn't mean I'm not a human being

MICK MILLS
upset at the abuse he received on not joining Sunderland

FOR THE RECORD

■ Injury-struck Watford advertised in The Times for professional footballers "… men or women … preference given to applicants with two arms and two legs in working order."

■ Alan Smith lost three teeth during Leicester's 2-2 draw with Stoke on September 24. They were retrieved from the pitch and replaced in hospital.

■ The second round of the League Cup saw the competing clubs seeded for the first time.

■ Ken Bates, the Chelsea chairman, called an extraordinary meeting on September 26 to remove Dave Mears and Viscount Chelsea from the board. He was angry that Mears had sold Stamford Bridge to Marler properties.

■ Tottenham Hotspur beat Nottingham Forest 2-1 on October 2 in the first of 10 live matches due to be shown on television.

■ John Greig resigned as the Rangers manager on October 28. He was replaced by Jock Wallace of Motherwell.

Hands across the terraces: Ken Bates at Stamford Bridge

Platini ends France's agony

IN THE finals of the European championships Michel Platini conclusively demonstrated that he was one of the world's greatest players. He led France, the host nation, to victory not only with dazzling skills and vision – he also scored nine of their 15 goals.

Dizzy Swansea on the slide

Turbulent year: Toshack left, returned and was then sacked

France had shown in the World Cup in Spain two years earlier that they were a side of great attacking flair but were still haunted by the memories of their catastrophic defeat at the hands of West Germany in the semi-final in Seville. France's fluent football had given them a two-goal lead in extra time but, inexplicably, instead of shutting up shop they went in pursuit of more goals. Instead they conceded two goals and lost the penalty shoot-out. In the European championships they also played with a swagger, rifling their way into a semi-final with Portugal in Marseille. It proved to be as dramatic as the World Cup. Once again the match went into extra time, but now France fell behind – for the first time in the match – to a goal from Jordao in the 97th minute. Now the French had to show tenacity. With six minutes remaining Domergue levelled, and then, with the dreaded penalty shoot-out looming, Platini fired a Tigana cross into the Portuguese net barely a minute from the end. Their opponents in the final were Spain, who had knocked out Denmark 5-4 in a penalty shoot-out.

The final in Paris on June 27 was to be the acid test. France had never won a major tournament: they had been humiliated by Brazil in the semi-final of the 1958 World Cup. The nation held its breath while the sporting press, especially L'Equipe, raked over the ashes of such disappointing defeats. The fears transmitted themselves to the players and suddenly the elan disappeared from their game and at the interval the match was goalless. But in the 16th minute of the second half fate, for once, blessed France. A curling free kick from Platini on the edge of the area was falling neatly into the arms of Luis Arconada, but bizarrely the Spanish goalkeeper allowed it to slip out of his hands and into the net. Spain simply fell apart.

With six minutes to go France were down to 10 men when Le Roux was sent off for his second bookable offence. Spain, sensing their opportunity, mounted attack after attack. Seconds before the final whistle, with virtually the whole of the Spanish team in the French half, Tigana cleared the ball over their heads and into the path of the onrushing Bellone. His chip over Arconada settled matters.

It had been a poor final, but the right team were European champions, and the right man, Platini, the man of the tournament.

SWANSEA'S downward spiral was happening almost as quickly as their previous climb to the heights. Newly relegated from the First Division they dropped straight out of the Second Division, failing to win an away match all season and never being placed higher than 20th in the table.

Their struggles on the field were matched by the problems off it. The chairman and vice-chairman resigned on October 16 and Doug Sharpe took over a club that was more than £1.5m in debt. Sharpe's first job in charge was to stave of the bankers, who demanded that Swansea raised nearly £500,000 in a few weeks. John Toshack, the manager,

resigned within a fortnight and although Doug Livermore took over temporarily Swansea had difficulty in finding a permanent replacement. Colin Appleton turned them down, so Toshack was re-appointed on December 21. But there was little he could do to stop the rot. Every player was up for sale in an attempt to raise money and three of them, including the veteran striker, Bob Latchford, were given free transfers to cut the wage bill.

The former forward even made a comeback as a sweeper in a rare victory on December 31. But when he refused to resign on March 5 he was sacked and left Swansea for the second and final time.

France's finest hour: Platini lifts the European championship cup

Form book finally ends minnows' majestic haul

BOURNEMOUTH set the theme for a topsy-turvy year in the FA Cup in the Third Round on January 7 when the Third Division club knocked out Manchester United, the holders, 2-0. It was the first time that Bournemouth had reached the Fourth Round in 24 years. Telford continued the shocks with 4-1 victory at Rochdale to became the first non-League club for three seasons to make the Fourth Round. In all, nine First Division clubs fell at the first hurdle (admittedly five of them against First Division opponents).

So it went on. In the Fourth Round, Brighton, last season's Cup finalists but now of the Second Division, proved last year's FA Cup elimination of Liverpool was no fluke by doing it again, this time at the Goldstone ground. With the big guns dropping like flies, the way was open to the minnows. And it was little Plymouth Argyle who came through on the rails.

On March 14 Plymouth beat Derby 1-0 in a Sixth Round replay with an Andy Rogers goal direct from a corner. They were only the sixth Third Division club to have reached the semi-finals of the FA Cup. There they met "super" minnows Watford who, although they had finished First Division runners-up the previous season, had never captured a major honour and were enjoying only their second season in the top flight.

Thus, despite the presence of 20,000 Argyle fans – nearly four times their average attendance – at Villa Park on April 14, the West Country club succumbed to a George Reilly goal in the second half. Everton, Watford's opponents at Wembley on May 19, were appearing in their first final since 1968 but their eighth overall. History, and form, finally asserted itself and Watford were swept away 2-0 as Everton collected their fourth FA Cup trophy.

Finishing touch: Andy Gray scores Everton's second goal against Watford

Changing the guard at Palace: Coppell becomes their eighth manager

Changing his mind at Palace: Bassett quits after four days

Millwall riot sparks blazing hooligan row with Thatcher

These people are society's problems and we don't want your hooligans at our sport

FA secretary
TED CROKER
to Margaret Thatcher after the
Luton-Millwall riot

HOOLIGANISM had been a running sore for over a decade, but although extensively reported in the media few people had actually witnessed it first hand. Then, on March 13, Millwall fans ran amok at Luton during an FA Cup quarter-final. Crucially, the riot was shown live on television and the entire nation, including Margaret Thatcher, the Prime Minister, watched in horror.

Hundreds of Millwall fans ripped up plastic seats, hurled some of them on to the pitch and used the rest as shields, weapons and batons as they engaged in a full-scale battle with 200 police-men. Nearly all of the television audience had probably never seen anything like it before.

The referee had to take the players off the pitch for 25 minutes while the police dealt with the mob. Luton did eventually win 1-0 to go through to meet Everton in the semi-final, but that was largely ignored as the riot made headlines worldwide.

To cap the riot on the pitch, the Millwall hordes rampaged through the town, causing thousands of pounds of damage to shops, houses and cars. And they wrecked the train back to London. Forty-seven people, including 31 policemen, were injured. The day after the mayhem at Luton, the Uefa executive awarded the 1988 European championships to West Germany. Bert Millichip, the FA chairman, claimed that England's application failed because of the riot.

On March 28, Thatcher conducted an hour-long ministerial meeting on hooliganism and, unhappy with football's failure to tackle the violence, summoned football's chiefs to Downing Street to explain themselves. Whereupon they did themselves, and football, no favours. On April 1, of all days, Ted Croker, the FA's secretary, told the Prime Minister: "These people are society's problem and we don't want your hooligans at our sport." The net effect of this complacency was that the government passed a bill banning the sale of alcohol at football grounds and set in motion plans for a national identity card system.

Some clubs did respond to the crisis. Despite howls of protests from the other clubs, Luton banned away fans from Kenilworth Road. And Chelsea, another club notorious for hooliganism, tried to tackle the problem, albeit in a muddled and haphazard way.

Ken Bates, their controversial chairman, banned a section of the press from Stamford Bridge for reporting hooliganism at Chelsea, erected an electrified fence to prevent pitch invasions and announced he was starting an ID card scheme.

The fence fell foul of the Greater London Council and was never switched on and the ID system was abandoned as unworkable. The press were eventually readmitted when Bates discovered it was impossible to stop them reporting from the terraces.

But although Bates was misguided, his heart was in the right place. In July the FA, incredibly, cleared Millwall of any blame for the Luton riot.

Pitched battle at Kenilworth Road: police struggle to control hundreds of Millwall fans

Terrace of shame: the trail of destruction left by the mob who had ripped up seats

Merseyside pendulum swinging Everton's way

HOWARD KENDALL had been steadily building a good side since his arrival at Goodison Park, and Everton at last were ready to emerge from the shadow of their great rivals Liverpool.

The first hint of what was about to come came in the Charity Shield when Everton won 1-0 with Bruce Grobbelaar conceding an own goal. By the end of October it was clear how far the pendulum had swung. Everton won 1-0 at Anfield and moved into fourth place while Liverpool slipped down to 18th.

Moran fouls Reid to become the first person sent off in an FA Cup final

Apart from a brief period over Christmas and the New Year, Everton were never out of first place from the start of November to the end of the season. And from December 26 to May 8 they strung together a remarkable sequence, winning six matches in a row, drawing two, and then running up 10 consecutive victories. The title was theirs on May 6, with five matches still to play.

The key to their success was the relentless pressure that the team exerted. Even when an opponent had the ball, he was given little time to do anything. Peter Reid was Everton's mainspring in midfield, and his industry deservedly brought him a first full cap for England and the acclaim of his fellow professionals, who chose him as their player of the year.

Everton's easy ride in the League was matched by their progress in the European Cup Winners' Cup. They did not meet a side of note until the semi-finals, but Bayern Munich were polished off 3-1 at home and Rapid Vienna were overrun 3-1 in the final in Rotterdam on May 15.

Everton had a majestic treble in their sights. But the Bradford inferno cast a pall over the FA Cup final on May 18. Even when Kevin Moran became the first man to be sent off in a final Everton could not press home their advantage. A man short, Manchester United battled on gamely to win a muted match 1-0 in extra time.

The many sides of Anton Johnson

ANTON JOHNSON was finally banned for life from any involvement with football clubs. The only surprise on February 11 was that it had taken the Football League so long to catch up with him. Johnson, a self-proclaimed millionaire who favoured a full-length wolfskin coat, dark glasses, big cigars and a Rolls-Royce, had broken just about every rule in the League's book since he had become involved in football in 1979.

The first club to suffer from his questionable dealings were Rotherham. When Johnson bought the club it was profitable. He left them deep in debt and the subject of League investigations over illegal payments.

Johnson also used a Guernsey-based company to take over Bournemouth while he was still involved with Rotherham. The use of this company allowed him to conceal his involvement in two clubs at the same time, which was not allowed under League rules. Amazingly, by 1983, Johnson was able to boast: "I have helped in the purchase of a dozen clubs."

Bournemouth, too, rued the day that Johnson became involved. But unfortunately other clubs seemed to fall for the brash claims (most of which were unfounded) of an inveterate self-publicist.

When Johnson breezed into Southend in 1983 he was hailed as the saviour of an almost bankrupt club – particularly when he was instrumental in appointing Bobby Moore as chief executive.

Soon, though, everything went sour as Southend, too, discovered discrepancies in their finances. Johnson was questioned by the police and the League finally acted, sending in a team of accountants to examine the books. They discovered such a tangle of questionable transfers and missing money that they were left with no option but to ban Johnson.

Johnson: banned

265

Celebration ends in tragedy –

IF HOOLIGANISM was the most visible blot on football's tattered reputation, the state of our stadiums was the other. Many were antiquated, decaying and unsafe. Just how unsafe became tragically clear on May 11 at Valley Parade, the last day of the League season, when Bradford City were playing Lincoln and were celebrating their Third Division championship and promotion to the Second Division. Just before half-time a fire started in the wooden main stand. Within minutes the blaze spread all along the stand and the celebrating fans were caught in a death trap. Many escaped on to the pitch, but 56 people died and hundreds suffered burns, some very serious.

The pitch had provided the only safe means of exit and if the spectators had been caged in (one of the methods used to curb hooliganism) then the

Death trap at Valley Parade: terrified fans flee on to the pitch, their only safe means of exit, to try to escape the flames

Telford and York take the whole country by storm

TELFORD took the giant-killing honours with a Cup run that took them all the way to the fifth round, with League opposition at every stage and a draw that was not kind to them. The Gola League side travelled to Third Division Lincoln in the first round, held them to a draw and then won the replay. The second round sent them to another Third Division club, Preston, who were despatched 4-1.

At least Telford were given a home tie in the third round. But instead of one of the glamour clubs they had to face yet another Third Division team. Bradford, who topped the table, were sent packing 2-1.

Even then Telford did not get any reward, being sent to one of the Fourth Division's pacesetters, Darlington. Another replay was needed before Telford got a chance to cash in with another trip, to Everton.

Telford finally met their match at the First Division leaders, but they were not disgraced in a 3-0 defeat and went home considerably richer than when they had started their trek around the country.

The greatest upset of the competition came in the fourth round. Arsenal had wobbled at the previous stage, needing two matches to get past Hereford. Their luck ran out at Bootham Crescent on January 26, when Keith Houchen scored the only goal, a penalty, to give Third Division York an historic victory. It was the seventh time since the war that Arsenal had been knocked out of the Cup by a team from a lower division.

56 perish in Bradford inferno

death toll could have been in the thousands. Still, it was the worst sporting disaster ever to occur in England.

The cause of the fire was eventually diagnosed as years of accumulated rubbish under the 76-year-old stand, which was almost certainly set alight by a discarded cigarette or dropped match. That the rubbish had been ignored for so long was a damning indictment of how football clubs viewed safety and the welfare of their paying customers.

On the very same day hooliganism raised its ugly head and claimed a life. A wall collapsed, killing a young boy, and 96 policemen were injured when Leeds fans rioted at a match in Birmingham. The two incidents, 100 miles apart, were a sorry reminder of the state in which English football now found itself.

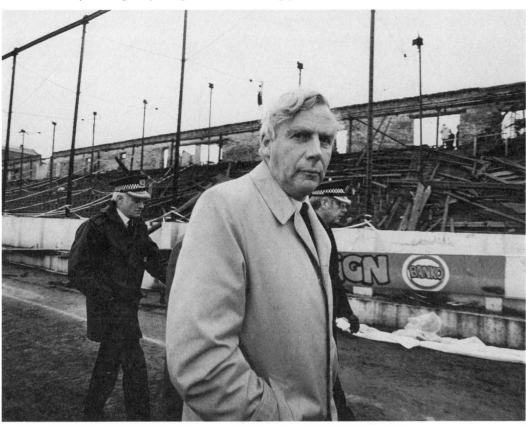

The aftermath: Judge Popplewell inspects the charred remains of the wooden main stand

TV money foolishly rejected

FOOTBALL seemed to think that television had bottomless pockets. So, on January 17, with the contract to show matches being renegotiated, club chairmen turned down £16m over four years. They were certain that they could get more money.

But the men who ran the game did not realise that their product had been devalued by the years of hooliganism. A bad winter and a large number of postponed matches had also affected clubs' cashflow.

Despite a warning from the Football League about the financial consequences of their rejecting the deal, the clubs refused to change their mind when they met again on Febru-ary 14. With the television companies adamant that they were not going to raise their offer, the prospect of a television blackout was looming.

Finally both the BBC and ITV ran out of patience. On May 2, they gave football a one-month deadline to reach agreement. Even then, the clubs were prepared to cut off their nose to spite their face.

The 1985-86 season duly started without any television coverage as the talks dragged on. In the end, though, football had to give in. And their intransigence had cost them a fortune. When agreement was finally reached football was forced to settle for a mere £1.3 m.

Strachan: tug-of-war transfer

39 killed in Heysel stampede

THE disaster at Bradford 18 days earlier and the mayhem at Luton in March had not prepared anybody for the criminal tragedy at the Heysel stadium in Brussels on May 29. The occasion, the European Cup final between Liverpool and Juventus, was the climax of the season, but just as we were about to enjoy the summit of European football the game reached its nadir.

Before the match even started Liverpool fans charged Juventus fans, who attempted to run away to safety. But an old wall collapsed and in the ensuing panic the Italians fell over each other and some were crushed to death. Thirty-eight people died that day (one more died in hospital later) and more than 400 were injured. The appalling scenes were watched by a global television audience dumbstruck with horror and incomprehension. How could such a thing have happened? Sadly, the answer is easy and a damning indictment of every aspect of the way football was run.

The stadium, a run-down, antiquated dinosaur, should never have been chosen as the venue for such an important and volatile match. And the corner of Z terrace was a death trap with two adjacent walls at one end providing no safe means of exit. Ticket control was non-existent and many Italian fans easily acquired tickets for the neutral Z section. It was into this section that the Liverpool fans charged when they easily broke out of their restricted X and Y terraces. Security and policing were pitiful. Liverpool fans, once inside, were able to hand their tickets over the wire to others outside. Some simply crawled in under the fence. The police precautions, such as they were, had not even anticipated that violence might occur before the kick-off. There was no attempt to search spectators for weapons or to prevent alcohol being brought into the ground. Many of the fans were drunk, and many had sticks, bottles and iron bars. There was no closed circuit television and the emergency services were woefully inadequate.

The failure of the Belgian police to have properly researched patterns of English hooliganism was incredible. No English police force would ever have made the dreadful mistakes the Belgians did, they would have spotted the problem much earlier and dealt with it; for all the warning signs were there.

The first Liverpool charge, after the usual bout of taunts and insults, happened at 6.30pm as eight policemen looked on. The fatal charge was the third,

Failing to segregate fans and allowing Italians into neutral sections created the conditions for mayhem

Debris of a disaster: stewards survey Z terrace, where the wall had collapsed on terrified Juventus fans

half an hour after the first, as the Liverpool fans weighed in with rocks, fists, beer cans and fireworks. The belated police intervention only made matters worse as police beat the panicking fans with batons to clear the terrace while fans lay dying. Amazingly, the match went ahead after a one hour 25 minute delay although West German television had the sensitivity to pull the plugs. And many of the fans in the stadium and the players were unaware of the scale of what had occurred. In England the television commentary swung from discussion and news about the mounting death toll to normal commentary on the game.

Although it almost went unnoticed, Liverpool lost 1-0 to a hotly contested penalty conceded by Gary Gillespie outside the area, and converted by Michel Platini. After the dust settled, everybody blamed each other as nobody would take responsibility. Politically it eventually brought down the Belgian government. In football, punishment was more swift. Within days the FA withdrew all English clubs from European competition for a year. It was not enough. Uefa banned all English clubs from European competition indefinitely, with Liverpool receiving an extra three-year ban to apply when English clubs were let back in. Fifa banned all English clubs worldwide, but in July reduced this to Europe, including Scotland, Ireland and Wales.

In Downing Street, Margaret Thatcher, the Prime Minister, was appalled at the scenes she had watched on television and the international damage it would do to Britain. Her efforts to force football to put its house in order were redoubled and the identity card scheme, which football claimed was unworkable, became the linchpin of her solution to hooliganism.

Shamefully, four of the six English clubs who had qualified for European competition (Everton, Manchester United, Norwich and Southampton) went to the High Court to get the ban lifted. They claimed it was unfair on them as they had

Dundee United left with nothing

DUNDEE UNITED did not win anything but, in a season where the honours were spread between Glasgow and Aberdeen, they certainly were in with a shout in all the competitions. Despite a poor start to the League – taking only nine points from their first 10 games – they rallied, beating Aberdeen twice in 10 days, to finish third to Aberdeen and Celtic for the second year in succession.

Dundee United's 1-0 defeat of Aberdeen at Pittodrie on December 22 ended a run of 24 home League matches without defeat. And which was the previous team to have a won League match at Pittodrie?

Dundee United in September 1983. Dundee United also put paid to Aberdeen's hopes of a fourth successive Scottish Cup when they beat them 2-1 in a semi-final replay at Tynecastle in April.

But despite these sterling performances against the runaway champions – Aberdeen led from start to finish and won the Premier League with a record number of points – it was the Old Firm that left Tayside without any Scottish silverware. Dundee United lost the League Cup final to Rangers by a solitary goal from Iain Ferguson and then the 100th Scottish Cup final to Celtic 2-1, having scored

the opening goal themselves.

In a season of remarkable performances by this canny side ably led by Jim McLean and Walter Smith, Dundee United saved probably their best for the third round Uefa Cup ties against Manchester United. In a thrilling match at Old Trafford in the first leg they were 1-0 down at half-time to a Strachan penalty before two goals from Hegarty and Sturrock meant that Manchester United went to Tannadice all square at 2-2. However, a McGinnis own goal spoilt the party and Dundee United went out 5-4 on aggregate in another wonderfully contested match.

A Juventus fan uses a plank to attack the barbed-wire perimeter fencing

Anti-climax: Juventus fans witness the return of the Cup at Turin airport

not been party to the events at Heysel. Liverpool took separate legal action. Only Spurs refused to be involved. The ban was upheld, the judge agreeing that

everything should be done, and be seen to be done, to ensure that such a tragedy never happened again. Sadly the football authorities did not heed him.

BOBBY ROBSON
Before Taylor, England were fine – but nobody noticed

Chris Nawrat

IT WOULD have been forgivable if, in the dark days of 1993, Bobby Robson had gloated over, or even taken some satisfaction in, the plight of Graham Taylor. His successor as the England manager had been bequeathed a team of world-class players, a team that had reached the World Cup semi-finals, yet Taylor had somehow perpetrated the impossible.

For only the third time since England had deigned to enter the World Cup in 1950 they had failed to qualify for the finals. Only Sir Alf Ramsey (in 1974) and Don Revie (in 1978) had committed such a gaffe. Ramsey was sacked, Revie fled to the riches of the Arabian deserts. Taylor, to his credit, eventually fell on his sword. And Robson, to his credit, kept his vow of silence.

It was a remarkable act of self-restraint. Robson, it should be remembered, had been the most vilified England manager ever. The tabloid press took a macabre delight in twisting the knife every time England had a poor result: "Plonker"; "In the name of God go"; "In the name of Allah go" (after a 1-1 draw away to Saudi Arabia); "England Mustafa New Boss" and "Desert Prats", were just some of the headlines during Robson's tenure. The hate campaign reached its nadir with revelations about extra-marital sexual liaisons.

Somehow Robson weathered all the storms whipped up by the media. They wounded him, upset him, but he stood firm. "It's the most difficult part of my life," he said. "It's very hurtful and you know it's going to hurt your family. I try not to read the papers too much. If it's abusive, I don't read it."

When Graham Taylor suffered much the same tabloid abuse, with much more justification as England suffered the embarrassment of defeat at the hands of the United States and conceding an eight-second goal to San Marino, Robson kept his own counsel. He could have said that after Ramsey, he was the best manager England ever had. He didn't. He could even have pointed out that, technically, Ramsey never actually qualified for the World Cup finals. (In 1966 England were the hosts, and in 1970 they qualified as the defending champions).

So let history say it for him. Under Robson England qualified for two successive World Cup finals. In 1986 England were top of their qualifying group, unbeaten with a goal difference of 19. In 1990 England were again unbeaten, second in their group without having conceded a goal – the only country to keep a clean sheet.

Then, when Robson's teams were on the world stage, they reached the quarter-finals and semi-finals respectively. By contrast, Scotland, having qualified seven times, have yet to get past

Hair's breadth from glory: Robson motivating his players before the shoot-out with West Germany

BOBBY ROBSON

Born February 18, 1933, Sacriston, County Durham

PLAYING CAREER
Fulham 1950-56
Signed in 1950 (152 games, 68 goals)
West Bromwich Albion 1956-62
Transferred for £25,000 (239 games, 56 goals)
Fulham 1962-67
Transferred for £20,000 (193 games, nine goals)
Internationals
Made his debut for England in November 1957 v France, and scored twice in the 4-0 victory. Received 20 caps and scored four goals

MANAGEMENT CAREER
Vancouver Royals Manager 1967-68
After an acrimonious break-up with the club he returned to Fulham
Fulham 1968-69
Appointed November, sacked January
Ipswich Manager 1969-82
Won the FA Cup in 1978; the Uefa Cup in 1981; League runners-up in 1981 and 1982
PSV Eindhoven Manager 1990-92
Won two League titles
Sporting Lisbon Manager 1992-93
Porto Manager 1994-
England
Manager of England July 1982 to July 1990
Record P 95 W 47 D 38 L 10 F 154 A 60

Moment of glory: Bobby Moore and Alf Ramsey get their hands on the World Cup

Journeyman: Greenwood had limited success

the first round. And who did Robson's teams lose to in 1986 and 1990? Argentina (courtesy of Maradona's cheating handball) and West Germany (via a penalty shoot-out), both of which went on to win the tournament. After Taylor's clangers, Robson's term of office now looks positively masterful.

History, of course, will not be so generous as to kindly overlook two disastrous European championship campaigns, 1984 and 1988, under Robson's management. In the first England failed to qualify, edged out by Denmark – a country not yet regarded as any kind of football power. In the second England stormed through to the finals in West Germany only to fall flat on their faces. They lost to Jack Charlton's Republic of Ireland, Holland and the Soviet Union to finish bottom of their group.

Strangely, a similar fate befell Graham Taylor in the European championships in Sweden in 1992, for which England had qualified without losing a match. Two goalless draws, no wins and only one goal. Once again this left England propping up the table. Robson, of course, bounced back. Taylor went under.

Quite why one England manager succeeds where another fails is a conundrum to which the mandarins of Lancaster Gate would dearly love to know the answer. Their appointment policy over the past 30-plus years shows no line of consistency whatsoever. If we ignore Walter Winterbottom (who never had control over team selection), Joe Mercer (who was a seven-match caretaker) and Terry Venables (who will not be truly tested until the European championships in 1996), England have had five managers: Sir Alf Ramsey, Don Revie, Ron Greenwood, Bobby Robson and Graham Taylor.

Of these five, three had been England internationals (Ramsey, Revie and Robson); three had been established First Division players (Ramsey, Revie and Robson); two were managers who had won the League championship (Ramsey and Revie); and three were managers who had won

other trophies (Revie, Greenwood, Robson).

Using just those bare statistics, Ramsey, England's most successful manager, has the best credentials. Despite never having managed a championship-winning team, Robson, with 20 caps, just edges out Revie, with six, by virtue of greater international experience as a player. Greenwood is way behind, with Taylor nowhere. Yet Revie was a disaster and Greenwood moderately successful.

Any analysis of the individual men's personalities gives little away as well. Robson and Taylor were ditherers? In his first eight matches Revie used 27 different players with only one ever-present. Taylor was frightened of flair players? They all were. Taylor dropped Paul Gascoigne and Chris Waddle (but persisted with John Barnes), but then Robson retired Kevin Keegan and Glenn Hoddle – whom Greenwood had hardly picked – Revie played Tony Currie just once and Ramsey discarded Jimmy Greaves.

And just to confuse the matter, there was one thing they all had in common: they had built their club successes on a tightly-knit camaraderie, a sort of family. Which is precisely the one thing

Ignominy: Taylor's team fell to earth

you cannot do in international management.

The job of England manager, which has often been described as being more onerous than the Prime Minister's, has been much misunderstood, particularly by its occupants. Ramsey was fortunate: the media were less intense in the 1960s; the pressure to succeed was not as compelling and the players were less demanding.

By the 1990s Taylor reaped the whirlwind that had (just) failed to sweep Robson away. The media pressure on the man in the hot seat borders on the unbearable. "You go into a press room and there's 250 journalists from all different countries," Robson told the author Johnny Rogan. "You've got 50 tape recorders on your desk and that's just the front row. There's five or six camera crews all filming live so if you stumble on a word it's all on tape. If Alf Ramsey moved into that now, he wouldn't believe it compared to what he had."

Taylor innocently thought that because he was brought up in a journalistic family he could sweet-talk his way past the press. He was wrong. Robson knew what the bottom line always was: "It's about results. You know what the job is? Winning."

The art of winning is arcane. Twice in the World Cup finals Robson lost the services of Bryan Robson, his captain fantastic, because of injuries. Robson is convinced that if, in the 1990 finals, he had been able to field a midfield of Bryan Robson, David Platt and Gascoigne, not only would they have beaten West Germany in the semi-final, Argentina would have fallen in the final and England would be the defending world champions.

Such a sweet outcome in Italy four years ago would have meant that Robson would have gone down in history as England's greatest manager and, of course, Graham Taylor would never have had to resign. He would have inherited an even better team from Robson, one that had automatically qualified for the 1994 World Cup finals. By such paper-thin scripts are destinies shaped.

Super League on the agenda

FOOTBALL finally gave in and accepted television's much-reduced offer midway through the season, but this did not stop the clubs' continual bickering. The arguments merely shifted to another power struggle.

Leading clubs wanted a greater say in how the game was run and talk of a breakaway Super League was rife. Even though Canon said they were not going to renew their backing of the League, and a group of sponsors warned the game that it had to get its act together before the money ran out, the wrangling went on.

Eventually the leading clubs got their way in April, although not until they had taken the Super League issue to the brink. The Second Division, fearful of losing their share of the television money, conceded that their voting rights should be reduced, and it was agreed that the First Division would shrink to 20 clubs over the next two seasons. To ease the realignment of the divisions, play-offs would be introduced.

At least the clubs realised that they were not going to be able to bully the television companies into submission. When the television contract came up for negotiation again in June, a £6.2m two-year agreement was reached in a matter of days.

Scotland, too had its share of the arguments. Unlike England, an agreement with television was in place in time for the start of the season. But within months there were arguments about the way the money was divided. By February nine of the 10 Premier League teams had joined forces and were threatening to set up their own league.

N Ireland and Scotland off to Mexico amid controversy

ALL the British teams bar Wales and the Republic of Ireland qualified for the World Cup finals in Mexico, England qualifying for the first time since 1970, coincidentally when the finals were also held in Mexico. England's cause was definitely helped by having Northern Ireland in the same Group. Billy Bingham's men beat Romania home and away while England could only draw both their matches with Romania.

Northern Ireland's qualification was not without a whiff of controversy. By November 13 an undefeated England had already qualified when they had thrashed Turkey 5-0 the month before, but Northern Ireland needed a point at Wembley to edge out Romania.

To British eyes an inspired 40-year-old Pat Jennings, who had not played League football for a year, in his 113th international (a world record), played a blinder to deny England in a goalless draw. To the Romanians it was a fix. But having lost twice to Northern Ireland themselves, it was more like sour grapes.

Wales were the team who had just cause for complaint for not being on the plane to Mexico. In the final match of the Group they had to beat Scotland at Ninian Park to qualify for a play-off against Australia or New Zealand, both minnows.

Wales were 1-0 ahead at half-time and the Scots were despondent. As the second half wore on Jock Stein, Scotland's manager, sensed the Welsh had settled for preserving their slender lead and Davie Cooper was sent on for Gordon Strachan. The Scots were immediately revitalised.

However the goal that levelled the scores and eliminated the Welsh should never have happened. With 10 minutes to go a dubious handball in the Welsh penalty area was adjudged by the French referee to be a penalty to Scotland. Cooper scored from the spot. Stein the maestro had pulled another masterstroke.

Sadly the match will be remembered for the death of the 62-year-old Stein, the most successful manager in Scottish history. Seconds before the final whistle he collapsed in the stadium's tunnel and died of a heart attack. Alex Ferguson, the successful manager of Aberdeen, stepped in as caretaker manager for the two-legged play-off against Australia (which Scotland won) and the finals in Mexico.

Cooper: vital penalty

Wembley wizard: Jennings kept England at bay to ensure Northern Ireland's World Cup qualification

United's flying start comes down to earth

MANCHESTER UNITED got off to such a flying start that people were soon assuming that they would run away with the First Division. United won their first 10 games to go nine points clear of Liverpool, and had Tottenham's long-standing record of 11 wins at the start of a season in their sights.

But a draw with Luton cost them the honour which, instead, went to Reading with 13 successive victories. But while Reading duly ran away with the Third Division, United's challenge faltered. They clung to the top of the First Division for the first half of the season, but they were dropping too many points and their early advantage was slowly whittled away.

Liverpool were reshaping their side and people were questioning whether Kenny Dalglish could make the transition from player to player-manager. There was even talk of this being London's year, with Chelsea and West Ham going well.

But it was Everton who showed first with an outstanding 2-0 victory at Anfield in February that put them in the driving seat. It looked as if

Everton were going to go one better than their neighbours for the second year running.

But you wrote off Liverpool at your peril. And the turning point came when Dalglish restored himself to the team. He had dropped himself early in the season and played very little since, prompting speculation that he was on the verge of giving up playing altogether.

Liverpool had seven matches left and they needed to win every one of them to stand any chance of catching up. Everton faltered, drawing at Nottingham Forest and losing at Oxford, and Liverpool pounced. Inspired by Dalglish they won all seven matches, only conceding one goal. Fittingly, it was Dalglish who scored early in Liverpool's last match, a far from easy trip to Chelsea, to take the title to Anfield for the sixteenth time.

Everton, too, had a tough last match at home to West Ham to decide who took second place. But West Ham's fixture backlog (10 games in under a month) caught up with them, and Everton easily prevailed in one of the most exciting finishes to the season for years.

Dalglish: came back to secure Liverpool's sixteenth title

FOR THE RECORD

■ Bobby Robson said that he was not happy with the League's refusal to postpone matches before England's World Cup qualifying games.

■ Roma were banned from European competition for a year when their president was convicted of trying to bribe the referee before they played Dundee United in 1984.

■ Jack Charlton quit as manager of Newcastle after fans called for his resignation during a pre-season friendly with Sheffield United.

■ Charlton agreed to move to Selhurst Park after the Greater London Council condemned the east terrace at The Valley. Their last match at The Valley, on September 21, attracted their largest crowd of the season. After the game, fans dug up the pitch for souvenirs.

■ Tottenham postponed two matches in October on the advice of police, who were worried about further disturbances in the wake of the Broadwater Farm riot.

■ A Leeds director resigned in protest when Eddie Gray was sacked as manager on October 11.

■ Bob Wilson, the 44-year-old television presenter, signed for Bristol Rovers as a standby goalkeeper in November.

■ Ken Wright scored three goals in four minutes, and five in total, as Raith beat Stenhousemuir 9-2 on November 2.

Scotland mourns Stein, a colossus of the game and the people's hero

JOCK STEIN, the manager of the Scotland national team and a football colossus, collapsed from a heart attack and died in the tunnel at Ninian Park on September 10. It was seconds before the end of Scotland's match against Wales which all but qualified Stein's team for the 1986 World Cup finals. The tragedy numbed the players and the whole of Scotland.

Stein was the most successful manager in Scottish history. Although a Protestant, he became the manager of Celtic, where he had been captain the 1950s, and guided them to capture the European Cup in 1967, the first British side to do so.

Under Stein's stewardship Celtic won 10 League titles, eight Scottish Cups and six League Cups between 1965 and 1978 before a car accident almost cost him his life. Before his tenure at Parkhead, he had managed Dunfermline from 1960 to 1964, winning the Scottish Cup in 1961. He spent 10 months at Hibs before joining Celtic.

After his accident Stein was briefly the Leeds manager before returning to Scotland later that year to manage the national side and take them to the 1982 World Cup finals in Spain.

Stein was born on October 5, 1922 in the Lanarkshire mining town of Burnbank, a fervent football community which has produced many top players. And two other legendary managers, Matt Busby and Bill Shankly, hailed from just a few miles away. Like Busby and Shankly, Stein was a man of the people and never forgot his roots.

Stein: Celtic's guru

THE
1985-86
SEASON

Wimbledon tough it out

WIMBLEDON'S remarkable rise continued apace, but the unfashionable team were making themselves few friends along the way. In August, Wimbledon were fined £3,000 by the FA because of their players' bad disciplinary record – they collected more than 250 disciplinary points in the previous season, the third time that they had topped this figure.

And in December the police warned the team about their behaviour, with allegations that Wimbledon players had made provocative gestures to the home crowd during a match at Barnsley's Oakwell ground. Then, in July, Wimbledon were fined a further £3,500 because, once again, of the number of players they had had booked and sent off.

Dave Bassett, the Wimbledon manager, was quick to defend his team, arguing that they were being unfairly penalised for their direct style of play. And though Wimbledon's approach was not pretty it was certainly more than effective.

They were unbeaten in their last 16 League matches, and the arrival from neighbours Millwall of John Fashanu, the club's record signing (albeit for a mere £125,000), provided the goals to propel Wimbledon into the First Division for the first time in their history.

Contrary to public opinion, I don't tell my players to kick the opposition in the nuts

DAVE BASSETT
Wimbledon manager

Venables hires Lineker in answer to Barcelona's Spanish inquisition

TERRY VENABLES had a topsy-turvy season with Barcelona. In March the Catalan club, despite having won the Spanish League the previous season, announced that Venables's contract would not be renewed at the end of June and the speculation was that he would be replaced by Howard Kendall. Unhappy with all the rumours, Venables responded by saying he intended to take a year off from the game. However, Arsenal made some not so discreet inquiries about his services which led to their coach, Don Howe, quitting in a huff.

Barcelona quickly changed their minds when Venables steered them to only their second European Cup final against the Romanian army side Steaua Bucharest, and confirmed Venables as their coach for the following season.

The final, in Seville in May, was a dreadful affair. The Spanish side, playing in their own

Team spirit is an illusion you only glimpse when you win

STEVE ARCHIBALD
of Barcelona

country, were under tremendous pressure to win and were the clear favourites. Yet on the night they froze. The Romanians went into their shell and stonewalled the Spanish for 120 minutes, and both sides failed to score.

In the penalty shoot-out the players' nerves were so frayed that only two of the seven penalties were scored, Steaua Bucharest surprisingly winning 2-0 to become the first east European side to lift the European Cup.

Not surprisingly Venables swooped during the World Cup finals to purchase a striker, and one that could also take penalties. Gary Lineker, of England and Everton, and the tournament's top scorer with six goals, joined Barcelona in July. It was believed that Lineker had cost the club in excess of £5.7m, with £4.2m going to Everton and £1.5m to the player.

Anxious moments for Venables and his assistant Alan Harris: under pressure at Nou Camp

'Rangers will sign Catholics' – Souness

RANGERS stunned everybody when they announced that Graeme Souness, then with Sampdoria, was to replace Jock Wallace as their player-manager. But there was a further shock in store at the press conference in April to announce his arrival. Souness pledged that the Glasgow club would now sign Catholics.

The statement created a furore in Glasgow where for 113 years the city had been divided by religious bigotry. Indeed, Rangers seemed to have an unwritten policy against fielding a Catholic player. Celtic, by contrast, had no such qualms about Protestants. Indeed Jock Stein, himself a Protestant, having been once asked who he would sign if offered a choice between two players of equal merit, one a Protestant and one a Catholic, replied: "The Protestant, because I know Rangers would never sign the Catholic."

But now, according to the former Liverpool player, all that was to change. "The best players will be signed, no matter what they are," Souness said. "It is not a thorny question as far as I

am concerned. How could I possibly have taken on this if I could not have signed Catholics? I am married to one and share my life with one. I could not have returned to Italy and told my wife I had the job, but there was a problem with Catholics."

Souness also vowed to go on a spending spree to find the best players and make Rangers one of the leading clubs in Britain. "I see this club as second only to Manchester United in Britain and bigger than Liverpool, Arsenal, Tottenham and anyone else."

However he was aware of the enormity of the task – Rangers had not won the title for nine years – and said: "To say I have been thrown in at the deep end is an understatement. I am envious of what Kenny Dalglish has done at Anfield and I want to follow in his footsteps. I believe I have taken on a harder job than he did because Liverpool were already a winning side."

Souness still had to see out the Italian season at Sampdoria before taking charge at Ibrox. Thirty-three in May, Souness cost Rangers some £400,000 in transfer fee and compensation.

Souness: "Thrown in at the deep end is an understatement"

Unhappy return: Bryan Robson (centre) was sent off in his comeback match

Hearts pipped at the post

IT WAS the cruellest of seasons for Hearts. The Edinburgh club took advantage of postponed matches to top the Premier Division on December 21 and tenaciously clung to the pole position until the very last Saturday with a 27-game undefeated run from October until May.

Then, away to modest Dundee, where a draw would have given them their first Premier Division title, they lost 2-0. Celtic, who had not been on top since the autumn, romped home 5-0 at St Mirren to steal the title on goal difference.

Aberdeen, who started well in the Premier Division, leading from October to mid-December, inexplicably slipped away, eventually finishing fourth. But the two Cups were a completely different story as they captured both. The League Cup was particularly sweet as it was the only domestic trophy that Alex Ferguson, their manager, had not previously won and Aberdeen did it without conceding a single goal. In the Scottish Cup Aberdeen compounded Hearts' misery at losing the championship by walloping them 3-0 in the final.

Bad weather and too many competitions cause chaos

THE FREEZING weather that gripped Europe in February reopened the debate about whether British football should have a mid-season break. But not everybody was in favour. When Millwall's FA Cup replay with Southampton was postponed for a second time George Graham, the Millwall manager, complained that football was getting too soft. "The pitch was fit enough for play," he said.

It was not long before the fixture lists were reduced to chaos. Matters were not helped by the invention of the Screen Sports Super Cup and the Full Members Cup, ostensibly to create more money-spinning matches. Critics accused the League of greed, and half of the clubs in the First and Second Divisions refused to enter the Full Members Cup. Those that took part saw little benefit and Coventry's match against Millwall drew just 1,086 spectators

Yet, at the same time, the Football League was insistent that the season had to finish on time to allow England to prepare for the World Cup. However, on April 1, the League finally had to concede that matches would have to be played after May 3, the original deadline.

Even then, many clubs suffered, particularly Darlington. Three days after the season should have ended their footsore team played their eighth match in 13 days and their second on successive nights – and they still had another two games to go.

Liverpool win Mersey final to double Dalglish's delight

THE CITY of Liverpool had never seen anything like it. They were used to the rivalry between Liverpool and Everton, but with both teams disputing the League title and both teams in the FA Cup final as well, the city went football crazy.

For weeks, the city was decked out in red and blue. And when Liverpool just pipped Everton in the League it only added to the excitement. Could Liverpool join the elite few who had done the Double? Or would Everton gain their revenge. It really did seem as if Liverpool was the centre of the footballing universe.

Tickets for the Wembley final were prized possessions. Some reports said that £6 standing tickets were changing hands for

£100, others put the price at nearer £1,000. But for most fans their tickets were priceless, not to be sold at any price.

And the game lived up to its billing, thanks to the master marksmen who had done so much for their teams. Gary Lineker struck first, tucking the rebound in after Bruce Grobbelaar could only parry his rasping shot. Everton were immediately inspired and played like a side possessed. Grobbelaar's goal was under siege and there was little Kenny Dalglish could do about it. Ian Rush, though, had other ideas.

Fed perfectly by Jan Molby, he ghosted through the Everton defence and round Bobby Mimms to put Liverpool back into the match. And five min-

utes later Rush combined with Molby again to set up Craig Johnston. Now it was Liverpool's turn to dominate and Everton's turn to suffer incessant pressure. With six minutes left Rush lashed another shot past Mimms to put the result beyond doubt.

It was the perfect end to Dalglish's first season as manager, and perfect proof that, despite what some pre-season doubters had thought, he was the right man to continue the great tradition started by Bill Shankly. And as Liverpool paraded the Cup around Wembley their supporters acknowledged the fact. Before they left the stadium they sang a moving tribute to the man who made it all possible – Shankly.

Perfect ending: Rush scored two goals and made one more in the thrilling FA Cup final

Rous, great reformer, dies

SIR STANLEY ROUS, the grand old man of British football died on July 18 at the age of 91.

Rous, the son of a grocer, began his love affair with football at an early age. He started his village's team while he was still at school and went on to play in goal for Lowestoft. But it was as an official rather than as a player that he made his mark.

After the first world war Rous became the senior sports master at Watford Grammar School and still found time to become a top-flight referee. He was a linesman at the 1926 Cup final and also took charge of the 1934 final. Rous's officiating was also respected throughout Europe, where he was the referee for 36 international matches.

Rous was one of six candidates to become secretary of the Football Association in 1934, and he was surprised to be appointed. But it soon became clear that the FA had made the right choice. In no time at all, Rous had rewritten the rules of the game and revolutionised the way that the linesmen and referee controlled matches, introducing yellow and red cards.

Rous's patient diplomacy was responsible for the home nations rejoining Fifa in 1947, and his tireless work for both Fifa and Uefa led to him being elected president of Fifa in 1961. But Rous was more than just an efficient administrator; one profile described him as "a man who resides at the mountain top, his views wide and all-embracing, his horizons limitless. Football is his game and the world his playing pitch."

Rous's work in modernising the game earned him respect wherever he went, and when he "retired" in 1974 he was immediately elected as an honorary life president of Fifa. He continued to be a keen spectator at football matches until just before his death, and hundreds of dignitaries from around the world attended a gala dinner to celebrate his 90th birthday.

Denis Follows, who succeeded him as the FA secretary, summed up Rous's contribution to world football when he said: "The secretary is the servant of the association and we all know what happened; the servant became the master."

Dalglish: the record-breaker who instantly made his mark as a manager

■ Kenny Dalglish won his 100th cap for Scotland on March 26.

■ Oxford United, in their first season in the First Division, won their first major trophy when they upset QPR 3-0 in the League Cup final on April 20.

■ Fifa lifted its ban on English clubs playing friendlies in Europe but, in May, Uefa decided not to readmit English clubs to the three European competitions.

■ Tottenham sacked Peter Shreeve and his assistant John Pratt on May 13. Three days later, David Pleat was appointed manager.

■ George Graham was appointed Arsenal manager in place of Don Howe on May 14.

■ Chris Woods moved from Norwich to Rangers on July 1 for £600,000, the British record fee for a goalkeeper. Rangers continued their spending spree when they signed Terry Butcher for £725,000, a Scottish record, later in the month.

■ Andy Roxburgh, who had never managed a club, was surprised to be named Scotland manager on July 16.

■ The Inland Revenue were granted a winding-up order against Middlesbrough on July 30.

■ There were two big transfers in the close season when Ian Rush was sold to Juventus for £3m and Gary Lineker joined Barcelona. The fee for Lineker was £4.2m and he got a £1.5m signing-on fee, spread over six years.

Spending spree: Rangers made Woods Britain's most expensive keeper

THE THIRTEENTH World Cup confirmed Diego Armando Maradona as the greatest player on earth. Sadly for the most popular sport on the globe it also confirmed him as the greatest cheat. Worse, the most blessedly gifted footballer since Pele was unrepentant, and boasted about his sin, calling it "the hand of God".

Maradona's disgrace was perpetrated in the quarter-final match against England. In the 51st minute Maradona and Peter Shilton, England's goalkeeper, rose together in the penalty area to meet a misdirected, lofted clearance from Steve Hodge. Maradona failed to get his head to the ball so he deliberately used his hand, flipper-like, to propel the ball over Shilton and into the England net. Instantly the Argentinian superstar danced away, arms aloft to celebrate his "goal". Inexplicably, the linesman did not raise his flag, and the Tunisian referee, Ali ben-Naceur, gave a goal despite Shilton's vehement protestations.

Everybody in the stadium and the billions watching on television knew what Maradona had done. Even he knew himself. That was what gave such offence, particularly when he tried to shrug off what had happened when the world's press interrogated him. "It was a little bit of Maradona's head, a little bit of the hand of God." Balderdash. It was all the hand of Maradona. But given the adulation he received in South America he probably thought that he *was* a god, and the rest of us poor, foolish mortals.

The England team were punch-drunk by the referee's decision. Thus, four minutes later, when Maradona did display his divine talent they literally stood by in astonishment. From a position wide on the right, and in his own half, Maradona took off to score a stupendous solo goal as he waltzed his way through virtually the entire England team. Peter Beardsley, Peter Reid, Gary Stevens, Terry Butcher and Terry Fenwick were all bamboozled before Maradona contemptuously put the ball past Shilton. As an Italian journalist remarked: "England were still in a state of shock, like a man who has just had his wallet stolen."

To their credit, England rallied, despite the manifest injustice done to them. With nine minutes remain-

WORLD CUP 1986

Maradona blasphemed his God-given talent

Hand of God: Maradona's cheating tarnished Argentina's triumph

ing John Barnes, who had come on as a substitute for Trevor Steven to add firepower to England's attack, in true winger's fashion ran straight at the Argentinian defence, rounded the full-back and pulled back the perfect cross for Gary Lineker to head home. Six minutes later Barnes, with a similar scintillating run, broke the Argentine defence yet again, but this time Lineker could not quite reach the cross for justice to be done.

England's path to the quarter-finals had not been a smooth one. Bryan Robson, their captain, had been carrying an injury whose full extent had not been known. England began their campaign by losing a scrappy game 1-0 to Portugal. Their bad start bordered on the cat-

astrophic in their second game when Robson dislocated his shoulder, Ray Wilkins was sent off for petulantly throwing the ball at the Paraguayan referee five minutes before half-time, and England could only draw 0-0 with Morocco. Ironically, this forced Bobby Robson, the England manager, to reshape his team, particularly in midfield, and it worked to his advantage.

The revamped team with Reid, Steven and Hodge in place trounced Poland 3-0 with a Lineker hat-trick to comfortably qualify for the next round, where Lineker, with another two goals, and Beardsley with one, easily eliminated Paraguay to set up the fateful clash with Argentina.

Northern Ireland and Scotland, the other British representatives, were unable to make it past the first phase. Northern Ireland always had an uphill task in a group that contained Brazil and Spain. Their only point came from a 1-1 draw with Algeria.

Scotland, too, were in a powerful group, nicknamed the group of death. But, unlike England, they were not able to reorganise in the face of adversity. Scotland had, in fact, inadvertently reshaped their team before the tournament started, by dropping Alan Hansen. Kenny Dalglish, his Liverpool teammate, miffed at Hansen's omission, then realised that he was carrying an injury.

Scotland lost their first match 1-0 to Denmark and then enjoyed their best game against West Germany where, shades of 1982 against Brazil, they briefly led courtesy of a goal from Gordon Strachan. In their final match, they could only draw 0-0 with a violent Uruguayan team who had a player sent off in the first minute. Had Scotland beaten the 10 men they would have reached the second round as one of the third-placed teams.

Fifa had been tinkering with the structure of the competition yet again, and had decided to abandon a second phase played on a group basis in favour of reinstating the knockout element after the first round. But the only way of reducing 24 teams to 16 was by allowing the four best third-placed teams from the first round to qualify.

Not only did this make this first round even more meaningless than in 1982 – now 36 matches would only eliminate eight countries – it also created anomalies. There could be no complaint about Belgium and Poland qualifying in third place with three points. But both Bulgaria and Portugal finished with two points and a goal difference of minus two. Bulgaria qualified because they finished third in their group, Portugal went home because they were fourth in their group. Worse, Uruguay finished with an inferior record to Portugal's (two points but a goal difference of minus five) but still qualified because they finished in third place.

Not that Uruguay lasted long. Argentina dispatched them in the second round 1-0 en route to a final showdown with West Germany,

Mixed fortunes: Strachan scored Scotland's only goal; Lineker was the tournament's leading scorer and Pumpido denies Rummenigge in the final

who had been getting stronger as the tournament progressed. However Franz Beckenbauer, their coach, kept insisting that they weren't good enough to win the tournament. In the first hour it looked as if he was right as Argentina, the hot favourites, established a seemingly impregnable 2-0 lead.

Lothar Matthäus, who had been given the job of marking Maradona, gave Argentina their first goal when he brought him down from behind. Jorge Burruchaga floated the free-kick into the area and José-Luis Brown outjumped Schumacher on the far post. The second was equally clear cut. Enrique put Jorge Valdano away on the right and, once again, Schumacher was found wanting. Despite Beckenbauer's doubts about his team, they then showed great resolve to get back on level terms. Rudi Völler flicked on a cor-

ner for Karl-Heinz Rummenigge in the 73rd minute. Nine minutes later, in a similar move, it was Völler's turn to finish off a corner with a header.

But Argentina and Maradona were not to be denied. Two minutes later, the Argentine captain split the West German defence with a pass giving Burruchaga oceans of space to stroke home the winner.

So Maradona and Argentina

won the World Cup. History will not quite remember it that way. For sure, the record books will show Argentina, captain Diego Armando Maradona, as the 1986 World champions. But people will not put great store by that triumph. Nor will they recall that Maradona was especially brilliant. Their abiding memory will be that he was a cheat. That should haunt Maradona for the rest of his days.

Atkinson out, Ferguson in

MANCHESTER UNITED'S terrible start to the season did not take long to cost Ron Atkinson his job. During Atkinson's time in charge United had never finished lower than fourth in the League, but only three wins from 13 matches left them 19th in the table.

The final straw came when United were humbled by Southampton in a third round replay in the League Cup on November 4. After the 4-1 defeat Atkinson admitted that he had hit rock bottom in his five-year tenure at Old Trafford and said: "We need to get some First Division respectability and I still believe that is possible with the staff we have got. I thought we would get a result at Southampton but things didn't work out. That's history now."

But within two days Atkinson was history in the most expensive sacking in English football. Tommy Docherty, perhaps still bitter at having to leave Old Trafford under a cloud, was quick to dance on Atkinson's grave. He said: "The sacking of Ron Atkinson is the best thing that could happen to Manchester United and it didn't come a day too soon. I don't like to see any manager get the sack, but I can't say I feel sorry because I hate the man.

"His downfall has been all of his own doing. I dislike him because of his flash personality. And to my mind it's that sort of attitude which has finally got him the sack."

Atkinson was replaced by Alex Ferguson, the successful Aberdeen manager who had

previously rejected offers from Rangers, Arsenal and Tottenham, but admitted: "The Old Trafford job was one I simply could not turn down."

The change cost United more than £1m in compensation to Atkinson, his coach Mick Brown and Aberdeen, plus a £400,000 contract for Ferguson.

But despite inheriting an ageing team, Ferguson was upbeat about the future. "The League title has got to be the players' objective and they could even do it this season," he said. "I have never thought in terms of being second or third. My job is to win every game here. That's the way I intend to attack the job, and I'm sure the players do not need to be told what the target is."

Despite losing his first match in charge, Ferguson soon won the respect of the players: "He put his finger on things quickly and made a very good impression – he was a breath of fresh air," Kevin Moran said.

United recovered to finish in 11th place, but Ferguson knew he still had a lot of work to do if he was going to mount a serious challenge for the League title. At the end of the season he told the board that they needed nine new players to win the championship.

Atkinson: the most expensive sacking in English football

Liverpool fans in court

THE HEYSEL tragedy continued to haunt English football as the case involving 26 Liverpool fans dragged through the courts.

The fans first appeared before magistrates in September, but the proceedings against them were adjourned twice. Finally, the presiding magistrate said that there was a case to answer and that they should be extradited to Belgium to face charges of involuntary manslaughter.

But the fans appealed to the High Court and succeeded in having the ruling overturned on a technicality, when Lord Justice Watkins said that the correct procedures had not been followed. MPs were outraged. Alf Dubs, Labour's home affairs spokesman, said it was a "disgraceful" decision. "We have been made to look fools and the Belgians will think we

are not serious about tackling the problem."

But the Belgians were not deterred by the setback. Represented by the Director of Public Prosecutions, they appealed to the House of Lords. On June 30, the fans, who had been on bail, were taken into custody. And a fortnight later five Law Lords unanimously allowed the appeal and said that the fans should be returned to Belgium.

Lord Bridge of Harwich said it was "absurd" to insist on strict adherence to a treaty signed in 1902 when such a grave crime was involved. This time it was the fans' families who were outraged. They claimed that the decision was political and also unfair as Juventus fans would escape punishment because there was no extradition treaty between Belgium and Italy.

Ferguson: had rejected offers from Rangers, Arsenal and Spurs

Souness brings success, strife and Sassenachs

GRAEME SOUNESS'S first season as the manager of Rangers was probably the most extraordinary in the history of the Ibrox club. At the end of it Rangers had won their first League championship for nine years, but not without mishaps and controversy along the way.

Souness had made his debut as player-manager in the League on August 9, away to Hibernian. Unfortunately the fiery Scot was involved in a full-scale brawl and was sent off. Nine players were booked as Rangers lost 2-1. Rangers were promptly fined £5,000, and Hibernian £1,000, by the Scottish FA.

Rangers' unhappy start continued through to the end of November as they won only 11 matches out of 19, and at one stage they were nine points behind the League leaders, Celtic. And on January 31 Rangers appeared to have a hit an all-time low when little Hamilton knocked them out of the Scottish Cup 1-0 at Ibrox, of all places.

However it may have been a blessing in disguise as Rangers were able to concentrate on the League where they had been whittling away Celtic's lead. Between November 29 and the last game of the programme on May 9 Rangers only lost one League match – to Celtic at Parkhead. Eventually Rangers won the title comfortably, six points ahead of their Old Firm rivals.

Dramatic though this turnaround was, even more surprising were Souness's forays into the transfer market. For once Scotland, which for more than a hundred years had witnessed an exodus of their best players to England, saw the trend reversed as Rangers lured no fewer than six Englishmen north of the border (Colin West from Watford, Chris Woods from Norwich, Terry Butcher from Ipswich, Neil Woods from Doncaster, Graham Roberts from Spurs and Jimmy Phillips from Bolton).

And in the close season he added Trevor Francis from Atalanta and Mark Falco of Spurs to bring the number up to a record eight. Souness may not have yet fulfilled his pledge to sign Catholics, but he was signing the next worst thing – Sassenachs.

Opening shot: Souness is sent off as George McCluskey of Hibs is carried off

Heading in the opposite direction: Souness with Roberts, one of the many Englishmen he signed

FOR THE RECORD

■ Middlesbrough, in the hands of the Official Receiver, had to play their first home match of the season at Hartlepool because they were locked out of Ayresome Park. The club was rescued when a new consortium agreed to pay all the outstanding debts.

■ Manchester United fined seven of their players a total of £12,000 for being late for dinner on the club's pre-season tour of Denmark.

■ Harry Haslam, the former Luton and Sheffield United manager, died on September 11, aged 65.

■ Aston Villa sacked Graham Turner on September 14, the day after the first team had been thrashed 6-0 by Nottingham Forest and the reserves had been walloped 7-0 by Manchester United.

■ There was another fire at Bradford on September 20, when Leeds fans overturned a fish and chip stall which caught alight.

■ Fulham suffered their record defeat on September 23, 10-1 at the hands of Liverpool in the League Cup.

Harvey: replaced Kendall

Everton win the pass-the-parcel contest but suddenly lose Kendall

DESPITE the vain attempts of the likes of Tottenham, Wimbledon, Nottingham Forest and Arsenal to vie for the League title, once again it became a private Merseyside duel. And for the second time in three years Everton won the League championship, and yet again at a canter – nine points ahead of Liverpool. So for the third year in succession the two Merseyside clubs had occupied the top two positions in the First Division championship.

Not that this was quite clear when the season started with the First Division leadership changing hands like a game of pass the parcel. Tottenham Hotspur were the first to hold pole position before giving way to Wimbledon

at the beginning of September.

Purists howled at the thought of biff and bang merchants even contemplating the championship, but then Forest took top spot and stayed in the top three until the New Year before faltering. Arsenal also had their share of title pretensions – leading from mid-November to the end of January.

But come the New Year the Liverpool giants stretched their legs and put together a string of form that left all the others in their wake. Kenny Dalglish's Liverpool went 12 League matches without defeat, winning 10, to gallop their way to top place. But five defeats in their final nine matches realistically killed off their last

hopes of the championship.

Everton's run was even more remarkable: of their last 29 League matches they only lost four, slowly moving from midtable to the front. Howard Kendall, their manager, had admirably proved the old adage that the First Division title race is a marathon, not a sprint.

Then, in June, Everton fans were shocked to learn that Kendall, who had guided their club to the European Cup Winners' Cup, two League titles and the FA Cup in six years, was leaving to coach Spanish club Athletic Bilbao. Colin Harvey, Kendall's assistant coach and midfield colleague in Everton's 1970 championship-winning side, took over as manager.

Mergers bypassed as Londoners unite to stay divided

MERGER MANIA swept London but the boardroom plans were soon scotched by rival fans, who were united by their common desire to see their teams saved.

The first two clubs to contemplate an amalgamation were Wimbledon and Crystal Palace. The idea was prompted by Wimbledon suffering a low level of support and a ground that was little changed from the club's days in the Southern League. Sam Hammam, Wimbledon's Lebanese managing director, saw the formation of a south London "super club" based at Selhurst Park and the sale of Plough Lane as a logical step forward.

But when the news broke in February both sets of fans were violently opposed to the idea. Wimbledon's fans staged a pitch invasion and Ron Noades, the Crystal Palace chairman, admitted that he had received death threats. Chris Wright, the leader of the Palace Action Group, even went so far as to say: "If Sam Hammam buys Palace he will think the streets of Beirut are quiet compared to what will happen in SE25."

The plan was short-lived, and

We will not be moved 1: QPR fans protest against the proposed merger with Fulham

called off by Noades when more than 90% of the Palace fans voted against the idea in a ballot in the club's programme.

On February 28 there were also simultaneous protests at QPR and Fulham, where both matches were held up for 20 minutes. The target of the fans' ire was a proposed shotgun wedding between the two clubs.

Like Hammam, David Bulstrode of Marler Estates, who owned Fulham, said that he was going to merge the club with QPR and move to Loftus Road. Jim Gregory, the QPR chairman who had sold out to Bulstrode, was promptly greeted with banners that read "Jim 'Judas' Gregory sold the QPR family for 30 pieces of silver –

traitor", and "Marler – football's Aids virus."

The Football League's management committee was forced to call an emergency meeting, which decided to block the merger. But in the end Bulstrode decided to save them the trouble by calling the move off himself and selling Fulham to a consortium led by Jimmy Hill.

Brave Luton ban away fans

ON THE face of it, Luton Town's decision to ban away fans from matches at Kenilworth Road seemed an excellent idea. In the 1984-85 season not only had there been the appalling scenes when Millwall fans invaded their pitch, fought with police and ran amok through the town, there had also been 190 arrests and 96 casualties throughout the season. The toll went down to 102 in 1985-86. However once the ban was imposed in 1986-87 there was not one single arrest made inside or outside the ground. But there was an almighty row.

The argument against the ban on away fans was three-fold. First, it penalised the innocent as well as the guilty. Second, it deprived the game of its atmosphere and third, it also deprived the away team from valuable vocal support. Luton's counter to this was that it made the game safer, the local residents were not plagued by hooliganism and the club saved a fortune in policing costs.

The Football League's opening salvo was to instruct Luton to lift the ban for League Cup matches. David Evans, the chairman, refused. The scheme, using identity cards, got underway four days later with a home match against Southampton. Unfortunately there were problems with the computerised turnstiles and many supporters missed Luton's fourth-minute opening goal. Critics gloated.

The row blew up in September when Luton insisted that Cardiff City supporters would not be allowed into their ground for their forthcoming League Cup match, notwithstanding a League regulation that stipulated the home club had to provide 25% of the available tickets for away supporters. Luton were expelled from the competition. Luton then said they would play behind closed doors as this would not breach League regulations. By October 6, after a meeting of all 92 clubs, the League suggested the match should be played at a neutral venue, but Luton refused and withdrew from the competition.

We will not be moved 2: David Evans stands firm over the ban on away fans

Two days later the FA muddied the waters still further by announcing that Luton could compete in the FA Cup without away supporters but only if they allowed other clubs to ban their supporters as well. Upset with this decision, there were idle murmurings that various League clubs would boycott the FA Cup.

By December tempers were frayed on all sides and Luton offered a partial relaxation of their ban: 500 tickets would be offered to certain clubs, increasing to 1,000 if there was no trouble. But when Luton drew Liverpool at home in the FA Cup tempers almost boiled over. The BBC came to the rescue and screened the game live on a Sunday.

Now the fracas turned into a farce. Liverpool were held to a goalless draw and Luton contrived to miss the replay at Anfield when their plane was unable to take off. Kenny Dalglish, the Liverpool manager, demanded an inquiry. When Luton did play a fortnight later they thrashed Liverpool 3-0 and Dalglish complained they should not even have been in the competition, having missed the original replay. The gods struck again when Luton were drawn to play QPR – at home. Fortunately for all concerned Luton lost the replay and the row subsided.

On June 4, despite the support of the Bedfordshire police for the scheme, Luton quietly announced they would discontinue their ban on away supporters and a brave, but foolhardy, attempt to tackle hooliganism ended.

The mighty fall sad victims to first play-offs

THE FIRST end of season play-offs in modern history brought only grief to two formerly mighty clubs, both of whom sunk to depths they had never reached before.

Sad Sunderland slipped into the Third Division for the first time in their history despite beating Gillingham 4-3 at Roker Park in front of their biggest crowd of the season. But that result, in the second leg, left the score 6-6 on aggregate and Sunderland went down on the away goals rule.

Bob Stokoe, their caretaker manager, immediately quit, despite having only been in charge for less than a month. Stokoe, who was brought in as caretaker manager to try to stave off relegation when Lawrie McMenemy left, said: "The most important thing is not my future, but that of Sunderland. I was brought in to help them survive and we have just failed. I've put in my heart and soul, but I think it's fate in some ways."

Phil Neal, the Bolton player-manager, was also fated to see his club slip into the Fourth Division for the first time in its history. Neal did stay with his club, though he decided to give up as a player. "The legs won't go any more," he said.

There was happier news, though, for Charlton, who kept their place in the First Division after beating Leeds in a replay; Swindon, who returned to the Second Division after nearly 20 years, again after a replay, and Aldershot, who won promotion to the Third Division against Wolverhampton.

Dundee United's trophy cupboard still bare

DUNDEE UNITED won many friends, but sadly no trophies. They became the first Scottish side to reach the final of the Uefa Cup, and with the big guns knocking each other out progressed smoothly to the Scottish Cup final against St Mirren. Under the inspirational management of Jim McLean they played neat, tidy, attractive football, and although their League aspirations had faded shortly after the New Year, they surely expected one piece of silverware.

By comparison with the Scottish Cup, their path to the Uefa Cup final had been strewn with giants. They eliminated Hadjuk Split 2-0, then Barcelona – under Terry Venables and last year's European Cup finalists – 3-1, which included a memorable 2-1 victory in the Nou Camp.

Their away performance in the second leg of the semi-final was perhaps even more remarkable. Having been held 0-0 at Tannadice they swept past Borussia Moenchengladbach 2-0 to reach the final against Gothenburg. A battling performance – particularly from their goalkeeper Billy Thompson – saw them lose only 1-0 in Sweden, but in the second leg they were never allowed to recover from Gothenburg's first-half goal and eventually lost 2-1.

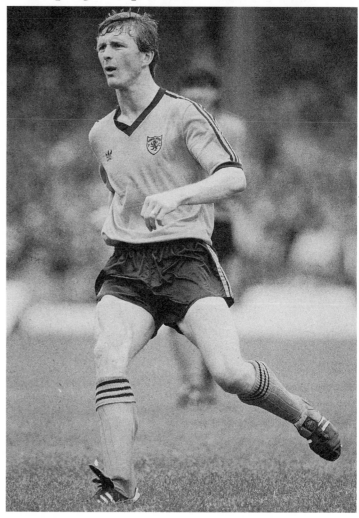

Paul Hegarty: One of Jim McLean's stalwarts in a frustrating season

Three days earlier, despite being favourites, they had lost a lacklustre Scottish Cup final to St Mirren in extra time. It was the first time that St Mirren had won the Cup since 1959. And so to everyone's surprise, Dundee United's cupboard was bare.

Torquay's bizarre escape as police dog bites a player

AUTOMATIC relegation from the Fourth Division made for a nail-biting finish on the last day of the season. And, in a bizarre twist to the tale, Torquay escaped the drop thanks to one of their players being bitten by a police dog.

With just eight minutes remaining Torquay trailed Crewe 2-1, and their biggest crowd of the season were resigning themselves to the drop. Jim McNichol went down injured and Ginger, a police dog, forgot his training and rushed on to the pitch. He sunk his teeth into the helpless Torquay defender and the referee was forced to halt the game for five minutes while McNichol received treatment to the wounds.

The stoppage threw Torquay a lifeline and with just seconds remaining in injury time Paul Dobson scored an equaliser. The 2-2 draw was enough to condemn Lincoln, who lost 2-0 at Swansea, to the GM-Vauxhall Conference on goal difference. Their place was taken by Scarborough.

Lew Pope, the Torquay chairman, said: "I'm going to buy Ginger the biggest steak in Torquay."

Dobson: life-saving equaliser

Coventry break Spurs' perfect record

COVENTRY, who had never appeared in an FA Cup final in their 104-year history, confounded Tottenham who had never lost any of their seven finals. Very much the underdogs, Coventry fought bravely and gamely to twice come from behind to eventually triumph 3-2 in extra time. But although it was a match full of drama and courage, it was also a match strewn with errors.

Tottenham had opened the scoring in the second minute when Chris Waddle picked up a woefully inadequate clearance and produced one of his dazzling bursts to cross the ball high to the far post. In darted Clive Allen to glance his 49th goal of the season. But, within seven minutes, Coventry, the poor relations of the expensively-assembled London side, were level. A cross from Gregory Downs was not cleared by either Ray Clemence or Steve Hodge and the nippy Dave Bennett whipped the ball away and thumped it home.

Defensive frailty was the culprit again four minutes from half-time when Hoddle's free-kick sailed over the stranded Steve Ogrizovic for the hapless Brian Kilcline to put through his own net as Gary Mabbutt thundered in. Yet Coventry never gave up and 18 minutes after the break had forced another equaliser when Bennett's cross eluded the Spurs defence and Keith Houchen headed home. And so to extra time.

This was to prove exceptionally cruel to Gary Mabbutt. In his attempt to clear Lloyd McGrath's cross he merely deflected the ball into his own net after six minutes. Thus a Tottenham side that included Osvaldo Ardiles and Glenn Hoddle surrendered their historic record.

It was a remarkable triumph for a modest, provincial club and just reward for the canny management duo of George Curtis and John Sillett. Forget that they had only finished tenth in the League, now it was Coventry that had never lost an FA Cup final.

From villain to hero: Kilcline scored an own goal but still collected the Cup

Hot shot: Clive Allen, Footballer of the Year, finished with 49 goals

DIEGO MARADONA
The demi-god who proved to have hands of clay

John Duncan

IF ONLY Steve Hodge had belted the ball into touch. If only Peter Shilton had gone for his punch with more conviction. If only it was possible to remember Diego Maradona for the second goal he scored against England in the World Cup quarter-final of 1986 and not the first.

But temptation was not something Maradona was used to resisting. Rising with Shilton he disguised his deception with practised skill, his crime exposed only by constant replay, his guilt hinted at by a momentary worried backwards glance at the referee. But however it was achieved the result will always stand, a fact of modern football that Maradona, the brightest star of an era where results and the riches that come with them meant everything, knew well.

Kindhearted souls might say that Maradona never had a chance, that he was the world's greatest player at a time when greed was good, that he was the victim of a burgeoning media market whose appetite could never be satiated. The best player and perfect representative of a discredited decade.

Diego Armando Maradona's first exposure to the potential of his own talent came at the age of

seven, when he began juggling oranges with his feet on a late-night Argentinian variety show. Born in 1960 to a poor family, he used the same skills entertaining the crowd in the half-time intervals of League matches.

He was signed by Argentinos Juniors at the age of 10, played a full season aged 16 in 1976 and helped the side earn promotion to the First Division. He was picked for the national team at the age of 17, but was dropped at the last minute from the Argentine squad for the 1978 World Cup. In 1981 he went to Boca Juniors (40 matches, 28 goals) who naturally enough won the title, before setting out on the world stage in 1982 having secured a move to Barcelona. He was still only 22 years old.

The world lay at Maradona's left foot. Two goals against Hungary in the first stages of the World Cup finals marked a few hatchet-men's cards. In the quarter-final groups he was struck in the face as he tried to turn the brutal Claudio Gentile, who escaped without punishment. Against Brazil he was constantly provoked until he was eventually shown the red card for his retribution, a chest high, studs raised assault.

Hand of God? The controversial goal

Perhaps this was the point when Maradona decided that skilfully executed cheating paid. His World Cup was over. The brutality was not.

Andoni Goicoechea, aka the Butcher of Bilbao, has a boot in a glass case in his living room. He doesn't need a plaque. Everybody who visits knows that this was the tool which Goicoechea used to destroy the ankle ligaments of Maradona in September 1983. That left the then Barcelona player with three steel pins in his leg. In one way or another, everybody wanted a piece of the best player in the world.

It was Terry Venables who rescued Maradona. With every 100-peseta thug in the Spanish League out to cripple him, virtually bankrupt, brash and unpopular in Barcelona despite his 22 goals in 36 games, Venables sold him to Napoli and saved his career.

On July 5, 1984, 60,000 people turned up to see Maradona in Napoli colours for the first time in a training session. The desperate southern Italian club, second-raters throughout their 58-year history, had got their man by agreeing to allow Maradona to pursue any external commercial interests he wanted.

The investment provided excellent returns. Maradona cost 13 billion lire; during his seven years at the club Napoli made profits of 200 billion lire. After whetting Neapolitan appetites Maradona returned to the international spotlight for the 1986 World Cup in Mexico.

Rarely can a single player have dominated a tournament as thoroughly. Argentina were an otherwise ordinary side, prodded to victory by the goals, crosses and powerful bursting runs of one man.

"Arsenal could have won the 1986 World Cup with Maradona," Bobby Robson said at the time. The crosses for all three goals against South Korea, a left-foot shot steered past Galli against Italy, the most perfect of crosses for

Out of favour: Maradona was jeered by the crowd after Argentina lost the World Cup final

Argentina's second goal against Bulgaria.

"The best one-footed player since Puskas," Sir Stanley Matthews said in Mexico. "In 1986," Franz Beckenbauer, the West German manager said, "there were moments when he reached the level of Pele."

Mexico's heat and altitude suited Maradona perfectly. Invisible for long stretches, he emerged from hiding to turn a game in an instant with a breathtaking piece of skill. Or skullduggery. Dismal, unadventurous England were holding out in the quarter-finals until Maradona attacked at the heart of their defence, the ball was lifted skywards by Hodge and Maradona punched the ball past Shilton.

"A little bit the hand of God, a little the head of Diego," he said in Spanish afterwards. The phrase gains a lot in translation. Five minutes later he gathered the ball inside his own half, brushed off Beardsley and Reid, ghosted past Butcher and Shilton and scored. It was one of the best World Cup goals ever. But it will never be his most famous.

The semi-final. Maradona burst into the area to reach a through ball (left-footed) before three converging Belgians. 1-0. He twisted past three more to shoot (left-footed). 2-0. In the final, West Germany were forced to employ Lothar Matthäus, their most creative midfielder, to snuff him out. With Maradona quiet and a 2-0 lead squandered, Maradona received a loose bouncing ball on the halfway line, twisted backwards and (left-footed), with two Germans within a yard of him, sent Burruchaga through to score the goal which won the Cup.

The Italian championship duly arrived, Maradona inspired, in 1987. Naples went berserk for five days. A Neapolitan graveyard was daubed with the slogan: "You don't know what you missed." The next day the slogan had been overwritten. "Don't be so sure we missed it."

Happier days: A jubilant Maradona after the defeat of England in the 1986 World Cup finals

---

DIEGO MARADONA

Born October 30, 1960, Lanus, Buenos Aires

PLAYING CAREER

Argentinos Juniors 1976-80
116 matches, 28 goals

Boca Juniors 1981-82
40 matches, 28 goals
Honours Argentinian championship 1981

Barcelona 1982-84
36 matches, 22 goals
Honours Spanish Cup: Winners 1983

Napoli 1984-91
186 matches, 81 goals
Honours Uefa Cup: Winners 1989
Italian League championship 1987, 1990
Italian Cup: Winners 1987

Seville 1992-93
26 matches, 5 goals

Newell's Old Boys 1993-

Internationals Argentina debut 1977
Honours World Cup: Winners 1986; Finalist 1990

But the wave of euphoria quickly crashed on the treacherous shores of self-destruction. Intoxicated and suffocated by ever increasing adulation and press attention, Maradona could never show his face during the day. Bravado became arrogance and he took to Napoli's seedy nightlife with a vengeance. Napoli's indulgence of his whims (he once stayed fishing with his father in Argentina after the Italian season had begun) left him to slide unchecked into disrepute.

He found it increasingly hard to get up in the mornings so Napoli had to train in the afternoons. Maradona drifted into the milieu of the Camorra and a disappointing 1988 left Napoli's 1989 title expectations low. But with the club enjoying a commanding lead at the top of Serie A the illegal betting operations of the Mafia were in line for huge losses, having underestimated Napoli's chances at 5-1.

Mysteriously, Maradona's form and the lead evaporated, with Napoli's first European triumph in the Uefa Cup barely appeasing the suspicions of a city where corruption is endemic. The title came again in 1990, but Maradona's time in Italy was coming to a close.

With Maradona overweight, suffering from a huge blood clot on his foot, and forced to have cortisone deposits from previous painkilling injections surgically scraped from his ankle, Argentina stuttered to the second round of the World Cup in Italy. Outplayed and outclassed by the luckless Brazil in the knockout stages, Maradona summoned a late effort with three Brazilians marking him and sent Caniggia through for the 80th-minute winner.

He did little as his side scraped through on penalties against Yugoslavia, before imploring Neapolitans to support Argentina in the semi-final. "Napoli no es Italia." It was a big mistake. Argentina beat the hosts on penalties but Italian supporters had their revenge on Maradona in the final, greeting his tears after a brutal and dull final against West Germany with derision.

Napoli fell out of love with Maradona and the 1990-91 season saw a long messy divorce. A succession of fines, failure to travel abroad with the team, announcements of retirement, a court case detailing his connection with drugs and prosti-

tutes, before finally, on March 17, 1991, the decree nisi. Maradona failed a dope test, traces of cocaine were found, and he was banned from the game for 15 months.

Napoli fought for custody insisting he returned after his ban, but instead the Argentinian opted for a brief inglorious spell at Seville, before returning to Argentina to star for an under-achieving Argentinian side, Newell's Old Boys.

But there were still more twists in the tale. After Argentina were humiliated 5-0 in Buenos Aires in a World Cup qualifier there was a clamour for Maradona to be recalled to the national side. Although 33, overweight, unfit and having been sacked by Newell's Old Boys for refusing to train, his country still believed in the myth of Maradona the miracle worker.

The adoring Argentina public got their way. Maradona returned for the two play-off games against Australia and his left foot seemed as sweet as ever as Argentina qualified for the finals in America. Now Maradona went into overdrive and incredibly shed nearly two stone in three months. When he stepped out in the Foxboro stadium in Boston on June 21 for Argentina's opening game against Greece he seemed to have rolled back the years.

His passing was as immaculate as ever and his goal against the Greeks was a thing of sublime beauty. But, as ever, the beast was lurking beneath the surface. After his country's second match Maradona was given a routine dope test – which he spectacularly failed and the roof caved in all over again.

The Argentine Football Federation promptly banished him from the tournament and Fifa banned him from any involvement in football. Maradona fled home to Argentina in disgrace yet again. This time his career was well and truly over. Even the flawed genius, although protesting his innocence, recognised this and announced his retirement.

If only Maradona had not been so stupid and foolish; if only he had been able to resist temptation; if only … but sadly the kid who had fought his way out of the gutter and reached the dizzy heights had finally plumbed the depths of ignominy.

287

Liverpool 1987-1988				
P	W	D	L	Pts
40	26	12	2	90

(3 points for a win, with 21 clubs)

Leeds 1973-1974				
P	W	D	L	Pts
42	24	14	4	62

(2 points for a win, with 22 clubs)

We know Ian Rush lets his goals do the talking, but so far he hasn't spoken very much

GIANNI AGNELLI
Juventus president

Liverpool storm to the title

FORGET Ian Rush, languishing at Juventus, Liverpool had John Aldridge. And what a replacement! When the dust settled on the season Liverpool had won the championship with nine points to spare, broken myriad records en route and the Rush look-alike had proved he was a look-alike in the scoring department: 26 goals in the League (to finish top scorer) and four in the Cups. Not bad for a Merseyside lad who had graduated from South Liverpool FC to Newport County to Oxford United . . . to Liverpool FC.

As usual, Liverpool began their League campaign slowly. But, before anybody had quite realised it, they were building an unbeaten run of phenomenal proportions. By December 19 Kenny Dalglish's side had gone 19 League games without defeat from the beginning of the season, their best start to a First Division season since 1949-50. On Boxing Day they broke their own record and were 10 points clear of Nottingham Forest.

The records kept tumbling. On January 31 their FA Cup

Perfect replacement: Aldridge finished top scorer in the League

fourth round victory at Aston Villa was their ninth consecutive game without conceding a goal. On March 16 they completed 29 games without defeat, emulating the record set by Don Revie's Leeds in 1973-74. Four days later came their Waterloo as Everton, the defending champions, prevented their bitter rivals from taking pole position in the history books in a

match as keenly contested, and as stirring, as any Cup final.

Ironically, the goal that undid them was scored by Wayne Clarke, the younger brother of Allan Clarke who was a key member of the Leeds side in their fabulous, unbeaten run 14 years earlier. Liverpool were to lose only one more League game, before clinching their 17th League title on April 23.

Rangers grab the headlines, Celtic the Double

HARDLY a day went by without either Graeme Souness or Rangers hitting the headlines in the English, as well as the Scottish, press. Unfortunately this was frequently for all the wrong reasons as Souness and his players kept getting themselves into hot water.

The season was barely a few weeks old before Souness had been sent off for a foul against the Celtic striker Billy Stark in Rangers' 1-0 defeat at Parkhead. He also hurled insults at the referee. It was the third time he had been sent off in little over a year. The Scottish FA punished the player-manager with a five-match ban.

In the next Old Firm clash on October 17 a goalmouth fracas of unbelievable proportions led to Terry Butcher and Chris Woods, of Rangers, and Frank McAvennie, of Celtic, all being

shown the red card. The Strathclyde police stepped in this time and charged the trio, along with Graham Roberts of Rangers, with disorderly conduct likely to provoke a breach of the peace. All four players pleaded not guilty.

Video evidence was used during their trial and both Woods and Butcher were found guilty and fined £500 and £250 respectively. Roberts escaped with a not proven verdict and only McAvennie was found not guilty. Within days there were rumours that the three Rangers players – all English – wanted to leave Ibrox and return to the south. In May, after a dressing-room argument with Souness, Roberts was granted a transfer and by August the former Tottenham player had joined Chelsea.

Despite the bad publicity,

Souness was his usual busy self in the transfer market and seemed to have no problem luring English stars to Ibrox. Ray Wilkins (£200,000) joined from Paris St Germain, and Mark Walters (£575,000) of Aston Villa was snatched from under the noses of Everton. Ian Ferguson was added to Souness's impressive squad from St Mirren for £850,000, a record between Scottish clubs, as was Richard Gough (£1.5m) from Spurs, a record between English and Scottish clubs.

Despite the transfer frenzy, Rangers had little silverware to show from the season. In October they captured the Scottish League Cup in a thrilling 3-3 draw with Aberdeen by winning the first-ever penalty shoot-out in the final, 5-3. Then their season fell apart. Terry Butcher broke his leg in the 1-0 home

McAvennie stands up to Woods

defeat by Aberdeen and missed the rest of the campaign. And to add insult to injury, Celtic cantered to the Double.

All change at White Hart Lane

THE COMINGS and goings at Tottenham made it resemble a railway station rather than a football club as White Hart Lane experienced a season of total upheaval. First to depart was Richard Gough, their centre-half. The homesick Scot was transferred to Rangers for £1.5m in October.

Next was David Pleat, the manager, 18 months after he had arrived. *The Sun* newspaper had revealed in June that police had questioned him about kerb crawling when he was the Luton manager. The Spurs board were unhappy about the affair but stood by him. But then in October the same newspaper revealed that he was yet again caught in a vice swoop and Pleat was finished at Tottenham.

Terry Venables, the former Spurs player who had quit Barcelona in September after a string of bad results, was persuaded to take up the post – but not until December when he had finished his holiday in Florida – and Osvaldo Ardiles was appointed caretaker player-coach. On the field Tottenham were having a nightmare. Their 3-0 home defeat by Wimbledon on October 31 was their fifth successive loss and there was a clamour for Venables to cut short his vacation.

By November 23 Spurs had gone seven games without a win and Venables took up his post a week early. Unfortunately Tottenham's tale of woe continued with an embarrassing 2-1 defeat in the Fourth Round of the FA Cup by Third Division Port Vale. Tottenham's season was in tatters – they had slipped from second in the table in September and eventually finished 13th – and was only enlivened by more arrivals and departures.

Ardiles went on loan to Blackburn minutes before the March 24 transfer deadline and Ray Clemence, their goalkeeper, announced he would retire at the end of the season. Meanwhile Venables went on a £6.5m spending spree capped by the signing of Paul Gascoigne in July for £2m from Newcastle. Gascoigne, at 21 and as yet uncapped by England, was Britain's first £2m player.

Other signings included Terry Fenwick, Bobby Mimms, Paul Stewart and Paul Walsh. For the long-suffering Spurs fans it finally looked as if Venables had the club back on the rails.

Sacked: David Pleat

Appointed: Terry Venables (right) and Alan Harris

Merthyr send Atalanta home punch drunk

LITTLE Merthyr Tydfil enjoyed the greatest night in their history when they humbled Atalanta 2-1 in the first round of the European Cup Winners' Cup on September 16.

The collection of part-timers from the Southern League Midland Division knocked the Italian Second Division team out of their stride right from the start of the match and Kevin Rogers gave them the lead after 35 minutes. Although Atalanta equalised quickly, Merthyr kept up the pressure and Ceri Williams scored a deserved winner in the 82nd minute.

Williams said: "I'll probably wake up tomorrow with a hangover. I have to leave for work at 6am, but that won't stop me celebrating." Williams was not the only person suffering a bad head the next day. An Italian reporter wrote that his town was "suffering from a hangover of Alpine proportions".

But Merthyr's celebrations were short-lived. Atalanta scored twice in five minutes (although Merthyr claimed that the first goal was offside) in the second leg. Merthyr hurled themselves forward in search of the equaliser and Williams went heart-stoppingly close with a 20-yard volley but the dream result was not to be.

Merthyr's honourable performance showed once again that the underdogs could have their day. In the League Cup, Reading overturned Chelsea and Southend, despite having the worst defensive record in the League, ousted another First Division side, Derby.

There were even more shocks in the FA Cup. Non-League sides Yeovil and Sutton despatched Cambridge and Peterborough, and Sutton took Middlesbrough to a third round replay. However, the season's giant-killing honours went to Third Division Port Vale, who toppled Tottenham 2-1 in the fourth round.

Macdonald's Huddersfield humiliated

MALCOLM MACDONALD left Maine Road a shell-shocked man on November 7. He had only been in charge of struggling Huddersfield for less than a month and he had just seen his team, bottom of the Second Division, annihilated 10-1 by Manchester City.

"Yes, I think you could say that it was perhaps my most humiliating day within football," Macdonald said. "I am shell-shocked as is everybody else connected with the club. We started off so well in the first quarter of an hour and could easily have scored a couple of goals, that was the silly thing about it. Once Manchester City went in front for some reason we just went totally to pieces. It was altogether just a total shambles."

Jimmy Frizzell, the Manchester City general manager, put it another way. Asked whether he had discussed the match with Macdonald, he said: "No. I've nae got many teeth and I would'nae like tae lose those I have."

City rewrote the record books that day; the biggest winning margin in their history, Huddersfield's worst defeat ever and the first time three players had scored a hat-trick in the same match for 25 years. And they went on to hammer Plymouth 6-2 a few days later, with Tony Adcock scoring another hat-trick.

By the end of the season, with Huddersfield firmly rooted to the bottom of the table, 14 points adrift with a goal difference of minus 59, Macdonald had resigned in despair.

Wimbledon ace Liverpool

"GAME, set and match to Wimbledon". That was just one of a host of headlines the day after one of the biggest upsets in the history of the FA Cup final. Liverpool, runaway League champions, and odds-on favourites to complete their second Double in three years, stumbled and fell over little Wimbledon, who 11 years previously had been a Southern League side. It was either a fairy-tale or a nightmare, depending on your point of view.

The hero of the day was without a doubt Dave Beasant, Wimbledon's goalkeeper and captain. His penalty save in the second half deprived Liverpool of the equaliser they needed to get back into a game that was fast slipping away from them. The villain was Brian Hill, the referee, who blew for a free kick when he should have played advantage and awarded a goal. Bravely, he admitted as much after the game.

That decision almost certainly turned the match. In the 35th minute Peter Beardsley was fouled by Andy Thorn but still managed to find the net. The goal did not stand and Liverpool were awarded a free kick instead. The injustice clearly unsettled their composure and, while they were still arguing with the referee about his decision, Lawrie Sanchez headed home a Dennis Wise free-kick. It was to be the only score.

The fates had certainly decreed that it was not going to be Liverpool's day. In the 61st minute John Aldridge stepped up to take his 12th penalty of the season, having successfully converted the previous 11. Beasant dived the full width of the goal to deny him. It was the first time a penalty had ever been missed in a Wembley Cup final. For the next 30 minutes Wimbledon's resolute defence defied the Liverpool bombardment and Beasant became the first goalkeeper to captain a Cup-winning side.

Strangely it was Beasant's last game for the club. Within three weeks he was transferred to Newcastle for £850,000, a British record for a goalkeeper.

Beasant was the first goalkeeper to captain a Cup-winning side

Match winner: Beasant's penalty save broke Liverpool's heart

Forest just keep hold of Clough in lengthy tug-of-war with Wales

WALES'S failure to qualify for the European championship cost Mike England his job after nearly eight years and brought a new twist to the club versus country debate.

When England was sacked in February there were rumours that Wales might turn to Brian Clough. Intense speculation reached a fever pitch when Clough said that he was prepared to leave Nottingham Forest if they stopped him running the Welsh team on a part-time basis. Both Clough and his chairman, Maurice Roworth, had talks with the Welsh FA but, in the end, Forest refused to allow Clough to take the job and he did not quit.

Wales struggled to come up with an alternative. Swansea refused to let Terry Yorath divide his time between two teams; the veteran Bob Paisley was mentioned in passing; Tottenham would not let Terry Venables be approached; David Williams, the Norwich coach, took charge for one match but his club blocked any further involvement; Clough threw his hat back in the ring and Roworth vetoed the idea again.

In little more than two months Wales had gone full circle so they went back to Yorath. He was appointed, at first for three matches and, finally, permanently in July, but still only on a part-time basis.

Mike England: sacked by Wales

Maxwell turns his beady eye on Watford

IF THERE was one thing that Robert Maxwell loved it was wheeling and dealing. Owning Derby, where he was the chairman, and Oxford, where his son was in charge, and still having shares in Reading was not enough to sate his appetite for power.

Maxwell wanted more. So, in November, he reached a £2m agreement with Elton John to buy Watford as well. But as far as the Football League was concerned that was one deal too many. The League refused to sanction the sale, which prompted a vitriolic outburst from Maxwell.

He dubbed the League's management committee the "mismanagement committee" and said: "What we have is a professional game dominated by incompetent, selfish, bungling amateurs. It is time those who love the sport woke up and kicked them out."

Philip Carter, the League's president, wasted no time in hitting back. He said: "He's a bare-knuckle fighter lashing out in all directions because he can't get his own way. His comments are unfortunate and deplorable. I thought he was attempting to

Like a candle in the wind: Elton John's liaison with Maxwell did not last long

use bully-boy tactics. He has made many outrageous statements."

Relations between the two men hardly improved when the League won a temporary injunction stopping Maxwell's company buying Elton John's shares but abandoned the court case four days later. Then a secret deal between Maxwell

and Carter, in which Maxwell could buy Watford in exchange for selling his interest in Oxford, unravelled as well.

Maxwell lost his temper yet again and Carter, accused of going back on a signed agreement by the Derby board, had his presidency of the League called into question.

The storm only blew over on

December 20 when Maxwell abandoned his plans for Watford and agreed to sell his shares in Reading. And the League, who had admitted that their rules may not have been able to stop Maxwell had he persevered, quickly reinforced their regulations restricting people having an interest in more than one club.

Dutch paint a masterpiece as England prove to be fakes

HOLLAND'S 2-0 defeat of the Soviet Union in the final of the European championships at long last laid to rest the ghosts of Dutch football. Twice they had reached the World Cup final, in 1974 and 1978, and lost – first to West Germany and then to Argentina. Now they had finally succeeded in a major tournament, and with brio.

Their 2-1 victory over West Germany in the semi-finals – their first for 32 years – was sweet revenge for their 1974 disappointment and surely consoled Rinus Michels, their manager, for his dispiriting loss 14 years earlier. And their football – centred around the fabulous talents of Marco Van Basten, Ruud Gullit and Frank Rijkaard – was reminiscent of the Total Football played by the Holland team of the 1970s.

In Van Basten, Holland possessed the man of the tournament and his performance in the final was electric. In the 33rd minute he headed a cross neatly into the path of Gullit who nodded a perfect goal past the Russian goalkeeper, Dassayev. Twenty minutes later Van Basten produced the goal of the tournament when he latched on to Arnold Muhren's deep cross and thundered an unstoppable volley past the hapless keeper. But just as it seemed that Holland would coast to victory, shades of past failures re-emerged.

Hans Van Breukelen, the Dutch keeper, foolishly gave away an unnecessary penalty six minutes after Van Basten's strike and all the old fears of snatching defeat from the jaws of victory came flooding back. Particularly as Holland had lost to the Soviet Union 13 days earlier in a group match. Fortunately for Van Breukelen he managed to save Belanov's penalty and the danger had passed.

For Bobby Robson's England the tournament was an unmitigated disaster. After all the worries about whether they would qualify at all for the finals in West Germany, they had done so in style. Having travelled to Belgrade needing a point against Yugoslavia, they came home convincing 4-1 victors. But in the finals they were cruelly exposed and lost all their three matches.

The most humiliating defeat was at the hands of the Republic of Ireland, managed by Jack Charlton, who had once been rejected as the England manager. The Republic were somewhat fortunate to have qualified at all, Scotland effectively doing the work for them by unexpectedly beating Bulgaria in Sofia in the last of the qualifying matches. The Irish team, largely composed of Football League players many of whom were only "Irish" because of parents or grandparents born in the Republic, played a canny spoiling game that utterly confounded England.

Ray Houghton's fifth-minute header, after blunders by Kenny Sansom and Gary Stevens left John Aldridge clear to fire in a cross, knocked England back on their heels. Inept performances from England's forwards, most noticeably John Barnes and, inexplicably, Gary Lineker, combined with a string of spectacular saves from Pat Bonner, the Irish keeper, sealed England's fate.

Further defeats at the hands of the Soviet Union and Holland meant that Robson's team had to slink home with their tails between their legs. Ireland, by contrast, drew with the Soviet Union, only lost 1-0 to Holland, narrowly missed out on a place in the semi-finals and came back national heroes.

Gullit: fabulous talents recreated the age of Total Football

Bonner: string of saves

Shearer, at 17, was the youngest hat-trick scorer in the First Division

FOR THE RECORD

■ Steve Bull of Wolverhampton scored a total of 52 goals, breaking the club's record that had stood since the 1938-39 season.

■ Uefa limited clubs to using four foreign players in European competitions next season and ruled that England, Scotland, Wales and Northern Ireland had to regarded as separate countries when counting "foreign" players. However, the restriction was waived for players already registered with clubs.

■ Wimbledon were charged with bringing the game into disrepute when nine of their players dropped their shorts during a testimonial match. The club was fined £5,000 and each of the players were fined £750.

■ Four of England's leading clubs – Arsenal, Liverpool, Manchester United and Tottenham – opted out of the Full Members' Cup.

■ Alan Shearer was the youngest player, at 17 years and 140 days, to score a hat-trick in the First Division when Southampton beat Arsenal 4-2 on April 9.

■ Gary Pallister became the first Second Division player to appear for England since Peter Taylor in 1976 when he made his debut against Hungary on April 27.

■ Peter Shilton broke Terry Paine's record when he played his 825th League match on April 30.

■ The 26 Liverpool fans facing charges in connection with the Heysel disaster were finally extradited to Belgium on September 7.

■ The FA sought sponsors for the FA Cup but a £20m four-year deal with Fosters fell through because the FA were not prepared to rename the competition.

More hooliganism keeps clubs out of Europe

BOBBY ROBSON'S humiliation at the European championships was made a hundred times worse for England off the field. The disgraceful scenes of English fans running amok undoubtedly condemned English clubs to at least another year in the wilderness.

Within days, the FA had withdrawn their application for English clubs to be readmitted to Europe. They knew that there was no chance of the ban being lifted because Uefa had already made it clear that they were not going to consider the matter until the tournament had finished.

The arrest of 381 English fans in Germany made for a grim end to a season that had been lawless before the opening day. The first taste of things to come occurred in early August, before a ball had even been kicked in anger. A ferry was forced to return to England when Manchester United and West Ham fans, both heading for pre-season friendlies on the continent, started fighting in the middle of the North Sea, terrifying the other passengers.

Then Scarborough should have celebrated their first ever game in the League on August 15. But there was so much disorder that the start of the second half was delayed by more than 10 minutes as police struggled to regain control. Eighteen fans were jailed for their part in the affray and Wolves, the visiting team, were fined £5,000 and ordered to make their away matches all-ticket.

The police and courts were also kept busy by players, who could hardly be said to be setting the best of examples. As well as court cases stemming from the battle of Ibrox, police had to stop the fighting between Lincoln and Barnet players in a GM-Vauxhall Conference match. Andy Brannigan of Arbroath was convicted of assault for breaking a player's leg, and Chris Kamara of Swindon was found guilty of causing grievous bodily harm to Jim Melrose of Shrewsbury.

The FA banned Kamara for the rest of the season and its chairman, Bert Millichip, said football was able to keep its house in order without the need

Punished: Kamara was banned for the rest of the season

for police involvement. However, in a season when more than 100 players were sent off before the end of November, proposals to deduct points from clubs with a poor disciplinary record received short shrift from the Football League.

293

Coventry make history the wrong way round at Sutton

THE third round of the FA Cup always produces some upsets but January 7 produced a truly memorable shock. With all the clouds hanging over the game, there was evidence aplenty that romance was alive and kicking.

Sutton United had drawn the First Division highflyers Coventry at home. The mid-table GM-Vauxhall Conference team were the usual eclectic mix; an insurance executive, a bricklayer, a Cambridge graduate, a member of the Jamaican international side, and a manager with a penchant for the finer points of English literature.

And the portents were there. Last season Sutton had taken Middlesbrough to a third round replay and had only lost by one goal after extra time. Then, Barrie Williams, their manager, had quoted Shakespeare to inspire his team. This time he chose Kipling's "everlasting teamwork of every bloomin' soul."

And it was undoubtedly Sutton's more cohesive teamwork that made Coventry wilt at Gander Green Lane. Tony Rains, the Sutton captain, struck first with a header from a corner in the 42nd minute. "We worked on it this morning, and I missed," he admitted.

Coventry equalised early in the second half but Matthew Hanlan restored Sutton's lead after two minutes. It was another set piece from a corner and, again, it had not worked in the morning training session.

Coventry besieged the Sutton goal, and twice had shots cleared off the line in the last few minutes, but they had no complaints. Their manager, John Sillett, admitted: "It will be worse when we open the papers and realise we made history the wrong way round."

Sutton's historic victory, only the sixth time a non-League club had knocked out a First Division side since the Second World War, duly captured all the headlines, putting Bradford's 1-0 victory over Tottenham into the shade.

But not even Williams' inspiration could lift Sutton in the fourth round against Norwich, when the giant-killers were themselves killed off. Two goals in two minutes were the start of an 8-0 rout.

Words of wisdom: Rains was inspired by his manager quoting Kipling

Clough gives troublemakers a taste of their own medicine

BRIAN CLOUGH found a novel way to deal with fans invading the pitch after Nottingham Forest's 5-2 defeat of QPR in the quarter-finals of the League Cup on January 18.

The Forest manager, a long-time campaigner against hooliganism, rushed off the bench, grabbed two fans, clipped them round the ear and hauled them off the pitch. People watching the incident on television did not quite know what to make of it; some thought he was a hero for tackling the louts but others thought he was wrong to descend to their level.

The next day Clough admitted that he had been in the wrong, even though he had acted for the best of reasons. Honour was restored when he apologised to the two fans and they, in turn, apologised to the club for running on to the pitch.

Gotcha: Television shows Clough collaring one of the fans invading the pitch

The Forest fans made their feelings clear when they cheered Clough before the start of Forest's next home game.

The FA, though, took a dimmer view, fining Clough £5,000 and banning him from the touchline for the rest of the season. Once again, the Forest fans showed what they thought, cheering Clough as he took his place in the stand.

Seconds out: Jones and Davis come out fighting

WIMBLEDON brought a new meaning to pre-season friendlies in their warm-up game on the Isle of Wight on August 14. Vinnie Jones, who epitomised their fighting spirit, did not take long to get in the swing of things when he laid out a Shanklin defender, an offence that cost him his place in the Charity Shield team.

There was worse to come as the brawling on the field got to be nearly as bad as the violence off it. The season was less than a month old when Paul Davis of Arsenal flattened Glenn Cockerill, breaking the Southampton player's jaw. Cockerill decided not to press charges, but the FA hit Davis with a £3,000 fine and a nine-match ban. Arsenal's reaction was to ban television cameras from their ground because ITV film of Davis throwing the punch was used by the disciplinary hearing.

The police were, however, involved after an ill-tempered match between Rangers and Aberdeen in October. Terry Butcher, incensed at a tackle that put Iain Durrant out of action for the rest of the season, kicked down the door of the referee's dressing-room. Although the police took no further action, the Scottish FA decided to fine Butcher £500.

The following month Wimbledon were back in the headlines for all the wrong reasons when John Fashanu allegedly punched Viv Anderson after Manchester United lost 2-1 in the League Cup.

Anderson hardly did his cause any good when, in his autobiography, he came out strongly in favour of professional fouls. But hopes that the FA were taking a tougher line on misconduct were dashed when Fashanu only received a three-match ban and £2,000 fine, and Anderson was banned for one match and fined £750.

Mark Dennis, too, was perceived to have got off lightly when he was charged with bringing the game into disrepute for the sixth time. He received the minimum ban of three matches, plus a £1,000 fine.

■ Liverpool had the best of the deal when Ian Rush returned to Anfield from Juventus for £2.8m on August 18. The transfer was almost £500,000 less than Juventus had paid to sign Rush from Liverpool.

■ Fourteen Liverpool fans were convicted of manslaughter in Belgium in cases arising from the Heysel riot. They were jailed for three years, with half of the sentence suspended, but allowed to return home on bail while they decided whether to appeal. Ten other fans were also cleared because of a lack of evidence.

■ The League finally reached a £44m agreement with ITV on August 8 when Gordon Taylor, the secretary of the players' union, agreed to halve the share of the money the PFA wanted to 5%. Even then, the players almost doubled the amount they received compared with the previous deal.

■ Russia won the gold medal at the Olympics by beating Brazil 2-1 in extra time.

■ Jackie Milburn, the legendary Newcastle player, died of cancer on October 9, aged 64.

Crowds line the street to mourn Newcastle's Jackie Milburn

Gotcha: Davis was hit with a £3,000 fine and a nine-match ban

All hell breaks loose as Rangers sign a Catholic

GRAEME SOUNESS and Rangers stunned all of Scotland when they actually did the unthinkable: on July 10 they signed a Catholic, Mo Johnston. Souness had vowed he would when he took the helm at Ibrox three years previously, but so far his major excursions into the transfer market had been to lure Englishmen north of the border.

Johnston's transfer was controversial twice over. Aside from being a Catholic, he was a former Celtic player who had agreed to rejoin them from Nantes on May 12 for £1.2m. And Celtic had even paraded him before the Scottish Cup final. Miraculously Souness had managed to incense both sets of rival fans in Glasgow.

Bigoted Rangers' supporters demonstrated outside Ibrox and burnt scarves, programmes and tickets in protest. Over at Parkhead, Celtic's management could not believe what had happened. Johnston, the 27-year-old Scottish international striker they had sold to Watford, having agreed to join Celtic then refused, had been instructed by Fifa's general secretary, Sepp Blatter, to stick to his verbal agreement. Johnston claimed that he had not signed a contract.

The £1.5m transfer brought Souness's dealings to £11m. To Protestant bigots he was a traitor. To the cynics the surprise was that Johnston was not English.

The day football killed itself

You'll never walk alone: the goal at the Kop end draped with flowers and mementoes

Lest we forget: Grobbelaar and Nicol at the requiem mass in Liverpool Cathedral

> *Football is irrelevant now, nobody is even asking after the other scores*
>
> KENNY DALGLISH
> immediately after
> the Hillsborough disaster

BRITAIN'S worst sporting tragedy occurred at one of football's showpiece events: the FA Cup semi-final, and millions around the world watched in horror as 95 spectators, including women and children, were killed and hundreds injured.

However, unlike the Heysel disaster, hooliganism was not responsible, this time the blame had to be laid squarely at football's door. For despite the deaths that had occurred at Ibrox in 1971 and Bradford and Heysel in 1985, England's stadiums were still death traps and football's administrators had done little, if anything, to deal with the problem.

Thus, at 2.50pm on April 15 at the all-ticket match between Liverpool and Nottingham Forest at Hillsborough the police allowed between 3,000 and 4,000 Liverpool fans, restless at the length of the queues and anxious about the approaching kick-off, to rush into the Leppings Lane End of the stadium.

In the surge that ensued thousands of the spectators were crushed against the perimeter fencing behind the Liverpool goal and, in the panic, were unable to escape. At the time most people were unaware of the scale of the disaster, believing that it was just a case of rowdyism. After six minutes the referee stopped the match as fans tore down advertising hoardings to use as makeshift stretchers and the full horror of the scene became apparent.

The catalogue of errors that led to this was legion. Liverpool had been allocated 24,000 tickets when their average attendance was 40,000 whereas Forest had been given 30,000 when their average was 17,000. There was a breakdown in communications with the emergency services and ambulances and medical equipment arrived late because they were not informed of the scale of the problem. And so on.

But the principal reason for the tragedy lay in the attitude football had to its stadiums. Instead of treating them as places of entertainment, they were more like prisons with fans on the terraces caged in, as if they were all hooligans. This was compounded by the woefully inadequate emergency medical facilities and poor communication between the police and stewards.

The day after Hillsborough, The Sunday Times roundly condemned all the football authorities, accusing them of complacency, and called for modern, all-seat stadiums to replace the death-traps that spectators had to endure. "Clubs that do not do so do not deserve to be in first-class football," the newspaper said. "Otherwise football will continue to be a slum sport played in slum stadiums and these tragic events will be repeated."

An inquiry was set up, under Lord Justice Taylor, and eventually his report was to echo these thoughts and recommend mandatory all-seat stadiums for clubs. But for the 95 dead and the hundreds of other victims it was too late.

Atkinson kicks off merry-go-round

SOME of the biggest names in management went through a topsy-turvy season in which they experienced the highs and lows of the game in rapid succession.

Ron Atkinson looked to be headed for the big time when he moved from West Brom to take charge of Atletico Madrid. But he quickly discovered that Spanish football club presidents are a fickle bunch, and none more so than the explosive Jesus Gil.

Third place in the League was not good enough and, despite having a two-year contract worth more than £500,000, Atkinson was fired after just 96 days. He was replaced in the hot seat by Colin Addison, who had moved from West Brom with him. Addison fared a little better, managing to stay at the club until the end of season.

As Atkinson was returning home, Malcolm Allison was heading to Europe to try to revive his career with the struggling Portuguese club Farense. But his reign was even shorter, a mere two months. Allison, though, still had big ambitions, even though he ended up at a little club, Fisher Athletic. He boasted that he would take the GM-Vauxhall Conference team into the League.

Jock Wallace, too, was on his way back to England from the continent. Amazingly, in January, Colchester, then bottom of the Fourth Division, managed to lure the former Rangers manager out of retirement in Spain. His was ultimately the only success story, although it took him a while to get to grips with the ailing club.

It took Wallace a month to end a sequence of 18 matches without a win, but in mid-April Colchester still looked like favourites for the drop. Somehow though, he worked a little bit of magic and the last five games were all won as Colchester scrambled their way to safety.

How the mighty have fallen: Allison went from the heights of Farense to the depths of Fisher Athletic

Moynihan: stubborn

Identity card row threatens clubs' swift return to Europe

THE DOOR finally started to open to allow English clubs back into Europe when Uefa's executive committee said that they were prepared to lift the ban for the start of the 1990-91 season. However, their decision in April was conditional upon government approval.

Although Colin Moynihan, the Minister for Sport, said that while he would try to have Liverpool readmitted to Europe at the same time as other English clubs, he was still insistent that identity cards must be in force for the start of next season.

When football said that it could not afford a national scheme the government threatened to impose a levy on transfer fees. And when the draft legislation was published football was shocked. Graham Kelly said the proposals were "horrendous" and Jack Dunnett, the League president, said the proposals could cost more than £30m. Even the referees wrote to Moynihan rejecting the idea.

But the government was unmoved, with Moynihan accusing football of ignoring offers from companies who were prepared to run a membership scheme at no charge. With neither side prepared to budge it was clear that there was still a long way to go before England's isolation would be ended.

Tottenham reshuffle their pack

THE to-ings and fro-ings at Tottenham just kept on happening, with a series of spectacular transfers after the season had finished.

Talk of Gary Lineker returning to England had swirled around the country in November. Johan Cruyff, the Barcelona coach, was said to have offered Lineker to Manchester United for £2.5m. United said they could not afford that much, Arsenal said they were not interested, and Rangers, with their reputation for spending enormous sums on English players, were then installed as the favourites.

Within a week the price had risen, with Aston Villa reportedly being told that Lineker would cost them £3m, with £2m going to Barcelona as the transfer fee and £1m going to Lineker to make up for what he would have earned in Spain.

Just as quickly as it had started the speculation died down, at least until April. Lineker was dropped and Terry Venables went to Barcelona to talk to the player he had taken to Spain in the first place. Venables succeeded in bringing Nayim to White Hart Lane on loan but he had to wait a little longer to land the star prize.

Lineker rejected a better offer from Monaco before committing himself to Tottenham in June in a £1.5m deal that included Nayim. But Venables soon recouped the money, with enough to spare to pay Lineker's £5,000 a week wages for several years, when he sold Chris Waddle to Marseille for £4.5m, a British record.

And Venables's rebuilding process did not stop there. His final move of a hectic month was to allow the long-serving Ossie Ardiles to go to Swindon as their player-manager.

Going: Waddle went to Marseille for £4.5m, a British record

Coming: Lineker turned down Monaco to return to England

Stevens' blunder cost Rangers a clean sweep

RANGERS utterly dominated the season and only a crass error by Gary Stevens denied them an historic treble. After three games of the season Rangers went to the top of the Scottish Premier League with a 5-1 victory over Celtic at Ibrox. Thirty-three games later they were still there as League champions, without ever having been dislodged or really threatened.

The poor early-season form of Celtic, who finished third, left them with far too much to do – and only Aberdeen, the run-ners-up by six points – offered much of a challenge. Rangers' strength lay in the expensively purchased pool of players at Souness' disposal.

Rangers' first trophy, the League Cup, had been acquired much earlier, on October 23, when they duly disposed of Aberdeen 3-2 in a thrilling final. Aberdeen had twice drawn level before, in extra time, Ally McCoist delivered the coup de grace in injury time.

The Cup final was less of a spectacle, but extremely gratify-ing to Celtic. Four minutes from half-time Joe Miller pounced on a silly backpass by Stevens for the only goal of the game. The Rangers players wept openly on the pitch as the fabulous treble eluded the best team in Scotland.

There was one consolation for Graeme Souness. After a take-over by the multi-millionaire David Murray, he became a member of the Rangers board with a 10% stake in the club, estimated as being worth £600,000.

Murray: bought Rangers

Title won with last kick

Final play: Michael Thomas scores the most dramatic goal in League history to snatch the title

FOR THE RECORD

■ Three brothers, Danny, Rodney and Ray Wallace, played for Southampton on October 22. It was the first time in 68 years that three brothers had played in the same First Division side. And Woking played two pairs of brothers when they lost to Cambridge in the first round of the FA Cup.

■ Steve Bull scored his 100th goal for Wolves on December 31. On May 1, when he took his total for the season to 52, he became the first player to score 100 goals in two seasons since George Camsell in 1928.

■ Newport County were finally wound up on February 27. They were then expelled from the GM-Vauxhall conference for failing to complete their fixtures.

■ A record five penalties were awarded in the match between Crystal Palace and Brighton on March 27, including three in five minutes. Palace missed three of their four penalties.

■ Rangers' first team lost 2-1 to Gretna on January 9 in a match to raise money for the Lockerbie disaster fund.

■ Bradford and Swansea staged a tug-of-war in court for the services of Terry Yorath, who was also the part-time Wales manager. The case was finally resolved when Yorath bought out the remainder of his contract with the Welsh club.

■ Ted Croker retired as secretary of the FA on February 10.

■ The Welsh FA admitted that they were so short of money that they could not afford to buy caps for the players in the non-League international against England. However, the team were allowed to keep their shirts as a memento.

■ Don Revie, the former Leeds and England manager, died on May 26.

■ Peter Shilton equalled Bobby Moore's record of 108 international appearances when England beat Poland 3-0 in a World Cup qualifying match on June 3.

■ Laurie Cunningham, the former England player, was killed in a car crash in Madrid on July 15.

THE LAST week of the season – extended to May 26 because of the Hillsborough disaster – was as dramatic as anything that could have been scripted by Hollywood. Liverpool, who in February had been 19 points behind Arsenal, simply had to beat Everton in the Cup final, beat West Ham at home and not lose by two goals to Arsenal at Anfield to become the first side to win the Double twice. Daunting as it sounds, Liverpool took to their tasks with relish.

The Cup final, on May 20, was an emotional affair as the two Merseyside clubs mourned the Hillsborough dead. The rival fans mingled before and during the match, maintained a minute's silence and sang You'll Never Walk Alone with Gerry Marsden.

Winning the FA Cup had become an obsession at Anfield as all at the club saw it as a token, but important, tribute to the Hillsborough victims. And John Aldridge, with a fourth-minute goal, seemed to have won it for them. But, with seconds remaining, Everton equalised when Bruce Grobbelaar failed to clear a shot and Stuart McCall nipped in.

Ian Rush, who had been brought on for Aldridge, restored their lead in the fourth minute of extra time with a classic striker's goal. Eight minutes later McCall volleyed a clearance straight into the back of the net and it was all square again.

Within two minutes Everton's hopes were dashed. Rush, who had been struggling all season, got the neatest of headed flicks on to John Barnes's cross and the first half of the Double was complete. West Ham were duly thrashed 5-1 two days later and only Arsenal, who had not won at Anfield for 14 years, remained.

Thus, on May 26, the League championship came down to the last match of the season. And to cap this most extraordinary of seasons it was a match between the first and second sides in the table – only the second time in the 101-year history of the Football League that this had happened.

The Match of the Century certainly lived up to its billing: it was like chess on speed. George Graham chose to play a sweeper system to deny Liverpool the space they needed to make full use of Barnes, and Kenny Dalglish used Aldridge and Rush (replaced by Beardsley) to probe the Arsenal defence. The pace was relentless and both sides strove for the ultimate prize. At half-time the match was scoreless and Liverpool were 45 minutes away from the Double.

But seven minutes into the second half Alan Smith scored a disputed goal from an indirect free-kick when a linesman briefly raised his flag and the nerve-tingling drama was going to go to the wire.

With 90 minutes gone, and the 40,000 crowd whistling like fury, Lee Dixon cleared the ball from deep in the Arsenal defence to Smith, who lobbed it into the path of the onrushing Michael Thomas. He evaded two challenges and, having waited for Grobbelaar to commit himself, flicked the ball past him to score the most dramatic goal in League history.

LIVERPOOL
Red machine ran as smooth as clockwork

Garth Crooks

LIVERPOOL were always difficult; on and off the field. I remember, as a Tottenham player, one incident after a match when both sets of players were having a "friendly" drink together that made this crystal clear.

"Glenn Hoddle's not good enough to get in our side," were the words that stopped the conversation dead in its tracks. There was no doubt who the offender was. Graeme Souness, who as a player was an uncompromising brute. His charming smile and his off-the-field politeness were the nets in which he would ensnare you.

The jibe spun a sober Tottenham contingent around on their heels. Cold stares waited impatiently for some form of elaboration in the hope that it might reduce the rising temperature in the bar. Souness left the area in the conspicuous manner in which he arrived. I soon realised that the intimidation we had witnessed was all part of the Anfield roadshow.

It all started under the charismatic Bill Shankly – the master of intimidation. Few managers possess it – he invented it. Not long after Liverpool had been dubbed the Red Army, a term used to give clarity to the type of environment to which you were about to be exposed, Shankly had retired and Liverpool had passed on the leadership to Bob Paisley with no apparent join.

It seemed as though Paisley only needed time to become familiar with Shankly's filing system to add to the family silver. The next 10 years saw

Start of an era: the 1965 Cup final

Paisley transform Liverpool from a formidable club side to one of the most dynamic clubs in Europe, completing his first championship and Uefa Cup double in his second season.

Yet at this stage few could appreciate or predict what Shankly had started. The sheer emotion generated by the Anfield crowd was indicative of him. Those scenes of the mercurial Scot, hands aloft in the centre circle receiving homage as though he were the Messiah are legendary. Even against mediocre sides it was impossible to get into the ground after 2pm on a Saturday, such was the euphoria.

Match officials would forget which decision they had made and why they had made them when caught in the Anfield cauldron. Visiting teams knew that under no circumstances could their defenders afford to be clumsy in the vicinity of the penalty area, for fear of the famous Anfield cry of "handball!" or "penalty!" It never ceased to amaze me how the players and fans could achieve that infamous Anfield appeal in total unison; meanwhile, match officials responded instinctively as though they had been struck by lightning.

Yet whenever players and officials came on to the pitch for the traditional pre-match walkabout you knew, at that precise moment, there was nowhere on earth they would rather be.

The Kop were famous among the pros for churning out lyrics, Lennon and McCartney style, but with a more cruel twist than their virtuoso compatriots. I remember when I played for Manchester United. "Whose up Mrs Brown? Whose Up Mrs Brown?" sung to the famous Cockney tune of Knees up Mother Brown, was the chorus that greeted us during one particular walkabout.

The object of derision was Tommy Docherty, the former manager of Manchester United who had just been dismissed by his employers because of an affair with the wife of the club's physiotherapist, Laurie Brown.

The sentiments sent my blood cold. This was not due to the fact that I was particularly friendly with Docherty. It was due to the unmerciful way the Kop used humour and verse as a poisoned cocktail to deal with their adversaries.

This satirical sword had the potential to inflict tremendous psychological damage to the opposition. But, as the famous emblem hanging over the tunnel stated: "This is Anfield". Before you got to their generals, you had to deal with the infantry.

Driving force: Dalglish

THIRTY GOLDEN YEARS

1959: Bill Shankly appointed the Liverpool manager

1962: Second Division champions

1964: First Division champions

1965: FA Cup winners

1966: First Division champions, European Cup Winners Cup beaten finalists

1969: First Division runners-up

1971: FA Cup beaten finalists

1973: Uefa Cup winners, First Division champions

1974: FA Cup winners, First Division runners-up, Bill Shankly retires and Bob Paisley takes charge

1975: First Division runners-up

1976: Uefa Cup winners, First Division champions

1977: European Cup winners, First Division champions, FA Cup beaten finalists

1978: European Cup winners, First Division runners-up, League Cup beaten finalists

1979: First Division champions

1980: First Division champions

1981: European Cup winners, League Cup winners

1982: First Division champions, League Cup winners

1983: First Division champions, League Cup winners, Bob Paisley retires and Joe Fagan takes over

1984: European Cup winners, First Division champions, League Cup winners

1985: European Cup beaten finalists, First Division runners-up, Joe Fagan retires and Kenny Dalglish is appointed player-manager

1986: FA Cup winners, First Division champions

1987: First Division runners-up, League Cup beaten finalists

1988: First Division champions, FA Cup beaten finalists

1989: FA Cup winners, First Division runners-up

Still going strong: Liverpool made a habit of winning trophies at home and abroad

For the past 30 years Liverpool have carefully appointed their generals. Keegan, Toshack and Hughes were the players on whom Shankly bestowed his dream. Paisley gratefully capitalised on the sound foundations built by Shankly, winning his first European championship in 1977 against the West German champions Borussia Moenchengladbach. Liverpool, through their carefully selected appointees, had discovered the secret to success, guarding it jealously with the mask of footballing simplicity.

A feature that has raised eyebrows in the world of football has been the enormous lengths Liverpool have gone to to ensure a player is of the right psychological make-up. Much of their success is due to getting this part of the purchase right.

Keegan's departure to Hamburg forced Liverpool to replace him with what they considered to be the best around. Having spent an entire season monitoring his attitude, Kenny Dalglish was their choice and a superb one it was too. In his first season Dalglish scored the winner to secure Liverpool's second European Cup triumph with a superbly taken goal against Bruges.

After championships in 1979 and 1980, Paisley became the first British manager to win three European Cups when Liverpool beat Real Madrid 1-0 in Paris. Three consecutive League championships and League Cups followed and, between 1986 and 1990, a further three championships, including the League and Cup double. Liverpool had become the most formidable team in Europe.

I had witnessed the cohesive force that made Liverpool special. On tour, their emphasis on team spirit bordered on paranoia – strangers were not welcome. Night after night the entire team would congregate in the lobby, singing traditional team songs passed down from previous Liverpool sides; pulling funny faces as hotel guests watched, astonished to see star players like Hansen and Lawrenson, Dalglish and Souness join in the merriment as their international images went up in smoke. The point was clear – one in, all in – there were no stars.

This same spirit ran through Anfield like a dose of salts and was clearly evident in 1985 and again in 1989 when disaster struck. A catalogue of administrative failures resulted in insufficient segregation during the 1985 European Cup final between Liverpool and Juventus at the Heysel Stadium. Persistent charging by opposing fans caused a wall to collapse, killing 39 people. Liverpool fans were singled out, held responsible and their team banned from Europe. What Liverpool had not realised was that Uefa had just cut their lifeline.

The shock of that decision turned into excruciating pain four years later when, in 1989, during the FA cup semi-final against Nottingham Forest, a cloud descended over the entire city, as 95 men, women and children were crushed to death. The city, its players and families closed ranks and mourned their dead.

Something spiritual happened to the club that day, setting Liverpool FC and their city apart from the rest of the country. Amid cries for the FA Cup to be abandoned the city insisted, in honour of its dead, that the competition continue. The club rose like a phoenix out of the ashes as they attempted to become the first club to win the famous League and Cup double twice. It was befitting that Liverpool and Everton should have both walked out together to contest the 1989 FA Cup final.

Liverpool's victory over Everton was like a sedative to the club and, providing that they were winning, it continued to be so. Yet one sensed that the burden they were carrying was too much.

Six days later Arsenal played Liverpool at Anfield, needing a two-goal victory to clinch the championship. The ground was, once again, the hotbed it always was and Liverpool were on for an historic double. However, Arsenal had other ideas. With seconds to go Michael Thomas snatched the second goal for Arsenal and with it the League championship. Suddenly 1989 would be remembered for all the wrong reasons.

Kenny Dalglish's transition from player to manager was indicative of the club's astuteness. However, it often seemed that the hope of at least half of the city fell on to the shoulders of their beloved team.

Pressurised and frustrated, Dalglish announced his retirement from the game only to return six months later as the manager of Blackburn Rovers. It was at this point that the cracks in the Shankly dynasty became visible.

For Hillsborough to strike so soon after Heysel was a devastating blow to a club that found itself having to adjust to the staple diet of domestic football. Not only was the club weak, it was vulnerable. The appointment of Graeme Souness as manager in 1990 highlighted their insecurity. Souness's attitude at Rangers was bullish to say the least. A peacetime prime minister may have been much better suited rather than one always ready for war.

Notably, the singing of the traditional songs accompanied by the stupid faces are no longer witnessed in the hotel lobbies, or anywhere else. The same players that were once not good enough to play for Liverpool are now wearing the famous red shirt and, sadly, it appears that the Liverpool dynasty is, at the moment, on hold, desperately in need of another Shankly.

Smooth succession: Moran, Paisley and Fagan were all products of the famous Boot Room

Swindon suffer heavy losses after betting scandal exposed

SWINDON, under the inspirational leadership of Ossie Ardiles, were pushing hard for promotion to the First Division when the roof fell in on their world.

The FA announced that it was investigating claims that the Swindon chairman, Brian Hillier, and manager, Lou Macari, had bet against their team before they lost an FA Cup match to Newcastle in 1988. Hillier admitted that the bet had been made, but said it was only insurance to cover money that Swindon would lose by not reaching the next round.

Both Hillier and Macari were found guilty of bringing the game into disrepute in February. Hillier was banned from football for six months (a sentence subsequently increased to three years), the club was fined £7,500 and Macari was fined £1,000. Within a week Macari, who by then was the manager of West Ham, had resigned from Upton Park.

The FA's investigation of Swindon also unearthed alarming evidence of unlawful payments to players and the manipulation of transfer fees. On May 1, Hillier, Macari, Colin Calderwood, the club captain, and Vince Farrar, Swindon's former chief accountant, were arrested. Hillier, Macari and Farrar were all charged with tax offences and released on bail.

Amid all the off the field turmoil, Ardiles had taken Swindon to the play-offs, where they beat Sunderland to win a place in the First Division for the first time in the club's history. But when Swindon admitted 36 breaches of League regulations on June 7, their punishment was harsh.

The League promoted Sunderland in their place, and relegated Swindon to the Third Division, giving their place in the Second Division to Tranmere. Swindon were horrified and appealed. They won some respite when the League restored them to the Second Division, a decision that infuriated Tranmere.

Hillier, Macari and Farrar were sent for trial at Winchester crown court. The case lasted five weeks and Macari was acquitted, but both Hillier and Farrar were convicted: Hillier of conspiracy to defraud the Inland Revenue and Farrar of conspiracy and false accounting. Farrar received a six-month suspended sentence and Hillier was jailed, initially for a year although the sentence was halved on appeal.

Out and down: Hillier, the Swindon chairman, was convicted of fraud

Macari: fined £1,000

Hapless Hartlepool take a hammering but refuse to lie down

PITY poor Hartlepool. They lost their first three games of the season, conceding 10 goals and failing to score even one. Then things went from bad to even worse in September.

A trip to Stockport turned into a nightmare. Hartlepool were three goals down by half-time and sunk 6-0, with Brett Angell scoring four of the goals.

Just to prove that it was not a freak result they caved in 6-0 again a fortnight later, this time at home to Doncaster, for whom Lee Turnbull got a hat-trick.

The rot continued into November when hapless Hartlepool went to Aldershot. It was the same old story: 3-0 down at half-time, beaten 6-1 and another hat-trick conceded to

Steve Claridge. Not surprisingly, Hartlepool, with only two wins to their name, were bottom of the Fourth Division.

Bobby Moncur, their manager, had had more than enough humiliation and he offered to resign. He was talked out of it by the club's chairman. But a fortnight later, after Hartlepool had gone out of the FA Cup in the

first round 2-0 at home to Huddersfield, and lost again in the League, he finally quit.

Things looked up a bit after Christmas, when Hartlepool even managed to win two matches in a row. They took their revenge on Stockport 5-0 and managed to finish the season a respectable 12 points clear of relegation.

Heroics guarantee Italian trips

DESPITE the odd hiccup along the way, England, Scotland and the Republic of Ireland qualified for the World Cup finals in Italy, all finishing runners-up in their groups.

Wales and Northern Ireland fared less well. Wales had a good excuse, they were in with West Germany and Holland, but two home draws did not help their cause. Northern Ireland's faint hopes were dashed in Dublin in October when Jack Charlton's Republic side beat them 3-0. Two goals from John Aldridge in Malta in November ended any doubts. It was the first time the Republic had qualified for the finals and followed on from their success in qualifying for the European championships two years earlier.

England virtually clinched their Italian berth with a stirring 0-0 draw in Sweden (the group's other qualifiers) in September. The hero of the night was England's captain, Terry Butcher, who played on despite having 10 stitches inserted during the half-time interval. The newspapers next day all carried gory photographs of Butcher with a blood-stained shirt and bandage round his head.

A month later, in Poland, another hero emerged, the goalkeeper Peter Shilton. He made four magnificent saves to keep the game scoreless and guarantee England's qualification.

Scotland lived on their nerves throughout the campaign and a feeble 3-0 defeat by France had left them needing a point at Hampden against Norway if they were to edge out France. Ally McCoist brilliantly scored the goal they needed to give them a cushion when he flicked the ball over Eric Thorsvedt. And they needed the cushion. With a minute left Scottish goalkeeping blunders returned to haunt them as Jim Leighton misjudged a speculative, long-range shot and the Norwegians equalised.

In the draw in December, England were seeded and would play all of their matches in Cagliari, on the island of Sardinia. This conveniently meant any hooligan problems would, initially, be kept off the mainland. Unfortunately the other countries in England's group were the Republic, Egypt and Holland. This raised fears of clashes with Dutch hooligans. Once again Scotland drew the short straw: Brazil, Sweden and Costa Rica.

Butcher: bloody battler

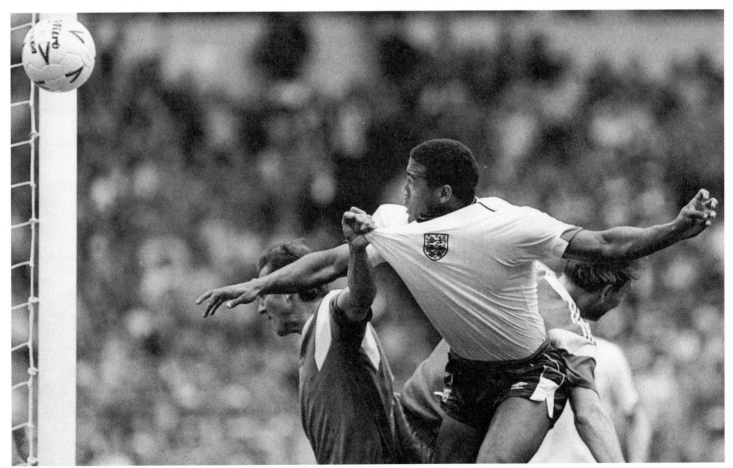

Tug of war: the close attentions of a Polish defender are sufficient to distract Barnes, who headed just wide of the post

Palace turn the tables on Liverpool

LIVERPOOL were red-hot favourites to sweep past Crystal Palace in the FA Cup semi-final at Villa Park on April 8. After all they were the Cup holders, top of the First Division and had thrashed Palace 9-0 at Anfield in September when eight different players had scored, a League record. By contrast Palace were deep in the relegation mire. But then Wimbledon had been massive underdogs in the 1988 final against Liverpool.

And this was a different Palace: only six players who had been humiliated in the autumn took the field in Birmingham. In particular Steve Coppell had broken the record for a goalkeeper when he paid Bristol Rovers £1m for Nigel Martyn.

After a quarter of an hour the match seemed to be following the script as Ian Rush put Liverpool ahead. Then they lost Rush and Gary Gillespie because of injury and in the second half Palace tore into them. Mark Bright equalised within seconds of the re-start and Gary O'Reilly put them ahead with 20 minutes remaining.

The pendulum swung Liverpool's way with McMahon's equaliser and a Barnes penalty. The drama was not over however: Andy Gray headed the equaliser two minutes from time. Extra time was to see Liverpool off as Alan Pardew headed in a corner to send Palace into their first final.

The second semi-final was as startling with Manchester United held 3-3 by plucky Oldham and then going through 2-1 in the replay. Could Palace pull it off again in the final? With seven minutes remaining it seemed so. The introduction of the partially fit Ian Wright 20 minutes from time, when United were 2-1 ahead, proved to have been a Coppell masterstroke.

Within three minutes Wright shredded the United defence for the equaliser. Two minutes into extra time Wright produced another gem for the lead. But, unlike Liverpool, United refused to buckle, pouring forward in search of the equaliser. Chance after chance was missed, until Hughes finally scored to take the Cup final into its fourth replay in a decade.

Like Brighton in 1983, Palace had missed the boat. The replay, five days later, was a scrappy affair. Alex Ferguson, United's manager, dropped his goalkeeper Jim Leighton for the on-loan Les Sealey. Lee Martin scored the only goal in a match mostly memorable for a series of niggling incidents. United's triumph meant they had emulated Tottenham and Aston Villa's record of seven FA Cups.

Just in time: Wright came on to score the equaliser for Palace

Rough and tumble: Andy Gray and Danny Wallace tangle for the ball in the drawn FA Cup final at Wembley

United bamboozled by Knighton's bid

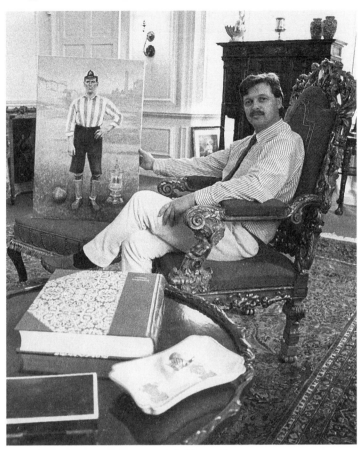

Room of his own: Knighton lords it in his castle

MANCHESTER UNITED'S image as the most prestigious club in Britain took a hefty dent on the opening day of the season when Michael Knighton made a surprise entrance on to the Old Trafford pitch. The property owner, decked in Manchester United training kit, blew kisses, saluted the crowd, juggled the ball and fired shots into an empty net.

It transpired that Martin Edwards, United's majority shareholder, had agreed secretly to sell his shares to Knighton in exchange for £10m cash and £10m to spend modernising the stadium. Knighton, then, was now the owner of Manchester United. Disbelief greeted the announcement and scepticism was rife that Knighton did not actually have the money. And so it proved.

The entire deal collapsed in embarrassment over the next three months as the cash failed to materialise and the press poured scorn on the new "owner". Knighton claimed that the newspapers were hounding him and had represented him as a Frankenstein that was out of control.

One by one his backers pulled out. In desperation Knighton approached the Rangers chairman, David Murray, for help. Then Robert Maxwell, Eddie Shah and others. No help was forthcoming. Knighton's relationship with Edwards became so frosty that Edwards took out an injunction to prevent him from showing any documents relating to the private financial details of the club to potential investors.

The whole affair had turned United into a laughing stock. In October Knighton was forced to withdraw from the affair when the whole United board threatened to resign. Knighton's consolation was a non-executive seat on the board and the joke was over.

Taylor orders safety first

LORD JUSTICE TAYLOR produced a sweeping condemnation of English football in his final report on the Hillsborough disaster, which was published on January 29. He was widely praised for the thoroughness of his investigation and for consulting everybody involved in football, from fans to the people who ran the national game.

Taylor lamented the fact that his was the ninth report on safety this century yet grounds were still incredibly squalid. He said football was blighted by old and crumbling stadiums with poor facilities, and lacked proper leadership. Although he condemned hooliganism, he pointed out that fans were fenced in and treated like prisoners of war.

In all he made 76 recommendations, the most important of which were that all-seat stadiums should be introduced to First and Second Division grounds by 1994 and the rest of the League by 1999. He also said that a national identity card scheme was unworkable and dangerous, because it would create a crush of fans outside of grounds.

Football immediately accepted all of his points as did the government, which gave up its long-running battle to enforce membership cards. Taylor's proposals were incorporated into the Football Spectators Act, which established a Football Licensing Authority to make sure the changes were carried out.

But it was not long before football was complaining about the cost of implementing the changes. The authorities said the total bill would top £100m, and many smaller clubs could be forced out of business.

The government was insistent that football had to find the money itself. However, in the Budget on March 20 they did relent slightly by cutting the amount of betting duty levied on the football pools by 2.5%, on condition that the money was used to finance ground improvements.

305

Hearts thwarted in audacious takeover of Hibs

HEARTS, who had finished third and qualified for Europe, put forward in June a radical proposal: a merger with their Edinburgh rivals, Hibernian. Hearts' £6.12m bid for the Easter Road club was a calculated attempt to form one strong Edinburgh club to break the Glasgow duopoly.

Hearts had a point. In the 45 years since the Second World War, there had been only 12 occasions when a club other than Rangers or Celtic had won the championship. And the last time Hibs had won the title was in 1952, Hearts 1960.

But this bold and ambitious plan was doomed from the outset. The fans mounted protests and marches with banners proclaiming "Hands off Hibs". The Hibs board voted unanimously to reject the offer. The Hibs supporters even campaigned for people who held accounts with the Bank of Scotland (who were backing the Hearts bid) to close them. So in July Hearts bowed to the inevitable and pulled out.

Hot-head Souness sets Rangers on fire

RANGERS began the season in dreadful fashion, winning only two of their first eight League matches, and were bottom of the table for three consecutive weeks after four games. But Graeme Souness's team turned that round in dramatic fashion and by mid-December they headed the Premier League table and stayed there to the end of the season, comfortably taking the title seven points clear of Aberdeen.

Off the pitch, however, Souness did not have such an easy time of it. In December he had a heated altercation with the Hearts captain, Dave McPherson, after Rangers had beaten them 2-1 at Tynecastle. The police reported the incident to the Scottish FA. Souness's complaint was that players were deliberately exaggerating fouls in order to get players sent off. Then in May he was fined a record £5,000 for breaking a touchline ban imposed earlier. The ban was also extended until the end of the 1991-92 season.

This was Souness's third touchline ban, each of them stemming from his failure to adhere to the first ban in 1989. However, Souness was caught bang to rights as video evidence clearly showed him shouting to his players from the tunnel in February.

While Rangers had difficulty controlling their fiery manager, Celtic, their cross-town rivals, had difficulty controlling their form. Leading the table at the end of October, they eventually slumped to fifth and were edged out of Europe by Dundee United. It was the first time that Celtic had missed European

Top dogs: Ally McCoist parades Rangers' 40th championship trophy at Ibrox

qualification for nine years.

Not that Celtic had particularly enjoyed their campaign in the European Cup Winners' Cup, going out in the first round 6-6. Trailing 2-1 to Partizan Belgrade from the away leg, they contrived to score five goals at Parkhead – four of them from their Polish striker Darius Dziekanowski – and concede four, the last coming within 90 seconds of the final whistle. The 5-4 score meant the Yugoslavs

went through on the away goals rule.

There were goals galore at Parkhead in September, but at Hampden in May Celtic and Aberdeen managed to play 120 minutes of stultifying, goalless football in the Scottish Cup final. However, because of the imminent World Cup, the Scottish FA had decreed there was to be no replay so the final went to a penalty shoot-out for the first time.

It then took 20 penalties before there was a result. Celtic missed their first, Aberdeen their fourth. With 18 kicks taken neither keeper had yet touched the ball, but on Aberdeen's 10th attempt the Dutch keeper, Theo Snelders, acrobatically deflected Anton Rogan's kick. Brian Irvine coolly slotted home and Celtic had triumphed 9-8. More of such nonsense would be seen in Italy in the World Cup finals.

Tabloid vendetta drives Robson out

THE tabloid papers' constant sniping at Bobby Robson finally drove to him resign as England manager and move abroad to coach PSV Eindhoven.

The speculation about Robson's future started in March, with a report that he would have to win the World Cup to stand any chance of keeping his job. More fuel was added to the fire when another paper claimed that sources in the FA said that it had already been decided that Graham Taylor would be the next England manager.

Eindhoven had approached Robson through an intermediary in April and said that the job in Holland was his if he wanted it. Robson's response was that his first loyalty was to England, and he was not prepared to talk to anybody until the World Cup was over. But Bert Millichip, the FA chairman, could not give Robson any assurances about his future, so he gave Robson permission to talk to Eindhoven.

Even then, despite the fortune he was offered, Robson wanted to stay with England.

I was just a victim of the tabloid newspaper war. I had watched this cancer spread over the eight years I had been in the job. It was ugly and damaging, and so often the reports were untrue

But at a second meeting with Millichip the FA did not offer to extend his contract. So, on what Robson described as "one of the saddest days of my career", he told the FA he would be leaving after the World Cup.

It did not take long for the news to leak out of the FA and Robson woke on the morning of May 24 to find his house besieged by reporters. At the press conference to confirm his departure Robson lashed out at the tabloid press, accusing them of printing scurrilous rumours. He left for Italy bitter at the treatment he had received over the years from the media and

Robson: embittered

knowing that he had his work cut out to stop the events of the past few weeks affecting his team's morale.

30 seconds of madness that seemed to last all season

TELEVISION viewers watched in amazement as the match between Arsenal and Norwich on November 4 degenerated into an all-out brawl. Norwich, who led 2-0 at half-time, were unhappy that Arsenal were awarded a penalty in the last seconds of the match. When Lee Dixon scored, to give Arsenal a dramatic 4-3 victory, the scuffling started.

Within seconds, almost all the players were involved in the fracas and police had to restore order. Amazingly, the referee, George Tyson, said that he was not going to take any action. The FA were not as lenient. Describing the incident as "30 seconds of madness", they fined Norwich £50,000 and Arsenal £20,000.

The FA were soon collecting another £20,000 each from West Ham and Wimbledon. They were involved in another mass brawl during their League Cup match on November 22, which West Ham won despite having Julian Dicks sent off.

Two days later, a pair of managers were also in trouble. John Bird of York and Ray McHale of Scarborough were both sent off for squaring up to each other and trying to trade punches. That indiscretion brought them both a three-month touchline ban.

And just when it looked as if England had convinced the rest of the world that it had its hooliganism problem under control, all the good work was undone when Leeds fans ran amok in Bournemouth on the last day of the season.

There were 120 arrests for rioting, looting and assault before, during and after the Second Division match on May 5. The local police were furious, saying that they had

Flash point: O'Leary manhandles Bowen and the fighting soon spread

warned the League not to stage the game on a bank holiday weekend. The chief constable of Dorset said police should be given the power to change fixture lists, and the League admitted that they were wrong not to heed the police advice.

LEAGUE TABLES AND RESULTS 1980 – 1990

	1980-81	1981-82	1982-83	1983-84	1984-85
WORLD CUP		Italy 3 / West Germany 1			
EUROPEAN CHAMPIONSHIP				France 2 / Spain 0	
EUROPEAN CUP	Liverpool 1 / Real Madrid 0	Aston Villa 1 / Bayern Munich 0	Hamburg 1 / Juventus 0	Liverpool 1 AS Roma 1; Liverpool won 4-2 on penalties	Juventus 1 / Liverpool 0
EUROPEAN CUP WINNERS CUP	Dynamo Tbilisi 2 / Carl Zeiss Jena 1	Barcelona 2 / Standard Liege 1	Aberdeen 2 / Real Madrid 1	Juventus 2 / Porto 1	Everton 3 / Rapid Vienna 1
UEFA CUP	Ipswich Town beat AZ Alkmaar 3-0 2-4	IFK Gothenburg beat SV Hamburg 1-0 3-0	Anderlecht beat Benfica 1-0 1-1	Tottenham Hotspur beat Anderlecht 1-1 1-1 (4-3 on penalties)	Real Madrid beat Videoton 3-0 0-1
FA CUP	Tottenham Hotspur 3 / Manchester City 2, after 1-1	Tottenham Hotspur 1 / Queen's Park Rangers 0, after 1-1	Manchester United 4 / Brighton & Hove Albion 0, after 2-2	Everton 2 / Watford 0	Manchester United 1 / Everton 0

FIRST DIVISION

1980-81
	P	W	D	L	F	A	Pts
Aston Villa	42	26	8	8	72	40	60
Ipswich	42	23	10	9	77	43	56
Arsenal	42	19	15	8	61	45	53
West Brom	42	20	12	10	60	42	52
Liverpool	42	17	17	8	62	42	51
Soton	42	20	10	12	76	56	50
Nottm F	42	19	12	11	62	44	50
Man Utd	42	15	18	9	51	36	48
Leeds	42	17	10	15	39	47	44
Tottenham	42	14	15	13	70	68	43
Stoke	42	12	18	12	51	60	42
Man City	42	14	11	17	56	59	39
Birmingham	42	13	12	17	50	61	38
Middlesbro	42	16	5	21	53	61	37
Everton	42	17	13	15	55	58	36
Coventry	42	13	10	19	48	68	36
Sunderland	42	14	7	21	52	53	35
Wolves	42	13	9	20	43	55	35
Brighton	42	14	7	21	54	67	35
Norwich	42	13	7	22	49	73	33
Leicester	42	13	6	23	40	67	32
C Palace	42	6	7	29	47	83	19

1981-82
	P	W	D	L	F	A	Pts
Liverpool	42	26	9	7	80	32	87
Ipswich	42	26	5	11	75	53	83
Man Utd	42	22	12	8	59	29	78
Tottenham	42	20	11	11	67	48	71
Arsenal	42	20	11	11	48	37	71
Swansea	42	21	6	15	58	51	69
Soton	42	19	9	14	72	67	66
Everton	42	17	13	12	56	50	64
West Ham	42	14	16	12	66	57	58
Man City	42	15	13	14	49	50	58
Aston Villa	42	15	12	15	55	53	57
Nottm F	42	15	12	15	42	48	57
Brighton	42	13	13	16	43	52	52
Coventry	42	13	11	18	56	62	50
Notts C	42	13	8	21	61	69	47
Birmingham	42	10	14	18	53	61	44
West Brom	42	11	11	20	46	57	44
Stoke	42	12	8	22	44	63	44
Sunderland	42	11	11	20	38	58	44
Leeds	42	10	12	20	39	61	42
Wolves	42	10	10	22	32	63	40
Middlesbro	42	8	15	19	34	52	39

1982-83
	P	W	D	L	F	A	Pts
Liverpool	42	24	10	8	87	37	82
Watford	42	22	5	15	74	57	71
Manchester	42	19	13	10	56	38	70
Tottenham	42	20	9	13	65	50	69
Nottm F	42	20	9	13	62	50	69
Aston Villa	42	21	5	16	62	50	68
Everton	42	18	10	14	66	48	64
West Ham	42	20	4	18	68	62	64
Ipswich	42	15	13	14	64	50	58
Arsenal	42	16	10	16	58	56	58
West Brom	42	15	12	15	51	49	57
Soton	42	15	12	15	54	58	57
Stoke	42	16	9	17	53	64	57
Norwich	42	14	12	16	52	58	54
Notts C	42	15	7	20	55	71	52
Sunderland	42	12	14	16	48	61	50
Birmingham	42	12	14	16	40	55	50
Luton	42	12	13	17	65	84	49
Coventry	42	13	9	20	48	59	48
Man City	42	13	8	21	47	70	47
Swansea	42	10	11	21	51	69	41
Brighton	42	9	13	20	38	68	40

1983-84
	P	W	D	L	F	A	Pts
Liverpool	42	22	14	6	73	32	80
Soton	42	22	11	9	66	38	77
Nottm F	42	22	8	12	76	45	74
Man Utd	42	20	14	8	71	41	74
QPR	42	22	7	13	67	37	73
Arsenal	42	18	9	15	74	60	63
Everton	42	16	14	12	44	42	62
Tottenham	42	17	10	15	64	65	61
West Ham	42	17	9	16	60	55	60
Aston Villa	42	17	9	16	59	61	60
Watford	42	16	9	17	68	77	57
Ipswich	42	15	8	19	55	57	53
Sunderland	42	13	13	16	42	53	52
Norwich	42	12	15	15	48	49	51
Leicester	42	13	12	17	65	68	51
Luton	42	14	9	19	53	66	51
West Brom	42	14	9	19	48	62	51
Stoke	42	13	11	18	44	63	50
Coventry	42	13	11	18	57	77	50
Birmingham	42	12	12	18	39	50	48
Notts C	42	10	11	21	50	72	41
Wolves	42	6	11	25	27	80	29

1984-85
	P	W	D	L	F	A	Pts
Everton	42	28	6	8	88	43	90
Liverpool	42	22	11	9	68	35	77
Tottenham	42	23	8	11	78	51	77
Man Utd	42	22	10	10	77	47	76
Soton	42	19	11	12	56	47	68
Chelsea	42	18	12	12	63	48	66
Arsenal	42	19	9	14	61	49	66
Sheff Wed	42	17	14	11	58	45	65
Nottm F	42	19	7	16	56	48	64
Aston Villa	42	15	11	16	60	60	56
Watford	42	14	13	15	81	71	55
West Brom	42	16	7	19	58	62	55
Luton	42	15	9	18	57	61	54
Newcastle	42	13	13	16	55	70	52
Leicester	42	15	6	21	65	73	51
West Ham	42	13	12	17	51	68	51
Ipswich	42	13	11	18	46	57	50
Coventry	42	15	5	22	47	64	50
QPR	42	13	11	18	53	72	50
Norwich	42	13	10	19	46	64	49
Sunderland	42	10	10	22	40	62	40
Stoke	42	3	8	31	24	91	17

SECOND DIVISION

	1980-81	1981-82	1982-83	1983-84	1984-85
Champions:	West Ham United	Luton Town	Queen's Park Rangers	Chelsea	Oxford United
Also promoted:	Notts County, Swansea City	Watford, Norwich City	Wolverhampton Wanderers, Leicester City	Sheffield Wednesday, Newcastle United	Birmingham City, Manchester City
Relegated:	Preston North End, Bristol City, Bristol Rovers	Cardiff City, Wrexham, Orient	Rotherham United, Burnley, Bolton Wanderers	Derby County, Swansea City, Cambridge United	Notts County, Cardiff City, Wolverhampton Wanderers

THIRD DIVISION

	1980-81	1981-82	1982-83	1983-84	1984-85
Champions:	Rotherham United	Burnley	Portsmouth	Oxford United	Bradford City
Also promoted:	Barnsley, Charlton Athletic	Carlisle United, Fulham	Cardiff City, Huddersfield Town	Wimbledon, Sheffield United	Millwall, Hull City
Relegated:	Sheffield United, Colchester United, Blackpool, Hull City	Wimbledon, Swindon Town, Bristol City, Chester	Reading, Wrexham, Doncaster Rovers, Chesterfield	Scunthorpe United, Southend United, Port Vale, Exeter City	Burnley, Orient, Preston North End, Cambridge United

FOURTH DIVISION

	1980-81	1981-82	1982-83	1983-84	1984-85
Champions:	Southend United	Sheffield United	Wimbledon	York City	Chesterfield
Also promoted:	Lincoln City, Doncaster Rovers, Wimbledon	Bradford City, Wigan Athletic, Bournemouth	Hull City, Port Vale, Scunthorpe United	Doncaster Rovers, Reading, Bristol City, Aldershot	Blackpool, Darlington, Bury

LEAGUE CUP

1980-81	1981-82	1982-83	1983-84	1984-85
Liverpool 2 / West Ham United 1, after 1-1	Liverpool 3 / Tottenham Hotspur 1	Liverpool 2 / Manchester United 1	Liverpool 1 / Everton 0, after 0-0	Norwich City 1 / Sunderland 0

SCOTTISH CUP

1980-81	1981-82	1982-83	1983-84	1984-85
Rangers 4 / Dundee United 1, after 0-0	Aberdeen 4 / Rangers 1	Aberdeen 1 / Rangers 0	Aberdeen 2 / Celtic 1	Celtic 2 / Dundee United 1

SCOTTISH PREMIER DIVISION

1980-81
	P	W	D	L	F	A	Pts
Celtic	36	26	4	6	84	37	56
Aberdeen	36	19	11	6	61	26	49
Rangers	36	16	12	8	60	32	44
St Mirren	36	18	8	10	56	47	44
Dundee	36	17	9	10	66	42	43
Partick	36	10	10	16	32	48	30
Airdrie	36	10	9	17	36	55	29
Morton	36	10	8	18	36	58	28
Kilmarnock	36	5	9	22	23	65	19
Hearts	36	6	6	24	27	71	18

1981-82
	P	W	D	L	F	A	Pts
Celtic	36	24	7	5	79	33	55
Aberdeen	36	23	7	6	71	29	53
Rangers	36	16	11	9	57	45	43
Dundee	36	15	10	11	61	38	40
St Mirren	36	14	13	9	49	52	37
Hibernian	36	11	14	11	38	40	36
Morton	36	9	12	15	31	54	30
Dundee	36	11	4	21	46	72	26
Partick	36	6	10	20	35	59	22
Airdrie	36	5	8	23	31	76	18

1982-83
	P	W	D	L	F	A	Pts
Dundee	36	24	8	4	90	35	56
Celtic	36	25	5	6	90	36	55
Aberdeen	36	25	5	6	76	24	55
Rangers	36	13	12	11	52	41	38
St Mirren	36	11	12	13	47	51	34
Dundee	36	9	11	16	42	53	29
Hibernian	36	7	15	14	35	51	29
Motherwell	36	11	5	20	39	73	27
Morton	36	6	8	22	30	74	20
Kilmarnock	36	3	11	22	28	91	17

1983-84
	P	W	D	L	F	A	Pts
Aberdeen	36	25	7	4	78	21	57
Celtic	36	21	8	7	80	41	50
Dundee	36	18	11	7	67	39	47
Rangers	36	15	12	9	53	41	42
Hearts	36	10	16	10	38	47	36
St Mirren	36	9	14	13	55	59	32
Hibernian	36	12	7	17	45	55	31
Dundee	36	11	5	20	50	74	27
St J'stone	36	10	3	23	36	81	23
Motherwell	36	4	7	25	31	75	15

1984-85
	P	W	D	L	F	A	Pts
Aberdeen	36	27	5	4	89	26	59
Celtic	36	22	8	6	77	30	52
Dundee	36	20	7	9	67	33	47
Rangers	36	13	12	11	47	38	38
St Mirren	36	17	4	15	51	56	38
Dundee	36	15	7	14	48	50	37
Hearts	36	13	5	18	47	64	31
Hibernian	36	10	7	19	38	61	27
Dumbarton	36	6	7	23	29	64	19
Morton	36	5	2	29	29	100	12

SCOTTISH FIRST DIVISION

	1980-81	1981-82	1982-83	1983-84	1984-85
Champions:	Hibernian	Motherwell	St Johnstone	Morton	Motherwell
Also promoted:	Dundee	Kilmarnock	Hearts	Dumbarton	Clydebank
Relegated:	Stirling Albion, Berwick Rangers	East Stirling, Queen of the South	Dunfermline Athletic, Queen's Park	Raith Rovers, Alloa	Meadowbank Thistle, St Johnstone

SCOTTISH SECOND DIV

	1980-81	1981-82	1982-83	1983-84	1984-85
Champions:	Queen's Park	Clyde	Brechin City	Forfar Athletic	Montrose
Also promoted:	Queen of the South	Alloa	Meadowbank Thistle	East Fife	Alloa

SCOTTISH LEAGUE CUP

1980-81	1981-82	1982-83	1983-84	1984-85
Dundee United 3 / Dundee 0	Rangers 2 / Dundee 1	Celtic 2 / Rangers 1	Rangers 3 / Celtic 2	Rangers 1 / Dundee United 0

1985-86 · 1986-87 · 1987-88 · 1988-89 · 1989-90

	1985-86	1986-87	1987-88	1988-89	1989-90
WORLD CUP	Argentina 3 West Germany 2				West Germany 1 Argentina 0
EUROPEAN CHAMPIONSHIP			Holland 2 USSR 0		
EUROPEAN CUP	Steaua Bucharest 0 Barcelona 0; Bucharest won 2-0 on penalties	Porto 2 Bayern Munich 1	PSV Eindhoven 0 Benfica 0	AC Milan 4 Steaua Bucharest 0	AC Milan 1 Benfica 0
EUROPEAN CUP WINNERS CUP	Dynamo Kiev 3 Atletico Madrid 0	Ajax 1 Lokomotiv Leipzig 0	Mechelen 1 Ajax 0	Barcelona 2 Sampdoria 0	Sampdoria 2 Anderlecht 0
UEFA CUP	Real Madrid beat Cologne 5-1 0-2	IFK Gothenburg beat Dundee United 1-0 1-1	Bayer Leverkusen beat Espanol 0-3 3-0; Leverkusen won 3-2 on penalties	Napoli beat VFB Stuttgart 2-1 3-3	Juventus beat Fiorentina 3-1 0-0
FA CUP	Liverpool 3 Everton 1	Coventry City 3 Tottenham Hotspur 2	Wimbledon 1 Liverpool 0	Liverpool 3 Everton 2	Manchester United 1 Crystal Palace 0, after 3-3

FIRST DIVISION

1985-86
```
              P  W  D  L  F  A Pts
Liverpool    42 26 10  6 89 37 88
Everton      42 26  8  8 87 41 86
West Ham     42 26  6 10 74 40 84
Man Utd      42 22 10 10 70 36 76
Sheff Wed    42 21 10 11 63 54 73
Chelsea      42 20 11 11 57 56 71
Arsenal      42 20  9 13 49 47 69
Nottm F      42 19 11 12 69 53 68
Luton        42 18 12 12 61 44 66
Tottenham    42 19  8 15 74 52 65
Newcastle    42 17 12 13 67 72 63
Watford      42 16 11 15 69 62 59
QPR          42 15  7 20 53 64 52
Soton        42 12 10 20 51 62 46
Manchester   42 11 12 19 43 57 45
Aston Villa  42 10 14 18 51 67 44
Coventry     42 11 10 21 48 71 43
Oxford       42 10 12 20 62 80 42
Leicester    42 10 12 20 54 76 42
Ipswich      42 11  8 23 32 55 41
Birmingham   42  8  5 29 30 73 29
West Brom    42  4 12 26 35 89 24
```

1986-87
```
              P  W  D  L  F  A Pts
Everton      42 26  8  8 76 31 86
Liverpool    42 23  8 11 72 42 77
Tottenham    42 21  8 13 68 43 71
Arsenal      42 20 10 12 58 35 70
Norwich      42 17 17  8 53 51 68
Wimbledon    42 19  9 14 57 50 66
Luton        42 18 12 12 47 45 66
Nottm F      42 18 11 13 64 51 65
Watford      42 18  9 15 67 54 63
Coventry     42 17 12 13 50 45 63
Man Utd      42 14 14 14 52 45 56
Soton         2 14 10 18 69 68 52
Sheff Wed    42 13 13 16 58 59 52
Chelsea      42 13 13 16 53 64 52
West Ham     42 14 10 18 52 67 52
QPR          42 13 11 18 48 64 50
Newcastle    42 12 11 19 47 65 47
Oxford       42 11 13 18 44 69 46
Charlton     42 11 11 20 45 55 44
Leicester    42 11  9 22 54 76 42
Man City     42  8 15 19 36 57 39
Aston Villa  42  8 12 22 45 79 36
```

1987-88
```
              P  W  D  L  F  A Pts
Liverpool    40 26 12  2 87 24 90
Man Utd      40 23 12  5 71 38 81
Nottm F      40 20 13  7 67 39 73
Everton      40 19 13  8 53 27 70
QPR          40 19 10 11 48 38 67
Arsenal      40 18 12 10 58 39 66
Wimbledon    40 14 15 11 58 47 57
Newcastle    40 14 14 12 55 53 56
Luton        40 14 11 15 57 58 53
Coventry     40 13 14 13 46 53 53
Sheff Wed    40 15  8 17 52 66 53
Soton        40 12 14 14 49 53 50
Tottenham    40 12 11 17 38 48 47
Norwich      40 12  9 19 40 52 45
Derby        40 10 13 17 35 45 43
West Ham     40  9 11 20 40 52 42
Charlton     40  9 15 16 38 52 42
Chelsea      40  9 15 16 50 68 42
Portsmouth   40  7 14 19 36 66 35
Watford      40  7 11 22 27 51 32
Oxford       40  6 13 21 44 80 31
```

1988-89
```
              P  W  D  L  F  A Pts
Arsenal      38 22 10  6 73 36 76
Liverpool    38 22 10  6 65 28 76
Nottm F      38 17 13  8 64 43 64
Norwich      38 17 11 10 48 45 62
Derby        38 17  7 14 40 38 58
Tottenham    38 15 12 11 60 46 57
Coventry     38 14 13 11 47 42 55
Everton      38 14 12 12 50 45 54
QPR          38 14 11 13 43 37 53
Millwall     38 14 11 13 47 52 53
Man Utd      38 13 12 13 45 35 51
Wimbledon    38 14  9 15 50 46 51
Soton        38 10 15 13 52 66 45
Charlton     38 10 12 16 44 58 42
Sheff Wed    38 10 12 16 34 51 42
Luton        38 10 11 17 42 52 41
Aston Villa  38  9 13 16 45 56 40
Middlesbro   38  9 12 17 44 61 39
West Ham     38 10  8 20 37 62 38
Newcastle    38  7 10 21 32 63 31
```

1989-90
```
              P  W  D  L  F  A Pts
Liverpool    38 23 10  5 78 37 79
Aston Villa  38 21  7 10 57 38 70
Tottenham    38 19  6 13 59 47 63
Arsenal      38 18  8 12 54 38 62
Chelsea      38 16 12 10 58 50 60
Everton      38 17  8 13 57 46 59
Soton        38 15 10 13 71 63 55
Wimbledon    38 13 16  9 47 40 55
Nottm F      38 15  9 14 55 47 54
Norwich      38 13 14 11 44 42 53
QPR          38 13 11 14 45 44 50
Coventry     38 14  7 17 39 59 49
Man Utd      38 13  9 16 46 47 48
Man City     38 12 14 12 43 52 48
C Palace     38 13  9 16 42 66 48
Derby        38 13  7 18 43 40 46
Luton        38 10 13 15 43 57 43
Sheff Wed    38 11 10 17 35 51 43
Charlton     38  7  9 22 31 57 30
Millwall     38  5 11 22 39 65 26
```

SECOND DIVISION

1985-86	1986-87	1987-88	1988-89	1989-90
Champions: Norwich City Also promoted: Charlton Athletic, Wimbledon Relegated: Carlisle United, Middlesbrough, Fulham	Champions: Derby County Also promoted: Portsmouth Relegated: Sunderland, Grimsby Town, Brighton & Hove Albion	Champions: Millwall Also promoted: Aston Villa, Middlesbrough Relegated: Sheffield United, Reading, Huddersfield Town	Champions: Chelsea Also promoted: Manchester City, Crystal Palace Relegated: Shrewsbury Town, Birmingham City, Walsall	Champions: Leeds United Also promoted: Sheffield United, Sunderland Relegated: Bournemouth, Bradford City, Stoke City

THIRD DIVISION

1985-86	1986-87	1987-88	1988-89	1989-90
Champions: Reading Also promoted: Plymouth Argyle, Derby County Relegated: Lincoln City, Cardiff City, Wolverhampton Wanderers, Swansea	Champions: Bournemouth Also promoted: Middlesbrough, Swindon Town Relegated: Bolton Wanderers, Carlisle United, Darlington, Newport County	Champions: Sunderland Also promoted: Brighton & Hove Albion, Walsall Relegated: Rotherham United, Grimsby Town, York City, Doncaster Rovers	Champions: Wolverhampton Wanderers Also promoted: Sheffi Utd, Port Vale Relegated: Southend United, Chesterfield, Gillingham, Aldershot	Champions: Bristol Rovers Also promoted: Bristol City, Notts County Relegated: Cardiff City, Northampton Town, Blackpool, Walsall

FOURTH DIVISION

1985-86	1986-87	1987-88	1988-89	1989-90
Champions: Swindon Town Also promoted: Chester City, Mansfield Town, Port Vale	Champions: Northampton Town Also promoted: Preston North End, Southend United, Aldershot *Scarborough replaced Lincoln*	Champions: Wolves Also promoted: Cardiff City, Bolton Wanderers, Swansea City *Lincoln replaced Newport*	Champions: Rotherham United Also promoted: Tranmere Rovers, Crewe Alexandra, Leyton Orient *Maidstone replaced Darlington*	Champions: Exeter City Also promoted: Grimsby Town, Southend United, Cambridge United *Darlington replaced Colchester*

LEAGUE CUP

1985-86	1986-87	1987-88	1988-89	1989-90
Oxford United 3 Queen's Park Rangers 0	Arsenal 2 Liverpool 1	Luton Town 3 Arsenal 2	Nottingham Forest 3 Luton Town 1	Nottingham Forest 1 Oldham Athletic 0

SCOTTISH CUP

1985-86	1986-87	1987-88	1988-89	1989-90
Aberdeen 3 Hearts 0	St Mirren 1 Dundee United 0	Celtic 2 Dundee United 1	Celtic 1 Rangers 0	Aberdeen 0 Celtic 0; Aberdeen won 9-8 on penalties

SCOTTISH PREMIER DIVISION

1985-86
```
              P  W  D  L  F  A Pts
Celtic       36 20 10  6 67 38 50
Hearts       36 20 10  6 59 33 50
Dundee       36 18 11  7 59 31 47
Aberdeen     36 16 12  8 62 31 44
Rangers      36 13  9 14 53 45 35
Dundee       36 14  7 15 45 51 35
St Mirren    36 13  5 18 42 63 31
Hibernian    36 11  6 19 49 63 28
Motherwell   36  7  6 23 33 66 20
Clydebank    36  6  8 22 29 77 20
```

1986-87
```
              P  W  D  L  F  A Pts
Rangers      44 31  7  6 85 23 69
Celtic       44 27  9  8 90 41 63
Dundee       44 24 12  8 66 36 60
Aberdeen     44 21 16  7 63 29 58
Hearts       44 21 14  9 64 43 56
Dundee       44 18 12 14 74 57 48
St Mirren    44 12 12 20 36 51 36
Motherwell   44 11 12 21 43 64 34
Hibernian    44 10 13 21 44 70 33
Falkirk      44  8 10 26 31 70 26
Clydebank    44  6 12 26 35 93 24
Hamilton     44  6  9 29 39 93 21
```

1987-88
```
              P  W  D  L  F  A Pts
Celtic       44 30 10  4 78 24 70
Hearts       44 23 16  5 74 32 62
Rangers      44 26  8 10 85 34 60
Aberdeen     44 20 17  7 56 25 57
Dundee       44 16 12  8 67 48 44
Dundee       44 18  7 19 71 63 43
Hibernian    44 12 19 13 41 43 43
Motherwell   44 13 12 19 37 56 36
St Mirren    44 10 15 19 41 64 35
Falkirk      44 11 11 22 42 74 33
Dunfermline  44  9 10 25 45 81 28
Morton       44  3 10 31 27 100 16
```

1988-89
```
              P  W  D  L  F  A Pts
Rangers      36 26  4  6 62 26 56
Aberdeen     36 18 14  4 51 25 50
Celtic       36 21  4 11 66 44 46
Dundee       36 16 12  8 44 26 44
Hibernian    36 13  9 14 37 36 35
Hearts       36  9 13 14 35 42 31
St Mirren    36 11  7 18 39 55 29
Dundee       36  9 10 17 34 48 28
Motherwell   36  7 13 16 35 44 27
Hamilton     36  6  2 28 19 76 14
```

1989-90
```
              P  W  D  L  F  A Pts
Rangers      36 20 11  5 48 19 51
Aberdeen     36 17 10  9 56 33 44
Hearts       36 16 12  8 54 35 44
Dundee       36 11 13 12 36 39 35
Celtic       36 10 14 12 37 37 34
Motherwell   36 11 12 13 43 47 34
Hibernian    36 12 10 14 34 41 34
Dunfermline  36 11  8 17 37 50 30
St Mirren    36 10 10 16 28 48 30
Dundee       36  5 14 17 41 65 24
```

SCOTTISH FIRST DIVISION

1985-86	1986-87	1987-88	1988-89	1989-90
Champions: Hamilton Academical Also promoted: Falkirk Relegated: Ayr United, Alloa	Champions: Morton Also promoted: Dunfermline Athletic Relegated: Brechin City, Montrose	Champions: Hamilton Academical Runners-up (not promoted): Meadowbank Thistle Relegated: East Fife, Dumbarton	Champions: Dunfermline Athletic Runners-up (not promoted): Falkirk Relegated: Kilmarnock, Queen of the South	Champions: St Johnstone Runners-up (not promoted): Airdrie Relegated: Albion Rovers, Alloa

SCOTTISH SECOND DIV

1985-86	1986-87	1987-88	1988-89	1989-90
Champions: Dunfermline Athletic Also promoted: Queen of the South	Champions: Meadowbank Thistle Also promoted: Raith Rovers	Champions: Ayr United Also promoted: St Johnstone	Champions: Albion Rovers Also promoted: Alloa	Champions: Brechin City Also promoted: Kilmarnock

SCOTTISH LEAGUE CUP

1985-86	1986-87	1987-88	1988-89	1989-90
Aberdeen 3 Hibernian 0	Rangers 2 Celtic 1	Rangers 3 Aberdeen 3; Rangers won 5-3 on penalties	Rangers 3 Aberdeen 2	Aberdeen 2 Rangers 1

WORLD CUP 1990

Penal code puts football in the dock

IF the finals of the World Cup are supposed to be football's showcase then the 1990 tournament in Italy was an unmitigated disaster. The statistics tell the story: in 52 matches 115 goals were scored but there were 164 cautions and 16 dismissals. In the last seven matches, from the quarter-finals to the final, only two were decided by goals scored from the run of play, the rest were won either by penalties or by a penalty shoot-out. Football had become a travesty of itself.

However, in the midst of all this depressing cynicism, England did rather well and progressed to the semi-finals – their best performance since 1966, and at the end of the tournament were given the Fair Play award. Their success was something of a surprise, particularly to the press.

In the 18 months prior to the finals Bobby Robson, the England manager, had been the victim of a sustained witch-hunt in the tabloids that would have destroyed lesser men. Even the quality newspapers contributed to the hysteria and hardly a single reporter gave England a prayer. So biased were the journalists that, even as England came within a whisker of reaching the World Cup final, they were still carping about the team and its performance. Meanwhile back home millions watched England's success on television with rapture.

And the Republic of Ireland's. Jack Charlton's odd assortment of Irish and Football League players did spectacularly well to reach the quarter-finals in their very first appearance in the World Cup finals. Admittedly, given their playing resources, their style frequently resembled an average First Division side but their only defeat was to Italy, one of the favourites, in the quarter-final and that was to a single goal from Toto Schillaci.

Sadly Scotland maintained their usual record: for the seventh time they failed get past the first phase; they experienced yet another embarrassing defeat, 1-0 to Costa Rica; and a stirring display against Brazil almost got them into the second round until a late goal put them on the plane home.

England began with the normal hiccups, drawing against the Republic of Ireland and Holland, the European champions, and only qualified for the second round by scraping a 1-0 victory over Egypt. The victory over Belgium that took them to the quarter-finals was inspired by Paul Gascoigne, arguably the player of the tournament. In the last minute of extra time he picked up a ball just outside the England penalty area and ran straight at the heart of the Belgian midfield. Desperate not to concede a goal, the Belgians conceded a free-kick instead. Gascoigne grabbed the ball, looked up, and then put it over the Belgian defence for David Platt to steal in and volley the ball home.

Cameroon, England's quarter-final opponents, were the shock side of the tournament. In the opening match they had stunned Argentina, the defending champions, by beating them 1-0 despite being reduced to nine men. They didn't lie down in front of England either. Platt had put England ahead midway through the first half, but 15 minutes into the second half Roger Milla, Cameroon's star player despite being 38, was brought down and Kunde converted the penalty. Four minutes later Cameroon went ahead and England seemed incapable of finding the equaliser. With nine minutes remaining, England seemed destined to experience their most embarrassing result since they were beaten by the United States in 1950.

However Cameroon gave away a foolish penalty which Gary Lineker coolly struck home, and in extra time they repeated their mistake, brought Lineker down in the penalty area again, and the Spurs striker put England into the semi-final against West Germany in Turin.

And inevitably Lineker was England's saviour again. The Germans had fortuitously taken the lead in the 59th minute when Andreas Brehme's free-kick was deflected over Peter Shilton by Paul Parker. Ten minutes from time Parker made amends by supplying the cross for Lineker to equalise and take the match into extra time.

With no more goals – although both teams hit the post – the tie was decided on penalties, as had the other semi-final the previous day. West Germany scored from their four attempts but Chris Waddle and Stuart Pearce both missed and England were eliminated 4-3.

Strangely the abiding memory of the match will probably not be those two costly misses but Gascoigne's tears. The young Spurs midfielder had already been booked earlier in the tournament and when he was booked again – for talking back to the referee after a foul – he burst into tears as he realised he would automatically miss the final.

Not that he would have missed much. West Germany's opponents were Argentina, but not the free-flowing, attack-minded Argentina of 1986 and 1978. This was a cynical and ruthless Argentina orchestrated by their captain, the fading Diego Maradona, into a team that played something that had only a passing reference to football as the world understands it.

Their progress to the final was a tactician's delight and a football purist's nightmare. They had played six games and won only two. They qualified for the second round as one of the four third-placed teams with the best records. In the quarter-finals and semi-finals, against Yugoslavia and Italy, they only won through on penalty shoot-outs. The physical side of Argentina's play deprived them of three key players for the final, Caniggia, Olarticoechea and Giusti – all ineligible because of bookings or dismissals.

The final, in Rome on July 8, summed up the whole tournament. It was a tedious bore where the Argentinians were clearly playing for the penalty shoot-out and the Germans were waiting for the Argentinians to misbehave and be penalised by the referee. West Germany's gamesmanship proved superior.

In the 68th minute Jurgen Klinsmann was routinely tackled by Monzon. However the German's theatrics were convincing enough for the Mexican referee to dismiss the Argentinian. Five minutes from time Rudi Voeller collapsed in a heap in the penalty area after a challenge from Sensini and a generous penalty was awarded which Brehme converted. It was the only goal of the game.

Ten minutes earlier Calderon had similarly been brought down in the German area, but without reward. To round off the match, and the tournament, three minutes from time Dezotti was sent off when trying to get the ball from Kohler, who was obviously time-wasting. In the ensuing bedlam Maradona was booked for dissent.

There is little doubt that the spectre of the penalty shoot-out haunted this tournament and ultimately turned it into a horror show. Fifa may argue that it is the only feasible way to break a deadlock and that the paying spectators expect to see a result. However, as the tournament unfolded it was transparent that the intention of certain teams was simply to prevent the other side scoring and gamble on the penalty decider. It is interesting to note that in the knock-out phases of the World Cups from 1954 to 1970, where there were no penalty shoot-outs, there was not a single draw in 40 matches.

Leading lights: Milla (Cameroon), Schillaci (Italy), Gascoigne (England), Klinsmann (Germany) and Maradona (Argentina)

Turning points: Lineker scores the equaliser against Cameroon and Brehme's penalty gives West Germany the World Cup

FOR THE RECORD

FIRST ROUND

GROUP A
	P	W	D	L	F	A	Pts
Italy	3	3	0	0	4	0	6
Czech	3	2	0	1	6	3	4
Austria	3	1	0	2	2	3	2
United States	3	0	0	3	2	8	0

GROUP B
	P	W	D	L	F	A	Pts
Cameroon	3	2	0	1	3	5	4
Romania	3	1	1	1	4	3	3
Argentina	3	1	1	1	3	2	3
Soviet Union	3	1	0	3	4	4	2

GROUP C
	P	W	D	L	F	A	Pts
Brazil	3	3	0	0	4	1	6
Costa Rica	3	2	0	1	3	2	4
Scotland	3	1	0	2	2	3	2
Sweden	3	0	0	3	3	6	0

GROUP D
	P	W	D	L	F	A	Pts
W Germany	3	2	1	0	10	3	5
Yugoslavia	3	2	0	1	6	5	4
Colombia	3	1	1	1	3	2	3
UA Emirates	3	0	0	3	2	11	0

GROUP E
	P	W	D	L	F	A	Pts
Spain	3	2	1	0	5	2	5
Belgium	3	2	0	1	6	3	4
Uruguay	3	1	1	1	2	3	3
South Korea	3	0	0	3	1	6	0

GROUP F
	P	W	D	L	F	A	Pts
England	3	1	2	0	2	1	4
R of Ireland	3	0	3	0	2	2	3
Holland	3	0	3	0	2	2	3
Egypt	3	0	2	1	1	2	2

SECOND ROUND

Cameroon 2   Colombia 1 aet
HT 0-0   Att. 50,026
Czechoslovakia 4   Costa Rica 1
HT 1-0   Att. 47,673
Argentina 1   Brazil 0
HT 0-0   Att. 61,381
West Germany 2   Holland 1
HT 0-0   Att. 74,559
Republic of Ireland 0   Romania 0
Republic of Ireland won 5-4 on
penalties   Att. 31,818
Italy 2   Uruguay 0
HT 0-0   Att. 73,303
Yugoslavia 2   Spain 1 aet
HT 0-0   Att. 35,500
England 1   Belgium 0 aet
HT 0-0   Att. 34,520

QUARTER-FINALS
Argentina 0   Yugoslavia 0
Argentina won 3-2 on penalties
Att. 38,971
Italy 1   Republic of Ireland 0
HT 1-0   Att. 73,303
W Germany 1   Czechoslovakia 0
HT 1-0   Att. 73,347
England 3   Cameroon 2 aet
HT 1-0   Att. 55,205

SEMI-FINALS
Argentina 1   Italy 1
Argentina won 4-3 on penalties
HT 0-1   Att. 59,978

West Germany 1   England 1
West Germany won 4-3 on penalties
HT 0-0   Att. 62,628

THIRD PLACE PLAY-OFF
Italy 2   England 1
HT 0-0   Att. 51,426

FINAL
West Germany 1   Argentina 0
HT 0-0   Att. 73,603

Teams
West Germany Illgner, Berthold (sub:
Reuter), Kohler, Augenthaler, Buchwald,
Brehme, Hassler, Matthaus, Littbarski,
Voller, Klinsmann
Argentina Goycochea; Ruggeri (sub:
Monzon), Simon, Serrizuela, Sensini,
Basualdo, Burruchaga (sub: Calderon),
Troglio, Lorenzo, Maradona, Dezotti

Leading goalscorers 6 Salvatore Schillaci
(Italy); 5 Tomas Skuhravy
(Czechoslovakia); 4 Michel (Spain), Roger
Milla (Cameroon), Gary Lineker (England),
Lothar Matthaus (West Germany)

Total goals scored 115
Average per game: 2.21

Sendings-off Andre Kana Biyik
(Cameroon) v Argentina.
Benjamin Massing (Cameroon) v
Argentina; Referee: Michel Vautrot (France).
Eric Wynalda (United States) v
Czechoslovakia; Referee: Kurt
Roethlisberger (Switzerland).
Vladimir Bessonov (Soviet Union) v
Argentina; Referee: Erik Fredriksson
(Sweden).
Eric Gerets (Belgium) v Uruguay; Referee:
Sigfried Kirschen (East Germany).
Peter Artner (Austria) v United States;
Referee: Jamal Al Sharif (Syria).
Khaleel Ganim Mubarak (United Arab
Emirates) v Yugoslavia; Referee: Shizuo
Takada (Japan).
Yoon Deuk-yeo (South Korea) v Uruguay;
Referee: Tullio Lanese (Italy).
Rudi Voller (West Germany) v Holland;
Referee: Juan Carlos Loustau (Argentina).
Frank Rijkaard (Holland) v West Germany.
Ricardo Gomes (Brazil) v Argentina;
Referee: Joel Quiniou (France).
Refik Sabanadzovic (Yugoslavia) v
Argentina; Referee: Kurt Roethlisberger
(Switzerland).
Lubomir Moravcik (Czechoslovakia) v
West Germany; Referee: Helmut Kohl
(Austria).
Ricardo Giusti (Argentina) v Italy; Referee:
Michel Vautrot (France).
Pedro Damian Monzon (Argentina) v West
Germany; Referee: Edgardo Codesal
Mendaz (Mexico).
Gustavo Abel Dezotti (Argentina) v West
Germany.

Number of players used by finalists
17 West Germany; 20 Argentina

● No captain has ever lifted the World Cup
trophy twice. Diego Maradona skippered
the 1986 winners and was captain of the
1990 runners-up. Karl-Heinz Rummenigge
has led two losing teams in the finals.

Arsenal march steadily to the title despite their trials and tribulations

Faeroes from zero to hero

THERE are upsets and shocks most seasons, but then along came the sensational Faeroe Islands. The islands in the far north of the Atlantic, a semi-autonomous part of Denmark with a population of barely 50,000, were playing their first ever competitive international.

The team of fishermen and farmers had to play their home match against Austria in Sweden because the islands only had artificial pitches, which were not allowed in the qualifying stages of the European championship.

Everybody expected the part-timers to be the whipping boys of Group Four. But, on September 12, in front of a mere 1,544 spectators, they embarrassed Austria 1-0 with a goal from Nielsen in the 61st minute. Nobody could believe it, least of all the Austrian manager Josef Hickersberger, who returned home and promptly resigned.

Anybody who thought the result was a fluke only had to go to Belfast in May. Northern Ireland took the lead just before half-time but the Faeroese fought back to earn a 1-1 draw and prove that they were anything but a joke side.

In Group Seven, England looked far from convincing as they drew twice with the Republic of Ireland and only just managed to win in Turkey with a scrambled goal from Dennis Wise on his debut. So the international honours belonged to Wales, who finished the season firmly atop of group five with three wins and a draw from four matches, including a creditable 1-0 victory over West Germany in Cardiff on June 5.

Bad blood: McClair tackles Adams in the match that erupted into a 21-man brawl

ARSENAL ultimately won the League at a canter with a record-breaking performance, but their season was not without its ups and downs. And for much of the time it looked as if the downs were going to outnumber the ups.

There was a shameful start to the campaign at Old Trafford when the match on October 20 dissolved into a brawl. The only one of the 22 players on the pitch not involved in the fighting was David Seaman, and it was the second time in as many seasons that Arsenal had been involved in such disgraceful scenes.

Retribution was swift. Arsenal fined George Graham and five players two weeks' wages, the FA fined both clubs £50,000 for bringing the game into disrepute, and Arsenal were docked two points and Manchester United one.

Then Arsenal were walloped 6-2 at home by Manchester United in the League Cup. And, just before Christmas, to add to the misery at Highbury, Tony Adams was jailed for nine months, with five months suspended, for drink-driving.

In between all these distractions, Arsenal were putting together a remarkable run of form in the League. They surpassed their best ever start to the season, and were not beaten in the League until February 2,

when they lost their 24th match to Chelsea. It was the only League match they were to lose all season, a performance that has only been bettered by Preston's 22 matches without defeat to win the first ever title back in 1888-89.

The final turning point came on March 3, when Arsenal won at Anfield. With Liverpool in disarray after the sudden departure of Kenny Dalglish, the bookmakers were soon refusing to accept any more bets on Arsenal winning the title. They ended the season seven points clear, even though the two points they had deducted meant that they had not led the table until January.

Super League on the cards

FOR a few brief months it looked as if club chairmen had finally managed to reach some sort of agreement on the future of the game. In August they agreed to return to a 22-team First Division and expand the League to 94 clubs, and a deal with ITV and BSB meant that there would be 115 live matches on television.

But nothing ever changed. No sooner had the season started than the bickering resumed. As the rows rumbled on, nobody could really work out exactly what it all meant, other than, as usual, the League and the FA were at each other's throats and the clubs were fighting among themselves over money.

At the heart of the matter was the question of who should run the national game. The dispute finally boiled over in April when the FA announced plans for an 18-team Super League, to start in the 1992-93 season.

The idea was that this would help the national side by cutting the number of matches played during the season. But the FA could not even agree among itself, with some people arguing that there should still be 22 clubs in the top flight because this produced more money-spinning fixtures.

Not surprisingly, the League was aghast, and its president, Bill Fox, accused the FA of trying to hijack the First Division.

But the League was forced to admit that it was powerless to stop any breakaway, although it threatened clubs with heavy fines if they did jump ship.

Finally, in June, the League told the FA to abandon its plans or face court action. The clubs responded by formally giving notice of their intention to resign from the League, so the case duly went to court.

The League lost its case, bringing the advent of the Premier League closer. But the only thing that was really clear at the end of a season of skirmishes was that there would be still more turmoil the following season before the matter was finally resolved.

Dalglish cracks under the pressure

KENNY DALGLISH was a man of few words as a manager, and he left the rest of the country speechless as well when he announced that he was re-signing as Liverpool manager.

Dalglish's decision, on February 22, seemed to be inexplicable. The player that Anfield had idolised had maintained Liverpool's great tradition, winning the Double in his first season in charge and guiding Liverpool to three League titles and two FA Cups during his six-year reign. And Liverpool were once again on top of the First Division and had just played a

pulsating 4-4 draw with Everton in the FA Cup fifth round replay.

The Liverpool board had no inkling of what was about to happen when it gathered for a routine meeting. One by one they did their best to persuade Dalglish to stay. But at the end of an emotional meeting that lasted all day he was insistent, the constant striving for success had created pressures that he could no longer bear.

Ronnie Moran was appointed caretaker manager, but he said that he did not want the job permanently. Graeme Souness was

the obvious favourite, but he said he was not interested: "I would never contemplate leaving Ibrox." John Toshack, of Real Sociedad, and George Graham, of Arsenal, also ruled themselves out.

So Liverpool tried Souness once again. This time, lured by a five-year contract worth £350,000 a year, he agreed to join Liverpool on April 16. The Kop were delighted and Rangers were unhappy at losing their leading light. David Murray, their chairman, said: "I think he is making the biggest mistake of his life."

Liverpool stunned: a grim-faced Dalglish announces his resignation

Souness: lured back

If he has resigned because of the pressures, the rest of us have no chance

HOWARD WILKINSON

313

Maradona the most hated man in Italy

Maradona: disgraced exile

DIEGO MARADONA'S stormy spell in Italy ended in disgrace when he fled the country in the wake of a drugs and sex scandal.

The Napoli forward's antics had already so alienated his club's supporters, and the rest of the country, that he was voted the most hated man in Italy. In the poll in December the Argentinian received a worse rating than even Saddam Hussein.

Maradona's response was to threaten to quit if his club did not allow him to leave at the end of the season. In the end, though, matters came to a head when Maradona was linked with a vice ring and then tested positive for cocaine after a League match.

Facing suspension by the Italian FA, and the prospect of being sent to jail, Maradona decided that he had overstayed his welcome and returned to Argentina on April 2.

Rangers snatch League in an ultimate High Noon shoot-out

WALTER SMITH was a very relieved man on May 11, the very last day of the season. And extremely grateful to his English centre forward Mark Hateley. His two goals at Ibrox saw off Aberdeen's late dash for the title and confirmed Rangers as champions. The finale was as extraordinary as Arsenal's triumph in the English League two years earlier when they snatched the championship from Kenny Dalglish's Liverpool.

Coincidentally it was Dalglish who accidentally put Smith in the most awkward of situations, having to beat the League leaders in the last match for the title. It was Dalglish's shock resignation at Liverpool in February that led to Graeme Souness's own shock resignation from Rangers on April 16 to take over the helm at Anfield. Rangers had only four League matches remaining.

At Christmas Rangers had looked certain League champions. But a bad spell from the end of February to the beginning of April – when they won only two games in six – had seen Aberdeen creep up on them.

Then a 3-0 defeat at Motherwell in the penultimate game saw them lose pole position for the first time since December, and by the narrowest of margins. Aberdeen and Rangers were level on points and level on goal difference. However, the north-east club got the nod by virtue of having scored two more goals!

The deciding match was billed as a High Noon shoot-out and was an exciting affair as Rangers pulled out all the stops in front of their anxious fans. Hateley's double strike rewarded them as Aberdeen went down 2-0.

The Scottish Cup final a week later also proved to be a thrilling affair. Motherwell had rocked everybody by knocking out Aberdeen away and then disposing of Celtic in a replay having twice been behind. Dundee United, their opponents, had had a much easier run although they only scraped past East Fife when a late goal in extra time earned them a replay. And then they won that in extra time.

The drama of the earlier rounds was relived at Hampden Park. Motherwell went ahead against the run of play in the first half, but by full-time the sides were level at 3-3. Then just as it looked as if the final would go to a replay up popped Kirk in the final minute to give Motherwell their first Scottish Cup since 1952.

Finishing touch: Hateley's two goals gave Rangers the title

Smith: baptism of fire

We're back with a bang as Hughes and United proudly conquer Europe

Captain fantastic: Bryan Robson led United to victory in Rotterdam

MANCHESTER UNITED made it a triumphant return for English clubs to European competition when they beat mighty Barcelona in Rotterdam 2-1 to lift the European Cup Winners Cup. It was also a night of delicious ironies. Mark Hughes, who had been deemed a failure at Barcelona, scored both United's goals. Alex Ferguson, the manager who had brought him back to Old Trafford three years earlier, also equalled Johan Cruyff's record of winning the competition with different clubs. Ferguson's Aberdeen had taken the trophy in 1983, beating Real Madrid in the final.

United had rocked Barcelona back on their heels from the kick-off by mounting attack after attack. By the 68th minute the Catalan defence seemed shell-shocked and when Steve Bruce headed a Bryan Robson free kick goalwards, Hughes had a simple tap-in.

Six minutes later the Welsh international was on target again when he escaped his marker, went wide of Busquets, the goalkeeper, and thumped the ball past him from the tightest of angles.

In the 80th minute a Ronald Koeman speciality, from a free kick, reduced the arrears, but despite a nervous 10 minutes United clung on to win their second European trophy.

FOR THE RECORD

■ Gary Lineker won Fifa's £20,000 fair play prize for never being booked or sent off during his career.

■ Paul Gascoigne became the first player to be sent off in a League match shown live on television when he was dismissed for dissent against Manchester United on January 1.

■ Chelsea were fined £105,000 for making illegal payments to players.

■ Bernard Tapie, the Marseilles president, was banned for a year for allegedly bribing players and intimidating referees.

■ England were one of eight countries bidding to stage the 1998 World Cup.

■ Bad weather on February 9 meant that only 12 matches in total were played in England and Scotland, the lowest number since 1979.

■ Ossie Ardiles took over as manager of Newcastle when Jim Smith resigned on March 26.

■ Abel Resino, the Atletico Madrid goalkeeper, set a world record when he went 1,275 minutes without conceding a goal.

■ Uefa, under pressure from the EEC, agreed to allow clubs to field five foreign players in League matches next season.

■ Liverpool were readmitted to European competition on April 19.

Woeful Worthing walloped

FEBRUARY was not a good month for Worthing. Already struggling in the Vauxhall League First Division they conceded 23 goals in less than a week, going down 10-0 at Whyteleafe in the League and losing 13-0 at Carshalton in the Loctite Cup.

Their manager, Joe Boon, was remarkably philosophical, saying: "The defeat at Carshalton was not as bad as it sounds. But we gave away five bad goals."

His chairman, John Mayer, was also resigned to the club's fate. "We have spent all our money on improving our ground, and there's nothing left to pay the players. Our sponsors have pulled out, and we get gates of only 150," he said.

Not surprisingly, the club finished rock bottom of the Division, 23 points adrift with only two wins and four draws from 42 matches and a goal difference of minus 129, having conceded 157.

Familiar territory: the Worthing goalkeeper is beaten yet again

Derby trigger mad transfer merry-go-round

THE END of the season brought a frenzy of activity in the transfer market, with a series of spectacular sales during the summer.

Derby, who were desperate to reduce their wage bill after being relegated to the Second Division, set the ball rolling when they sold Mark Wright and Dean Saunders to Liverpool in quick succession in July. Wright moved for £2.2m on July 12 and Saunders followed him two days later for a British record £2.9m. Graeme Souness was obviously determined to rebuild his team as he quickly sold Peter Beardsley to Everton for £1m and Steve Staunton to Aston Villa for £1.1m, and used some of the money to bring Mark Walters to Anfield from Rangers for £1.25m.

In between times, Nottingham Forest bought Teddy Sheringham for £2m; Celtic signed Paul Elliott for £1.4m and Tony Cascarino for £1.1m; Manchester United signed Paul Parker for £2m; Manchester City spent £2.5m for Keith Curle and collected £1.3m for Mark Ward; and transfer tribunals ordered Leeds to pay £1.6m for Rod Wallace and £1.3m for Tony Dorigo.

But all of these deals were eclipsed by Aston Villa. Having spent £1.6m to bring Dalian Atkinson back from Spain they recouped all the money and plenty more as well with the sale of David Platt to Bari. The British record was raised even higher by the £5.5m price tag and it seemed that for a few heady weeks that money was no object in the multi-million pound pursuit of success.

Superstition works for Spurs

WITH the very existence of the club in doubt throughout the season, Tottenham experienced drama and crisis on the pitch as well. Driven by superstition – the year ended in a '1' when Tottenham historically had won the FA Cup – and the desperate financial mess they were in, Spurs put together a successful Cup run that bordered on pure fiction.

Paul Gascoigne, pure genius and childish scoundrel, was the lead character. Going into the semi-final he had scored five crucial goals and against Portsmouth and Notts County had virtually single-handedly retrieved victory from certain defeat. Then, on Sunday April 14, Tottenham faced Arsenal in first semi-final to be held at Wembley. With millions watching around the globe, Gascoigne had a ready-made world stage on which to make his mark.

And in the fifth minute Gascoigne demonstrated why Lazio were prepared to pay £8.5m for him when he took one of most audacious free kicks ever seen. From fully 35 yards out Gascoigne thundered a dipping, swerving shot that flew past the Arsenal wall and evaded the groping fingers of David Seaman.

Then, six minutes later, he combined with Paul Allen on the right wing with a breathtaking exchange of passes that caught the Arsenal defence at

Daft as a brush: Gascoigne self-destructs in the Cup final

Platt: British record

sixes and sevens. Allen's cross was met by Gary Lineker's toe. The match was effectively over. Arsenal pulled one back in the second half, but Lineker restored the two-goal lead when he ran at the Arsenal defence, Tony Adams lost him, and Seaman, uncharacteristically, failed to halt the danger.

Although Gascoigne was only half-fit – he had had a stomach operation a month earlier – and he only played for an hour, he was the winning inspiration for Spurs. He chased everything, harried and injected the vital urgency that lifted Spurs past their north London rivals, whose hopes of the Double were now dashed.

In the final, on May 18 against Nottingham Forest, Gascoigne again made his mark – but this time as the villain, not the hero. From the kick-off he had played like a maniac. He had badly fouled Gary Parker in the opening minutes and was fortunate not to be booked.

In the 15th minute he committed an horrendous scything tackle on Gary Charles just outside the Spurs penalty area. Gascoigne was left writhing in agony and had to be taken off with an injured knee. Once again he was fortunate not to receive harsher punishment from the referee.

But his team were punished. From the resultant free-kick Stuart Pearce shot through the

Tottenham wall to take the lead. Television evidence showed that the gap had been created by Forest's Lee Glover pushing Gary Mabbutt aside, but the goal stood.

Tottenham's misfortunes continued as the match went on: Lineker had a goal disallowed for offside that TV proved was legitimate; he then missed a penalty having been brought down in the area by Mark Crossley, the Forest keeper, who was neither cautioned nor sent off.

However, Paul Stewart rectified things with a well-taken equaliser in the 55th minute and the final drifted into extra time. Bizarrely, Brian Clough, who had never won the FA Cup, did not come on to the pitch to advise, exhort or comfort his young players. Instead he chatted to a policeman. By contrast, Terry Venables was visibly encouraging and counselling his team in the centre of the pitch.

Inevitably, this day of craziness continued to the end. The unfortunate Des Walker headed into his own net attempting to clear a flicked-on corner and handed Spurs their eighth FA Cup, a record. Much had been at stake, and although Gascoigne's injury threw into doubt his lucrative transfer to Italy, Spurs could now look forward to a Charity Shield appearance and a European campaign. It was news that would please their creditors.

Tottenham's nightmare ended by dream ticket

AFTER a year of uncertainty, Tottenham were finally rescued on June 22 when Terry Venables, the manager, and Alan Sugar, the Amstrad giant, formally took over the club for £7.2m. They were called the Dream Ticket and it appeared the nightmare of Tottenham FC, which had debts of some £20m, going out of existence was finally over.

The nightmare had started in September when it was revealed that Irving Scholar, the then chairman, had conducted secret negotiations with Robert Maxwell, the newspaper tycoon, to take over ailing Spurs. The debt was put at £12m.

Scholar had agreed with Maxwell that he would put £13.2m into the club. Worse, Scholar had borrowed £850,000 from Maxwell to make the final payment to Barcelona for the transfer of Gary Lineker, and he had not informed the rest of the Spurs board about his negotiations.

These extraordinary goings-on forced the Stock Exchange to investigate Spurs as they were a publicly quoted company. Six weeks after they began their scrutiny, the Exchange suspended all dealings in Tottenham's shares and Scholar was forced to resign as chairman.

Just before Christmas it was revealed that Venables was attempting to put together a consortium to take over the club, but finding suitable backers was proving difficult. As the months wore on there were rumours and counter rumours about the future of the club.

In March Lazio of Rome confirmed they had offered £8.5m for Paul Gascoigne and it appeared that, given their financial straits, Tottenham would have to bow to the inevitable.

Throughout the season Maxwell's interest in Spurs waxed and waned, but just as the Dream Ticket seemed set to clinch the deal he made a last-minute bid that almost came off. However Scholar, the majority shareholder, was persuaded by Sugar and Venables to sell to them and the predatory Maxwell was seen off.

It was an historic moment: successful businessman and successful manager in partnership at a leading football club. Their first task was to clear the debt and balance the books. Sugar warned the relieved fans that it would be some time before Tottenham ventured into the transfer market as a buyer.

Forced out: Irving Scholar's secret talks precipitated the crisis

Dynamic duo: Terry Venables and Alan Sugar snatched control of Tottenham from under the nose of Robert Maxwell

PAUL GASCOIGNE
The naughty boy
who has never grown up

Louise Taylor

PAUL GASCOIGNE

Born May 27, 1967, Gateshead

PLAYING CAREER
Newcastle United 1984-88
92 League appearances (9 as a substitute),
  21 goals
Tottenham Hotspur 1988-92
91 appearances (1 as substitute)
19 goals in the League, 8 in the League Cup,
  6 in the FA Cup
Honours FA Cup: Winners 1991
Lazio 1992 to present
Internationals England debut June 1989 v
  Denmark in Copenhagen (as a substitute)
Honours World Cup: Semi-final 1990

PAUL GASCOIGNE is England's troubled talent. If he plays well everybody rejoices, if he reaches for the self-destruct button the country is concerned. And with good reason, for Gascoigne rarely does things by halves.

On song in Lazio's or England's midfield, he challenges critics to describe him as anything other than the greatest British footballing talent of his generation. But they know that nobody is more capable of blowing – and really blowing – golden opportunities than Gascoigne.

After treating Tottenham fans to a virtuoso performance in the 1991 FA Cup semi-final against Arsenal – who could forget his glorious 35-yard goal from a right-footed free kick – the Wembley stage seemed set for a splendid swan-song in the final against Nottingham Forest. A new life in Rome with Lazio beckoned, but two lunatic tackles in the first half put it very much on hold.

The second reckless lunge, at Gary Charles, left Gascoigne facing complicated cruciate ligament surgery on his right knee. The best prognosis was a year out of football, and everybody knew his suffering was totally self-inflicted.

Five months on, the convalescent, still wanted by Lazio, was enjoying some play time on his native Tyneside. He watched his former Newcastle teammates take on Derby from the packed St James's Park terraces. His knee survived the madcap jostling at the Gallowgate end, but emergency surgery was needed after an incident in a nightclub well after chucking-out time in the nearby pubs. Once again, Gascoigne had taken one risk too many.

As he did in a training session in April 1994, when he broke his right leg in two places with a reckless tackle. Once again, Gascoigne's mercurial career was put on hold. Lazio had welcomed their great Geordie hope in the summer of 1992. Whether through arrogance, ignorance or nonchalance, Gascoigne arrived embarrassingly overweight and unfit. The Italians were insulted, just like the television reporter whose microphone he would belch into and the physiotherapist whose treatment table he would urinate upon. Then there were the photographers he punched.

Soon, Lazio would be irritated and exasperated by Gascoigne's turbulent relationship with his on-off girlfriend Sheryl Kyle, a glamourous divorcee and a mother of two. Trust Gascoigne to fall for a woman to whom he is physically attracted to the point of obsession but whose dislike of football and jealousy provokes frequent rows of soap-opera scale. No sooner did they kiss and make up than it all seemingly ended in tears again.

Talking of tears, Gascoigne became a cult figure, an icon even, when he started crying after being booked during England's match against Germany in the semi-finals of the 1990 World Cup. The country sobbed with him, devastated that the discovery of the tournament would be suspended for the final.

In the event, England lost on penalties and the referee, Jose Wright, confirmed that the caution that made the tears flow was as much for backchat as a foul on Thomas Berthold. When you are one yellow card away from missing the World Cup final, winding-up the referee represents self-destruction written in 6ft-high capitals.

Even so, Gascoigne's performances against Holland and Belgium had been world class. He had done much to redeem Bobby Robson's bruised reputation as the England manager. It was all a long way from 1982 when a puppy-fat padded 15-year-old had been rejected by Robson after a trial with Ipswich. Later, Robson would recognise "Paul's flair, imagination and spontaneity".

A year and two CSEs (grade four English and environmental studies) after his trial at Ipswich, Gascoigne signed for Newcastle. It was every Dunston boy's dream come true.

But not Colin Suggett's. The Newcastle coach at the time recalls a hyperactive, impossibly cheeky, overweight teenager who compulsively guzzled Mars bars and McDonalds. The "alcoholic refuelling" would come later – in those days Gascoigne was flat on his back after three shandies.

Suggett advised Jack Charlton to release this disruptive influence. But Gascoigne charmed the manager out of it before bewitching St James's Park with his body swerves, free kicks and radar passing. Few players possessed half as many tricks.

Perhaps part of Gascoigne's problem is the extraordinary ease with which he mastered the

Over the top: Gascoigne's reckless challenge at Wembley almost ended his career

England expects: Gascoigne, so often a match winner, leads an attack against Turkey

Heartbreak: the 1990 World Cup semi-final

game. Perhaps it explained his compulsion to flirt with danger – as on the day he arrived at Lazio's training ground doing 80mph on a motorbike and not wearing a helmet.

Gascoigne's capacity to disarm would see him putting an arm around Margaret Thatcher and getting his next England manager, Graham Taylor, drunk on brandy. Taylor, like most managers to cross Gascoigne's path, frequently had his patience pushed to the limit. Stories of the prodigy's penchant for binges and puerile pranks with Jimmy "Five Bellies" Gardner and his other Geordie muckers abound.

But the bottom line for managers is that matches must be won and Gascoigne is a match winner. As Glenn Roeder, the Watford manager and a friend of Gascoigne's put it: "Paul's only Achilles heel is pace. He has perfect balance, vision, a football brain, awareness of what is going on around him, a fantastic first touch, and dribbling and shooting skills."

Most footballers are lucky to have one or two such gifts. And Gascoigne is also sufficiently muscular and sufficiently mean to look after himself. But if Gascoigne is a man on the pitch he all too often reverts to childhood off it.

Until his involvement with Kyle, he could not sleep unless the lights and the television were left on. Added to an apparent inability to be alone, this indicates incredible insecurity. Perhaps the brain haemorrhage his father suffered when Gascoigne was 11, or the trauma of seeing Steven Spraggon, his best friend's brother, killed by a car when he was 12 explains this.

In some respects Gascoigne can still behave like a 12-year-old. He relishes cutting the toes off teammates socks and makes cappuccino coffees with shaving foam. Personally chaotic, he frequently forgets his passport and admits to not knowing how much his bank account contains. It is a brand of unworldliness reserved for pop stars and top footballers.

Like so many gifted men, Gascoigne constantly demands reassurance. Terry Venables, the manager who brought him to Tottenham, appreciates this. "I used to talk to Paul on a friendly basis, to let him know I was thinking of him. He is the type of guy who needs to know you are concerned about him.

"You have to find the root of his problems. He may have come to me with a sore thumb and asked why he was feeling bad. The real reason wouldn't be the sore thumb. I always tried to get behind the superficial problems."

Clearly, sergeant-major Suggett style disciplinarians bring out the worst in Gascoigne. And in turn he is adept at drawing out the dark side of managers. Many Newcastle fans feel that Kevin Keegan's Midas touch could be tarnished if he were tempted to bring this black sheep back to Tyneside.

Some people say that Venables was too soft on Gascoigne at Tottenham. But, so far, he is the one person to have man-managed Gascoigne with any degree of success. The installation of his old mentor as the England manager was supposed to be the best thing that could happen to Gascoigne. Now we will have to see if he can bounce back from another career-threatening injury.

Italian adventure: Gascoigne has been through turbulent times while playing for Lazio

Birmingham fans run riot

St Andrews witnessed the worst disturbances seen at an English football match for several years when the Third Division match between Birmingham and Stoke on February 29 was halted by a pitch invasion.

The incident was sparked by Stoke scoring a late and controversial equaliser. When Birmingham then had a shot cleared off the line hundreds of their fans swarmed on to the pitch, and one of them attacked the referee, Roger Wiseman.

Samesh Kumar, the Birmingham chairman, appealed to the fans to calm down and when he was ignored it was announced that the match would not continue. But, 20 minutes later, when police had cleared the ground, the remaining 35 seconds of the game were played.

Terry Cooper, the Birmingham manager, was horrified by the events and threatened to quit. He said: "I have to ask: 'Do you really want to be a manager of a club like this?' I don't know what the FA will do. If they dock points that's a season down the drain."

Birmingham's cause was hardly helped by Kumar, who said that one the reasons for the disturbance was "some scandalous decisions" made by Wiseman. That outburst led to him being charged with misconduct by the FA. The club were fined £50,000 and ordered to play two matches behind closed doors.

Wiseman, too, had had enough. Three weeks after the match he withdrew from the list of referees, citing the mental stress that he was under as the reason.

Careless United hand Leeds the championship on a plate

The Manchester United faithful had waited 25 years for their eighth League championship and throughout the season they were always the clear favourites to lift the title. Then in one fateful spell over Easter they hit relegation form, not championship form, when they only won four out of their last 14 League matches and handed the title to Leeds, who had dogged them throughout the campaign.

Not that Leeds were unworthy champions; after all, they were unbeaten at home and only lost four League matches. Howard Wilkinson had built a resilient side, which with the flair of Gordon Strachan – ironically a Manchester United cast-off – and in the last third of the season Eric Cantona, the French international, were virtually impossible to contain.

United had got off to a flying start, unbeaten in their first 12 League matches, but Leeds would never lie down, and were United's nemesis all season. The two sides built up a huge lead over the chasing pack and then seemed to be constantly swapping top place each week.

Their intertwining reached comic levels in January when they were drawn against each other in both Cups and had to play a League match as well. These three fixtures were scheduled over 11 days and billed as "The Battle of the Titans". United won both Cup games (and went on to win the League Cup) but in hindsight probably did their chief rivals a favour.

In football parlance, they left Leeds no choice but to concentrate on the League.

Which they did and United didn't. On April 16, Manchester United were on top of the table, two points clear of Leeds with a game in hand. Then on April 18 they drew with lowly Luton and over the next nine days their title aspirations turned into dust.

They lost 2-1 to Nottingham Forest at home, squandered their game in hand by falling 1-0 to relegated West Ham and then lost 2-0 at Anfield on April 26. On the same day Leeds won 3-2 at Sheffield United by virtue of an own goal by Brian Gayle. A week before the end of the season, the impossible had happened: the championship had not gone to Old Trafford, but returned to Elland Road for the first time since 1974 and the days of Don Revie.

Turning the tables: Strachan masterminded Leeds's late charge to the title

In the bag: Leeds celebrate their first championship since 1974

Dalglish is Blackburn's star turn

BLACKBURN ROVERS pulled off a spectacular coup when, barely an hour before their match against Plymouth on October 12, they announced that Kenny Dalglish was their new manager.

Dalglish had been lured out of retirement by Jack Walker, a lifelong Blackburn fan who had spent millions of pounds of his personal fortune on the club. The former Liverpool manager said: "Obviously, seven months ago football was not the most important thing in my life. I'd had enough and needed to recharge my batteries. But the time is right to come back. People will ask why I should have come to Blackburn, but they've impressed me as a club with ambitions to get into the Premier League."

Walker wanted nothing but the best for his beloved club, and for him money was no object. Dalglish was given a three-year contract worth £1m and told he had at least £10m immediately available to strengthen the team.

The club was immediately revitalised and from January to mid-March topped the Second Division. But then a disastrous

New broom: Dalglish swept Blackburn into the Premier League

run of six defeats looked as if it would end Walker's dream of Premier League football for the moment. They only just made the play-offs, where they squeezed past Derby 5-4 on aggregate to face Leicester in the decider at Wembley. There, Mike Newell's penalty put them back in the top flight for the first time since 1966.

Dalglish wasted no time in putting Walker's money to work, and in July he broke the British transfer record when he bought Alan Shearer from Southampton for £3.6m. That brought Dalglish's spending to more than £6m and made it perfectly clear he was determined that Blackburn were going to be among the country's best.

Premier League feud ends in peace

THE long-running battle over the Premier League finally came to an end, but not before everybody involved had spent yet another season in interminable wrangling.

The season did not start well, with the Football League in total disarray over what to do. Any hope of there being any constructive debate was soon dashed when clubs threatened to isolate the Premier League and Sir Bert Millichip, the FA chairman, responded by threatening to suspend the entire League. And the players said they would consider a strike if they did not get a big enough say in how the game was run.

The fateful decision to go ahead with the Premier League was finally taken by the FA

Council on February 20. That should have been the end of the matter but the PFA revived their strike threat.

So the arguments dragged on until the end of April, when the PFA won a 50% increase to £1.5m in the share of the money they received from television. That, finally, should have been the end of the matter.

But television and money added a further twist to the tale. On May 18 the FA announced a record-breaking deal with the BBC and Sky, worth £304m over five years. Sky would show 60 live matches a season on Sundays and Mondays, and the BBC would show highlights on Saturdays and during the week. However, ITV, complaining about the way deal had been done,

went to court and it was a further month before the dispute was settled.

Amazingly, at the end of all the in-fighting, very little appeared to have really changed. The First Division would become the Premier League, with 22 clubs due to reduce to 20 by 1995. The Second, Third and Fourth Divisions thus confusingly became the First, Second and Third Divisions.

There would be other cosmetic changes: the Premier League would allow a third substitute on the bench, and half-time would be extended to 15 minutes. The only thing that did seem to be different was the colour of the shirts the referees would wear: green in the Premier League and purple elsewhere.

The magic touches of Hateley and McCoist do the trick for Rangers

Midas touch: McCoist was the first Scot to win the Golden Boot

RANGERS eventually swept all before them, winning the Scottish Cup and the championship by nine points. But halfway through the season things did not look so clear cut.

In September Rangers had lost the semi-final of the League Cup 1-0 to Hibs – who went on to win their first trophy for 19 years – and were trailing to Hearts in the League. However, it proved to be just another sluggish start for the Ibrox club. From November 30 to the end of the season Rangers strung together a fabulous run, winning 20 of 24 League matches and only losing once.

Their large squad of international players was an obvious advantage, but the prolific scoring of Mark Hateley and Ally McCoist made Rangers virtually unbeatable. Between them they notched up a breathtaking 54 League goals, McCoist becoming the first Scot to win Europe's prestigious Golden Boot. And in July Rangers had another boost when Trevor Steven returned from Marseille for £2.4m. He had joined the French club only the previous August for a fee of £5m, a Scottish record.

By contrast, Celtic had a terrible season. They were knocked out of the League Cup on penalties by Airdrie, of all people, and beaten 1-0 in the semi-final of the Scottish Cup by Rangers, who were down to 10 men.

Then, in the last match of the season, Celtic needed only to draw with Hibs to finish runners-up and so qualify for the Uefa Cup ahead of Hearts. They lost 2-1, their first defeat in 17 League matches, and Hearts beat Falkirk 2-0 to snatch second place by one point. The gods did smile on Celtic in the end though: because of the expansion of the number of countries wishing to enter the competition Uefa granted Scotland an extra place and Celtic were reprieved.

Souness bungles publicity after heart surgery

GRAEME SOUNESS had always been the epitome of a professional – never smoking, hardly drinking, and keeping himself fit. So, hours after they had drawn with Portsmouth in the FA Cup semi-final on April 6, the Liverpool team were stunned when they were told that their 39-year-old manager had been taken to hospital because he needed an immediate triple heart bypass operation.

While he was recuperating, his judgment, for once, deserted him. Souness allowed the Sun to take pictures of him kissing his girlfriend as he recovered in hospital. Tactlessly, the photographs were published on the same day as a memorial service for the fans who had died at Hillsborough.

The people of Liverpool had never forgiven the Sun for its tasteless reporting of the tragedy, and were furious that Souness had dealt with the very paper that was still hated on Merseyside. There were continued calls for Souness to be sacked.

On the way back: Souness recovers in hospital after a successful triple heart bypass operation

Brilliant McManaman's switch puts Sunderland's lights out

THE DAY before the FA Cup final Graeme Souness defied the doctors and left hospital after his heart operation. It was just the fillip Liverpool needed.

Souness received a stirring welcome at Wembley, but Ronnie Moran, his assistant, was still in charge of the team to play Sunderland. And the massed fans from Wearside sensed that they might be able to pull off another famous upset.

Second Division Sunderland had already collected three First Division scalps: West Ham, Chelsea and Norwich in the semi-final. And Liverpool had looked far from convincing in the competition. They were taken to replays by Bristol Rovers and Ipswich and only just scraped past Portsmouth in the semi-final, which went to a penalty shoot-out.

The introduction of a shoot-out if the replay finished level had already accounted for several other clubs. Manchester United became the first First Division team to be eliminated this way when they went out to Southampton in the fourth round.

Sunderland harried Liverpool right from the kick-off, preventing them from getting fully into their stride, and deserved to be level at half-time. Both teams missed good chances, and Liverpool claimed that they should have been awarded a penalty just before the interval.

It was then that Moran made the switch that was to transform the match. Steve McManaman had only come into the side the day before, when John Barnes failed a fitness test, and at half-time Moran switched him from the left flank to the right.

Within two minutes of the restart he had burst down the right touchline, withstood a push in the back from a defender and lifted the ball into the penalty area. Michael Thomas waited for the ball to bounce and then unhesitatingly unleashed a brilliant volley. Tony Norman stood no chance of stopping the shot and Liverpool were ahead.

With McManaman continuing his incisive runs Liverpool soon settled into their smooth passing game. Thomas was the provider of the second goal, whipped in by Rush in the 67th minute, and Moran finally allowed himself a jig of delight on the touchline.

However, his greatest day ended on an odd note. It had been decided that tradition would be overturned and the losers would go up to the royal box first. Somebody, though, forgot to put the medals in the right order. So when a dejected Sunderland team trooped up the steps they were presented with the winners medals and they had to swap them afterwards with Liverpool, who were given the losers medals.

FOR THE RECORD

■ Tragedy struck the French Cup semi-final between Bastia and Marseille when a temporary stand collapsed, killing a number of spectators.

■ Three Leicester fans won compensation when they sued Millwall over the poor view they had had at The Den.

■ Belgium's highest court confirmed the convictions of Uefa and its general secretary Hans Bangerter on charges arising from the Heysel disaster.

■ Leeds banned 19 fans for life after they were convicted of offences arising from the disturbances in Bournemouth last season.

■ The FA rejected a £2m offer from Bass to sponsor the FA Cup semi-finals and final.

■ Doncaster Belles won the inaugural women's National League with 11 straight victories.

McManaman: the inspiration

Hail the conquering hero: Rush scores Liverpool's second goal at Wembley

Lineker goes to spread the word in Japan

BLACKBURN were not the only club prepared to spend big money in the pursuit of success. And perhaps the least expected move came in November when Grampus Eight, of the burgeoning Japanese League, signed Gary Lineker. The deal meant that Lineker would leave Tottenham at the end of the season, but it was not a happy time for him. His baby son was taken ill and diagnosed as having a rare form of leukaemia.

Lineker's teammate Paul Gascoigne was also back in hospital, but his suffering was all of his own making. Gascoigne was involved in a fracas in a Newcastle nightclub and damaged his knee again, putting back his recovery by several months and casting another cloud over his move to Lazio.

But it was not all doom and gloom at White Hart Lane. The club were able to announce that their debts had been cut from £21m to £5m and their finances were back under control, clearing the way for their shares to be re-listed on the Stock Exchange.

Lineker: learning Japanese

Taylor hits rock bottom in England's European fiasco

European misadventures: Taylor and McMenemy did not like their trip to Sweden

THE European championships saw Graham Taylor's career as the England manager hit rock bottom. Despite struggling to qualify, England had travelled to Sweden with confidence; they were in the weaker of the two groups and their captain Gary Lineker, with 48 international goals, seemed certain to equal and surpass Bobby Charlton's record of 49.

Three matches later, England had drawn two, lost one, Lineker had not scored a single goal and, to rub salt in the wound, had been substituted 29 minutes from the end of the final match against Sweden which England had to win to qualify for the semi-finals.

Bafflingly, Taylor had chosen to end Lineker's international career – he had announced he would retire after the championships – in a most humiliating way. Worse, Taylor's gamble failed as Sweden won 2-1 to leave England at the bottom of their group.

If it had not been for Lineker England would not have been there in the first place. A series of indifferent performances against the Republic of Ireland and Turkey in the qualifying group had meant that England needed a point against Poland in Poznan on November 13 if they were to pip Jack Charlton's Irish team for the trip to Sweden.

With 15 minutes remaining England were trailing to a first-half 40-yard goal from Szewczyk that had been deflected by Gary Mabbutt. Then Lineker won a corner from which he conjured an amazing volley to snatch a precious equaliser.

England were not alone in their misery. Italy and Spain had failed to qualify and war-torn Yugoslavia were excluded in line with UN sanctions over human rights. Denmark replaced them at 11 days notice, and proved to be the revelation of the tournament. In their first match – against England – the Danes achieved a creditable 0-0 draw, and might even have won.

Strangely, the usual European superpowers, France, Holland and Germany, all came unstuck as the tournament unfolded. Germany were extremely fortunate to reach the semi-finals. They beat Scotland 2-0 despite being outplayed, and then the Scots did them a huge

favour by beating CIS 3-0.

France were as dismal as England, failing to win a single match. Holland, who had won their group convincingly, were Denmark's opponents in the semi-finals. The Dutch, twice behind, rallied to snatch a 2-2 draw. But, after a goalless 30 minutes of extra time, stuttered in the penalty shoot-out. Peter Schmeichel saved Holland's second kick, from Marco van Basten, and when nobody else missed, put Denmark into the final against Germany, the world champions.

Nobody really gave the Danes a chance; after all, they were only the substitutes for Yugoslavia and they had been hit by injuries. But in the 18th minute John Jensen stunned the Germans by taking the lead. Despite German pressure the Danes played a cool game of defence and counter attack and achieved the seemingly impossible when Kim Vilfort scored from a Christiansen header 12 minutes from time. Denmark, 2-0 victors over Germany, and European champions? As Schmeichel said: "We still don't understand what we have done."

Keegan just staves off relegation after Newcastle kick Ardiles out

OSSIE ARDILES should have known better than to listen to his chairman. It always seems that managers of struggling clubs get the sack just after being told that their job is safe.

And there was no doubt that Newcastle were struggling. By the start of February they were 23rd in the Second Division. Ardiles, who had been brought to the club to return them to the big time, was under increasing pressure as Newcastle faced up to the prospect of going down to the Third Division for the first time in their history.

But on February 2, Sir John Hall, the Newcastle chairman, was unequivocal: "Let's kill off once and for all the rumours that his job is on the line. If he leaves it will be of his own volition."

Three days later Ardiles was sacked and replaced by Kevin Keegan. Hall insisted that he had meant every word of what he had said and everybody assumed that the decision to sack Ardiles had been forced on the club by their backers, Newcastle Breweries.

Keegan won his first match in charge, 3-0 against fellow strugglers Bristol City. But it was not long before it looked like things were going to turn sour for the former Newcastle idol as well.

After Newcastle's victory over Swindon on March 14, Keegan rushed from the ground and headed for Heathrow, prompting speculation that he had resigned. Hall promptly announced that he was putting up £$\frac{1}{2}$m of his own money to buy players to strengthen the debt-laden team. All Keegan would say, cryptically, about his relationship with the club was: "I don't understand it. It's not like it said in the brochure."

It looked as if Keegan's arrival and Hall's money were too little to late, particularly when Newcastle were thrashed 6-2 at Wolverhampton. With

Keegan: great escape

two matches to go Newcastle were still in line for relegation but then successive victories over Portsmouth and Leicester enabled them to beat the drop. Hall, who by now had taken con-

trol of the club was satisfied and Keegan was rewarded with a three-year contract.

About face: three days after being reassured that his job was safe Ardiles was summarily sacked by Newcastle

THE
1992-93
SEASON

*Something special
has gone out of every
footballer's life*

DAVID PLATT

ON FEBRUARY 24 English football lost one of its greatest players and important role models when, at the age of 51, Bobby Moore OBE passed away, nine days after announcing that he was suffering from cancer.

Immediately the tributes poured in – from all over the world. For, although Moore would be best remembered for captaining England to the World Cup in 1966, he was also a wonderful ambassador for the game and represented all that was sporting and fair.

As a defender he was scrupulously clean, but brilliantly effective. His ability to read a move and intercept the ball was breathtaking; to an attacker it was as if you had had your pocket picked without knowing how or why.

Pele said of him: "Moore was my friend, the finest, the most honourable defender I ever played against." The duel between the two in the 1970 World Cup finals was one of the finest examples of physical and cerebral chess ever seen on a field.

Moore spent the bulk of his club career at West Ham (544 appearances) before transferring to Fulham (124) in 1974. At West Ham, despite perennial struggles against relegation, he helped mastermind the East End club to the first trophies in their history, the FA Cup in 1964 and the European Cup Winners' Cup in 1965, coincidentally both at Wembley. Fate of course decreed that a year later he would climb the same 39

Moore: the epitome of fair play

Happier days: Moore at the height of his career with the World Cup trophy at Wembley in 1966

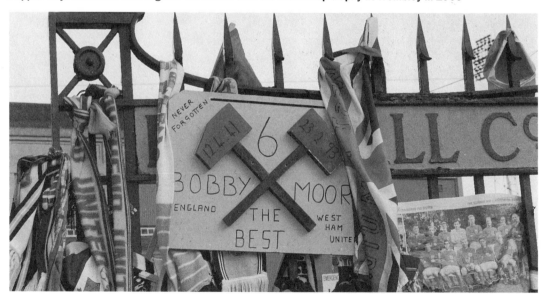

The tributes poured: "He will never grow old in people's minds" — Ken Bates

steps to lift yet another trophy, this time the ultimate prize, the World Cup.

Moore's death stunned the nation and reminded them of the past and what was lost. As Ken Bates, the Chelsea chairman, said: "He will never grow old in people's minds, in the same way that President Kennedy won't. Camelot has always seemed real because we remember Kennedy as a young man and it's going to be the same with Bobby Moore."

England repeatedly shoot themselves in the foot

THE WRITING was on the wall for Graham Taylor and England's hopes of qualifying for the 1994 World Cup after a series of embarrassing results.

In October, at Wembley, England dropped a precious point to Norway, who had established themselves as the front-runners in group two by thrashing San Marino 10-0, when they allowed Rekdal to equalise Platt's 55th minute goal with 14 minutes left.

Then, despite two encouraging results (a 4-0 roasting of Turkey and a 6-0 annihilation of San Marino) in April England let slip a two-goal lead, once again at Wembley, against Holland for another draw. Holland's equaliser came from the spot five minutes from time after Des Walker had foolishly given away a penalty.

But worse was to come. In Chorzow, in May, only Ian Wright's 84th-minute equaliser saved England from a potentially lethal defeat by Poland.

Taylor blamed the players and said they were "running around like headless chickens".

Four days later in Oslo, Taylor made four changes and a wholesale tactical switch only to be humiliated 2-0 by Norway. In fact, the scoreline flattered England as they played utterly inept football. There were widespread calls for Taylor's head as English football seemed to have reached its nadir.

It hadn't. On June 9, in Boston, it reached rock bottom.

Famous in Anglo-American history for the Tea Party in 1773 that led to the colony throwing off Imperial rule, Boston threw another party that sent shivers down England's spine.

"There can't be a lower point for any manager, and yes, it is a national disgrace," Taylor said. "This result is now in the history books – I suppose it will haunt me from now on." Without a doubt "USA 2 England 0" will be forever inscribed on Graham Taylor's heart.

Yankee Doodle Dandies: the Americans were euphoric at inflicting a humbling defeat on England

FOR THE RECORD

■ Peter Shilton was sent off for the first time in his career on August 28, in his 971st League game.

■ Hereford set an unenviable record when they had four players sent off in their match against Northampton on September 6.

■ Barclays announced in October that they would not be renewing their sponsorship of the League.

■ Ian Rush passed Roger Hunt's record of 286 goals for Liverpool on October 18. And Guy Whittingham broke Portsmouth's record with 42 in the League and 44 in all.

■ Chelsea secured their future in December when a bank bought Stamford Bridge and granted them a 20-year lease.

■ Adrian Blake, the Kingstonian goalkeeper, was hit by a coin thrown from the crowd and had to be substituted during the FA Cup first round replay with Peterborough, who led 3-0 at the time and went on to win 9-1. The FA ordered the match to be played again behind closed doors and Peterborough won 1-0.

■ Ted Croker, the former secretary of the FA, died on Christmas Day, aged 68.

Video nasty gets Vinnie a clip round the ear

WHEREVER Vinnie Jones went trouble seemed to follow. This time he got into hot water in the film studio for his appearance in a video, Soccer's Hard Men.

In the video, Jones said: "If you are going over the top on me you have got to put me out of the game because I'll be coming back for you, whether it's in the next five minutes or next season."

Sam Hammam, the Wimbledon chairman, branded Jones a "mosquito brain" and the rest of the country condemned a tape that seemed to glorify the worst aspects of behaviour on the pitch.

Although Jones apologised, the FA handed down a record £20,000 fine and a six-month ban suspended for three years in

November. Hammam, though, thought the FA had gone over the top and accused them of applying double standards, singling out Jones for punishment while being more lenient with other offenders.

Even after this incident Jones could not stay out of trouble. Summoned to Lancaster Gate on March 29 because he had exceeded 40 disciplinary points, he failed to turn up at the appointed hour and was banned indefinitely.

Jones claimed that he had got the time of the hearing mixed up, and made sure he arrived early for the rescheduled case a fortnight later. A four-match ban was imposed and, not before time, the FA told Jones to "grow up".

Jones: "mosquito brain"

> *It's quite difficult dealing with Mr Flashman because if you speak your mind he tends to sack you*
>
> EDWIN STEIN
> the Barnet assistant manager sacked a mere three times

Clough leaves the helm as Forest's ship sinks

Bowing out: Clough salutes the Forest fans for the final time

Barnet rise above the strife

MAIDSTONE, struggling in the Third Division with small crowds and huge debts, had their first match of the season called off and were given until the following Monday to guarantee that they would be able to fulfil all of their fixtures. Unable to come up with the necessary backing, they resigned from the League on August 17.

And it was not long before speculation was swirling around another Third Division club, Barnet. Within days of Maidstone's demise, the north London club were banned from the transfer market because they had not paid their players' wages.

Two months later the issue was still not resolved and it took the intervention of both the League and the PFA to head off a threatened walk-out by most of the squad. Barnet's shaky financial position was hardly helped when they were fined £50,000 for breaches of League regulations.

Things had got so bad by late March that, when salary cheques had bounced once again, the Cardiff chairman gave the Barnet players £1,000 to tide them over after the two clubs met at Ninian Park. And the League, with their fine still unpaid, finally ran out of patience and threatened to expel Barnet.

That prompted Stan Flashman, the controversial Barnet chairman, to resign, citing "health reasons". But, as his parting shot before he left, he sacked his manager, Barry Fry, for the eighth time.

Fry, who had already been dismissed and reinstated earlier in the season, was offered his job back by the new chairman. Hardly surprisingly, he opted to join Southend instead, saying: "Being manager of Barnet was like living with a double-decker bus on your head. When I left it was like it had been driven off."

Amazingly, despite having to have their wages paid by the PFA yet again, the players seemed to be unaffected by the financial turmoil. They finished third in the Third Division to claim the last automatic promotion place.

Parting shot: Flashman quit as the chairman and sacked Fry yet again

BRIAN CLOUGH finally bowed to the inevitable and announced his retirement on April 26. "Old Big 'ead" had spent 18 years calling the shots at Nottingham Forest, but it had been painfully apparent all season that Clough was starting to lose his grip.

Forest had had a terrible start to the season, losing six of their first seven matches and only winning three games before Christmas. Despite trying to play some attractive football, they never looked like being able to drag themselves clear of relegation.

Clough had signed a one-year extension to his contract in November, but behind the scenes a storm was brewing. The board was split into pro and anti-Clough factions, and Clough was shocked by newspaper allegations about his alleged excessive drinking.

Finally, just after being made a Freeman of Nottingham, the 58-year-old Clough said that he would retire at the end of the season. The fans flocked to the City ground to pay their last respects on May 2, a match that Forest lost to Sheffield United to condemn them to the First Division.

Even the United fans saluted the man who many people thought was the greatest manager never to lead England. "Clough for England," they chanted without any hint of irony.

It was a sad end for a man who had taken Forest from the obscurity of the Second Division to the heights of the League title and two successive European Cups.

But Clough could not resist one last wisecrack. "I didn't expect today to be so emotional, but I ain't going to miss the job at all," he said.

United's championship at last

ALEX FERGUSON did not want a repeat of last season, when Manchester United let the title slip from their grasp. So when his team hit a patch of poor form, drawing five matches in a row and losing the next two, he decided it was time for a foray into the transfer market.

He pounced on November 26, signing the mercurial Eric Cantona from Leeds for £1.2m, a price that was widely regarded as a bargain. The deal marked a turning point in the fortunes of both clubs – Leeds struggled for the rest of the season while United got steadily better.

Cantona was soon scoring goals for Manchester United as they set off in pursuit of Norwich, who had opened up a clear gap at the top of the table. And it was a lack of goals that was to prove Norwich's undoing as they finished the season in third place, having conceded four more goals than they managed to score.

As Norwich slipped back, the battle between United and Aston Villa was intense. The spectre of another late failure was revived when United went four matches without a win in

Silver lining: Ferguson's title success lifted last year's cloud

March. But Ferguson was not going to make the same mistake twice.

United won their last seven matches while Villa were the team that faltered. They handed the title to United on May 2 when they lost to Oldham. Ferguson was playing golf at the time and the news was broken to him by another golfer, who went up to the United manager on the last green and said: "Excuse me Mr Ferguson, you are the champions."

The celebrations at United's home match against Blackburn the next day were enormous. Old Trafford had waited for this moment since 1967 and the legendary Sir Matt Busby was there to applaud Ferguson, the first manager to win a league title in both Scotland and England.

Morrow crocked as Arsenal crack both Cups

STEVE MORROW'S first appearance in a Wembley final was a dream that turned into a nightmare.

The full-back was still struggling to become established in the Arsenal side and had already spent several spells on loan to lower division clubs. And he probably only owed his place in the team to play Sheffield Wednesday in the League Cup final to injuries to more established players.

But Morrow did an excellent job in helping to stifle the threat posed by Chris Waddle, John Sheridan and John Harkes. Although Harkes gave Wednesday the lead in the ninth minute, Arsenal were level before half-time when Paul Merson volleyed the ball powerfully past Chris Woods.

With Arsenal starting to dominate the midfield, Merson hit a cross that was not cleared properly. Morrow popped up to give Arsenal a 2-1 victory. After the match, Tony Adams hoisted Morrow aloft to celebrate the young player's vital first goal for his club.

Then disaster struck. Morrow fell awkwardly from his captain's shoulders and there was a sickening crack as he hit the ground and broke his arm.

The injury cost Morrow a chance of a return to Wembley when the two clubs met again in the FA Cup final on May 15. The final was a muted affair, with Ian Wright giving Arsenal the lead and David Hirst scoring an equaliser in the second half.

The replay was little more attractive. Wright gave Arsenal

the lead but Waddle took the match into extra time. With a penalty shoot-out looming Andy Linighan, who had never been popular with the Arsenal fans, headed the winner a minute before time to silence his critics.

Norwich were not complaining either. The strike by their former player put Arsenal into the European Cup Winners Cup, handing the last Uefa Cup place to Norwich, the first time they had played in Europe.

There was also a first for Arsenal, who became the first English side to win both Cups in the same season. It was also historic for George Graham, who became the first person to win the League and both Cups as a player and a manager – all six honours coming with Arsenal.

Morrow: fall guy

Bribery scandal wipes out Marseille's triumphs

WHEN Basile Boli scored the only goal of the match as Marseille beat AC Milan in the European Cup final all of France celebrated. They were the first French team to bring home the trophy from a competition that the French had been instrumental in creating in the 1950s.

So the scandal that engulfed Marseille was even more shocking to France. The first rumblings had been heard before the final on May 26, with allegations surfacing that Marseille had bribed Valenciennes players to go easy in a League match the week before. Marseille won 1-0 to secure the title.

At first, Marseille denied the charge. But, in July, their midfield player Jean-Jacques Eydelie confessed that he had acted as a go-between for payments to three Valenciennes players. His admission opened the floodgates and implicated Marseille's general secretary, Jean-Pierre Bernes, the right-hand man of their president, the flamboyant Bernard Tapie.

Fifa and Uefa demanded action, but the French federation said that they could do nothing until the investigations were complete. As the case dragged on through the summer Uefa did not want the reputation of the European Cup harmed so they excluded Marseilles from defending their crown days before they were due to play AEK Athens in the first round.

Tapie went to court to get the decision overturned but dropped the case when Fifa warned that France was running the risk of exclusion from all international competition.

The French federation finally decided to suspend Bernes and three players, and strip Marseille of their League title. But Marseille's real punishment was the amount of money they would lose by being excluded from Europe.

A club that had made a fortune, and was able to spend a fortune on players and wages, suddenly found itself on the financial rocks and having to sell players just to survive. Tapie said that £15m was needed and that he was going to resign as soon as his successor could be found.

Europe eludes Rangers

Fighting draw: Rangers came back from a 2-0 deficit against Marseille

FOR ONCE, Rangers' foray into Europe came close to fulfilling the form they constantly demonstrated in Scotland. They easily qualified for the Champions League of the European Cup, and in doing so had the added pleasure of eliminating Leeds United, the English champions, by comfortably beating them 2-1 home and away in the unofficial "British championship". However, Leeds were extremely fortunate to be playing the Scottish champions at all.

In the previous round, having lost 3-0 away to Stuttgart, Leeds had fought back tenaciously at Elland Road to win 4-1 and had seemingly been knocked out on away goals. Then it transpired that the German side had inadvertently fielded four foreign players, one more than is permitted, and Leeds were awarded the tie 3-0. In the ensuing replay at Barcelona, Leeds won 2-1.

In Group A of the Champions League, where the four teams met each other home and away, Marseille were Rangers' biggest hurdle. And after 75 minutes of the home match against the French champions Rangers trailed 2-0 and seemed to be dead and buried. But goals from McSwegan and Hateley earned them a draw and a fighting chance of reaching the European Cup final for the first time. Marseille and Rangers sailed past Bruges and CSKA Moscow, the other clubs in the Group, to set up a winner-takes-all match in France on April 7.

Once again Rangers exhibited sterling courage to come back from a goal down, but the draw was never going to be enough. In the last match Marseille beat Bruges in Belgium to clinch a place in the final against AC Milan, where the French club unexpectedly won 1-0.

There was consolation for Rangers in Scotland where they swept everything before them with imperious power. They won the Premier League title for the fifth consecutive season, won both Cups by beating Aberdeen 2-1 twice to complete the Treble and broke numerous records en route. But still the Holy Grail of the European Cup eludes them.

Rearguard action: Tapie withdrew his case when Fifa upped the stakes

Venables and Sugar: a tale of two sweethearts who fell out of love

ON MAY 14, the day before the FA Cup final, it was apparent that Tottenham's so-called dream ticket of Alan Sugar and Terry Venables that had snatched the club out of the grasp of Robert Maxwell two years earlier had turned into a nightmare. In a sensational move, Sugar, the chairman, had Venables voted off the board and sacked as Tottenham's chief executive.

Sugar's dramatic coup stunned everybody. On the face of it, the break-up between the two men who had been hailed as saviours seemed inexplicable, particularly as the club's financial plight seemed to have been turned around in September when a trading profit of £2.9m, compared to the previous £3.1m loss, had been announced.

However, the source of the bad blood between Sugar and Venables soon leaked out. According to Sugar: "Venables behaved as if I was some kind of rich lunatic, a rich nutter who had put his money in and was supposed to sit over there and mind his own business."

It was Sugar's unease about Venables' encroachment on the commercial side and the character of some of the people he had employed at the club that provoked the rift. In particular, Sugar was disturbed by Venables' association with Eddie Ashby, an undischarged bankrupt with a string of failed companies behind him, who Venables had hired as "general manager" and who had been involved in the sale of Paul Gascoigne to Lazio. Venables' refusal to get rid of Ashby precipitated Venables' dismissal.

Venables did not take his sacking lightly and went to the High Court to seek reinstatement. Tottenham fans rallied to his cause as Sugar was seen as the villain of the piece. There were demonstrations outside the court with placards such as: "T yes, Sugar no", and Sugar's life was made a misery with anonymous abusive phone calls and death threats. Even a boycott of Tottenham's matches the following season was planned by the supporters.

However, two things turned Sugar's position around. First, the allegations in court in June that Brian Clough, the Nottingham Forest manager, had wanted a "bung" from Tottenham during the Teddy Sheringham transfer. And second, the astute appointment later that month of Osvaldo Ardiles as manager. Ardiles, a World Cup winner with Argentina in 1978, and a Spurs immortal, was just the palliative the angry Spurs fans needed, and the discontent melted away.

As did Venables' court action when the judge ruled that Sugar's decision to sack Venables was within his powers and he refused to force Sugar to reinstate him.

Venables: losing battle

Acrimonious divorce: Alan Sugar won the war of words in the High Court to decide who ran Tottenham

331

BRIAN CLOUGH
The maestro who bowed out on a low note

Alex Spillius

WHAT is our lasting memory of Brian Clough? Of a nonconformist genius, or of a sad, apparently alcoholic man in a green track-suit top unable to summon his once mighty powers? Any answer will say something about the respondent, about whether he or she leans towards optimism or pessimism. Towards fond, selective recollection or realism. Probably most of us would mix a bit of both.

But what a pity the question can even be asked. Had it been put before the beginning of the 1992-93 season responses would have been unequivocally positive. Apart from maybe those who had felt the rough end of Clough's egoism in person. For the public he was a joy: eccentric, provocative, witty and wondrously gifted. The idioms of Clough's teams were style, flair and irrepressibility, and they even won things. To the supporters and many citizens of Derby and Nottingham his status edged on divinity.

Some favourite Clough moments. On a television panel during the 1986 World Cup Mick Channon was bleating on: "We've got to get bodies in the box. The French do it, the Brazilians do it, the Italians do it..." Clough interrupted: "Even educated fleas do it." (The remark was even funnier as Channon didn't have a clue what Clough was referring to – the Louis Armstrong song, Let's Do It.) Clough on politicians: "There are more hooligans in the House of Commons than at a football match." And on signing the striker Nigel Jemson: "I haven't seen the lad, but my coaches have and he also comes highly recommended by my greengrocer."

Clough became a fixture in the public mind during a TV discussion before England's 1-0 defeat by Poland in 1973 – which had extinguished England's hopes of qualifying for the World Cup finals the following year – when he called the Polish goalkeeper, Jan Tomaszewski, a "clown". Despite the fact that Tomaszewski disproved him with a string of miraculous saves, from then on the nation knew who Brian Clough was, which can be said of very few in football.

The man was outrageously controversial and we loved him for it. Even those who did not share his left-wing views would have been impressed by his chest-beating support for Labour when most football men were blandly Conservative. Later, stories emerged about fish and chips for striking miners, of spontaneous donations to charity and of chocolates and flowers for players' wives.

As a manager he was unrivalled at making a silk purse out of a sow's ear, of turning ordinary players into stars. His footballers have often had trouble pinpointing his power over them: partly it was inspired by fear, partly by respect for his quickness of mind and partly by his encouragement to play the game the natural way. His best teams had the perfect balance of powers: the straightforwardness of Larry Lloyd in defence, the industry of Ian Bowyer in midfield, the trickery of John Robertson on the wing, the deft improvisation of Trevor Francis in attack. At times he had money to spend – but only after he had earned it for Forest with trophies – though many of his expensive purchases failed: Justin Fashanu, Gary Megson and Asa Hartford among others.

Clough, with his partner Peter Taylor, brought inconceivable success to not one but two provincial cities with weak football traditions, and their record deserves reciting: one League championship with Derby; promotion from the Second Division with Nottingham Forest, followed by two League Cups, one League championship and, incredibly, two European Cups. (Strangely, the FA Cup always eluded Clough). When the final whistle blew after the second European triumph, over Hamburg, Clough, unpredictable as ever, didn't jump for joy but calmly rose from the bench with the look of a man who had finished a quietly satisfying day at the office.

It was no coincidence that after Taylor's acrimonious departure in 1982 Clough and Forest went on to win just two more League Cups, a comparative decline. Forest continued to delight, but Clough was never able to acquire a striker to match Francis, and his team, like the man, were highly entertaining but soft-centred. Also for the first time since those disastrous 44 days as manager of Leeds in 1974, Clough was left to soldier on alone. It wasn't just Taylor's

Exciting prospect: Clough was a prolific scorer in his brief career with Sunderland

Going down: Clough stares relegation in the face

diligence as a coach that was missed; the bitterness of their falling out debilitated Clough, crushingly saddened by a man who was once his best friend, but prevented by his pride of effecting a rapprochement.

After Taylor left it seemed Clough was cruising and somewhat waywardly at that. He seemed to lose the ambition to build a team with a genuine chance of regaining the championship – though League Cups were easy. He began an exclusive column for the Sun, an odd move for a Labour supporter. In 1977 he had been passed over for the England job in favour of Ron Greenwood; perhaps his comment a few years earlier that "I would like the supreme job of dictating football" had not helped. Clough was not called "Old Big 'Ead" for nothing, and the grey men of Lancaster Gate were not prepared to handle such an arrogant maverick. By the time Bobby Robson succeeded Greenwood, Clough was too much of an outsider – but it still hurt.

Clough had never endured adversity stoically. His playing career was tragically ended at the age of 27 by an horrendous injury after scoring 251 goals in 274 games for Middlesbrough and Sunderland. Clough never felt comfortable around injured players ever again. Although he won just two England caps, the frequent comparisons made at the time with Jimmy Greaves were valid.

Crowning glory: Forest won the European Cup in 1979 and retained it in 1980

Clough had great things ahead of him.

Taylor, who had befriended Clough at Middlesbrough, later recalled the three months Clough spent out of work immediately after he was sacked as Sunderland's youth team coach in 1965: "If it had been any longer, he'd have gone to pot. He was a no-hoper: jobless, boozing heavily and on his way out." The way back was offered by Fourth Division Hartlepools, where Clough became manager. With hindsight, his behaviour as described by Taylor was an omen of his problems in the twilight of his career.

Clough's magic as a manager did not disappear overnight, rather it faded as as his behaviour went from amusing to bewildering. In 1989 he hit a supporter who was invading the pitch, then literally kissed and made up in front of the TV cameras. More and more often he coped with the gremlins by being more outrageous and pecking TV interviewers became almost commonplace. Clough went through a phase of forbidding physios to treat players on the field. Darren Wassall came off during a reserve game complaining of an injured hand. Clough spat on the defender's injured limb and told him: "There, that's better." A distraught Wassall soon left Forest for Derby.

During the 1992-93 season Clough had clearly lost his way. Wassall, Des Walker and Teddy Sheringham were sold without replacements being found. As Forest struggled unhappily into bottom place, Robert Rosario, a striker with a one-in-eight strike rate, was signed, and Nigel

Clough, his son, was inexplicably moved to centre-back. Clough Snr's retirement at the end of the season was inevitable, but the announcement was messily brought forward by revelations in two Sunday tabloids about his drinking problems.

After 18 years Clough left amid tears and an affection reserved for a loved one, though his team were relegated by a distance. But then Clough was surely always going to go with a bang as well as whimper.

Controversy still dogged him after he had quit the game. A television documentary alleged he had acquired 2,000 League Cup final tickets which had found their way on to the black market and that he had demanded cash payments for Forest to appear in testimonials. In the High Court during the Terry Venables-Alan Sugar case it was also alleged that he liked a "bung" when buying and selling players.

Any mud that stuck after these allegations will surely fall off in time, and the memory will grow sweeter. Nothing will take Clough's record away from him, while the legacy of fine football he left at Forest will, with wise guardianship, outlast his lifetime. In the post-war pantheon of managers, he is up there with Matt Busby, Stan Cullis, Bill Nicholson, Bob Paisley, Alf Ramsey, Don Revie, Bill Shankly and Jock Stein. All are treasured for different reasons, but more than anything else Cloughie will be recalled with a smile, as an original; and life, let alone football, has few enough of them.

OLD BIG 'EAD'S ACHIEVEMENTS

Born March 21, 1935, Middlesbrough

PLAYING CAREER

Middlesbrough 1953-61

213 League appearances, 197 goals

Scored 100 goals in the League in fewer games than anybody else

Sunderland 1961-65

61 League appearances, 54 goals

Leading scorer in the Football League in the 1957-58 season (40 goals) and in 1958-59 (42 goals)

Leading scorer in the Second Division in 1959-60 (39 goals)

Internationals Played for England Under-23 (three times), England B (once) and appeared in two full internationals

MANAGEMENT CAREER

Hartlepools United Manager 1965-67

Aged 29, he was the youngest manager in the League

Derby County Manager 1967-73

Honours League Championship: Winners 1972

Second Division: Winners 1969

Brighton and Hove Albion Manager 1973-74

Leeds United Manager July 20, 1974-September 1, 1974 (44 days in charge)

Nottingham Forest Manager 1975-93

Honours European Cup: Winners 1979, 1980

FA Cup: Finalists 1991

First Division: Winners 1978; Runners-up 1979

League Cup: Winners 1978, 1979, 1989, 1990; Finalists 1980

Promoted from the Second Division in 1977

Double act: Clough and Taylor revived Forest's fortunes before their bitter split

THE 1993-94 SEASON

Toshack quits Wales after only 47 days

THE writing was on the wall for Terry Yorath when Wales just missed out on qualifying for the World Cup finals yet again. Determined to do better in the European championship, Wales turned to John Toshack.

However, the way Toshack replaced Yorath split Welsh football. Toshack agreed to run the national team while still managing Real Sociedad. Toshack was unaware of the furore until his first match in charge. During Wales's 3-1 defeat by Norway he was jeered by the fans, who chanted Yorath's name.

Toshack promptly quit after just 47 days in charge, complaining bitterly about the politicking, which he described as a "dirty war". He said he had been misled about Yorath's departure. "I have realised some things I did not know before and I have no intention of continuing. I want to wash my hands of the whole affair."

Exit Taylor, enter Venables

NOT since the dark days of the 1970s, when England twice failed to qualify for the World Cup finals, had the international side plumbed such depths. When Graham Taylor's team faced Holland in Rotterdam in October a draw would probably have secured their passage to America. Instead they went down 2-0 and left themselves with virtually no chance of qualifying.

Taylor and England had their excuses: Ronald Koeman should have been sent off when he brought down David Platt when he was in a clear goal-scoring position just outside the penalty box. However the German referee, Karl Assenmacher, decided otherwise. And Koeman, to add insult to injury, promptly went on to score the killing first goal from a free kick.

England's qualification now demanded that they won by seven goals away to San Marino and Holland lost to Poland. Mathematically possible, but in reality a pipe-dream. The pipe-dream became a nightmare in November when San Marino embarrassingly took the lead after eight seconds. It was only their second goal in the group. England eventually won 7-1 and Holland duly dispatched Poland to grab the second qualifying place behind the group leaders Norway.

Within days Taylor did the honourable thing and fell on his sword. But who was to succeed him? Steve Coppell instantly became the favourite and just as quickly ruled himself out: "I don't want the job and I don't envy who gets it." Suddenly it seemed that the managership of England was a poisoned chalice. Don Howe, Kevin Keegan and John Lyall were just some of the putative candidates who did not want to be in the frame.

Dave Bassett, the Sheffield United manager, wondered: "Who will the FA pick next? Probably Walt Disney." Roy Hodgson, Switzerland's manager, was also thought to be on the short-list. But he promptly kicked the idea into touch: "You have got to be joking. Even the Pope would have second thoughts about taking the England job."

In desperation the FA turned to Jimmy Armfield to head-hunt the new England boss. Despite his acrimonious feud with Alan Sugar and the questions surrounding his business dealings, Terry Venables was Armfield's, and the public's, choice. Indeed there was nobody else left to turn to.

Venables started out on the right foot by recalling Peter Beardsley and picking a crowd-pleasing team who duly beat the European champions Denmark 1-0 at Wembley in March. A 5-0 thrashing of Greece, and a goalless draw with Norway, when England were unlucky to have a goal disallowed, followed in May. Suddenly life after Taylor did not seem so bad.

The first nail in England's coffin: Ronald Koeman takes advantage of the referee's leniency to punish England

Busby goes to heaven

SIR MATT BUSBY, the man who had single-handedly created the legend of Manchester United, died on January 20 at the age of 84. Busby had revelled in the fans delight when United won the title last season, their first championship since he had been in charge in the club's glory days in the 1960s.

Alex Ferguson, the United manager who had done so much to restore United's fortunes, said: "He was the outstanding man of them all – even Bill Shankly and Jock Stein sought his advice and experience."

It was a fitting tribute to a man who, like Shankly and Stein, was a product of the close-knit Scottish mining community that had spawned three of the greatest managers of all time.

Busby had played for Manchester City before the war and when he left the army he took charge of an ailing Manchester United. The struggling team were deep in debt and the ground was a bomb-damaged ruin. With no money to spend, Busby pulled on his tracksuit and concentrated on developing the talent at the club.

He turned the club around so quickly that they won the FA Cup in 1948 and the League in 1952, their first championship in more than 40 years. But Busby knew that his side was ageing, and with United languishing at the bottom of the table he replaced almost half of his team overnight with untried reserves.

The Busby Babes were born and they grew up fast, with successive League titles in 1956 and 1957. Tragically, the heart was torn out of the team by the Munich air disaster in 1958, when eight United players were killed and Busby was lucky to escape with his life.

Miraculously, Busby rebuilt United again, winning the FA Cup in 1963 and the championship in 1965 and 1967. His crowning glory came in 1968 when he finally laid the ghosts of Munich to rest with the defeat of Benfica at Wembley in in the European Cup final.

Spurs fall on hard times

THE TROUBLES that bedevilled Tottenham would just not go away. The feud between Alan Sugar and Terry Venables dragged on throughout the year and almost cost Spurs their place in the Premier Division.

During the two men's battles, evidence of financial irregularities came to light. Tottenham thought they were doing the right thing by reporting the cases to the FA, but their openness rebounded on them.

The transgression involved undeclared loans that were never intended to be repaid, and other payments to players. The FA regarded this as a serious breach of their rules and established a special commission to investigate.

At the end of a lengthy inquiry, Tottenham, who had admitted 34 charges of making irregular payments, were horrified when they were fined £600,000, banned from the FA Cup for a year, and told they would begin next season with 12 points deducted.

Sugar pointed out that the people responsible were no longer at the club and that the loss of points and the exclusion from the FA Cup would mean

Sugar: shocked and horrified

that the people who would really suffer were the fans.

Tottenham appealed and, after a degree of horse-trading, the 12-point penalty was reduced to six, with the fine increased to £1.5m and the FA Cup ban left in place. Sugar said: "I find it quite shocking really. If any other Premier League club has got anything to disclose to the authorities it is going to be a brave man that comes forward now. Looking on the positive side, we are not going to be relegated. We have lost two games and that's all. Arsenal had points deducted once and went on to win the League."

. . . but find rich pickings

TOTTENHAM'S response was swift and devastating. In 48 hours at the end of July they signed two World Cup stars, Ilie Dumitrescu from Romania for £2.6m and Jurgen Klinsmann from Germany for £2m. The two transfers astonished football.

It was a coup reminiscent of 1978, when Keith Burkenshaw, then the Spurs manager, snapped up the two Argentine World Cup stars Riccardo Villa and Osvaldo Ardiles for £750,000. Now, Ardiles, the Tottenham manager, was grabbing similar headlines.

With Klinsmann aboard, Tottenham have, with Teddy Sheringham, a £4.1m strike force that matches Blackburn's Alan Shearer and Chris Sutton, assembled at twice the price.

"Inside England, the prices are really stampeding; they

don't reflect the quality of players in general," Ardiles said. "Abroad, the price reflects the player's ability more." He was not the only British manager to be that astute.

In the close season, a flock of overseas players moved to British clubs. Rangers were the biggest purchasers, bringing the Frenchman Basile Boli from Marseilles for £2.7m and the Dane Brian Laudrup from Fiorentina for £2.2m. Forest and Arsenal were not far behind; Forest signed the Dutchman Bryan Roy from Foggia for £2.5m and Arsenal bought the Swede Stefan Schwarz from Benfica from £1.75m.

Brian Robson, newly installed as the Middlesbrough manager, snapped up Jaime Moreno for a paltry £250,000 – the first Bolivian to play in English football.

Brady, Jordan and Macari walk Celtic plank

WHILE RANGERS just marched imperiously on, Celtic were steadily falling apart. The crisis was brought to a head on the eve of the club's annual meeting in October – Liam Brady walked out on the club and his assistant Joe Jordan followed a day later.

They had been hailed as saviours when they took charge 18 months before but their attempts to revive the club's fortunes had been bedevilled by internal politics.

The board turned to another Celtic hero, Lou Macari. His first game in charge delighted the fans, a 2-1 victory over Rangers. The suffering supporters soon had more to cheer about when the board they hated were swept aside by a consortium led by Fergus McCann.

However, the mood of optimism was short-lived. By the end of yet another barren season McCann had acrimoniously sacked Macari and controversially replaced him with Tommy Burns, the Kilmarnock manager.

Milan's dream final is Barcelona's nightmare

IT WAS the dream final that everybody wanted, Barcelona versus Milan for the European Cup. Everybody expected a thrilling match between two evenly-matched teams, and the spectators duly got a feast of football. What they did not to expect to see was a 4-0 demolition of Johann Cruyff's multi-million pound side.

The match was virtually over by half-time after Daniele Massaro gave Milan a 2-0 lead. His fellow striker Dejan Savicevic ran the Barcelona defence ragged and two minutes into the second half he audaciously lobbed the backpedalling Andoni Zubizarreta from outside the penalty area. Marcel Desailly, who had won the European Cup with Marseille the year before, added to Barcelona's misery in the 58th minute.

The Spanish press hailed Milan's victory as an historic defeat for Barcelona, who had been taught a lesson as Milan's hegemony was confirmed. Cruyff's response was to sign a new contract with Barcelona and begin dismantling his squad. Zubizarreta was packed off to Valencia, Michael Laudrup went to Real Madrid and Julio Salinas joined Deportivo La Coruña.

By a late twist of fortune, Barcelona already knew they would have an opportunity to redeem themselves in the European Cup. They had already snatched the Spanish League title at the last gasp. Deportivo needed to win their last match to take the championship but with the score 0-0 Miroslav Djukic missed a penalty in the last minute. It was the second year in a row Barcelona had taken the title in the very last match of the season.

Eclipsed: Romario, a World Cup star, failed to shine in the European Cup

Nightmare goal ends Rangers' dreams of glory

IT SHOULD have all been so easy. Rangers had won the championship for the sixth year in a row, retained the League Cup and only Dundee United stood between them and a second successive clean sweep of the Scottish honours. And Dundee United were hardly the most difficult opponents. They had finished mid-table in the League, only winning 11 matches, and had lost the last six Cup finals they had appeared in.

But Rangers were undone by one of the most bizarre goals ever seen at Hampden Park. Dave McPherson attempted a suicidal back pass which forced Ally Maxwell, the Rangers goalkeeper, to rush his clearance.

He miskicked the ball, which flew straight to Christian Dailly, the Dundee United forward. Dailly's shot trickled towards the net but, amazingly, rebounded off the far post. Craig Brewster could not believe his luck and he raced in to score the easiest goal of his life.

If there was ever a club where something strange was going to happen it had to be Dundee United. Ivan Golac was hardly the archetypal manager. His idea of the right way to prepare for a big match was to take his players out for a drink and a walk round the park to admire the trees.

Unorthodox as the technique was, Dundee United's 1-0 victory prompted Walter Smith, the Rangers manager, to threaten a root and branch clear-out of his team. And within weeks he had signed Basile Boli and Brian Laudrup.

Finishing touch: Craig Brewster salutes his manager

Cantona conjures up Double despite a month of madness

Killing blow: Cantona sends Kharine the wrong way to score his first penalty

On the surface, Manchester United's progress to the Double seemed to be serene. But at one point, after an incredible period of turmoil, they looked as if they would finish the season having won nothing.

After losing to Chelsea in September they seemed to be almost unstoppable in the League. By January they had opened up a 16-point gap over Blackburn and most people would have handed them the title there and then.

When they were beaten by Chelsea at Old Trafford in March, their first defeat at home for 17 months, their unbeaten run in the League was a record 34 matches. It was the start of a month of madness.

The team seemed to lose its collective head with four players sent off in the space of five matches. Eric Cantona was dismissed twice in successive games, Peter Schmeichel got his marching orders in the quarter-finals of the FA Cup and Andrei Kanchelskis was shown the red card in the League Cup final.

Aston Villa won 3-1 at Wembley to end United's hopes of becoming the first English side to complete the treble, a feat Alex Ferguson had accomplished in Scotland with Aberdeen. And with so many of their key players suspended, United were almost eliminated from the FA Cup by Oldham, one of the weakest teams in the Premier Division. With seconds remaining, Oldham were about to pull off the upset of the season but Mark Hughes conjured up a brilliantly taken goal to force the tie into a replay.

All the time, Blackburn had been closing the gap in the League. They had whittled away United's advantage so effectively that the two clubs were only separated by goal difference. But, showing the hallmarks of true champions, Ferguson steadied his team's jangling nerves. United moved into overdrive and it was Blackburn's turn to falter. United retained the title with a match to spare and finished seven points ahead of Blackburn.

United met Chelsea, their nemesis in the League, in the FA Cup final. In the first half it looked as if Chelsea were going to be the victors yet again. After the interval, however, United raised their game. Helped by two penalties scored by Cantona, the second a very questionable award because the offence appeared to be committed just outside the area, Chelsea were swept away 4-0.

Having won the Double for the first time in the club's history, only one challenge remains for Ferguson – to emulate Matt Busby and win the European Cup. Particularly because this year's campaign ended in disaster when United were ignominiously bundled out of the European Cup by Galatasary.

The Turkish side drew 3-3 at Old Trafford and drew the ill-tempered second leg 0-0 to go through on away goals. The ugly side of Cantona came to the fore when he started a brawl in the tunnel and claimed that the referee had been bought.

"Hump it, bump it, whack it might be one possible recipe for a good sex life, but it won't win us the World Cup"

KEN BATES

Tragedy: Escobar dead

Escobar: a £500,000 reward was offered for the conviction of his killers

WHEN Andres Escobar unluckily scored an own goal as Colombia lost to the United States it was an expensive mistake. The defeat made it virtually certain that Colombia, one of the pretournament favourites, would not reach the second round of the World Cup finals. But nobody could ever have imagined that he would pay for the mistake with his life.

Nine days later Escobar had returned home and was leaving a restaurant in Medellin with his fiancee. He was attacked by three men, one of whom said: "Thanks for the own goal" before repeatedly shooting Escobar in the chest and face. As each bullet hit his body, the attackers shouted: "Goal".

Escobar died instantly and there was outrage in Colombia.

At his funeral 100,000 Colombians cried for "justice" as they filed weeping past his open coffin. A £500,000 reward was offered for the arrest and conviction of the killers.

Andy Townsend, the Republic of Ireland midfielder, spoke for everybody at the World Cup when he said: "It makes you wonder what it is all about. When lives are being taken because of football it makes you wonder if it is all worthwhile."

The tournament, already rocked by the Maradona scandal, had to come to terms with an even greater tragedy. An American television commentator said: "We thought we were going to watch another sports tournament. But instead we are seeing all of life, the good, the bad, and the very ugly."

Scandal: Maradona failed drug test

IT WAS a bombshell as great as the Ben Johnson scandal at the 1988 Olympics. Diego Armando Maradona, the greatest player since Pele, had failed a routine drug test and was expelled from the World Cup finals in the United States.

At first Maradona protested his innocence saying that the drug that had been found in his urine sample after the match against Nigeria was simply a cold cure. While it is true that ephedrine, the banned substance, is present in common cold cures, Dr Michel d'Hooghe, Fifa's medical expert, took great pains to refute Maradona's defence.

The doctor explained that a full analysis had revealed that Maradona had been taking five banned drugs and if Maradona had been taking medicine for a cold there were better products. "We did not find one pill containing the five products so we suppose it must be a cocktail," he said.

When the Argentine Football Federation learnt of the news they acted swiftly and threw Maradona out of the tournament. Fifa banned Maradona from any involvement in football and decided to review the situation once the World Cup was over. But there was little sympathy for Maradona. "He broke the rules and that is the end of it," Guido Tognoni of Fifa said. "It would not matter if it was only a small dose. You cannot be half pregnant. You either are or you aren't."

Not for the first time Maradona fled to Argentina in disgrace. The affair was horribly reminiscent of 1991, when he had tested positive for cocaine after a League match in Italy and had been banned from football for 15 months. Facing prosecution on charges of possessing and distributing cocaine, and involvement in a vice ring in Naples, he had sneaked out of the country just before a warrant was issued for his arrest. No sooner had he returned home than he was arrested in Buenos Aires for taking cocaine.

When the news of the latest scandal broke Maradona had claimed: "I did not take drugs. I have never needed stimulants for showing my skill." He suggested that he was a victim of conspiracy and said: "Fifa beat me over the head without any compunction."

However two days later Maradona admitted that he had "forgotten to tell" the team doctor that he was taking pills. "I took those pills as if they were aspirin," he said. "Thousands of players do it but the cost is always higher when Maradona does it."

To everybody's surprise Maradona quickly returned to the World Cup to commentate for an Argentinian television station on his country's second-round match against Romania. With their playmaker gone, his former teammates were also heading home after their 3-2 defeat and Maradona accepted the inevitable and announced his retirement.

The Buenos Aires newspaper, La Prensa, summed up the whole sorry mess: "Maradona will never show his magic again. The biggest soccer star of modern times slammed the door on his sporting life, leaving us in a fog of scandal."

Maradona: disgraced game again

Kidderminster are the first to put the big boys on the block

To boldly go: Humphreys took Kidderminster into the fifth round

KIDDERMINSTER had never reached the third round of the FA Cup before, and their greatest day was given even more spice when they were drawn against their near-neigbours Birmingham. To add to the excitement, Kidderminster's manager, Graham Allner, had been signed as a schoolboy by Birmingham but then rejected.

Birmingham took the lead in the ninth minute and were rampant for much of the match. But they wasted their chances, including missing a penalty. Kidderminster only managed a handful of attacks, but they made them tell. Goals from Cartwright and Purdie earned the GM-Vauxhall conference team a home tie against Preston.

This time Kidderminster had the best of the play and a goal from Humphreys ensured that they were one of the few non-League sides to have ever reached the fifth round, where they bowed out 1-0 to West Ham.

The fourth round proved to be an amazing graveyard for the big-name, big-money clubs. Cardiff beat Manchester City and then there were two days of mayhem in the replays. Blackburn, second in the Premier League and with a team valued at £12.9m, lost 1-0 at home to Charlton (£290,000). Arsenal (third, £8.8m) were trounced 3-1 by Bolton (£1.4m) at Highbury in extra time; Newcastle (fourth, £6.9m) lost 2-0 at Luton (£250,000) and Leeds (seventh, £9.9m) lost 3-2 in extra time at home to Oxford (£935,000). In total, £38.5m of Premier League talent had been made to look very foolish by less than £3m of players from the lower divisions.

Arsenal sing the same old song and still hit the winning note

GEORGE GRAHAM, who had won every domestic honour with Arsenal, finally collected his first European trophy as a manager. He had played in Arsenal's only other European triumph, the 4-3 defeat of Anderlecht in the 1970 Fairs Cup final.

This time Graham inspired his below-strength team to beat Parma, the holders and favourites, 1-0 in the European Cup Winners Cup in Copenhagen. It was a classic Arsenal performance of resolute defence and containing football. Indeed, before the game kicked off, prescient fans sung the club's new anthem "One-Nil to the Arsenal".

In the 20th minute Alan Smith provided the one when he latched on to a failed overhead clearance. The nil came from Arsenal's immaculate back four, in which their captain Tony Adams was outstanding. Bob Wilson, watching Adams at breakfast on the morning of the game, said: "He strolled in like John Wayne. His face was fixed like a mask and it never broke again until the final whistle. You could see him thinking 'This is the day of battle.' He devotes himself to Arsenal. He is their rock."

One-Nil: Smith scores the goal to give Arsenal their European triumph

339

WORLD CUP 1994

Beauty beat the beast, thanks to Brazil and Fifa

FOOTBALL is about romance and dreams, or it is nothing. After the horrors of 1990 it seemed destined for nothing. But in 1994, despite the disgrace of Diego Maradona failing a drug test and the tragedy of Andres Escobar's murder, the beautiful game was born again. The midwives were Fifa, who used their legislative powers to privilege adventurous play. And, to everybody's satisfaction, Brazil delivered.

They had to. A generation had passed since Pele, Tostao, Rivelino, Gerson et al had last brought the ultimate trophy to the land of the samba. Destiny decreed that Brazil 1994 – Romario, Bebeto, Jorginho, Aldair et al – had finally to fulfil their roles as heirs apparent. They did, in style. Not the 1970 style, eschewing defence and simply relying on scoring more goals than their opponents. This was a modern Brazil: flair was tempered with a competitive and organised strategy that disappointed their attack-crazy fans at home, but won fans worldwide. They coasted serenely to the dream final against Italy.

By contrast their opponents had ridden their luck to have progressed so far. Italy were the worst of the third-placed teams to qualify for the second round. Indeed, their record was worse than the United States and Saudi Arabia. They were seconds away from being eliminated by Nigeria in the second round before Roberto Baggio baled them out. Their luck held again in the quarter-final against Spain, when Julio Salinas missed an easy opportunity and then, with seconds left, the referee missed Mauro Tassotti breaking Luis Enrique's nose in the Italian penalty area.

Sadly for a tournament characterised by exciting football, Italy retreated into their craven shell for the showpiece occasion frequently having their entire team camped in their own half. Frightened to take on the ebullient Brazilians at their own game, Italy played for the breakaway, extra time and the lottery of penalties. They got their comeuppance. After 120 minutes, the greatest show on earth came down to a penalty shoot-out and it was their very own genius, Roberto Baggio, who blasted his shot over to give Brazil an unprecedented fourth World Cup.

Generation game: the Cup returned to Brazil after 24 years

It was a fitting finale: Italian fear had fallen to Brazilian courage and the soul of football was alive and well. Billions of people breathed again, the beautiful game was in safe hands.

Fifa must get much of the credit for this resurrection. They introduced three points for a win in the first round; outlawed the tackle from behind; insisted on a liberal interpretation of the offside rule; forced "injured" players off the field to avoid time-wasting and instructed referees to follow these new guidelines or be banished from the tournament. By and large, the revolution worked. Admittedly some referees were over zealous in their application of the coloured cardboard, but then they, too, got their own red card.

Self-professed experts had dismissed Fifa's initiative as something concocted by meddling bureaucrats. How wrong they were. For the first time forwards were able to ply their trade without fear of defenders scything them down.

True, there were myriad yellow and red cards (227 and 15). But, equally true, attacking football was to the fore precisely because of the fear of punishment. This was not Fifa taking a sledge-hammer to crack a nut – this was taking a scalpel to excise a cancer.

Apart from the final, only two other matches ended in 0-0 draws, and 141 goals were scored. The Americans, who were written off as football dunces, were gripped by the excitement and the spectacle – the 52 matches were watched by 3,567,415 spectators at an average of 68,604 per game. Two billion people watched the final on television and the organisers made a profit of $20m on a $4bn turnover. And this was the tournament that the prophets of doom said was going to be a disaster.

England, along with Northern Ireland, Scotland and Wales, failed to qualify. This was the first time since the Home countries had entered the World Cup in 1950 that all four were absent. The Republic

of Ireland, managed by Jack Charlton – a World Cup winner for England in 1966 – were left to carry the flag for the British Isles.

Ireland were duly, and unsurprisingly, adopted by the English media as "our" team. No fewer than 20 of the 22-man squad were playing in the English League (the other two played in Scotland), and were so Irish that the majority of them probably thought brogue was a kind of shoe you bought in posh shops. By and large, it was a journeyman squad of English pros, with Irish grandmothers, who battled hard but were found wanting on the world's biggest stage.

The manager didn't help. Charlton, a dour centre-half for Leeds in the 1960s and 1970s, cut much the same figure as an international manager in the 1980s and 1990s. In a World Cup that was a beacon for the game, Ireland were the only team to play boring, negative football. And Charlton gave the worst possible example to his players. He bitched about the rule changes. He bitched about the supply of water for his players in the desperate heat and humidity in America in the summer. He even argued about a delayed substitution when the paperwork was cocked up. So much so that he received a touchline ban and a £10,000 fine from Fifa.

To the English media, and his similarly fawning fans in Ireland, Jack was standing up to the Fifa mandarins. In reality he was being the same curmudgeonly so-and-so as Don Revie had been in Leeds' dark days. All mouth and no trousers. In the spring, Fifa had invited all the coaches at the World Cup to a briefing where every rule change and procedure for the tournament would be discussed and explained. Who didn't turn up? Charlton. Little wonder Fifa took a dim view of his constant complaints.

Charlton also never realised what tournament he was in. As the other coaches and countries quickly adapted and played attacking football, Charlton's Ireland were Leeds' stick-in-the-muds, trying to win games without really trying to score. Thus, having beaten Italy 1-0 in the opening game, they supinely lost to Mexico 2-1. They rescued themselves with a goalless draw with Norway only to be overrun 2-0 by Holland in the second round.

Their "proud" record under Charlton beggars belief: in two World Cups they have won only two matches out of nine – one of them in a penalty shoot-out – and scored a miserly four goals. Eamon Dunphy, a perennial thorn in Charlton's flesh, summed up their performance in America neatly: "At a tournament notable for its quality, Ireland stood out as beggars at the banquet."

Others relished the feast. Notably the United States who beat Colombia, one of the pre-tournament favourites, to qualify for the second phase where they only went down 1-0 to Brazil. But it was the forgotten states of the post-Communist Balkans that provided the real World Cup fireworks. Bulgaria and Romania did a little more than emerge from Stalinist backwaters, they exploded on to the world scene. Romania reached the quarter-finals. Bulgaria, who had never won a match in five World Cup finals, were inspired by Hristo Stoichkov into the semi-finals.

When Fifa finally decide how to allocate the extra places for the 32-country World Cup in France in 1998 they *must* privilege Europe. The evidence from this tournament is undeniable: playing on the other side of the world in the worst possible conditions for them, Europe still managed to provide seven of the last eight contenders. Only Brazil were good enough to survive in the European pressure cooker.

Sweet and sour: Romario (above left) and Roberto Baggio were the players of the tournament. But it was a disconsolate Baggio who lost the Cup

FOR THE RECORD

FIRST ROUND

GROUP A	P	W	D	L	F	A	Pts
Romania	3	2	0	1	5	5	6
Switzerland	3	1	1	1	5	4	4
United States	3	1	1	1	3	3	4
Colombia	3	1	0	2	4	5	3

GROUP B	P	W	D	L	F	A	Pts
Brazil	3	2	1	0	6	1	7
Sweden	3	1	2	0	6	4	5
Russia	3	1	0	2	7	6	3
Cameroon	3	0	1	2	3	11	1

GROUP C	P	W	D	L	F	A	Pts
Germany	3	2	1	0	5	3	7
Spain	3	1	2	0	6	4	5
S Korea	3	0	2	1	4	5	2
Bolivia	3	0	1	2	1	4	1

GROUP D	P	W	D	L	F	A	Pts
Nigeria	3	2	0	1	6	2	6
Bulgaria	3	2	0	1	6	3	6
Argentina	3	2	0	1	6	3	6
Greece	3	0	0	3	0	10	0

GROUP E	P	W	D	L	F	A	Pts
Mexico	3	1	1	1	3	3	4
Ireland	3	1	1	1	2	2	4
Italy	3	1	1	1	2	2	4
Norway	3	1	1	1	1	1	4

GROUP F	P	W	D	L	F	A	Pts
Holland	3	2	0	1	4	3	6
Saudi Arabia	3	2	0	1	4	3	6
Belgium	3	2	0	1	2	1	6
Morocco	3	0	0	3	2	5	0

SECOND ROUND
Spain 3   Switzerland 0
HT 1-0 Att. 53,141
Italy 2   Nigeria 1 aet
HT 0-1 Att. 54,367
Germany 3   Belgium 2
HT 3-1 Att. 60,246
Bulgaria 1   Mexico 1
Bulgaria won 3-1 on penalties
HT 1-1 Att. 71,030
Holland 2   Ireland 0
HT 2-0 Att. 61,355
Brazil 1   United States 0
HT 0-0 Att. 84,147
Sweden 3   Saudi Arabia 1
HT 1-0 Att. 60,277
Romania 3   Argentina 2
HT 2-1 Att. 90,469

QUARTER-FINALS
Italy 2   Spain 1
HT 1-0 Att. 53,644
Bulgaria 2   Germany 1
HT 0-0 Att. 72,416
Brazil 3   Holland 2
HT 0-0 Att. 63,998
Sweden 2   Romania 2
Sweden won 5-4 on penalties
HT 0-0 FT 1-1 Att. 81,715

SEMI-FINALS
Italy 2   Bulgaria 1
HT 2-1 Att. 77,094
Brazil 1   Sweden 0
HT 0-0 Att. 84,569

THIRD PLACE
Sweden 4   Bulgaria 0
HT 4-0 Att. 83,716

FINAL
Brazil 0   Italy 0
Brazil won 3-2 on penalties

Teams
Brazil Taffarel; Jorginho (Cafu), Aldair, Marcio Santos, Branco, Mazinho, Mauro Silva, Dunga, Zinho (Viola), Romario, Bebeto
Italy Pagliuca; Mussi (Apolloni), Baresi, Maldini, Benarrivo, Berti, Albertini, D Baggio (Evani), Donadoni, R Baggio, Massaro
Referee S Puhl (Hungary)

Penalty shoot-out
Italy Baresi missed, Albertini scored, Evani scored, Massaro saved, R Baggio missed
Brazil M Santos saved, Romario scored, Branco scored, Dunga scored

Leading goalscorers 6 Hristo Stoichkov (Bulgaria), Oleg Salenko (Russia); 5 Romario (Brazil), Roberto Baggio (Italy), Jurgen Klinsmann (Germany); 4 Martin Dahlin (Sweden), Gabriel Batistuta (Argentina), Florin Raducioiu (Romania), Kennet Andersson (Sweden)

Total goals scored 141
Average per game: 2.71

Sendings-off Marco Etcheverry (Bolivia) v Germany; Referee: A Brizio Carter (Mexico).
Nadal (Spain) v South Korea; Referee: P Mikkelsen (Denmark).
Ioan Vladoiu (Romania) v Switzerland; Referee: N Jouini (Tunisia).
Luis Cristaldo (Bolivia) v South Korea; Referee: L Mottram (Scotland).
Gianluca Pagliuca (Italy) v Norway; Referee: H Krug (Germany).
Sergei Gorlukovich (Russia) v Sweden; Referee: J Quiniou (France).
Rigobert Song (Cameroon) v Brazil; Referee: A Brizio Carter (Mexico).
Tsanko Zetanov (Bulgaria) v Argentina; Referee: N Jouini (Tunisia).
Leonardo (Brazil) v United States; Referee: J Quiniou (France).
Fernando Clavijo (United States) v Brazil.
Gianfranco Zola (Italy) v Nigeria; Referee: A Brizio Carter (Mexico).
Emil Kremenliev (Bulgaria) v Mexico; Referee: Jamal al-Sharif (Syria).
Luis Garcia (Mexico) v Bulgaria.
Stefan Schwarz (Sweden) v Romania; Referee: P Don (England).
Jonas Thern (Sweden) v Brazil; Referee: J Torres Cadena (Colombia).

● An Albanian lost his wife when, short of money, he gambled her on the result of the Argentina versus Bulgaria match. He then complained to the police when his wife left him for the winner of the bet.

● *"Either you mean what you say or you crack jokes, and Fifa never crack jokes."* Guido Tognoni on the disciplinary crackdown.

LEAGUE TABLES AND RESULTS 1990 – 1994

	1990-91	1991-92	1992-93	1993-94
WORLD CUP				Brazil 0 Italy 0; Brazil won 3-2 on penalties
EUROPEAN CHAMPIONSHIP		Denmark 2 Germany 0		
EUROPEAN CUP	Red Star Belgrade 0 Marseille 0; Belgrade won 5-3 on penalties	Barcelona 1 Sampdoria 0	Marseille 1 AC Milan 0	AC Milan 4 Barcelona 0
EUROPEAN CUP WINNERS CUP	Manchester Utd 2 Barcelona 0	Werder Bremen 2 Monaco 0	Parma 3 Antwerp 1	Arsenal 1 Parma 0
UEFA CUP	Inter Milan beat AS Roma 2-0 0-1	Ajax bea Torino 2-2 0-0; Ajax won on away goals	Juventus beat Borussia Dortmund 3-1 3-0	Inter Milan beat Casino Salzburg 1-0 1-0
FA CUP	Tottenham Hotspur 2 Nottingham Forest 1	Liverpool 2 Sunderland 0	Arsenal 2 Sheffield Wednesday 1, after 1-1	Manchester United 4 Chelsea 0

FIRST DIVISION – PREMIER DIVISION (1992)

1990-91

	P	W	D	L	F	A	Pts
Arsenal	38	24	13	1	74	18	83
Liverpool	38	23	7	8	77	40	76
C Palace	38	20	9	9	50	41	69
Leeds Utd	38	19	7	12	65	47	64
Man City	38	17	11	10	64	53	62
Man Utd	38	16	12	10	58	45	59
Wimbledon	38	14	14	10	53	46	56
Nottm F	38	14	12	12	65	50	54
Everton	38	13	12	13	50	46	51
Tottenham	38	11	16	11	51	50	49
Chelsea	38	13	10	15	58	69	49
QPR	38	12	10	16	44	53	46
Sheff Utd	38	13	7	18	36	55	46
Soton	38	12	9	17	58	69	45
Norwich	38	13	6	19	41	64	45
Coventry	38	11	11	16	42	49	44
Aston Villa	38	9	14	15	46	58	41
Luton	38	10	7	21	42	61	37
Sunderland	*38*	*8*	*10*	*20*	*38*	*60*	*34*
Derby	*38*	*5*	*9*	*24*	*37*	*75*	*24*

1991-92

	P	W	D	L	F	A	Pts
Leeds Utd	42	22	16	4	74	37	82
Man Utd	42	21	15	6	63	33	78
Sheff Wed	42	21	12	9	62	49	75
Arsenal	42	19	15	8	81	46	72
Man City	42	20	10	12	61	48	70
Liverpool	42	16	16	10	47	40	64
Aston Villa	42	17	9	16	48	44	60
Nottm F	42	16	11	15	60	58	59
Sheff Utd	42	16	9	17	65	63	57
C Palace	42	14	15	13	53	61	57
QPR	42	12	18	12	48	47	54
Everton	42	13	14	15	52	51	53
Wimbledon	42	13	14	15	53	53	53
Chelsea	42	13	14	15	50	60	53
Tottenham	42	15	7	20	58	63	52
Soton	42	14	10	18	39	55	52
Oldham	42	14	9	19	63	67	51
Norwich	42	11	12	19	47	63	45
Coventry	42	11	11	20	35	44	44
Luton	*42*	*10*	*12*	*20*	*38*	*71*	*42*
Notts C	*42*	*10*	*10*	*22*	*40*	*62*	*40*
West Ham	*42*	*9*	*11*	*22*	*37*	*59*	*38*

1992-93

	P	W	D	L	F	A	Pts
Man Utd	42	24	12	6	67	31	84
Aston Villa	42	21	11	10	57	40	74
Norwich	42	21	9	12	61	65	72
Blackburn	42	20	11	11	68	46	71
QPR	42	17	12	13	63	55	63
Liverpool	42	16	11	15	62	55	59
Sheff Wed	42	15	14	13	55	51	59
Tottenham	42	16	11	15	60	66	59
Man City	42	15	12	15	56	51	57
Arsenal	42	15	11	16	40	38	56
Chelsea	42	14	14	14	51	54	56
Wimbledon	42	14	12	16	56	55	54
Everton	42	15	8	19	53	55	53
Sheff Utd	42	14	10	18	54	53	52
Coventry	42	13	13	16	52	57	52
Ipswich	42	12	16	14	50	55	52
Leeds	42	12	15	15	57	62	51
Soton	42	13	11	18	54	61	50
Oldham	42	13	10	19	63	74	49
C Palace	*42*	*11*	*16*	*15*	*48*	*61*	*49*
Middlesbro	*42*	*11*	*11*	*20*	*54*	*75*	*44*
Nottm F	*42*	*10*	*10*	*22*	*41*	*62*	*40*

1993-94

	P	W	D	L	F	A	Pts
Man Utd	42	27	11	5	80	38	92
Blackburn	42	25	9	8	63	36	84
Newcastle	42	23	8	11	82	41	77
Arsenal	42	18	7	7	53	28	71
Leeds	42	18	16	8	65	39	70
Wimbledon	42	18	11	13	56	53	65
Sheff Wed	42	16	16	10	76	54	64
Liverpool	42	17	9	16	59	55	60
QPR	42	16	12	14	62	61	60
Aston Villa	42	15	12	15	46	50	57
Coventry	42	14	14	14	43	45	56
Norwich	42	12	17	13	65	61	53
West Ham	42	13	13	16	47	58	52
Chelsea	42	13	12	17	49	53	51
Tottenham	42	11	12	19	54	59	45
Man City	42	9	18	15	38	49	45
Everton	42	12	8	22	42	63	44
Soton	42	12	7	23	49	66	43
Ipswich	42	9	16	17	35	58	43
Sheff Utd	*42*	*8*	*18*	*16*	*42*	*60*	*42*
Oldham	*42*	*9*	*13*	*20*	*42*	*68*	*40*
Swindon	*42*	*5*	*15*	*22*	*47*	*100*	*30*

SECOND DIVISION

1990-91	1991-92	1992-93	1993-94
Champions: Oldham Athletic Also promoted: West Ham United, Sheffield Wednesday, Notts County Relegated: West Bromwich Albion, Hull City	Champions: Ipswich Town Also promoted: Middlesbrough, Blackburn Rovers Relegated: Plymouth Argyle, Brighton & Hove Albion, Port Vale	Champions: Newcastle United Also promoted: West Ham United, Swindon Town Relegated: Brentford, Cambridge United, Bristol Rovers	Champions: Crystal Palace Also promoted: Nottingham Forest, Leicester Relegated: Birmingham, Oxford, Peterborough

THIRD DIVISION

1990-91	1991-92	1992-93	1993-94
Champions: Cambridge United Also promoted: Southend United, Grimsby Town, Tranmere Rovers Relegated: Crewe Alexandra, Rotherham United, Mansfield Town	Champions: Brentford Also promoted: Birmingham City, Peterborough United Relegated: Bury, Shrewsbury Town, Torquay United, Darlington	Champions: Stoke City Also promoted: Bolton Wanderers, West Bromwich Albion Relegated: Preston, Mansfield Town, Wigan Athletic, Chester City	Champions: Reading Also promoted: Port Vale, Stockport

FOURTH DIVISION

1990-91	1991-92	1992-93	1993-94
Champions: Darlington Also promoted: Stockport, Hartlepool, Peterborough, Torquay Elected to the League: Barnet	Champions: Burnley Also promoted: Rotherham Town, Mansfield Town, Blackpool Elected to the League: Colchester	Champions: Cardiff City Also promoted: Wrexham, Barnet, York City *Wycombe W replaced Halifax Town*	Champions: Shrewsbury Also promoted: Chester, Crewe, Wycombe

LEAGUE CUP

1990-91	1991-92	1992-93	1993-94
Sheffield Wed 1 Manchester Utd 0	Manchester United 1 Nottingham Forest 0	Arsenal 2 Sheffield Wednesday 1	Aston Villa 3 Manchester United 1

SCOTTISH CUP

1990-91	1991-92	1992-93	1993-94
Motherwell 4 Dundee United 3	Rangers 2 Airdire 1	Rangers 2 Aberdeen 1	Dundee United 1 Rangers 0

SCOTTISH PREMIER DIVISION

1990-91

	P	W	D	L	F	A	Pts
Rangers	36	24	7	5	62	23	55
Aberdeen	36	22	9	5	62	27	53
Celtic	36	17	7	12	52	38	41
Dundee	36	17	7	12	41	29	41
Hearts	36	14	7	15	48	55	35
Motherwell	36	12	9	15	51	50	33
St J'stone	36	11	9	16	41	54	31
Dunfermline	36	8	11	17	38	61	27
Hibernian	36	6	13	17	24	51	25
St Mirren	36	5	9	22	28	59	19

1991-92

	P	W	D	L	F	A	Pts
Rangers	44	33	6	5	101	31	72
Hearts	44	27	9	8	60	37	63
Celtic	44	26	10	8	88	42	62
Dundee	44	19	13	12	66	50	51
Hibernian	44	16	17	11	53	45	49
Aberdeen	44	17	14	13	55	42	48
Airdrie	44	13	10	21	50	70	36
St J'stone	44	13	10	21	52	73	36
Falkirk	44	12	11	21	54	73	35
Motherwell	44	10	14	20	43	61	34
St Mirren	*44*	*6*	*12*	*26*	*33*	*73*	*24*
Dunfermline	*44*	*4*	*10*	*30*	*22*	*80*	*18*

1992-93

	P	W	D	L	F	A	Pts
Rangers	44	33	7	4	97	35	73
Aberdeen	44	27	10	7	87	36	64
Celtic	44	24	12	8	68	41	60
Dundee	44	19	9	16	56	49	47
Hearts	44	15	14	15	46	51	44
St J'stone	44	10	19	15	51	66	39
Hibernian	44	12	13	19	54	64	37
Partick	44	12	12	20	50	71	36
Motherwell	44	11	16	15	48	61	36
Dundee	44	11	12	21	48	68	34
Falkirk	*44*	*11*	*7*	*26*	*60*	*86*	*29*
Airdrie	*44*	*6*	*17*	*21*	*35*	*70*	*29*

1993-94

	P	W	D	L	F	A	Pts
Rangers	44	22	14	8	74	41	58
Aberdeen	44	17	21	6	58	36	55
Motherwell	44	20	14	10	58	43	54
Celtic	44	15	20	9	51	38	50
Hibernian	44	16	15	13	53	48	47
Dundee	44	11	20	13	47	48	42
Hearts	44	11	20	13	37	43	42
Kilmarnock	44	12	16	16	36	45	40
Partick	44	12	16	16	46	57	40
St J'stone	*44*	*10*	*20*	*14*	*35*	*47*	*40*
Raith	*44*	*6*	*19*	*19*	*46*	*76*	*31*
Dundee	*44*	*8*	*13*	*23*	*42*	*57*	*29*

SCOTTISH FIRST DIVISION

1990-91	1991-92	1992-93	1993-94
Champions: Falkirk Also promoted: Airdrie Relegated: Clyde, Brechin City	Champions: Dundee Also promoted: Partick Thistle Relegated: Montrose, Forfar Athletic	Champions: Raith Rovers Also promoted: Kilmarnock Relegated: Meadowbank Thistle, Cowdenbeath	Champions: Falkirk Runners-up (not promoted): Dunfermline (*League reorganised into four divisions*)

SCOTTISH SECOND DIV

1990-91	1991-92	1992-93	1993-94
Champions: Stirling Albion Also promoted: Montrose	Champions: Dumbarton Also promoted: Cowdenbeath	Champions: Clyde Also promoted: Brechin City	Champions: Stranraer Runners-up (not promoted): Berwick

SCOTTISH LEAGUE CUP

1990-91	1991-92	1992-93	1993-94
Dunfermline 2 Hibernian 0	Hibernian 2 Dunfermline 0	Rangers 2 Aberdeen 1	Rangers 2 Hibernian 1

Bibliography

Those wishing to read more about the events we chronicle should find these books, among the many we consulted, to be particularly useful.

100 GREAT BRITISH FOOTBALLERS Trevor Brooking; Queen Anne Press; 1988

A GAME OF TWO HALVES edited by Stephen F Kelly; Mandarin; 1992

A HISTORY OF BRITISH FOOTBALL Percy M Young; Arrow Books; 1973

A STRANGE KIND OF GLORY Eamon Dunphy; Heinemann; 1991

ALEX FERGUSON, 6 YEARS AT UNITED Mainstream Publishing; 1992

ALL PLAYED OUT Pete Davies; Heinemann; 1990

AGAINST THE ODDS Bobby Robson with Bob Harris; Stanley Paul; 1990

AN EVERTON DIARY Peter Reid with Peter Ball; Queen Anne Press; 1988

AN ILLUSTRATED HISTORY OF BALL GAMES Nigel Viney and Neil Grant; William Heinemann; 1978

AND THE SPURS GO MARCHING ON Phil Soar; Hamlyn; 1982

ANUARIO DEL FUTBOL El Pais; 1994

ARSENAL OFFICIAL HISTORY Phil Soar and Martin Tyler; Hamlyn; 1989

ASSOCIATION FOOTBALL, VOLUMES 1-4 edited by AH Fabian and Geoffrey Green; Caxton; 1960

ASSOCIATION FOOTBALL AND ENGLISH SOCIETY 1863-1915 Tony Mason; Harvester Press; 1980

BACK PAGE FOOTBALL Stephen F Kelly; Macdonald Queen Anne Press; 1988

BEHIND CLOSED DOORS Irving Scholar; Andre Deutsch; 1992

BOBBY MOORE Jeff Powell; Everest; 1976

BOBBY MOORE, A TRIBUTE edited by David Emery; Headline; 1993

BOBBY MOORE, THE LIFE AND TIMES OF A SPORTING HERO Jeff Powell; Robson Books; 1993

BOOK OF WORLD FOOTBALL Brian Glanville; Dragon; 1972

BOYS OF '66 Martin Tyler; Hamlyn; 1981

CHAMPIONS OF EUROPE Brian Glanville; Guinness; 1991

CLOUGH Tony Francis; Stanley Paul; 1989

CUP FINAL EXTRA Martin Tyler; Hamlyn; 1981

DALGLISH Stephen F Kelly; Headline; 1992

DON'T SHOOT THE MANAGER Jimmy Greaves with Norman Giller; Boxtree; 1993

EVERYMAN'S DICTIONARY OF DATES revised by Audrey Butler; J M Dent; 1987

FAMOUS SPORTING FIASCOS Stephen Winkworth; Sphere Books; 1984

FOOTBALL! Nicholas Mason; Temple Smith; 1974

FOOTBALL AND THE DECLINE OF BRITAIN James Walvin; Macmillan; 1986

FOOTBALL IS MY PASSPORT Billy Wright; Stanley Paul; 1957

FOOTBALL PLAYERS' RECORDS 1946-92 Barry J Hugman; Tony Williams; 1992

FOR THE GOOD OF THE GAME John Harding; Robson Books; 1991

FULHAM'S GOLDEN YEARS Ken Coton; Ashwater Publishing; 1992

GAMES AND SETS, THE CHANGING FACE OF SPORT ON TELEVISION Steven Barnett; BFI Publishing; 1990

GAZZA AGONISTES Ian Hamilton; Penguin; 1993

GLASGOW RANGERS PLAYER BY PLAYER Bob Ferrier and Robert McElroy; Crowood; 1990

GLENN HODDLE, AN AUTOBIOGRAPHY Pelham Books; 1982

GLORY GLORY Bill Nicholson; Macmillan; 1984

GLORY GLORY MAN UNITED Bryan Robson; Collins Willow; 1992

HEART TO HEART Mike Aitken and Wallace Mercer; Mainstream; 1988

HEROES AND VILLAINS Alex Fynn and Lynton Guest; Penguin; 1991

HOOLIGANS ABROAD John Williams, Eric Dunning and Patrick Murphy; Routledge & Kegan Paul; 1984

HOTBED OF SOCCER Arthur Appleton; Rupert Hart-Davis; 1960

HOWARD KENDALL'S EVERTON SCRAPBOOK Souvenir Press; 1986

ILLUSTRATED ENCYCLOPAEDIA OF BRITISH FOOTBALL Phil Soar; WH Smith; 1990

JOCK STEIN Ken Gallacher; Stanley Paul; 1988

JUST LIKE MY DREAMS John Lyall; Penguin; 1990

LIVERPOOL Matthew Graham; Hamlyn; 1985

LIVERPOOL IN EUROPE Stephen F Kelly; Collins Willow; 1992

LIVERPOOL IN EUROPE Steve Hale and Ivan Ponting; Guinness; 1992

MANCHESTER UNITED: THE BETRAYAL OF A LEGEND Michael Crick and David Smith; Pelham Books; 1989

MORE CELTIC GREATS Hugh Keevins; Sportsprint; 1990

MORE RANGERS GREATS Dixon Blackstock; Sportsprint; 1991

MORE THAN A MATCH Lee Chapman; Random House; 1993

NEWS OF THE WORLD FOOTBALL ANNUALS Invincible Press

OUT OF TIME Alex Fynn and Lynton Guest; Simon & Schuster; 1994

PAUL GASCOIGNE, THE INSIDE STORY Jane Nottage; Collins Willow; 1993

PEARS CYCLOPAEDIA Christopher Cook; Pelham; 1990

PELE: MY LIFE AND THE BEAUTIFUL GAME Pele with Robert L Fish; New English Library; 1977

PERSONNA YEAR BOOK OF SPORTS Robert Martin; Pelham; 1969

PLAYFAIR WINNERS ANNUAL 1991-92 Edward Abelson; Queen Anne Press; 1991

PUFFIN BOOK OF FOOTBALL Brian Glanville; Puffin Books; 1970

ROTHMANS FOOTBALL YEAR BOOKS Queen Anne Press

SCOTTISH FOOTBALL Kevin McCarra; Polygon; 1984

SICK AS A PARROT Chris Horrie; Virgin; 1992

SOCCER Derek Henderson; Hamlyn; 1980

SOCCER, A PANORAMA Brian Glanville; Eyre and Spottiswoode; 1969

SOCCER FIRSTS John Robinson; Guinness Publishing; 1986

SOCCER SHORTS Jack Rollin; Guinness Publishing; 1988

SPORT IN BRITAIN, A SOCIAL HISTORY Tony Mason; Cambridge University Press; 1989

SPORTS QUOTES OF THE EIGHTIES Peter Ball and Phil Shaw; Mandarin; 1990

SPURS, A COMPLETE RECORD Bob Goodwin; Breedon Books; 1988

STANLEY MATTHEWS David Miller; Pavilion; 1989

SUNDAY TIMES: THE SPORTING DECADE – 1980s Chris Dighton; Macdonald Queen Anne Press; 1990

SUNDERLAND AND THE CUP Arthur Appleton; Frank Graham; 1974

THE 1991 INFORMATION PLEASE SPORTS ALMANAC edited by Mike Meserole; Houghton Mifflin, Boston

THE BOOK OF SPORTS QUOTES Jonathon Green and Don Atyeo; Omnibus; 1979

THE COURAGE BOOK OF GREAT SPORTING TEAMS compiled by Chris Rhys; Stanley Paul; 1985

THE COURAGE BOOK OF SPORTING HEROES compiled by Chris Rhys; Stanley Paul; 1984

THE DAILY TELEGRAPH FOOTBALL CHRONICLE Norman Barrett; Carlton; 1993

THE DONS Jack Webster; Stanley Paul; 1990

THE DOUBLE AND BEFORE Danny Blanchflower; Four Square; 1961

THE ENCYCLOPAEDIA OF SPORT edited by Charles Harvey; Sampson Low, Marston and Co; 1959

THE EUROPEAN CHAMPIONSHIP John Robinson; Marksman; 1988

THE FOOTBALL ENCYCLOPAEDIA edited by Frank Johnston; Associated Sporting Press; 1934

THE FOOTBALL FACT BOOK Jack Rollin; Guinness Publishing; 1990

THE FOOTBALL LEAGUE 1888-1988 Bryon Butler; Macdonald Queen Anne Press; 1987

THE FOOTBALL MAN Arthur Hopcraft; Sportspages; 1988

THE FOOTBALL MANAGERS Johnny Rogan; Macdonald Queen Anne Press; 1989

THE GLORY GAME Hunter Davies; Mainstream; 1990

THE GLORY, GLORY NIGHTS Colin Gibson and Harry Harris; Cockerel Books; 1986

THE GOLDEN AGE OF FOOTBALL Peter Jeffs; Breedon Books; 1991

THE GOOD, THE BAD AND THE BUBBLY George Best; Pan; 1990

THE GUINNESS BOOK OF SOCCER FACTS AND FEATS Jack Rollin; Guinness Superlatives; 1979

THE GUINNESS DICTIONARY OF SPORTS QUOTATIONS Colin Jarman; Guinness; 1990

THE GUINNESS FOOTBALL ENCYCLOPAEDIA edited by Graham Hart; Guinness; 1993

THE GUINNESS FOOTBALL FACT BOOK Jack Rollin; Guinness Publishing; 1993

THE GUINNESS INTERNATIONAL WHO'S WHO OF SPORT Peter Matthews; Ian Buchanan and Bill Mallon; Guinness; 1993

THE GUINNESS RECORD OF THE FA CUP Mike Collett; Guinness; 1993

THE GUINNESS RECORD OF WORLD SOCCER Guy Oliver; Guinness; 1992

THE HILLSBOROUGH STADIUM DISASTER The official report by Lord Justice; HMSO; 1990

THE HUTCHINSON ENCYCLOPAEDIA Guild Publishing; 1988

THE ILLUSTRATED FOOTBALLER Tony Ambrosen; Breedon Books; 1989

THE LEEDS UNITED STORY Jason Tomas; Arthur Barker; 1971

THE NEW SCOTTISH FOOTBALL FACT BOOK compiled and edited by Forrest HC Robertson; Sports Data Services; 1985

THE OFFICIAL HISTORY OF THE FOOTBALL ASSOCIATION Bryon Butler; Macdonald Queen Anne Press; 1991

THE ONLY GAME Roddy Forsyth; Mainstream; 1990

THE OXFORD COMPANION TO SPORTS AND GAMES edited by John Arlott; Oxford University Press; 1975

THE SIXTIES REVISITED Jimmy Greaves & Norman Giller; Queen Anne Press; 1992

THE SOCCER TRIBE Desmond Morris; Jonathan Cape; 1981

THE SPORTSPAGES ALMANACS Matthew Engel and Ian Morrison; Simon and Schuster

THE STORY OF THE WORLD CUP Brian Glanville; Faber and Faber; 1993

THE SUNDAY TIMES CHRONICLE OF TWENTIETH CENTURY SPORT Chris Nawrat, Steve Hutchings and Greg Struthers; Hamlyn; 1992

THE SUNDAY TIMES SPORTS BOOK John Lovesey, Nicholas Mason and Edwin Taylor; World's Work; 1979

THIS ONE'S ON ME Jimmy Greaves; Coronet; 1979

THREE SIDES OF THE MERSEY Rogan Taylor and Andrew Ward; Robson books; 1993

TOTTENHAM HOTSPUR PLAYER BY PLAYER Ivan Ponting; Guinness; 1993

TRAUTMANN Alan Rowlands; Breedon Books; 1990

WAR GAMES: THE STORY OF SPORT IN WORLD WAR TWO Tony McCarthy; Queen Anne Press; 1989

WEST BROMWICH ALBION, THE FIRST HUNDRED YEARS G A Willmore; Readers Union; 1979

YOU'LL NEVER WALK ALONE Stephen F Kelly; Macdonald Queen Anne Press; 1991

Acknowledgements

The publishers would particularly like to thank the staff of the Times Newspapers Picture Library and Dawn Wyman of the Hulton Deutsch Collection for their invaluable help in providing pictures for this book. Every effort has been made to trace copyright-holders but if errors or omissions are brought to our attention we shall be pleased to correct them in future editions of the book.

Action Images 177 top, 293 top, 330 bottom
Allsport 6 bottom left, 101 bottom, 271 top left, 288 bottom, 313 top, Shaun Botterill 320 bottom, 327 top, 336 bottom, 340, Simon Bruty 305 bottom, Chris Cole 338 bottom, Phil Cole 335 centre, Jan Collsioo 161 bottom left, Nick Potts 335 top, Pressens Bild 101 top, 101 centre, 137 bottom left, 161 bottom right, Ben Radford 341 bottom, Anton Want 339 top
Associated Press 61 left, 97 bottom right, 108 left, 117 top, 117 bottom left, 134 bottom, 140 bottom, 157 bottom, 232 bottom, 244 top, 259 top, 269 bottom
Associated Sports Photography/George Herringshaw 193, 222 bottom right, 229 bottom, 233 bottom, 323 left, Nigel French 325 top
Tony Bartelo 328 bottom
British Library 5l top
Caledonian Newspapers Limited 140 top, 143 bottom, 28l bottom
Calyx Photo Services 293 bottom
John Cocks 11 left
Colorsport 2-3, 7 top, 7 centre, 7 bottom, 15, 16 right, 19 top, 21 bottom, 22 bottom, 23 left, 23 right, 26 top, 26 bottom, 30 top, 30 bottom, 31 left, 55 top, 60 left, 93 top right, 93 bottom, 97 top, 100 top, 115 top, 130 bottom right, 131, 132, 135 top, 150 bottom, 163, 166 top, 166 bottom, 167 left, 173, 174 left, 183 bottom left, 183 bottom right, 185 bottom, 189 top, 190, 191 top, 191 centre, 191 bottom, 192 top left, 192 top right, 201 bottom, 203 bottom, 205 centre, 206 bottom left, 209 right, 210, 212, 213 bottom left, 213 bottom right, 221 left, 221 top right, 221 centre left, 221 centre right, 221 bottom left, 221 bottom right, 222 top, 232 top, 248 top, 248 bottom, 249 left, 249 right, 270, 277 top left, 278, 279 top, 279 centre, 279 bottom, 311 top left, 311 top right, 311 centre top left, 311 centre top right, 311 centre bottom, 311 bottom, 319 bottom, 334, 335 bottom, 336 top, 337 bottom, 338 top, 339 bottom, 341 top, Andrew Cowie 337 top, Colin Elsey 242 top, Olympia 100 bottom, Varley 161 centre
Copyright Assignments (Norwich) Bryn Colton 328 top
County Press, Wigan 187 top, 189 bottom,

198 bottom, 209 left, 224 left, 236, 256
Alan Cozzi 329 bottom
Daily Record 8
Tony Edenden/Sportsfocus 284 top
Colin Elsey 141 right
Empics Neal Simpson 320 top
FIFA 48, 62, 63 top, 63 bottom, 77 centre top, 77 centre bottom, 77 bottom, 88 top, 88 bottom, 89 top, 89 centre left, 89 centre right, 89 bottom
Fotosports International 192 bottom, 202 bottom, 214, 231 bottom
Glasgow Herald 22 top
Global Sports Photos 243 top
Barry Greenwood 305 top
Hailey Sports Photographic 253 bottom, 273 left, 283 right
Steve Hale 292 right
Tommy Hindley/Professional Sport 285 right, 297 top
Hulton Deutsch Collection 1, 11 right, 13 bottom, 14 top, 14 bottom, 27, 29, 34 top, 34 bottom, 35, 36 bottom, 37, 38 left, 38 right, 39 top, 39 bottom, 40, 4l, 42, 43 left, 44 left, 44 right, 45 top, 45 bottom, 50 top, 50 bottom, 53 top, 54 top right, 54 bottom right, 55 bottom, 59, 60 right, 6l right, 64 top, 64 bottom, 65 right, 69 bottom, 70 top, 70 bottom, 72 top, 72 bottom, 73 bottom, 74 top, 77 top, 78 left, 79 bottom, 80 top, 80 bottom, 81 top, 81 bottom, 86 top, 86 bottom left, 86 bottom right, 90 top, 91 centre left, 91 bottom left, 91 bottom right, 93 top left, 95 top, 95 bottom left, 97 bottom left, 99 right, 102 bottom, 104, 105 top left, 108 right, 109 right, 110 bottom, 111 bottom, 114 bottom, 116, 117 bottom right, 118 top, 118 bottom, 119 top left, 120 top, 121 top, 121 right, 122 left, 123 right, 124, 125 top, 127 bottom right, 128 top, 129 top, 130 bottom left, 133 bottom, 134 top, 135 bottom, 137 centre, 137 bottom right, 144 right, 146, 147 left, 147 right, 148 top, 149 top, 149 bottom, 151 top, 153 bottom left, 153 bottom right, 156 bottom, 161 top, 162 top right, 162 bottom, 164 top, 164 bottom, 167 right, 171 bottom left, 177 bottom, 179 left, 180 top, 182, 183 top left, 184 bottom, 188 left, 188 right, 196, 197 top right, 199 top, 201 top, 202 top, 206 top, 208 bottom, 215 left, 217 top left, 217 bottom left, 219 bottom, 224 bottom right, 226 left, 227 top left, 227 bottom, 230 top, 230 bottom, 239 top, 239 centre, 241, 242 bottom, 250 top, 300 bottom, Rob Gallagher 318, 319 top left
The Illustrated London News Picture Library 12 top, 13 top, 20, 28
Imperial War Museum 32
ITV 294 bottom
Stewart Kendall/Sportsphoto Agency 260 left, 292 left, 332 right
Kicksports Foto 294 top

M. Larkin 103 bottom right
Mark Leech 211 bottom, 233 top, 244 bottom, 260 right, 282 top, 295 left, 298 left, David Davies 257 bottom left
Liverpool Daily Post and Echo 301 top
London Express News Service 265 bottom
London News Service Mark Morris 323 right, Paul Vicente 321 bottom
Eamonn McCabe 209 centre
Manchester Evening News 21 top
Mercury Press Agency 313 left
Monitor Press Features 133 top
North London Photo Service 205 left
Photographic News Agencies 102 top, 110 top, 126
Picture Services A. Harris 127 bottom left, S. Martin 91 centre right
Popperfoto 16 left, 17 top, 17 bottom, 18 top right, 31 right
Press Association 12 bottom, 73 top, 125 bottom left, 125 bottom right, 128 bottom, 130 top, 133 centre, 135 centre, 137 top, 137 centre top, 139, 141 left, 145 top, 148 bottom, 154 top, 157 top, 168 left, 170 bottom, 172 top right, 174 right, 175 bottom, 176 bottom, 178 right, 179 right, 181 top, 186 left, 187 bottom, 194 top, 194 bottom, 197 top left, 207 left, 219 top right, 224 top right, 226 right, 229 top, 240 bottom left, 245 bottom, 247 top, 250 bottom, 257 top, 258 top, 264 top, 28l top, 282 bottom, 283 left, 285 left, 290 top, 295 right, 301 bottom, 303 top, 326 top, Fiona Hanson 302 left
Press Association/Reuter 76, 82 bottom, 85 bottom right, 96, 97 centre, 98 bottom, 103 top, 109 left, 111 top, 112 right, 113 bottom, 119 top right, 120 bottom, 121 bottom left, 122 right
Press Portrait Bureau 79 top, 103 bottom left
Professional Sport Ltd 261 bottom
Pro-Shot 322 top
Duncan Raban/All-Action Photographic 277 top right, 280 top
Raymonds, Derby 138 centre, 138 bottom
Reed International Books Ltd 9 top, 9 centre, 9 bottom
Reuter 314 top
Scotsman Publications 87 bottom, 245 top
Sport & General 18 left, 85 bottom left, 127 top, 129 bottom, 172 bottom, 246 bottom, 254, D. Bennett 228 right
Sportapics 277 bottom
Sporting Pictures (UK) 200 right, 204, 211 top, 215 bottom right, 217 bottom right, 227 top right, 237 bottom left, 237 bottom right, 240 top, 262 top, 273 right, 274 left, 291 top, 314 centre, 333 bottom
Syndication International/Hulton Deutsch 18 bottom right, 90 bottom, 98 top, 123 left, 138 top, 142 bottom, 143 top, 150 top, 162 top left, 168 right, 169 top, 169 bottom, 208 top, 216, 223 bottom, 225, 228

left, 251 bottom, 253 top, 255 top left, 258 bottom, 263 bottom left, 266, 268 top, 287, 288 top, 289 right, 296 top, 296 bottom, 298 top right, 327 bottom, 332 left, 333 top
Bob Thomas Sports Photography 4, 19 bottom, 207 right, 213 top, 219 top left, 223 top, 231 top, 240 bottom right, 252 bottom, 255 top right, 257 bottom right, 267 bottom, 274 right, 275 left, 286 top, 289 left, 302 right
Times Newspapers Picture Library 36 bottom, 43 top right, 43 bottom right, 51 bottom, 52 left, 52 right, 53 bottom, 54 left, 58, 63 centre, 65 top left, 65 bottom left, 68, 69 top, 71 top, 71 bottom, 74 bottom, 82 top, 83 bottom, 84, 85 top, 92, 99 left, 105 top right, 105 bottom, 112 left, 114 top, 142 top, 145 bottom, 151 bottom, 154 bottom, 155 top, 156 top, 165 top, 171 top, 171 bottom right, 175 top, 176 top left, 176 top right, 180 bottom, 181 bottom, 183 top right, 184 top, 185 top, 186 bottom right, 200 left, 215 top right, 217 top right, 218 top, 237 top, 243 bottom, 246 top, 255 bottom, 271 top right, 29l bottom, 303 bottom, 304 top, 306, 307 top, 307 bottom, 314 bottom, 315 top, 316 bottom, 317 top, 319 top right, 322 bottom, Frank Baron 268 bottom, 269 top, Roy Beardsworth 321 top, Martin Beddall 317 bottom, David Davies 313 right, Ted Ditchburn 325 bottom, T. Dixon 178 left, Stewart Fraser 165 bottom, Greenwood 91 top, Harris 94, 95 bottom right, Warren Harrison 238, Frank Herrmann 195 top, 218 bottom, Tommy Hindley 251 top, P. Jay 275 right, D. Jones 197 bottom, Karadia 267 top, H. Kerr 198 top, Tom Kidd 330 top, Paul Lewis 263 top, F. McKechnie 298 bottom, Denzil McNeelance 297 bottom, John Manning 252 top, Dud Miller 264 bottom, Risley 83 top, 87 top, Hugh Routledge 271 bottom, 299, 312, 324 bottom, 331 top, Peter Simpson 265 top, Chris Smith 276, 286 bottom, 300 top, 304 bottom, 316 top, Ian Stewart 203 top, 263 bottom right, 272 bottom, 290 bottom, 324 top, 329 top, Tom Stoddart 280 bottom, Travis 195 bottom, Simon Walker 331 bottom, Warhurst 113 top, 119 bottom, Mike Wilkinson 272 top, Ian Wright 206 bottom right
UPI 115 bottom, 144 left, 152, 153 top, 155 bottom, Roy Letkey 261 top, Jeff Widener 259 bottom, Roland Witschel/DPA 262 bottom
United Sports Picture Agency 239 bottom
Universal Pictorial Press & Agency 78 right, 172 top left, 222 bottom left, 284 bottom, 326 bottom
Varley Picture Agency 199 bottom
Dave West 315 bottom